ROSCOE CONKLING
OF NEW YORK

Voice in the Senate

ROSCOE CONKLING
From *Harper's Weekly*, Vol. 32, No. 1636 (April 28, 1888)

ROSCOE CONKLING OF NEW YORK

Voice in the Senate

by DAVID M. JORDAN

Cornell University Press

ITHACA AND LONDON

First published 1971 by Cornell University Press.
Published in the United Kingdom by Cornell University Press Ltd.,
2–4 Brook Street, London W1Y 1AA.

International Standard Book Number 0-8014-0625-0
Library of Congress Catalog Card Number 76-148021

PRINTED IN THE UNITED STATES OF AMERICA
BY VAIL-BALLOU PRESS, INC.

TO BARBARA

CONTENTS

CONTENTS

ILLUSTRATIONS

PREFACE

On June 4, 1888, some weeks after Roscoe Conkling's death, the New York *Herald* wrote: "Mr. Conkling's memory may be safely trusted to the American people. They are fully acquainted with his few foibles and his many great qualities. They recognize him as a steadfast friend and an uncompromising foe, too chivalrous to do a mean action himself and too proud to forgive it when done by another."

In this judgment, the *Herald,* one of the few newspapers to support Conkling during his lifetime, missed its mark. Conkling, together with most of his fellows at the summit of American political life in his day, has been all but forgotten. This is unfortunate, because in many respects the present structure of American society began to take shape in the Gilded Age, the years following the Civil War.

Roscoe Conkling was one of the most singular characters of the time, and one of the most tragic. A man of great intellect, a commanding presence on the stump, a domineering leader both in the caucus room and on the Senate floor, and a lawyer of great ability, he yet came to be scorned and hated by his fellow citizens, and he severely damaged that Republican party which he believed to be one of the great political creations of history. How this happened I have attempted to spell out in the pages that follow. Why it happened has been the subject of some speculation on my part. Further analysis of Conkling's behavior from a psychoanalytical point of view would, I believe, be fruitful.

There have been two earlier biographies of Roscoe Conkling, neither of them wholly satisfying. The Senator's nephew and sometime secretary, Alfred R. Conkling, wrote a sketchy and extremely laudatory biography shortly after his uncle's death. Many years later, in 1935,

Donald Barr Chidsey wrote a popular account of Conkling. I have attempted to fill in some of the gaps left by these works.

One of the problems in dealing with Conkling is the sparseness of source material. The Senator wrote no memoirs, left no journals or diaries, and collected no letters. There are Conkling letters around, and though I have searched diligently and turned up many, I cannot claim to have found them all. Unlike many of his contemporaries, such as Garfield, Reid, and even Arthur, Conkling was not much of a letter writer. Many of his surviving letters merely refer back or ahead to personal meetings just held or planned. Unlike John Sherman, Conkling carried on no voluminous correspondence from Washington with local legislators or other political leaders in his home state. Sherman had to write letters to keep in touch with his constituents in Ohio; Conkling had only to get on a train to New York.

Other than the scattered letters, both his own and those of his fellows, the major sources for Conkling's life are the daily and weekly newspapers and journals, the *Congressional Globe* and *Congressional Record,* government publications, and the writings and reminiscences of his contemporaries. The latter are of course flawed by the usual biases, petty vindictiveness, and lapses of memory; but they do occasionally provide illuminating glimpses of Conkling. The *Globe* and the *Record,* of course, permit him to speak in his own words. These words, the raw sound of a political moment (though sometimes slightly edited by the speaker before publication), may actually give a better picture of the man than scrupulously crafted pages of self-justification written many years after the event. In any case, Conkling neither believed in self-justification nor indulged in it. The reconstruction of his life must be done with no retrospective help from the Senator himself.

In writing this book, I have had help, albeit not much from Conkling. Its nucleus was a senior thesis written many years ago for the Princeton University history department, entitled "The Downfall of the Conkling Machine," for which I had the advice and guidance of Professor Francis Loewenheim. Needless to say, the present work in no way resembles that earlier effort.

I have spent much profitable time in the vast open-stack collections of Princeton University's Firestone Library. The people in the Manuscript Division of the Library of Congress were of much assistance to me in many visits there. The Uticana Room and the microfilm collection of old Utica newspapers of the Utica Public Library were of great value.

Further help with the Utica background was provided by Janson L. Cox and his successor, Susan C. Crosier, directors of the Oneida Historical Society at "Fountain Elms" in Utica. The staffs of the Free Library of Philadelphia (particularly Robert F. Looney of the Print and Pictures section) and the Yale University Library were very helpful, as was that of the New-York Historical Society. Thanks also should go to Gerald D. McDonald and the Manuscript Division of the New York Public Library, which I used extensively along with the library's general collection. Professor Harold J. Jonas gave his encouragement, for which I am grateful. Professor W. David Lewis of the State University of New York at Buffalo read the manuscript and made numerous valuable suggestions. Some of the most active assistance I received came from Herbert Finch and the staff of the Collection of Regional History at Cornell University.

I would like to express my gratitude, too, to the many friends who have put up with Conkling quotations and anecdotes over the last few years, and to my good friend Scott McMillin of Cornell University. My special thanks go to the gracious ladies who typed the manuscript, primarily Mrs. Elizabeth Monteleone, as well as Mrs. Dorothy Gottschall, Candy Golden, and my sister Jane Jordan.

Finally, no one suffered with me more over the preparation of this book than my wife Barbara and, to a lesser extent, my oldest daughter, Diana. They accompanied me on many journeys to Utica, Washington, New York City, and other places, and my wife was sometimes hard-pressed to explain to friends our vacation jaunts to the banks of the Mohawk River. They joined me in periodic visits to the southeast corner of Madison Square in Manhattan to gaze at the Conkling statue enjoyed by the pigeons there. And they put up with my growling and grumbling while I worked on the manuscript. To their patience and forbearance can be attributed much of whatever merit this book may possess.

DAVID M. JORDAN

Jenkintown, Pennsylvania

ROSCOE CONKLING
OF NEW YORK

Voice in the Senate

"For I do not remember how many years, Mr. Conkling was the supreme ruler of this State; the Governor did not count, the legislatures did not count; comptrollers and secretaries of state, and what-not did not count. It was what Mr. Conkling said."

—ELIHU ROOT

"Like Roderick of the Glen, a bugle blast from the Utica statesman is worth ten thousand men to the Republican hosts of this State."
—New York *Herald,* September 23, 1877

"As a politician of power and prominence, he is really a compound of collectors, appraisers, gaugers, and weighers. He is made up of them, and draws his whole sustenance from them."
—*The Nation,* October 4, 1877

CHAPTER 1

————◀•••▶————

A PROMISING YOUNG MAN

"Lord Roscoe," many called him, and he carried himself like a member of the higher peerage. Roscoe Conkling steps from the pages of history angry, haughty, larger than life. Although he was vindictive and overbearing, he was handsome, intelligent, and capable of orating for hours at a time without losing either a word of his memorized speech or a listener; gaudy as a peacock, he makes the political leaders of our era pale into shadows in comparison. He was not a pleasant man, but he stirred strong emotions, and he had a considerable impact on American history.

Mention of the post–Civil War period produces a negative reaction in most Americans. After the heroism, the bloodshed, the cowardice, above all the towering drama of the war, the political battles of the Gilded Age frequently seem a bit petty, even tawdry. Grant as President, chief executive over a corrupt administration, seems a completely different person from Grant the fearless and decisive general. President Grant has received a universally bad historical press. Hayes has received almost no press at all. Where history marks Abraham Lincoln as a martyr to the Civil War and the passions of rebellion, and John Kennedy stands as a martyr to the Cold War and America's involvement with the world, Garfield's martyrdom to an unseemly patronage squabble is an embarrassment to the American historical sense. Arthur is treated by history as an accident, cited only to show that a president can sometimes rise above his background.

In addition, examination of the details of the economic and industrial development of the United States during these years, the vast and rapid expansion taking place behind the façade of the political activities, too often reveals that leading public figures, both in politics and business, could not stand up to very severe scrutiny. When Speakers,

1

senators, cabinet members, even presidents are tainted with traces of the corruption spread by single-minded entrepreneurs, history tends to turn its face modestly away.

Yet, the story of this continental nation is a continuum. Much of modern America, its economics, its racial attitudes, and its politics, was shaped in the years from the end of the Civil War to the election of Cleveland, just as twenty-first-century America is being shaped now. And the warriors in those almost forgotten political battles, venal or hypocritical though some may have been, stamped the times with their collective imprint.

There were some pretty good—and colorful—battlers among them— Blaine and Cameron and Oliver P. Morton, Bayard of Delaware, Horace Greeley, Sam Tilden, sulphur-tongued Charles Sumner, Carl Schurz, railroad magnates like Tom Scott and C. P. Huntington, the money barons Gould and Cooke, Tweed and Kelly of Tammany, and a squadron or two of generals on both sides who turned politician (and some generals who were never anything but politicians). There were customs collectors and land speculators, ministers and professional veterans, the Boys in Blue. Among this galaxy of stars of brighter or darker magnitude, a man who stood out as one of the most spectacular and powerful figures of the age was the Republican boss of New York, Roscoe Conkling.

A man with stiff pride to match his imperious bearing, the statesman from Utica dominated the Empire State's politics for more than a decade and, for a considerable portion of that time, dominated the United States Senate as well. Conkling's epic battles with Hayes and Garfield helped to redress the balance of powers between president and Congress after the almost disastrous tilt of the Andrew Johnson era. He caused, though certainly not by design, a major revamping of the selection process for federal employees. And his long and bitter feud with James G. Blaine helped to weaken the Republican party to the point where the Democrats, though stained with rebellion, could effectively restore a two-party system.

Conkling operated on a grand scale. He carried on a notorious love affair with the most famous beauty of the time, in the process cuckolding a former Senate colleague, until the liaison was cut short by a true *opéra bouffe* ending. When critics deplored the influence of political "machines," his was the one they meant. He grandly waved aside two proffered nominations to the United States Supreme Court, one for the chief justice's robes. He was the darling of the galleries, with his flamboyant style of dress and speech, and he was the pivot of attention for great numbers of people who detested him and everything he stood for in politics. They hated him, but they missed him when he was gone —he took with him a sense of order in New York politics, leaving chaos behind—and they attributed all manner of schemes and stratagems to him long after he had ceased to care.

Conkling's political downfall was spectacular, and it took the most famous storm in American history to kill him. Public attention followed him, and, although his friendships were few, he was feared or respected by many.

This, then, was Roscoe Conkling—a man of curious appeal, handsome, proud, the center of attention everywhere he went, but who, for all his abundant color and flash, was a man of political substance.

Alfred Conkling, the future senator's father, was, in a sense, a tragic figure. Although he ended his years in obscurity, known primarily as "Roscoe Conkling's father," he had once been a man of prominence. His was the fifth generation of American Conklings, marking its descent from Ananias Conkling, a glass worker who emigrated from England between 1635 and 1637.[1] Born in 1789 in Amagansett, Long Island, the senior Conkling, following his graduation from Union College in Schenectady, married Eliza Cockburn, "the belle of the Mohawk." By this time, he had moved to the more northerly realms of Albany and the Mohawk Valley, where he became an active politician, involving himself primarily with those who would in subsequent years of that fluid political era become Whigs. The young lawyer, highly regarded as a rising member of the bar, was elected to Congress and served in Washington from 1820 to 1823, though he was not happy in the House.

On August 27, 1825, President John Quincy Adams named Alfred Conkling a federal judge for the Northern District of New York. Here Conkling was to serve for twenty-seven years, until he resigned from the bench in 1852 at the request of his friend Millard Fillmore to serve as minister to Mexico in the wake of the Mexican War.

Leaving the court was a mistake for Conkling. After a turbulent tenure in Mexico City, ended when the Democratic administration of Franklin Pierce replaced him, Judge Conkling moved on to Omaha, in

[1] I. B. Conkling, *The Conklings,* pp. 17, 91. Complete bibliographical information is given in the Selected Bibliography following the text.

the rough-hewn Nebraska Territory, where he practiced law. Ultimately, however, he returned to New York, living on in Utica until his death in 1874 at the age of eighty-five.[2]

During his happier days in New York, the judge had sired seven children, four sons and three daughters. The youngest of his sons was born on October 30, 1829, and named after William Roscoe, an English historian and minor poet, whose works Mrs. Conkling was said to have been reading at the time of her pregnancy.[3]

Roscoe was born in Albany, and he spent his early childhood in the capital, until the family moved in 1839 to Auburn, at the foot of Owasco Lake. That same year, young Roscoe suffered a broken jaw when he was kicked in the face by a horse. There were apparently no lasting physical effects from the injury, as the boy grew to a handsome manhood. Unfortunately, there exists virtually no evidence of the influence of his early childhood on Conkling's adult personality.

In 1842, Roscoe, who was never an enthusiastic scholar, was sent to Mt. Washington Collegiate Institute in New York City, under the watchful eye of his oldest brother, Frederick, already a resident of the great metropolis. Roscoe may have been a problem to his parents; sending a worrisome child away to school is a customary reaction. He attended the New York school for only a year, and it is most likely that the major benefit gained from his stay was obtained outside the classroom. The city exerted a powerful magic upon a youth with a keen mind and a taste for excitement. Although Conkling as an adult was generally linked in the public mind with Utica, he actually spent considerably more time in New York City and lived there after he left the Senate.

At the age of fourteen, Roscoe returned home to enter the Auburn Academy. In the three years he attended Auburn, the young man's taste for politics, for the influence of power, and the intricacies of political maneuver was whetted to an overpowering degree. The motivating force here, as in New York, was not his schooling; it was the life which he observed around him. For his father, the judge, was still

---

[2] See H. J. Jonas, "Alfred Conkling," pp. 295–305, for most of the background on Alfred Conkling. Elizabeth Cady Stanton, the suffragette, drew a poignant picture of the "proud, reserved judge . . . unaccustomed to manifestations of affection and tender interest in his behalf" on frequent visits to the Peterboro, N.Y., home of abolitionist Gerrit Smith. E. C. Stanton, *Eighty Years,* p. 52.

[3] A. R. Conkling, *Roscoe Conkling,* p. 8.

considered one of the most powerful leaders of the Whig party in the northern and central parts of New York. Among the men who visited Judge Conkling and his family were great figures like Congressman John Quincy Adams, a former president and secretary of state; former President Martin Van Buren, not a Whig but progressively more unhappy with the "slavocracy" controlling his Democratic party; former Chancellor James Kent of New York, a giant of American jurisprudence; and the crafty Whig political strategist, Thurlow Weed, the editor of the Albany *Evening Journal*.[4] Heady company indeed, for the bright and headstrong Roscoe!

In Auburn, of course, the reigning political luminary was Weed's protégé, the formidable William Henry Seward. At this time, Seward had just returned to the private practice of law following the completion of his term as governor, but he was preparing as well for his elevation to the United States Senate in 1848 and perhaps one day to the presidency. Seward was a good friend of Judge Conkling and also of the judge's youngest son.

In addition to the great names of the day who made stops at the Conkling household, there were of course many lesser figures from the local political scene who consulted with the judge from time to time. These men too would take a few moments to stop and discuss local political affairs with young Roscoe. Thus, when he began his own political career, he was knowledgeable far beyond his years.

Picture a handsome young man of sixteen, with somewhat more than the usual degree of vanity and lust for the limelight, with a good, quick intelligence, who has been exposed throughout the formative years of his adolescence to politics and politicians, not just the ordinary run of local job-seekers and influence-peddlers, but men who have been at the summit—or expected to be there shortly—men who have wielded the ultimate levers of power. Then picture the same young man as he finishes his education at the Auburn Academy and contemplates his next step. Not surprisingly, Roscoe Conkling, self-willed and decisive, determined that that next step would not be college, which was a disappointment to the judge, who had been the first college graduate in the Conkling family. No classical education for the young man, who was drawn as if by a magnet to a sphere promising a more immediate outlet for his energies. Young Roscoe in 1846 entered the offices of Spencer and Kernan in Utica, to read law. A pattern of rebellion

4 *Ibid.*, p. 14.

emerges, as Roscoe Conkling early made it clear that he would be his own master: no college career, and his legal training would take place eighty miles away from home. Later, of course, he was to regret in an offhand sort of way passing up "the advantage of a University education." But this was an afterthought, really; he never looked back.[5]

Joshua A. Spencer and Francis Kernan were two of the most famous lawyers in upper New York state. Spencer was called "perhaps the foremost advocate that ever lived in the United States," a trifle broad, perhaps, but one gets the picture of a man who could handle himself in a courtroom. Both were active in politics. Spencer was a Whig leader in Oneida County, while Kernan was an active Democrat. Kernan, thirteen years Conkling's senior, was to be involved politically with Roscoe for nearly all of his life. Spencer died in 1857, but Roscoe Conkling did not forget him; in later years, Conkling said, "Whatever success I may have had in life I owe in a great measure to Mr. Spencer." Spencer seems to have replaced Judge Conkling as the paternal force in Roscoe's life.[6]

Spencer and Kernan did not pay law clerks and, since young Conkling was almost entirely without means of his own, he borrowed from his brother an amount sufficient to enable him to complete his legal studies. This loan was repaid to Frederick out of the first fees Roscoe earned as a member of the bar. With this assistance, the young law student was able to take a room as a boarder.[7]

An old-time courthouse habitué recalled at the time of Conkling's death his first vision of the future Senator, still a law clerk, arriving in Rome to search for the courthouse, looking "like a tall, blond young lady" with "a tall silk hat, a frock coat with velvet collar; his cheek was as fresh as a rose, and he had long red ringlets clustered about his neck." Though the red ringlets did not last long, Conkling always remained a striking figure.[8]

As his law study neared its completion, young Conkling formed a brief partnership with Thomas R. Walker, the mayor of Utica. Conkling was admitted to the bar early in 1850, and he pleaded and

[5] *Ibid.;* W. D. Shipman, "A Memorial," p. 77. It was said that Conkling's formal schooling was "supplemented by a wide range of general reading, and by the daily influence of a cultivated and refined home life."

[6] A. Chester, ed., *Legal History of New York,* III, 231; M. M. Bagg, ed., *History of Utica,* p. 544.

[7] H. W. Scott, *Distinguished Lawyers,* p. 189; Utica City Directory, 1847–1848.

[8] R. G. Ingersoll, *Memorial Address,* p. 94.

won his first court case before his father, who fixed a high standard for him, shortly thereafter.[9]

The town in which Roscoe Conkling had chosen to settle was the trading center and the largest mill town of the Mohawk Valley. Utica, just twenty miles east of the geographic center of New York, had originally been the site of the only ford across the Mohawk River for many miles. At this ford a settlement, at one time named Whitestown, had sprung up. Not far removed was the hub of a network of trails leading to the portage at Rome to the northwest, Oneida Castle to the west, and east to the settlements on the Mohawk and the Hudson. Utica sat at the western end of the Mohawk highlands and just south of the central Adirondack foothills.

Utica's 1830 population of 8,300 grew rapidly with the development of easier transportation and the consequent expansion of industry. In 1836, the Chenango Canal and the Utica and Schenectady Railroad were completed. Though the seventy-eight miles from Schenectady to Utica took six and a half hours by train, this access to the area facilitated greater industrial opportunity. A varied manufacturing business grew up in the city, and in 1847, the textile industry, which was to become the main staple of Utica's economy, blossomed with the opening of woolen mills and, in the following year, cotton mills. Utica was booming and growing fast, but its expansion was based on substantial business and solid, hard-working people.[10]

This then was the town where Roscoe Conkling opened his office for the practice of law, on Genesee Street, the main commercial thoroughfare, just up the hill from Baggs Square, near the river, the heart of Old Utica. Now a town of well over 17,000, it had been settled primarily by people of English, Welsh, Scotch-Irish, and German stock, many with backgrounds in puritan New England; because it was expanding and flourishing, it was a town where an intelligent, ambitious young man could make his mark in a hurry—in law or in politics. Roscoe Conkling clearly intended to make his.

Young Conkling did not wait until his admission to the bar to become active in Whig politics, with the help of Joshua Spencer. Conkling had studied the art of oratory, and Spencer encouraged him to take

[9] Oneida *Morning Herald,* Nov. 28, 1849; A. R. Conkling, p. 19.

[10] Writers Program, *New York,* pp. 353–355, together with information furnished by the Oneida Historical Society, for data on Utica.

advantage of public speaking opportunities. The young law clerk was eager to do so. He loved the power he had, standing on a platform, with rapt listeners before him. His greatest moments, throughout his life, were to come in speeches, whether on the stump, in Congress, or before the United States Supreme Court. Opponents mocked the boasts of Conkling's supporters that this speech or that was "his greatest effort," but it was nevertheless true that he delivered as many notable orations as any speaker of his day.

Conkling considered himself a "Seward Whig." He had strong feelings about slavery and the free-soil movement which would impel him ultimately into the Republican party. In 1848, Conkling stumped the county with "stirring and effective appeals in behalf of the Whig cause" for the ticket of Zachary Taylor and his father's friend, Millard Fillmore of New York.[11]

In 1849, Conkling, in recognition of his services, was chosen a delegate from his ward in Utica to the Whig convention at New Hartford for the First Assembly District of Oneida County, to select delegates to the state and judicial conventions. He was subsequently elected a delegate to the judicial convention meeting at Syracuse, with instructions to support Oneida's own Joshua Spencer for judge of the state Court of Appeals. At the judicial convention itself, young Roscoe, still under twenty, was now functioning on a state-wide level for the first time. The judicial convention contained few of the senior leaders of the party but a large number of rising young Whig lawyers. He could now meet on a first-name basis young politicos from Buffalo and Troy, from Broome County and Brooklyn. Some of these politicians, and we can be sure that Conkling measured them with a cool and critical eye, would be around for a long time; and functions such as this convention afforded a great opportunity to watch and to judge such men, to observe the stresses which bore upon them, the vices which might undermine them, the habits of mind which motivated them, even the loyalties which might one day make them valuable allies. Undoubtedly Conkling himself did not go unnoticed. In the business sessions, he not only

[11] Oneida *Morning Herald,* Oct. 31, 1850. Though both Seward and Fillmore were numbered among Alfred Conkling's friends, they were unfriendly rivals in New York Whiggery. Seward's doctrine of a "higher law" than the Constitution and his willingness to inflame sectional differences further rather than to yield anything to the South in composing those differences was to contrast sharply with Fillmore's warm advocacy of the Compromise of 1850 in the crucial days when he was elevated to the presidency by Taylor's sudden death in July 1850.

helped Spencer win his nomination for the Court of Appeals but also, after three or four inconclusive ballots, he successfully moved the unanimous nomination of Joseph Mullen of Jefferson County for judge of the Fifth Judicial District of the Supreme Court. The bare news story reveals nothing of the dickering and ultimate bargain producing this result, but it is clear that Roscoe was serving his political apprenticeship.[12]

In April 1850, Calvert Comstock submitted his resignation as district attorney of Oneida County, and the selection of a successor devolved upon the Whig governor, Hamilton Fish, another friend of Judge Conkling. The post was one avidly sought by political-minded Whig lawyers, and there was considerable pressure on the governor. On April 22, 1850, in what has been called the "most noteworthy" appointment of his two-year tenure as governor, Fish named twenty-year-old Roscoe Conkling as district attorney. Later, Fish was to write to Judge Conkling that "the friends of some of the unsuccessful candidates at the time were very severe in their censure of me," although "the appointment has vindicated itself." [13]

Conkling applied himself vigorously to his new position, no doubt with an eye to the November election for a full term. The disposition of criminal matters in a lively, booming county, not too restrained by the genteel manners of the metropolis, was an important duty, particularly since the prompt imposition of law and order was not one of the more marked features of America's drive westward. At the close of Conkling's first criminal term as district attorney, the Whig paper in town, the Oneida *Morning Herald,* reported on May 16, 1850, that the new prosecutor had "more than met the expectations of his friends by the able, energetic and remarkably successful manner in which he has discharged his severe and responsible duties. Of the fourteen indictments tried by jury, convictions were had on all but two." Even the Rome *Sentinel,* the Democratic paper in the county's other sizable town, said that "he made a good District Attorney; his experience and practice just fitted him for that office." [14]

On October 12, 1850, the Oneida Whigs, in convention assembled at Rome, nominated Roscoe Conkling for a full term as district at-

[12] *Ibid.,* Sept. 21, 22, 27, 29, 1849.

[13] A. Nevins, *Hamilton Fish,* I, 32–33; Oneida *Morning Herald,* April 25, 1850.

[14] Quoted in Utica *Morning Herald,* Oct. 18, 1859.

torney. It was not unanimous, but then Roscoe always seemed to generate some opposition.[15]

The local Whig paper dutifully praised Conkling: "Roscoe Conkling, Esquire . . . has filled the post for which he is nominated, for several months, with great ability and to the entire satisfaction of all. He is an active Whig and an able lawyer." His name, though still no doubt that of "the son of Judge Conkling," was spreading through the state. From his birthplace, Albany, in Thurlow Weed's journal: Conkling "is a young man, but one of great promise in the political and professional field." From his old hometown, Auburn: Conkling "gives promise of being one of the greatest ornaments to the bar, in the State." [16]

The campaign of 1850 in Oneida was one of considerable movement but little substance, with the opposition to Conkling based mainly on his youth. In Washington, however, the struggle which wrenched from a reluctant Congress what we know as the Compromise of 1850 cost Whig votes around the country, and Roscoe Conkling felt its effect. In the November election that year, Samuel B. Garvin, the Democratic candidate, was elected district attorney with 8,070 votes, to 7,454 for Conkling. The defeated incumbent, hardly a has-been at twenty-one, went back to the practice of law.[17]

Roscoe Conkling quickly became one of the most prominent members of the Oneida County bar. He did not, however, enjoy any great popularity among his legal brethren. Even at this early stage of his career, Conkling had developed a talent for cruel, biting sarcasm and outright invective, personal qualities which would, down through the years, cost him friends and create needless enmities. His reputation as a fine trial lawyer grew, and with the increasing reputation came increased fees. Conkling was never a legal scholar, but he was not just a flamboyant advocate trying court cases by ear. He always believed in careful preparation of a case, and was particularly skillful in organizing the trial of a cause which required certain technical knowledge. His intelligence was challenged by the need for grasp of an unfamiliar

[15] Oneida *Morning Herald,* Oct. 14, 1850.

[16] Quoted from Albany *Evening Journal* and Auburn *Daily Advertiser* in Oneida *Morning Herald,* Oct. 23, 1850.

[17] Oneida *Morning Herald,* Oct. 31, Nov. 14, 1850. Garvin, curiously, moved to New York in the 1860's and was appointed by Governor John Hoffman to fill the vacancy caused by the election of District Attorney A. Oakey Hall as mayor of the city; Bagg, ed., p. 559.

area, and he would respond to the challenge with a driving campaign of self-education in that particular field, handwriting analysis, anatomy, cotton mill procedures, whatever, until he could conduct a dialogue with experts on fairly even terms. "He had," as his nephew said, "great confidence in himself." Roscoe excelled particularly at cross-examination of witnesses and the final argument.[18]

In December 1853, in a case which helped to make him famous throughout central New York, Conkling successfully defended Sylvester Hadcock, accused of forgery, in the Herkimer County Courthouse. The prosecuting attorney was Joshua Spencer, Conkling's old mentor. Conkling procured an acquittal by proving his client's illiteracy and by a typically impassioned appeal to the jury to return the defendant to the bosom of his large and needy family.[19] We can only guess, over a century later, which of these two features actually gained the acquittal.

Roscoe, at this time, was living in Bagg's Hotel, in Baggs Square, a short walk from his office.[20] He was charging fifty- and seventy-five dollar fees for his cases now, and he knew he was good. His personal traits were now becoming indelible parts of him. His use of sarcasm and ridicule have been mentioned, and the growing self-confidence. He was a handsome young man and an elegant dresser—some called him a dandy. He was fond of poetry, particularly Byron. He did a great and varied amount of reading, but whether it was for love of literature or to improve and diversify his speech-making ability is not clear. Most likely, the two reasons were blended; if one does not *like* to read, one will not read much, no matter what the practical rewards may appear to be. He read the great English political philosophers, along with Shakespeare, Milton, and Macaulay. He had a prodigious memory and committed to it vast quantities of literary material, which he could reproduce verbatim when needed.[21]

Conkling was a passionate advocate of physical conditioning, an outgrowth perhaps of his vanity. He was an enthusiastic horseback rider and boxer; his critics no doubt would maintain that the latter interest was a manifestation of Conkling's readiness to do battle at any time. Probably it was; his aggressive nature never changed. (It led

[18] A. R. Conkling, pp. 20, 23; Scott, p. 190; Shipman, p. 78. Shipman said that in the years after he left the district attorney's office Conkling "attained an eminence rarely reached by any one of his years."

[19] Scott, p. 191.   [20] Utica City Directory, 1851–1852, 1852–1853.

[21] A. R. Conkling, p. 21.

him into both law and politics.) He drank little, and he loathed tobacco and the use of it, by anyone, in his presence. If he entered a room in which another person was smoking, Conkling would throw open the nearest window, to allow the noxious fumes to escape.[22]

While the young man was hardening into the mold of the adult, and the young lawyer was increasing his professional competence and his income, the young Whig politician was hewing to the line of party regularity. In 1852, Conkling stumped around Oneida County for General Winfield Scott, "Old Fuss and Feathers," in the last presidential campaign waged by the expiring Whig party. It was a scurrilous campaign, with Scott's effort too inept for a public which was ready now to try a politician rather than another general, and Democrat Franklin Pierce carried New York and the nation. In far-off Mexico City, this was to signal the close of the diplomatic career of Conkling's father. In the United States, sectionalism, antislavery doctrines, and the free-soil movement would soon do in the Whigs, who had never been much for ideology anyway. They never got over Andrew Jackson dying, and the disastrous effect of winning a couple of presidential elections.

The Whig party was dying, but it was not yet dead. In New York in 1853, it was still alive because the Democratic party had been and remained bitterly split, between its Hunker and Barnburner elements. One of the prime candidates for the nomination for attorney general when the Whig state convention opened on October 5 was Roscoe Conkling, twenty-four years old. The leading aspirant for the slot was "the brilliant but indolent" Ogden Hoffman of New York City. Hoffman, now sixty years old, had served in Congress in Van Buren's administration, had been U.S. attorney in New York for Harrison and Tyler, and was considered by some to be the greatest criminal trial lawyer of his time. He was an extremely popular man of great reputation, but Conkling had certain strength of his own, and it took three ballots before Hoffman received a majority of the convention. The exposure did not hurt Conkling.[23]

The following year, when the Whigs convened at Syracuse on September 20, Roscoe Conkling was a vice-president of the convention.[24] Significantly, however, Conkling spoke of that convention as belonging

[22] *Ibid.*, pp. 36, 45.

[23] D. S. Alexander, *Political History*, II, 187–188; A. C. Flick, ed., *History of New York*, VII, 76.

[24] Alexander, II, 201.

to the Republican party—the new political amalgam forming in that turbulent year of 1854 from Conscience Whigs, Free-Soilers, and abolitionists, devoted to halting the extension of slavery and to moderating the influence of King Cotton in Washington. Conkling always considered himself an original Republican. He had no difficulty in springing nimbly from the dying Whigs to the newly born Republicans, and in the process he established himself as one of the leaders of the new party in Utica and Oneida County.

In October 1854, Conkling tried one of the biggest cases of his budding career. He represented an orphaned eighteen-year-old choir singer, a young beauty named Martha Parker, charged with "want of chastity" by the pastor of her church, the Reverend F. A. Spencer. Miss Parker brought suit against her supposed spiritual leader for slander, with Roscoe Conkling as counsel for the plaintiff. The defense interposed was that of truth of the charge, which, together with Conkling's presence, guaranteed a spectacular trial. The trial lasted for three days, and in his two-hour closing address to the jury, Conkling successfully attacked the credibility of the star witness for the defense, a man who claimed to have had sexual relations with young Martha, and attacked as well the faithlessness of the defendant to his spiritual vows: "How shall I describe the enormity of such a violation of the laws not only of man but of the King of Kings by one who, when he thus bids defiance to reason and to right, must have heard, ought to have heard, the pleadings on Calvary, the warnings on the Mount of Olives, and the thunders of Mount Sinai still ringing in his ears?" [25]

The Reverend Mr. Spencer could not match the thunders of Mount Sinai: he was found liable. The record verdict of $2,500 given by the jurors was gratifying not only to the young plaintiff but also to her attorney, whose renown spread.

On June 28, 1855, the twenty-five-year-old lawyer married Julia Catherine Seymour of Utica. Miss Seymour, two years older than Conkling, was a member of one of the most prominent families in the Mohawk Valley. Francis Kernan, who knew her well, thought her "marriageable," said that she was "amiable," but doubted that she had "much force of character." Indeed, self-effacement seems to have been her prime quality. The leading ornament of the Seymour family was Julia's brother Horatio, who had just completed a term as governor of

[25] A. R. Conkling, pp. 50–51.

New York. Seymour, a long-time lieutenant of the Albany Regency—
the Democratic organization of Martin Van Buren, Silas Wright, and
William L. Marcy—had been defeated for re-election in 1854, but he
was subsequently to serve a distinguished term as war governor of the
state and to run a close race as the Democratic candidate for the presidency in 1868. Horatio was the antithesis of the young Republican his
little sister brought into the family; he was dignified, possessed of an easy
culture, courteous, and gracious; he was nineteen years older than
Conkling, and he was to find his brother-in-law a constant, even osten-
tatious, opponent. Seymour was strongly opposed to his sister's marriage; later developments show how much wiser Julia would have been
to listen to the governor's advice.[26] In 1855, however, the marriage
appeared to local society as a happy union of Governor Seymour's
sister with Judge Conkling's son. A biographer of Seymour has said
that Conkling "supplied the House of Seymour with all those masculine
virtues which the whimsical Horatio was supposed to lack." [27]

The external change in Conkling's mode of living was not precipi-
tous, however, as he moved Julia into his boarding house in downtown
Utica. While she sat home, Roscoe pursued the demanding and time-
devouring practice of a prospering young attorney, and increasingly
involved himself in politics. The relationship was starved of care and
attention from the start; probably the self-centered Conkling was unable to give of himself that portion required for a successful marriage.

More and more of Conkling's attention was devoted to the workings
of politics. This was an age without pervasive electronic media, without
organized spectator sports, and without elaborate devices for mass en-
tertainment. Many people, of course, were far too occupied in providing
food for their tables and a roof for their heads to have any great need
for diversion. Many Americans, though, were interested in politics.
The great issues of slavery, Mexico, economic expansion, and the territories excited and stirred the American people. Newspapers of all
political persuasions expended much space and effort on scornful and
hard-worded denunciation of their political opponents. Many of the
brightest and ablest men of the country, as well as some of the most
knavish, played their parts in the political struggles of the day.

Roscoe's influence in Republican affairs in the city and Oneida

[26] Francis Kernan to Hannah Kernan, Jan. 9, 1855, Francis Kernan Papers;
S. Mitchell, *Horatio Seymour,* p. 574.
[27] Mitchell, p. 255.

County kept growing. He soon was one of the best-known Republicans in the area, but, more important, he had probably the best political mind in the Mohawk Valley and no one could match his driving ambition. This is crucial because, in a limited political sphere, self-confidence and ambition, if sensibly controlled, can carry all before them.

In 1856, Thurlow Weed decided the time was not yet ripe for the accession of Seward to the presidency, so the Republican party nominated for its first presidential run the mercurial John Charles Frémont, the "Pathfinder," who enjoyed a wide and colorful national reputation and whose name fit in admirably with the party's campaign slogan, "Free soil, free speech, free men, Frémont." That the erratic Frémont had no other visible qualifications to be president of the United States at one of the crucial points in the nation's history, that he had indeed several very serious disabilities—impetuosity, poor judgment, and rash opportunism, among others—did not make him less attractive in the eyes of the new Republican leaders, who needed a glamorous candidate with a name already familiar to the electorate.

To succeed the lackluster and ill-starred Pierce the Democrats selected the old wheel horse of so many Democratic administrations, "Old Buck," James Buchanan of Pennsylvania. Buchanan had nursed presidential ambitions for years; indeed, as secretary of state, his fever for the presidency had been only too obvious and irritating to Polk. Buchanan, while certainly not the attractive figure Frémont was, had the virtue (deceptive though it may have been) of appearing stable and safe, no inconsiderable quality in those anxious times. Besides, Buchanan had been absent as minister to the Court of St. James during the fiery debates on the Kansas-Nebraska Bill, so he bore none of the deep scars and bruises left on the major participants.

A third candidate in the race that fall was former President Millard Fillmore of Buffalo. Fillmore deserved the nomination of the Whig party in 1852 after he had succeeded Zachary Taylor, but he had been thrown over in favor of Scott because of Seward's unceasing animosity, as well as abolitionist fury at his signature of the Fugitive Slave Law as part of the Compromise of 1850. In 1856, Fillmore appeared as the presidential candidate of the nativist American party.

Roscoe Conkling now took to the hustings for John Charles Frémont and the Republicans. Conkling worked ardently for the Pathfinder; he undoubtedly earned much satisfaction from Frémont's victory in New York State by 81,000 votes.[28]

28 A. R. Conkling, p. 64.

In the nation as a whole, however, Buchanan swept in with a sizable electoral vote edge, although with less than a majority of the popular vote.[29] The presence of Fillmore in the race unquestionably hurt Frémont. However, the Republican party had been blooded, it had survived, it had in fact performed creditably. The country was given four years to ponder whether Frémont's wild indiscretion could have been worse than Buchanan's narrow and indecisive legalism.

On February 25, 1858, the Republicans of Utica nominated Conkling as their candidate for mayor, giving him 28 votes in the local nominating convention to 7 for his opponent. The Utica *Herald* said that Conkling "commands the confidence of our staid and conservative citizens, and will excite an enthusiasm in our young men that will make him victor at the polls by a goodly majority." [30]

The nominee, however, announced that he accepted the honor only with reluctance; duty alone forced him from his homestead and private concerns to the aid of his fellow citizens. Having made this conventional and customary bow to the concept of being "called" to the office, Conkling was ready to go to work. The party organ announced that Conkling had consented "to accept the nomination for Mayor, in response to the imperative demands of the Republicans of the city. . . . His name is creating a healthy enthusiasm." [31]

The campaign, of blessedly short duration (five days), was lively while it lasted, with the Democrats charging that Conkling would not have time to devote to the position. The Republicans retorted that, while indeed Conkling *did* have a large law practice, "he has measured somewhat the duties of the station, and will enter upon it with a determination to perform them and to perform them thoroughly." [32] Ellis Roberts, the young editor of the *Herald,* a close friend of Conkling, pushed hard for his election, and the paper thundered out salvos against the opposition.

When the votes were counted on March 2, 1858, Conkling had been elected to public office for the first time. He carried six of Utica's seven wards and received 1,865 votes to 1,501 for his Democratic opponent, Charles S. Wilson.[33] Conkling, it might be noted, was elected to office by the actual vote of the electorate on only four other occasions, and

[29] Buchanan 1,838,169; Frémont 1,341,264; Fillmore 874,534.
[30] Feb. 26, 1858.   [31] *Ibid.,* Feb. 27.   [32] *Ibid.,* March 1.
[33] *Ibid.,* March 3.

Chester Alan Arthur, first lieutenant of the machine. (The Bettmann Archive, Inc.)

Alonzo B. Cornell. (Collection of Regional History and University Archives, Cornell University.)

James G. Blaine, the "Magnetic Man." (The Bettmann Archive, Inc.)

James A. Garfield, during Civil War service. (The Bettmann Archive, Inc.)

Senator and Mrs. William Sprague, in happier days.
(The Bettmann Archive, Inc.)

William M. Evarts. (The Free Library of Philadelphia.)

Thomas C. Platt, as a young politician. (The Free Library of Philadelphia.)

Levi P. Morton, financier and political worker. (The Free Library of Philadelphia.)

he never ran for office in a constituency larger than Oneida County. His long Senate career, of course, was made possible by vote of the New York legislature.

One week later, on March 9, 1858 (the good citizens of Utica were refreshingly businesslike; within a span of two weeks they nominated, elected, and inaugurated their city executive), Roscoe Conkling was sworn into office. As mayor, he earned his $250 annual salary by serving as a member of the common council and functioning as the executive head of the city. Conkling's one-year term of office was not one of great moment or controversy—it was said that "public improvements were very much curtailed and the administration seems to have been conducted on an economical plan"—until, as usually happens, outside political factors made their influence felt.[34]

In September, spurred on no doubt by the fact that Mayor Conkling was the most likely Republican candidate for Congress, the Democrats, who held an 8 to 7 majority on the common council, called upon the mayor to publish the list of secret watchmen he had employed to expose a series of arsons. Whatever embarrassment they hoped to cause the young mayor exploded in their faces as Conkling, four days before the Republican nominating convention, announced that only three watchmen had been employed by the city, while he personally had patrolled Utica's streets at night with several other aldermen. The Democrats left Conkling alone for a while after that.[35]

While Conkling was doing battle with the Democrats in the sessions of the Utica Common Council, he was engaged in a more serious contest with fellow Republicans. Orsamus B. Matteson, a wealthy lawyer and president of the Bank of Central New York, was the incumbent congressman for Oneida County, completing his fourth term, but Matteson had managed to alienate virtually all segments of his party, inspiring grave doubts about his probity, having been censured by the House for his corrupt connection with a land grant bill for the Des Moines Navigation and Railroad Company. He was, by mutual and unanimous consent, retiring from the office. The selection of his successor, on the Republican side, narrowed to two Utica lawyers, Conkling and Charles H. Doolittle.

For the week or so before the county convention met in Rome on September 21, Republicans in the towns of Oneida County held their caucuses and chose their delegates. In this context, Conkling could

[34] Bagg, ed., p. 292.　　[35] Utica *Morning Herald,* Sept. 18, 1858.

not be stopped. He had been making the rounds of just such meetings for over ten years. Once again, he and his friends fanned out through the county, sitting down in the small rooms and large halls where the caucuses were held, telling the farmers, storekeepers, doctors, and mill-workers why Roscoe Conkling should be Oneida's man in Congress. As the towns and villages met and selected, it became clear that Conkling would be the nominee.

When the convention gathered, Congressman Matteson had a letter read reaffirming his intention to step down (a superfluous, but face-saving action). Thereupon Ward Hunt of Floyd, an able lawyer and an ex-Democrat, later to be a close friend of Conkling and eventually an associate justice of the United States Supreme Court, nominated Doolittle, and Dr. L. W. Rogers of Utica proposed Conkling. It was no contest; the mayor won on the first ballot, 62 to 23. In a story prob-ably more legendary than factual, it is said that some delegates wanted to nominate Conkling for his size and strength, to handle the fiery Southerners in the House. We may be sure, however, that such an idea would have been brought to the attention of any delegates who would find it appealing.

In Conkling's acceptance address, he indicated his awareness of the rift in the party's ranks by making a serious call for unity, pledging that "no Republican shall find cause to grieve for the vote he may cast for me." Three rousing cheers were given the nominee as he left the platform.[36]

It was clear that more than three rousing cheers would be needed to send Conkling to the House of Representatives. The Republican party, while not actually split, at least suffered from some lingering disaffec-tion, and the Democrats had nominated Judge P. Sheldon Root, a strong candidate who had been in the public eye for almost thirty years. The Democrats nationally were suffering from the bitter and widening split between Buchanan and Douglas, but no one knew what effect this might have on the race in Oneida County, where the parties were traditionally rather evenly divided. The Republicans' troubles mounted when Matteson, unable to abide the thought of Conkling suc-ceeding him, threw his support behind Judge Root, his former law partner.[37] This might have been disastrous in a "swing" county like

---

[36] *Ibid.*, Sept. 22.

[37] Interestingly, Root had been Horatio Seymour's law partner many years before, from 1834 to 1837; Bagg, ed., pp. 550–551.

Oneida, but Conkling by a prodigious application of energy was able to overcome it. Unfazed by Root's refusal to debate him, Conkling stumped around Oneida County night after night, speaking in hot, crowded halls to the farmers, mechanics, millworkers, and small businessmen who made up his electorate. Such an effort, customary in the eyes of mid-twentieth-century Americans, was rare in 1858. We should remember, too, that he was not motoring, but riding on horses, in stages, or, on rare occasions, on a bouncy, bumpy train. As the campaign neared its end, Conkling was even able to venture outside his district to help the successful gubernatorial bid of Edwin D. Morgan.

The Democrats charged that Conkling had failed to vote for Frémont, a patently silly attack, and accused him of being "an office seeker." The Republican organ gallantly replied, "This is so absurd with those who know Mr. Conkling that it will only be laughed at." [38] Meanwhile, the Republican press launched a violent attack upon the vulnerable Matteson, so discrediting the incumbent that his support of Root became a liability to the Democratic candidate.

On November 2, 1858, by a majority of 2,793 out of a little under 20,000 votes cast, Conkling defeated Judge Root, at the same time running over 200 votes ahead of Governor Morgan. Conkling had won the largest majority ever achieved for a local candidate in Oneida County. The Utica *Herald* crowed: "The county of Oneida feels proud of her newly elected Representative, and the more so for his sterling and unwavering devotion to Republican principles." [39]

Conkling had shown himself to be a tireless and talented campaigner, a rising star in New York's Republican party—but Buchanan's troubles with Kansas, and Yankee impatience with the insolent fire-eaters of the slave power, the Yanceys and the Rhetts, certainly had not hurt him.

The Thirty-sixth Congress would not convene until more than a year after Conkling's election. In the meantime, he still had several months left of his term as mayor of Utica. As it turned out, he had longer to serve than he thought. On March 4, 1859, when council met to canvass the returns of the recent election for mayor, both Charles S. Wilson, the Democrat, and John C. Hoyt, the Republican, turned up with 1,739 votes apiece. The city attorney, asked who was now mayor by the council, reported on March 18 that since the city charter provided

[38] Utica *Morning Herald*, Oct. 1, 1858.   [39] *Ibid.*, Nov. 5, 6.

that the mayor served until his successor was qualified, there was therefore no vacancy and "Hon. Roscoe Conkling is legally Mayor of the City for the present year." The unhappiness of the Democratic majority at this ruling can only be imagined.

The Democrats of the council, who had planned to elect one of their number to the vacancy they expected to exist, now found themselves stymied by Conkling's presence; they set about hounding him out of office. They embarked upon a calculated program of harassment, opposing and taunting him at every turn. That first meeting, on March 18, they succeeded in reducing to anarchy. But Conkling persevered.[40] He stayed on as Utica's chief executive, enduring the badgering of the Democrats, which tapered off as they realized that he would *not* be driven out, managing the affairs of the city as frugally as possible, and skipping as many meetings as seemed politically prudent. Finally, as the time came for Conkling to leave for Washington, he resigned. To the council on November 18, 1859, Conkling wrote: "I hereby resign the office of Mayor, and leave you with the hope that your future action may in all things redound to the honor and prosperity of the city." [41] In other words, he had done his duty to the city by serving and to the Republican party by keeping the mayoral office out of Democratic hands for eight and one-half months, and now he was going on to more important matters.

Roscoe Conkling, his wife, and his infant daughter Bessie left Utica on the 12:38 train for Washington on November 21, 1859, after a "large number of friends took leave of him at the Depot." [42] It could be said that in a figurative sense *he* at least never came back. He was physically present in Utica from time to time, but henceforth the nation would hear his voice, would indeed feel the impact of his personality. Utica would be on the fringe.

[40] *Ibid.*, March 5, 19, 21, 1859.   [41] *Ibid.*, Nov. 19.   [42] *Ibid.*, Nov. 22.

CHAPTER 2

ONEIDA'S CONGRESSMAN

The new congressman from the Oneida district set up residence at the Willard and took stock of his situation. To the natural strangeness of a new position in a new city was added the tension and ill-feeling engendered by slavery and sectional conflict. The House convened and Conkling was sworn in on December 5, 1859.[1]

Sectional virulence lost no time in asserting itself as the dominant motif of the Thirty-sixth Congress. The 109 Republicans in the House did not form a majority, as there were 101 Democrats and 27 Know-Nothings. Two months were consumed in choosing the Speaker. Throughout the long contest, Conkling supported the Republican choice, John Sherman of Ohio, but Sherman was unable to win sufficient votes from outside his party or his section. Finally, out of sheer weariness, the House compromised somehow on a new member, William Pennington, a Newark lawyer who had been governor of New Jersey almost two decades previously.

As the speakership fight was blowing up into a major storm, on December 6, Conkling apparently played a part in a near riot on the floor of the House. Thaddeus Stevens, the grim and bitter abolitionist, back in the House after six years' absence, asserting leadership over the Republican forces, stirred up the fight. After listening to a stream of insults and threats from the Southern hotheads, Stevens rose to tell them that things had changed:

All is right with them, for they have tried it fifty times and fifty times they have found weak and recreant tremblers in the North who have been affected by it, and who have acted from those intimidations. They are right, therefore, and I give them credit for repeating with grave countenances

[1] A. R. Conkling, p. 91.

21

that which they have so often found to be effective when operating upon timid men.

The Southerners muttered among themselves and then, as if to give the lie to Stevens's intimation that they were bluffing, Martin Crawford of Georgia led a half dozen of them toward Stevens. It is at this point, legend has it, that the brand-new member from Utica rose up, planted himself in front of the aged and crippled Stevens, and glared defiantly at the advancing flower of Southern chivalry. As the story goes, Crawford and his cohorts halted and then retreated to their seats. Stevens, to cap his triumph, then finished with, "That is the way they used to frighten us. Now you see exactly what it is, and what it has always been." [2]

Conkling's maiden effort as a speaker in the House came on March 20, 1860, on the unsuccessful claim of one A. J. Williamson to the seat from New York City then held by the spectacular Daniel E. Sickles, a Democrat. There was a dispute as to the return filed by the county board of canvassers in 1858, with the result that the state board had issued no certificate. The matter had been inflamed by Sickles' 1859 killing of his wife's lover, the son of Francis Scott Key, for which he was subsequently acquitted on the ground of temporary mental aberration.

Conkling spoke for about twenty minutes, primarily on the legal merits of the affair, defending the course of both the state board and of Williamson, the contestant, in bringing it before Congress. It was said that Conkling "stripped the case from all the fog with which it had become enveloped" with his clear and lawyerlike approach to the question. The New York *Tribune* said, "No more successful first effort has been witnessed for years, and with so little parade and preparation." [3]

The new legislator received more good press for his participation in debate on a bill for construction of a telegraph line to the Pacific

[2] R. Korngold, *Thaddeus Stevens,* pp. 102–103; *Cong. Globe,* 36th Cong., 1st sess., pp. 24–25.

[3] March 21, 1860; Conkling's part in the debate is in *Cong. Globe,* 36th Cong., 1st sess., pp. 1259–1264; Utica *Morning Herald,* March 24, 1860. It should be noted that Sickles kept his seat. He went on to become a dashing Union Army general, winning praise at Chancellorsville and criticism at Gettysburg. He was later a controversial minister to Spain for Grant, 1869–1873, returned to Congress many years later, 1893–1895, and lived till 1914.

Coast. Conkling's speech of April 12, 1860, in defense of the measure was called one of his "clear and compact, convincing arguments." [4]

A few days dater, on April 17, Roscoe delivered a long, carefully prepared address attacking the Supreme Court for its decisions, through Chief Justice Roger B. Taney, in the Dred Scott Case and in *Ableman v. Booth*,[5] a case decided March 7, 1859, upholding the supremacy of the United States over state governments regarding the enforcement of the Fugitive Slave Law. The occasion for Conkling's oration was a message from President Buchanan in the course of which the unfortunate chief executive advised Congress that Taney's decision had settled the question of slavery in the territories once and for all. This was a point that no good free-soil Republican conceded for a moment, and Conkling's speech was applauded by his party. His speech was strong but marked by what the correspondent of the New York *Evening Post* called "gentle courtesy," a rare commodity in a Conkling speech.[6]

Conkling started with good free-soil doctrine, saying that "with an unalterable determination that slavery shall never range this continent, there lives a hope that even in its abiding places it will wither and die." But the Supreme Court, he said, "asserts that every acre of the Territories is already the rightful prey of slavery. . . . My business today is with the power of the Supreme Court, not with its wisdom." He addressed himself to the binding effect of Supreme Court decisions upon Congress, a coordinate branch of government, and he said, as do many critics of the Court today, "Why, Sir, the infallibility ascribed to the Supreme Court makes the Constitution nothing but wax in the hands of Judges; it amounts to a running power of amendment." He then developed his point that "the judgments of the Supreme Court are binding only upon inferior courts and parties litigant" and that its decisions are "not obligatory upon Congress" but are addressed to "the discretion of Congress." Whenever Congress determines that a judgment is "subversive of the rights and liberties of the people, or is otherwise hurtfully erroneous," Congress has the duty to disregard it.[7]

Conkling's speech was praised by the Albany *Journal* as "a con-

[4] N.Y. *Tribune*, April 13, 1860. Conkling's speech, with an amusing colloquy with Stevens about the sixty presidential candidates in the Senate, is in *Cong. Globe*, 36th Cong., 1st sess., p. 1695.
[5] Also *U.S. v. Booth*, 21 Howard 506. [6] April 19, 1860.
[7] *Cong. Globe*, 36th Cong., 1st sess., app., pp. 233–236. Conkling's Court speech is discussed in C. Warren, *Supreme Court*, II, 347–349.

vincing exposure of the Democratic pretense . . . expounded in the Dred Scott Decision," and by the New York *Evening Post* as "a legal argument" and "an eloquent speech for other than legal men." The hometown paper, its editor partial to his friend in Congress, called the talk "an exposition of a great public question . . . from the more broad plateau of Justice and enlightened Patriotism." [8]

The Democrats could hardly allow Conkling to occupy the broad plateau of enlightened Patriotism all by himself, so on April 25, 1860, Congressman John W. Noell of Missouri in reply attacked Conkling for raising "on the floor of Congress the standard of rebellion to the decrees of the Court." He chided the young lawyer that "every man who has read the hornbooks of the profession ought to know that, when we enact a law, its validity and constitutionality must be determined by the Judiciary." [9]

The debate on the Dred Scott decision simmered and sizzled throughout the session. Conkling had made his contribution with a closely reasoned and ingenious argument against the Court's power, but his position was not the prevailing one in the time of John Marshall, or of Roger Brooke Taney, and the same position, advanced by latter-day politicians unhappy with Supreme Court decisions, does not prevail today.

Shortly thereafter, the eyes of the nation swung to Chicago, where the young Republican party was to nominate its presidential candidate and, in view of the wide and bitter split in the Democratic party, probably the next president of the United States. This assemblage in the immense temporary structure called the Wigwam was planned to be the culmination of Thurlow Weed's years of effort for his ally, William H. Seward. The time had come, so the theory ran, for the great New York leader, the espouser of a "higher law," the herald of an "irrepressible conflict."

When the balloting was completed on May 18, however, the party's choice was not Seward but Abraham Lincoln. Even Thurlow Weed could not control this convention. Conservatives felt that Seward's past inflammatory speeches showed a dangerous radicalism. He was deeply mistrusted in the pivotal states of New Jersey, Pennsylvania, and In-

[8] Albany *Journal*, N.Y. *Evening Post*, and Utica *Morning Herald*, April 19, 1860.
[9] Warren, II, 348–349.

diana, and, particularly in the last two states, where the new party had Know-Nothing, nativist antecedents, Seward was thought to be too friendly with the Roman Catholic church. Andrew Curtin and Henry S. Lane, the candidates for governor in the two states, toured the hotel lobbies working against Seward. After Pennsylvania's first-ballot vote for its favorite son, Simon Cameron, these two states voted almost solidly for Lincoln. They carried many other delegates with them, delegates who felt that for success in November the national ticket must help carry the October state elections. Seward, according to the men from the two key states, would drag the ticket down to defeat in October; losses in these two states in October would presage defeat nationally in November. Besides, the party had lots of candidates— Bates, Chase, Lincoln—who looked like winners. In addition, Lincoln's managers, led by Judge David Davis, made whatever deals or promises they thought necessary to pick up added delegates. Weed, boiling with frustration, was unable to combat this thinking, and Seward, the Republicans' most famous and respected leader, was regretfully jettisoned; the delegates nominated the lesser-known lawyer from Illinois.[10]

The next order of business was the unification of all parts of the party behind the ticket of Lincoln and Hannibal Hamlin of Maine. In Oneida County, this meant a great Republican rally in Utica on June 4. A good political rally was a major social event, frequently combined with other pleasant activities of a nonpolitical nature. The large crowd was very happy to hear from its Congressman, who said, "For six long months have I been in a city where political and sectional animosities and partisan hatred, such as the institution of slavery alone can engender, have poisoned the very fountains of good neighborhood, and led men, and even women, to forget the ordinary emotions of good feeling and courtesy." And before Roscoe worked into his glorification of Lincoln, he allowed himself a bow to the thought which many shared at the time, particularly in upstate New York: "If the question at Chicago had been who shall be President, instead of who shall be the candidate, beyond all question the choice would have fallen upon New York's illustrious statesman." [11] No doubt he was right. In Utica, it certainly did not hurt to say it.

But Lincoln was safe: if the presidential nominee committed no

[10] The progress of the convention is described in A. K. McClure, *Our Presidents,* pp. 155–162, and many other sources.
[11] Utica *Morning Herald,* June 5, 1860.

egregious blunders, he would carry state after state while Douglas and John C. Breckinridge split the normal Democratic vote. The Democrats were set on a course of self-destruction which must carry through to its end—the election of a Republican to the White House. (That this triumph of the new sectional party should then lead to a further result —severance of the Union—was openly discussed and advocated in the South.) Roscoe Conkling was rightfully more concerned with his own re-election; with all due respect to Pennsylvania and Indiana, Seward heading the ticket would have helped Conkling more than the man from Springfield.

Conkling deserved re-election. He had worked hard in Washington in his short period of time there, learning his way around (even if he did once complain of "all of these complications, these indirect, silent, invisible schemes, by which the floor is mortgaged and farmed out").[12] He was no firebrand, though he had to deny, a month after taking his seat, that he had delivered a challenge to Barksdale of Mississippi.[13] His major efforts on the floor of the House had been legal expositions of his point of view rather than inflamed partisan diatribes, which were all too common in that first session of the Thirty-sixth Congress. Although he was generally a follower of the grim Stevens, he was not an unremitting party-liner. Roscoe Conkling never submitted to anyone else's lead. In even his closest political association, with Grant, Conkling was as much leader as follower.

The Republican convention for Oneida County met at Rome on September 4, 1860, and renominated Conkling without opposition. His re-election campaign was not particularly noteworthy, but it was successful. As one of the more prominent young members of the House, he was called upon to make some speeches outside of his district, with the result that his effort in Oneida was a bit spotty. He had trouble keeping some of his local speaking engagements, and a number of good Republicans in towns throughout the county were disappointed not to hear their congressman (and best orator) on occasions when he was promised to them.[14] At those meetings, however, where Roscoe did speak, he was at his best, scoring the Southern fire-eaters, the

---

[12] *Cong. Globe,* 36th Cong., 1st sess., p. 1442, March 20, 1860.

[13] *Ibid.,* p. 439, Jan. 13, 1860. After Conkling's denial, Barksdale rose to corroborate him.

[14] He missed scheduled speeches, for example, in Clayville, Boonville, Waterville, and Lee Center; Utica *Morning Herald,* Oct. 18, 20, 24, 26, 1860.

spineless Supreme Court, the ineffectual Buchanan, and calling for Oneida to give a big majority to the Railsplitter from Illinois at the head of the ticket.

Conkling's opponent was the mayor of Utica, DeWitt Clinton Grove, the editor of the local Democratic paper, the Utica *Observer*. Grove's only apparent impact was to turn an unfortunate accident into the most interesting story of the campaign. It seems that on Wednesday night, October 31, a fifty-year-old blacksmith named Thomas Bates, apparently drunk, was put off the 8:30 train from Rome to Utica after an argument with the conductor; the train was a mile or two outside of Rome, near Oriskany, and Bates then wandered across the tracks and was struck by a train coming up from Utica. He died November 9. Grove circulated the story that Conkling, who had been on the train from Rome, had made some unkind remarks about Bates and then had him removed from the train, thus causing the poor man's serious injury and probable death. In light of Conkling's personality, the story would have had a certain plausibility. In any event, the Republican press promptly came up with statements and letters from all sorts of people who had been on the train (it must have been very crowded) and could verify Conkling's unimpeachable conduct. Indeed, according to the conductor, Conkling even offered to pay the man's fare if that was the problem. The Republicans managed to smother the whole affair with such a mass of laudatory material that any unfavorable implications were completely lost. It may even have been a net gain for Roscoe.[15]

The party organ was worried about Conkling's frequent absences from his district during the campaign and felt it necessary to call on "brother Republicans" to "give at least one half day to looking after the interests of Roscoe Conkling!" [16] There was little need for worry. On election day Conkling piled up a large majority of 3,572, more even than Lincoln's. As the *Herald* said, "Well done for Old Oneida." [17]

Roscoe Conkling would return to Washington for a second term, more experienced, older, and armed with a vote of confidence from his constituents. He would be serving with a Republican administration in which his old friend Governor Seward would be playing an important

---

[15] The Bates affair can be followed in the Utica *Morning Herald,* Nov. 1 through Nov. 5, 1860. The day after Bates's death the *Herald* charitably noted that he "had been conspicuous on many occasions in temperance meetings."

[16] Utica *Morning Herald,* Nov. 5, 1860.   [17] *Ibid.,* Nov 7.

role. It became increasingly apparent, however, that Lincoln's regime would face problems different in nature from its predecessors, the "doughfaced" Democratic administrations that tried, with varying degrees of success, to keep a lid on the slavery and free-soil controversies. This would be an administration faced with that most horrifying of all problems, well-armed sectional rebellion. As events in the South raced ahead of the ineffectual Buchanan during the long and agonizing interregnum, it was clear that Conkling would return to a Congress charged with helping the president conduct a civil war.

CHAPTER 3

REBELLION AND
CIVIL WAR

As the second session of the Thirty-sixth Congress convened in
Washington, the somber duty confronting its members was to attempt
in some manner to hold the Union together. The duty devolved upon
Congress because the tortured administration of James Buchanan could
no more preserve the Union after the Democratic debacle at the polls
than it could avoid the policies which produced that defeat. Buchanan's
administration was led by Southerners who hesitated not at all in joining the secessionist ranks, and the president, paralyzed by his own in-
decision, did little to stop the march of secession. Only the fortuitous
appointments of Joseph Holt, Edwin M. Stanton, and John A. Dix to
the crumbling cabinet, succeeding the departing Southerners, shored
up the administration at all. The president-elect, Lincoln, had no real
authority to act and little inclination to speak until he had the means
to bulwark his words. There existed great concern throughout the
land that the still untested Lincoln would not in any event have the
capacity for firm action. The long period from November to March
witnessed a national government rendered nearly powerless while the
states of the lower South seceded and seized federal installations and
arms.

Congress, however, took some initiative as Buchanan fussed and
fretted over whether he had the authority to take steps to protect the
Union and the government's property. John J. Crittenden of Kentucky,
a revered elder statesman honored for his prior efforts on behalf of the
preservation of the Union, presented to the Senate on December 18 a
proposal which he hoped would settle sectional differences in a manner
satisfactory to the South without yielding any basic interests of the
Northern states. The major feature of his compromise was a proposition

to be incorporated in the Constitution that the line of the Missouri Compromise, 36° 30', be extended across the territories to the Pacific, with slavery to be protected everywhere south of the line. This, interestingly, had been James K. Polk's suggestion in the closing days of his administration when the New Mexico territories were newly won, but it had been rejected in the Compromise of 1850, which was silent on the subject of slavery in the new territories. Climate and geography had been counted on to keep the soil of New Mexico free.

Two days later, on December 20, South Carolina passed its ordinance of secession, the bitter fruit of Calhoun's theory and years of inflammatory politics, and the crisis of the Union had truly come to pass. The following day, the Republicans in the Senate killed the Crittenden Compromise, on the advice of the president-elect. Lincoln recognized the proposal as a renunciation of the right ever to do away with slavery; while he was prepared to seek ways to abolish slavery gradually, if necessary, he would not yield on his insistence that it must be recognized as a temporary institution.

In the House, Roscoe Conkling, in a manner conciliatory and conservative, favored portions of the Crittenden Compromise, though he voted against a proposed constitutional amendment which would have guaranteed slavery in the South and in the territories for all time. Conkling had no illusions, however, that "anything could be done here . . . to arrest the revolution now prevailing in some portions of the country." Southern politicians had worked for years to turn their communities against the new party in the North, he said, and now, "ten thousand springs of falsehood and perversion have filled the very atmosphere with noxious vapors." [1]

South Carolina was out, while compromise efforts were just getting started. As the efforts at conciliation successively bloomed, withered, and died, and the president wrung his hands in the White House, the other states of the Deep South listened to the commissioners posted to them from South Carolina. On January 9, 1861, Mississippi seceded, followed the next day by Florida, and the day after by Yancey's Alabama, over some opposition. On January 19, Georgia's convention passed its ordinance of secession by a bitter 164 to 133; a week later Louisiana voted itself out, and on February 1, Governor Sam Houston was unable to prevent Texas from leaving the Union he had fought so long and hard to permit it to enter; Houston himself was then forced from office. With a month more of lameduck government in Washing-

[1] *Cong. Globe,* 36th Cong., 2d sess., p. 649, Jan. 30, 1861.

ton, seven states had already left. The Border States and the states of the upper South waited for Abraham Lincoln.

Buchanan, meanwhile, faced the vexing question of protecting United States property in the rebellious area. This was an issue he never did come firmly to grips with, as the Southerners seized forts, arsenals, post offices, and custom houses within their domain. Buchanan made a half-hearted effort to reinforce Fort Sumter in Charleston Harbor, and he worked out quasi truces for Sumter and Fort Pickens in Florida, but basically he left this problem for his successor.

Conkling scored Buchanan, charged with the preservation of the national defenses, for his course; to perform his duty, he said, the president "needed no courts to issue process and no marshal to execute it. Nothing was needed but firmness and integrity. Either one alone would have been sufficient; but he chose to leave the country 'naked to its enemies.'" Conkling painted a vivid word-picture of Buchanan, "petrified by fear, or vacillating between determination and doubt, while rebels snatched from his nerveless grasp the ensign of the Republic, and waved before his eyes the banner of secession and rebellion." [2]

The South Carolinians left Sumter temporarily unmolested, assuming that Lincoln would eventually order its evacuation. Thus, as the first Republican administration took office, the question of peace or war, of a consensual separation or forcible repression, focused on Charleston —the ancient center of secessionist theory from the day of Calhoun and Hayne, the seedbed and inspiration of the present movement which had sundered a great nation. All would watch Charleston to see if Lincoln would, as Horace Greeley urged, "let the erring sisters go in peace." After a month of consideration, consultation, and attempts at reconciliation, Lincoln took the step clearly foreshadowed in his inaugural address; he attempted the relief of Sumter, and Beauregard's subsequent bombardment and capture of the fort touched off the war. Lincoln would preserve the Union, by force, if necessary; the states of the upper South regretfully joined their slaveholding fellows in the Confederacy, and America was engaged at last in what Seward had once called an "irrepressible conflict."

Back in Albany, the legislature had to elect a United States Senator. Seward's term was expiring, and he was moving up to the president's cabinet. Though Seward was gone, his mentor Weed was still the power

[2] *Ibid.*, p. 650.

in Republican New York. With a safely Republican legislature, Weed would fill the Senate vacancy.

The old Albany newspaperman selected as his candidate for Seward's slot one of the leaders of the New York City bar, William Maxwell Evarts. Evarts was later to become one of the most prominent men in American public life, one who would cross swords on many occasions with Roscoe Conkling. He was not comfortable with politicians, and he blithely broke many of the rules of the political game. Probably Evarts would have been uncongenial to Thurlow Weed. In any event, Weed was never able to put him to the test, for the choice was not to be uncontested; Horace Greeley, the famous editor of the most famous newspaper in the United States, the prestigious New York *Tribune*, had decided he was going to the Senate. The old "firm" of Seward, Weed, and Greeley which had controlled the Whig and Republican parties in New York for a period of years had broken up; Whitelaw Reid said that Greeley "was very sore at being treated not as an equal and comrade [by Seward and Weed], but as a convenience to the machine." [3]

By 1861, Thurlow Weed had been in a position of political leadership for over thirty years, during which time his power over candidacies, patronage, and legislation had been immense. His Albany *Evening Journal* was scanned by activists of both parties for indications of political trends, straws in the New York political winds, and for the rise and decline of individual politicians. While the sidetracking of Seward at Chicago had been a severe disappointment and curb to his plans, Weed had no intention of yielding his powers to Horace Greeley—or anyone.

Greeley, who had started publishing the *Tribune* on April 10, 1841, as a low-priced, mass-circulation Whig daily, with the support of Weed and Seward, was long consumed by a desire for public office. Although he had written in 1841, "An Editor who is good for much *in* his profession will rarely seek to exchange it for an office," he spent years struggling for elective positions. In 1848, he had been elected to Congress for a three-month term to fill a vacancy and had immediately undertaken to reform the House and most of its practices, which very shortly made him the most unpopular man on Capitol Hill. Most members of Congress viewed him as a madman. Greeley, the preposterous-looking vegetarian, an odd genius with a great bald head fringed with

[3] R. Cortissoz, *Whitelaw Reid,* I, 200.

a ridiculous set of whiskers, considered himself called to public duty, though the public time after time turned him down for the offices he sought; but he kept on trying, to his ultimate ruin.[4]

Evarts, who had been chairman of the New York delegation to the 1860 Republican National Convention, was a tall, thin, bony man, with a large and prominent nose. A reporter once called him "by all odds the ugliest man known to fame."[5] Evarts, who considered himself a representative of "the better element" in politics, had no concept of the arts of public appeal—he was always taking unpopular stands on issues (as counsel to Andrew Johnson at his impeachment trial, for instance). Yet, as Weed's candidate, he should have been the senator.

The infighting was fierce in a Senate battle which was long considered an epic in New York political annals. A third candidate in the race was Ira Harris, a nondescript fifty-nine-year-old judge, whose chances were so slight that he placed himself wholly at the disposal of Thurlow Weed. The boss held Harris in reserve in case of trouble. For weeks before the Republican legislative caucus the canvassing was carried on with threats, cajolery, horse-trading, whispers, and appeals. The matter was not resolved by the time the caucus started, and the formal balloting increased the tension.

Greeley and Evarts seesawed back and forth on successive ballots, and as Harris's votes slowly dropped away and other scattered votes were attracted to the two major candidates, both their totals inched higher. As the ninth ballot approached, it appeared that Greeley was about to go over the top and obtain a majority. At this moment, Weed ordered the Evarts men to go over immediately to Harris, who still had a small nucleus of his own. On the ninth ballot, Greeley was contained, with Harris taking a slim lead. On the tenth, Harris was elected, Greeley was defeated, and Weed put the best face he could on things when he wrote, "Paid the *first* installment on a large debt to Mr. Greeley."[6]

Nevertheless, the Senate election demonstrated the existence of a

---

[4] G. Van Deusen, *Horace Greeley*, pp. 51, 185, 126–128. Andrew Johnson called Greeley "a sublime old child," p. 349.

[5] F. G. Carpenter, *Carp's Washington*, p. 26.

[6] Van Deusen, p. 257. See also Van Deusen, *Thurlow Weed*, pp. 262–264. It was said that when the word to switch from Evarts was given out, one of Weed's henchmen came to the dictator and asked him if he knew Harris personally and if Harris was safe. Weed is said to have exclaimed, "Do I know him personally? I should rather think I do. I invented him!"

major rift in the Republican party in New York and marked the end of Thurlow Weed's unchallenged control. The party was available for capture by someone who could fix upon the appropriate means.

The election of Ira Harris to the U.S. Senate in 1861 had yet another meaning. Six years later, when the young congressman from the Oneida district was to aspire to the same Senate seat, he would find it occupied by a bland and colorless individual with little political strength of his own. If either Evarts, with his sharp legal mind and outstanding oratorical ability, or Greeley, with the most powerful newspaper in the nation at his disposal, had been the incumbent, Roscoe Conkling might well have decided to stay in the House for a while longer.

An incident reported to have occurred early in 1861 provides an insight into the development of Roscoe Conkling's political personality. A delegation of three prominent Republicans from his home district came to Washington with the names of acceptable candidates for federal positions in Oneida County. Not unnaturally, the first person they sought out was their young congressman. When informed of the purpose of their visit, Conkling chilled them with: "Gentlemen, when I need your assistance in making the appointments in our district, I shall let you know." Whereupon his callers turned on their heels and fled from his presence, properly chastened, thenceforth to be his bitter opponents.[7]

The story, if true, illustrates a number of things. It demonstrates, first, how unpleasant Roscoe Conkling could be, and with what little apparent concern for the long-range consequences of such a course (though in this particular situation he was no doubt aware that his callers were interested in building up their own political base, not his). The story shows as well that he had by now developed a proprietary interest in his seat and did not intend to share any of the functions of it with anyone. In some districts, at this time, attention was paid to the rotation of congressional honors among party men; no one in Oneida was ever permitted to speak of rotating Roscoe Conkling out of his House seat. Finally, it gives a good indication that at the very outset of the war Conkling appreciated the power and importance of patronage. We cannot know for sure if he had a prevision of the vast burgeoning of the federal civil service immediately ahead, although from some of his speeches it can be inferred that he realized a full-

[7] A. R. Conkling, p. 120.

scale war would bring about extensive changes in the makeup and structure of the federal government. We can be sure that Roscoe Conkling intended to keep in his own hands the levers of power that federal patronage gave.

On another occasion observers witnessed him indulging in cutting sarcasm, at the expense of a colleague, from which there could be no conceivable gain other than self-gratification. Conkling stood up in the House and, for no apparent reason, said that he had read in the *Congressional Globe* of a few days before "a very plausible, fascinating argument, which . . . must have electrified the House, to say nothing about the galleries, when, in truth and in fact, I was here myself until the House adjourned on that day, and that gentleman did not address the House at all, and nobody made any such speech, or any part of it." Then "that gentleman," the Honorable Reuben E. Fenton, Republican from the Chautauqua district of New York, rose with offended dignity and pointed out that he had gotten unanimous consent of the House to have his speech printed, a practice not unknown then, although not as common as it is now. We will hear a good deal more of Reuben E. Fenton, and so would Roscoe Conkling. Such an encounter certainly did not endear him to the ambitious Fenton, though its occurrence indicates that the two had probably already begun to cultivate a mutual dislike.[8]

Although the Civil War was starting, Conkling personally was thriving as a prominent member of the party governing the United States during its most turbulent time. He did not go into the Army, though he surely could have had a high commission, and in later years he was sometimes coupled with his enemy Blaine as having been "invincible in peace and invisible in war." Yet Conkling had no illusions about the nature of the war to be fought, as his speeches show; he knew it would be bloody and dirty, with little martial glory. He knew he could be more effective for the Union cause as a powerful member of the House than as a target for a rebel sharpshooter. No one ever questioned his physical courage. Still, he marched to the beat of his own drummer, no one else's.

The congressman from Oneida certainly made a formidable figure when he got to his feet in the House chamber. He was very tall, about six feet three, erect and muscular, with wavy sandy-blond hair, a full pointed beard, and, falling across his broad forehead, a golden Hype-

8 *Cong. Globe,* 36th Cong., 1st sess., pp. 2260–2261, May 22, 1860.

rion curl. It was with this curl that political cartoonists for years identified Conkling; no matter how indifferently drawn a figure might have been, if it had a curl falling across the middle of the forehead, it was Roscoe Conkling. His attire verged on the exotic; he favored bright ties and fancy waistcoats and frequently wore light-colored trousers under a black cutaway coat. He took great care and pride in his personal appearance, recognizing that it constituted a part of his political equipment. Back home in Utica, although Conkling was still living in boarding houses, he and Julia were looking around for a proper home, one befitting an important congressman.

The Thirty-seventh Congress convened in its first session on July 4, 1861, to sit for little more than a month and to vote the administration the sinews of war. Lincoln wanted men and money, and he counted on his party's leaders in Congress to make sure that he got them. The president, virtually a newcomer to Washington, his single term in the House almost forgotten now, was a stranger to Congress and to most of its members; he depended upon the Republican leaders—and to a lesser extent, the War Democrats—to recognize the exigencies of the country's situation and to act accordingly.

In the House of Representatives, the president's reliance was necessarily upon the acknowledged leader of that body, the fierce abolitionist from Lancaster, Pennsylvania, Thaddeus Stevens. Tall, cadaverous, and crippled, Stevens conducted the business of the House with a brusque efficiency, only occasionally leavened with a dry, cutting wit. He was determined that the United States would fight secession and the slave power with all the force at the nation's disposal, and he planned to ensure to the administration all the resources necessary.

Stevens was aided in his domination of the House by the new Speaker, his colleague from Pennsylvania, Galusha A. Grow. Among the other Republican lieutenants of the Lancaster legislator were two transplanted Yankees from Illinois, Elihu B. Washburne and Owen Lovejoy (whose abolitionist brother Elijah had been shot to death in 1837 by a proslavery mob), flinty Justin S. Morrill of Vermont, and Conkling of New York.

Conkling took an active role in the shaping and molding of the vital revenue measures which the House considered and finally passed. His position was not one, however, of unquestioning adherence to the legislation as reported by Stevens. The initial effort produced by the Ways and Means Committee provided for a direct tax, apportioned among the states, bringing in $50,000,000. The basis of assessment was to be real estate, and Conkling, coming from a district with a considerable agricultural interest, was aroused: "I am opposed to a gigantic scheme of this sort . . . imposing so enormous a burden chiefly upon the rural districts, upon agricultural property, excluding entirely from its operation . . . the personal property of the country. I protest against taxing farms until everything else is taxed." Conkling then assured that he was "ready to vote all the money needed to throttle rebellion, to trample to death this painted lizard called secession," but he certainly did not want the farmers of the country to pay for the war alone![9]

Stevens, Secretary of the Treasury Chase, and the legislative leaders in both houses, including Conkling, worked over the measure until a majority was assured. The direct tax on land was scaled down to $20,000,000 to meet rural objections, additional tariffs on enumerated items were enacted to make up revenues, and a direct income tax was imposed. On July 29, 1861, Conkling spoke again on the matter of war needs and revenue measures, demonstrating that he had developed a realistic picture of the job ahead while many of his colleagues were still in the "On to Richmond!" stage:

I believe every gentleman in this House understands that war is not a question of valor, but a question of money; that it is not regulated by the laws of honor, but by the laws of trade. I understand the practical problem to be solved in crushing the rebellion of despotism against representative government is, who can throw the most projectiles? Who can afford the most iron or lead? Who, by mastership in managing finance, shall attain supremacy in the great grapple for the mastery going on today upon this continent?

Conkling went on to say that the most obnoxious parts of the bill as far as he was concerned had been eliminated and he was now willing to pass it, "trusting the Senate to scrutinize it as far as they can." He then voted "aye" with the majority which passed the revenue bill, 77–60.[10]

The congressman took little active part in the measures augmenting the military establishment of the nation, although he supported the ad-

[9] *Ibid.*, 37th Cong., 1st sess., p. 272, July 25, 1861.
[10] *Ibid.*, p. 327, for Conkling's speech. The vote is on p. 331.

ministration on them. Conkling strongly opposed a resolution giving a House select committee power to investigate any and all government contracts until the end of the Thirty-seventh Congress: "It is very gross for this House to assume . . . that not only one department of this Government, but all the departments of this Government are to be so managed that we are called upon to appoint a roving commission." [11] Such a position was curiously kind-hearted and trusting, an unusual one for any congressman to take, then or now, and it appears particularly incongruous in one who was to be for most of his public career a jealous guardian of congressional as opposed to executive prerogatives. The resolution was adopted anyway.

In one of the few nonwar subjects brought before the House, the New Yorker introduced on July 17 a resolution to appoint a select committee to consider the subject of a general bankruptcy law, "a dry, precise matter of law—a subject of some labor." The resolution was agreed to, and for the next year or so, Roscoe Conkling was considered the House's resident expert on bankruptcy laws. Conkling never did get a bankruptcy law drawn to his satisfaction passed, and in time his interest in the subject waned.[12]

On August 6, 1861, this early session of Congress adjourned, and the members went home, to watch the administration fumble with the problem of getting its armies underway, properly equipped and intelligently commanded, to assess the capabilities of Abraham Lincoln, and, most importantly, to learn what their constituents thought about the great events taking shape around them.

When the members returned to the capital in December for the second session, many months had passed, but the rebellion seemed no closer to its end. The nation had watched with mounting frustration as the days went by with very little indication of activity on the part of the Union Army.

This army, in the East, was now under the command of one of the strangest military figures of our history. George Brinton McClellan had taken command of the Army of the Potomac in late July, 1861, while Congress was still in session, and high hopes had been placed in the self-assured general who had done well in a difficult early campaign in western Virginia. By December, however, people were beginning to wonder about McClellan. He conceived his duty to be to develop the

[11] *Ibid.*, p. 168, July 17, 1861.   [12] *Ibid.*, pp. 129, 224–225.

Army of the Potomac into a strong fighting weapon and, at the appropriate moment, to hurl it at the enemy, thus destroying him in the vital eastern sector. Even McClellan's severest critics concede that he did a good job in molding an effective military instrument. He never could convince himself, however, that the opportune moment for the use of that instrument had arrived. He always saw a larger Confederate army over the hill somewhere between himself and Richmond. He held on to these delusions even when scouting reports indicated the contrary; Joseph E. Johnston, commanding the Confederates before McClellan, knew his army was in jeopardy if McClellan ever moved. But McClellan did not move. He persisted in building up his army, demanding more and more troops to match the overwhelming rebel legions that might fall upon him at any moment, and nurturing his martyr complex, a lone victim of the Washington politicians, the press, and the military establishment. He alone was destined to save the nation, and jealous, petty men were frustrating him in his efforts to do so.

As the public watched the army grow, as it felt the heartbeat of the nation pump faster with commercial and industrial energy, as its tax bills increased, it wondered why there were no battles, why the South was not driven to its knees. Finally, in October, a small, bloody, and disastrous engagement was fought at Ball's Bluff, forty miles from Washington. Brigadier General Charles P. Stone led a Union Army across the Potomac to a fiasco; the manner of the defeat, caused by stupidity of command, was felt throughout the North to be a disgrace. Large numbers of men were lost at the water's edge milling about looking for boats to take them back across to safety; some were drowned when their boats capsized and sank. Stone was later arrested and blamed for the defeat; McClellan's fatal lack of initiative contributed to it as well.

The members of Congress had been home, among their constituents, during McClellan's irresolute summer and fall; they had been close to the people when the dreadful news of Ball's Bluff—an inconsequential battle, but the only one there was—was reported through the North. Congress heard the troubled complaints of the nation, and the government at Washington would soon hear them also.

On December 3, 1861, the day Congress reconvened, Roscoe Conkling offered the House a resolution: "Resolved, that the Secretary of War be requested, if not incompatible with the public service, to report to this House, whether any, and if any, what measures have been taken to ascertain who is responsible for the disastrous movement of our troops at Ball's Bluff." [13]

The war department apparently decided that this congressional intrusion into the business of the army could be brushed away with little difficulty. A message was returned to the House that McClellan felt an investigation was indeed incompatible with the public service. The adjutant general, who prepared the answer, reckoned without Roscoe Conkling, who had informed himself on the subject, was concerned about it, and was not about to be swept aside by the echelons of the war department. Conkling, on January 6, 1862, insisted that the answer was not responsive to the question. The question, he said, asked primarily whether or not any measures had been taken, in relation to the battle. It was a matter more of method than of substance. Was the war department interested in digging out the mistakes of its generals and possibly learning from them, preventing repetitions? Of course, as Conkling worked into his theme, his rhetoric took off into the blue, as it was wont to do; the battle, he said, was "the most atrocious military murder ever committed in our history as a people." Conkling then rehearsed in detail the tragedy of the battle, with appropriate notice given to the gory and maudlin. His speech triggered a lengthy debate on the whole subject of Ball's Bluff and the ongoing conduct of the war.[14]

The importance of Conkling's persistent attention to this tragic but otherwise relatively unimportant encounter lay in the fact that Conkling's resolution, in conjunction with similar efforts in the Senate, led ultimately to the creation of a joint congressional watchdog committee to oversee the administration and the military as they fought the Civil War. The Joint Committee on the Conduct of the War for the balance of the conflict looked over the shoulders of Lincoln, Cameron, Stanton, the generals, even occasionally Gideon Welles and the Navy people; it offered comments and suggestions on what it saw; it made demands. It made a great many mistakes and quite a few faulty judgments. It was frequently irresponsible. Yet it furnished much of value, and it saw to the correction of many abuses. More importantly, the committee represented the people of the country, checking on the experts in a brand-new endeavor, in which it quickly became obvious that much of the expertise of the departments and of the military was designed for some other kind of arena, irrelevant to a great nation at war with itself. The simplest man in the street could observe the awful blunder-

[13] *Ibid.*, 2d sess., p. 6.   [14] *Ibid.*, p. 189.

ings of a Pope or Burnside and feel that somehow such men must be prevented from leading American soldiers. The joint committee was this feeling institutionalized.

Conkling busied himself with other activities which he felt would be useful to the war effort. On December 9, 1861, saying, "there is a multitude of harpies, which no man can number, preying upon the vitals of the Commonwealth," Conkling introduced a bill to subject to military courts-martial and punishment certain persons engaging in economic crimes against the government, running the gamut from speculation to bribery.[15]

The next day he offered a resolution asking the attorney general to report his views as to the best means of obtaining a retrocession of that part of Virginia formerly a part of the District of Columbia.[16] On January 14, Conkling opposed an appropriation of $35,000 for the U.S. exhibition at the London World's Fair. He felt that "we have something a good deal more important to do with our money. . . . We have a world's fair now in session on this continent. We are all on exhibition before the world." [17]

Conkling supported a measure to abolish the franking privilege for congressmen, holding that the availability of free mailing inspired all sorts of unnecessary publications by government functionaries. He said this placed a great burden upon congressmen, who had to get this great volume of paper out to their districts, and besides, no one ever read it anyway. Roscoe was chided by his colleague, Pomeroy of New York, who said that "he should represent a rotten borough instead of one of the constituencies of Yankees, who will always be asking questions about mouse-traps and everything else that concerns their taxes and their interests." Conkling meekly replied that he had only said "the franking privilege had made the mails . . . plethoric with public documents which I thought had not been read." [18]

In a number of ways, Roscoe Conkling made it clear that he was not enthralled with the idea that a congressman was supposed to take care of his constituents, as individuals, in Washington or from Washington. He was quite willing enough to legislate for them as a whole, but dealing sympathetically with individuals or small delegations making personal contact with him was even then, as it would always be, a dis-

15 Utica *Morning Herald,* Dec. 10, 1861.   16 *Ibid.,* Dec. 11.
17 *Cong. Globe,* 37th Cong., 2d sess., p. 332.   18 *Ibid.,* p. 258, Jan. 9, 1862.

tasteful and difficult chore, one he would quickly dispense with, if possible. One day, he complained that "in one way or other, while one hundred thousand people are entitled to the member's undivided time and service here, a few persons manage to employ, in the transaction of their private affairs, a large part of the time which belongs to the whole constituency." [19]

Whether it was getting books, looking up information, steering someone to the proper department, or even just being cordial to visiting constituents, Roscoe Conkling did not like dealing with human beings. He knew how to handle a crowd; he was an orator. But he confessed, on occasion, that he did not feel comfortable with individuals, even when he was sympathetic to their problems; with no gift for small talk, he simply did not know what to say to people. It is small wonder, then, that Conkling preferred the Senate, insulated from the people by the legislature, to the House, where people with all their problems and "private affairs" thought their congressman belonged to *them*.

As January of the second year of the war began to slip away, the House of Representatives considered a momentous bill, one designed to help the nation pay for the war but with serious implicit fiscal consequences. On January 22, 1862, the Ways and Means Committee, led by its determined chairman, Stevens, brought forth a bill proposing the issuance of $150,000,000 of "legal tender paper" directly by the government and to be given credit by government fiat. Salmon P. Chase, the Secretary of the Treasury, was not convinced of the soundness of the idea, although he concurred in the experiment, and a number of others felt it to be a dangerous innovation, one to which they could give no assent. Among them was Roscoe Conkling.

He fought hard against the measure. Aware of the doubts of Chase, Conkling on January 29 asked "whether the present Secretary of the Treasury is in favor of making paper a legal tender; and also whether he is prepared to recommend to Congress the adoption of that measure." [20] On February 3, Conkling proposed a substitute for the committee's bill, calling for the issuance of $500,000,000 of 6 per cent bonds payable in twenty years, at rates no lower than the equal of par 7 per cent stocks, together with a short-term, one-year issue of $200,000,000 United States notes, redeemable in coin and with no interest.[21] This was not really a satisfactory substitute, but Conkling felt almost anything would be better than going to a paper standard.

[19] *Ibid.,* p. 252.   [20] *Ibid.,* p. 549.   [21] *Ibid.,* p. 615

The next day, Chase sent the House a letter reluctantly approving the legal tender bill, and the weight of Stevens' whip began to tell. But Conkling continued the fight: the government's credit, he said, "consists of the ability and integrity to pay all debts and perform all promises with scrupulous exactness and punctuality. . . . Do we not know that we have no right to authorize the utterance of a dollar of paper, without accompanying it with a tax for its ultimate redemption? We do know it." [22]

As Stevens drove the House toward a vote on his measure, he took time, on February 6, to attack Conkling's proposal to issue the 7 per cent equivalent bonds redeemable in gold and turn these over to the banks of Boston, New York, and Philadelphia in exchange for bank notes no longer redeemable in specie. The Pennsylvanian said:

Sir, this proposition seems to me to lack every element of wise legislation. Make a loan payable in irredeemable currency, and pay that in its depreciated condition to our contractors, soldiers, and creditors generally! The banks would issue unlimited amounts of what would become trash, and buy good hard money bonds of the nation. Was there ever such a temptation to swindle?

He further proposes to issue $200,000,000 United States notes, redeemable in coin in one year. Does not the gentleman know that such notes must be dishonored, and the plighted faith of the Government broken? No one believes that we could then pay them, and it would run down at once. If we are to use suspended notes to pay our expenses, why not use our own? [23]

Conkling was on his feet again, joining in the last-ditch fight along with Justin Morrill and Owen Lovejoy; "I agree with some other gentlemen who said that this bill was a legislative declaration of national bankruptcy." After proclaiming the "French proposition about virtue—that it is the first step that costs," and predicting the future issuance of more and more paper, Conkling retired from the fight, voting in the minority as the bill was passed, 93 to 59.[24]

Conkling was to be a consistent battler for sound money throughout his public career, both in the House and in the Senate. His criticism of the inflationary course of American financing throughout his years in Washington was economically sound, and many of his warnings

[22] *Ibid.*, p. 633; John Sherman later wrote that "whatever may have been the constitutional scruples of Secretary Chase in respect to the legal tender clause, he yielded to it under the pressure of necessity." J. Sherman, *Recollections,* I, 274.

[23] *Cong. Globe,* 37th Cong., 2d sess., p. 688.   [24] *Ibid.,* pp. 691, 695.

were to prove quite accurate. In 1862, however, the legal tender device was probably the best to be initiated under the circumstances; America's supply of hard money was totally inadequate for the needs of the war, and heavier taxes would have seriously impaired necessary popular support for the administration's course.

Congressman Conkling did on occasion find more gratifying activities in the House than the defiance of a Republican administration and Republican congressional leadership involved in fighting the legal tender bill. On February 24, 1862, he introduced a resolution giving thanks to Generals Halleck and Grant "for planning the recent movements within their respective divisions, and to both those generals, as well as to the officers and men under their command, for achieving the glorious victories in which those movements have resulted." [25]

Conkling's resolution in the House represented the first public acclaim for Grant, the hitherto unknown soldier from Galena, Illinois. Although this resolution was produced by one who was to become one of Grant's closest political friends, its genesis obviously was a desire to recognize the generals, any generals, who had finally brought about some notable Union victories. From the form of the Conkling offering, it is apparent that Grant's name was thrown in with that of the more famous Halleck, whose considerable military reputation had not yet crumbled.

Conkling made himself helpful in other ways. President Lincoln sent a message to Congress on March 6, 1862, asking for a joint resolution offering aid to any state adopting a plan of gradual abolition of slavery. On March 10, at the president's request, Conkling asked leave to offer such a resolution: "That the United States ought to cooperate with any State which may adopt gradual abolishment of slavery, giving to such State pecuniary aid, to be used by such State in its discretion to compensate for the inconveniences, public and private, produced by such change of system." When objection was made, Conkling said: "This resolution is in the exact words of the President of the United States, as sent here with the message in which he recommends its passage. It relates to a subject in regard to which almost every member, if not every one, has made up his mind; and those who have not made up their minds will not have their conclusions settled by any discussion which may occur on this resolution."

[25] *Ibid.*, p. 930.

The next day, in spite of Thaddeus Stevens calling it "the most diluted milk-and-water gruel proposition that was ever given to the American nation" (he did not believe in giving slaveholders any recompense for the release of their chattels), the Lincoln-Conkling resolution passed the House, 89 to 31. Its ultimate effect upon the course of emancipation was small.[26] The fact that Lincoln favored Conkling with the task of introducing the graduated emancipation resolution naturally reflects favorably upon the congressman, but it is also a mark of Conkling's relative conservatism on the abolition question. This was a resolution the president would not dare to entrust to such fierce radicals as Stevens or Lovejoy, but he found Conkling to be less doctrinaire and more flexible on the subject.

During the balance of the session, Conkling took an active part in the consideration of a vast number of measures concerned primarily with the war effort. He had an enthusiastic, snarling run-in for a few days in late April and early May with two of his fellow Republicans, Henry L. Dawes and Elihu Washburne, over the committee to investigate government contracts. Conkling was still opposed to it, and particularly to the way its work was being conducted. Some harsh words passed on the floor of the House, and finally on May 6, Washburne apologized for "personal remarks and imputations on the gentleman from New York . . . I ask the House to forget that they were ever made." Conkling then said, "I am glad that reflection has induced the statement to which the House has just listened," and that if he, on his part, had wounded the feelings of any member, "I regret it." So much for formal apologies, but Conkling never spoke to Washburne again.[27]

Congress ultimately adjourned, of course, sending its members back home to get themselves re-elected. Since Congress had assembled, there had been some good news, almost all of it from the west. In addition to the victories at Fort Henry and Fort Donelson in February, the victory at Island No. 10 had cleared the Confederacy from the upper Mississippi, a hard and bloody battle (though hardly a Union victory) had wasted the Confederate troops at Shiloh, and Farragut's naval action had captured one of the great cities of the South, New Orleans.

[26] *Ibid.,* pp. 1149, 1179. Also discussed in Nicolay and Hay, *Abraham Lincoln,* V, 214, and S. W. McCall, *Thaddeus Stevens,* p. 216.

[27] *Cong. Globe,* 37th Cong., 2d sess., p. 1973. On Conkling's long hostility to Washburne, see Blaine to W. Reid, May 15, 1880, Reid Papers.

Even with the victories and the advances, however, long casualty lists flowed back to the loyal states. From action in the eastern sector the casualty lists were as long or longer; yet there were no victories to show for the effort. From Virginia came news of Jackson's spectacular campaign in the Shenandoah Valley against the Union generals Banks and Frémont, McClellan's defeat at the Battle of Seven Pines, and his inconclusive and generally disappointing Peninsular Campaign. In late August, the braggart Pope led his army into a disaster at Second Bull Run, and in September, Lee struck north through Maryland, although this thrust was blunted by the stand-off at Antietam. The Union Army was clearly no closer to Richmond, but the shock of death and disability spread through more and more Northern households. A lot of political fence-mending was called for; the populace had suffered through the loss of loved ones, through inflation and rising prices, through the exactions of the tax collector. The military defeats produced widespread war-weariness.

Roscoe Conkling was the principal orator at the annual fair at Trenton Falls, back in Oneida County, on September 18, 1862. He started by dwelling upon the duties owed to the country at this perilous time, to furnish men to carry on the war, to sustain the credit of the government, and to "appreciate the solemn nature of our political duty, and rightly perform it," i.e. re-elect Republican congressmen. He then moved into the more usual subject of such county-fair speeches, the great contributions and superior virtues of agriculture and its practitioners. It was said that his remarks were received "with great favor by his immense audience." [28]

Several days before the county convention, the *Herald* called for Conkling's renomination and, showing the direction of the wind of public opinion, even in "old Oneida," said that "Mr. Conkling among distinctive Republicans in Congress, is known as a conservative and not as a radical. While he goes with his party, he acts rather with the moderate than the extreme wing. When Lovejoy and Sumner and that class of men, hold a private caucus, our representative has not been invited." [29]

When the convention assembled at Rome on September 26, Conkling's nomination by acclamation was followed by an acceptance speech "even more pointed and ringing than usual." [30] The Democrats ran

---

[28] Utica *Morning Herald*, Sept. 19, 1862.   [29] *Ibid.*, Sept. 20.
[30] *Ibid.*, Sept. 27. Conkling's speech is printed at length in the *Herald* two days later.

against Conkling his old tutor, Francis Kernan, a formidable opponent. Even worse, Utica's most prominent citizen, his brother-in-law Horatio Seymour, was the Democratic candidate for governor, on a straight-out antiadministration platform, against General James S. Wadsworth of Geneseo, the Republican. Wadsworth, an uncompromising radical, had been nominated over the opposition of Weed, and his selection signaled the effective end of Weed's control of the New York Republican party.

The Democrats attacked Conkling's speech in the House on January 30, 1861, on compromise measures to hold the Union together, as an "incendiary harangue." Conkling, they said, had not really been interested in preserving the Union short of war. The Republicans retorted that "he went to the very verge of proper concession to those who were yet law-abiding citizens, and who professed to desire to remain loyal and faithful to the Union."

The opposition gleefully quoted the harsh remarks Washburne had made against Conkling on May 4, and all the Republicans could do in reply was to point out that Washburne had apologized for them two days later. More sinister, a group of Republicans more anti-Conkling than pro-Kernan, led by those whom the congressman had once rebuffed in Washington, moved over to the Democratic side to defeat Roscoe, working both overtly and covertly, and having considerable effect. Meanwhile, the Republicans were tearing into Kernan and Seymour with a ready spirit, on the basis of their opposition to the war and necessary war measures.

Some of his problems Conkling could do little about. His older brother Frederick had been a member of Congress from New York City in the Thirty-Seventh Congress. Most of the time the two brothers voted alike, but occasionally they disagreed. One such difference came when Frederick voted "nay" on a measure to enlarge the Erie Canal. This meant nothing in New York City, but in Oneida County, canal country, it was an issue which was to bedevil Roscoe throughout the canvass, with people getting the erroneous impression (helped along by the Democrats, of course) that Roscoe had voted against such a proposition.

The Republicans extolled Conkling for his reputation "as an opponent of all sorts of jobbery and corruption." They said that he "is a consistent and warm personal friend of President Lincoln," a trifle exaggerated, perhaps, but they could show that in the only instance where Lincoln wanted a specific resolution introduced—compensated emancipation—he selected Conkling to introduce it.

Conkling went to the usual large rallies, and in Utica he "spoke for nearly an hour in his happiest and most eloquent vein, holding his hearers spell-bound till midnight," after which he left the hall and spoke outside to those who could not get in. Even those who might vote against him, to protest the conduct of the war, were glad to wait for hours to hear their congressman orate.

As the day of election approached, the *Herald* warned against false Republicans who, out of personal pique against Conkling, would undermine the administration. "Their opposition to Mr. Conkling is personal in the lowest and meanest sense." [31]

When the votes were counted, Kernan had carried the county, 9,943 to 9,845; Conkling was defeated. This, in spite of Wadsworth's Oneida victory over Seymour by 481 votes. But the day was a dark one for the Republicans; Seymour was elected governor by 10,000 votes, and the Democrats made gains throughout the Northern states. The *Herald* disconsolately surveyed the wreckage in Oneida County:

Oneida County has swung away, we trust but temporarily, from her Republican moorings. Those who in other days have been active in the Republican ranks, yesterday were found active on the side of the enemy. Some of them worked openly for Mr. Kernan, and let the rest of the Democratic ticket have an easy course. Others of them, while pretending to favor the Republican ticket, were secretly assailing it in the most effectual manner. Add to this that men were told that the election of the Democratic candidates would stop the draft and stop taxes, that money was poured out like water for Seymour and for Kernan, and the causes of the disastrous defeat of yesterday are explained.[32]

The general dissatisfaction with the war, the killings, the defeats, the inflation, undoubtedly contributed most to the erosion of Conkling's prior majority. It must be admitted, however, that he managed to generate a lively guerrilla warfare against himself by disgruntled and unhappy former followers.

Throughout the third session of the Thirty-seventh Congress Roscoe Conkling was a lame duck, with some of the loss of influence that the term implies. The sessions of Congress were timed differently then than they are today. A congressional session was convened every year on the first Monday of December, sitting until its business was done or its term had expired. The third session of the Thirty-seventh Congress was called to order on December 1, 1862, while the initial sitting of

[31] *Ibid.,* Oct. 7, 21, Nov. 1, Oct. 29, Nov. 4.   [32] *Ibid.,* Nov. 5.

the Congress elected at the 1862 election did not take place until December 7, 1863—thirteen months after the election.[33] Thus, by the time Kernan took his seat, slightly over half of the period between his election and the next one had already passed. Roscoe Conkling did not waste that time.

The very day that the third session convened, Conkling introduced a resolution looking to the placing of gunboats on Lake Ontario and possibly the other Great Lakes, as well as establishing water communciations for warships between other waterways and the Great Lakes. Never again would there be any confusion in the minds of the Oneida electors about Roscoe Conkling's concern for the maintenance and enhancement of the Erie Canal.[34]

On January 7, 1863, he introduced his bankruptcy bill, for which his colleagues on the select committee were only too willing to give him all the credit. He said that "we are the only commercial state, I believe the only one in Christendom, without a system of bankruptcy." The measure was denounced by Westerners as a Wall Street bill, and it was tabled on February 3. An ambitious Republican in New York, though, could do worse than introduce bills denounced as aiding the Eastern financial interests.[35]

Conkling had another run-in with Fenton on December 11, 1862. Fenton offered a resolution directing the Navy to furnish a convoy for protection against the *Alabama* (the marauding Confederate warship built in Liverpool and the source of much friction with Britain) to any ships containing corn, flour, and other commodities "intended as a free offering by the citizens of the United States to the starving poor of England." Conkling rose indignantly to state that he had given notice several days before that he was going to offer a bill for the very same purpose. "I do not claim any patent for it at all," he boomed, as he demonstrated why he did exactly that, "but this, as I understand it, is merely a House resolution. . . . I suggest to my colleague that it will not answer the purpose he had in view at all." Fenton's resolution thereupon died, although Conkling's subsequent offering on the subject was defeated four days later.[36]

---

[33] This state of affairs, mandated by Article I, Section 4, of the Constitution, stayed in effect until passage and ratification of the Twentieth Amendment, in 1933.

[34] *Cong. Globe,* 37th Cong., 3d sess., p. 2, Dec. 1, 1862.   [35] *Ibid.,* p. 223.

[36] *Ibid.,* p. 73. Conkling's measure, defeated 71–46 after Owen Lovejoy objected that "if England can build an *Alabama,* she can send armed vessels for the purposes specified," was in *ibid.,* pp. 92–93.

Conkling fought another losing battle against the issuance of more paper money. This rear-guard action was not as determined as that of 1862, because it was clear that more paper would have to be issued and that the House would go along. Conkling's attitude was that of a Cassandra vindicated: "The experiment has not perhaps weakened the belief then expressed, that it would prove a capital if not a fatal error to cut loose from a specie basis and soar aloft upon the wings of unbridled expansion." He recalled his argument that the first step would lead to the next and the next, "that necessity would goad the Government from one issue to another." He detailed the 50 per cent depreciation of the paper already issued and asked "whether it is in any sense unavoidable that we should put out $300,000,000 more?" Conkling recited for the House the fate of the unbacked paper money of the Continental Congress in the Revolutionary War: "And what became of it? It sank so low that it was not worth a rye straw nor a rush; it was not worth a shilling a peck, despite all their enactments." [37]

Notwithstanding all the effusions of Conklinian logic, sarcasm, and rhetoric, Congress moved ahead in its preset course with the further issues of paper, determined to finance the war and leaving the consequences to the postwar period, when all manner of vexing questions would face the American government. With this last struggle behind him, Conkling bowed out of the House of Representatives, determined to return to the great stage upon which he had played a small but increasing part.

Conkling returned to Utica to rescue, as best he could, his law practice. His legal career, during his years in the House and the Senate, was necessarily sporadic, dwindling to virtually nothing when he was most prominent. Though he replied in 1873 to an inquiry "whether I practice law in vacation, etc. . . . . that I do," he really did not practice much. One of Roscoe's best friends later said that his political life, from the age of twenty-nine to fifty-one, "took the very heart and marrow out of his professional career," not only depriving him of "the wholesome discipline which his ardent and exuberant nature so much needed to compact his faculties and steady and clarify his judgment," but also "relaxing the habit of close legal reasoning." [38]

[37] *Ibid.*, p. 365, Jan. 16, 1863, and p. 1322, Feb. 27.
[38] Shipman, p. 79; Conkling to unnamed addressee, May 17, 1873, Conkling Letters.

Conkling did have a few notable cases in these years, even while he was in Congress. In 1861, he received much acclaim for his successful defense of Reverend Mr. Henry Budge, tried for the murder of his wife. The case was a sensational one in central New York, and its defense required Conkling to make a minute study of the science of anatomy, because success hinged upon the remote possibility of confuting the expert testimony of the physician who had conducted an autopsy four months after the death, originally labeled suicide. Conkling hired a New York City pathologist as tutor, procured a serviceable cadaver, and went to work to learn anatomy. The doctor later said that Roscoe absorbed in a few days what it had taken him thirty years of professional practice to learn, an exaggeration perhaps, but testament enough to Conkling's quick and retentive mind. With this new knowledge, Conkling was able to conduct a withering cross-examination of the prosecution's star witness, the doctor, destroying his testimony in a taut confrontation in which one slip by Conkling, one indication that he did not really know what he was talking about, could have ruined his whole defense and restored the doctor's authority with the jury. Conkling was sure-footed and his command of medical jargon was perfect; as a result his overpowering closing speech won an acquittal.

Roscoe was also able to procure a favorable verdict for another client, the publisher of the *Christian Intelligencer,* in defense of a libel action. The plaintiff, the author of a book called *Biblical Science,* felt that he had been treated unjustly by a severe review of his book in the *Intelligencer.* Conkling was able to get a disagreeing jury the first time the case was tried, and a verdict for the defendant the next time. He showed an encyclopedic mastery of the Bible in his defense, thus helping to overcome the plaintiff's contentions.[39]

While the displaced congressman attempted to take up the thread of his professional career, he made a major adjustment in his personal life. In 1863, he purchased a two-story post-Colonial stone house, a square gray residence dominating John Street and downtown Utica from its eminence in Rutger Park. The house was once known as "Miller's Folly," because of its remoteness from the village when old Judge Morris S. Miller started it in 1820. By 1863, the section was fashionable, and the entry of the Conklings and Seymours certainly enhanced its desirability. Here Roscoe Conkling installed Julia and his young daughter Bessie. Symbolically, perhaps, he also kept a room at Bagg's Hotel,

[39] A. R. Conkling, pp. 121–132; Scott, pp. 192–193.

downtown. The discreet estrangement from quiet, refined Julia had already begun. It was treated circumspectly, never announced, never really made final, but it just happened. The house in Rutger Park was never really to be his home; there was always someplace else—Bagg's Hotel, Wormley's or the Willard in Washington, the Fifth Avenue Hotel in New York City, the Delevan House in Albany—where Conkling was more alive, more vital, more in his own element, than he ever was in the genteel atmosphere of Rutger Park, where he was always in a sense a visitor at Mrs. Conkling's home.[40]

Though Roscoe made a living from the law, in late 1862 he ventured into cotton speculation in the Memphis area with his friend Charles A. Dana, soon to be assistant to Secretary of War Stanton. Each man put up $10,000, while a third partner invested his expertise in cotton. Dana procured letters of recommendation from Stanton to the generals commanding in the areas where he would be dealing. Expectations were high, but the firm was soon put out of business by a War Department ban on the cotton trade. Conkling was free to concentrate on getting back into Congress.[41]

There is a story told by Chauncey Depew of the New York Central, later a persistent gadfly and critic of Conkling, of a visit paid to him by Conkling and Ward Hunt after Conkling's loss of his seat. At the time, Depew was secretary of state of New York, his post not having been up for election in 1862, and Roscoe had apparently determined that the leading obstacle to his own renomination for Congress in 1864 was a certain Erastus Clark, one of the leading citizens of Utica. Roscoe asked Depew to appoint Clark a deputy secretary of state, in order to remove him from Utica. Depew agreed to do it, and Conkling allegedly arose and in his most ornate and orotund tones said, "Sir, a thing that is quickly done is doubly done. Hereafter, as long as you and I both live, there never will be a deposit in any bank, personally, politically, or financially to my credit which will not be subject to your draft." [42]

In 1863, Conkling mended his political fences. The Loyal Leagues

[40] Writers Program, p. 358; Utica City Directory, 1863–1864.

[41] C. A. Dana, *Recollections* (1963 ed.), pp. 38–39. Dana was one of those who wrote to Stanton that the trade was injuring morale in the army

[42] C. M. Depew, *My Memories of Eighty Years,* pp. 82–83. Conkling, in a letter of Dec. 11, 1863, to T. B. Carroll, said that the reason he went after the job for Clark was that the man was unemployed, impoverished, in frail health, and the sole support of a wife and five children. This does not sound much like a congressional competitor; Conkling Papers, New-York Historical Society.

of New York met at Mechanics Hall in Utica, and when Conkling was called upon for a speech at the close of the regular business, he responded with a one-hour effort, following which the convention "adjourned in the best humor." On September 30, he sent a message to a Union mass meeting in New York, scoring the recent course of Governor Seymour which led to the famous Draft Riots. He spoke at Union rallies at Oneida on October 24 and at Camden on October 31. In addition he agreed to serve on a committee of four for the district to facilitate the enlistment of volunteers for the army.[43]

In 1863, after notable and decisive Union victories, it suddenly became possible to see through to a successful termination of the war. The spectre of invasion firmly rebuffed at Gettysburg was matched by the protracted but ultimately successful siege of Vicksburg. The 1864 campaigns of Grant and Sherman brought victory closer. The war machine continued to consume huge numbers of men, however, and the North suffered under increasing casualty lists.

The name of the party was now, temporarily, Union rather than Republican; the split between War Democrats and Peace Democrats, most strikingly personified by Roscoe Conkling's brother-in-law Horatio Seymour, had caused the former to desert their old political home base; while they would hesitate to join the Republican party, they could with good conscience ally themselves with Lincoln in a party to save the Union.

As 1864 drew on, the president had several political worries to go with all his military ones. The Virginia campaigning was bloody and destructive (in one month in the spring Grant lost 60,000 men), and revulsion against the losses was spreading through the North. The siren songs of the Peace Democrats were finding listeners; four years and still no end—why not negotiate some kind of peace with the Confederacy? Lincoln was urgently concerned with the possibility of losing the presidential election to a Peace Democrat. On the other end of the political spectrum, the radicals were unhappy with Lincoln, unhappy with his pocket veto of the Wade-Davis bill for a radical reconstruction planned by Congress, unhappy with his reluctance to turn the war from one to save the Union to one to free the slaves, possibly just unhappy with the fact that Lincoln was not a vindictive man

---

[43] Utica *Morning Herald,* Oct. 21, 25, 31, 1863; N.Y. *Times,* Oct. 1, 1863. The Ninety-Seventh Regiment, from Boonville, was known as the Conkling Rifles.

and that his reconstruction would not be that of the South-haters.

The Union party at Baltimore in June nominated Lincoln for a second term, giving him as his running mate a War Democrat from Tennessee, Andrew Johnson. In mid-August, a group of radicals led by Congressman Henry Winter Davis of Maryland, Charles Sumner, Horace Greeley, and possibly even Salmon P. Chase, attempted to arouse a sufficient storm against the president to "force him to withdraw from the ticket." The conspirators were, however, turned down by several prominent persons from whom they expected help. Among these were Thurlow Weed, who said that his objection to Lincoln was that "he has done too much for those who now seek to drive him out of the field," and Roscoe Conkling, who "refused bluntly to sign their call." Greeley had tried as early as April to recruit Conkling for this effort, without any apparent success.[44] These unexpected refusals, together with the news in the first days of September that Atlanta had fallen to Sherman after the long drive down from Chattanooga, caused the radicals' effort to collapse; the malcontents were forced to unite behind Lincoln.

On September 22, the Union county convention met at Rome to select a candidate for Congress. Erastus Clark, deputy secretary of state courtesy of Chauncey Depew, moved Conkling's nomination by acclamation, but there was opposition. A delegate from Boonville "urged the nomination of some other man, on the ground that the interests of the party and the cause required it." He said that Conkling had not supported the administration in Congress and that "his appointments had been for private ends . . . to build up a personal party."

Conkling's friend Ward Hunt replied. He said that two years before, A. D. Barber and Palmer V. Kellogg (two of the gentlemen who had once visited Conkling in Washington to talk about appointments) "from personal and interested motives only" had "conspired by corrupt means, by the use of money, to defeat him." Hunt defended Conkling on the question of appointments and further, he said, Conkling did not even want to run again, really. Then, in a gesture bearing all the earmarks of a Conklinian ploy, he pulled out a letter from the president, in answer to one of his own, saying "that I am for the regular nominee in all cases; and that no one could be more satisfactory to me as the nominee in that District, than Mr. Conkling. I do not mean to say

<hr>

[44] Nicolay and Hay, IX, 366–367; letters of Greeley to Conkling, April 5, 11, 1864, Greeley Papers, New-York Historical Society.

there are not others as good as he is, in the District; but I think I know him, to be at least good enough."

After this, a vote was taken, with Conkling winning 77 votes to 8 for Charles H. Doolittle. The surprises were not yet over, however. Roscoe entered and made a speech declining the honor, saying, "My private affairs and professional business were too far destroyed during my past service in Congress, not to admonish me that I can ill afford now to re-enter public life. . . . My interest and inclination are so much averse to a continuance in political life, that you must allow me to retire."

The nomination was then reaffirmed by acclamation, showing incidentally that Conkling and his friends had such firm control of the convention that there was no chance of his declination being taken seriously, and many of the delegates crowded around Roscoe, insisting that he be the candidate. After a little more of this, insuring more solid party backing, Conkling came back on and agreed to bow to the requirements of his friends and run.[45]

The Utica *Herald* later declared that it was two years of misrepresentation that Lincoln was opposed to Conkling "which induced inquiry of Mr. Lincoln, and it was false statements concerning the correspondence which brought it out at the convention." Whatever it was, the very fact of the letter, dated August 16, would appear to be a clear indication that Lincoln shared no apprehension that Conkling was involved in the radical cabal against him.[46]

The Democrats unanimously renominated Francis Kernan, and the stage was set for a repeat of the 1862 election. There were differences, however. Sherman's capture of Atlanta, Sheridan's victories in the Shenandoah Valley, Grant's strangulation of Lee's Army of Northern Virginia—all these were plus factors for Conkling, in contrast to the handicap he had borne in 1862 compounded of McClellan's inactivity, military losses, and the draft.

Conkling was left free to concentrate on his old mentor, the incumbent congressman. He scoffed at "the party and press who must scowl and grumble while loyal men celebrated, whose success depended upon

[45] Utica *Morning Herald*, Sept. 23, 1864.

[46] *Ibid.*, Sept. 30. Samuel Eliot Morison, in his *Oxford History of the American People* (New York: Oxford University Press, 1965), p. 693, names Conkling as a conspirator against Lincoln's renomination. Yet Conkling told Henry Raymond on May 25 that upstate sentiment was almost unanimously with Lincoln; F. Brown, *Raymond of The Times*, pp. 250–251.

defeat in the field." It was an outright struggle of support for the administration against the Peace Democrats. Conkling and Kernan spelled out the issue clearly in Oneida, and on the state-wide level Reuben E. Fenton made the issue clear in his campaign for governor against the incumbent, Horatio Seymour, who had been for two years the most articulate and influential opponent of President Lincoln's course. Fenton, a former Democrat, had stayed clear of the sniping and backbiting of the Weed-Greeley guerrilla warfare, and he went into the campaign with a reasonably united party behind him, though he had not been the choice of the radicals for the nomination. They, along with Roscoe Conkling, had wanted Wadsworth again, but the latter had the misfortune to get himself killed in the Wilderness in May.[47]

Conkling toured his county as he had not done two years before; he visited nearly every hamlet and crossroads in Oneida as well as covering the larger towns and Rome and Utica. He spoke out for the Lincoln-Johnson ticket, recited in his own inimitable style his record of support for the president, and blasted Kernan for his obstruction and his encouragement of the forces of secession.

A few days before the election, the Utica *Observer* charged that the Conkling people were trying to stir up prejudice against Kernan's Catholicism. The *Herald* replied that no one had mentioned it before and the Democrats were trying to pick up Catholic votes. The *Observer* again trotted out the Washburne diatribe at Conkling in 1862, and the *Herald* responded again with Washburne's apology. Conkling worried that the Democrats and their allies would have more money available and that this might hurt. Amid such customary electioneering, the campaign ground to a halt as election day approached.[48]

When the votes were tallied, it became apparent relatively early in the evening that Conkling had reclaimed his seat. By nine o'clock, Roscoe had launched into a two-hour speech for his followers, to "utterly indescribable" applause. Then he was serenaded by two thousand supporters with Chinese lanterns and a band outside his rooming house,

[47] Utica *Morning Herald*, Sept. 26, 1864. After Wadsworth's death, Conkling's choice was General John A. Dix. See Conkling to Henry Raymond, Sept. 15, 1864, and C. A. Dana to Raymond, July 21, 1864, Jones Papers; and Conkling to Greeley, April 25, 1864, Greeley Papers, New York Public Library; and Greeley to Conkling, April 26, 1864, Greeley Papers, New-York Historical Society; N.Y. *Times*, Sept. 7, 8, 1864.

[48] Utica *Morning Herald*, Oct. 24, 22, Nov. 1, Sept. 26, 1864; letter, Conkling to S. Draper, Oct. 27, 1864, Conkling Letters.

so he gave another speech "in a hoarse voice." [49] Conkling had won the election by a majority of 1,150 votes.

Elsewhere, in contrast to the gloomy 1862 elections, it was a glorious evening for the Republican, or Union, party. Abraham Lincoln carried the state of New York over his Democratic opponent, the reluctant George B. McClellan, by 6,749 votes, and the spread of his nation-wide 400,000 majority gave him a lopsided victory in electoral votes. Fenton was now governor-elect of New York, ousting Seymour with a majority of 8,293. The Union party won the state senate in New York and comfortably carried the assembly. And the New York con-gressional delegation, the largest in the nation, in the Thirty-ninth Congress would consist of twenty Unionists and only twelve Demo-crats. In this group would be the re-elected Roscoe Conkling, with "a majority which proves the confidence of the county in his integrity, the respect entertained for his ability, and the popular determination to maintain a man who does not allow himself to be used by lobbyists and schemers." [50]

It was now Conkling's turn to watch the months pass by while he waited until the following December to take his seat. These months were packed with momentous events. Shortly after the election, Sher-man cut loose from his lines of communication stretching back to Ten-nessee, disappeared from the view of the Northern public, and started his march from Atlanta to the sea, cutting a wide swath of devastation across Georgia. Hood's army was all but crushed by the Union armies of Schofield and Thomas at Franklin and Nashville. The unceasing pressure of the Army of the Potomac brought Lee's army near the breaking point, and on March 4, 1865, with victory at last in sight, Abraham Lincoln swore the oath of the presidential office for the second time, offering "with malice toward none; with charity for all . . . to bind up the nation's wounds."

As March passed into April, Lee's desperate army broke out of Richmond, heading west in an unsuccessful attempt to move around Grant's forces and go south by rail. Soon nearly surrounded, Lee on April 9 surrendered his army to Grant at Appomattox Court House, and the few remaining Confederate commands followed his lead. North-

[49] Utica *Morning Herald,* Nov. 10, 1864.
[50] H. A. Stebbins, "Political History," p. 45; Utica *Morning Herald,* Nov. 9, 1864.

ern joy was turned to deepest sorrow, however, as Booth's bullet cut down Lincoln within the week, leaving the United States government, staunchly Republican—whatever the temporary label—and hostile to the vanquished but unrepentant South, in the hands of a Southern Democrat. Andrew Johnson was a long distance, politically, emotionally, and socially, from the Yanceys, Rhetts, Davises, Ruffins, and Cobbs who epitomized the Southern Democracy before the war. The Republican politicians of the North, however, were to discover rather quickly and to their surprise that Andrew Johnson was no radical Republican either. He may have been the one person in the nation most unsuited for the position at that particular time, especially given his own distinctive personality.

Back in Utica, on the night of April 3, a great and spontaneous outpouring of people gathered in Baggs Square to celebrate the news of Lee's pull-out from Richmond and its capture by the Union Army. "Loud calls were made for Roscoe Conkling," the press reported, but this time the citizens were denied the pleasure of an oration; the congressman-elect was out of town. He was in Washington, and very shortly in Richmond. The pot of gold at the end of the rainbow for four long, bloody years, the erstwhile Confederate capital drew important visitors like a magnet after its fall, and Conkling was one of the first, arriving on April 5, accompanying Charles Dana on a fact-finding visit ordered by Stanton.[51]

A few nights later, on April 14, at about the same time that Abraham Lincoln was heading toward Ford's Theatre, the mayor of Utica named Conkling to a committee of eminent citizens to plan Utica's great celebration of the war's end, set for April 20. The next morning, in shock at the news of the president's death, the committee disbanded. As part of a much sadder assignment, Conkling found himself head of a committee of Utica's leaders, including the president's old adversary, his brother-in-law Seymour, to accompany the train bearing Lincoln's remains back to Springfield as it covered the distance from Albany to Utica on April 26. Though Conkling was not granted his request that the train stop in the city for longer than the scheduled twenty minutes, the loyal citizens of Utica took the occasion to pay their respects.[52]

Conkling must have tried to recollect whatever he could of the blunt-

[51] Dana, pp. 229–230.
[52] Utica *Morning Herald*, April 4, 11, 15, 16, 26, 27, 1865.

talking Tennesseean who was now to be president, from the days in the early part of the war when Andy Johnson had been a heroic figure around Washington because he stayed on when almost all the other Southerners had departed to the Confederacy. Almost certainly, though, Conkling could have had only a dim acquaintance with Johnson, and the chief executive must have appeared to him as an unknown quantity.

Powerless to participate in the large events at Washington before December, Roscoe Conkling involved himself in central New York in a matter destined to have ramifications far beyond anyone's conceptions. On April 4, 1865, Major John A. Haddock, the acting assistant provost marshal general for western New York and a close associate of General James B. Fry, the provost marshal general, was placed under arrest at Elmira. This was a result of a noisome scandal which had been developing in the region as a series of collusive conspiracies between the provost marshal's office and "bounty brokers" gradually became public knowledge. The provost marshal was responsible for recruiting and for administering the draft, and his office was bound to be vastly unpopular even if administered properly. From Elmira and its environs, Haddock ran his office in a disgraceful fashion, with false quotas, inflated payments to certain favorites, uncertainties, and deceptions, and he did not quite make it through to the end of the war.

Stanton and his assistant secretary, Dana, selected Conkling as special counsel to prosecute Haddock. There were some efforts on the part of Conkling's friends later to say that he took the job reluctantly, but this contention does not really bear up under scrutiny, nor need it. It was a job that needed doing, and Conkling performed it with great ability. He had been interested for some time in the operation of the provost marshal's office in his area; he had on a number of occasions protested the acts of its agents, clashing with General Fry and with Haddock.[53]

The court-martial of Haddock began at Elmira in May, 1865, and lasted four months. Some said that Conkling was almost too eager for a conviction. However, in his summation speech, he said: "Give me a certificate of my zeal, that I may leave it as a legacy to my children; and bid them say of me, 'He did his utmost to gibbet at the crossroads of public justice all those who, when war had drenched the land with

[53] A. R. Conkling, pp. 217–218; Utica *Morning Herald,* April 7, 1865.

blood and covered it with mourning, parted the garment of their country among them, and cast lots upon the vesture of the Government, even while they held positions of emolument and trust.' " [54]

Through Conkling's efforts, Haddock was convicted and fined $10,-000. This outcome pleased the congressman-elect, but he brooded over the fact that Fry, the man he felt was really responsible for the disgrace at Elmira, was not touched. He would bide his time, and James B. Fry's turn would come. When it did, the unexpected developments would shake the Republican party for years.

[54] A. R. Conkling, pp. 242–243.

CHAPTER 4

BLAINE THE FOE

In December 1865, the new Congress convened. Roscoe Conkling had not been forgotten during his enforced absence; in a move indicative of the high regard in which Thaddeus Stevens held him, Conkling was named to the Ways and Means Committee, "by common consent the highest ranking committee in the House."[1] A colleague on the committee was an easy-going, pious, and somewhat unctuous ex-general from Ohio, James Abram Garfield, starting his second term in the House. Another second-termer with whom Roscoe was to become more familiar was a former newspaperman representing a district in Maine, James Gillespie Blaine. Other interesting newcomers included William B. Allison of Iowa and a former soldier from Ohio named Rutherford Birchard Hayes (though Hayes remained fairly obscure throughout his term). The older group of politicians, the ones who had been unable to prevent a fratricidal war, were gradually passing from the picture; there was a new, younger element that would make the future headlines.

On the first day of the session, December 5, Roscoe Conkling offered a resolution, asking the Committee on Military Affairs to determine whether the office of provost marshal general "cannot now advantageously be dispensed with." The House routinely approved the resolution and passed on to other business. But Conkling had served his notice that he was not yet through with General Fry.[2]

Not only was Conkling a member of the Ways and Means Committee, but now the leadership had him named to the newly created Joint Committee on Reconstruction. For the Congress, while not very unified on how to bring about the reunion of seceded states, was very

[1] L. Sage, *William Boyd Allison*, p. 76.
[2] *Cong. Globe*, 39th Cong., 1st sess., p. 9.

definite on one matter: Congress was going to do it, not Andrew Johnson.

The new president attempted to present Congress with a *fait accompli* when it convened in December. Andrew Johnson was either foolish or naive or both; he clearly had not been paying attention to the rumbles of congressional discontent about postwar planning while Lincoln was alive. He ignored the Wade-Davis Bill and the feelings it represented and plunged ahead on his own. He had been busy during those months since his accession, and he felt that Reconstruction had by December been largely accomplished under *his* aegis. Johnson had put into effect his theory that the Southern states need only elect governments loyal to the Union to be eligible for restoration to all the rights of statehood. The South, baffled and stunned in its defeat, had no alternative to accepting Johnson's plan as the considered opinion of the national government, though its leniency was startling. The president repeated many times that "treason is a crime and must be made odious," but his demands upon the South were so few as to belie his words. The period between the end of the war and the convening of Congress was the crucial one, for during this time the prostrate South would have doubtless complied with whatever terms its conqueror laid down. When no real terms were forthcoming, Southern spirit revived, and an air of tentative defiance took shape. By the time Congress met, all the Southern states *had* reorganized under the Johnson plan, even to the point of electing their senators and representatives to Congress, many of whom were ex-Confederate officers or prewar proslavery congressmen. The Republicans controlling the Thirty-ninth Congress could hardly have been expected to welcome their erring brothers back just as if the years since 1861 had never passed. In retrospect, though they may have been misled, Southerners should have seen that they were courting trouble. Not only did they elect to Congress men who *had* to be unacceptable to the North, they also passed a series of laws—the famous "black codes"—which, no matter how necessary they may have appeared in the South, could only appear to the North as efforts to reimpose slavery in all but name upon the freedmen.

The radicals, those Republicans who favored stern treatment of the South to achieve the changes in Southern society necessary to give the freedman his place, were far from a majority in Congress or the public at large. The majority was composed of men unsure of how to treat the conquered South, men who were not implacable adversaries of the

Southern people, but who wanted some assurances that the aims of the war, hazily defined though they may have been, were not to be thrown away in the rush to normalize relations after the fighting stopped. This majority was not prepared for an influx of swaggering ex-rebels or the reinstitution of some form of serfdom over the blacks.

The Joint Committee on Reconstruction, sometimes called the Committee of Fifteen, which was to deal with all questions of the reestablishment of the seceded states in the Union, originally included a majority of such relatively conservative men among its members. Its chairman, the eminent Senator William Pitt Fessenden of Maine, was one, and so was Roscoe Conkling of New York. There were three Democrats (to twelve Republicans) on the committee, but there were also a number of convinced radicals, such as Jacob Howard, a senator from Michigan, George S. Boutwell of Massachusetts, George Williams of Oregon, and Stevens.

The committee met almost daily for many months after its establishment, taking voluminous testimony on conditions in the South; during this period the president's unyielding resistance to all congressional initiatives, combined with the intemperate tone of many of his utterances, contrived to drive away from him many who had fully expected to support his positions.

The violence of the radical reaction against Johnson was probably increased by the initial radical assumption that Johnson was one of them, signified by the exclamation of Senator Ben Wade of Ohio when he and his fellows met with the president shortly after the assassination. "Johnson," said Wade, "we have faith in you. By the gods, there will be no trouble now in running the government." What Wade and the radicals had failed to understand was that they and Johnson were united on only a very few points: the preservation of the Union against rebellion, support of the Thirteenth Amendment, and detestation of the planter aristocracy of the South. Beyond these areas, however, all was in conflict, and the wartime coalition quickly broke apart.[3] As the Southern states proceeded to elect their prewar or wartime leaders, as they passed their "black codes" to eliminate the bone and marrow of freedom from the emancipated slaves, and as Johnson gave his sanction to their actions, by recognition and by wholesale pardons of rebel leaders—so did the assumption of congressional leadership over Reconstruction become more certain. The president's unwavering po-

[3] K. M. Stampp, *Era of Reconstruction,* pp. 52–53.

sition that Congress had no right to legislate relative to the Southern states while they were unrepresented was equivalent to a total abdication of any presidential control over Reconstruction.

The theoretical justification for the varying courses advocated by the president and congressional leaders rested on differing ideas of what the ordinances of secession passed in 1861 had legally accomplished. Johnson's constitutional theory of secession was that the Southern states had never really been out of the Union and therefore needed only to elect governments recognizing their adherence to the United States; this would restore them to their rightful places in the Union, and that would be the end of that. It was this theory which the president applied during 1865 before Congress convened, and he held to it with unyielding rigidity thereafter.

The radicals had different ideas on what had happened in those dark days of early 1861. Thaddeus Stevens took the position that secession had been accomplished, that the Confederacy had been treated as a foreign power during the war with all the rights of a belligerent, and that the Southern states were now "conquered provinces," subject to whatever terms the victors chose to impose. Senator Charles Sumner of Massachusetts professed a "state suicide" theory, not quite as extreme as Stevens's in principle, but differing little in the practical outcome of congressional rights. His idea was that the enactment of an ordinance of secession extinguished a state government, which then reverted to the status of a territory. A territory, of course, could not become a state until it complied with such regulations as Congress might enact, at such time as Congress chose to grant statehood. At this point in the Sumner theory, the Southern states were in roughly the same position as the "conquered provinces" of Thaddeus Stevens, though not subject to the confiscations which Stevens desired.

The theoretical position which came to be accepted by a majority of Congress was enunciated by Congressman Samuel Shellabarger of Ohio, as well as by Chief Justice Chase. This theory held that secession was impossible and therefore void but that some states could lapse from the guaranteed republican form of government. When this happened, Congress was then entitled to take jurisdiction over the lapsed state and prescribe the steps for reinstating a proper government. This was the position subscribed to by most of the more conservative members, including Roscoe Conkling. In any event, no matter what the theory, Congress would call the tune for the restoration of the South, and Andrew Johnson would dance to it or he would not dance at all.[4]

It should be kept in mind, however, as we consider the period of Reconstruction that the victorious North, for all the bellicose and heated oratory of the radical Republicans, imposed an astonishingly mild peace upon its rebellious sisters. Seldom in world history do examples occur to match the leniency shown by the Union after a protracted, bloody civil war. There were no treason trials or reparations, only short-lived restrictions on the political rights of even the Confederate leaders, a military occupation which was relatively ineffective, and an ultimately futile effort to insure the freed black man the rights of citizenship. Indeed, a case can be made that had Andrew Johnson exacted somewhat stiffer terms in the summer of 1865 the South would have complied willingly, the North would have been satisfied, and the unhappy developments of the later military Reconstruction would have been avoided.

While the former Confederate states were still out of the Union, however, the Committee on Reconstruction had an urgent piece of business to transact, a matter of legislation that we know today as the Fourteenth Amendment. The purpose of this amendment was to set forth constitutional terms for readmission to the Union and to protect the rights of the freedmen. It served ultimately to engraft into the Constitution a definition of citizenship which would include the liberated slave, together with a protection against passage by any state of discriminatory laws, and an exclusion of blacks from the basis of representation in Congress in any state which barred them from voting.

Conkling's role in congressional affairs at this time was a curious one. He was regarded as, and considered himself, one of the more important members of the House, but his part in Reconstruction matters often seemed peripheral. He, as one of the most influential members of the Committee of Fifteen, took an active but not decisive part in framing the Fourteenth Amendment; his particular interest was in the provision on representation. This was not really the most important or substantive part of the proposed amendment, but it looked at the time as if it would be most significant in terms of political mechanics. That was always important to Roscoe Conkling. His draft of the section would exclude from the numerical basis of representation all persons of a race or color whose civil or political rights and privileges

[4] *Ibid.,* pp. 86–87. See also E. L. McKitrick, *Johnson and Reconstruction,* pp. 93–119.

were denied them. On January 17, he explained his idea: "The entire object is to devise such a mode of adjusting representation that if race or color is made a ground for withholding political or civil rights the consequence shall be to deduct the whole of that race from the enumeration upon which political power is based."

Conkling considered this altered basis of representation one of the essential prerequisites of Southern restoration; he also listed renunciation of the right of secession, repudiation of the Confederate debt, guarantees of civil rights, and disqualification of Confederate leaders. None of these could be considered unreasonable requirements; yet some experts felt the speech showed Conkling sliding into the radical camp.[5]

On January 20, in committee, Conkling suggested another change to tailor the new amendment to Northern realities, moving to replace "citizens" in the representation section with "persons." The reason was that "many of the large States now hold their representation in part by reason of their aliens" who could be included under "persons" but not under "citizens." [6]

Two days later, Conkling defended the majority's representation amendment, now changed to provide for exclusion when the "elective franchise" was withheld from any race, in debate on the floor with Andrew Rogers of New Jersey, one of the three Democrats on the joint committee. Conkling pointed out that, without a constitutional change, the Southern states, which had until then counted three-fifths of their slave populations in their congressional enumerations, would be entitled to count five-fifths of their free black populations, even though those free blacks had no more political rights than had the pre-war slaves. The result would be to give the seceded states twenty-eight additional representatives. Conkling decried this: "Twenty-eight votes to be cast here and in the Electoral College for those held not fit to sit as jurors, not fit to testify in court, not fit to be plaintiff in a suit, not fit to approach the ballot-box. . . . Shall such be the reward of those who did the foulest and guiltiest act which crimsons the annals of recorded time? No, sir; not if I can help it."

Conkling then presented a table showing the different modes of apportioning representation and the results thereof, state by state. Then

[5] J. B. James, *Fourteenth Amendment*, pp. 56–58; *Cong. Globe,* 39th Cong., 1st sess., pp. 233, 278, 252.

[6] James, p. 59; *Cong. Globe,* 39th Cong., 1st sess., p. 359.

came a jarring note. Blaine of Maine interrupted with another set of tables which he claimed were more accurate; Blaine was concerned that New England could *lose* representation under the proposal. Roscoe, miffed, said that Blaine's figures were not correct, while his were. He then continued his debate with Rogers, who asked about an educational qualification for voting. Conkling answered that if it were not actually aimed at a single race it would not cause any reduction of representation. He concluded that "the amendment is common to all States and equal for all," while conceding that "its operation will of course be practically only in the South"; the Northern states had so few Negroes that they could be excluded (as most were) without affecting representation at all.[7]

The following day, James G. Blaine got the floor again to press home his argument for the accuracy of the tables he had presented. He said:

The gentleman from New York controverted this proposition and I now reassert it. . . . But as the gentleman from New York, in introducing his figures, did not use them in support of the suffrage basis, of course I have no issue with him . . . and so far as his argument went in that way it went against the conclusion he was contending for, presenting anew the spectacle of the waterman in the Pilgrim's Progress, who got his living by vigorously rowing in one direction while steadily looking in the other.

CONKLING: I desire to answer not so much the argument as the witticism of my friend from Maine.

BLAINE: Oh, no; no wit, either perpetrated or intended.

CONKLING: Well, Mr. Speaker, we considered it very witty over here; but then we are so far off.

BLAINE: Glad the gentleman thinks my wit will carry a long distance.

CONKLING: In answer to what we deemed over here the witticism of the gentleman, I wish to say that I had a particular purpose in introducing the figures and statement that I did. . . . It is very common in the country to charge that nothing can be done here which in any way militates against the interests or the aggrandizement of New England. It is said that New England is the focus of fanaticism.

BLAINE: I thought the gentleman only rose for explanation.

CONKLING: I am going to make a very brief explanation. New England is the place where the man said the sun riz and sot in his back yard, and it is alleged that such regard is had to it here that we cannot do anything here that militates against New England, and that various persons here— myself among the number—are opposed to the suffrage basis merely be-

7 *Cong. Globe,* 39th Cong., 1st sess., pp. 357–359.

cause it takes away some part of the power of fanatical New England. Now, I desire to relieve the proposition before the House of any imputation that it comes here or is supported in the interest of New England and in preference to the other proposition, because the other proposition hits New England. I deny that it hits New England and I deny that this proposition benefits New England; in other words, I support this proposition on account of its own merits and not for local or electioneering purposes.

BLAINE: I am very much obliged to the gentleman for the patronizing care with which he looks after the interests of fanatical New England.[8]

Conkling's resolution was ultimately reported back to the committee for sharpening; when the committee eventually produced its amendment in final form, Conkling called it "the best, the wisest, the most effectual, the most all-sufficient plan and proposition of reconstruction that we ever had, that the ingenuity of any man ever suggested."[9] The Senate did not quite agree with him; the Republican caucus in that house rewrote the measure again, giving it the form in which it would finally be submitted and ratified.

The important outcome of the debate on the representation tables was a heightened sense of rivalry on the part of two young congressmen with clearly antagonistic personalities. A few days before that tangle, Conkling had risen on the floor of the House to correct a mistake in reporting by the Associated Press of a resolution offered by him, when Blaine again inserted himself into the matter to ask that the resolution be read, as he had a question about it. Conkling squelched that by saying that "it is not necessary to take up time to read it, as the gentleman would have seen had he been within hearing when I commenced my remarks."[10]

Senator Stewart of Nevada later said that Conkling and Blaine were "both ambitious and full of fight. . . . They were, however, very jealous of each other, and whenever I heard they were going to have a personal controversy I went over to the House to hear them spar. Their debates were historic, and prevented each of them from ever occupying

[8] *Ibid.*, pp. 376–377.

[9] *Ibid.*, 40th Cong., 2d sess., p. 2608, May 27, 1868. Interestingly, the "Journal of the Committee of Fifteen," edited by B. B. Kendrick, demonstrates that Conkling took virtually no part in any discussion of what turned out to be Section 1 of the Fourteenth Amendment, the only section with lasting effect. Indeed, on several occasions he voted against it.

[10] *Cong. Globe,* 39th Cong., 1st sess., p. 278, Jan. 17, 1866.

the Presidential chair. Conkling was the more dignified and commanding, but Blaine more aggravating and personal." [11]

Everyone in Congress was by now aware that a real donnybrook
could break forth between these two at any time. At a formal dinner
in Washington, someone had alluded to Conkling with poetry:

> No pent-up Utica contracts our powers,
> But the whole boundless continent is ours.

Conkling attributed the lines to Addison and was furious when Blaine
corrected him and said they were from Sewell's "Epilogue to Cato."
The two had an angry exchange, and Conkling's love for Blaine was
not increased when research proved the latter correct.[12] Thad Stevens
felt, however, that as long as Conkling and Blaine kept in line on the
important party issues they could maintain their private feud on the
side. For the Republican party, in the long run, old Thad was tragically
wrong.

Even at this time, and on into February, there was still a possibility
in people's minds—a hope, perhaps—that Andrew Johnson and the
Republican majorities in Congress could work out a means of co-
existence; they were, after all, constitutionally charged with the task
of governing the same country. In mid-February Congress was to make
a decision in a matter dear to the president's heart, and Johnson had to
approve or reject a pet bill of the Congress. Here was an opportunity
to work out at least an armed truce, if no more.

The Committee on Reconstruction had before it for consideration
the readmission of Tennessee—the president's own state, in which he
was of course intensely interested. Meanwhile, Congress had passed
and sent to the president's desk a bill extending the life of the Freedmen's Bureau for an indefinite period. Continuation of the bureau, a
wartime agency to offer aid and comfort to the bewildered ex-slave,
was considered indispensable by the Republicans, for the enactment of
the "black codes" in the Southern states had demonstrated what could
be expected for the Negroes of the South without federal assistance.

11 W. M. Stewart, *Reminiscences,* p. 206.
12 M. A. Dodge, *James G. Blaine,* p. 152. The two men bet a basket of champagne on the correct attribution. Conkling paid up, but he refused to attend the
party Blaine threw to drink it.

Tennessee, of course, had been the least disloyal of all the seceding states, had been largely occupied by the Union Army since early in the war, and was conceded by most Northerners to be ready for readmission.

In the Committee of Fifteen, the most moderate of the four subcommittees to which had been assigned the various Southern states [13] reported a plain resolution simply readmitting Tennessee to the Union on a parity with all the other states. That was on February 15. Two days later, though, Senator George Williams of Oregon moved that the subject of Tennessee be referred for review to a select three-man committee to be appointed. When this motion carried 8 to 7, Fessenden (who had cast the deciding eighth vote) named to the select committee Conkling, Williams, and Boutwell, the latter two hard-line radicals. The recommendations of the select subcommittee were somewhat more rigorous than the original resolution, but the moderating hand of the Utica congressman could still be seen. Before she could be readmitted, Tennessee must, by a majority of her voters, repudiate the rebel debt while guaranteeing payment of that of the Union, disavow the right of secession, and agree to the disfranchisement and disbarment from any political activity for five years of all who aided or adhered to the rebellion. The delay factor and the disfranchisement section were the features of the Conkling committee report which caused consternation. What the whole business clearly showed, however, was that even many conservative Republicans were not yet ready to start readmitting rebel states unconditionally. Some amendments to the report were proposed, and the whole matter was put aside for a couple of days, to await developments.

The day the Conkling report was presented, February 19, Johnson fired off his veto of the Freedmen's Bureau Bill, which Congress was unable to pass over his veto. It is not clear that one necessarily followed from the other, though the trifling with Tennessee's readmission has been cited by Reconstruction historians as the cause of the president's final intransigence.[14] Perhaps it was the action of two days before, when the committee refused to readmit Tennessee with no strings at-

[13] This committee consisted of Senator James Grimes of Iowa, and congressmen Henry Grider of Kentucky and John A. Bingham of Ohio. Conkling's subcommittee had in charge Virginia, North Carolina, and the ancient bastion of secession, South Carolina.

[14] H. K. Beale, *Critical Year*, pp. 80–83; Kendrick, ed., pp. 67–69.

tached, which turned Johnson away. Most likely he would have vetoed the Freedmen's Bureau Bill anyway, as an unconstitutional federal interference with the right of the states to take care of their blacks in their own way. He also made it clear in his veto message that he would approve no legislation bearing upon the South while that section was unrepresented in Congress.

However it came about, the point of no return had been passed between Andrew Johnson and the Congress—and the Freedmen's Bureau veto had created more radicals out of Republican conservatives. So did Johnson's lengthy response, three days later, to a Washington's Birthday serenade at the White House. The president called Sumner, Stevens, and Wendell Phillips "traitors" and claimed that they were plotting his assassination. Andrew Johnson—humorless, stubborn, egotistical, defensive, neither fish nor fowl between Northern Republicans and Southern Democrats—was his own worst enemy. He presented Stevens with more supporters than the congressman could ever have won on his own. Henceforth between president and Congress there would be war.

On a slightly lower level, Roscoe Conkling's congressional career was proceeding, enveloped in the usual cloud of asperity. He even ran afoul of Stevens on January 19, when he expressed doubt on the wisdom of spending $105,000 to purchase a possible site for a naval shipyard. He said that those pushing the project "fail to show with sufficient clearness to satisfy my mind that it is necessary at all; and therefore I am constrained to vote against it."

With heavy-handed irony, Stevens retorted: "I understand that wherever there is any doubt the gentleman will vote against an appropriation. Now, I suppose that there is no appropriation to which some men will not object. Then the gentleman will not vote for any appropriation."

Conkling, undaunted, responded that "I give the benefit of that doubt to the side of economy and retrenchment." [15]

And indeed, Conkling was developing a reputation for himself as an advocate of economy in government and a ready opponent to many proposals for federal spending on unnecessary projects. Economy and governmental retrenchment were linked in his mind as means to his

[15] *Cong. Globe,* 39th Cong., 1st sess., p. 328.

ultimate goal for the nation—a return to specie currency and retirement of the paper issued during the war.

Conkling tangled as readily with colleagues from his own state as with outsiders. On April 16, he engaged in bitter, personal debate with Henry J. Raymond of New York, formerly one of the Republican leaders of the House, but now under a shadow in his own party for his continued support of Andrew Johnson. Conkling charged Raymond, who was editor of the New York *Times,* with responsibility for a "malicious and venomous" article about him in that paper, though Raymond disclaimed any knowledge of it.[16]

The next day, Conkling nagged at Robert Schenck of Ohio, chairman of the Military Affairs Committee, over provisions of the Army Reorganization Bill, and when Schenck became exasperated, Conkling said, "I hope the gentleman from Ohio will not get too energetic." He ridiculed "that celebrated pelvic gesture by which the gentleman makes himself forcible" and said that "my friend's manner is rather appalling." [17]

Conkling enjoyed these minor skirmishes and the chances they afforded him to exercise his gift of sarcasm. But he was merely warming up for the big battle with Blaine which erupted a few days later.

Blaine of Maine: the "Magnetic Man." A friend once said of him, "I defy anyone, Republican or Democrat, to be in his company half an hour and go away from him anything less than a personal friend." [18] A native of Pennsylvania, Blaine had gone into journalism in Maine with the Kennebec *Journal* before the war. Since 1859, he had been acknowledged as the Republican leader of Maine, and he had been in the House since 1863. He was obviously a comer in the national Republican party, and everyone loved him. Well, almost everyone; Roscoe Conkling found his charm resistible.

The Army Reorganization Bill turned out to be the battleground for the two young congressmen. Blaine, a member of the Military Affairs Committee, could be said to have had a proprietary interest in Schenck's bill. On April 13, Conkling jumped all over an amendment offered by Blaine, changed the language around, offered his own amendment, and said: "I think that would meet the point on all sides, and leave it in much better shape than it is now."

[16] *Ibid.,* p. 1971.   [17] *Ibid.,* pp. 2001–2002.
[18] W. C. Hudson, *Random Recollections,* p. 128.

Blaine, angered, said, "I will accept that in lieu of my amendment, although I think it is mere surplusage." [19] They tangled over it again three days later.

On April 24, when the Army Reorganization Bill was again under consideration, Conkling rose and, in his usual slow, measured tones, stated: "I move to strike out section 20 of the bill. My objection to this section is that it creates an unnecessary office for an undeserving public servant; it fastens as an incubus upon the country a hateful instrument of war, which deserves no place in a free Government in time of peace."

Section 20 created a permanent bureau of the provost marshal general. It was naturally assumed that the appointee to the permanent office would be the wartime incumbent, who just happened to be General James B. Fry.

To counter a belief that General Grant was behind the provision for continuance of the office, Conkling read a letter from Grant dated March 19, saying in part, "I think there is no necessity for a Provost Marshal General." Having presumably neutralized the magic name of Grant, Roscoe worked back into his main theme:

The Provost Marshal's Bureau was a temporary expedient resorted to in an extreme emergency to bring volunteers hastily to the field. Its mission is ended, and it should be buried out of sight. . . . But there are yet other grounds of objection. I protest against any promotion or reward for the officer whose interests are involved in this section. . . . I protest, in the name of my people and in the name of the people of the western division of New York, against perpetuating a power under which they have suffered, beyond the capacity of any man adequately to state in the time allotted to me.

As he spoke, Conkling had no reason to notice that Blaine, hearing his voice, had descended from the gallery, where he had been conversing with a friend, to the floor, where he was waiting to speak in reply. Conkling continued:

Central and western New York have a right to feel and do feel deeply on this subject. My constituents remember . . . wrongs done them too great for forgetfulness and almost for belief by the creatures of this bureau and by its head. . . . By acts of their own, and by acts done by their superior at Washington, they turned the business of recruiting and drafting into one carnival of corrupt disorder, into a paradise of coxcombs and thieves.

[19] *Cong. Globe,* 39th Cong., 1st sess., p. 1950.

When Conkling had finished, Blaine got the floor. Since, as it later developed, Blaine hardly knew General Fry, the suspicion must be strong that the Maine man involved himself in this matter solely to irritate and aggravate his rival. He said that the committee's action was in conformity with an earlier letter of Grant to the committee, a letter "which came officially before the committee, and which was not smuggled in in the manner in which the letter read by the gentleman from New York comes before us." As Conkling steamed at that reference to the private character of the Grant letter *he* had read, Blaine went on:

Mr. Speaker, I do not suppose that the House of Representatives care anything more than the Committee on Military Affairs about the great recruiting frauds in New York, or the quarrels of the gentleman from New York with General Fry, in which quarrels it is generally understood the gentleman came out second best at the War Department. I do not think that such questions ought to be obtruded here.

Though the gentleman from New York has had some difference with General Fry, yet I take pleasure in saying that, as I believe, there is not in the American Army a more honorable and high-toned officer than General Fry. That officer, I doubt not, is ready to meet the gentleman from New York or anybody else in the proper forum. I must say that I do not think it is any very creditable proceeding for the gentleman from New York here in this place to traduce General Fry as a military officer when he has no opportunity to be heard. I do not consider such a proceeding the highest specimen of chivalry that could be exhibited.

After this, Conkling, who must have been startled at the sudden vehemence of the defense of General Fry, regained the floor:

Mr. Speaker, if General Fry is reduced to depending for vindication upon the gentleman from Maine, he is to be commiserated certainly. If I have fallen to the necessity of taking lessons from that gentleman in the rules of propriety, or of right or wrong, God help me.

I say to him further that I mean to take no advantage such as he attributes of the privileges of this place or of the absence of General Fry. On the contrary, I am ready to avow what I have here declared anywhere. I am responsible, not only here but elsewhere, for what I have said and what I will say of the Provost Marshal General.

I say further, that the statement made by the gentleman from Maine with regard to myself personally and my quarrels with General Fry, and their result, is false. He says I can—

Blaine was on his feet in an instant:

What does the gentleman mean to say was false?

CONKLING: I mean to say that the statement made by the gentleman from Maine is false.

BLAINE: What statement?

CONKLING: Does not the gentleman understand what I mean?

BLAINE: I call the gentleman to order. I demand he shall state what was false in what I stated. I have parliamentary right. I demand the gentleman shall state what was false in what I said.

Blaine knew he had a parliamentary leg up in Conkling's use of the word "false," and, although the Speaker ruled out of order his point of order that it was improper to say something was false without stating wherein it was false, he was soon back with a proper point of order based on the use of the word. Conkling snarled, "One who makes such points of order should be more careful how he makes them." He went on:

It is not my disposition, Mr. Speaker, to engage in personal controversy upon this floor, but when any member forgets himself so far as to impute unworthy motives and resentments to me, when my motives and resentments are wholly foreign to the matter before the House, he must expect a rebuff; and when he asserts offensively that I have had personal quarrels with a person whose administration and public acts are under consideration, and that I have been worsted in these quarrels, and that, too, before the Secretary of War and by the Secretary of War, and when that statement has no foundation in fact, I think the Chair and the House will agree with me that something is to be pardoned to the earnestness of the occasion. I said what I felt bound to say, speaking not only for my own constituents, but for other constituencies in New York whose representatives hear me. I could not remain silent when I know that in my own district and elsewhere men who stood up honestly and attempted to resist "bounty jumpers" and thieves were stricken down and trodden under foot by General Fry. I affirm that the only way to acquit him of venality is to convict him of the most incredible incompetency. I am responsible for that, sir, everywhere.

He then said that Blaine's statement had been, using parliamentary language, "erroneous and destitute of that which it should possess in order to render it admissible in debate." Blaine tried to get the floor back, and Roscoe said: "I decline to yield it to the gentleman from Maine."

Conkling went on to say that "in my judgment no officer of this Government holding a similar position has done so much harm and so little good as the officer of whom I am speaking." Then, looking directly at Blaine, "If that is offensive to anybody, so be it. To the particular individual to whom it may give worst offense, I will answer not here but elsewhere, when it becomes necessary." He then yielded the balance of his time to Spalding of Ohio.

In a few moments, however, Blaine had the floor again:

I stated when I was up before, and I left it to the gentleman from New York to answer whether I stated it correctly, that I had understood there were personal difficulties between himself and the Provost Marshal General. . . . I have understood that in those difficulties the gentleman from New York, as I said before, did not come out first best. I did not make this as an assertion. I left it to him to say whether it was so or not. Cerainly I did not violate any principle of propriety or of parliamentary etiquette. And, sir, even were I in full health, (and I ought to be in my bed today), I could not consent to go into this cheap sort of stuff about answering "here and elsewhere" and about "personal responsibility" and all that kind of thing.

Conkling was seething, but his rival had the floor and there was nothing to be done but sit and listen.

Sir, I do not know how to characterize it. When we had gentlemen here from the eleven seceded states, they used to talk about answering "here and elsewhere"; and it was understood that they meant a duel! I suppose the gentleman from New York means nothing of that kind; I do not know whether he does or does not; but that is the only meaning that can be attached to the phrase. When a man says that he is ready to answer "here or elsewhere," he means that he is willing to receive a note outside of the District of Columbia. Well, now, that is very cheap, and certainly beneath my notice. I do not believe the gentleman from New York wants to fight a duel; and I am sure he needs no assurance from me that I do not intend it. When I have to resort to the use of the epithet of "false" upon this floor, and this cheap swagger about being responsible "here or elsewhere," I shall have very little faith in the cause which I stand up to maintain.

After this, Mercur of Pennsylvania got the floor back, and this round of the Blaine-Conkling eruption subsided.[20]

The next day, however, Blaine triumphantly took the floor on a matter of personal privilege and crowed that Conkling had, in violation of the rule against correcting the *Globe* transcript of matters of per-

[20] The tiff can be followed in *ibid.,* pp. 2151–2153.

sonal controversy between members, changed his "not here but else-where" statement of the day before to something more circumspect. "The gentleman sought by an alteration to take away the entire point of my reply to him. I characterized some of his bravado as 'cheap swagger' when he talked about meeting me 'here or elsewhere' . . . a phrase well known in Congress; it is the phrase of bullyism. It was a phrase upon which I commented, and which I denounced and justly denounced, and which the gentleman had no right to alter at the *Globe* office."

Conkling, who really had altered the phrase, then rose to deny that the matter was one of personal controversy but was strictly a public matter: "I have made no alterations, none whatever, except those alterations which all gentlemen make, rejecting the surplusage and dif-fusive style which will always enter, more or less, into extemporaneous speaking. . . . The member from Maine, with frivolous impertinence, put into the debate an imputation upon my motives; and attributed to me dishonorable personal resentment." The "gentleman from Maine" is now the "member from Maine"; Conkling would not again give Blaine even the *pro forma* credit implied in the more usual title. Blaine, he went on, "says those are technical words. I did not know that they were technical words. I have heard them used here repeatedly."

After Blaine got back in with another thrust, Conkling haughtily replied that "the member's zeal outruns his discretion, which perhaps is not the first occurrence of that kind in his life." [21]

The matter simmered for a few days. On April 30, Blaine rose to ask the clerk to read a letter from General Fry, "for the double purpose of vindicating myself from the charge of having stated in debate last week what was false, and also for the purpose . . . of allowing fair play to an honorable man in the same forum in which he has been assailed."

When the Speaker asked if there was objection, all eyes turned toward Conkling, who said, "I infer that this has some reference to me. I shall make no objection provided I may have an opportunity to reply to whatever the letter may call for hereafter."

Thad Stevens then objected to the interruption of the consideration of the Rivers and Harbors Bill, so the matter was carried over. This gave sufficient time for a large congregation to gather for the expected fireworks. They were not disappointed.

[21] *Ibid.*, pp. 2180–2181.

Later on, Blaine got the floor, saying, "Whether I was in error or not I leave to those who hear the letter of the Provost Marshal General." The letter, a long one which he and Fry had composed together, ostensibly to thank Blaine for his defense of the week before, accused Conkling of all sorts of improprieties, including blocking prosecutions of bounty frauds at Utica and illegally accepting extra pay from the government while a member of Congress for his work as prosecutor in the Haddock court-martial. Blaine should have known better than to produce such a blast from an outsider against a member of the House, particularly such an important member as Conkling had become.

By the time all the accompanying documents, mainly communications back and forth among Conkling, Dana, and Stanton, had been read by the clerk, Conkling was prepared:

I appreciate the indifference with which the House must listen to an issue such as this, in its design on one side so personal and so individual in its character. . . . I was prepared for all the calumnies and all the responsibility that he must take who strikes at the thieves, marauders, and miscreants who have fattened upon the necessities and needs of their country. . . . I understand perfectly that I must be prepared for all comers of this description, and it was to this that I referred in my avowal of my readiness to maintain my allegations of wrong in the Provost Marshal Bureau at all times and places. I will not say "elsewhere" for fear of unsettling the nerves of some who hear me.

Conkling then went on at great length to state the circumstances of his employment in the Haddock affair. His engagement he enveloped in a great cloud of verbiage because he *had* received his fee from the government at a time when he was back in Congress, though his services had been performed while only a congressman-elect. He then had some passages read from the *Globe* making reference to Blaine's speech about what he called his "personal quarrels" with Fry, when Blaine interrupted: "I hope the gentleman will read the whole. If he will show me the word 'personal' in the speech to which he is replying, I will reward him. He cannot do it. He is putting his own interpretation upon it."

Conkling responded stonily, "Mr. Speaker, I hope the active member from Maine will preserve himself as free from agitation as possible."

After some further angry colloquy with Blaine, Conkling went on with his speech, arraigning Haddock and Fry, and asking the House's pardon that the members had to witness the spectacle of "the head of a bureau, a clerk in the War Department, sending here to be read such a pile of rubbish as that, a personal assault upon a member of this House." At his request a committee to investigate the whole matter was appointed.

Blaine could not leave well enough alone. A few minutes later, he rose and said that in spite of all Conkling had said he still was paid both salaries at the same time, "though I will say this much of him, if he will permit me, that I have no doubt he will restore it if convinced he has taken it improperly."

Stung again, Conkling took the field once more:

For fear that I omitted to state it, I beg leave to say that no commission, paper, or authority whatever was ever issued to me except the letter of retainer which has been read, employing me to act, according to its language, before military courts and other tribunals.

BLAINE: Mr. Speaker—

THE SPEAKER: Does the gentleman from New York yield to the gentleman from Maine?

CONKLING: No, sir, I do not wish to have anything to do with the member from Maine, not even so much as to yield him the floor.

BLAINE: All right.

Conkling spoke further of his capacity as counsel for the court-martial, and added:

Now, Mr. Speaker, one thing further: if the member from Maine had the least idea how profoundly indifferent I am to his opinion upon the subject which he has been discussing, or upon any other subject personal to me, I think he would hardly take the trouble to rise here and express his opinion. And as it is a matter of entire indifference to me what that opinion may be, I certainly will not detain the House by discussing the question whether it is well or ill founded, or by noticing what he says.

He then apologized to the House again for a matter caused "originally by an interruption which I pronounced the other day ungentlemanly and impertinent, and having nothing to do with the question."

Still, Blaine must score the final point.

It is hardly worthwhile to pursue this controversy further; but still the gentleman from New York cannot get off on the technicality which he has suggested. He says that a commission never was issued to him. I understand him to admit that if a commission had been issued to him he could not have taken pay for both offices. Now, everyone knows that those preliminary authorizations are the things on which half the business arising out of the war has been done. Men have fought at the head of battalions and divisions and Army corps without having received their formal commissions.

Then goaded beyond good sense and parliamentary courtesy, the man from Maine launched into the final assault, the consequences of which would haunt him for years.

As to the gentleman's cruel sarcasm, I hope he will not be too severe. The contempt of that large-minded gentleman is so wilting; his haughty disdain, his grandiloquent swell, his majestic, supereminent, overpowering, turkey-gobbler strut has been so crushing to myself and all the members of this House that I know it was an act of the greatest temerity for me to venture upon a controversy with him. But, sir, I know who is responsible for all this. I know that within the last five weeks, as members of the House will recollect, an extra strut has characterized the gentleman's bearing. It is not his fault. It is the fault of another. That gifted and satirical writer, Theodore Tilton, of the New York *Independent,* spent some weeks recently in this city. His letters published in that paper embraced, with many serious statements, a little jocose satire, a part of which was the statement that the mantle of the late Winter Davis had fallen upon the member from New York. The gentleman took it seriously, and it has given his strut additional pomposity. The resemblance is great. It is striking. Hyperion to a satyr, Thersites to Hercules, mud to marble, dunghill to diamond, a singed cat to a Bengal tiger, a whining puppy to a roaring lion. Shade of the mighty Davis, forgive the almost profanation of that jocose satire! [22]

Blaine sat down.

Senator Stewart said, "the House slightly hissed." [23] The Speaker said that if any member had called for order, he would have enforced the rules at once. A few moments later, the House adjourned.

Three months later, on July 19, the special committee detailed to hear the matter reported back that Conkling's conduct relative to the Haddock court-martial had "been above reproach," that he had been "not only innocent, but eminently patriotic and valuable step by step to his Government at a time of imminent peril." The committee also condemned Fry for his attack upon Conkling, and Stevens said, "I must do the gentleman from Maine, now absent, the justice to suppose that he was entirely uninformed of the contents of the letter, or he would never have presented it to the House," knowing full well that Blaine knew exactly what was in the letter.[24]

[22] This round of the Conkling-Blaine quarrel is in *ibid.,* pp. 2287, 2292–2299.
[23] Stewart, p. 206.   [24] *Cong. Globe,* 39th Cong., 1st sess., pp. 3942–3945.

So Conkling was vindicated; Fry was excoriated (Stevens asked why Fry was not in the penitentiary with his friends); and Blaine came in for a good deal of criticism, too. Unfortunately, however, Roscoe would never be able to shake off that image—the "turkey-gobbler strut." And he carried a burning hatred of Blaine to his grave. He once told George Boutwell of Massachusetts, "That attack was made without any provocation by me as against Mr. Blaine . . . and I shall never overlook it." He never did.[25]

Conkling worked hard during this session of Congress, particularly with the Committee on Reconstruction, but he had few other moments of public exposure on the large scale. He did at one point take issue with Stevens over the power of the secretary of the treasury to call in greenbacks. This was a subject in which he had as much interest as in his quarrel with Blaine. Conkling and Allison of Iowa took the position that this power, which Stevens opposed, already inhered in the secretary: "I entirely concur in the statement . . . by the gentleman from Iowa that the very power which the gentleman from Pennsylvania says would appal the country now exists." [26]

A matter which assumed considerable importance to the Republican majorities in Congress was that of the test oath imposed upon representatives coming to Washington from the reconstructed Southern states. The radicals determined that the Southern congressman-elect would not be permitted to judge for himself whether he was able to take the oath; the house involved would decide on the fitness of every individual applicant. Otherwise, hotheaded ex-rebels could come in and swear the oath falsely, and nothing could be done about it. This led to some complications.

On July 27, Conkling opposed a joint resolution to excuse from the "iron-bound" oath (of nonallegiance to the former rebel government) one of the new senators from Tennessee. David T. Patterson, Andrew Johnson's son-in-law, was conceded to have been a staunch Unionist during the war, but he had taken an oath to the Confederate government in order to retain his judgeship in eastern Tennessee. In this position, he had furnished aid and succor to the harassed Unionists of his region. Senator Lyman Trumbull offered a resolution to remove Patterson's disabilities and permit him to take a modified oath. Horace Maynard of Tennessee pushed this in the House, after it passed the

---

[25] G. S. Boutwell, *Reminiscences,* II, 264.
[26] *Cong. Globe,* 39th Cong., 1st sess., pp. 1456–1463; Sage, p. 80.

Senate, but he ran afoul of Roscoe Conkling, who felt that the Senate should bear the full responsibility if it wanted to excuse Patterson. Conkling said: "In the very first instance in which this safeguard is needed, the first in which it was to be relied upon, it is proposed that we shall throw it away." He moved to table the resolution, and his motion carried, 88 to 31. The Senate ultimately permitted Patterson to take the oath anyway.[27]

Finally, as another insight into Conkling's congressional behavior, on the "last night but one of the session," he objected vigorously to passing a bill giving about five thousand square miles of land to the San Francisco and Humboldt Bay Railroad. The bill was thereupon tabled. Conkling, both in the House and in the Senate, was not one of those who believed in indiscriminate handouts to railroads, and he was found opposing more grants than he supported. His post-Senate representation of Gould and a number of large railroads has caused some historians mistakenly to consider him an avid congressional advocate of largesse to the roads. Blaine was—it got him into trouble; Conkling was not.[28]

With the close of the session at the end of July, there was barely time for a few weeks of relaxation before the start of the 1866 campaign. With the heated battles of this year between president and Congress there was certain to be no letup in the pressure.

The Union county convention met at Rome, in the court house, on September 8. After Roscoe Conkling was unanimously nominated by a rising vote, he delivered a snarling acceptance speech that helped to set the tone for the bitter campaign of 1866. The depth of Republican feeling about Johnson (shared by doctrinaire radicals and many like Conkling who were not), the consciousness of betrayal, and the frustration of rage, show clearly through Conkling's phrases:

The President of the United States, as he goes on his deceitful errand, with an imperial condescension, a supercilious patronage, which seems to ape Louis Napoleon, repeats from place to place: "I shall place the constitution in the hands of the people."

[27] *Cong. Globe*, 39th Cong., 1st sess., pp. 4272–4273. Sumner had challenged Patterson's ability to take the oath in the Senate and demanded an investigation. When the probe developed Patterson's oath to the Confederate government, Trumbull introduced his resolution and got it through the Senate. A fitful debate in the House was ended by Conkling's decisive speech; H. Hyman, *Era of the Oath*, pp. 91–93.
[28] *Cong. Globe*, 39th Cong., 1st sess., p. 4202, July 26, 1866.

This angry man, dizzy with the elevation to which assassination has raised him, frenzied with power and ambition, does not seem to know that not he but the men who made the constitution placed it in the people's hands; but they did place the constitution in the people's hands, and they placed Andrew Johnson in the people's hands too; and when those hands shall be clenched at the ballot box, Andrew Johnson and his policy of arrogance and usurpation will be snapped like a willow wand. He must be dead to the throb of the public heart who does not feel the coming retribution from an indignant people, buffeted and betrayed.[29]

The campaign was kicked off in earnest with a mass meeting before a packed Mechanics Hall in Utica on September 13. Conkling gave a two-and-a-half hour speech, outlining the conflict between Johnson and the Congress, and was wildly cheered. The *Herald* said that if the Democrats "mean to win the Congressional race on this course, it is high time they trotted out their nag. If he isn't spavined already, he will be before he finishes his trial of strength and speed with Roscoe Conkling." [30]

On September 20, at Rome, the Democrats trotted out their nag, who turned out to be an old anti-Conkling Republican, Palmer V. Kellogg, one of the group that had journeyed to Washington to help Conkling with appointments some years before. Kellogg made little real impression on the electorate, and Conkling was left relatively free to help out around the state.

The Republicans (the "Union party" business was dying away now) renominated Fenton for governor. General Stewart L. Woodford, the candidate for lieutenant governor, a rising young politician from Brooklyn, was not well known. Roscoe Conkling turned out to be the major speaker for the Republican campaign that fall, and a prime cause of the party's victory. As usual, Julia saw little of her husband, even though Congress was adjourned. They loved him in his old home town of Auburn, where he opened his speech "with a touching reference to former days, to 'graves growing green, and heads growing gray.' " [31]

He blasted Johnson for his speaking tour of the North, the famous "swing around the circle." "Not satisfied with conniving at the robbery and murder of the Unionists, and the exaltation and reward of traitors at the South," said Roscoe, "he comes to buffet and slander the Union people of the North and to blacken the memory of their dead." His

---

[29] Utica *Morning Herald*, Sept. 10, 1866.   [30] *Ibid.*, Sept. 14.
[31] From the *Northern Christian Advocate*, quoted in Utica *Morning Herald*, Oct. 5, 1866.

keynote was that the whole issue of Reconstruction was a false one in the campaign, artificially blown up by scheming politicians like Johnson and the Democrats. The great need of the South, he said, was for the Southerners to go to work for themselves.[32]

In the last days of the campaign, the Democrats tried to gather together a workingmen's movement to support their candidate; this group sought replies from the candidates as to their views on the reduction of the daily hours of labor. Conkling scornfully answered that "expressions of opinion in the nature of pledges made by candidates for office on the eve of election" were not worth much; they should look at his votes in the House.[33]

When the votes were counted on November 6, Conkling had 12,470 to 11,053 for Kellogg. It was a Republican year. Johnson was crushed by a smashing Republican victory, and with top-heavy majorities against him in both houses the president's influence almost completely vanished. State-wide, Fenton overcame John T. Hoffman, a stalking-horse for the Tweed Ring, by 13,000 votes. Woodford won. The congressional delegation was made up of twenty Republicans and only eleven Democrats. And the state legislature was solidly Republican.[34] This was important, for it assured the election of a Republican to the United States Senate seat opening up in 1867. And it was important to Roscoe Conkling, for he had not made those tours around the state *solely* to defeat Andrew Johnson, or to build up the margin for Reuben E. Fenton.

Horace Greeley, who had senatorial ideas of his own, knew what Conkling was about. Greeley, who lost his own congressional race in New York City by 10,000 votes, saw to it that the *Tribune,* the most influential Republican paper in the country, did not endorse Conkling in his contest.

[32] A. R. Conkling, p. 278; Stebbins, pp. 127–129.
[33] Utica *Morning Herald,* Nov. 1, 1866; Conkling to Messrs. Trembly and Paxondale, Oct. 29, 1866, Conkling Papers, New-York Historical Society.
[34] Alexander, III, 166; Stebbins, pp. 136–137.

CHAPTER 5

SENATOR CONKLING

Ira Harris, elected to the Senate as Thurlow Weed's man in 1861, had served a nondescript, middling term through the most exciting period in American history. He accomplished little but did manage to become the butt of a story that Lincoln once said he never went to sleep at night without looking under the bed "to see if Judge Harris was not there wanting something for somebody." Harris had grown more radical as his term drew to a close, because he wanted to be re-elected for six more years, and this seemed to him to be the best way to go about it. No one really thought he meant it, however, when he started making noises like Sumner or Stevens or the other real radicals; Gideon Welles said Harris "has been a cunning manager, as he thought; has, against his own convictions, gone with the Radicals." [1]

If Harris wanted the Senate seat, he was not alone. His very obvious weakness helped to multiply the number of candidates. Shortly after the election of 1866, there were at least eight starters in the race. Harris, the incumbent, was one. Horace Greeley, naturally, was another, as was another editor, George William Curtis of *Harper's Weekly*.

Curtis was a rather strange figure for this kind of contest. He was a political idealist of strongly literary bent, but his writing was a bit too precious to qualify as good literature. He had been at Brook Farm, had studied at a German university, and had devoted years to travel and leisure. An ardent abolitionist and an early Republican while others still hesitated about jettisoning the Whig party, he was to become a staunch supporter of civil service reform. With the 300,000 readers of his journal, Curtis could exert considerable leverage, but he recognized

[1] G. Welles, *Diary*, III, 20. Senators, of course, have done this from time to time since the founding of the republic. The problem for Harris was that he was too transparent.

85

his problem in the Senate race: "I am not enough of a politician for the purposes of the men who make senators." [2]

Lyman Tremaine, who had been elected attorney general of the state in 1857 as a Democrat, was another candidate, though now as a Republican. Conkling had once said of Tremaine, "Bad as his politics are, sir, he is an accomplished lawyer." [3] He had become a Republican at the start of the war, had run for lieutenant governor with Wadsworth in 1862, and was elected to the assembly in 1865. He was a long shot for the Senate, but then who had ever heard of Ira Harris in 1861?

Charles J. Folger of Geneva was regarded as a strong candidate. Formerly a county judge, Folger was the leader of the state senate and a highly popular figure. He was known as a fine lawyer and a handsome and modest man. Years later he would serve as Arthur's secretary of the treasury.

Two Supreme Court judges, Ransom Balcom of Binghamton and Noah Davis of Erie County, were also candidates. Davis was a serious candidate because he was from the western part of the state, and that region felt it was entitled to the seat. But Governor Fenton quite obviously meant to go to the Senate two years hence, and he, as a westerner, might have trouble if the west already had one seat.

The other leading contender for Harris's seat, of course, was Roscoe Conkling.

The jockeying started immediately after the 1866 election. On November 15, Greeley's letter dated the day before appeared in the Newburgh *Journal,* announcing his candidacy for the Senate.[4] The famous editor, once called by Conkling "grotesque and harmless," was his own worst enemy. The city election in New York took place on December 4, and Greeley alienated many Republicans by his proposal that the party run a Democratic judge at the head of the ticket. This proposition reminded party leaders of Greeley's tactics of the year before when his support of a fusion candidate for mayor enabled Hoffman, Tweed's man, to beat Republican Marshall O. Roberts. Greeley's suggestion was rejected, but the maneuver hurt him with Republicans in the Senate considerations.[5]

Shortly before the Senate race was to be decided, Greeley brought forth a proposal for "universal amnesty and universal suffrage," a

---

[2] G. Milne, *George William Curtis,* p. 141.

[3] *Cong. Globe,* 36th Cong., 1st sess., p. 1263, March 20, 1860.

[4] Stebbins, p. 144.   [5] Van Deusen, *Horace Greeley,* pp. 346–347.

marriage of ideas he felt sure would bring him support from both radicals and conservatives. Instead, both groups were repelled.[6]

The field gradually narrowed. Curtis, afraid that he was distrusted as being "dainty and too respectable," [7] withdrew in favor of Conkling after declining to form a coalition against him with Davis. Tremaine also pulled out in favor of the congressman. Folger, frustrated in his efforts to translate personal popularity into commitments for the Senate seat, also left the field.

It quickly became clear that the Senator would be chosen from among Harris, Davis, and Conkling. There was great interest in the contest. The *Times* correspondent wrote from Albany on January 3 that "almost the first question which is asked the village or country statesman, on his arrival in this city, is about the candidate of his locality for United States Senator." Some were more interested than others. Conkling wrote to Julia from Albany:

Great sums of money are among the influences here. I have resolutely put down my foot upon the ground that no friend of mine, even without my knowledge, shall pay a cent, upon any pretext nor in any strait, come what will. If chosen, it will be by the men of character, and if beaten this will be my consolation. . . . The gamblers say that I can have $200,000 here from New York in a moment if I choose, and that the members are fools to elect me without it; only think of it! [8]

There was a lot of money floating around. One story that was passed about, no doubt with knowing winks, related the reaction of a veteran lobbyist to the report that a gentleman named Clarke, former controller of the currency, might be a dark horse in the race: "Oh, he don't stand any chance at all, but if he controlled the currency *now* he might make a sure thing of it." [9]

Day by day, the newspaper reports told of the fluctuating fortunes of the hopefuls. Conkling felt that Fenton's ostensible support of Davis had to be a blind, in view of Fenton's own ambitions, so he conducted

[6] *Ibid.*, pp. 348–349. Following Greeley's political, as distinguished from his journalistic, career is almost like following Harold Stassen's a century later. The same strongly beating liberal impulse, the same obvious sincerity, and the same frustration with the public's obtuseness shine through both characters, and, as with Stassen, so with Greeley, the reaction of the public and the politicians is to laugh. Nothing can be more devastating to political ambition.

[7] Milne, p. 141.

[8] A. R. Conkling, p. 287. The purchase of Senate seats from venal legislatures was just getting underway. The practice fitted the age.

[9] N.Y. *Times*, Jan. 4, 1867.

his canvass primarily against Harris; only in the caucus itself did he discern that Davis, not Harris, was the more powerful opponent. Fenton had reluctantly fallen in step behind Davis because he considered the Utica congressman the most dangerous threat of all. Fenton and Conkling had never liked each other, and the governor was quite aware of Conkling's abilities and ambitions.

One of the nerve-jangling features of the whole affair was that it was not known when the legislative leaders would call the caucus, for which only a few hours' notice was needed. Finally, at 7:00 P.M. on January 10, the caucus was held in the assembly chamber. Senator Folger was selected as chairman, and the members got down to the business at hand.

Ellis Roberts started by placing the name of his friend Conkling in nomination, and R. L. Burrows of Erie then did the same for Davis, urging his election on the ground that western New York had never been represented in the Senate. Harris, Balcom, and Greeley were nominated as well. Senator Andrew D. White, also the president-designate of the brand-new Cornell University, rose to say that he had hoped to nominate George William Curtis but since that gentleman had withdrawn he had looked around for a suitable substitute. And he was for Conkling: "In the last political canvass he made the first presentation of a great cause. He sounded the keynote which gave victory to the Republican party. What was wanted in the Senate was not judicial talent but a voice! (Applause.) Four millions of people wanted a representative that would be heard in the council of the nation. (Applause.)" [10]

White's speech made an impression, particularly that part about a voice. Edwin Morgan, the other senator, was no orator. and certainly Harris had never reminded anyone of Seward. Everyone knew that this was Conkling's special area of excellence.

They took one informal ballot, led by Conkling with 33, then Harris 32, Davis with 30, Balcom 7, Greeley 6, and a single vote for Folger. Greeley's name was hastily withdrawn before the first official call. On that ballot, Davis took the lead with 41, followed by Conkling's 39, as Harris fell to 24. On the next ballot, with Harris dropping away rapidly, Conkling climbed to 45, with Davis close behind at 44; Harris had 18 and Balcom only 2. Balcom's supporters then withdrew his

<hr>

[10] *Ibid.*, Jan. 11. White said, "I received congratulations from great numbers" for his speech; R. M. Ogden, ed., *Diaries of A. D. White*, p. 149.

name. On the third formal ballot, Conkling had 53, only two short of the number needed to win, while Davis had 50 and Harris 6. The following ballot was declared invalid, as there were one too many votes cast, probably by design to give the anti-Conkling forces time to save the day. On the fifth ballot, however, there was no stopping Roscoe. He piled up 59 votes, to 49 for Davis and one for Folger.

The nominee was greeted by supporters and opponents alike in his rooms at the Delevan House. Judge Davis came in and made a speech of congratulations, as did Lyman Tremaine, A. H. Laflin of the New York Custom House, and many others. Reuben Fenton did not come. They even carried Conkling through the corridors on their shoulders, which probably did not appeal to him, but it was all in the spirit of victory.[11]

Reaction to Conkling's triumph, ratified in the official election by the legislature on January 15, was varied, though mostly favorable in the "young and vigorous representative" line. Roberts' paper called it "a fit tribute to the integrity, fidelity and ability which he has displayed" in Congress. The *Tribune* called him "a most effective debater and canvasser" and Curtis, in *Harper's* on January 26, said Conkling was "young, fearless, devoted, able; of the profoundest convictions." Curtis must have winced every time he read that in later years.

Down in Washington, Gideon Welles, the secretary of the navy, wrote in his diary that "Conkling is vain, has ability with touches of spread-eagle eloquence, and a good deal of impetuous ardor. He may improve and he may not. At present he is an intense Radical. If he has real sense he will get the better of it with experience." [12]

But Welles was often somewhat grumpy and sour. Roscoe Conkling would start a new career in a place where he would no longer be interrupted by the Speaker's hammer telling him that his time had expired, a place where he would become famous, and be very much at home. He was in the United States Senate.

March 4, 1867. The new Congress convened as soon as the old one expired—the better to keep a weather eye on Andrew Johnson, the angry Tennesseean at the other end of Pennsylvania Avenue. Roscoe

[11] The coverage of the Senate election is primarily from the N.Y. *Times* and Utica *Morning Herald* from the beginning of January, 1867, to just after the election; see also Stebbins, pp. 144–156.
[12] Welles, III, 16.

Conkling marched to the front of the Senate with Edwin D. Morgan, his New York colleague, and, in those strong measured tones the Senate was to hear so often, took the first of his three oaths of office in the upper house. Among the other new Republican senators sworn in with Conkling were Oliver P. Morton, an angry paralytic, the former war governor of Indiana; James Harlan of Iowa, a former senator who had recently served as secretary of the interior (a short term marked by his economy-measure dismissal of an obscure clerk named Walt Whitman); Simon Cameron of Pennsylvania, Lincoln's first secretary of war, the old "boss" of the Keystone State, slightly gamy with a whiff of corruption about him; and Justin S. Morrill of Vermont, coming over with Conkling from the House to begin a Senate career of almost thirty-two years.

The Senate was strongly Republican, as was the House, and even so well known a newcomer as Roscoe Conkling must start out in the back row, where he sat between Patterson of New Hampshire and Garret Davis of Kentucky, a Democrat and war-time Copperhead.

Conkling did not take long to get involved in the business of the Senate. On March 9, he spoke on a measure to relieve impending starvation in certain parts of the South; though he was not convinced by the evidence presented, he said, "This is rather a fearful question upon which to make a mistake." His idea was to use Freedmen's Bureau money if needed, with that agency to ask for a deficiency appropriation to make up for it.[13]

A few days later, Conkling crossed swords with another freshman, Senator Charles Drake of Missouri. Drake, a little banty rooster of a man, was a radical leader of his state, though of somewhat limited abilities. The Republican leadership in Congress had by now completely seized the initiative on Reconstruction from the president, had successfully passed over a veto a basic plan of military Reconstruction of the South, and was now considering a supplement to that act. Conkling had taken very little part in the passage of the Reconstruction Act of March 2; he had been too personally concerned with his election and then his impending transfer to the Senate. The act was such a patchwork piece of legislation, though, that a second bill was seen to be necessary. The new senator from New York was determined to play an active role in this measure. Senator Drake had proposed an amendment to the Supplementary Reconstruction Bill providing that all read-

13 *Cong. Globe*, 40th Cong., 1st sess., p. 42.

mitted states must provide for the secret ballot in their constitutions and agree never to change such provisions. Conkling posed a situation where a readmitted state, as soon as it had its representation back, promptly changed its constitution to provide for viva-voce voting: "What is the Senator, or what are we going to do about it?"

Drake grandly replied, "I, for one, would be prepared to say that they should not have Senators or Representatives in these Halls as long as that violation existed."

Conkling: "That is, the Senator would turn them out on that violation of this act?"

Drake: "Certainly, without a moment's hesitation."

Conkling, with his man now well taken into camp, then turned from Drake to the front of the hall and intoned: "Well, Mr. President, I have only to say, if the senator will indulge me, that it would be rather an awkward thing to do in a good many respects." He then pointed out not only the practical but also the legal and judicial barriers. "The Supreme Court has decided, I think repeatedly, certainly in one case that I well remember . . . that any such compact would be utterly and absolutely void for all purposes."

A few moments later, Drake complained that Conkling "is evidently very complacent indeed with regard to his point. I judge, from the manner in which he put it and from the remarks which he made, that he thinks it is quite a clincher." Indeed he did, and indeed it was.[14]

A couple of nights later, on the same bill, Drake offered an amendment that if a majority of the registered voters in a Southern state voted *for* a constitutional convention it should be held, and if a majority voted *against* a convention it should not be held. When Conkling arose again to ask: "Suppose a majority of those registered do not vote either way, what will be the result then?" Drake had to admit sheepishly that this had "never occurred" to him.[15]

This was a question of some moment, the size of the vote needed for a reconstructing state to call a constitutional convention, and Conkling engaged in a stormy debate that Saturday night with Oliver Morton and Howard of Michigan. The Morton proposal would call a convention

14 *Ibid.*, p. 100, March 14, 1867. Drake, the son of one of the leading medical educators of the nineteenth century, was later appointed chief justice of the U.S. Court of Claims by Grant. Conkling was not overflowing with respect for Drake's intellect.
15 *Ibid.*, p. 155, March 16, 1867.

upon a favorable vote of a majority of those voting; Conkling wanted
an absolute majority of registered voters to be in favor:

I can conceive of nothing more repugnant to the idea which, as I understand it, has lain at the foundation of the action of the Union party of
this country for the last year in Congress and out than the notion apparently insisted upon here that we are to erect in these States governments based upon the absence of majorities, based upon the consent of
minorities, and that we are to throw away on the threshold all the opportunities that we have to erect governments there established upon principles
really republican.

Despite Conkling's pleas, the Senate adopted Morton's amendment
by a vote of 22 to 21. The radicals planned to reconstruct these states
with minority votes, because they feared that the white Southerners
might boycott the elections; this way, the newly enfranchised Negroes
could call the conventions. On the Supplementary Reconstruction Bill
as on other occasions, Conkling demonstrated that he was not a "whole-
hog" radical, and he frequently differed with the radical leadership on
the conditions to be imposed upon the returning states.[16]

He *was* fully conscious of the power of patronage. There was little
available as long as Johnson held the presidency, but Conkling knew
that state of affairs would not last long. Lyman Trumbull of Illinois introduced a bill on March 22, 1867, to amend the newly passed Bankruptcy Law by relieving the chief justice of the duty to appoint registers
of bankruptcy, leaving this function to the district courts. Conkling in
opposition said nobody expected the chief justice to know personally
the men he appoints; he "would call to his aid the Senators and Representatives from that State . . . and learn from them the qualifications
and the merits of the applicants in each particular locality." This seemed
eminently reasonable to the members of the Senate, few of whom
seemed to regard this as an improper function for the chief justice, so
Conkling's referral of the bill to committee killed it.[17]

The next day, Roscoe became involved for the first time with an
edifice and an institution which would in the long run become a primary
focus of his career. The House had been conducting one of its periodic
investigations of the New York Custom House. This dark granite building on Wall Street, between William and Hanover Streets, had long
been the subject of intermittent breast-beatings decrying the graft and

[16] *Ibid.,* pp. 148–149, 156, March 16, 1867.   [17] *Ibid.,* p. 277.

inefficiency surrounding it, and of course most of the charges were true. The New York Custom House collected more revenue than all the other ports of entry to the United States combined, and its presiding officer, the collector, received under the unique system of compensation in effect, based largely on shares called "moieties" of collected fines, a much larger annual income than his superior, the secretary of the treasury, larger even than that of the president.[18] The current incumbent in the collector's office was Henry A. Smythe, and Mr. Smythe was on the griddle before a House committee. All this would not have affected Senator Conkling, had it not been for someone dragging into the hearings in a most uncomplimentary vein (having to do with graft in the general-order business) two members of the Senate, Patterson of Tennessee and Doolittle of Wisconsin. While most of the senators rose to defend their colleagues against the very idea that a committee of the lower house could even mention senators in an investigation, paying very little attention to the actual allegations, Conkling rose for another purpose. The chairman of the House committee, the object of most of the senatorial invective, was Roscoe's political ally in central New York, Calvin T. Hulburd of St. Lawrence County. Conkling made a spirited defense of Hulburd, though he denied that he agreed with the imputations cast upon the two senators. The matter passed quickly, but Conkling had undergone his initiation in Custom House politics.[19]

As March passed into April, the Republicans were split as to whether Congress should stay in session. The early asembly was extraordinary, anyway, and many members felt that Johnson had been properly tied down by the measures passed and enacted over his veto; Congress could well adjourn to its regular session in December. Conkling believed this and said so; the radical leadership, pushed by those like Charles Sumner who felt that Congress might very properly stay in session all the time, finally compromised by recessing to July, not adjourning to December.

When the Senate convened on July 3, the Republican caucus adopted Conkling's resolution that the Senate do no business whatever except that found to be necessary to remove presidential obstructions in the way of enforcing the military and supplemental Reconstruction acts in the manner intended by Congress. Conkling beat down a resolution

18 L. D. White, *Republican Era,* p. 118. *The Nation* estimated, on Feb. 19, 1874, that the collector received about $50,000 a year.
19 *Cong. Globe,* 40th Cong., 1st sess., pp. 300–301.

by Sumner that the Senate not be restrained or the session curtailed.[20] The young senator from New York was moving up, and the nation was starting to notice him. He and Morton were quickly taking places in the Republican leadership. The Chicago *Republican* called Conkling "already the leader of the Senate," despite his years, and the Washington *Chronicle* said, "No new senator has ever made in so short a time such rapid strides to a commanding position in that body." [21]

Governor Reuben E. Fenton was at the moment the closest thing the New York Republicans had to a "boss" and he meant to keep it that way. A historian of New York politics later said. "From the moment Conkling became a senator the division of the party into two stout factions was merely a question of time." [22] Nevertheless, Fenton still had to await the expiration of Morgan's term, while Conkling was on the scene in Washington.

Conkling fought successfully against the extreme radicals in their efforts to prolong the Senate session, agreeing finally to recess to November 21, rather than to adjourn sine die. Sumner called the resolution a surrender, a proposal "to leave the President, a bad man . . . from the heats of summer to the cold of winter, to bestride this country like a Colossus." [23] Zach Chandler of Michigan, one of the radical leaders, a crude man, reputed to be a drunkard, made a violent attack upon conservatives who wanted to adjourn, singling out in particular the esteemed William Pitt Fessenden of Maine. Fessenden in reply said that he could endure "the denunciation of even so potent a man" as Chandler so long as he was sustained by the conservative leaders of the Senate, among whom he mentioned both senators from New York. So Conkling was able to thread a narrow line between the two sides of the party; each felt he was really one with them. Conkling's resolution for adjournment was passed 17 to 14.[24]

As a United States senator and, more urgently, as a politician aspiring to the leadership of his party in New York State, Conkling had to

[20] N.Y. *Times*, July 4, 1867.

[21] Both quotes were March 28, 1867, the Chicago one in A. R. Conkling, p. 291, and the Washington one in Alexander, III, 172.

[22] Alexander, III, 173.

[23] *Cong. Globe,* 40th Cong., 1st sess., p. 754, July 20, 1867.

[24] *Ibid.,* pp. 751–752, 754. Fessenden, one of the Senate's greatest intellects, had long been its leader on financial affairs and had served a year as secretary of the treasury under Lincoln.

start thinking about the annual gatherings of the Republicans. In 1867, the state convention was to be held in September in Syracuse, the commercial center on Lake Onondaga.

The state of New York had long been marked by a species of political absolutism. It was a large and varied commercial and industrial unit, and the near-even division of voters between its two major parties necessitated strong political organizations. These organizations were usually run on quasi-military principles of discipline and obedience, together with proper rewards for faithful service. The boss, and most of the time there was one, ran affairs absolutely; revolts were crushed ruthlessly. On the other hand, if a revolt against authority succeeded and a boss was overthrown, the new leader quickly moved to make the party over in his own image.

There had been a series of bosses in New York, from the beginning of the nineteenth century. DeWitt Clinton with his Federalist organization was the first, but he was ultimately eclipsed by the Albany Regency, the Democratic machine of Martin Van Buren. Van Buren, who was able to achieve the pinnacle of the presidency (only to find the rewards far inferior to the expectations), was surrounded by very able politicians like William L. Marcy, Silas Wright, and John A. Dix. The Regency had, in the Albany *Argus,* a party organ, but the most essential asset it controlled was patronage; until its breakup in the 1848 collapse of the Democratic party between Hunkers and Barnburners over slavery and free soil, all jobs for Democrats in New York State were funnelled through the Albany Regency.

The parallel organization on the other side of the political fence was the Whig following of Thurlow Weed. He, too, had his paper, the Albany *Evening Journal,* and his corresponding control over patronage and party rewards. Weed had brought his Whig machine practically intact into the new Republican party, thereby giving it an "instant" boss, along with a powerful vote getter in Seward.

In both parties, however, matters were in a state of flux in 1867. The Albany Regency had to all intents and purposes disappeared, and power in the Democratic party was diffused among warring leaders of the masses of New York City—Tammany Hall, Mozart Hall—and the upstate apparatus of the so-called Canal Ring, which exercised effective control over the Democratic parties in all the counties bordering the Erie Canal from Albany to Buffalo, and south to Elmira along the Chemung Canal. The ring, for whom Senator Jarvis Lord of Rochester served as a powerful voice in Albany, was an unhealthy amalgam of contractors who worked on the canals and politicians who thrived by its favor. The Canal Ring did not bother Tweed, and Tweed did not interfere with the ring. Samuel Tilden, who ultimately unified the party (with some exceptions), had not yet made his move.[25]

Weed's Republican dominance had withered because of his age, the failure of Seward to achieve the presidency, and the strategic mistake of sticking with Andrew Johnson. The fact that Harris, Seward's stand-in, had been virtually a cipher in the Senate had not helped either. Once Seward stayed on in the Johnson cabinet, however, he and Weed were politically dead in New York. As Johnson picked up his old Democratic ties, Unionist followers like Weed were lost. The old dictator did try to exert influence within the Democratic party, but his ancient adversaries brushed him aside easily. With Weed out of the way, the resourceful Reuben E. Fenton set about making himself the Republican leader of the state.

Fenton was a strange mixture of serious deficiencies and useful abilities. Men differed about him, to say the least. Consider these two statements, both by Republicans of similar political hue, both considered to be men of good will. Chauncey M. Depew of the New York Central Railroad: "He had every quality for political leadership, was a shrewd judge of character, and rarely made mistakes in the selection of his lieutenants." President Andrew D. White of Cornell: "There stood Fenton, marking the lowest point in the choice of a State executive ever reached in our Commonwealth by the Republican party." [26]

Reuben Eaton Fenton was born in 1819 near Frewsburg, in the western part of New York, and he spent all his life in the Chautauqua area. He was shrewd and thrifty, and he made a great deal of money buying and selling land. He was elected to Congress as a Democrat in 1852, but he was a Barnburner, or free-soil Democrat, and he eagerly joined the Republican party when it was founded in 1854. He served as a congressman until 1864, when he resigned to run for governor against Horatio Seymour; one of the marks of his eligibility was his freedom from the Weed-Greeley dogfights. Fenton was elected and then re-elected in 1866. It is instructive to note that in 1864, when he first ran for governor, Fenton was suspected by some "hard-peace" advocates of being too conservative; yet the conservative Republicans of

---

[25] Hudson, pp. 48–49.

[26] Depew, p. 34; A. D. White, *Autobiography,* I, 131.

New York on the whole supported Conkling in his struggle with Fenton. One should be wary of assigning ideology too important a role in intraparty feuding in New York.

Fenton's two terms as governor were marked by several major reforms in education and in the administration of state hospitals and similar facilities.[27] But Fenton was not an outstanding speaker in a day when oratorical ability was considered one of the highest qualities in a public figure; he was a trimmer, who endeavored constantly to catch the drift of public feeling and adapt to it. He had few strong political principles of his own; even his participation in the Liberal Republican movement of 1872 came about mainly because of his pique at Grant and Conkling. Many people thought him dishonest. It was noised about publicly, without denial, that Governor Fenton had accepted a bribe from Jay Gould to sign a bill favorable to the financier's railroad manipulation; whether true or not, the fact that people were prepared to believe the story tells us something about Fenton's public standing prior to his entry into the Senate. Even his closest friends never claimed that Fenton possessed any qualifications of the first order. What he did have was a will to political power, a winning personality which enabled him to recruit and hold followers, a crafty but clever political instinct which usually kept him from making serious mistakes, and the good fortune to be elected governor of New York at about the same time that Weed and Seward sank into oblivion. The New York *World* called him "a weak man"; others said he was without "statesmanlike qualities"; the reality of the situation in 1867, however, was that Reuben E. Fenton was, regardless of merits or demerits, the number one leader of the New York Republican party.[28]

Fenton's plan for the 1867 state convention was to have Lyman Tremaine named as chairman; the governor had enough delegates there to run things pretty well as he saw fit. There was, however, one hitch: Roscoe Conkling let it be known that he desired to be chairman. Fenton could control the convention so far as naming the relatively minor state officials for the ticket; could he control the delegates in a head-to-head joust with the popular and newly elected senator? Fenton supposed, too, that the other senator, Edwin D. Morgan, would throw what weight he had into the balance against him. Morgan knew whose seat Fenton was after, and Morgan was no Ira Harris. He was

[27] H. G. McMahon, *Chatauqua County*, pp. 151–155; Writers Program, p. 393.
[28] N.Y. *World*, Sept. 7, 1866; Alexander, III, 115.

a substantial statesman, a nationally prominent figure; his trouble lay in the shameful neglect of his political fences back home while he was in Washington. In fact, Morgan urged Conkling to steer a resolution through the convention endorsing the official conduct of the two U.S. senators should the convention go on record as approving Fenton's work as governor.[29]

The body assembled in Syracuse on September 25, and, to the surprise and consternation of the Fenton forces, Senator Edward Madden of Orange County rose at the very outset and presented a resolution that the committee on organization be requested to report for permanent chairman the name of Roscoe Conkling. Before most of the delegates were settled into their seats, the resolution carried, and Conkling was the chairman. Then he made a speech, which was, naturally, the high point of the gathering.

Not surprisingly, he spoke viciously about Andrew Johnson:

Millions of bullets had tried in vain; but assassination is a more exact science than war, more precise than Shylock's knife. Had murder done either less or more it had lost but by striking till it came to Andrew Johnson and sparing him it won. . . . We went to war to gain peace—lasting peace. We conquered, and the law of nations and of nature gave us the right to require security for the future. We had a right to make sure that the red eye of battle had closed never to open more upon fraternal strife. Congress upheld this right. A recreant Executive denied it.

After a long passage detailing the assembled wrongs of the president, Conkling delivered this thinly veiled warning: "It is not for me to express, nor even to form an opinion of, the grounds for impeachment which may exist. The duty I may in another place be called upon to do imposes silence and abstinence upon me, and besides, from the outset it has been my earnest hope that the country might be spared the anxiety and disturbance incident to deposing the chief officer of the Government." [30] The delegates loved it. It was the thing people remembered from the convention.

The actual nominations of the convention were controlled and dictated by Governor Fenton, in league with Horace Greeley of the New York *Tribune*. The conservative elements of the party were pretty much shut out by the convention, at Fenton's command. All this was of no

[29] J. A. Rawley, *Edwin D. Morgan*, p. 225.
[30] N.Y. *Times*, Sept. 26, 1867.

moment to Senator Conkling. He knew he was not yet strong enough to oust Fenton from power.

Fenton gained no lustre from the fact that his hand-picked ticket was swamped in the general election by 48,000 votes. Greeley, too, came in for his share of the blame; he was too prone to intraparty squabbling, and he made the mistake of injecting the temperance issue into the canvass. This always brought out a heavy Democratic vote in New York City.[31]

Shortly after the election in November, 1867, Congress reassembled in Washington, sniffing around the capital to see whether Andrew Johnson had ruined the country in the interim. What to do about Johnson —this was the big question facing the leaders of Congress as they reconvened. Thad Stevens had no doubt about the answer: impeach him. Ben Wade of Ohio, the president pro tempore of the Senate, agreed, though he, being next in line for the presidency with no vice-president around, was clearly an interested party. Indeed, the Cincinnati *Commercial* ran a long folksy article entitled "Senator Ben Wade at Home," which was reprinted verbatim by the New York *Times* on July 1, 1867, with the comment, "The principal object of the article is evidently to bring the distinguished statesman properly forward as a candidate for the Presidency." Wade was coarse and belligerent and, though a lawyer and former circuit judge back in Ohio, he demonstrated no comprehension of the meaning and principles of the Constitution. He had been almost as bitterly antagonistic to Lincoln as he was to Johnson, and no thinking person regarded him seriously as a candidate for president. Yet, there he was, the heir apparent, if only Johnson could be moved out of the way.

Talk of impeachment had been bruited about for some time. It must be presumed that most people took such talk with a large quantity of salt, for no president of the United States had ever come close to being subjected to such an indignity. The doubters failed to recognize, however, that no president had ever had so large a majority of hardened opponents against him in Congress as Johnson had, and that the balance between the executive branch and Congress was seriously out of order.

The skeptics wondered, too, why any further action needed to be taken against the president, since the Republican majorities in both

31 Van Deusen, *Horace Greeley*, p. 366.

impeachment ?
why ?

houses had rendered him virtually powerless. On party measures, they could pass any bill they desired, await the usual veto, and then promptly pass it into law over the veto. With the Tenure of Office Act and senatorial confirmation power, Johnson's hands were effectively tied in the matter of appointments and dismissals, too. But this view reckoned without the passions aroused by the war, still dying slowly, the Republican feeling that Johnson was cheating the loyal North of the legitimate fruits of victory, the incomplete nature of Southern submission, and the pure personal animosity which that scourge-tongued president had managed to arouse. Besides, Johnson still retained the power to administer the Reconstruction acts, and he did this in a way that was most displeasing to the congressional leadership.

There were from time to time proposals to impeach Johnson just on general principle, but Stevens and the hard-line leadership of the House knew they had to have some specifics, or they would lose some of the senators they needed to make up a two-thirds vote for conviction. Johnson proceeded to furnish them with the specifics.

Edwin M. Stanton, Lincoln's "architect of victory," was still secretary of war, but Andrew Johnson considered him an enemy. Stanton reported everything that transpired at cabinet meetings to the radical leaders of Congress; Johnson and everyone else knew that this was going on. That Stanton should stay on in the cabinet under such circumstances was an atrocious affront to the executive, but it was coolly calculated. Stanton's retention as secretary of war was one of the primary reasons for the passage of the Tenure of Office Act on March 2, 1867, over a veto of course. Under this legislation, the president could not remove a subordinate without the consent of the Senate. In August, 1867, Johnson called upon Stanton to resign, but the secretary refused. The president thereupon suspended him from office, pending the reconvening of Congress, with Grant, whose political views were unclear to all (including himself), named as secretary ad interim. Stanton did not acquiesce in the president's course, and he was encouraged by congressional leaders such as Conkling, who wrote him on August 14 that he had managed with "credit and good effect".[32] When Congress reconvened and refused to allow the dismissal of Stanton, the secretary resumed his post, and Grant vacated the office, much to Johnson's chagrin. Grant said he had never agreed to take the job permanently, and Johnson said he had. The recriminations between the two became

[32] B. P. Thomas and H. M. Hyman, *Stanton*, p. 554.

nasty. Finally, on February 21, 1868, the exasperated president removed Stanton, thereby flouting the Tenure of Office Act, which he and a great many experts in the field felt was clearly unconstitutional. There ensued a comic opera which was played out over physical possession of the war office between Stanton and the president's next choice, General Lorenzo Thomas, an armchair soldier who here made his only significant appearance in history. It made no difference. Stevens had his opening now, and Johnson was to be impeached.

On February 25, 1868, Stevens and John Bingham of Ohio appeared in the Senate to impeach the president. A committee of seven, including Conkling, was appointed to take the House message into consideration and to work out rules for the subsequent proceedings before the Senate.[33] There was a lot of talk in the Senate about whether that body should be recorded as sitting as a "high court of impeachment" or any kind of court. Roscoe Conkling said no, "We shall proceed as the Senate, performing a judicial function no doubt, but nevertheless the Senate." [34] His view prevailed, and the Senate did not call itself a court. Just words, perhaps, but they may have soothed some consciences; the Senate might make decisions on more political grounds than any court should. And this was to be a political trial. Evarts, the president's counsel, said, "The managers conduct the trial as if it was that of a horsethief." Gideon Welles said sourly, "A shameless, brazen effrontery and villainy mark certain Senators," mentioning among others Sumner, Cameron, and Conkling. "He is to be tried and condemned by these violators, conspirators, and perjurers." [35]

But Welles, of course, did not like the anti-Johnson tone of the whole affair, and he was very suspicious. One day, he passed Conkling and Ben Butler, one of the managers of the impeachment for the House, in conversation on a street corner—"an ominous and discreditable conjunction," he called it—and Welles was sure that they "showed in their countenances what they were talking about." [36]

He may have judged Conkling harshly. The senator gave little evidence of any overpowering interest in seeing Johnson convicted, asked only a few questions in the course of the trial, and had an influence only at the beginning when his motions denied to the president's law-

[33] *Cong. Globe,* 40th Cong., 2d sess., pp. 1405–1406.
[34] *Ibid.,* p. 1523, Feb. 29, 1868.
[35] Evarts to Edwards Pierrepont, April 16, 1868, Pierrepont Papers; Welles, III, 301.
[36] *Ibid.,* 336–337.

yers additional time which they wanted to work on their defense. During the course of the trial, Conkling voted to sustain Chief Justice Chase on evidentiary rulings which were overturned by the majority, rulings which favored the defense.[37] Conkling voted for conviction but he made no speech about it, and he did not file a separate written opinion as so many of his fellow senators did.

Though the Johnson impeachment has long been regarded as a discreditable piece of work, it might be noted that Johnson was an "accidental" president who had not been elected to the office, that he was a Democrat placed on the Union ticket by Lincoln for an emergency now past, and that the "sanctity of the office," after such dismal recent examples as Pierce and Buchanan, was not much of a consideration. The president's rough-and-tumble manner and intemperate tongue disgusted many congressmen, including some who were themselves no better. Johnson had clearly been repudiated by the people at the last election, and many politicians, Conkling among them, felt no compunctions about casting a political vote against a political adversary.

The long-sought vote on the eleventh article of impeachment, the one on which the House managers felt they had their best case, was taken on May 16. Tension ran high. Everyone knew that Ben Wade had already picked his cabinet, to be installed with him when Johnson was evicted from the White House. The Republicans had 42 of the 54 senators and needed 36 votes to convict. They knew that all twelve Democratic senators would vote for acquittal, and they knew that there were defections in their own ranks. Intimidation, cajolery, and coercion were the order of the day to bring waverers into line, although nothing has ever linked Roscoe Conkling with this effort. In fact, Conkling had been quite ill for several days before the vote. As the roll call began, no one really knew what was going to happen. As expected, the first Republican defectors were Fessenden of Maine and Fowler of Tennessee. James Grimes of Iowa, dying, had been carried in by four men, but he had himself raised to his feet to vote "not guilty." John Henderson of Missouri, a freshman, voted as expected to acquit. There was doubt about Conkling's colleague, Edwin D. Morgan, but he voted for conviction. Johnson always felt that Morgan voted this way for political expediency, with his own seat coming up the

<hr>

[37] *Cong. Globe,* 40th Cong., 2d sess., supp., pp. 11, 28, March 13, 24, 1868; J. Mushkat, "The Impeachment," p. 279. Mushkat's article is an editing of the journal of Congressman John V. L. Pruyn of New York.

next year, and that he would have voted to acquit if his vote had been necessary. Soon, the name of Edmund G. Ross of Kansas, the most uncertain vote of all, was called. When Ross voted "not guilty," the House managers knew their cause was lost. Two more Republicans, Lyman Trumbull of Illinois and Peter Van Winkle of West Virginia, were expected to cast their votes against conviction, and when they did so, the total vote was 35 guilty, 19 not guilty, with one more vote needed to convict.[38]

The managers postponed proceedings for a couple of weeks and later tried votes on two more articles, but these met with the same result, and the effort was abandoned. Johnson was not turned out; yet, as a vindictive Charles Sumner said, "he may go forth from this Chamber with a nominal acquittal; but he must go forth as a blasted public functionary." [39] True enough, but he was to all intents a blasted functionary before the impeachment; he served out the remaining months of his term in a peaceful oblivion.

On May 26, Stanton submitted his resignation. Johnson chose Seward to take over the war department as well as his own, but before sending this commission to the Senate, Seward felt that Republican senatorial sentiment should be checked. He went to Conkling, who agreed to check with his colleagues. On May 29, Roscoe wrote Seward that tempers were still high, that Johnson should be wary of playing games with Congress right after the acquittal, and that Seward's name would not be acceptable to the Republican leadership, a sad commentary on changing times and the fate of an erstwhile leader of the party.[40] Shortly thereafter, the President sent in the name of General John M. Schofield, hero of the Battle of Franklin, who was confirmed.

The Fortieth Congress, when it was not trying to evict the president, was bedeviled by currency questions just as its predecessors had been. The advocates of a return to specie payments were contradicted by those favoring the issue of more paper, while others threw up their hands and said to let the secretary of the treasury expand or contract as he saw fit. Senator Conkling, while taking an adamant position against any further issue of paper, was realistic enough to recognize that

---

38 Rawley, pp. 228–229; Mushkat, p. 282; *Cong. Globe,* 40th Cong., 2d sess., supp., p. 411.
39 *Cong. Globe,* 40th Cong., 2d sess., p. 2493, May 16, 1868.
40 Thomas and Hyman, p. 610; G. Van Deusen, *Seward,* pp. 481–482.

an immediate return to hard money would promptly bring about economic dislocation and depression.

In January 1868, he opposed a bill of Morton's to restrict the power of the secretary to contract the currency. "A large class of people," he said, would interpret this "as a permanent policy of anti-contraction" and another large class as "a measure unmistakably indicating an intention positively to expand and render still more redundant . . . the currency of the country." [41] Despite Conkling's opposition, the bill

In June, he opposed, again unsuccessfully, the National Bank Bill, which included a section authorizing the issue of $20,000,000 more of paper. Conkling still found himself on the losing side of the issue in his struggle for what he conceived to be "sound money," but he knew that he was right and that in time his party would come to see that.[42]

He was in a minority, too, in the matter of railroad grants. The congressional bounty to the many railway entrepreneurs who appeared with supplications was almost limitless. Blaine, soon to be Speaker at the other end of the Capitol, was most active in pushing through grants of land and funds for "deserving" railroad enterprises, and many in the Senate were fully as eager to help out. Conkling was not one of them, as he explained one day in the Senate:

I was one who believed, that it was desirable and well originally to foster by subsidies and lands the laying of a track of railroad from the Valley of the Mississippi to the Pacific Ocean. I voted for the original bills looking to the establishment of such a line of road, and with the lights before me, I should do so again. I was anxious to provide for a road connecting one side of this continent with the other side. But, sir, there is such a matter as too much of a good thing; and it does not follow that because it was wise to adopt measures which have already insured a railroad from Omaha to San Francisco, which is to be completed almost while we are talking about it, it is therefore wise to continue to subsidize companies, not only branches but parallel roads, to gridiron the entire West.[43]

It was at this time that Collis P. Huntington, the president of the Southern Pacific, wrote of Conkling, whom he considered a friend, that he was "so straight he leans backwards." Huntington from time to time tried to do things for Conkling, not to buy him, as he knew he could not do that, but to attract his good will; however, he found the New

passed the Senate.

[41] *Cong. Globe*, 40th Cong., 2d sess., pp. 526–527, Jan. 15, 1868.
[42] *Ibid.*, p. 3153, June 15, 1868.   [43] *Ibid.*, p. 1896, March 16, 1868.

Yorker "very sensitive," unlike many of his colleagues in the Senate.[44]

The problem of the South was still very much present. Since he was still opposed to the imposition of "fundamental conditions," Conkling took an active part in the debates which resulted in the readmission, finally, of Arkansas, North Carolina, South Carolina, Louisiana, Georgia, Alabama, and Florida, all in properly "reconstructed" form, in June 1868.[45] All of these states were now in line to send good Republicans to represent them in Washington; if the Southern accents of some of these men were somewhat newly acquired, at least there was no doubt of their fidelity to the principles and programs of the Republican leadership.

Finally, Conkling spent much of the session voting against appropriations and measures involving the expenditures of new funds; with proper retrenchment on the part of the government, he felt, a speedy return to specie payment would be easier. Indeed, near the close of the session, Senator James Dixon of Connecticut, a renegade Republican who had just been the target of some blistering Conklinian sarcasm, said of the New Yorker: "He has been here now I think about a year, and I have heard him discuss a great many subjects, but I think economy is his theme. As to the final result of all, he comes down to that, that is the refrain, 'economy.' " [46]

[44] Huntington to Charles Crocker, March 21, 1868, in D. Rothman, *Politics and Power,* pp. 196–197.

[45] The Arkansas bill passed the Senate, 34–8, on June 1, 1868, and the bill for the other states passed on June 10, by a vote of 31–5; *Cong. Globe,* 40th Cong., 2d sess., pp. 2750, 3029.

[46] *Ibid.,* p. 3360, June 22, 1868.

CHAPTER 6

A NATIONAL VIEW

Congress was anxious to adjourn in the early summer of 1868, because 1868 was the year the presidency was to be redeemed from Andrew Johnson. It was time to be about the work of redemption, to take to the hustings for Ulysses S. Grant.

There had been much tugging and hauling for the general's political soul since the end of the war, but there was never much doubt, once Grant found out that he was a Republican, that he would be the Republican nominee in 1868. The only question concerned the identity of the selection for vice-president. New York had its candidate for the second slot, but he was not Roscoe Conkling's candidate. The early state convention, held at Syracuse on February 5 to select delegates for the national convention, endorsed General Grant by acclamation and, carefully controlled by the boss, recommended Reuben E. Fenton for vice-president. Fenton was storing up future trouble for himself because many New York Republicans were unhappy at the governor's method of selecting delegates. Most of the more conservative Republicans in the state now looked to Roscoe Conkling as a potential leader against Fenton.

When the Republican National Convention met in late May, Ulysses S. Grant was nominated by a unanimous roll-call vote. That was easy. The real fight was for vice-president. This convention paid little heed to any supposed right on the part of the presidential candidate to pick his running mate, and Grant asserted no such right. There were four prime potentials for the second spot, though eleven men in all received votes on the first ballot. Chief among these was Ben Wade, previously considered a sure thing since he would be the incumbent president, but now losing strength rapidly since Johnson's acquittal a few days before. The plan had been for Wade to step down to the vice-presidency, but

106

the Senate had knocked a hole in that strategy. There were three other leading contenders: Senator Henry Wilson of Massachusetts, a long-time antislavery Whig and early Republican; Schuyler Colfax of Indiana, Speaker of the House, a former newspaperman, and a lay leader of the Methodist Episcopal Church; and finally there was Fenton. Though Wade led on each of the first four ballots, with Fenton close behind, it became quite clear that neither of these two nor Wilson had the strength to go over the top. On the fifth ballot the congenial Colfax surged ahead to a sudden but overwhelming victory. Fenton's cause had been aided not at all by New Yorkers who toured the delegations with the word that he was not nearly as strong in his home state as it might appear to outsiders. A number of those most active against the governor at Chicago later turned up in Roscoe Conkling's camp—when there was a Roscoe Conkling camp. Initially, they were merely against Fenton.

Though many experts felt that 1868 was to be a Republican year, the Democrats, in their convention in New York City in early July, put on the most surprising show. The Republican gathering had been cut and dried; no one could get too stirred up over the vice-presidential uncertainty. The Democratic party, though still in eclipse because of its loud opposition to the war, still managed to generate excitement and suspense at its nominating convention.

The leading contenders for the presidential nomination were former Congressman George H. Pendleton of Cincinnati, President Andrew Johnson, whom the Democrats had to applaud but certainly were not about to nominate, General Winfield Scott Hancock, and Senator Thomas A. Hendricks of Indiana, the leader of the small band of Democrats in the upper house. Pendleton, the vice-presidential candidate in 1864, had been a wartime Copperhead; he and Hancock, a legitimate Democratic war hero, not a reluctant dragon like McClellan, represented the extremes in the party. Behind the scenes there was a great deal of talk about the availability of Chief Justice Salmon P. Chase, still ostensibly a Republican but ready to return to his old affiliations with the Democracy, if it would only nominate him. Chase had avidly pursued the presidency for years, and an active stand-by canvass was conducted for him now. Horatio Seymour was for Chase, and so, for a time, was Samuel J. Tilden, the strong man of the New York delegation. Tilden later became cool to the Chase movement, though his preference for the nomination was unclear.

Twenty-two inconclusive ballots were taken. Pendleton surged to the fore and then collapsed, Johnson disappeared from sight, Hancock peaked and then receded, and Hendricks held an unimpressive lead. The time had come when the Chase boom was supposed to sweep suddenly across the convention. It never happened. An Ohio delegate stood up and threw the name of Horatio Seymour before the convention. For two years during the war, Seymour had given the Democrats what life and direction they had, and the party faithful now repaid him for it. State after state changed its count to Seymour. The New Yorker rose and pleaded that, "Your candidate I cannot be," but the tide was so far advanced that he could not roll it back. Tilden advised him that he must accept, and he did so, reluctantly. There is much evidence that Seymour was genuine in his desire to refuse the nomination and that he was swept to the head of his party's ticket by that rarest of political phenomena, a sincere and honest draft.[1]

On July 9, Roscoe Conkling, whose relations with Seymour had never been much more than "correct," wrote the following genuinely good-natured letter to his somewhat bewildered brother-in-law:

We think it will hardly do to send our congratulations by telegraph, lest you be injured by holding communication with the enemy. But we do congratulate you most heartily on the nomination and on the most complimentary manner of it. Some of the telegraph operators sent me each ballot from the start, and to-day I telegraphed from the Capitol to Julie, so that she too had the tidings at the moment. The whole thing has upset our house politically, Julie and Bessie being both out openly for the Democratic ticket.

Blair gives you no strength I think, but with or without him, in N.Y., any nomination possible would have been weak in comparison with your own, and if we have done anything deserving Democratic rule, by all means give us the President now suggested. So much I will stand by.[2]

On this gracious note, Conkling departed the political scene for a while. Leaving in mid-August, the senator took his first long trip away from the eastern seaboard. Accompanied by his Utica crony, Ward

[1] The voting in the two conventions of 1868 is set forth in McClure, pp. 210, 215–216. A more detailed description of the Democratic convention is in A. C. Flick and G. S. Lobrano, *Samuel Jones Tilden*, pp. 166–180.

[2] Conkling Papers, Library of Congress. Blair, of course, was Frank P. Blair of Missouri, a former radical Republican who, like most of the famous Blair family, ultimately drifted back to the Democrats, and had been nominated for vice-president with Seymour.

Hunt, and the famous Swiss naturalist, Professor Louis Agassiz of Harvard, who wanted to study glacial phenomena, and with several other friends, Conkling headed west. He did manage to mix a little politics in his tour, however. The first stop was at Harrisburg, where they visited Simon Cameron, and learned of the death of Cameron's old rival for Pennsylvania's Republican leadership, Thaddeus Stevens, bitterly disappointed to the last that the Senate had failed him in his bid to turn Andrew Johnson out of office.

From Harrisburg the party moved on to Galena, Illinois, where they stopped for a chat with General Grant, who did not know quite what he was doing as a candidate but was advised by the party leaders that he was doing it very well indeed. The tourists then journeyed to Dubuque, down the Mississippi to St. Louis, and then overland to Kansas City and Lawrence, Kansas, the old Free-State center of "bleeding Kansas" in the 1850's. Here Roscoe was prevailed upon to make a speech. At the terminus of the railroad at Fort Harker, Kansas, they were met by Conkling's friend, General Phil Sheridan, and then went on across the plains to Denver in carriages and on horseback, with the tall, strong, senator staying in the saddle all the way. They camped out on the plains at night, beneath the clear western sky and the stars. Conkling gloried in the open spaces, the panoramic vistas, the towering mountains, the rushing rivers. It made a deep impression upon him, and he often spoke of his vision of the West. But he was an Easterner born and reared, and he had a stake in the older section. Not for him to tear up his roots and drag them across a continent—but it was comforting to know that it was all there.

From Denver in the foothills of the Rockies, they moved west to Georgetown, high up in the mountains. They climbed Grey's Peak, with the senator leading the way. The party descended to Boulder, Colorado, and then traveled by stage to Cheyenne in the Wyoming Territory. From there they went by rail to Bitter Creek, Wyoming, west of the Continental Divide, in the old fur-trapping country, peopled forever by the shades of Bridger, Bonneville, Ashley, Sublette, and their cohorts. Then east again on the railroad and home to Utica. The senator's knowledge of America was greatly broadened, though perhaps without being perceptibly deepened.[3]

Conkling returned around the end of September. The Republican campaign was in full swing, and the senator was eager to assume a

[3] Conkling's western trip is described in A. R. Conkling, pp. 308–312.

leading role in it. Not only was his brother-in-law running for president against General Grant, but there was also an election for governor of the state of New York.

Fenton was not running for another term. His eye was on the Senate seat of Edwin D. Morgan, whose term expired in 1869, and he could not afford the gamble of another gubernatorial candidacy. When the Republicans met at Syracuse to select their state ticket, it was generally assumed that Congressman John A. Griswold of Troy, a personable and very popular ironmaker, a friend of Roscoe Conkling, would be nominated with no serious opposition. At the last minute, Horace Greeley sent John Russell Young, one of his star reporters on the *Tribune,* to Syracuse to procure the editor's nomination. Young recruited Chauncey Depew to make a nominating speech for Greeley, much against Depew's better judgment. The delegates treated Greeley's eleventh-hour candidacy as a joke, even though Depew made what was widely acclaimed as a memorable speech, and Griswold swamped the editor 247 to 95 on the first ballot. Alonzo B. Cornell, the son of the founder of the bright new university in Ithaca, was nominated for lieutenant governor.

Greeley, miffed and disappointed once again, later told Depew: "I cannot understand why I desired the nomination for governor nor why anybody should want the office. There is nothing in it. No man now can name the ten last governors of the State of New York." [4] This indulgence in sour grapes, of course, did not mean that Greeley had been cured of his office-seeking mania. The Democrats selected as their candidate the mayor of New York City, the loser to Fenton in 1868, Tweed's man, John T. Hoffman.

Conkling worked hard for Grant in the campaign. On September 28, he told a crowd in Utica that the Democratic platform was "a gigantic swindle." [5] On October 8, barely a week after his return from the West, Conkling addressed a large campaign meeting at Cooper Union. The *Times* called it "a highly respectable and intelligent audience, among whom were a large number of ladies." Naturally. The ladies always loved to watch and hear Roscoe, exuding animal vigor, even sexuality. The crowd first had to put up with a short talk by Senator Morgan, although his flaws as a speaker were generally forgiven in the universal respect accorded him. Then Conkling came on with one of his real

---

[4] Depew, pp. 88–89; also Van Deusen, *Horace Greeley,* p. 371.
[5] N. Y. *Times,* Oct. 1, 1868.

spell-binders, a long and carefully prepared message fusing the two leading questions, as he called them, of Reconstruction and finance. After Roscoe was finished, there was nothing to do but adjourn.[6]

Though Conkling worked long and hard to elect the Republican ticket in 1868, his speeches dealt with issues and platforms, not with personalities. On personalities, he was in a ticklish spot. The Republican press put out rumors of Seymour's insanity or impending insanity, and Conkling took it upon himself to deny publicly any imputation of madness in the Seymour blood, an imputation that reflected directly upon his own wife and daughter.[7] On the whole, Roscoe handled fairly well the delicate problem of giving complete support to his party's ticket without upsetting the precarious personal balance between himself and his brother-in-law, a relationship which was always a bit edgy and which became more so with the progressive estrangement between Roscoe and Julia. Conkling's speeches emphasized the virtues of Grant, the wickedness of President Johnson, the good work of Reconstruction, and the need for retrenchment and economy; he left Horatio Seymour alone.

The senator concentrated his campaign efforts in the central part of the state, with emphasis on Oneida and its neighboring counties. At one point in the canvass, he toured with Chauncey Depew, the amiable railroader to whom Conkling was allegedly indebted for the removal of Erastus Clark from the path of his congressional re-election. Depew tells an interesting story about Conkling on this trip.

The various committees on arrangements under whose auspices Conkling was to speak had been notified in advance that the senator would not speak outside but only within the confines of a hall. Those majestic, measured periods were far more impressive resounding off the interior walls of an auditorium than being blown to the winds in the open air. Besides, a speech of two hours or so without electrical amplification is very hard on the vocal chords under any circumstances, but much more so when delivered outside to a diffuse and scattered crowd. In any event, says Depew, when the speakers arrived in Lockport, they found that a mistake had been made. A vast crowd of 20,000 filled the fairgrounds, waiting, among the diversions of the county fair, to hear the Republican message. Conkling insisted upon his terms—no outdoor speeches. A rearrangement was hastily contrived; it was announced that Conkling would be speaking at the local opera house and

6 *Ibid.,* Oct. 9.   7 C. H. Coleman, *Election of 1868,* p. 258.

Depew was detailed to speak to those who were left at the fairgrounds. As might be expected, very few showed up at the opera house, as no meeting had been scheduled there, and Conkling gave no speech. In the meantime, Depew gave what he modestly described as a very effective talk to the throng at the fairgrounds. When Depew found the senator later, that personage was "very indignant." No doubt. One does not trifle with a proud and touchy United States senator in such a manner. Depew put it this way: "The cordial relations which had existed up to that time were somehow severed and he became very hostile." [8] Of course, Depew tended to be a political maverick who paid little heed to the obligations of party regularity, and such people never stayed for long in Roscoe Conkling's good graces.

Conkling not only made speeches for the 1868 ticket, he also was able to recruit Edwin M. Stanton, who had never been a strong Grant advocate, for some campaigning on behalf of the ticket. He wrote Stanton that Grant had spoken of the ex-secretary "with strong feeling of friendship" and convinced Stanton that he should lend his voice to the Republican cause. [9] Grant later appointed Stanton to the Supreme Court, though the old veteran died before he could take his seat on the bench.

Conkling's efforts bore fruit in his home area, for he was able to carry Oneida County for Grant against his brother-in-law, the county's most distinguished citizen. Seymour carried New York State as a whole, however, by 10,000 votes; he was the beneficiary of one of the most blatant frauds in American electoral history. The Democratic majority, which carried Hoffman to victory over Griswold by 28,000 votes, was manufactured by William M. Tweed out of a staggering use of "repeaters," wholesale naturalization of new citizens by Democratic judges in New York City, widespread voting by fictitious persons, and a dishonest count of the ballots in the city. [10]

Despite the loss of the Empire State, Ulysses S. Grant was elected president; his popular majority of roughly 310,000 was translated into an electoral college triumph of 214 to 80. The White House was safely redeemed, delivered into the strong hands of the hero of Appomattox. No one took the trouble to worry about what he might do with it.

On January 1, 1869, a bitter, snowy day, Reuben E. Fenton relinquished the governorship of New York after two terms, a period of

[8] Depew, pp. 75–76.   [9] Thomas and Hyman, p. 619.
[10] Stebbins, pp. 392–394.

four years in which he had worked assiduously to build a personal organization to maintain control of the Republican party of the state. Though the Democrat Hoffman was sworn in as the new governor, the Republicans still controlled the legislature. The senate was narrowly Republican, 17 to 15, but the assembly had a wider margin, 75 to 53. The test of Fenton's strength would come quickly, in the election of a United States senator.

Morgan wanted another term. There was really no reason why he should not have it, except that he stood in Fenton's way. Morgan was a solid person, "a figure to inspire confidence among business men." [11] Born in 1811 of Welsh farming stock, he rose from clerk in a general store in Hartford to partner in the business. He and two friends from Hartford opened a business in New York City in 1837, but their timing was bad, and the Panic of 1837 soon chased Morgan's partners back to Connecticut. He carried on alone, and soon made a great success as a commission merchant. He was shrewd, austere, and cautious, but when he made up his mind, he was bold and impatient for proper execution of his ideas. In 1843, he formed E. D. Morgan and Company, which grew into one of the nation's foremost import houses. Great personal wealth soon followed, together with an urge for involvement in politics.

Morgan moved through the Whig ranks in New York City, as an assistant alderman, then two terms as a state senator, until in 1853 he became Whig state chairman. From this vantage point, it was an easy step to chairman of the new state Republican party the following year, and in 1856 he was named the first national chairman. In 1858, Morgan was elected governor of New York, and he was re-elected in 1860; he carried out with distinguished ability the tasks of leading the nation's largest state in the crucial first two years of war. At the close of his term as governor in 1863, Morgan was elected to the U.S. Senate, and he had the further honor of declining with thanks Lincoln's invitation to become secretary of the treasury upon Chase's ascension to the Supreme Court. Morgan, a tall, massive, heavy-featured man, quiet but highly respected, was no political accident, no minor impediment to be swept aside by the crafty Fenton. There would be a fight.[12]

Morgan was no speaker, and he lost some strength among radical elements because he had supported Andrew Johnson longer than had many others. Besides, it was whispered that Morgan would have voted

11 Rawley, p. 9.
12 *Ibid.,* pp. 4–50, for biographical background on E. D. Morgan.

to acquit the wicked president if his vote had been necessary to do so. No one knew for sure, but it seemed possible and Fenton's people spread the word.

Morgan, though, wrote to his numerous friends all over the state, asking for their help in getting him re-elected. He contributed $5,000 to the 1868 campaign, to be used wisely in helping some marginal members of the legislature win their elections. His friend and former aide Chester A. Arthur, a sage young political head, was there in Albany to help him, and Conkling was active in his favor as well. (After all, Morgan was not going to be a boss, and if Fenton went down, the Chautauquan was through. That left an inviting prospect for Conkling.) Morgan's friends in Washington wrote letters urging his re-election, and newspaper stories casting doubt on Fenton's personal integrity started to appear as well. One of Fenton's problems was that people were generally disposed to believe such stories.

At first it was expected that the selection of a Speaker of the Assembly would indicate which way the winds were blowing; Truman G. Younglove was reputed to be Fenton's man; John H. Selkreg, Morgan's. Unexpectedly, when the Republicans met on January 4 to pick a Speaker, Selkreg withdrew his name, leaving Younglove unopposed. The *Times* said that, "under the circumstances," the selection of a Speaker could not be regarded "as a settlement of the Senatorial contest." Anyway, that journal opined hopefully, "It is not believed by the best portion of the Republicans that he will permit the Senatorial question to enter in any way into the formation of committees." Morgan was not concerned about Younglove; he had contributed to the new Speaker's campaign in 1868, and Younglove had won by only four votes. Morgan presumed that gratitude would keep Younglove neutral, at the least.[13]

But Younglove announced that he would not name the house committees until after the Senate seat had been decided, though he denied stoutly that his failure to name them was designed to influence the outcome of that battle. Nevertheless, many observers figured that the Speaker was now sitting with most of the cards in his hand; given the manner in which legislation went through the assembly, the way greased with lubricants of gold and silver, the chairmanship of a leading committee was considered to be a very lucrative plum.

The Republican caucus met on Saturday evening, January 16, and

[13] N. Y. *Times,* Jan. 5, 6, 1869.

Fenton's name was placed in nomination by Speaker Younglove. The game was over almost before it started. Under the watchful eye of the Speaker, hopeful house members cast their votes for Fenton, and Morgan went down, 52 to 40. Morgan was bitterly disappointed.

As for Fenton, he and his followers were jubilant. They had flexed their muscles and shown that they were the power in the Republican party in New York. One correspondent wrote from Albany:

The success of Fenton is construed by his friends here as a guarantee that they are to have all the fat berths, both Federal and State, in the gift of the party. They . . . seem to take it for granted that Fenton is to be omnipotent with the incoming President, and sole arbiter of the fortunes of all members of the Republican party in the State of New York.[14]

Roscoe Conkling was not happy, but he bided his time. He had measured Fenton, and he did not think his new colleague was big enough to master the Republican party in the state.

There still remained a few weeks of the final session of the Fortieth Congress, a few weeks with Andrew Johnson resident at 1600 Pennsylvania Avenue, before the great day of Republican restoration. In those few weeks, considerable legislative business was conducted. Important matters were in contention: the fate of the proposed Fifteenth Amendment to the Constitution, repeal of the Tenure of Office Act before Grant became president (with Johnson out of the way, there would be no need for it, said those who thought logically about politics), currency (as always), and the public credit. A sizable chunk of business for a lameduck session.

Conkling happily voted for a bill pledging payment of all government obligations in coin except where the issuing legislation expressly provided otherwise. The bill passed the Senate on March 3, the last day of the session, and Conkling said, "I rejoice that at last the day has come when Congress is about to say that taking honesty, integrity and the force of obligations as the rule, the Government of the United States is to acknowledge and pay that which it honestly owes." His happiness was premature.[15]

The constitutional amendment to guarantee the political rights of the freedmen had been the subject of a great deal of effort, time, and

[14] *Ibid.*, Jan. 18. The Senate election can be followed in the *Times,* Jan. 4–18, 1869, and is also covered in Rawley, pp. 231–233.

[15] *Cong. Globe,* 40th Cong., 3d sess., pp. 1653, 1834.

debate. Conkling mentioned this on February 17, as the Senate drove toward a vote on the amendment:

I should consider it . . . a great calamity after all the precious time that has been devoted to this subject . . . if we should submit an amendment which, assuming it to be carried, would be wholly inadequate to the object after which we are reaching. . . . I am ready to vote now, for any amendment, whatever its form may be, whatever its paternity may be, which will present to the states fairly . . . the question whether they will surrender or relinquish so much of their jurisdiction, or supposed jurisdiction, as enables them to discriminate against persons of a particular race in respect to voting and holding office.[16]

The Senate passed the amendment in its ultimate form, except that the guarantee extended to the right to vote *and* "to hold office." When Conkling and Stewart of Nevada, the Senate conferees, reported back to the Senate on February 26, the conference committee had deleted the phrase "or to hold office." This provoked a long and heated debate which lasted until 3:00 A.M. the next day. Conkling and Stewart felt confident that the right to vote comprehended the right to hold office, so they recommended acceptance of the conference report. A number of other senators, led by George Edmunds of Vermont, disagreed, and felt that the deletion of the office-holding phrase was a surrender of a substantive part of the amendment. But it was late in the session. Conkling pointed out that if the Senate refused to accept the conference committee's suggestion, it was most likely that no amendment would go to the states for ratification. The House had already agreed to the report, so, reluctantly and very late at night, the Senate did so as well.[17]

Efforts were being made to repeal the Tenure of Office Act, the statute used by the Republican majorities to cripple Johnson's power to remove unwanted subordinates. Some Republican leaders, notably Senator Oliver P. Morton, understandably regarded the act as so much excess baggage with the presidency safely in the hands of a well-advised Republican chief executive. Grant himself wanted it repealed. There were others, however, who differed. To them, it was senatorial prerogative that mattered, and the act was a not inconsiderable weapon in the unending struggle between Congress and the executive. The legislative branch was in the ascendancy now, and these men saw no reason why the situation should be changed. Republicans against Democrats was

[16] *Ibid.,* p. 1317.
[17] *Ibid.,* pp. 1623–1633, 1641; also Stewart, pp. 236–237.

all well and good, but a Republican president, if he were to become too powerful, could as easily thwart the aims and purposes of the Republican bloc in Congress as a Democratic president. The veterans of the radical squabbles with Abraham Lincoln could assure newcomers of this fact. To these leaders, it made little sense to throw away before the fact a tool which could be of use in dealing with a new and totally untried president. Roscoe Conkling here stood forth for the first time as a prominent defender of legislative privilege, even against a chief executive of his own party. Conkling was one of the staunchest defenders of the Tenure of Office Act.

On February 20, 1869, Conkling scoffed at the need for a change, telling the Senate that too much had been made of the act, that it was not really much of a restriction upon a president:

What is the law, that any man should charge it with standing in the way of administrative reform? During the session of the Senate . . . it imposes . . . not a feather's weight of fetter upon the Executive hand; all that could legally be done without the law can be done with the law. It operates during the recess of the Senate. How? Simply to restrain arbitrary and wicked favoritism and vengeance. . . . What, then, is the impediment in the President's way? Simply that he must have cause for removal, and must report that cause to the Senate. That is all.[18]

Conkling knew, of course, that he was dealing with a possibly explosive subject, since Grant was taking office with a sizable popular majority behind him, and he moved to blunt the thrust of Morton's argument that repeal was in order because of a Republican president:

Like the Senator from Indiana, I would remove from the path of the incoming Administration every obstacle. I wish to leave the President-elect free to the full and useful exercise of the good judgment and good qualities which we all ascribe to him. At the same time, I wish . . . to preserve the consistency of the Senate, to preserve the position which the Senate has maintained in the last and most dire emergency known in our jurisprudence.[19]

Conkling gauged well the sentiment of his senatorial colleagues; he was on numerous occasions in the future to hold out to them the dazzling prospect of maintaining the privilege of the Senate as the highest element in our federal government, and on this first such occasion he won his majority. Morton, seeing his bill to repeal languishing untended

[18] *Cong. Globe,* 40th Cong., 3d sess., p. 1412.   [19] *Ibid.,* p. 1415.

and unloved, offered a rider to the Legislative Appropriation Bill on March 2 to repeal the Tenure of Office Act. Conkling shouted that the motion was "out of order . . . when our business is to go forward in the remaining hours of this session and consummate the necessary appropriation bills." Morton's amendment went down, 26 to 22.[20]

The following day, the bill to repeal came up for a final vote, the day before Grant was to take office. Conkling knew where the votes were, and he listened with pleasure as the bill was voted down, 35 to 15. The Tenure of Office Act was still the law of the land, and a majority of the Senate had served notice that the political complexion of the resident of the White House was not that important when matters relative to the prerogatives of the Senate were at issue.[21] Only half the battle had been won, of course; it would shortly come up again with a new Senate and a new president.

Roscoe Conkling had learned his way around the Senate during a trying period when the American government was split as it had never been before. He would now have the opportunity to work with a member of his own party as president; the public, the press, and the Republican politicos of New York State would observe the results closely.

[20] *Ibid.*, pp. 1793–1794.   [21] *Ibid.*, p. 1867.

CHAPTER 7

TO THE VICTORS
BELONG THE SPOILS

Ulysses S. Grant took the oath of office as the eighteenth president of the United States on a blustery day in early March 1869, and the ceremony was quickly followed by a blizzard. The inaugural ball was a fiasco, with the storm adding confusion to inadequate planning. Grant's personal contribution to the jumble came hard on the heels of his inauguration, when he submitted his cabinet to Congress.

In his inaugural address, the new president had said: "It will be my endeavor to execute all laws in good faith, to collect all revenues assessed, and to have them properly accounted for and economically disbursed. I will to the best of my ability appoint to office those only who will carry out this design." [1]

Until the names were submitted, no one knew how Grant planned to carry out this vow. The president-elect had joked with the press about the secrecy surrounding his cabinet selections. Even Mrs. Grant, he said, knew nothing about them. He had declined to discuss the composition of his cabinet with any of the Republican leaders, and they were as anxious to learn of its makeup as was the general citizenry. When the nominations were submitted, they were jolted, more so even than the press and public. The initial public reaction was that the new president had picked some sort of "reform" cabinet, since it was clearly not composed of men the political pros would have selected. This first reaction quickly wore off, to be replaced by one of chagrin at the utter political naïveté displayed in the cabinet's creation. John Sherman wrote later that "his attempt to form a cabinet without consultation with anyone, and with very little knowledge, except social intercourse with the

[1] J. D. Richardson, ed., *Messages and Papers,* VII, 8.

persons appointed" planted seeds of doubt as to Grant's possible success in the civil office.[2]

The selections for the two top cabinet spots caused the most shock and dismay. For secretary of state, Grant named Elihu B. Washburne of Illinois, his congressional sponsor in the days when Grant was making his military comeback at the start of the war. Washburne was a party wheel horse in the House, but a man without any apparent qualifications for the leadership of the state department at a time when sensitivity and imagination would be needed to meet the world problems of a postwar America. It turned out to be Grant's plan to send Washburne to France as minister, after a one-week tenure as secretary of state to give him more prestige. This trifling with the office added no stature to the president.[3]

For the treasury, Grant selected Alexander T. Stewart of New York City, the entrepreneur of the world's largest retail establishment at Broadway and East Ninth Street, where he underpaid his help to an extent that raised eyebrows even at that time. Stewart, a canny Irishman, was one of the wealthiest men in the country, but he was, as a merchant, specifically barred by law from serving as secretary of the treasury. Roscoe Conkling, dissatisfied in any event with the appointment of a man who had only recently placed his influence behind Fenton in the contest with Morgan, mentioned numerous statutory provisions which were flouted by the nomination.[4] The most obvious was the provision of the Act of 1789 which established the office, providing that "no person appointed to any office instituted by this act shall, directly or indirectly, be concerned or interested in carrying on the business of trade or commerce." The uproar at the Stewart appointment was considerable.

As secretary of the navy, the new president named Adolph Borie, a millionaire Philadelphia merchant. Grant had played a mysterious little game with the press about a "Pennsylvania man" in the cabinet, but no one ever expected Borie to be the man. He was almost totally unknown to Washington, had had no contacts whatever with public life,

[2] J. Sherman, I, 449.

[3] A. Badeau, *Grant in Peace,* pp. 162–163; W. B. Hesseltine, *Ulysses S. Grant,* p. 140.

[4] N. Y. *Sun,* Jan. 27, 1869; see H. E. Resseguie, "Federal Conflict of Interest," pp. 276–277.

and learned of his appointment for the first time when he read it in a newspaper on the way home from the inauguration.[5] Both Borie and Stewart, however, had been generous contributors to Grant, and the new president wanted them in his cabinet. Grant, who had never had money, was throughout his presidency unduly impressed by those who did.

The other four appointments were not as controversial, evoking only wonder at the strange admixture of the cabinet. The name of John A. Rawlins, Grant's closest advisor, as secretary of war was not sent in for a week, in order to let Grant's friend Schofield hold over from Johnson's cabinet as a compliment. Rawlins had asked Grant for the war department, and the president-elect could not refuse him, though he had not planned on a cabinet spot for his friend. Jacob D. Cox in the interior department was another former general who had been governor of Ohio for two years but had been passed over for re-election because of his advocacy of racial segregation. He was recognized as an able administrator and no objections were raised to his selection, though he clearly brought no political strength to the administration. For attorney general, Grant named Judge Ebenezer Rockwood Hoar of the Supreme Judicial Court of Massachusetts. He was an excellent choice, but he quickly became anathema to the politicos. The final selection was John A. J. Creswell, a veteran politician from Maryland, once a secessionist, more recently an active radical, who was to serve as postmaster general.

Even the selections to which no insuperable objections could be raised were vulnerable to the charge of being obscure, unknown, hardly the men one would expect to be the colleagues of the chief executive and the heads of the great departments in Washington. Henry Adams, educating himself with observations of his government in its seat at the capital, said that "Grant's nominations had the singular effect of making the hearer ashamed, not so much of Grant, as of himself." [6] Nevertheless, the Senate, without much thought, confirmed the appointments unanimously.

On March 6, Grant compounded his folly. He sent a message to the Senate, reciting the provisions of the law barring Stewart from the treasury and asking: "In view of these provisions and the fact that Mr. Stewart has been unanimously confirmed by the Senate, I would

[5] Badeau, p. 163.   [6] H. Adams, *Education*, p. 262.

ask that he be exempted by joint resolution of the two Houses of Congress from the operations of the same." [7]

Congress refused to do any such thing, and on March 9 Grant withdrew his message from the Senate. In the interim, Stewart had worked out a plan, similar to that now used by wealthy officeholders, to transfer his business to trustees who would devote all profits to New York City charities. Grant at first accepted the idea with pleasure, reportedly calling it "the most magnanimous thing I have ever heard of in my whole life," but then, under pressure from the politicians, suddenly reversed himself and accepted Stewart's resignation. Stewart was replaced in the treasury by George S. Boutwell, former governor of Massachusetts, not Grant's choice but forced upon him by the Republican leaders, a nondescript public functionary of limited imagination but a radical and a reliable politician. Henry Adams said Boutwell's name "suggested only a somewhat lugubrious joke." [8]

Borie quickly relinquished his honors at the navy department and was succeeded by George Maxwell Robeson of New Jersey, another unfortunate choice.

After a couple of weeks, Washburne was given the French mission, and the helm of the state department was turned over to Hamilton Fish of New York. Fish, who had been a Whig congressman, governor, and U.S. senator before the Civil War, thought that he had retired from politics long before; yet he became the brightest adornment of the Grant administration. His conduct of American foreign policy during the next eight years was one of the solid achievements of Grant's tenure. Fish, it will be recalled, had appointed Roscoe Conkling to his first public office, and he remained on good terms with the senator. Though the secretary was no advocate of the methods of political control exercised by Conkling, the two men established a useful relationship. Conkling was able to keep Fish posted on developments and sentiment in the Senate, at a time when the normal channel for such information, the Foreign Relations Committee, was being choked by the developing intransigency and hostility of the committee's chairman, Charles Sumner. Additionally, Fish could detail to Conkling the think-

[7] Richardson, ed., VII, 8–9.

[8] H. Adams, p. 263. On the Stewart trusteeship plan, N.Y. *Herald,* March 9, 1869; Resseguie, pp. 290–292. Stewart suggested the free-trade advocate David Wells in his place, but Boutwell had already been selected. Ironically, Stewart wound up supporting Greeley in the 1872 election.

ing of the cabinet on matters of interest to the Senate and the senator. Also, the two men used each other as pipelines to Grant on various matters in which the president would be more inclined to heed one rather than the other.

Grant's cabinet troubles did not end when he straightened out the initial mess. He was to be plagued with them throughout his presidential career. The treasury department was a particular headache, but he was free of aggravation only with the state department. He made strange selections from time to time, he allowed his more able members to be driven from office by political pressures, and he had far more than the usual presidential allotment of incompetent and venal advisors.

The short first session of the new Congress met for a little over a month in March and April of 1869, while Grant tried to put his administration in order. With Colfax now elevated to the vice-presidency, Conkling's bitter rival, Blaine, was the new Speaker of the House, where he had more power than was good for him. Conkling's more immediate rival, Fenton, was now sharing New York's senatorial representation with him, and the former governor quickly shouldered ahead of Conkling in the race for Grant's ear. Fenton made it quite clear to the president that he was the Republican leader in New York State and must have control of New York patronage. Grant seems to have acquiesced in this assertion, and he was gratified by Fenton's efforts in the Senate on behalf of the ill-fated Stewart nomination. For the time being, Conkling would stay in the background, waiting for Fenton to make a false step.

At the start of every new administration, the major consideration facing both the new president and Congress was always the same—jobs. The government had a lot of jobs at its disposal, and the hungry Republican politicians in 1869 had a lot of prospective jobholders ready to fill them. But Grant still wanted the Tenure of Office Act repealed, and he tied repeal together with the distribution of patronage by the simple device of announcing that he would fill only offices which were vacant; he would create no vacancies. This imposed tremendous pressure upon the members of Congress, who were swamped with demands from office-seekers to repeal the law and break the patronage log jam. A bill for repeal had been introduced in the Senate shortly after the start of the session, but its prospects appeared no better than those of its predecessor in the previous Congress until the president took his stand.

The House, with nothing much to lose by it, passed a bill repealing the act. This left matters up to the Senate, where there was still much opposition to repeal but an understandable desire to get the patronage jobs filled and a reluctance to quarrel publicly with Grant at the outset of his term.

A disposition to compromise soon became evident. Even Roscoe Conkling relaxed his previous inflexible stand, when on March 10 he suggested some changes in the law during Grant's administration in order "to remove from the path of the Executive every hindrance such as has been referred to." [9]

Conkling took little public part thereafter in the debates on the measure, but he was active behind the scenes. He was strongly opposed to outright repeal, but he was resigned to some modification. He suggested suspending the operation of the act for Grant's term, while others proposed suspending it until the next session of Congress. This would get the jobs filled and preserve senatorial protection of the jobholders. Morton was strongly opposed to such a course, as was Grant; they wanted simple repeal of the act.

The Republicans in the Senate held a secret caucus on March 22, the proceedings of which were soon public knowledge. According to Gideon Welles, Conkling and Edmunds tried to bind those attending the caucus to abide by its decisions, but the advocates of repeal refused to go along with such a scheme. Welles reported that Conkling, whom he called "an egotistical coxcomb . . . who would, at any time, sacrifice the right to benefit his party," and Morton "are reputed to have had a sharp passage in caucus." [10]

The caucus worked out a compromise, giving the president power to dismiss either by securing the Senate's approval or by having a successor confirmed by the Senate. This amendment was adopted on March 24, but when the House refused to concur in the Senate amendments, a conference committee was appointed. The bill as it came from conference and was ultimately adopted provided that the president might suspend a jobholder during a recess and nominate a successor within thirty days after Congress reconvened. If the Senate declined to confirm, the president could send in new nominations until one was ratified. The two houses had divergent understandings on the consequences of the session ending before a nomination was confirmed, but in this state of affairs the bill was passed. Grant signed it shortly there-

[9] *Cong. Globe,* 41st Cong., 1st sess., p. 45.   [10] Welles, III, 558.

after, sadly disappointing many of his friends and supporters; they saw quite clearly that absolute repeal was easily attainable so long as he held the club of the unfilled jobs.[11]

Congress adjourned in April 1869, until the following December, and the American people could make their first assessment of the new president.

Ulysses S. Grant had been elected to office by a nation which had grown up with the mystique of George Washington—the great soldier who brought a sure hand to the civil affairs of the nation and set things right in a confused and muddled time. Now Grant was to do likewise. It quickly became evident, however, that Grant was no George Washington.

He was a small, shy man, barely five feet eight inches tall, with a brown beard and mustache and slightly graying hair. He had received an indifferent education at West Point, and his intellectual equipment was devoid of any cultural depth. He thought in military terms, and he had no real concept of the Constitution and its meaning for American government. The will of the people, as interpreted and expressed through Congress, represented to him the guiding light for the conduct of his office. That this also enabled him to adopt a very passive conception of his role was completely congenial to him, for he had a strong trace of slothfulness in his nature.

Adam Badeau, Grant's biographer and crony, told Henry Adams that he and Rawlins were the only ones who understood Grant. To Badeau, "Grant appeared as an intermittent energy, immensely powerful when awake, but passive and plastic in repose. . . . For stretches of time, his mind seemed torpid." During this time, Badeau went on, he and Rawlins and the rest of the staff would discuss ideas among themselves, in Grant's presence, and, "in the end, he would announce the idea as his own, without seeming conscious of the discussion; and would give the orders to carry it out with all the energy that belonged to his nature." The staff members "could never follow a mental process in his thought. They were not sure that he did think." [12]

Politicians calling upon Grant with propositions of one kind or another frequently received in reply only silence or incomprehensible

---

[11] Modification of the Tenure of Office Act can be followed in Hesseltine, pp. 150–153, and Binkley, *President and Congress,* p. 192.

[12] H. Adams, p. 264.

grunts, while the president chewed on his ever-present cigar. They were often distressed to learn later that something said or intimated by the president meant to Grant something far different from the interpretation placed upon it by his listener. This was a cause of great difficulty with political associates, a source of periodic criticism, and a basis for resentment by a man who was unable to tolerate criticism with equanimity.

It is too easy, though, to present a picture of Grant as a dolt. We cannot dismiss so summarily the man who took Vicksburg and gradually enveloped Lee's army at Richmond. His mind at times worked very logically and with great precision, and he was decisive and vigorous when a course of action had been determined. His tenacity was legendary. He was always courteous and, though basically shy, he could laugh heartily on appropriate occasions. But the qualities which made Grant a great general did not help him in the presidency. One of the assets which carried him to the heights in the war was a generous portion of good luck; as president, he never really had any.

Conkling in that summer of 1869 won a flashy case against Francis Kernan in *Smith v. New York Central Railway,* one of the last big jury cases he won before his political fame and the press of time eventually limited him to the more lucrative and specialized corporate and patent cases. The plaintiff's husband had been a New York Central engineer, commissioned to hurry a special train full of company directors and officials from Syracuse to Albany as quickly as possible. Erroneously instructed that the track had been cleared all the way to Albany, poor Smith was killed when he plowed into the rear of a slow-moving freight train just around a curve near Utica. Senator Conkling's two-hour summation dwelt at lachrymose length upon the contrast between the bejeweled railroad directors, drinking champagne, playing poker, and laughing in the expensive drawing rooms of the train, and the lowly engineer, driving to his death in the darkened cab, faithful to his orders to get to Albany as fast as possible. Conkling pointed to some of these same directors sitting in the courtroom as he intoned: "In eternity, the pebbles upon the grave of poor Smith will shine as brightly as do the diamonds upon the bosoms of these men!" The jury awarded the unheard-of damages of $18,000, and when Kernan spoke confidently of an appeal, old Commodore Vanderbilt, president of the line, ordered, "Pay it! If Conkling tries this case again he may get fifty thousand!" [13]

The law could not compete, though, with the glittering lure of national politics, especially as Conkling saw in Grant a man he could work with, a man who needed guidance through the unknown and unsuspected traps of government and politics, a man who needed control. And though Fenton controlled the patronage at the start of Grant's administration, Grant was noticing New York's senior senator. Fenton had a tendency to fawn, a penchant for obsequiousness, but Conkling, when he felt strongly on a subject, took his position, and worried nothing about the consequences. Grant liked that. He and Conkling drew closer together.

In the summer of 1869, in fact, Grant accepted Conkling's invitation to him and his family to stop and visit in Utica on their summer trip.[14] Though Grant was still treating formally with Fenton as the party leader, his regard for the former governor was starting to slip. Conkling's dominating personality, the strong intellect and proud bearing, began to weave a spell around Grant which was never broken.

In 1869, only minor offices were at issue in New York State, and the convention at Syracuse in September was left to its own devices, relatively uncontrolled. Grant's first hesitant attempts at Reconstruction had tarnished his image, and worse still, the convention met within days after the failure of Jay Gould and Jim Fisk to corner the gold market on Black Friday, September 24. The near success of the corner, the fumbling course of the administration and Boutwell, and the fact that Grant had foolishly allowed himself to be seen publicly in the company of Gould and Fisk combined to give the nation an uneasy feeling about the president's possible association with the abortive swindle. When the state convention met on September 30, Republicans felt a grim pessimism about the forthcoming election. Combined with their own troubles was the fact that Tweed's Tammany was riding at the peak of its power.

The Republicans, groping for unquestioned respectability, made the

[13] A. R. Conkling, pp. 319–322; Scott, pp. 193–194. Conkling wrote to Sidney T. Fairchild, a director of the line, on July 23, 1869, that neither he nor his clients had anything to do with an indictment for criminal negligence which grew out of the same incident; Charles S. Fairchild Papers.

[14] Conkling Papers, Library of Congress.

improbable selection of George William Curtis to head the ticket as the nominee for secretary of state. Curtis, citing editorial and family duties, declined the nomination, though this withdrawal led to much criticism of him within the party. When the candidate for comptroller also re-fused *his* nomination, Horace Greeley was substituted for that spot and accepted. *He* never declined any proffered nominations. In the subse-quent election, the Democrats won easily, capturing both houses of the legislature, and fastening the rule of Tweed and Hoffman more firmly upon the state. The results of Fenton's leadership of New York were not beautiful to behold, when viewed with Republican eyes.[15]

The second session of the Forty-first Congress convened on Decem-ber 6, 1869. Before it had recessed, a major shift in power in the Republican party of the state of New York had taken place, and a once promising political career had fallen into terminal disrepair. Roscoe Conkling was on his way to supreme power in the party in New York, while Fenton was washed away in a tide which eventually swept him into the backwater of Liberal Republicanism and oblivion.

The major national issue which was carried through in the session was, as it had been for so long, that of Reconstruction. Things were a bit different this time, however. By the time Congress adjourned, all of the Southern states were reconstructed and represented in Congress. The debates were long and acrimonious, the squabbles seemed endless, but they were at length resolved.

Conkling, on December 17, advised against making ratification of the Fifteenth Amendment a fundamental condition to the readmission of Georgia. He felt that insisting on ratification would furnish "a good deal of fixed ammunition" to be used "for very hurtful purposes," namely to maintain that Georgia had been coerced into ratifying and that therefore the *Northern* states, "in consequence and indirectly," had been deprived of their free volition.[16] This was an interesting point but, though certainly valid, it ran afoul of the radical intentions for recon-structing Southern states. With Morton pushing it, the precondition amendment carried the Senate, with Conkling voting "nay."

This question of "fundamental conditions" for the readmission of Southern states was an important one, and one on which the Repub-

---

[15] Van Deusen, *Horace Greeley,* p. 388; Milne, pp. 141–142. Fenton's friend Greeley even ran 4,000 votes behind the losing ticket.

[16] *Cong. Globe,* 41st Cong., 2d sess., p. 208.

lican majority, as we have seen, was split. The radicals who claimed the right to impose such conditions were led by Morton, Sumner, Drake, and Richard Yates of Illinois. The more moderate leaders were Conkling, Trumbull, Edmunds, and Carpenter. The issue came up on numerous occasions.[17]

The following month, in debate on the readmission of Virginia, Conkling debated Morton on a basic question of the relative rights of states and Congress, a question he had raised before. The issue was the power of Congress to expel in the event of Virginia's rescission of its ratification of the Fifteenth Amendment. Morton said, "I believe that if we have a right to reconstruct a State government that has been destroyed by rebellion we have a right to protect it after it has been reconstructed; that the right to reconstruct implies the right to protect the reconstructed state."

Conkling disagreed:

Why, sir, can it be that lawyers or laymen can differ in opinion upon the doctrine that after we have restored Virginia, after we have crowned her again with that sovereignty, that statehood, that relationship, call it what you may, which she has lost, we can dicate to her the action of her Legislature and can expel her representatives unless she attends to our behests? And I ask can lawyers doubt that an argument which will prove that conclusion will show that Maine or Missouri can be made to lie down upon the bed which we prescribe, and be stretched if they are too short, or shortened if they overmatch in length? [18]

On this, Conkling prevailed; the amendment Morton was supporting was defeated.

But the question was real. While congressional Reconstruction came to an end with the close of the session, the Republicans were very concerned with "protecting" the reconstructed states, as Morton phrased it; actually, what was to be protected was the Republican party in the South. The protection, of course, was ultimately carried out not with laws but with federal troops.[19]

In a phase of that concern, on March 18, 1870, Conkling reported for the Judiciary Committee on the qualifications of Major General Adelbert Ames to be a United States senator from the reconstructed state of Mississippi. The problem with General Ames, a Maine man

17 E. B. Thompson, *Matthew Hale Carpenter*, p. 133.
18 *Cong. Globe*, 41st Cong., 2d sess., pp. 353, 355–356, Jan. 11, 1870.
19 Hesseltine, p. 189.

who was the military provisional governor of the state, was that he did not quite meet the constitutional requirement of being "an inhabitant" of the state when he was elected. No one seemed to boggle at the idea of a military governor, with complete dominion over the legislature making the selection, being chosen as senator, but Conkling reported against General Ames on the "inhabitant" question. He excused himself to his party colleagues by saying that "the interrogatory submitted to the committee . . . is made of sterner stuff than political or personal preference," and on the merits, he said that Ames went to and remained in Mississippi strictly in obedience to military orders.[20]

After Conkling made a long speech on the meaning of the word "inhabitant," particularly in its constitutional sense, a long and heated debate ensued, lasting for several days. Morton led the pro-Ames senators, along with Jacob Howard of Michigan. A court listening to the evidence would have had to agree with Conkling and refuse Ames the seat, but this question was to be decided on political, not judicial, grounds. A vote was taken on April 1, and Ames was admitted, 40 to 12.

Morton was fully convinced that the greater good of the American people required Republican governments in the South and Republican representatives in Congress from the Southern states. Therefore, the Constitution was not to stand in the way of this result. George Frisbie Hoar later said of Morton:

He had little regard for Constitutional scruples. I do not think it should be said that he would willingly violate his oath to support the Constitution. But he believed that the Constitution should be interpreted in the light of the Declaration of Independence, so as to be the law of life to a great, powerful and free people. To this principle of interpretation, all strict or narrow criticism, founded on its literal meaning, must yield.[21]

Conkling, though he too desired the permanency of Republican rule in the South, was unwilling to join his more extreme party brethren in ignoring the dictates of the Constitution to achieve it. For this, he may be entitled to a little better historical press; unfortunately, Conkling is generally lumped in with his fellow Republicans for wanton abuse of the Constitution.

[20] *Cong. Globe*, 41st Cong., 2d sess., p. 2125, March 22, 1870.
[21] G. F. Hoar, *Autobiography*, II, 94.

Conkling tangled with Morton on another vital issue which cut more on geographical than party lines. He carried on a struggle for over two months on the issue of the income tax, an exaction of which New York, with one-eleventh of the country's population, paid one-third. The great financial and industrial interests of New York were opposed to continuance of the tax, and Conkling led their battle in the Senate. The old income tax, a war necessity, was scheduled to die in 1870, and Roscoe Conkling wanted to keep his foot on its neck so that it did not come back to life: "Disguise it as we may, the scheme is agrarian, sectional, and unfair." He fought it tooth and nail; it was "the unjust tax, the tax of doubtful constitutionality, the tax which the public faith stands plighted not to revive, the tax which is no longer needed." He called it a tax "well calculated to produce a nation of liars . . . grievous and demoralizing in practice." [22]

But Morton, from agrarian Indiana, liked the tax, and so did John Sherman of Ohio, who carefully cultivated his image as the financial authority in the Republican ranks of the Senate. Sherman said, "There never was so just a tax levied as the income tax . . . levied upon all alike according to their income." [23]

On June 24, the Senate approved Conkling's motion to strike out of the tax bill the provisions for a revival of the income tax. Morton railed against the vote as "a great mistake" and a "blunder." [24] Subsequently, after Morton got his troops under control, the income tax was voted back into the tax bill, and it was there when the bill was passed on July 6. Conkling reluctantly voted "aye" on final passage of the whole tax package. The income tax would remain in effect until 1872.

One other legislative item on which Conkling came to grief was a naturalization bill he was pushing "to put the heel of legislation upon frauds and outrages which turn popular elections in this country into a farce." [25] He was still burning over the extensive voting frauds in New York City in 1868 which turned the results of the election around and gave the state to the Democrats. One of the chief methods used in perpetrating the electoral abuses was wholesale naturalization of im-

[22] *Cong. Globe,* 41st Cong., 2d sess., p. 4761, June 23, 1870, and p. 2487, April 7, 1870.
[23] *Ibid.,* p. 4714, June 22, 1870.   [24] *Ibid.,* pp. 4808–4809.
[25] *Ibid.,* p. 4833, June 25, 1870.

migrants just before the election. The new "citizens" then gratefully turned out for Tweed and the Democrats. The Senate, however, was not yet prepared to enact sweeping changes in its naturalization laws to satisfy the grievance of a single senator, no matter how eminent. It did finally vote a watered-down measure for policing the polls at election time, which really satisfied no one but was taken by Conkling as an acceptable half loaf.

Floating in the background behind all the floor debates was the treaty for the annexation of San Domingo which had been negotiated by Grant's aide, Orville E. Babcock, with a gaggle of shady opportunists and cutthroats in the West Indies republic, a treaty which very few wanted except Ulysses S. Grant, whose reasons even today are not very clear. Grant said the people of San Domingo "yearn for the protection of our free institutions and laws, our progress and civilization," but this seemed highly dubious.[26] There appeared to be no compelling reasons why the United States should accept this backward half of the island of Hispaniola from a disreputable group whose title to dispose of the country was none too clear. Charles Sumner became almost apoplectic at the mention of San Domingo. The administration supporters in the Senate, most of them, dutifully voted for ratification of the treaty when it was finally pried loose from Sumner's Foreign Relations Committee, but they had little heart for it. No one wept for the treaty when it fell far short of the two-thirds approval it needed. *The Nation,* on June 16, said the whole thing made "the intelligent citizen wish St. Domingo, coffee, sugar, and all, at the bottom of the sea." Grant did not get the message, though; he would not let the project drop. It was to come back to haunt the Republican majority again.

President Grant, after Black Friday, the Tenure of Office Act, and San Domingo, began to think in political terms. The beautiful theory of "no policies against the will of the people" started to fade as he realized there was more than one way to express the will of the people. *His* blundering, naïve efforts seemed in most cases to result in disaster, and he could see the erosion of his popular esteem. Politics and political power and the desires of the Republican leaders now began to assume major places in Grant's thinking about his office and the performance of its functions. He shortly made one of the most politically telling

[26] Richardson, ed., VII, 61.

moves of his presidential career and, by so doing, won himself an un-flinching ally.

The most powerful nonelective political job in the nation below cabi-net level was that of collector of the Port of New York. The New York Custom House did such a booming business that it employed a sizable staff. It was an establishment in which, years before, a few dozen extra employees, hired on for political purposes only, were hardly noticed. When the few dozen were not noticed, it was only a short step to the addition of twenty or thirty more, until the New York Custom House payroll soon became the nesting place of ward-heelers, caucus-riggers and other assorted political handy men in large numbers. The time, energy, and salaries of these men were thus available resources of the ruling party.

Grant had appointed as collector to rule over this strange establish-ment a contributor named Moses Grinnell. Named surveyor, in charge of the inspectors, weighers, and gaugers was Alonzo B. Cornell, a young party wheel horse with good connections and a great deal of money, inclined toward Conkling. The naval officer, the third in authority, supervisor of a staff of clerks who calculated the duties, was a Fenton man named Edwin A. Merritt. As Merritt later put it: "I held that po-sition for about sixteen months, when Mr. Grinnell . . . was found not to be giving general satisfaction." [27] Mr. Grinnell, unfortunately, was using his position to collect customs duties, when almost all the experts in the field were agreed that collection of revenues was defi-nitely a secondary part of his job. It was time to look about for a suc-cessor, one who would utilize the Custom House in the right way and for the proper purposes.

The previous summer, when President Grant took up his vacation residence at Long Branch, New Jersey, he became acquainted with a fellow lover of horseflesh, a politician from New York named Thomas Murphy. Murphy, with a varied and somewhat dubious background, was said to have been a "shoddy contractor" during the war, and he had not always been steadfast in his political allegiances. But he was able to converse on equal terms with the president about horses, and was a congenial Irishman besides, so they became fast friends.

On June 20, 1870, the New York *Tribune* rebutted a rumor of the impending nomination of Calvin T. Hulburd as collector, and there

27 E. A. Merritt, *Recollections*, p. 79.

were stories that Fenton was pushing for the appointment of William H. Robertson. It was obvious that some kind of change was coming, and the nature of the change, when it occurred, would surely have great impact on Republican politics in New York.

On July 1, Grant sent to the Senate the nomination of Murphy for collector, with Grinnell moving down to naval officer and Fenton's close friend Merritt being displaced altogether. The *Times,* no partisan of either U.S. Senator, called the Murphy nomination "the sensation of the Capitol, especially among the New York members and politicians," and said that "Senator Fenton and his friends seem to accept it as a direct blow at them." The paper sadly speculated that "the anxiously sought-for harmony and unity among New York Republicans . . . is now further off than ever," and editorially it said, "There was no necessity for the step. The public have not been considered in it."

Greeley's *Tribune* was much more outspoken. Its correspondent spoke of the New York members holding "for an hour at least a sort of an informal indignation meeting." But Greeley knew that the sin to be decried was not the removal of Grinnell but the installation of Tom Murphy. Murphy was a well-known and vociferous foe of Greeley's friend, Reuben E. Fenton, and had been one of those touring the delegations at the 1868 national convention to demonstrate the fact that Fenton was not even the choice of his own state for vice-president. The *Tribune* went on:

The nomination of Thos. Murphy as Collector, and the removal of Genl. Merritt, raised a storm of indignation which was expressed in the most emphatic manner. Mr. Murphy was denounced as a Tammany Republican, an Andrew Johnson Republican, a Thurlow Weed Republican, a Conservative Republican, a bigoted Roman Catholic, a champion of Gen. Butler, and as generally unworthy the confidence of the Republican party of New York. The expression was general that he must not be confirmed. . . . The nomination of Mr. Murphy and the removal of Gen. Merritt are looked upon as the work of Gen. Butler and Sen. Conkling, and as a matter of course it is expected of Mr. Conkling that he will endeavor to secure the confirmation of Messrs. Murphy & Grinnell. Gen. Merritt is known to be the special friend of Senator Fenton, and therefore Fenton must work not only for the defeat of Grinnell, but also of Murphy.

What had Conkling to do with the Murphy nomination? Contemporary press reports had no hesitation in giving him the credit for the coup against Fenton. But fuller evidence makes it clear that it was Grant's own doing. He had become fed up with Fenton. When it was obvious that Fenton was losing favor at the White House, the senator became desperate and addressed an insolent letter to the president, making allusions to his own aspirations for the presidency in 1872, and offering to withdraw and turn New York over to Grant if agreeable understandings could be reached in regard to patronage! [28] Grant's reaction to this pompous idiocy was unmistakably clear. He remembered his friend Murphy, the horseman who disliked Fenton, and decided to install him in the most powerful position in the state. Conkling told his friend Stewart, the senator from Nevada, that "if it had been left to him he should not have selected Mr. Murphy. He said there was another person, a political friend, who had performed such services to the party and to the country as entitled him to the place." [29] Conkling said publicly, a couple of years later, that Murphy was appointed "not to gratify me or at my solicitation. . . . I did not suggest his appointment." [30]

Though Murphy was not initially Conkling's man, the senator was quick to note that political power in New York was in the balance; if Fenton chose to fight Grant's selection, what better way to cement relations with the national administration than to lead the fight for the president's nominee?

The *Tribune,* on July 4, after a day or so to scout around and see which way the wind was blowing, reported, "There is to be a very bitter fight between Senator Conkling and Gov. Fenton over the nomination." The account continued:

The feeling among the New York members, which manifested itself so strongly on Friday, has greatly subsided, and many of them, although strongly opposed to Mr. Murphy, think it their duty to support him as the choice of the President, and are of the opinion that more harm will be done the party in their state by making war on the President's nominee than by quiet acquiescence in the nomination. Senator Fenton dissents from this view.

The New York press had a field day with the "very sharp and earnest contest going on over the Collectorship." [31] The papers reported the gathering of crowds of New York politicians, come to Washington to

28 N.Y. *Times,* July 24, 1872.   29 Stewart, p. 254.
30 N.Y. *Times,* July 24, 1872.   31 *Ibid.,* July 7, 1870.

look after their own interests and those of their respective champions. One day the *Tribune* reported the appearance of two Methodist ministers in the Senate lobby, urging the rejection of Murphy on religious grounds.

The *Tribune,* on July 7, stated that "this change involves a Presidential slight and a loss of power which must be most distasteful to Fenton and his followers." It quoted a Fenton man who said that Grant "could not possibly have made a nomination more offensive to what is left of the Republican party than that of Tom Murphy for Collector!" *The Nation* said, "It may very well be doubted if his appointment will do anything but still further weaken the party." [32]

The following day, as it became apparent that the congressional session was nearing its end and the Murphy question would have to be resolved, the *Times* discussed its import in a lead editorial:

On both sides the contest at Washington has been conducted with the slightest possible reference to the wishes and welfare of this City, or even the welfare of the Republican party. The whole affair has narrowed down to a struggle for personal and partisan advantage between the two New York Senators. . . . How the vast and varied interests that are affected by the management of the Customhouse would be affected, neither the President nor the Senate seemed inclined to discuss. Whether Mr. Fenton should thwart Mr. Conkling, or whether Mr. Conkling should thwart Mr. Fenton, was the outward and visible issue to be determined. Behind both, wires were at work whose number and extent indicate the force of feuds which exist among New York Republicans.

On July 11, the Senate went into executive session to consider nominations for offices, and the first one to come up was Thomas Murphy. Fenton occupied the entire afternoon with his speech against Murphy, mainly a collage of newspaper clippings detailing what he felt to be Murphy's sordid and nefarious life. Interspersed were the senator's own editorial comments, what the *Times* called "a very severe arraignment of the personal and political character of the candidate." At six o'clock, by prearrangement with Conkling, Stewart of Nevada moved that a recess be taken until 8:00 P.M., when Conkling would be given an hour to reply and Fenton a further half hour.

When the Senate reconvened, Conkling commenced a devastating attack upon his colleague, "every sentence of which was replete with logic, sarcasm, reason, and invective." Conkling knew, as did many in

32 *The Nation,* July 7, 1870.

New York politics, of an unfortunate episode from Fenton's youth, when the future senator had been entrusted with $12,000 to carry from New York to Albany, had arrived in Albany reporting its loss, and had been chagrined to have investigation turn up the missing money secreted in his bedclothes. Fenton had been arrested and, after extensive inquiry, discharged. Conkling had with him this evening in the Senate the record of the criminal proceedings against Fenton. As he neared the end of his speech, he walked down the aisle to a spot directly opposite the seat of the Chautauquan.

"It is true," he said, "that Thomas Murphy is a mechanic, a hatter by trade; that he worked at his trade in Albany supporting an aged father and mother and a crippled brother. And while he was thus engaged there was another who visited Albany and played a very different role,"—drawing the court record from his pocket, and extending it toward Senator Fenton,—"the particulars of which I will not relate except at the special request of my colleague." Fenton's head dropped upon his desk, as if he had been struck down with a club. The scene in the Senate was tragic.[33]

A fellow senator who was present told Conkling, "If you had spoken of me in that way I should have killed you," to which the New Yorker just smiled.[34] But the stakes were high, and Roscoe Conkling had no doubt that Reuben Fenton would do the same to him given a chance. The Senate promptly confirmed Murphy.

Conkling and his cohorts celebrated that evening, and their numbers grew:

Parlors Nos. 34 and 36 at Willard's, the headquarters of the score or more New York politicians who have been here for a week in the interest of Murphy, are in a blaze of glory tonight. They are holding high carnival over their victory . . . and many times have they drunk, amid cheers, to what they denominate "The political death of Reuben E. Fenton." It is astonishing to see how many Murphy men there are since 9 o'clock this evening. It would seem, to hear them talk, that there never existed an anti-Murphy man, excepting Senator Fenton himself. Senator Conkling is the hero of the occasion, and to his speech in the Executive Session of the Senate today is attributed the overwhelming vote given to Mr. Murphy.[35]

The Nation commented on "the overwhelming defeat of Senator Fenton and the triumph of Mr. Conkling, who seems in his heart not

---

[33] Stewart, p. 257.   [34] A. R. Conkling, p. 374.
[35] N.Y. *Tribune,* July 12, 1870.

to dislike a fight, and who appears to have managed this one with great skill and ferocity." It withheld its congratulations, though it expressed its distaste for Fenton, because of the character of the immediate beneficiary of the battle, Tom Murphy, "a hack politician, unfit for any trust." [36]

Two days after Murphy was confirmed, General Horace Porter of Grant's staff wrote him that "my only desire is to see you distribute the patronage of your office as to render the most efficient service to the country and the cause of the Administration." [37] Murphy needed no reminding. He was devoted to Grant—and to Conkling. In New York, Roscoe Conkling, with the most powerful patronage instrument in the country in his hands, was now in line to become the boss.

[36] July 14, 1870.   [37] Nevins, *Fish,* II, 593.

CHAPTER 8

———◆◆◆◆▶———

THE CONKLING MACHINE

A few months later, with the power of the Custom House at his back, Conkling whipped Fenton again at the Republican state convention at Saratoga. In that gathering he left behind a trail of ill-feeling, outraged pride, and mortification. The convention was an astonishing show and, if the whirling and dodging of the senator seem hard to follow to a reader observing from the vantage point of a century, the confusion spread among the delegates on the scene can only be imagined.

As the delegates assembled at the famous spa in early September, they were well aware that the major issue was more than the selection of a candidate for governor. The struggle for mastery between the two United States senators pervaded all the deliberations of the convention. Reuben E. Fenton made it his business to be there early, to check with all his lieutenants, to clear matters ahead of time with retainers and followers of long standing, to cash in outstanding political I.O.U.'s, and to bolster the wavering and the dubious. Reassurance was needed, reassurance that everything was still all right even with a temporary setback, even though the detested Murphy had taken over the Custom House with all its jobs.

Conkling was there early, also, along with his new friend Tom Murphy. With Murphy, Conkling had picked up as a follower one who was to be far more valuable over the long haul, the collector's lawyer, Chester Alan Arthur of New York. Arthur had been associated with Conkling in the fight to save Morgan's Senate seat from Fenton early in 1869; Arthur's initial introduction into state politics came through Governor Morgan, in whose administration he had served. Arthur came to fight Fenton; he stayed to follow Roscoe Conkling.

Fenton's plan was to have his friend, the very popular Charles H. Van Wyck, selected as temporary chairman of the convention and himself as permanent chairman. This double-barreled salvo at the outset would serve as sufficient affirmation of Fenton's strength to keep any prospective wanderers in line. The scheme looked sound, and the wily Fenton felt confident. Van Wyck, a lawyer, former Union general, and a well-liked congressman, would be a formidable opponent for Conkling. The Conkling forces knew that Fenton had the votes; the only likely tactic was to dislodge them. Fenton's strategy was impeccable; his mistake was to overlook the sound political dictum that in a fight like this a wise manager rides herd on his votes until they are cast.

Conkling's candidate for temporary chairman, selection of which would be the first—and most important—battle of the conclave, was an unlikely one, George William Curtis of *Harper's*. But then Conkling was in an unlikely spot, and he needed all the help he could muster. The night before the convention, the senator and Tom Murphy went calling upon the Fenton delegates, to instruct them in the facts of life in the harsh world of New York politics. Fenton's prior control of the federal patronage did him no good; the two men made it quite clear to every jobholder that, Fenton man or not, his job was on the line in the morning; if he voted with Fenton, he would soon be seeking employment elsewhere. If he did not have a federal job, it was made plain that there would be a number of openings after the convention and if he were interested—well, President Grant would look after those who were his friends (Conkling's friends) in New York State. Conkling and Murphy made their rounds most of the night, and by morning it was apparent that their course had taken hold. Curtis beat Van Wyck, 220 to 150.

Conkling then utterly confounded his enemies by moving the selection of Van Wyck as permanent chairman—a better spot than the one Fenton had picked out for the congressman and, even more delicious, the spot that Fenton had picked out for himself. Conkling won Van Wyck's friends with this move and left the ex-governor isolated. So Conkling was two points ahead. But these positions were symbolic; a convention chairman had nothing but memories the day after adjournment. The main reason for the convention was to select a candidate for governor to run against John T. Hoffman. And the gubernatorial situation, as the delegates prepared for the balloting, was in a bewildering swirl. Conkling's political gymnastics of the next couple of hours would hardly clear up this situation.

Originally, Fenton's candidate was Marshall O. Roberts of New York

City, a wealthy steamship entrepreneur and banker, often on the fringes of New York politics. Roberts was no friend of Roscoe Conkling, so to head him off, Conkling let it be known that *his* candidate might very well be Horace Greeley! At the suggestion, probably, of Fenton, Roberts hastened to withdraw in favor of his good friend Greeley, and Fenton moved over to take charge of the Greeley candidacy; he certainly did not want Greeley beholden to Conkling for a nomination, not with such a powerful newspaper as Greeley possessed! The *Times* spoke of an understanding between Fenton and Roberts "by which the adroit Senator is to be put in a position to head off the Conkling movement in favor of Horace Greeley as a candidate and take all the credit of that brilliant idea to himself." [1]

Greeley thus apparently had *both* U.S. senators in his camp ahead of time, but it was obviously a fluid situation. Among the names suggested as possible nominees the morning of the convention were Greeley, Judge William H. Robertson of Westchester, General John C. Robinson, and the man reputed to be the president's choice, General Stewart L. Woodford, the lieutenant governor under Fenton. Where was Conkling? Just before the balloting started, he was heard telling some of his supporters to vote for George William Curtis—for the second time in one day! Fenton was baffled by his rival's actions, and Conkling's friends were not quite sure what he was doing, either. In the voting that followed, many delegates were inadvertently trapped in the wrong column, simply because the leaders were doing so much jumping around and it took too long for the word to trickle down to the followers.

On the first ballot, Woodford led with 153 votes, followed by Greeley with 143, and Curtis 104½. On the second ballot, Conkling switched his support ostensibly to Greeley, who was fading, and Curtis's votes fell away. Woodford led again with 170½, Greeley had 139, and Curtis trailed with 87½. After the second ballot, Conkling moved to adjourn. Fenton, seeing in this an act of desperation, blocked the motion, and then found himself outgeneraled for the final time by Conkling. On the third ballot, as Fenton swung behind Greeley, Conkling went over to Woodford and put him over the top with 258 votes, to 105½ for Greeley and 20 for Curtis.

As the final touch, Conkling secured more than two-thirds of the Republican state committee and had Alonzo B. Cornell made its chair-

[1] N.Y. *Times,* Aug. 31, 1870; *The Nation,* Sept. 15, 1870, for a review of the convention.

man. There was no doubt now that the Republican party organization in New York belonged to Roscoe Conkling.

There were bitter and prolonged recriminations after the Saratoga convention, mainly from Greeley, who never forgot his humiliation, one of the principal factors leading him into the Liberal Republican revolt of 1872, and also from Curtis, who never forgave Conkling. The *Times* summed up the convention as well as anyone:

The truth is, however, that so much superfluous strategy went on over his [Greeley's] head that he was inevitably sacrificed. Between two stools he fell to the ground. If Senator Fenton had contrived to afford him a fair chance the result might have been different. The rival Senators between them lost control of the situation, and the fault is not to be laid at the door of Senator Conkling, who can never be accused of acting in bad faith toward Mr. Greeley.[2]

Though Conkling may very well have lost control of events in the last hectic stages of the gubernatorial balloting, he wound up in the winner's circle because he was always a few jumps ahead of Fenton and, basically, because he had the Custom House, which meant the support of Grant.

The Nation, on September 15, said, "The Republican is a rare one who sees just how the party was benefited by the State Convention at Saratoga last week." Nevertheless, it was a convention long remembered in New York, not least of all by Roscoe Conkling.

Boss Conkling. No one called him that, of course; he was always "Senator." But people began to look at him with a changed viewpoint. He had succeeded to the place which Weed had held, which Fenton had come close to gaining, which such giants as DeWitt Clinton and Martin Van Buren had occupied back when the century was young. Elihu Root, in his mature years, wrote of his political youth: "For I do not remember how many years, Mr. Conkling was the supreme ruler in this state; the Governor did not count, the legislatures did not count; comptrollers and Secretaries of state and what-not, did not count. It was what Mr. Conkling said." [3]

One of Conkling's new admirers, an aspiring young politician from Owego, in Tioga County, named Thomas C. Platt, who first hooked up

[2] N.Y. *Times,* Sept. 10, 1870. The *Times* reporters and editorial writers enjoyed crowing over the political misfortunes of their great rival on the *Tribune.*

[3] E. Root, *Addresses,* p. 202.

with Conkling at Saratoga in 1870, said of him: "Conkling was then one of the handsomest men I ever met. He was over six feet tall, of slender build, and stood straight as an arrow. His hair was just turning gray. A curl, described as Hyperion, rolled over his forehead. An imperial added much to the beauty of his Apollo-like appearance. His noble figure, flashing eye and majestic voice made one forget that he was somewhat foppish in his dress." [4]

Though one of the Democratic leaders of the Senate said of him one day, "Youth and beauty are so entirely his that I never dreamed of applying the phrase 'senior senator' to him," Roscoe Conkling, in 1870, was forty-one years old.[5] He was a veteran of many years in Washington and a leader of the ruling party in the United States Senate. He was a confidant of the president and the head of the Republican party in the richest, most populous state in the Union. Surely, he was a man with a virtually limitless political future. Even Chauncey Depew of the New York Central, whose early friendship with the senator had long since cooled, said, "Roscoe Conkling was created by nature for a great career." That he missed it, he added, "was entirely his own fault. Physically he was the handsomest man of his time. His mental equipment nearly approached genius. He was industrious to a degree. His oratorical gifts were of the highest order, and he was a debater of rare power and resources. But," he went on, "his intolerable egotism deprived him of vision necessary for supreme leadership." In spite of his "oratorical power and his talent in debate," he made no lasting impression on the country. "The reason," Depew concluded, "was that his wonderful gifts were wholly devoted to partisan discussions and local issues." [6]

Perhaps. But then it could be said that the mark of Conkling's genius was his ability to make great national questions out of his local issues.

Opinions on Roscoe Conkling at this stage of his career varied. Henry Adams, for example, who loathed Conkling from the depths of his Brahmin soul, said that such leaders "could not be burlesqued; they were more grotesque than ridicule could make them." [7] Hamilton Fish, in a position where he had to make far more practical judgments than

[4] T. C. Platt, *Autobiography,* p. 55.

[5] *Cong. Globe,* 42d Cong., 2d sess., p. 166, Dec. 18, 1871. The quote was by Thomas F. Bayard of Delaware.

[6] Depew, p. 79.   [7] H. Adams, p. 261.

Henry Adams, felt differently. Fish was unhappy about the influence with Grant of some of the Republican senators—men like Morton, Zach Chandler, Matt Carpenter of Wisconsin, and Cornelius Cole of California. But there were a number of men whom Fish trusted, men he felt confident would not ensnare Grant in unforeseen traps, foremost of whom was Conkling. The secretary saw Conkling's faults, his bizarre disposition, his exotic posturings, but he also recognized in Conkling a counselor whose advice to Grant "would be unselfish and shrewd, though decidedly partisan." [8]

Georgie Frisbie Hoar, who cared not at all for the New Yorker, admitted that Conkling "never flinched in debate from the face of any antagonist. There was something almost sublime in his lofty disdain." Besides, continued Hoar, "he was on the side of the country in her hour of peril." Roscoe Conkling never really asked for recognition beyond that.[9]

Senator Thomas Hendricks of Indiana, the Democratic leader, in the course of debate with the senator from New York, said, "I suppose the idea of the Senator is that if you quarrel with a man once you have got to quarrel with him all your life." And though Conkling denied it, the entire course of his career proved that he really believed just that.[10]

He was a big favorite in the Senate, not particularly among his fellow senators, who knew that he was unmatched in his ability to harry, goad, and annoy an adversary in debate, but in the galleries, particularly the ladies' gallery, which was always packed when he was scheduled to speak. An unfriendly journal once quoted an auditor of a Conkling speech as saying "that as speaking he did not consider it good, but as acting he liked it. It is certainly very like some acting." [11] Adept at memorization, Conkling was able to concentrate on and indulge himself in the stagy mannerisms which endeared him to the galleries and so infuriated his critics. He spent a great deal of time writing, correcting, embellishing, and polishing a speech, and took long walks in the country to master it and commit it to memory. Later on, an admiring employee of the Republican state committee named Lawrence served as a listening post for the senator. Conkling orated to him by the hour, and when the senator eventually delivered his speech, it would be word for word as Lawrence had heard it.[12]

[8] Nevins, *Fish*, II, 589.   [9] Hoar, II, 59.
[10] *Cong. Globe,* 40th Cong., 2d sess., p. 1728, March 7, 1868.
[11] *The Nation,* Feb. 1, 1877. Thompson, p. 167.   [12] Depew, pp. 80–81.

Around Washington, Roscoe Conkling was reputed to be very dashing and successful with the ladies. The rumors increased as it became obvious that he and his wife Julia were growing more distant as the years passed. Tales of the senator's infidelity were widespread. At one time, it was said, the editor of a weekly paper in Washington prepared a long article detailing Conkling's extramarital activities. Conkling got wind of it, confronted the editor, and insisted on reading the proofs. When he finished, he asked the editor, evenly, "Do you intend to print this article?"

"I do," replied the newspaperman.

"Then I will kill you," said Conkling, without hesitation.

The editor's assistant, who was present and told the story, said: "I saw the fear of imminent death seizing the soul of my chief. There was in Mr. Conkling's voice something so unspeakably fierce and cruel and in his savage gaze something so appalling that few men, I think, could have withstood him." The article was never printed, and the proofs were destroyed.

Few people in Washington loved Roscoe Conkling, but everyone took him seriously. His flamboyant attire and his exaggerated oratorical mannerisms might be ridiculed behind his back, but few men were able to stand up to his "cruel and savage gaze" without flinching.[13]

Conkling paid little attention to the formalities of organized religion; he said, "The Episcopal church is the church to which I go." He had, in earlier years, been a regular communicant at Trinity Church in Utica, but his adherence was now irregular and *pro forma* only.[14]

He was apparently devoted to his daughter Bessie, who served as his main link to the house in Rutger Park, and he was now the most prominent politician in the family, since Seymour's defeat in 1868. But politics and the attractions of Washington drew him increasingly away from his family. Though his famous liaison with Kate Chase Sprague had not yet begun, he found Washington and New York City (when Congress was not in session) far more congenial than distant, unexciting Utica.

[13] C. E. Russell, *Blaine*, pp. 116–117. Russell cites no source for the story of Conkling and the editor, so it must be presumed that he, as an old Washington reporter, had it direct from the editor's assistant, certainly the original source. From a biographer's point of view, it is unfortunate that the article was never published.

[14] *Cong. Globe*, 41st Cong., 3d sess., p. 1892, March 2, 1871; J. R. Harding, *Trinity Church, Utica*, p. 114. Seymour, his brother-in-law, and his crony Ward Hunt were both vestrymen of the church, but Conkling had no taste for such activity.

One of Washington's leading reporters told a story of Conkling's passion for physical fitness, combined with his relish for combat. In the brick house on Fourteenth Street where he boarded, Conkling had set up a private gymnasium. Here he worked out daily. His favorite exercise was with boxing gloves and a punching bag. One evening after dinner, Conkling showed his gym to a guest, Senator Matt Carpenter, and asked him if he would like to box a bit. When Carpenter agreed, Conkling cuffed him about in fine style. Carpenter later hired a professional boxer named Jem Mace to visit Conkling's establishment with him. When Roscoe again asked Carpenter to box, the senator from Wisconsin declined but suggested that Mace, whom he introduced as a "constituent," might spar with Conkling. The two squared off, and Mace promptly battered Conkling to the floor, while Carpenter stood by and roared. The reporter did not describe Conkling's reaction to this ruse, but it can certainly be imagined.[15]

No matter what his personal foibles, Conkling had shown the political nerve and muscle to take over as undisputed leader of the Republican party in the state of New York. One of the very good reasons Conkling's power was so imposing was the coterie of able political pros he had gathered around him. His three chief lieutenants, led by Chester Alan Arthur, together with A. B. Cornell and Tom Platt, were supplemented and bolstered by a strong second line of political craftsmen, men like Richard Crowley, L. P. Morton, George Sharpe, and Louis F. Payn.

Arthur, like Conkling, was a successful lawyer, but his type of practice was totally different. Where Conkling was the flamboyant advocate, the rousing trial attorney, Chester Arthur was the quiet, calm office counselor, drafting wills and business contracts for his steady clients, keeping them out of lawsuits, and keeping out of court himself as much as possible. Even with his political involvement, Arthur continued an active law practice through the years; he did not leave the law behind until he had the necessity forced upon him at Garfield's death.

Arthur was born in North Fairfield, Vermont, October 5, 1830, the first son of a Baptist minister. Chester's father dragged his family from pulpit to pulpit throughout Vermont and upstate New York until, in 1844, he became pastor of the Baptist church in Schenectady. Here Chester enrolled at the local lyceum and, a year later, at Union Col-

15 Carpenter, pp. 257–258.

lege, already established as one of the leading colleges in the East. His career there was not particuarly noteworthy, though he was able to graduate in the rolls of Phi Beta Kappa.

Following his graduation in 1848, young Arthur studied law while teaching school to support himself. His studies drew him in the direction of New York City, where he was admitted to the bar in 1854. His political tendencies, acquired from his father, were antislavery, and he became a Whig and ultimately a Republican.

Arthur joined the local militia and became judge advocate general of the second brigade of the New York militia, combining his military endeavors with his legal training. In 1860, after he had worked for the successful reelection of Governor Morgan, the governor appointed him engineer in chief on his military staff. After the Civil War started, Morgan named the hard-working young lawyer assistant quartermaster general of New York, in which position Arthur labored long and well. The hard-pressed Morgan, desperately seeking able associates to help him master the complexities of running the largest state in the Union while keeping New York's levies in the field adequately supplied, appreciated Arthur's talent, hard work, and loyalty. In 1862, he was promoted to quartermaster general. Arthur left this position on January 1, 1863, when the Democrat Seymour took over the executive mansion, but he contributed much of himself during the trying times of the Morgan administration.

Upon his retirement from state service, Arthur was able to apply himself to the law and politics and to develop in addition a cultured taste for the good life of New York society. He moved his family into a new home on Lexington Avenue at Gramercy Park in 1867, and he was elected to the very distinguished Century Club. He was an inveterate fisherman, and he loved to take angling jaunts into the Catskills or the Adirondacks or, when everything was just right, to the Thousand Islands. It required a lucrative income to support Arthur's standard of living, but in his quiet, unobtrusive manner he had built a very fine practice.[16]

After the war, Arthur considered himself a conservative Republican, as was his patron Morgan. In 1866, Arthur stuck with Seward and Weed in their support of President Johnson. However, in the Syracuse

---

[16] Much of the background material on Arthur's pre-Conkling life is from G. F. Howe, *Chester A. Arthur,* pp. 1–35. Some of Howe's extremely favorable judgments on Arthur, however, must be regarded with skepticism.

convention of 1867, Roscoe Conkling, newly elected to the Senate, allied with Morgan, and looking for friends in his upcoming battle with Fenton, was quite willing to become the sponsor of the return to the fold of the New York City conservatives, including Arthur. When Fenton caused their repudiation by a convention that he controlled, many New York conservatives, including Chester Arthur, formed an alliance in the succeeding months with Roscoe Conkling. Arthur's association with Conkling grew through his connections with Morgan and Murphy, and after the Saratoga convention of 1870, Arthur was Conkling's man.[17]

Arthur was a shrewd, imaginative, and meticulous political manager; he was a master organizer, a necessity for Conkling's new organization. His dignity and calm courtesy kept him above much of the camaraderie and fellowship of the political club. The "boys" felt that he was one of them, though a little superior to them, and everyone, friend and foe, found him genuinely likable.

The name Cornell was a magic one in New York State in the middle of the nineteenth century. Everyone knew the rags-to-riches story of Ezra Cornell, the former millhand who worked out a feasible means of insulating telegraph wires on poles, thereby insuring the success of Samuel F. B. Morse's fabulous invention. Ezra Cornell built the first experimental telegraph line from Baltimore to Washington and led the way in the construction of additional lines throughout the East. He founded the Western Union Telegraph Company, and he became marvelously wealthy. He served as a Republican in the state senate, where he became friendly with Senator Andrew Dickson White. He and White led a successful fight to appropriate the Morrill Land Grant subsidy for the state to a new college to be founded in his adopted home town of Ithaca. Cornell himself made lavish gifts of cash, but even more importantly, he set himself to devoting the remainder of his active life to the firm establishment and growth of the school, which came to bear his name.

His son Alonzo, born in Ithaca in 1832, became an active Republican politician and, in time, one of Roscoe Conkling's key machine keepers. Ironically, this son of the founder of a great university disregarded his father's exhortations and abandoned his formal education at the age of sixteen, dropping out of the Ithaca Academy to go

[17] P. R. Levin, *Seven by Chance*, p. 160; Howe, p. 37.

to work in the telegraph office. "I *cannot* set down and study and keep my mind on my book for any length of time," Alonzo wrote his father in the fall of 1847.[18]

Young Alonzo was tremendously self-confident; he was sure he could run his own office, and he had no hesitation in giving his father business advice. After working in Troy and Montreal, he was placed in charge of the office in Cleveland and did well; Ezra's partner wrote, "There is a good deal of the right sort of grit in him, and he *will* be somebody." [19] Ezra soon found that, while his son was very free with advice, both technical and administrative, it was, on the whole, good advice. Alonzo was a successful businessman; he operated a line of steamboats on Cayuga Lake, and he became vice-president and cashier of the First National Bank of Ithaca, and ultimately vice-president of the Western Union Telegraph Company. He was also active in politics.

In 1864, he became Republican chairman of Tompkins County and was marked as one of the rising young men of New York politics. Two years later, his father's name was prominently mentioned as a candidate for governor, but the forces of incumbent Governor Fenton were too numerous. It fell then to Alonzo to move for Fenton's nomination by acclamation.[20] In 1868, however, young Cornell was the nominee of the Republican party for lieutenant governor. He lost in November, but the tour throughout the state served as valuable exposure for the future role he was to play. As a prior opponent of Fenton, Cornell was a natural and early adherent of the Conkling opposition wing. With the Grant administration, Cornell was named surveyor of the New York Custom House, a strategic position, and the New York *Times* called him "a young man of energy, capacity and integrity." [21] By the time of Conkling's 1870 battles against Fenton, Cornell was a well-entrenched ally.

Alonzo B. Cornell was not generally well-liked. Tall and stout, with thick features, the one word most frequently attached to him was "cold." He was strong-willed and stern, the keeper of his own counsel. He was criticized for his lack of imagination and limited vision, but he served a definite function in Conkling's organization. In the Saratoga convention of 1870, after the senator had put the Fenton forces to rout and dominated the selection of the new state committee, Conkling saw to it that Cornell, whom he had known since the 1863 state convention,

18 P. Dorf, *The Builder,* pp. 116, 126.   19 *Ibid.,* p. 136.
20 *Ibid.,* p. 320.   21 March 26, 1869.

was selected as chairman, a post he was to retain for eight years. Cornell was tough and thick-skinned, and he kept the state committee in hand.[22]

The third member of Conkling's first string was Thomas Collier Platt, born in 1833 at Owego, in Tioga County in the "Southern tier." Platt's political career came as a decided detour from a life in the ministry planned by his puritanical father. Platt later said, "I had such a surfeit of churchgoing in my youth that if it could be averaged up and spread out, it would do for all my life." His father sent him to Yale to attend to his clerical studies, but ill-health forced him to quit. The townspeople said that young Tom was "a rather bloodless, wobbly-legged, flat-chested squawky-voiced boy." [23]

Back in Owego, he learned how to put up prescriptions, because, as he later explained, "For years I had nursed the longing to become a druggist." He went into partnership with a friend and from 1856 to 1872, when Platt was elected to Congress, the Platt and Hull Drug Store was the center of political life in Tioga County.[24] Platt served a two-year term as county clerk from 1859 to 1861. He was a good politician, tactful, an easy mixer, and he moved ahead in the party. By the late sixties, he was Tioga County Republican chairman. As one of the leaders of the Southern tier, he came to the attention of the senator from Utica. He liked Conkling, and Conkling liked him, though Platt's affection was based, as was everything with him, on careful calculation. "From the day I met Conkling we were on confidential terms. I had been selected by him to look after the Southern tier counties, and I made frequent trips to Washington to consult with him. Though to strangers he appeared cold and austere, to me he was companionable and sought my advice on practically every phase of New York political conditions." [25]

Platt was crafty, ambitious, and unburdened with ideology or sentiment. He could do the glad-handing and back-slapping which made Arthur uncomfortable, which Cornell found repellent, which Conkling

[22] Most of the background material on Alonzo B. Cornell is from an autobiographical fragment in the A. B. Cornell papers, Cornell University Library, as well as from Dorf, *The Builder,* an excellent biography of his father.

[23] H. F. Gosnell, *Boss Platt,* p. 13; W. A. White, "Platt," p. 145.

[24] Platt, p. 3.

[25] *Ibid.,* p. 60; Platt's *Autobiography,* written from a long perspective, inflates considerably his importance in Roscoe Conkling's scheme of things.

would never have considered. Besides, Platt had a great fund of political knowledge, and he knew local politicians from all over the state.

Arthur, Cornell, and Platt were the three men who gradually developed as Conkling's chief assistants, the men who ran the state party while Conkling stayed close to Grant and developments in Washington. Despite surface similarities such as relative age and the odd fact that each of them married a woman named Ellen, they were basically very different. Arthur, genial but dignified and reserved, was unlike Cornell, cold and silent, who was again very different from the more outgoing and down-to-earth Platt. But Roscoe Conkling was not forming a friendship league; he was building a political organization, a machine, which had to be strong enough to withstand the buffeting of time and trouble. These were strong, able men, and they served their purposes well.

Other interesting and talented men were machine leaders, too. One of these was Thomas L. James of Hamilton, who had been a printer and newspaper publisher, a collector of canal tolls, and a sometime employee of the New York Custom House. Befriended by Conkling many years before, James was absolutely devoted to the senator. In 1873, Grant named him postmaster of New York. Four years later Hayes reappointed him. James had a great talent for honest and efficient administration, and his conduct of the largest post office in the nation won him many accolades.[26] It was a source of chagrin to opponents that such a dedicated and able public servant could be a follower of Roscoe Conkling.

A wealthy businessman named Levi P. Morton, generally known as "L. P.," was another member of the group. Morton was born the son of a poor Calvinist minister in Vermont in 1824, and he grew up in rural poverty. His first jobs were as clerk in country stores, but he was a shrewd and able young man, with a good business head, and he eventually moved on to New York, where he established a commission business in wholesale dry goods. At the start of the Civil War, his firm was one of those which went into bankruptcy as a result of the sudden withdrawal of lucrative Southern business, but in 1863 he opened a private banking house which soon prospered. The firm's success made Morton very wealthy, and his urbane manner and warm personality brought him a host of friends, among them Ulysses S. Grant. Morton became a staunch backer of the president, and, in New York, this soon

26 See, for example, N.Y. *Times,* Aug. 27, 1875.

drew him into the group surrounding the pro-Grant leader, Senator Conkling.[27]

A young lawyer named Richard Crowley, state senator from the Niagara district and a friend of Collector Murphy, was another steadfast follower of the senator. Crowley's wife once wrote that "in the brilliant and now ended career of Roscoe Conkling, he had no friend more loyal than Richard Crowley." In March of 1871, Grant appointed Crowley to the position of United States attorney for the Northern District of New York (a district running from Albany to Buffalo, and from the Pennsylvania line to Canada), a post he held for eight years, until his election to Congress.[28]

Stewart Woodford, Grant's friend and the gubernatorial nominee of 1870, quickly became part of the organization, in which he was the second-best orator. There were others: adroit political manipulators like Louis F. Payn of Columbia County, harbor master of New York, a friend of Platt and an accomplished lobbyist at Albany, and George Sharpe, who later became surveyor at the custom house. There were lawyers like young Elihu Root and Elbridge G. Lapham, an older, more mediocre man. There were judges such as Charles Folger of the Court of Appeals. George Washington Dunn, the sheriff of Broome County and publisher of the Binghamton *Republican,* the leading party organ of the Southern tier, contributed his considerable support to Conkling. Financiers like Henry Clews, a Wall Street banker who grew fat on the bond issues of the Reconstruction governments of the Southern states, were with Conkling, as was William Waldorf Astor, later, as Baron Astor, the founder of the British branch of his famous family. The new organization attracted other ambitious political functionaries like Silas Dutcher, Stephen B. French, and John F. Smyth. There were many other political leaders across the state who adhered to Conkling's machine, along with hundreds of anonymous weighers, gaugers, postmen, and toll collectors who organized the precinct meetings which selected delegates to district gatherings where delegates to state conventions were picked.

Horace Greeley once wrote that, while traveling through the state, he "came upon hundreds of Senator Conkling's New York Custom House officials—supposed to be guarding the waterfront—far in the

[27] For details on Morton's early life, see R. McElroy, *Levi Parsons Morton,* pp. 1–49.

[28] J. Crowley, *Echoes of Niagara,* pp. 177, 169.

interior, traveling upon trains everywhere in connection with their party duties at local nominating conventions, committee meetings, and caucuses under the command of Conkling." [29]

Conkling's opponents charged that, in the selection of employees for the custom house and other federal patronage establishments,

the first question relates to their politics. Does John Smith, for example, belong to the party in power? Is he a working man at the polls? Is he a good ticket-peddler? Can he run a party caucus? How many votes can he influence? These are the questions which, under the Conkling regime, take precedence of all others. The appointee to the service must be a good party man, an active politician himself, or the protégé and friend of some one who is such. He may be a scamp; but if he is all right in the political and party sense, this one fact will cover a multitude of sins.[30]

The patronage employees were assets to the organization in two ways; first, many of them were able to draw a living from the federal treasury while devoting their time and efforts to the advancement of political aims, and, second, these salaries themselves were subject to assessments of anywhere from 2 to 6 per cent by the Republican organization, to provide the fuel for running the machine. "The millions paid out of the Federal Treasury in this State were to him as a military chest," it was said of the senator some years later, "From them political zeal, skill, and efficiency were rewarded." [31]

The whole thing was tied together by Conkling. The senator made frequent visits to New York City, always on weekends and sometimes more often than that when schedules in Washington permitted. The Fifth Avenue Hotel, where Conkling stayed in New York, became the center of party affairs.[32] The organization showed little interest in anything but its own perpetuation. The plans and programs that were worked out concerned the winning of elections, or controlling caucuses, or making sure that the right people were in the right jobs. Rarely did Conkling and his lieutenants discuss positive legislative or administrative initiatives, and Conkling's efforts in these areas in the Senate, spotty though they were, seem to have been completely independent of the machine in New York. The machine leaders were interested only in keeping their power intact and in preventing the Democrats or rival Republicans from seizing any of it.

[29] M. Josephson, *The Politicos,* p. 92.   [30] *The Independent,* July 21, 1881.
[31] N.Y. *Times,* June 1, 1881.   [32] Gosnell, p. 56.

CHAPTER 9

CLEANSING THE PARTY

With Woodford as its candidate for governor, and with a new leader in Roscoe Conkling, the Republican party of New York State went forth in the fall of 1870 to battle the Democracy. However, 1870 was the last brazen triumph of the Tweed Ring. John T. Hoffman was re-elected governor, and A. Oakey Hall—"Elegant Oakey"—was re-elected mayor of New York. Sixteen of the thirty-one New York congressmen were Democrats, and the party of Tammany won control of the legislature as well.

Conkling took an active part in the campaign, which helped him in consolidating his rule of the party. Fenton played almost no role, and there were grave suspicions about his disgruntled supporters. Tom Platt claimed that the party was defeated "through the treachery of the Fenton men in New York," many of whom held "lucrative municipal places under Tammany Hall by grace of the notorious William M. Tweed." [1]

Even President Grant got wind of what happened. He wrote to Conkling on November 18: "I have no doubt but benefits have accrued to the Republican party, in New York, from the change of officials there. There were not quite enough of them made in my opinion after the fight." [2]

One of the sources of Tweed's strength in the metropolis was this fifth column in the opposition party, a group generally known as the "Tammany Republicans," which insured Tweed whatever majority he desired in the city. Republican election officials in the pay of Tammany Hall naturally offered no resistance to Democratic doctoring of vote returns. After the election of 1870, Conkling gave the word to cut out

[1] Platt, p. 56.   [2] Conkling Papers, Library of Congress.

this cancer in the Republican body, to clean up New York's Republican organization. If this could be done, he felt, the party's position would be excellent; "The health of our party, and its strength for the future," he wrote, "seem to me better now than for a long time." [3]

New York City had a population of not quite one million in 1870, but its metropolitan area doubled that. It was a gaudy, roistering, vulgar city, full of toughs, bums, "swells," whores, sweatshops, speculation, manipulators, and wealth. It was this era that filled the town with grotesque and tasteless architecture—"early General Grant"—and the development of industry led to an accentuation of the vulgarities of the age. Gould and Fisk and the sanctimonious Daniel Drew symbolized the shoddy, shady financial morals of the day; the followers of Tweed, accomplished thieves like Peter B. "Brains" Sweeny and Richard "Slippery Dick" Connolly, were their counterparts in politics. Not content with absolute mastery over the Democratic party of New York, Tweed was able to debauch the city Republican organization, the Republican general committee, as well.[4]

The effort to revamp the New York City Republican party began at the 1870 Saratoga convention. Horace Greeley urged the necessity of "such a . . . purification of the party in this City as would relieve it from the incubus of Tammany Hall and its treacherous Republican allies." With this impetus, after the defeat at the polls in the fall, petitions were presented to the state committee calling for a thorough reorganization. The state committee agreed to undertake the job. Strangely enough, Greeley, by this time, had been elected chairman of the Republican general committee; that group, dominated by Tweed's Republican officeholders and hangers-on, declined to be reorganized. The state committee asked Greeley to take charge of the reorganization, Cornell writing that he hoped "for a general acquiescence from all Republicans in favor of this reorganization." The editor, who had urged the reform in the first place, now refused. It was perplexing; Roscoe Conkling wrote that Greeley "contributes industriously to a state of things which . . . he affects to deplore." Cornell, the state chairman, then named William Orton and Jackson S. Schultz to do the job. Orton and Schultz established a complete new structure, with

---

[3] Conkling to E. Pierrepont, Nov. 19, 1870, Pierrepont Papers.

[4] Van Deusen, *Horace Greeley*, pp. 339–340. On one famous occasion the corpulent Fisk, having been exposed in a swindle, said blithely, "Nothing is lost save honor."

new committeemen where necessary and new delegates to the central committee. There was no doubt that some of the purged officials were eliminated more for allegiance to Fenton than to Tweed, and a fight at the next state convention was assured.[5]

The state convention was called for September 27, 1871, at Syracuse, and it promised to be a rouser. The *Times* said its "first duty" would be "to establish a Republican organization in this City which shall be without taint of Tammany influence. This will be immediately presented by the contesting New York delegations." The delegates gathered, along with large numbers of other interested participants, and the hotels filled to overflowing. Reuben Fenton, a surprise attendant, checked into the Empire House; word had been passed that he would not be there. He told a reporter that he had "happened along this way 'accidentally.'" Everyone speculated about what would happen with the New York delegates. The *Times* figured on a compromise:

As between Conkling and Fenton, the friends of Conkling will have a clear majority in the Convention, and can have everything their own way if they choose, but Senator Conkling, who is a delegate himself, cordially seconds the efforts of those who are striving for harmony. The New York trouble will probably be settled by the admission of both delegations, each delegate being allowed half a vote. The action of the State Committee in the reorganization will be approved, and the new State Committee be authorized to perfect the organization in New York by a union of the two existing organizations on such terms as they may deem advisable in their discretion.[6]

Invariably, year after year, the newspapers assured their readers before state conventions that Senator Conkling would be reasonable in the interests of harmony and party unity. Consistently, year after year, they guessed wrong. The only harmonious conventions he had were the ones in which there was no opposition to his control at all. This one was a wild affair.

Weiting Hall, where the convention met, was packed, and the building's owner wisely took out special insurance against damage. The seats on the stage were occupied by toughs and hoodlums brought up from New York City, and the contesting delegations appeared ready to settle their differences by physical means. It looked like a brawl

[5] N.Y. *Times,* Aug. 29, 1871; Cornell to H. Greeley, March 14, 1871, Cornell Papers; Conkling to Pierrepont, Feb. 11, 1871, Pierrepont Papers.
[6] Sept. 26, 27, 1871.

right from the start. Cornell recruited the police to eject the interlopers from the stage, and the convention was ready to begin.

Clearly, the credentials committee was going to be all-important in settling the claims of the New York rivals. Since the credentials committee would be appointed by the temporary chairman, the first order of business was the election of this official.

Cornell called the convention to order at noon, and George Sharpe promptly nominated Andrew D. White, the president of Cornell University, for temporary chairman. Edwin Merritt nominated Depew, but Cornell ruled the nomination out of order since Depew was not a delegate. Disorder and fighting broke out on the floor, and it took some time for the police to stop the melee and bring the convention under control. When the crowd settled down again, a Fenton follower named G. Hilton Scribner was placed in nomination. Cornell then called the roll. As the delegates responded, a small but firm majority was established by the Conkling element, and this put White over the top. As the newly elected chairman moved to the rostrum, he was handed a list of names by Cornell. This was to be the credentials committee. Upon taking the chair, White then read off the list unchanged, despite audible protests from the Fenton people. White later said, "I received this list, not only with implied, but express assurances that the agreement under which I had taken the chairmanship had been complied with; —namely that the list represented fairly the two wings of the party in convention. . . . I had no reason then, and have no reason now, to believe that the State committee abused my confidence." [7]

Though White felt sure that the committee was evenly apportioned between the two wings of the party, other observers saw clearly that twelve of the fourteen members of the committee were Conkling supporters. Conkling had cautioned Cornell well in advance of the necessity for careful construction of this committee.[8] The majority of the committee reported that the new city organization should be stamped the valid one but that both sets of delegates should be seated in the convention, with half votes. The minority report denied the authority of the state committee to meddle with the Greeley group at all, and demanded that the Tammany Republican delegation be seated. A hot debate ensued.

State Senator Hamilton Ward proposed a compromise; seat both

[7] A. D. White, I, 166.
[8] Conkling to Cornell, Aug. 28, 1871, Cornell Papers.

delegations in the convention, giving each delegate a half vote, and direct the state committee to blend the two organizations into one united party group. The sentiment of the convention swung behind this way out of the trouble, and White prepared to put Ward's proposal to a vote. Suddenly, from the back of the hall, the voice of Roscoe Conkling cut dramatically through the din as he shouted, "Not yet the question, Mr. President!" and strode to the platform.

Sharply, harshly, the senator proceeded to cut the compromise proposal to pieces. He would have no part of any weak-kneed half measure. He asked to have the two reports of the credentials committee voted upon, and he demanded that the work of reorganization in New York City not be thrown away little more than a month before the election.

A horde of ballot-box stuffers, pirates and robbers have clutched by the throat the greatest city in the western world. A horde of pirates, whose firm name is Tammany Hall, and I stand here to say that beyond presenting in its own organization the most hideous spectacle in modern history, it has debauched, tampered with, and to a large extent controls that glorious organization which is the brightest in the annals of political parties.[9]

The compromise was dead. Conkling recognized that acceptance of the Ward proposal made possible a divided delegation to the national convention in 1872, while reorganization as decreed by the state committee practically assured a solid delegation for Grant. As far as the senator was concerned, a solid Grant delegation was more important than the illusory party harmony desired by some newspaper editors. He wrote John Sherman, "We have done nothing harsh to the anti-administration minority, but the least and mildest thing which would prevent a split in our organization with trouble for the future, and probably a double delegation in the next national convention." [10]

The Ward proposal was defeated, the majority report was adopted by over forty votes, and the Fenton and Greeley men from New York

[9] N.Y. *Times,* Sept. 28, 1871. Conkling had planned to take no part in the New York City debate; Conkling to Cornell, Sept. 18, 1871, Cornell Papers. The imminence of the unwanted compromise forced him to scrap his plans.

[10] Conkling to Sherman, Oct. 13, 1871, Sherman, I, 479. Conkling wrote to Andrew D. White, on Nov. 23, 1872, after Grant was safely re-elected, that "the firm impartial hand with which you held the State Convention last year was the hinge on which the result in the state, if not in the nation, turned." He went on to set forth in sequence what would have happened "had the Tammany Greeley organization in N.Y. been permitted to survive." A. D. White Papers.

City walked out of the convention. One of their number, licking his wounds the next day, wailed: "We have met in this Convention the Collectors of ports, internal revenue officers all over the State. We have met Postmasters in solid phalanx; the District Attorneys, the registers in bankruptcy, and the bankrupts also." Tom Platt sized it up about right: "This established Conkling firmly in control of New York State." [11]

While the state committee was developing its new organization in New York City, the final session of the Forty-first Congress developed some fireworks of its own.

San Domingo blazed back into public attention again. The president made it clear that he was not finished with his various projects for the lease of Samaná Bay or the annexation of the entire island republic. Charles Sumner, the long-time chairman of the Senate Foreign Relations Committee, a pompous, self-inflated personage of overbearing manner, called once by Conkling "the great orb of the State Department, who rises periodically in his effulgence and sends his rays down the steep places here," was opposed to any consideration of Grant's schemes for San Domingo.[12] Many senators were opposed to the whole idea of San Domingo, and even more were put off by the manner of the introduction of the question, particularly the extraordinary usurpation of authority by General Babcock, Grant's aide. None went to the bitter extremes of Sumner in opposing it. Perhaps the man could not help it; in 1856, his intensely personal and vituperative manner of speech had won him a brutal caning on the Senate floor by Preston Brooks of South Carolina after a fiery speech on the troubles of Kansas. In 1870, Sumner may have felt that similar retaliation by Grant's supporters might once again elevate him to that high place in public sympathy which his earlier beating had won. He dealt with no hot-headed Southerners this time, however; cold-blooded politicians knew how to handle Sumner when once he had delivered himself into their hands.

On December 12, 1870, Morton presented a resolution, which all understood was offered on behalf of the administration, to send a

[11] N.Y. *Times,* Sept. 29, 1871; Platt, p. 59. The Syracuse convention can be followed in the daily newspapers, particularly the *Times* and the *Tribune,* and also in Platt, pp. 58–59; A. R. Conkling, pp. 339–342; Alexander, III, 256–261; and Van Deusen, *Horace Greeley,* pp. 393–395.

[12] *Cong. Globe,* 40th Cong., 2d sess., p. 3393, June 23, 1868.

three-man commission to San Domingo for investigation of the resources and possibilities of the place. This was in response to Grant's request in his annual message of December 5, "to appoint a commission to negotiate a treaty with the authorities of San Domingo for the acquisition of this island." [13]

Morton had done a good part of his duty to his chief by submitting the watered-down resolution, which called only for investigation, not negotiation. No one was wildly anxious to go much farther with it. For two weeks the Morton resolution was debated in bitter executive sessions, with Sumner leading virulent opposition to it. Charles Sumner took the floor in open session on December 21.

"Mr. President," he began, "the resolution before the Senate commits Congress to a dance of Blood. . . . It is a new step in a measure of violence. Several steps have already been taken, and Congress is now summoned to take another." Several senators who were on Sumner's side in opposing annexation wondered, listening to the Massachusetts senator, whether they and Sumner were even talking about the same subject; they had the impression that Morton's resolution called only for an investigating commission. "As a Senator, as a patriot, I cannot see my country suffer in its good name without an earnest effort to save it." Sumner attacked the dealings of Babcock and President Baez of the Dominican Republic, and he scored the pledge made by Babcock in his protocol with the Dominicans that Grant would "privately" use all his influence to win Congress's consent to annexation. "There was the promise," Sumner proclaimed. "Senators about me know how faithfully the President has fulfilled it, how faithfully he has labored, privately and publicly, even beyond the protocol."

The Massachusetts statesman referred scornfully to rumors that Grant wanted to make a change in the Foreign Relations Committee by removing him, or Carl Schurz, or Patterson of New Hampshire, and he wound up with a fervid, impassioned, embittered plea of protest, after stating to his amazed listeners that he had never said unkind words about the president, even in executive session. This startled those who had just sat through two weeks of Sumner's violent attacks upon Grant in the closed sessions.[14]

[13] Richardson, ed., VII, 100.

[14] Sumner's "dance of blood" speech is in *Cong. Globe,* 41st Cong., 3d sess., pp. 226–229.

Following Sumner's address, the Senate recessed until the evening, when Morton led off for the administration forces with a point-by-point reply to Sumner's charges, stating, "It seems to me that he has overdrawn this thing in a manner that can only be described as ridiculous or ludicrous." [15]

Nye of Nevada and Chandler of Michigan followed, each tearing into Sumner with his own brand of oratorical venom, and, after Sumner replied to Chandler, came what the galleries had been waiting for; the tall, blond senator from New York received the floor and started to speak.

Conkling warmed to his subject slowly, a luxury he was permitted under Senate rules:

Mr. President, during this debate I have held my peace till now. I should be silent still but for the violence done this day to justice and to fairness, but for the wrong heaped upon one, foremost, not in the easy greatness of things written and said, but in the arduous greatness of things done; one who has excelled not in swollen periods, but in brave, honest deeds which have covered his name with imperishable renown.

He moved into the merits of the resolution before the Senate. "It was alleged that the treaty was hedged about with jobs on every side," he said. Accordingly, the president was asking, not for annexation or even a commitment to such a proceeding, but "to allow disinterested witnesses to visit San Domingo and bring back intelligence which may show that the President and others have been assailed, not with the weapons of the warrior, but with the weapons of the assassin." Sumner, Conkling went on, would deny the president the right of sending an unbiased commission "to report whether it be true that aggravated and agglomerated fraud besmears the treaty and the very soil of Samaná."

"Why, sir," Conkling continued, "if the charges made by the Senator today against the President be true, it would be necessary to convict him of being a fool in order to acquit him of being a knave. And yet the honorable member from Massachusetts says he has said no word against the President!"

Conkling denied that Grant had attempted in any way to change the composition of the Foreign Relations Committee. He himself, though, was quite willing to have a change made, and he called for Sumner's deposition: "Speaking for myself, upon my own responsibility, I say

[15] For Morton's speech, see *ibid.*, pp. 236–238.

that the time has come when the Republican majority here owes it to itself to see that the Committee on Foreign Relations is reorganized and no longer led by a Senator who has launched against the Administration an assault more bitter than has proceeded from any Democratic member of this body."

Senator Conkling went on at some further length, discussing the proposed commission of inquiry, but finally concluded on a surprisingly mild note by stating, "I am not anxious to debate the merits of San Domingo now." [16]

Sumner attempted a short rebuttal to "the piled-up agony of the Senator from New York," but the handwriting was on the wall for the proud but confused idealist from Massachusetts. His days as chairman of the committee which he loved so well were clearly numbered.

Meanwhile, Morton was determined to get a vote on his resolution that evening. After 1:00 A.M., Allan Thurman of Ohio, one of the ten Democrats in the Senate, taunted the majority members on their internal blood-letting: "Gentlemen of the Republican party, are you satisfied with this day's debate?" [17] But the battle went on and on, until finally, at 6:37 A.M., a weary Senate passed Morton's resolution for a commission of inquiry. It can be safely assumed that there was little eager anticipation of the commission's return.

Early in the new year of 1871, there took place on the floor of the Senate the first of many attacks upon Conkling's control of the New York Custom House. On December 14, 1870, Fenton had presented an innocent-looking resolution calling for an investigation into the collection of the revenues at Boston, New York, Philadelphia, Baltimore, New Orleans, and San Francisco. "Upon its face," said Roscoe Conkling, "it seemed an ordinary and a meritorious resolution, putting no one on trial and having no private or sinister aim." From it came a two-man subcommittee, Senator James Patterson of New Hampshire and Congressman Porter Sheldon, a lame-duck representative from Fenton's own Chautauqua district and a loyal follower of the deposed leader. Patterson and Sheldon spent most of their time in New York, and their findings trickled back to the capital.

On January 23, 1871, Lyman Trumbull of Illinois spoke about reports in the New York press that Murphy was "turning out competent and efficient clerks . . . for the purpose of putting in persons who can perform more political service and less public service to the country."

[16] Conkling's speech is found in *ibid.,* pp. 244–247.   [17] *Ibid.,* p. 255.

Conkling promptly responded that such reports were "without foundation, speaking very moderately of them." [18]

The next day, Patterson appeared to deliver a speech about his investigation, after which Conkling got the floor. The New Yorker began in a vein which startled some of his colleagues, when he said:

Perhaps in one respect there is not in this body a more disinterested and unbiased witness touching the New York custom-house in its present management than myself. I shall prove this when I state that since the present collector of the Port of New York was appointed I have never verbally or in writing, directly or indirectly, recommended to him or requested of him the appointment or the retention in office or the removal of a single person.

Conkling then reviewed the history of the investigation, including its sponsorship by Fenton, "not friendly to the chief officers of one of the places mentioned in the resolution," and the nature of the proceedings. "The importers find fault," he said scornfully. "As a general truth I should say that it shows a collector of customs to be efficient rather than lax if those who pay duties find fault." The only other charge made by Patterson, he said, was that inspectors accept presents from importers in exchange for expediting matters and small accommodations. This has always happened, said Conkling: "It is the misfortune, the fatal infelicity of all human government, that it must be administered by men." Needy men will accept small gifts. "It is to be deplored, of course."

Conkling then forced Patterson to admit that the committee had no evidence showing any impropriety of any sort on the part of Murphy, Cornell, or Grinnell.

The truth will appear that the present collector of the port of New York has devoted himself, not only with assiduity, but with conscientious determination, to eradicating abuses of long growth, and that in the particulars in which he is now challenged he has given the best and the most successful administration of the office we have had for years.[19]

Then it was Reuben Fenton's turn to deny any desire for a "controversy at this time with him" over the "practices of the Administra-

18 *Ibid.*, p. 667.

19 Conkling's speech is in *ibid.*, pp. 690–691. Some six years later, on May 17, 1877, Collector Chester Arthur wrote to John Jay on the virtual impossibility of preventing the offering and acceptance of gratuities for expeditious service; Arthur Papers, New-York Historical Society.

tion" but to complain of "proscription within the party organization for a difference of opinion relating to its organization and preferences for men." More specifically, Fenton went on, "Under the administration of the present Collector, all persons who are known to me or my friends as of a particular classification or shade in the Republican politics of New York have been put out and others put in, who, to say the least, do not in a higher degree enjoy the confidence and respect of the public." [20]

The controversy concluded the next day, when Fenton read a letter from his friend Congressman Sheldon, denying any hostility against Murphy. Conkling brushed Sheldon's letter aside and went after Fenton for his remark of the day before that Murphy was firing his friends, Conkling challenged Fenton to give one name, and Fenton refused to do so, saying the time and place were not appropriate for such a discussion. Conkling then triumphantly stated: "I say upon my veracity and responsibility as a Senator that in no single instance to my knowledge or belief has any man been removed from office in the State of New York during the present Administration because of his being the friend or adherent of my colleague." [21]

In Utica, in 1871, a shingle was hung out in front of Conkling's law office on Tibbitts Block, announcing the presence within of the firm of Conkling, Holmes, and Coxe. Sidney T. Holmes had a very short association with the senator, and the suspicion must be strong that the whole idea of the law firm was to use Conkling's name to produce some clients for his young nephew, his sister's son, Alfred C. Coxe, who had studied law with him. Coxe was no dunce, to be sure, as his distinguished later career on the United States district and circuit courts demonstrated, but the name of his famous uncle on the door no doubt helped to bring people into the office. Roscoe was not there in body very often, however, continuing to spend most of his year in Washington and New York. From 1872 to 1875, the firm name was Conkling, Lord, and Coxe, with Scott Lord, a Democratic politician and sometime congressman from Geneseo, replacing Holmes. After that, the senator's name appeared alone, with an office maintained for form's sake at 77 Genesee Street until 1882. He still maintained his legal residence at the gray stone house in Rutger Park. It was said that he had women, but he

20 *Cong. Globe,* 41st Cong., 3d sess., p. 692.
21 *Ibid.,* pp. 723–724.

was always discreet enough that there was never more than rumor for public consumption, at least until he met Kate Chase Sprague. He saw little of his wife, who, it was said, "accepted his philandering propensities in the spirit of the age." [22]

[22] I. Ross, *Proud Kate,* p. 233. Scott Lord wrote to Francis Kernan on December 11, 1871, asking for the latter's advice on Lord's leaving Geneseo, New York, to accept the proposition to come to Utica and Conkling's firm; Kernan Papers. Presumably, Kernan gave a good recommendation.

CHAPTER 10

ONCE AGAIN, GRANT

The results of the dismal (to Republican eyes) election of 1870 became manifest on March 4, 1871, when the Forty-second Congress met for the first time. The large Republican majority in the House was cut down to a relatively small edge, though the Senate was still safe. Both houses, however, were full of Republicans who were out of sympathy with the Grant administration. This was particularly so in the Senate, where party members like Sumner, Schurz, Fenton, Tipton of Nebraska, and Trumbull were threatening to go out of bounds altogether. In the House, a strong sentiment for tariff revision was apparent, the result of the free-trade doctrines of the eminent economist David Wells. This trend worried the president and his monied friends, along with many of the leading Republican politicians, who were staunch supporters of protection. The day was saved, however, and protection left undisturbed: the outbreak of disorders in the South enabled Grant and the Republican leadership to devote the entire short session to the South and the Ku Klux Klan.

The Klan, springing from humble and not necessarily racist origins in Pulaski, Tennessee, in 1886, had been reorganized into the "Invisible Empire of the South" at Nashville the following year, with the aim of disciplining the emancipated blacks and restoring them to an attitude of proper humility. Thereafter it was saddled with the blame (correctly so, in many cases) for all the floggings, lynchings, intimidations, and varied atrocities visited upon the freedmen and their white allies. From the carpetbag governments a cry arose for help to halt the depredations and restore good Republican order to the conquered region.

On March 23, Grant reported to Congress that "a condition of affairs now exists in some of the States of the Union rendering life and property insecure and the carrying of the mails and the collection of the

revenue dangerous." Therefore he urgently recommended "such legislation as in the judgment of Congress shall effectually secure life, liberty,
and property and the enforcement of law" in the South. And he added,
pointedly, "There is no other subject upon which I would recommend
legislation during the present session." [1] The result was the passage of
the Ku Klux Act, permitting the use of the army and suspension of the
writ of habeas corpus, with which the federal government hoped to
restore order.

During this first session of the new Congress, the Dominican commissioners returned and filed their report with the president. In the
touchy state of affairs on Capitol Hill, a reopening of the San Domingo
squabble was the last thing desired by the Republican leadership, and
this time General Grant cooperated. On April 5, he submitted the report to Congress, saying that it "more than sustains all that I have
heretofore said" on the bounties and blessings of San Domingo. Grant
pointed out that rejection of the treaty amid the general cries of "corruption on the part of the President" made investigation imperative,
and he said the report of the commissioners "fully vindicates the purity
of the motives and actions of those who represented the United States
in the negotiation." With this, he said, "ends all personal solicitude
upon the subject." He suggested that no action be taken on the subject
at the current session beyond printing the report and making it available to the public, a recommendation with which the leadership was
only too happy to comply. And he concluded by saying that, though he
had incurred the hostility of those who deemed their "opinions and
wishes treated with insufficient consideration," yet could he "bear with
patience the censure of disappointed men." [2] Thus Grant masterfully
disposed of the festering issue of San Domingo. Neither Conkling nor
any of Grant's most faithful supporters expected to see the annexation
of San Domingo return to vex their conduct of Senate business again,
and finally they were correct.

Though San Domingo remained out of the American republic, Grant
was able to exact a measure of revenge at the expense of the treaty's
most violent adversary. When the Forty-second Congress convened,
the Republican caucus in a bitter session voted by an overwhelming
majority to replace Sumner as chairman of the Foreign Relations Committee, redeeming Conkling's threat of the previous December. There
was opposition on the Senate floor from Sumner's faithful satellite, Carl

---

[1] Richardson, ed., VII, 127–128.   [2] *Ibid.*, VII, 128–131.

Schurz, but the deed was quickly done. Thus, Sumner became a second-class citizen in the United States Senate in which he had served so long and in which he was still perhaps the most famous member. Grant's enemies railed against the deposition—young Whitelaw Reid of the *Tribune* boasted of "rapping" Conkling "pretty vigorously over the head" on the subject—but to no avail.[3] To make the cup more bitter, Sumner's cherished committee was entrusted to the veteran mediocrity from Pennsylvania, Simon Cameron. The old-timers were dropping away, and Grant's lieutenants held the reins of the Senate.

At about this same time, an episode took place which earned Conkling a persistent and lifelong enemy. President Grant called a special session of the Senate on May 10 for the consideration of the Treaty of Washington, the treaty negotiated with Great Britain for the disposal and assessment of American claims for damages caused by the Confederate raider *Alabama,* built in Britain in violation of her neutrality. Painstaking precautions were followed in order to keep the terms of the pact secret until the Senate passed upon it. On May 11, however, the New York *Tribune,* boasting of the trouble and expense involved in procuring a copy, published the treaty in full. The Senate in its collective dignity was outraged, and an investigation was ordered. Matthew Carpenter and Conkling conducted the inquiry. The two Washington reporters for the *Tribune* refused to divulge the source of the leak, so the Senate, at the urging of Conkling and Carpenter, took the two correspondents into custody for contempt. This foolish step highlighted Roscoe Conkling's complete disregard for public opinion and the power of the press. The newspapermen were confined to a rather luxurious "jail," in the keeping of the Senate sergeant at arms, and they were treated royally for the few days they were held. In the face of the immediate and predictable storm of criticism in the nation's press, the Senate quickly backed down and released the men. The chief targets, naturally, were Conkling and Carpenter, and the loudest screams came from Reid of the *Tribune,* recently arrived from Cincinnati to become Greeley's right arm. He heaped abuse upon the two senators, calling them "common jailers," among other things. Conkling reacted characteristically; he never had any use thereafter for the brash young editor, and he scorned his paper. "The truthlessness and malice of

[3] Letter of Reid to John Bigelow of April 10, 1871; J. Bigelow, *Retrospections,* IV, 488.

that journal," he wrote, "is so habitual and so well understood that it makes no impression on me." Reid's biographer says that "the ridicule with which he flayed Conkling in the course of upholding his correspondents accounted for some, at least, of the enmity which that individual long cherished for him in political affairs." [4]

The year 1871 was an important one in New York, for it marked the overthrow of the infamous Tweed Ring. The better elements in New York City, inspired by the lead of the New York *Times* and cartoonist Thomas Nast of *Harper's Weekly,* and spearheaded by Samuel J. Tilden, organized the Committee of Seventy to redeem the city. Through 1871, the revelations in the columns of the *Times,* the weekly cartoons by Nast, and finally the attacks by the committee, the Republicans, and, belatedly, the honest Democrats took their toll on the Ring. Roscoe Conkling congratulated the *Times* on its "brilliant dashing foray" which "will change great currents and upset a venal dynasty." Tilden attempted to purge the party of its dishonest Tammany elements in the Democratic state convention of 1871, but he was prevented by Tweed's control of the conclave. One speaker went so far as to call the stories of frauds in New York City "the mere dreams of Republican imagination," drawing great applause as Tilden winced.[5]

Though Tweed continued defiant, calling his tormentors in the Democratic party, Tilden, Seymour, and Kernan, "three troublesome old fools," [6] grand jury investigations were added to the attacks upon the city government. Mayor A. Oakey Hall, a respectable but pliant tool of Tweed, was severely censured by a special grand jury for his conduct of city hall. Richard B. Connolly, the city comptroller, one of the original conspirators with Tweed and Peter Sweeny, upon learning that he was to be made a scapegoat for the evils of the Ring by Mayor Hall, immediately opened communications with Tilden and the reformers. Tweed's organization seemed to be splitting apart, and Nast's cartoons

---

[4] R. Cortissoz, I, 188; Thompson, pp. 149–153. Conkling to E. Pierrepont, Dec. 12, 1871, Pierrepont Papers. The only New York paper the Senator read regularly was the *Herald;* Conkling to Benjamin K. Phelps, April 4, 1877, Conkling Letters. The two jailed *Tribune* correspondents were Zebulon L. White and H. L. Ramsdell. Reid joined the *Tribune* in 1868 as Greeley's assistant and became managing editor the following year.

[5] Alexander, III, 271; Conkling to George E. Jones (publisher of the *Times*), July 28, 1871, Jones Papers.

[6] N.Y. *Tribune,* Oct. 6, 1871.

continued to receive wide circulation. Tweed was reported to have said at this time: "Let's stop them damn pictures. I don't care so much what the papers write about me—my constituents can't read; but damn it, they can see pictures." [7]

With the election coming on, Conkling was confident. "This state is ours," he wrote, "unless the people are discouraged from voting in the country by the belief that with Tammany to count, it matters not what majority roll up above the Highlands." [8] Tammany, though, was in deep trouble; the Republican ticket, selected at the Syracuse convention controlled by Roscoe Conkling, carried the state, and the legislature was returned to Republican hands. The senate (though Tweed himself was re-elected) was now solidly Republican, 24 to 8, and the assembly was held by the Republicans with a 97 to 31 majority. Though remnants of the Tweed Ring remained (Hall was still mayor of New York City, and Hoffman, a satellite rather than an insider in the Ring, continued as Governor), its hold on the city was broken. Its leaders were arrested or fled the country, and the immense, systematic plunder of the public treasury was stopped. Not only was relative honesty restored to the government of New York City, it appeared that this salutary result was obtained in conjunction with the re-establishment of Republican control in the state.

Time was to show, however, that the overthrow of Tammany had elevated to an eminent public position the sour-visaged corporation lawyer who, when he finally decided to attack Tweed frontally, contributed much to the triumph. Samuel J. Tilden earned a national reputation overnight and was the prime beneficiary of Tweed's downfall.

With a presidential election coming, the session of Congress which convened on December 4, 1871, was concerned largely with political activity, since there was little push from the executive for legislative urgencies. The political sounds emanating from Capitol Hill were counterpointed by the shuffling and scuffling of would-be presidential candidates, all of which was turned into as bizarre an outcome as American presidential history has ever seen.

The basic fact of political life for 1872 was that a segment of the Republican party was disaffected with an incumbent president who was sure to be renominated. In Missouri, in 1870, the split had become

[7] A. B. Paine, *Th. Nast,* p. 179.
[8] Conkling to Sherman, Oct. 13, 1871; J. Sherman, I, 479.

official with the formation of the Liberal Republican party, a third party which had carried the state behind Carl Schurz and Governor B. Gratz Brown against the Democrats and administration Republicans. Disappointed figures like Sumner and Fenton, men whose power and influence had for one reason or another waned under the Grant administration, were ready to join professional dissidents like Schurz in a national Liberal Republican party. Senators like Lyman Trumbull of Illinois and others, honestly disillusioned with Grant and disappointed that he did not see fit to listen to their counsels, were ripe for a Republican alternative. The large body of Wellsian tariff reformers, convinced that tariff reform under Grant, with *his* legislative leaders, was an idle dream, but not yet ready to cast their lot with the Democracy, also sought a plausible middle ground. And one of the most powerful Republican newspapers, Greeley's New York *Tribune,* was calling for change. The problem of the Liberal Republicans was a simple one. Who could be their candidate?

For the administration party, there was no question and no choice. For 1872, the word was Grant. The president liked it in the White House; it was comfortable and, as he functioned, not too taxing. It was apparent that he was not any longer the pure-white above-politics leader that he had been in 1868; his record was marred by Black Friday, San Domingo, a questionable Southern policy, some strange appointments to office, and a marked willingness to play power politics when the time seemed suitable. He would have to be re-elected on a partisan Republican platform, because he was now a partisan Republican.

Though Grant's popularity had noticeably slipped, the Democrats were in the frustrating position of being unable to do very much about it. They had no plausible candidates. The Senate, one of the potential breeding grounds for presidential candidates, was virtually dry as far as the Democrats were concerned. They were in such a tiny minority that their leaders, such as Allan Thurman of Ohio and Thomas F. Bayard of Delaware, found it almost impossible to make any kind of impression upon the national mind. The House was barely beginning to creep back to a semblance of two-party balance, and there was no one there to oppose Grant. Horatio Seymour was used up, and even Chief Justice Chase was approaching the end of his illustrious career. Tilden's star was just starting to rise, but he was still known mainly as Tweed's tormentor, not quite a sufficient base for a presidential nomination. The few Democratic governors offered no hope; the only one who had been groomed for a shot at the White House in 1872 was New York's John T. Hoffman, but the Tweed revelations left him out. The Democrats slowly accustomed themselves to the idea that if the Liberal Republicans got off the ground and actually ran someone for president of the United States, the party of Jefferson, Jackson, and Douglas might have to fall in line behind that nominee. It was a sobering thought.

The first order of the day, as it was so often, was the New York Custom House. Shortly after the 1871 election, on November 18, Murphy resigned as collector. Murphy's total ignorance of the business of the collection of revenues, protests at the monopoly of the "general-order" business enjoyed by the firm of Leet and Stocking, and the vocal unhappiness of the New York merchants with his administration made Murphy's departure inevitable. He felt justifiably proud of the results of the recent election as well as the consolidation of Republican power in the hands of Conkling and the administration adherents. In addition, Murphy was gratified to see his own close friend and attorney, Chester Arthur, selected as Conkling's choice for his successor. Grant wrote Murphy thanking him for "the efficiency, honesty, and zeal" with which he had carried on the office. This commendation excited both indignation and mirth.[9]

The collector's office was a crucial one for Conkling in building and maintaining his organization. It was essential that the right person be in the job, and Arthur was ideal. He was honest and efficient, candid and courteous, and unlike Tom Murphy he had none of the air of the party hack. Yet, despite the efficiency with which he ran the place, Arthur was able to make it serve its political needs.

Though criticism of the appointment was ostensibly aimed solely at its political implications, some of it, particularly from the increasingly embittered Horace Greeley, hit Arthur himself rather solidly. "The General," said the *Tribune* on November 21, "will be in the Custom-House a personal burlesque upon Civil Service Reform. . . . He is a devoted servant of the Murphy clique." The next day, Greeley's paper said, "The collector is Tom Murphy under another name. . . . He was Mr. Murphy's personal choice, and he was chosen because it is

[9] C. Bowers, *The Tragic Era*, p. 373.

believed he can run the machine of party politics better than any of our great merchants."

Whitelaw Reid, by now a confirmed Conkling foe, wrote a diatribe against the administration to his friend John Bigelow: "There is an utter surrender of the civil service to the coarsest use for factional purposes by the coarsest men. Mr. Grinnell goes out to make room for Mr. Murphy. When we drive Mr. Murphy out his counsel and personal representative takes his place." [10]

The muttering and murmuring about Murphy's administration continued after he was gone, and the flame was fanned by a speech in the Senate on December 13 by Carl Schurz. The Missouri senator spent some time detailing the testimony taken previously by Patterson's committee on the monopoly of the "general-order" business by Leet and Stocking. This was a messy bit of scandal in which Colonel George K. Leet, formerly a member of Grant's staff, upon production of a letter of introduction from Grant to Collector Grinnell, was able to receive the exclusive franchise for overnight storage of goods coming into the custom house, for which he charged exorbitant rates. Schurz called this "a system of shameless and wanton robbery imposed on the merchants of New York." He said it reminded him "of the robber knights of the Rhine . . . who stretched a chain across that river and made the shipper who went up or down pay toll" for the privilege of passing by.

"The fact remains," Schurz went on, boiling with righteous indignation, "that this scandalous system of robbery . . . is sustained against the voice of the merchants of New York . . . against the judgment and the voice of the Secretary of the Treasury himself." He reached a crescendo as he asked, "What is the mysterious power that sustains it?" As the galleries hushed, Schurz answered his question: "The conclusion is inevitable that it is a power stronger than decent respect for public opinion, nay, a power stronger than the Secretary of the Treasury himself." Schurz appealed to his colleagues to appoint a new, high-powered investigating committee, to delve to the bottom of the great New York Custom House frauds and, incidentally, to furnish ammunition to the anti-Grant forces for the coming campaign.

Conkling, who detested Schurz, was on his feet to deny that any such committee was needed; the whole issue arose from political motives: "If the Senator is so sure he knows of a great wrong needing laws to

[10] Reid to Bigelow, Dec. 30, 1871; Bigelow, IV, 571.

abate it, why does not the arm of legislation interpose against that 'mysterious power' which, pointing upward with certain nebulous and mysterious expressions, the Senator insinuates presides over the customhouse and Treasury Department, and paralyzes and arrests the efforts of reform?" [11]

It was an election year, though, and pressures for some kind of a look at the New York Custom House, from the anti-Grant senators, from the still angry merchants and importers of New York, and from uncommitted Republican politicians, were strong. James Garfield, in the House, wrote of his indignation at the administration senators in this debate, "superserviceable lackeys that sneeze whenever their master takes snuff." So on December 18, 1871, with Conkling's approval, an investigating committee was appointed, which held hearings through the first three months of 1872, submitted majority and minority reports in June, and saw the whole question die for lack of interest, just as Conkling suspected it would.[12]

On December 12, 1871, Charles Sumner introduced in the Senate a resolution proposing a Constitutional amendment providing for a single term for the president of the United States. Though the amendment, by its wording, would not apply to the holder of the office at the time, its adoption would naturally constitute a studied rebuff to Grant at a time when he clearly was planning to stand for a second term. Roscoe Conkling would have none of that. Conkling was a friend and counselor of the president, an advocate of his policies, and a valiant defender of his national image. In August, Conkling had written about Grant to his friend John A. Griswold, saying: "He has made a better President than you and I, when we voted for him, had any right to expect; and he is a better President every day than he was the day before. He has given the country the best practical administration, in many respects, we have had for a quarter of a century and the people know it." [13]

When the Sumner amendment came on the floor, Conkling made a long and ardent speech in opposition to the scheme. First he dealt with the motives of the Massachusetts senator: "This proposed amendment" is simply "a make-weight, an expedient, to affect the re-election of President Grant."

[11] *Cong. Globe,* 42d Cong., 2d sess., pp. 94–96.
[12] C. C. Tansill, *Thomas Francis Bayard,* pp. 61–63. The Garfield quote, from a letter of Dec. 16, 1871, to Whitelaw Reid, is in the Reid Papers.
[13] A. R. Conkling, pp. 336–337.

Sumner had bolstered his case with the arguments of civil service reform, but Conkling quickly took care of that: "In the name of civil service reform . . . we are to disable nobody but the one man who, from time to time, may by actual trial be found capable and acceptable. What would be thought of such a suggestion applied to the common affairs of life?"

By now, the senator had warmed to his subject, as he dragged out the armaments of language, language which would have its echoes in his famous 1880 nominating speech.

After all the depths and shoals of calumny have been sounded, after false-hood and vulgarity have been poured out till grossness itself is sated, after every weapon in the poisoned armory of rancor has been plied, after the resources of civilized and of savage warfare have been exhausted, what must be the hold of a candidate on the affections and respect of his country-men when the last chance of his overthrow is by constitutional amendment?

Despite the assaults of "presses and demagogues," Conkling continued, Grant remains "secure, as no predecessor for forty years has been se-cure, against detraction and defeat." As Conkling reached his conclu-sion, the cheering from the galleries was a bitter sound in the ear of Charles Sumner. "Flaws and foibles they may find, but the heart and judgment of the nation are with the unyielding soldier who made war victorious, and the quiet man who makes peace safe for all; and his name and transcendent deeds will live in grateful memory, when those who would blast his fame have moldered in forgotten graves, and when their epitaphs have vanished utterly." [14]

After this treatment, the one-term amendment died a quick and un-lamented death.

In mid-February, a bitter debate erupted in the Senate, again touched off by Sumner, on the administration's alleged violation of the neutrality laws during the Franco-Prussian War. The charge made by Sumner, no doubt with a nice calculation of the domestic political effect, was that of shipping arms to France. Most of the American people had watched with satisfaction as Bismarck's diplomacy and von Moltke's armies dealt a crushing defeat to the Second Empire of Louis Napoleon; the pretentious emperor was an unpopular figure in the United States— even before his ill-advised Mexican adventure with Maximilian—and

[14] *Cong. Globe,* 42d Cong., 2d sess., pp. 354–358, Jan. 11, 1872.

his sudden capture and downfall were greeted with hearty approval by most citizens on this side of the Atlantic. There were sizable blocs of German-American voters in several of the Northern states, while Franco-American voters were rather scarce. Thus, a charge of favoring the French, if it could be sustained, could have serious political repercussions.

Sumner made the charge; Sumner moved for an investigation; but it was his faithful follower, the lean and bearded Carl Schurz, peering through his spectacles, and popularly invested with great power over "the German vote," on whom attention focused. Schurz was a hero of the ill-fated 1848 Revolution in Germany, and he had led with some distinction Union armies composed mainly of German-Americans in the Civil War. He was one of the most famous Germans in America, and he it was who carried the burden of the debate for the anti-Grant elements. Conkling and Morton led the administration forces, and, though the debate scarred two weeks of the session—Conkling called it "a saturnalia of licentious talk"—and though almost all of the members took part in the proceedings, the passages between Conkling and Schurz attracted the bulk of attention.

On February 15, during one of Schurz's opening speeches on the subject, Conkling harried the Missouri senator with questions and interruptions. At one point in the proceedings, Schurz asked Conkling's attention to a statement he was making, saying in a mock-apologetic manner, "I am sorry to trouble him so much." Conkling shot back, to the accompaniment of laughter from his administration cohorts, "I beg to assure him he has not troubled me yet." [15] By the time the debate was over, Roscoe Conkling could no longer make such a statement.

Conkling broadened Sumner's request for an investigation into the administration by adding to it a resolution to inquire whether any member of the Senate had been in contact with the French government, "or any emissary or spy thereof," citing as his support for such an inquiry an old statute of 1799 providing for a fine or imprisonment for citizens of the United States having intercourse with foreign agents on matters in which the United States might be interested. This was aimed directly at Schurz, who had been admittedly in contact with certain French agents, from whom he had received information allegedly relating to the sales of arms. Schurz took immediate and excited umbrage at such an extension of the scope of the inquiry, the original aim of

[15] *Ibid.,* p. 1046.

which was solely to embarrass Grant and provide ammunition for the fall campaign; Conkling was able to take satisfaction from the evident reaction his resolution produced.

"But let us have investigation on all sides," he said. "Let there be no dark place, no nook, no corner anywhere. The American honor has been assailed; the American name has been hawked at; grave and offensive charges have been spread before the world. Let us know the truth no matter at what cost of convenience." [16]

The following day, Schurz took up the battle once again, protesting that he and his allies were "met by one of the spokesmen of the Administration, flourishing the statute in his hands, threatening them with fine and imprisonment! Indeed a most glorious spectacle!" But Carl Schurz was not daunted. "If the Senator from New York thinks that he can in this way throw fear into my soul, he will easily discover that he is mistaken. On the paths of duty that I have walked I have seen men much more dangerous than he; and before a thousand of them my heart would not quail."

He then turned to the claim that the investigation was meant to curry favor with the German vote and the scornful assertion of Conkling and Morton that he pretended to carry the German vote in his pocket:

Both Senators have taken the trouble to inform this body that no man in this country owns the German-born citizens of this Republic. That is most certainly true, and I am proud of it, for I am one of them; and I am sure nobody owns me. (Laughter.) No, sir, no man owns the German-American citizens of this country. No politician owns them, no Senator does; not even the President of the United States; but least of all are the Germans of this country owned by that class of politicians who desperately cling to the skirt of power through whatever mire that skirt may be trailed. (Applause in the galleries.) [17]

Schurz listened with satisfaction as the galleries cheered him, and he considered the speech a great triumph. But Roscoe Conkling had no intention of letting things rest. The next day he charged back into the fray, saying that he could not "refrain from commenting upon the somewhat airy exhibition made by the Senator from Missouri yesterday." He fenced with Schurz on the exact language the Missourian had used in his statement about facing men much more dangerous than Conkling, his heart not quailing, and when Schurz finally repeated what

[16] *Ibid.,* app., p. 66, Feb. 19, 1872.   [17] *Ibid.,* app., p. 74.

he had said, Conkling said, "Mr. President, personal courage, if it be true, does not blurt or swagger; personal courage is not froth; and men eminent for the intrepidity and boldness of their character do not strut or perch themselves upon an eminence and boast of it." [18]

Schurz answered this attack by saying, "If I did or said anything yesterday that looked like strutting, then I most sincerely beg the Senate's pardon; for I certainly do not want to encroach upon the exclusive privileges of my honorable and distinguished associate from New York." [19] The galleries applauded, missing the irony that this sally should come from one who was easily Conkling's equal, if not his superior, as a posturing prima donna.

Though the talk dragged on, the fireworks between Conkling and Schurz were over. The debates in the Senate were all that ever really developed from the French arms question; there was no investigation worthy of the name. The major achievement of Sumner and Schurz in introducing the matter into the political arena was to inflame further the growing dissension between the two wings of the Republican party.

The Liberal Republicans did get their third-party movement off the ground. Schurz, fittingly, as a nonconformist and rebel of long standing, considered himself the patron saint of the new party, and as the group's national convention at Cincinnati on May 1 drew near, there were even some bona fide presidential candidates. The most likely choice, it was thought, was the eminent Charles Francis Adams, Brahmin to the core, bearer of a proud name and a proud tradition of public service, and honored for his contribution to the national welfare as minister to the Court of St. James in the trying days of the Civil War.

The possible nomination of Adams was so ominous to the Republican hopes that Conkling himself approached Adams in April to sound him out on the idea of running as Grant's vice-presidential candidate. Colfax had indicated that he would not seek a second term, so his slot was available to offer to potential opponents. To no avail. Adams turned Conkling down cold.[20]

The other figure most prominently mentioned for the Liberal Republican nomination was the corpulent David Davis of Illinois. Lincoln's old political advisor was now an associate justice of the United States Supreme Court but still very much interested in political

[18] *Ibid.*, p. 1156.   [19] *Ibia.*, p. 1157.
[20] C. F. Adams, *Charles Francis Adams,* pp. 391–392.

affairs. Davis was felt to be conservative enough that the nation's business elements would not be alarmed by his candidacy, and he had already been nominated for president in February by the Labor Reform party, one of several *ad hoc* groups which sprang up in 1872.[21]

The convention which met in Cincinnati was a weird conglomerate. It included tariff reformers, disgruntled political pros like Fenton, starry-eyed idealists, and the famous "Quadrilateral" of well-known newspapermen—Samuel Bowles of the Springfield *Republican,* Henry Watterson of the Louisville *Courier-Journal,* Murat Halstead of the Cincinnati *Commercial,* and Horace White of the Chicago *Tribune.* The four editors expected that they would control the proceedings. There was also a handful of designing power-seekers with very definite ideas about what they wanted the convention to produce. These latter were exemplified by the two Missourians, Governor B. Gratz Brown and Senator Frank Blair. Add to this mixture young Whitelaw Reid, playing the kingmaker, moving from group to group with the message of Horace Greeley's availability and desirability, and the rare blend of this convention becomes clear.

As it developed, Adams's absence (he had gone off to Europe), the machinations of Reid, Fenton, and Brown, and the political naïveté of the reformers and the newspaper editors together produced an astonishing ticket. Though Schurz in his keynote address had hailed the convention as a gathering of those who would no longer "permit themselves to be driven like a flock of sheep," he soon found to his dismay that he had lost control. Though it took six ballots, the convention ultimately chose as its candidate for president of the United States the highly improbable—some called him "impossible"—Horace Greeley.

The new party's only chance for victory lay in combining anti-Grant Republican votes with those of the Democrats. So the Liberal Republicans selected for their leader a man who furnished the opposition with a thirty-year body of writings on the depravity of the Democrats, both as a party and as individuals. They asked the tariff reformers to accept as their candidate a man who, while he had swung wildly from one extreme to the other on many issues, had always stood unflinchingly for protection. They asked Southern Democrats to swallow a fervent abolitionist, and they asked the country at large to support a man who, though acknowledged to be a brilliant newspaper editor, was generally regarded as an eccentric, if not a crackpot. Greeley was a man widely

21 McClure, pp. 227–230.

noted for his personal oddities, his penchant for fads and fancies, his erratic political behavior, and his volubility. The contrast with the "strong, silent" Grant was pronounced, but it was not clear that such a perfect disparity was all that desirable. Many of the delegates were appalled when they found what they had done. Greeley's running mate was B. Gratz Brown, and some said it served the Missouri governor right.

The Republican National Convention, freed by desertion of all dissident elements, met in Philadelphia on June 5, nominated Grant without opposition, and selected Henry Wilson of Massachusetts to run for vice-president in place of Colfax, even though the Indiana statesman had suffered second thoughts about relinquishing his office. The platform set forth in glowing terms the Republican accomplishments and boasted, "This glorious record of the past is the party's best pledge for the future." [22]

A month later the Democrats convened in Baltimore. It was an unhappy gathering. The Democrats were faced with the necessity of naming as their choice a man who had called them "traitors, slave-whippers, drunkards and lecherous beasts," but accept him they had to do. Zebulon Vance of North Carolina gulped and said, "If the Baltimore convention puts Greeley in our hymn book, we will sing him through if it kills us." [23]

Even Grant saw humor in the predicament of his opponents. As the Democratic convention was starting, the president wrote to Roscoe Conkling about it: "The Baltimore Convention is now in incubation. Before she hatches, and we see what the offspring looks like, or rather how it is received by its parents, it is hard to judge how much fondling it will receive. I have no doubt but it will look like a full moon, with spectacles on the man in it, but whether it will be caressed as much after hatching as during incubation I doubt much." [24]

The Democracy adopted the Liberal Republican platform verbatim by a vote of 670 to 62, over the vocal opposition of Senator Bayard of Delaware, and it then went on to nominate Greeley and Brown with very little open dissent.[25]

---

[22] *Ibid.*, pp. 234–236.   [23] J. F. Wall, *Henry Watterson*, p. 111.

[24] Conkling Papers, Library of Congress. Evarts called it "this new experiment whether 'the pen is mightier than the sword.' " Evarts to Pierrepont, June 21, 1872, Pierrepont Papers.

[25] McClure, pp. 237–238.

Subsequently, a rump Democratic convention, meeting at Louisville, repudiated Greeley as a Democratic nominee, proclaiming that "the Democratic party is held together by the cohesion of time-honored principles which they will never surrender in exchange for all the offices which presidents can confer." This group chose the famous New York lawyer, Charles O'Conor, as a candidate.[26]

The field was thus set for the race.

The tone of the campaign that followed may be indicated, first, by a line from one of Henry Watterson's editorials in the Louisville *Courier-Journal*, on July 3: "We do know that Grant is an iron-hearted, wooden-headed nutmeg, warranted to kill" and, second, by Conkling's characterization of Greeley, in his Cooper Union speech on July 23, as "grotesque and harmless . . . a man of oddities, flattered by many and most of all himself." [27] Worse things than this were said about Greeley by his former party colleagues during the campaign (indeed, Greeley complained that "I hardly knew whether I was running for President or the Penitentiary").[28]

Grant was certainly not going to do any speaking. On July 15, in accepting an invitation from his friend Conkling to visit in Utica, the president had written that "it will be better that I should not attend any convention or political meeting during the Campaign. It has been done, so far as I remember, by but two Pres. candidates heretofore and both of them were public speakers, and both were beaten. I am no speaker and don't want to be beaten." [29]

So, it was up to the senator from New York to set the keynote of the campaign for the Republican party. This, Conkling did cheerfully. He found it most congenial to have all of the Republicans who had given him trouble, who had harassed and opposed him, suddenly arrayed against him outside the party walls, in the enemy camp where he always thought they should have been. Schurz, Sumner, Reuben Fenton, Chauncey Depew, Whitelaw Reid—a group like this supporting a presidential ticket led by Horace Greeley; nothing could have seemed more delicious to Roscoe Conkling.

To the five thousand jammed into Cooper Union that warm July evening, he expounded the Republican message in his own matchless style. He always spoke slowly and emphatically, standing ramrod

[26] *Ibid.*, pp. 238–239.   [27] Wall, p. 109; N.Y. *Times,* July 24, 1872.
[28] Alexander, III, 301.   [29] Conkling Papers, Library of Congress.

straight, one foot slightly in advance of the other, with his head thrown back, the better to roll forth the thunderous sentences. This night he was at his best. He reviewed the criticisms made by the Liberal Republicans against Grant and his administration, and he reviewed the records of the critics as well, citing Schurz and Fenton as examples of men who had sought offices for their relatives. "The hungry 'Reformers' of today fattened and exulted then. It was, in their estimation, high merit and statesmanship for Senators and others to crouch and prowl day and night around the sources of power."

He came to Ulysses S. Grant:

Yet this man, honest, brave, and modest, and proved by his transcendent deeds to be endowed with genius, common sense and moral qualities adequate to our greatest affairs; this man . . . who snatched our nationality and our cause from despair, and bore them on his shield through the flame of battle, in which, but for him, they would have perished . . . this man, to whom a nation's gratitude and benediction are due, is made the mark for ribald gibes and odious groundless slanders. Why is all this? Simply because he stands in the way of the greed and ambition of politicians and schemers.

Conkling described Greeley at length. Long behind him were the friendly relations he had preserved with the editor before his senatorial election. Now, as he detailed the eccentric career and ideas of the Liberal Republican nominee, Conkling summed up the question facing the electorate: "The issue is narrowed to a single inquiry: which is personally the safest, fittest man for the Presidency?" [30] On the terms as *he* defined them, Roscoe Conkling was willing to let the people make their decision. The five thousand left Cooper Union that night, exhausted by the mental exertion demanded by the orator, but exultant that they had received the ministration of the true political doctrine.

Later on, in the fall, Conkling barnstormed throughout New York State, spreading the message about Grant and zestfully lambasting his old intraparty foes who were now marching arm in arm with the Democrats. In addition to the great interest Conkling took in the successful outcome of the Grant canvass, it was very much to his benefit to roll up a handsome margin in New York; the legislature elected in 1872 would select a United States senator in 1873. At one point in the campaign, some talk was circulated that the name of Edwin D. Morgan might be submitted to the caucus the next January, but the former

[30] N.Y. *Times,* July 24, 1872.

governor and senator quickly and obediently squelched whatever movement might have been getting underway, saying, "I am in favor of the
re-election of Mr. Conkling." [31]

The Republican state convention met in Utica in late August to
select a state ticket. There was no outright "organization" choice for the
gubernatorial nomination. Conkling was far more interested in getting
Grant re-elected than in hand-picking a governor. Among the names
mentioned were Morgan, Judge William H. Robertson of Westchester,
General John A. Dix, former Mayor George Opdyke of New York, and
General John C. Robinson. Opdyke was eliminated by the organization
because he had been mayor during the "draft riots" of 1863. Otherwise,
matters were rather unclear as the convention approached. The *Times*
said, "For once a Republican Convention shall not be dominated by
such arts as Fenton has made familiar in our state politics, but left
free to act upon its own judgment." [32]

John Adams Dix, then seventy-four, was a hoary veteran of New
York and national politics, with legal, business, and military careers
thrown in for good measure. He had fought in the Battle of Lundy's
Lane in the War of 1812, had later entered the field of law, and had
become active in Democratic politics in Cooperstown. He had been a
leader of Van Buren's Albany Regency. He had served as New York's
adjutant general and secretary of state and had been United States senator from 1845 to 1850. Dix's free-soil sentiments drove him out of harmony with many Democratic leaders, though he filled in as secretary
of the treasury in Buchanan's cabinet from January 1861 to Lincoln's
inauguration. In those dark days, Dix received the plaudits of the
Northern people for his stern message to the collector at the New Orleans Custom House: "If anyone attempts to haul down the American
flag, shoot him on the spot!" Dix was commissioned a major general
and served commendably throughout the war in Maryland and the East.
After the war, supporting Johnson, he was appointed minister to France
and filled that post from 1866 to 1869. Though he did not feel much
allegiance to party lines, Dix commanded great personal popularity,
also without regard to party lines. The *Times* wrote that Dix "would
probably have received the nomination without any serious contest but
for his extreme age, and the grave doubt which exists that for that
reason he may not be willing to assume the office." [33] Given the known

[31] Rawley, p. 244.   [32] N.Y. *Times,* Aug. 19, 1872.
[33] *Ibid.,* Aug. 20.

reluctance of Dix, it was felt that the probable choice of the convention would be ex-Governor Morgan.

On August 20, however, the day before the convention, Dix wrote a letter declining to run, and Morgan announced that he would not accept the nomination. Though this seemed to leave the path open for Judge Robertson, the *Times* ran an ominous editorial squib: "The correspondents say that a number of the delegates talk of nominating Senator Robertson, of Westchester, for Governor. We hope that wiser counsels will guide the Convention." [34]

The delegates who read this were thrown into a panic. Politicians put much store in the influence upon the public of the party-oriented newspapers in a time when other mass media were lacking, and the Republicans of New York had long counted upon having at their back the editorial resources of the two most influential papers in the state, the *Tribune* and the *Times*. In 1872, they knew that Reid had taken the *Tribune* into the opposition camp in support of its former editor, and they were loath to incur the active displeasure of the *Times* by nominating a candidate for governor whom the paper would not support. The cryptic remark about "wiser counsels" opened the gubernatorial question for rethinking.

When the convention gathered the next day, it still appeared that Robertson would win, with no other possible names being considered, though there was much backstage talk among the delegates about the threat posed by the *Times* remark. Just before the close of nominations, however, a delegate proposed the name of John A. Dix. Henry Clews of Wall Street, an amateur follower of Conkling, seconded the nomination "in behalf of the bankers and business men of New York." The convention went wild, and before control could be re-established, Dix had been selected by acclamation.[35]

Robertson was a hard-headed, unforgiving sort, and he knew that somehow or other he had just been done out of an excellent chance to become governor of New York. When he looked around to see where he could fix the blame for this unhappy state of affairs, he observed that Dix, who had been nominated, was a friend of Roscoe Conkling (though not a close one by any means, and certainly not a slavish political follower of the senator), and, more clearly, that Clews, the seconder, was an adherent of Conkling and, even more damning, was Conkling's house guest for the duration of the Utica convention. Clews

[34] *Ibid.*, Aug. 21.   [35] *Ibid.*, Aug. 22.

was clearly Conkling's agent in snatching the nomination from Robertson's grasp. So, in Robertson's mind, it always remained, and the Westchester politician became an unrelenting enemy of Roscoe Conkling.

Clews, however, always maintained that he had been acting strictly on his own in endorsing the name of Dix and that Conkling had known nothing about his plans. Conkling apparently had no particular favorite for the nomination, though Dix was clearly congenial to him. He may very well have disliked Robertson even then, though there is no real evidence of that. Basically, the senator felt that the ticket would rise or fall on the strength of General Grant, not the candidate for governor.[36]

Whether Clews or Conkling had the idea to buck Robertson made no difference in the long run, because Robertson assigned the credit to Conkling. Since he was also very ambitious, there is little doubt that he would have become an opponent of the senator before too long in any event.

The Democrats selected Conkling's old mentor and opponent, Francis Kernan, to run for governor, and they let the Liberal Republicans have the nomination for lieutenant governor. This slot was filled by Chauncey Depew. It made little difference. After a campaign of abuse and invective rarely matched, generated mainly by Greeley's turncoat status, Grant won big. He carried the nation by some 700,000 votes and won a huge majority in the electoral college. He took New York by 53,000 votes, topped even by the Dix majority of 55,000, and swept in a solid Republican legislature.

It was a glorious moment for Ulysses S. Grant and for his mighty bulwark in New York, Roscoe Conkling. The glory was slightly clouded when Greeley, broken by the campaign and its outcome, went mad and died within a few weeks of the election. Nothing could dim the fact, however, that the Republican party was still in command, nationally and in the state of New York. Conkling summed it up in a letter to a friend: "We had an annoying opposition to encounter to be sure, but *that* army will never fight again." [37]

[36] H. Clews, *Twenty-Eight Years*, p. 308.
[37] Conkling to Pierrepont, Nov. 20, 1872, Pierrepont Papers.

CHAPTER 11

———◆◆◆◆———

HARD TIMES

The year 1873 was to usher in a new and golden era for the Republican party. On New Year's Day, the New York *Times* surveyed the scene and editorialized: "Considering the condition and extent of the Republic, the violent passions which have rent and torn it, the vast and varied interests affected by its political institutions, and the growing intelligence and independence of the electors, the position of the Republican Party is proud beyond all precedent." Grant was safely reelected, the Democrats were vanquished, the Republican party was cleaner and purer than it had ever been because of the desertion of the perfidious Liberals, and the party's leaders were to go on to greater and more brilliant triumphs. It was a glorious world!

One of the first of the leaders to receive his reward would be Roscoe Conkling. His Senate term expired on March 3, 1873, so the seat had to be filled for the next six years. There was little doubt who would fill it. The *Times* said, "The victory of November will not be complete until after Mr. Conkling has been chosen to again fill the high place where he shed such lustre upon his State, and earned such enduring honor for himself." [1]

Conkling's partisans had control of the state legislature. On January 6, A. B. Cornell, newly elected to the house, was named Speaker. Two days later, at 7:30 P.M., the Republican caucus met to select the senator. It was all cut and dried. There was a series of eulogistic speeches, extolling the virtues, the accomplishments, and the party loyalty of Roscoe Conkling, and then the caucus voted unanimously to make him its selection.

The *Times* the next day delivered to Conkling a resounding and unsolicited tribute:

[1] N.Y. *Times,* Jan. 7, 1873.

A man who has to defend a cause against enemies is likely to make many enemies himself, and it would be far from complimentary to Senator Conkling to say that he has no enemies. In truth, the "independent Republicans"—the men who wish to slay the party while pretending to embrace it—hate him to a man. The *doctrinaires* dislike him, because he is thorough-going, and has no sympathy with people whose heads are in the clouds. Men like Fenton have an antipathy toward him, because he is honest while they are knaves. On the other hand, Mr. Conkling enjoys the confidence of the great bulk of the Republican Party, and in this State that confidence will be manifested by his re-election as United States Senator.

Conkling was officially elected by the legislature on January 22, 1873, and the *Times* the next day said, "We anticipate some brilliant work from him during the next few years."

The bright future of the Republican party turned dark very quickly. Charges of corruption in connection with something called "Credit Mobilier" had been brushed aside before the election as so much "campaign oratory." Investigation soon proved, however, that the charges were only too true, and many of the leading figures of the party were severely damaged by the revelations—saved from ruin, in fact, only by an incredible whitewash job by the House committee investigating the affair.

Credit Mobilier of America was a corporate front used by the leaders of the Union Pacific Railroad to strip the company of its great assets, mostly furnished by the United States government. Credit Mobilier was formed as a construction company, and it contracted to build the road across the continent at a hugely exorbitant price, transferring from the Union Pacific to the building corporation, whose shareholders were virtually the same, the permanent endowment granted the road by Congress. In 1868, in order to forestall congressional challenge to the swindle, Congressman Oakes Ames of Massachusetts, the guiding spirit of Credit Mobilier, undertook to distribute shares in the company to congressional leaders where he felt the most good would be done. The New York *Sun,* late in the 1872 campaign, made the initial charges concerning Credit Mobilier, and an inquiry was begun. As it progressed, its revelations were sensational. The *Times* correspondent sent home from Washington a dispatch on January 8, 1873, in which he wrote incredulously: "If such men as Blaine, Dawes, Boutwell,

Bingham, Garfield, Wilson, Colfax, Patterson, Allison and others are corrupt, then there is no longer virtue resident anywhere in the halls of Congress."

And so it certainly appeared. For Garfield, Allison, Vice-President Colfax, Vice-President-elect Henry Wilson, John Bingham, William "Pig Iron" Kelley of Philadelphia, Senator James Patterson of New Hampshire, Senator James Harlan of Iowa, all Republicans, and James Brooks, the Democratic leader of the House, were rather clearly implicated in the mess. Most became involved when they permitted Ames to sell them stock for extremely low prices, with a large dividend already declared on the stock and another one promised within a very short time. It is hard to interpret Ames's dealings with his colleagues as anything other than bribery. Kelley and Garfield, the unctuously pious future president, had not even paid a *low* price for the stock; they paid nothing. Ames held it for them until the dividends paid for it in full. Garfield compounded his sin by denying that he had ever had the stock; even the accommodating House committee, though it was ready to excuse his transgressions, could not accept his story of non-involvement.

What was the outcome of all this? Ames, when the dirty linen started to come out, apparently told the truth (thereby incriminating his fellow statesmen, which was, after all, the unforgivable crime). So he and Brooks, who happened to be the only Democrat involved in the affair, were "condemned" by the House, and no action at all was taken with Garfield, Allison, and their colleagues. A resolution to impeach Colfax was introduced, but it died in the House. In the Senate, Patterson, whose term was expiring, was censured, and Harlan was rebuked by the Morrill Committee, which investigated senatorial involvement in the scandal.

Roscoe Conkling was involved only very peripherally. Because his name had been mentioned in passing in the House proceedings the Morrill Committee brought in a finding that "Mr. Conkling does not appear to have been connected in any way with the stock of the Credit Mobilier or of the Union Pacific Railroad Company, and consequently is in no way affected thereby." [2]

The Morrill Committee's work appears to have been a more measured and conscientious job than that of the corresponding House committee, but the idea that the members of the Senate were more virtuous

2 *Ibid.*, Feb. 28.

than their brethren in the House is not a natural conclusion. Oakes Ames was in the House and had much easier access to his colleagues there than to the members of the Senate.

The House whitewash of the Republican leaders was not very convincing to Washington observers, and the Credit Mobilier scandal was the first of a series of revelations which scarred Grant's second term. Oddly, the activities which caused the uproar in most instances occurred during his first term or, as in the case of Credit Mobilier, during Johnson's administration. In almost every case, though, some part of the Republican party was incriminated.

While the investigations into Credit Mobilier proceeded, the Forty-second Congress nervously carried on its work in its dying month. The jumbled, confusing, ceaselessly riven affairs of Louisiana occupied much attention, as they would from time to time until the state was finally turned back to its white Democratic leaders to assure Hayes's inauguration. For years the names of such as Kellogg, McEnery, Warmoth, Pinchback, and their fellows in the political wars of the state were staples of congressional debate.

On January 7, 1873, Conkling supported a resolution to inquire into the Louisiana election of the previous November before counting that state's electoral votes. The election had been scandalous, as Louisiana elections generally were, and the stench from this one had penetrated all the way to Washington. The resolution passed, and an investigation was held, but before any benefits came from it, things bubbled over again. A federal judge of dubious repute installed the Republican pretender to the governorship by simple judicial mandate, and the Democrats howled. Allen Thurman of Ohio, the Democratic leader of the Senate, an able lawyer noted for the red bandana handkerchief he used as an inveterate snuff taker, spoke in opposition to the pretensions of a federal judge, whom he called "a little judge of a court that we may abolish tomorrow," interfering in such a manner. Conkling responded for the Republicans, sneering at Thurman's exposition of "the very latest Democratic gospel of the respect due to the judgment of courts." He contrasted Thurman's stand with the abject deference demanded by Democrats to Taney's prewar decisions.[3]

No matter the outcome of debate on any particular facet of the struggle, Louisiana remained an open sore on the body politic, as

3 *Cong. Globe,* 42d Cong., 3d sess., pp. 639–640, Jan. 16, 1873.

contending elements of equally disreputable schemers—Republicans, Democrats, blacks, whites, carpetbaggers, scalawags, turncoats, generals, grafters, all mixed up into unrecognizable groups—struggled for control of the state and the right to steal from its treasury.

The final contribution of the Forty-second Congress to American history was the infamous Salary Grab. Responding initially to public sentiment to increase the compensation of the president to a level more commensurate with his responsibilities, the movement for pay increases was quickly taken over in the House by Congressman Benjamin F. Butler of Massachusetts with the idea of declaring a grand bonus for the members of Congress. As the New York *Times* declared on February 10, 1873, "The country will be painfully surprised when it realizes just what shape the question of the increase of salaries has taken in Congress." The measure proposed to raise congressional salaries from $5,000 to $7,500 per year; this part of the bill was not particularly shocking and was regarded in many respectable quarters as a proper thing to do. Congressional salaries were certainly not princely at $5,000. The rabbit which Butler pulled from his congressional hat was that the increase was to be retroactive for the past two years; thus each member would be voting himself a windfall of $5,000 in one lump sum. Lameduck members would pick up the bonus and then head home from Washington without rendering so much as one day's service for it.

The House passed the measure, along with a companion bill raising the presidential salary from $25,000 to $50,000 per annum, and sent both along to the Senate. On March 1, Senator Edmunds moved that the Senate concur in the House bill; the swaggering, high-living Matt Carpenter of Wisconsin pushed for approval. Conkling rose in indignation and spoke in opposition to the bill and managed to stall it for a couple of days. On March 3, however, the last day of the session and of the Congress, the Senate concurred in the House bill, without change, 36 to 27. Roscoe Conkling, to his credit, voted "nay." President Grant promptly signed the pay-raise measures, thus doubling his own salary, effective the following day. The press tore into Congress for its greed, calling the bill "a plunderers' measure," and concluding, "Let Republicans and Democrats alike own the facts with shame." [4]

And so the Forty-second Congress came to a close, with more than a majority of its members feeling that they had put across a financial

[4] N.Y. *Times*, March 10, 1873. See also Nevins, *Fish*, II, 612.

coup for their own benefit, at the expense of the public. The amazing aspect to be kept in mind is the conjunction in time between the Credit Mobilier investigation and the Salary Grab bill. The sheer brass of Butler and his cohorts can hardly be credited. The American people looked forward with less than wild enthusiasm to the morrow's initiation of four more years of Grant, who, after all, had signed the thing. Probably no other president-elect has suffered so much loss of public esteem between election day and inauguration day as Grant did in those four months.

Grant's second term began on a bitterly cold March 4, 1873, a day so frigid that the weather, combined with the usual bungling inaugural planning, made the day a total loss. The same may be said about the entire second term of Ulysses S. Grant. Certainly, even Grant's supporters found it hard to say very much in his favor. Blow after blow smashed into his administration—economic, political, moral—but the silent soldier at the head of the government barely reacted at all.

This second term marked the beginning of a real split in the Republican party, much more serious than that of 1872. Sumner, Schurz, Trumbull, Greeley, Fenton—the men of the Liberal Republican bolt—were deficient in political muscle, for all their vocalizing and rhetoric. They were, to a degree, war-time men whose time was past. In addition, they walked out of the party, instead of trying to capture it. The chasm in the Republican ranks which widened in the years after Grant's second election was between two groups of powerful leaders, each seeking to gain control. The split was polarized, basically, around Conkling and Blaine. The conflict broadened over the years, to come to a crashing climax in the events of 1880 and 1881. The strict patronage politicians—Conkling, Morton, the Camerons, Zach Chandler of Michigan, Matt Carpenter, John Logan of Illinois—these men and their satellites were arrayed against another group, led informally by Blaine, which sought to disassociate itself as much as it dared from the incumbent Republican administration. Though some of these men (such as Blaine, Garfield, and Allison) were themselves tainted, they were able, along with others like John Sherman and George F. Hoar, to move some distance away from Grant. To Conkling, in particular, any movement to push Grant to the background smacked of political treason as base as any perpetrated in 1872. Though the press rocked from time to time with cries of "Caesarism" against the president, Roscoe Conkling believed that U. S. Grant, complete with Fort Donelson, Vicksburg, Richmond, and Appomattox, was a priceless possession of the Republican party.

George Frisbie Hoar later wrote: "Selfish men and ambitious men got the ear of that simple and confiding President. They studied Grant, some of them, as the shoemaker measures the foot of his customer." [5] This was no doubt true, and the records reveal that some of the men who won Grant's confidence abused him dreadfully. It is not just that such criticism should be leveled without qualification at Roscoe Conkling. Hoar had no love for Conkling; he described him as "unfit to be the leader of a great party." [6] It is not clear, though, that Hoar meant to include the New Yorker in his condemnation. Conkling's patronage politics in New York brought no particular credit to Grant, but it was not what cost him a high place in presidential ratings. Conkling never abused the president's trust in matters of personal honesty, and he led Grant's forces as well as could be done in the Senate. Though Conkling himself brought forth no striking measures of legislation, he was Grant's chief adviser in the two matters of the second term which produced the most long-lasting praise for the president, the veto of the inflation bill in 1874 and the Electoral Commission Act in 1877. Certainly Roscoe Conkling had great influence with Grant, who once said of the senator: "I regard him as the greatest mind in public life or that has been in public life since the beginning of the Government." [7] He did not presume on that influence to the president's disadvantage.

Following the inauguration, the Senate convened in special session for most of the month of March. The oath of office was administered to Conkling despite the inadvertent absence of his formal credentials. Others were not so fortunate. Under the prevailing constitutional provision that senators were to be elected by the state legislatures, a pernicious use of great amounts of money in such elections had come to be almost standard operating procedure. This factor was present even in Roscoe Conkling's first election to the Senate in 1867. It soon became almost commonplace to devote many senatorial business hours to hearing contests for seats, with charges and countercharges of bribery, extortion, and the like.

Two such debates took place during this short session. In one, concerning an Alabama seat, Conkling led the fight for the Republican

[5] Hoar, I, 197.   [6] *Ibid.*, II, 55.   [7] *The Nation*, Oct. 7, 1880.

contender, George E. Spencer, a carpetbagger from Iowa, against a Democrat named Francis Sykes. After a spirited passage, Spencer predictably was sworn in, the New York *Times* stating with some bias that "Sykes had no credentials that any but partisans could recognize." [8]

The other case which festered throughout the month-long special session was the possible expulsion of Senator Alexander Caldwell of Kansas, a wealthy railroad man, for alleged bribery in procuring his election. The facts of the situation seemed to show that Caldwell had at the least allowed bribery on his behalf. The major issue before the Senate seemed to be whether one could expel a man when he won by more than the number of bribed voters. It was not a very edifying debate. Morton, surprisingly, joined with the Democrats and Liberals to push for Caldwell's expulsion, while Conkling, Carpenter, and Logan led his defenders. Caldwell eventually resolved the issue by resigning. One of the high points was another bitter, shouting altercation between Conkling and Schurz which brought many senators to their feet and forced the vice-president to gavel for order. [9]

Another matter which irritated the senator from New York in the special session was that of committees. The Democrats, who had numbered only ten senators in the previous Congress, now had twenty-four members, counting the Liberals, who certainly were not being included among the Republicans. Since the opposition now made up two-sevenths of the Senate, the Democrats insisted upon two members (out of seven) on the important Senate committees, rather than the one they had had previously. In the Republican caucus, Conkling, backed by Edmunds, took the position that they should still get no more than one. However, when the Democratic leadership refused to designate any assignments, the Republicans compromised: they enlarged the committees to a membership of nine and gave the opposition the second seat. Conkling sniffed disdainfully at such tender treatment of the minority. [10]

The good times ended that summer. Prosperity came to a screeching halt, as the United States made another sharp turn in the boom-and-bust business cycle. Financial panic started it, but that soon led to a

---

[8] *Cong. Rec.,* 43d Cong., spec. sess., p. 29; N.Y. *Times,* March 8, 1873.

[9] The Schurz-Conkling tussle took place March 20, 1873, and is found in *Cong. Rec.,* 43d Cong., spec. sess., pp. 132–134.

[10] N.Y. *Times,* March 11, 1873.

general business decline and depression. History knows it as the "Panic of '73," but the hard times lingered on for four or five years.

The crash had many causes, both domestic and foreign. Overseas, a series of European wars, speculation, and overexpansion contributed to the problems of the United States, but there were causes aplenty in this country. Currency and credit inflation and governmental extravagance played their parts, but the prime factor may have been the excessive absorption of capital into railroad investments; capital which should have been circulating at large was tied up in long-range building programs with no early returns. Additionally, the railroads were often badly built and badly located, with no public demand for the services they were prepared to furnish. The United States suffered from an adverse trade balance, too. In such circumstances, not much was required to push the country over the brink to financial chaos and depression.

Just before the tight little financial world of Wall Street blew up, Conkling, Sherman, William Windom of Minnesota, and Simon Conover of Florida were touring as a special Senate committee to investigate the improvement of facilities for water transportation, with particular emphasis on the Great Lakes. [11]

When the group arrived in Buffalo on September 18 the stunning news reached them that the financial house of Jay Cooke and Company, the most prestigious in the country, had been forced to close its doors. Cooke had hosted President Grant for breakfast that very morning at his "Ogontz" estate outside of Philadelphia without breathing a word of the situation to the chief executive. In the preceding ten days two other firms had failed, but these straws in the wind had been largely ignored; however, when the great financier of the Civil War ordered his house shut down, the panic was on.

The senators of the water transportation committee hastened home, their services as a special committee terminated by the news.[12] For Sherman and Conkling, particularly, there would be trying times: Sherman, because he was generally considered the Senate's leader on financial questions; Conkling, because he was the Senate's most single-minded exponent of sound, hard money, and a depression, if it fol-

[11] *Ibid.*, Sept. 17.

[12] J. Sherman, I, 489. For the Grant-Cooke breakfast at Ogontz, see E. P. Oberholtzer, *Jay Cooke*, II, 421–422. Chapter 18 of the Oberholtzer book deals with the causes of the Panic of 1873, with particular reference of course to the involvement of the Cooke interests.

lowed the crash (as it in fact did), would produce a plethora of inflationary "funny money" theories.

The New York *Times* tried to minimize the effect of the Cooke collapse:

The "street" is indulging in the costly luxury of its annual panic. Yesterday two large firms, one of them the best known probably of all our banking-houses, were compelled to suspend. Messrs. Jay Cooke & Co. and Messrs. Geo. Opdyke & Co. have yielded to nearly identical influences. Both had advanced money largely to new railroads, and both were caught by the feeling of distrust of this class of enterprises which has come over the community. . . . On the general course of business it is observable that the frantic excitement in Wall Street has little or no effect.[13]

The paper's editorial observation was not as acute as it might have been. Days of chaos quickly followed on the heels of "the frantic excitement in Wall Street," as the Stock Exchange was forced to close for ten days, panic and uncertainty swept the country, and countless concerns and individual entrepreneurs were forced into bankruptcy. Full-scale business depression soon followed. It was a deep and searing depression, probably the worst in American history to that time. It brought idleness, hunger, destitution, violence, and crime, as the victims of uncomprehended economic forces turned from the customary channels of life in attempts to relieve their sufferings. They turned also to new, more radical political and social ideas and to the purveyors of economic panaceas. The basic quality of American life was materially affected by the depression of the seventies.

For business leaders and industrial magnates, however, unlike ordinary citizens, the depression was a temporary inconvenience, the result of errors of judgment. It was regarded as a period of "penance for economic sins." Besides, it offered opportunities for low-cost expansion and modernization of plants and facilities. Such future notables of capital as Carnegie, Rockefeller, and Armour were able to take giant steps forward during the seventies.[14]

For the next four or five years, as the depression deepened and continued, it was a motivating force, either directly or otherwise, of many public activities. Because of it, elections were won or lost, legislative initiatives were made or rejected, public figures advanced or receded in

[13] N.Y. *Times,* Sept. 19, 1873.
[14] T. C. Cochran and W. Miller, *Age of Enterprise* (Harper Torchbooks ed.), p. 137.

esteem. Roscoe Conkling was frequently criticized for failing to take sufficient cognizance of the depression; he had his own matters of interest, however, which took primacy over the business conditions of the country. Too, he felt a basic reluctance to tinker with the commercial mechanism of society; undisturbed, it would eventually right itself. There was really little need for legislation designed to end the depression.

Within days after the money market collapsed, the state convention of the Republican party convened in Utica. It was predicted ahead of time that "no convention was ever so free in its action as that of tomorrow promises to be. There is no 'slate,' and nobody has endeavored to form any combinations." [15] It *was* a harmonious convention, as predicted, for the organization had it well in hand. Conkling wanted to make sure that two incumbents who had gone with Greeley in 1872 were dropped from the ticket, and this was done. The major action taken by the convention was a resolution calling for congressional legislation repealing the Salary Grab and providing for repayment of the bonanza provided in that measure.

This resolution, which fit precisely with a measure which Conkling had prepared for submission to the next session of Congress, was attacked savagely by *The Nation* on October 2. E. L. Godkin's liberal journal, a resolute and tireless opponent of Roscoe Conkling, his political methods, associations, and objectives, in this case struck very wide of the mark. Platforms, Godkin said,

whatever else they are, need not record the spitefulness or personal animosities of one man. . . . Senator Fenton, who is wise in his generation, some time since saw that there would be violent popular disapproval of the "back pay" enactment, and returned his money to the Treasury; while Mr. Conkling, less prudent or more willful, refused to take notice of the storm until he found that nothing less than obedience would serve. He is now said to be the author of the resolution which condemns the action of Congress in passing the obnoxious measure. It, at all events, fits his personal case as precisely as if it had been made with a view of apologizing for his recalcitrancy.

It was almost as if Godkin chose, as an intellectual exercise, one of the worst possible cases to see if he could still turn it into abuse of Conkling. It did not work. Conkling had in fact voted against the

15 N.Y. *Times,* Sept. 24, 1873.

Salary Grab, both in preliminary voting and on final passage. He had never drawn the so-called "back pay" from the treasury, unlike Fenton, who then wrote what the *Times* on September 26 called "a sham letter returning the back pay." In addition, Conkling *was* prepared to press for congressional enactment of a measure to secure the back pay to the treasury, instead of trusting to a series of self-serving letters from people like Fenton at such times as they "saw that there would be violent popular disapproval of the 'back pay' enactment." From time to time over the years, Godkin got in some telling blows at the senator, but this was decidedly not one of them. The Democrats quickly dropped the Salary Grab as an issue against Roscoe Conkling.

As the month of October slipped into November, conditions in the country deteriorated, and it became obvious to the voters that the post-war prosperity was ending. Lashing out at the first convenient scapegoat, the electorate of New York State brought down the Republican party from its eminence in Albany. The Democratic party carried the state election of 1873, leaving Governor Dix with a Democratic legislature. As the election returns came in throughout the nation, bringing few good tidings for the Republicans, it became clear that the depression would bear heavily upon the members of Congress when they came together in December.

CHAPTER 12

———◄•••►———

THE CHIEF JUSTICE—
AND HIS DAUGHTER

Another matter pressed urgently upon the president before the reassembling of Congress. On May 7, 1873, Salmon P. Chase—Free-Soil Democrat, radical Republican, senator, governor, cabinet minister, indefatigable seeker after the presidency, and, for the last nine years of his life, chief justice of the United States, suffered a stroke and died. Grant, who had such a hard time with appointments to major offices, was faced with another headache.

He first determined that he would let the position remain vacant until Congress reconvened, thus giving the rumor mills six or seven months to speculate as to Chase's successor. The names most prominently mentioned were associate justice Samuel F. Miller of Iowa, the dominant personality on the existing Court, Evarts, Lyman Trumbull, E. Rockwood Hoar, and former Associate Justice Benjamin R. Curtis. There were political disabilities which would work with Grant against Evarts, Trumbull, and Hoar. Trumbull, after all, had supported Greeley for president the year before, and Hoar, the former attorney general, had previously been rejected by the Senate when named an associate justice because he had been politically uncooperative while in Grant's cabinet. Evarts, though a pillar of the American bar and probably the choice of the legal profession, had always been a political maverick, evidenced by his representation of Andrew Johnson and his service as attorney general for that president.[1] Evarts' personal choice was Rockwood Hoar, but Grant set him aside. Hoar, on the other hand, wrote to Evarts that "if fitness governs, you will be the foremost, and if it

[1] Warren, II, 552–553. There was also talk, not serious, of William S. Groesbeck of Ohio.

does not, I should be sorry to think I was in competition on any other principles." [2]

None of these men suited the president. Finally, Grant turned, as he did so frequently, to the man he apparently wanted to appoint from the beginning, Roscoe Conkling. He wrote to Conkling on November 8:

When the Chief Justiceship became vacant I necessarily looked with anxiety to some one whose appointment would be recognized as entirely fitting and acceptable to the country at large. My own preference went to you at once. But I determined—and announced—that the appointment would not be made until the meeting of Congress—that I thought a Chief Justice should never be subjected to the mortification of a rejection. The possibility of your rejection of course was not dreamed of. But I think the conclusion of waiting for confirmation was right in principle.

I now wish to state to you that my first convictions on the subject of who should be Judge Chase's successor have received confirmation by time; and I tender the nomination to you, to be made on the meeting of Congress, in the hope that you will accept, and in the full belief that no more acceptable appointment could be made.[3]

Though the New York *Tribune,* two days after Grant's letter, was still saying that "the stories of an offer of the Chief-Justiceship to Mr. Conkling, or to any one, are unfounded," there had been some inklings ahead of the fact. Indeed, as far in advance as October 2, *The Nation* said: "The gossip about the Chief-Justiceship grows louder, and points more plainly than before to Mr. Roscoe Conkling as the probable nominee for the office." Editor Godkin used this gossip as a springboard for another attack on the senator. "His ability," he said, "is that of an ardent, indefatigable stump-speaker and party manager. Indeed, the stump has in our time produced no such fustian as he pours from it." He ridiculed the idea that Conkling could even be considered a politician:

To politics, in any good sense of the word, Mr. Conkling has not contributed a single useful or fruitful idea; he is not the author of a single measure of value or importance; he has made no speech which any sensible man can bear to read—so that his political claims to the chief place on the bench of the greatest tribunal in the world are as paltry as his professional ones.

After the offer to Senator Conkling became known, the press was

[2] C. L. Barrows, *William M. Evarts,* pp. 225–226.
[3] Conkling Papers, Library of Congress.

basically critical of it. Conkling had few friends in the press (newsmen received the same haughty, aloof treatment from him that the rest of the public got). Those admirers he had were hard-pressed to answer the demands of his detractors that they point to the hallmarks of an outstanding legal career. They confessed that the senator had been too busy dealing with the great public questions to devote much time to a strictly private law practice. Besides, they said, John Marshall was a politician, too.

Harper's Weekly, surprisingly mild, said, "Senator Conkling, whose name is now oftenest mentioned in connection with the office, is forty-five years of age, and has quite as much reputation as a lawyer as either of the Chief Justices at the period of their appointment, and is probably a better speaker than any of them were at any period of their careers." [4]

The Independent, a religious weekly with a wide influence, damned Conkling with faint praise when it said that "the President might have done much worse, and . . . he also might have done much better." It went on:

Independently of his prominence as a successful politician in the Republican party and what is no more than a fair reputation as a lawyer, Senator Conkling does not by his antecedents or acquirements present anything like a first-class grade of qualifications for the high office. We are aware that he is the personal friend of the President, and that the latter has many reasons to appreciate his strong and earnest party support; yet these considerations should not control the appointment.

While the journal conceded that Conkling might make a good judge, it asked whether he possessed "the judicial mind in an eminent degree." [5]

The Nation called Conkling "the kind of man that General Grant's recent appointments would lead us to think he would select in the present instance," and it worried that "there are a great many 'political considerations' hanging around Mr. Conkling." [6]

While the press and the country considered the worthiness of the Conkling selection, as well as its effect upon the Supreme Court and the

---

[4] *Harper's Weekly,* Dec. 13, 1873.

[5] *The Independent,* Nov. 27, 1873. This was a common reaction—Garfield expressed the same fear, though he conceded that Conkling "if he would forego all political ambitions would make an able Chief Justice." H. J. Brown and F. D. Williams, eds., *Diary of J. A. Garfield,* II, 249.

[6] *The Nation,* May 22, 1873.

Republican party, no one apparently ever expected Roscoe to turn the offer down. But he did.

It took some time for Grant's letter of November 8 to catch up with the senator, but he finally received it on the 15th. He then spent some time in what he called "due reflection" upon the matter. Among others, he talked it over with Arthur, Cornell, and Platt on several occasions, as he wrestled with what must have been an extraordinarily difficult decision. Few men in our nation's history have been tendered the chief justiceship; fewer still have declined the honor. For a lawyer, it represents the pinnacle of the profession. For a politician, too, it stands as a position in which, within the framework of Constitution, statute, precedent, and logic, policy decisions of the highest nature can be made. The lifetime tenure of the office presents the chance to cut loose from the strains and divisions of partisan politics.

The first consideration which faced Conkling, however, was one of partisan politics; with the New York legislature now in Democratic hands, he would not even be able to select his successor in the Senate, and his seat would fall to the enemy. This should have been a minor consideration, of course, but it would not have seemed so to the Cornells and the Platts.

Besides, divorcing himself from party politics was not an entirely congenial thought to Conkling. The combat of partisan warfare had been embedded in him from youth, and all other aspects of his life occupied secondary positions. The goal of the presidency still stood before him, at such time as Ulysses S. Grant chose to leave the office; in the meantime, Conkling would stay in the Senate, in the thick of the hard political battles he loved so much. There he would be needed: by the country, whose currency was about to come under attack once again, and by the president, who was entitled to rely upon his firm support.

He wrote to the president on November 20 from Utica:

You offer me the Chief Justiceship—and this confidence outweighs all the honors of the place. . . . My transfer now from the Senate to the Bench, involves considerations not only beyond my own interest and wishes, but I think even beyond those before you; and after much thought I am convinced that in view of the whole case you would agree with me that another appointment should be made. . . . I ask you to let your choice fall on another, who, however else qualified, believes as man and lawyer, as I believe, in the measures you have upheld in war and in peace.[7]

[7] Conkling Papers, Library of Congress.

The first sentence of Conkling's letter offers a key to his thinking: he conceived of the chief justiceship as an "honor" but apparently gave little thought to the idea of himself functioning in such a position. He recognized that he was probably incapable of the detachment necessary to the bench. To his friends, Conkling explained his decision to decline the appointment: "I could not take the place, for I would be forever gnawing my chains." [8]

After Conkling turned down the proffered appointment, Grant stumbled around in inept confusion. He first approached Fish, but the elderly secretary discouraged his nomination. Ben Butler pushed the name of Caleb Cushing, a 73-year-old Massachusetts politician-lawyer of erratic principles, who had been a "dough-faced" member of Pierce's cabinet and had chaired the breakaway 1860 Democratic convention which nominated Breckinridge for president. Though Cushing had since become a Republican, he was deeply mistrusted by the Senate, and Grant wisely elected not to send in his name. What Grant did, though, was probably worse; he nominated his attorney-general, George H. Williams of Oregon. Williams had been a failure as chief legal officer of the government and was not even reckoned a good lawyer. There were also serious doubts about his honesty, and it was known that he had been using the justice department contingency fund for private purposes.

The reaction against Williams was very unfavorable, from the public and the legal profession, with Conkling and Frederick Frelinghuysen of New Jersey leading the opposition in the Senate. It was rumored that Conkling was making ready a bill to abolish the chief justice as a presidential appointment and have him selected from among their number by the associate justices. Finally, on January 8, 1874, Williams recognized that he was beaten and requested the withdrawal of his name.

The president was now frustrated and angered by the situation, so he impulsively sent to the Senate the name of Caleb Cushing, without consultation with anyone. This nomination, of course, made things worse. All of the fears expressed to Grant during his earlier consideration of Cushing were now shown to be justified, and the Senate was united against the appointment. The president at last consulted with the leaders of the upper chamber. It was finally decided that the selection should be

[8] Platt, *Autobiography*, pp. 67–68. Garfield in his diary compared Conkling to the Younger Pitt, who "declined any but the first place," and suggested that "perhaps this is Conkling's reason." Brown and Williams, eds., II, 249.

Morrison R. Waite, a highly respected but relatively unknown lawyer from Toledo. Before Waite was named, Grant made one last try for Conkling, through the medium of a letter from Timothy Howe and Hannibal Hamlin to Cornell, saying, "we have the best of evidence that the President would like to renew the offer to Mr. C." But the next day, January 19, Cornell wired Howe that "circumstances render it inadmissable for the person you name to do as you propose." Accordingly, Waite was nominated and confirmed. Grant had at last come up with a chief justice.[9]

One writer commented on Conkling's refusal to succeed Chase by saying, "Though he did not accept the revered Chief's position, he did accept his place in the heart of the daughter." [10] For several years, in fact, the keen-eyed in Washington social circles had noted the attentions paid by Roscoe Conkling to Kate Chase Sprague, the daughter of the chief justice. Such court would naturally have been observed and commented upon, for Kate Sprague was a beauty, and Conkling was one of the most flamboyant and picturesque leaders in the capital.

Kate was more than a beautiful girl; she was also an astute politician. She came by this trait naturally enough. When she was sixteen years old, she returned home from her New York boarding school to assume the position of mistress of the household of her widower father, then the governor of Ohio. She established a stylish, sophisticated routine in Columbus, and she impressed visitors with her dazzling beauty and her bright intelligence.

In 1859, the worldly Carl Schurz had occasion to stay overnight at the governor's home, and at breakfast the next morning he met Kate, then nineteen:

[She] let herself down upon her chair with the graceful lightness of a bird that, folding its wings, perches upon the branch of a tree. She was . . . tall and slender, and exceedingly well formed. Her features were not at all regularly beautiful according to the classic rule. Her little nose, somewhat audaciously tipped up, would perhaps not have passed muster with a severe critic, but it fitted pleasingly into her face with its large languid

[9] Grant's fumbling course in picking a chief justice after Conkling turned him down can be followed in Nevins, *Fish*, II, 660–666, and Warren, II, 553–556. The Howe-Hamlin-Cornell exchange of Jan. 18 and 19, 1874, is in Conkling Papers, Library of Congress.

[10] M. M. Phelps, *Kate Chase*, p. 244.

but at the same time vivacious hazel eyes, shaded by long dark lashes, and arched over by proud eyebrows. The fine forehead was framed in waving gold-brown hair. She had something imperial in the pose of her head, and all her movements possessed an exquisite natural charm. No wonder that she came to be admired as a great beauty and broke many hearts.[11]

The perfect bust and figure, the saucy nose, the hazel eyes and golden-brown hair—all these are mentioned time and again, all these and particularly the proud bearing. When Chase came to Washington in 1861 to take his place in Lincoln's cabinet, his daughter Kate quickly established herself as the reigning beauty of the capital. She could converse on equal terms with the political figures she met and captivated, and she served as an additional and very acute pair of eyes and ears for her father, to whom she was devoted.

In November 1863, in a marriage that many said was dictated by ambition for her father, Kate wed Senator William Sprague of Rhode Island in a lavish Washington ceremony, which was followed by a sumptuous reception for over five hundred guests, including President Lincoln, who made sure to kiss the bride.

Sprague, the handsome young heir to a family textile business worth many millions, was considered a fine catch in 1863. In addition to his fortune, he possessed a good record as the youthful war governor of Rhode Island in 1860–1861, as a dashing Union general, and as a newly elected senator with a bright career ahead. Shortly, however, Kate found to her humiliation that he was a drunkard.

Nevertheless, the Sprague millions provided solace to Kate. She furnished a magnificent mansion at Narragansett Pier, called "Canonchet," with a lavish and opulent hand, and in Washington, particularly after the war, she was able to entertain in high style. Seldom, though, did she share the company of her husband, whose Senate career took a decided downward turn in the spring of 1869, when he startled the Senate with reckless speeches attacking money and business and charging that the Senate itself had been corrupted by the same agents. Though he had just been elected to a new term and stayed on to 1875, Sprague thereafter took little part in the business of the Senate and carried no influence whatever.

In the meantime, Sprague's wife was the center of Washington society. It was said that Kate was courted as much after her marriage as

[11] C. Schurz, *Reminiscences*, II, 169.

before, but she never lost her poise or her heart until Roscoe Conkling came along.

It was the spring of 1870 when it became obvious that Conkling and young Mrs. Sprague were seeing each other. She was reported to have sent flowers for his Senate desk, and from this and other manifestations of regard the town gossips started to link the two. Besides, everyone in Washington knew of the problems between Kate and her husband, and most were aware of Conkling's polite estrangement from Julia, who seldom strayed from Utica.

Neither Kate nor Roscoe cared much for public opinion, and after the chief justice's death the two were seen in public together more and more frequently. Conkling counseled Kate on financial matters; her father had left a meager estate and her extravagance, her husband's mismanagement, and the prevailing hard times had combined to wipe out the Sprague textile empire. She needed help, and Roscoe provided it. He succeeded in having the Chase family home in Washington exempted from taxes, in memory of her father's great services to the country. She needed companionship as well, and Roscoe provided that, too. There is no documentary evidence of sexual relations, since neither boasted or wrote memoirs, but there seems little reason to doubt that the two slept together over a long period of time. Kate yielded herself to Roscoe completely; he was "the man in her life who seemed to be irresistible to Kate. He understood her ambition and shared her iron will. In Conkling, Kate had met her master." [12]

[12] I. Ross, *Proud Kate,* p. 231. For background on Kate Chase, her marriage to William Sprague, and her liaison with Conkling, see Ross, *Proud Kate,* pp. 31–235; Bowers, pp. 252–255; and Phelps.

CHAPTER 13

---◆◆◆◆►---

A NATION'S CREDIT

Congress came together for its annual session on December 1, 1873, and Roscoe Conkling braced himself for the onslaught of depression-induced panaceas to cheapen the currency of the nation. Conkling knew that Grant was a babe in the woods in fiscal matters. His constitutional advisers on monetary policy were little better. Boutwell's tenure in the treasury had been marked by a relentless drive to reduce the public debt, heedless of any other considerations. Other than that, he had shown no initiatives at all, and few were saddened when he resigned to enter the Senate. The new Secretary, William A. Richardson, who had been Boutwell's assistant, was a weak reed for the president to lean on. Already people were dismayed at the fumbling and irresolute course pursued by Richardson since the market crashed. With no firm policy set by the administration, with conditions in the country continuing to deteriorate, Congress would set the pace for action, would indeed set out what that action would be.

"Inflation" was the word of the moment, "inflation" to put into circulation enough money so that everyone should have some, so that everyone could pay his bills and buy groceries and put a proper roof over his head. If there were just more money, things would get better, business would improve, and prosperity would return. The key to inflation was the greenback dollar, the paper money issued, over Roscoe Conkling's opposition, to pay for conducting the Civil War. There had been a peak figure of four hundred million greenback dollars in circulation, but by virtue of the contraction act this amount had been reduced to $356,000,000. When the panic struck, as a reflex reaction Secretary Richardson had re-issued, without warrant of law, $26,000,000 worth of paper. This was the background as Congress met, with inflationists demanding the issuance of more and more paper.

Conkling made his position clear from the outset. On February 19, 1874, the senator warned, in language reminiscent of his wartime lectures to the House, "against all schemes for wholesale issues of irredeemable paper money. . . . Reason and experience convince me that we shall launch Government and people on a sea without shore or bottom when we legislate the nation out upon a sea of unlimited irredeemable paper money. . . . Paper money not to be paid or redeemed," he said, "is a falsehood and a fraud. It can never be true, and therefore it can never be right or safe."

Conkling's conclusion demonstrated that even a great depression was not cause enough to turn his back on his monetary philosophy: "Now that no war threatens us, and no overmastering necessity is to be pleaded, guilty and mad will be the hour when Congress can find no better way to conduct the finances of the nation than to print an unlimited issue of irredeemable promises to pay." [1]

Conkling was the only one of the leading administration spokesmen in the Senate who stood foursquare against inflation. Morton and Logan, coming from the predominantly debtor-populated Midwest, felt that some inflation was necessary, and even John Sherman, who prided himself on his unshaken devotion to sound money, wobbled and fudged a bit this time, though the ultra-inflationists soon drove him back into opposition.

The so-called Ferry bill, as it was reported to the floor of the Senate by Sherman's Finance Committee, provided for greenbacks in the amount of $382,000,000, with gradual repayment of these notes in coin or five-per-cent bonds, after January 1, 1876. In other words, Sherman would legalize, ex post facto, Richardson's illegal re-issue of $26,000,000 worth of greenbacks. Even this was too much for Conkling, while it was far short of enough for the ultras. [2]

In the debate which the bill touched off, extending over several months, party solidarity quickly disintegrated. The currency question, hard money or soft, was one which cut across party lines. The Republican caucus was unable to enforce any party stand on the measure, and the Democrats did not even try. The bill was battled out on the floor. The fight was bitter, with Conkling leading the hard-money opposition, aided mainly by Carl Schurz, of all people.

In the final outcome, Sherman's limitation of $382,000,000 was shoved aside. "Several amendments," Sherman said, "were offered and

[1] *Cong. Rec.*, 43d Cong., 1st sess., p. 1637. [2] J. Sherman, I, 495.

adopted which enlarged the maximum of notes to $400,000,000 and greatly weakened the bill as a measure of resumption of specie payments. Instead of a return to specie payments, it provided for an expansion of an irredeemable currency." [3] While it may have been stretching things for Sherman to talk of his original proposal as "a measure of resumption of specie payments," it was undoubtedly true that the bill which passed the Senate on April 6 was expansive and inflationary. The sober business judgment of the country was appalled. *The Nation* said the Senate's action showed that "that body is given over completely to inflation in its maddest form." The ultras were even dissatisfied with the final limitation which they won, but they accepted it out of realism. The bill passed the Senate, 29 to 24, with Conkling voting "nay" in company with such Democratic leaders as Bayard of Delaware.[4]

The House passed the Ferry bill, virtually without debate, on April 14, by a vote of 140 to 102, and sent it on to the president. What Grant, with his somewhat child-like ideas of finance and currency, would do with the bill raised considerable speculation. He was under pressure from many sides, pressure greater, he said, "than he had ever before experienced," to sign the bill for a temporary alleviation of the financial distress in the country and also to save the Republican party in the national elections of 1874 and 1876, when the Democrats were confident they would ride the depression into the White House. On the other side, Conkling counseled with the president, striving to instill in Grant his own theories of finance and national credit.

Grant hesitated and wavered and wondered; he kept silent, as always, and he used up most of the time given him by the Constitution for consideration of a bill passed by the Congress. As the days passed, apprehension and excitement over the fate of the bill grew. Even Roscoe Conkling did not know how the president would come out. Grant wrote for himself messages both approving and rejecting the measure, to see which was more convincing. The arguments of Conkling and his more conservative advisers finally won out, and on April 22, 1874, the president sent to Congress the veto message, expressing his "regret at not being able to give my assent to a measure which has received the sanction of a majority of the legislators chosen by the people," but calling the bill "a departure from true principles of finance, national interest,

---

[3] *Ibid.*, I, 504.

[4] As an illustration of the mixed-party support which carried the Ferry Bill, 57% of the Republicans joined 48% of the Democrats in the Senate to approve it; Rothman, p. 78. *The Nation*, April 2, 1874.

national obligations to creditors, Congressional promises, party pledges (on the part of both political parties), and of personal views and promises made by me in every annual message sent to Congress and in each inaugural address." [5]

Conkling, overjoyed, wrote a note to the president, "to express my admiration for your latest proof that you are as great as any duty ever set before you." [6] The public credit was saved, according to fundamentalist principles of economics, though it was saved at the cost of prolonged suffering among the impoverished citizenry.

It remained only to kill the bill officially, by making sure the Senate failed to vote to override the veto. On April 28, when the question of acting upon the veto came up, Conkling said scornfully: "Indeed, except that the Constitution requires the Senate to reconsider the bill, it would not be worth while ever to act on it again." He then voted against the bill again as the 34 to 30 vote to override fell far short of the necessary two-thirds.

"Turning now from things of the past," Conkling said when he regained the floor the same day, "I wish to say a word about things of the present and the future." The senator from New York reasoned that the economy would straighten itself out, once the question of possible legislation was resolved. "Business halts and waits for final action in Congress," he said. "We ought to act promptly, or learn and declare promptly that no action will occur at the present session." [7]

What Congress finally achieved was a legitimization of Richardson's release of the $26,000,000 of greenbacks. This was basically the extent of congressional reaction to the Panic and the hard times flowing from it, and even this was, in Roscoe Conkling's opinion, more than was necessary.

During this session of Congress, as in so many, the New York Custom House became once again a subject of inquiry and interest. This, despite the fact that Collector Arthur was receiving the general approbation of the business community. Indeed, at the start of the year, *Harper's Weekly,* not a pro-Conkling publication, called Arthur "one of the most efficient and acceptable officials who have filled that position," remark-

[5] Richardson, ed., VII, 268–269. See A. S. Draper, "Grant's Veto," p. 474, and J. A. Kasson, "A Veto by Grant," p. 949, for description of the pressures on Grant and the president's reaction to them.

[6] Conkling Papers, Library of Congress.

[7] *Cong. Rec.,* 43d Cong., 1st sess., p. 3426.

ing that he had "introduced into the various departments under his control reforms that have been of practical advantage to our merchants, and equally serviceable to the government." No more, it was said, can "political roughs . . . extort places in the Custom-house as a reward for fraud and trickery at caucuses and the polls." [8] This, it should be noted, was praise indeed from *Harper's,* whose editor, George William Curtis, was one of the most tireless and uncompromising advocates of civil service reform.

Nevertheless, a recent extreme case had pointed up the inequity and hardship sometimes imposed by the so-called "moieties" system in the custom houses of the nation, and Congress was now reacting to the public outcry against that system. In 1872, Collector Arthur had, in accordance with the law, summoned William E. Dodge, a partner in the well-known importing house of Phelps, Dodge and Company, and presented him with charges of undervaluing, for customs purposes, imports coming into the Port of New York. The law as it then read provided that the entire value of any shipment of which a part had been undervalued was subject to forfeiture as a penalty, and the shipment in question had been valued at $1,750,000! Horrified at this potential liability, the company eventually worked out with the collector a compromise penalty figure of $271,019.23, and paid it, with half going to the government and half being split up among the special treasury agent involved in the case and the three chief officers of the port. From the latter half, sizable legal fees were allegedly paid to Roscoe Conkling and to Ben Butler of Massachusetts for their professional services in construing the statute. After making the payment, Phelps, Dodge officials discovered to their dismay that the total undervaluation was only $6,658.78; worse, the duties of which the government was deprived, the actual cash loss to the revenue service by reason of the undervaluations, were $1,664.68. Yet the company had paid a penalty of over one hundred sixty-eight times that amount, and half of it had gone into the pockets of the government officials who had been on the spot when the windfall took place! [9]

Though Arthur, his associates, and their counsel had done everything strictly in the manner set forth by the statute covering the situation, still the merchants had the unmistakable feeling that Congress had never contemplated such a grotesque result.

Throughout June of 1874, a long and extended debate took place in the Senate on the reform of the custom house laws of the United States

[8] Jan. 17, 1874.   [9] Howe, pp. 49–50.

as well as repeal of the moieties system, the arrangement whereby half of the penalty collected went to the local officers. On June 10, Conkling announced to the Senate, "I am ready to vote, I mean to vote to dispense altogether with the moiety system so called." [10] Despite this manly affirmation of intention, though, things were not quite so simple. The Port of New York collected the great bulk of the customs revenue of the country, and it was the chief officers of its custom house who gained the most by the moieties system. Naturally, with this money coming in to Arthur, George Sharpe, and their associates, a certain percentage of it found its way into the party coffers to help maintain the hegemony of the Republican party (and more particularly the Conkling machine) in New York State. If this steady, ready source of income were cut off, Conkling's organization would suffer *pro tanto*. It was not a thing to be done hastily or carelessly. Unfortunately, the manifestations of public disapproval of the system (not because the party was making a lot of money, but because of the unfair way it was coming out of the importers) were strong and clear, and the system was doomed. Unfortunately, also, particularly in light of the Phelps, Dodge case, there was not much that a senator could say in favor of retaining the existing procedure and sound convincing about it. Hence Conkling's statement of June 10. He then followed the classic parliamentary procedure of voting on most preliminary roll calls against the bill and of introducing successive amendments to the measure to try to draw its teeth. He also took the opportunity to put in a good word for his lieutenants, referring at one point to Arthur and "the very high character which he deserves not only for integrity but for manhood in all regards." [11] Finally, as Conkling had foreseen, the vote on passage of the bill came up and he resignedly joined in the final majority of 39 to 3.

The money would be missed, but it was not an overwhelming loss. Conkling and his men still held the custom house in a firm grip; if one of the fringe perquisites had been lost, it mattered little when the basic strength of the establishment still inured to the machine.

The senator could see, of course, that times were changing. It was now nine years since the end of the war, and the old iron spirit which had prevailed in Washington in those exciting months and years after

[10] *Cong. Rec.*, 43d Cong., 1st sess., p. 4814.
[11] *Ibid.*, p. 4711, June 9, 1874. Arthur, on June 3, suggested that perhaps Senator Sherman's committee would like to hear his assistant collector on the moieties bill; Arthur to Conkling, Arthur Papers, New-York Historical Society.

Appomattox was fading away. As the war spirit died, as the substantive differences between the parties disappeared, it was more and more the interests of business and industry which dominated Washington life. The men of strong convictions, the doctrinaires, were vanishing.

On March 11, the death of Charles Sumner was announced to the Senate, and the next day Conkling spoke of the "vacant chair . . . long held by a Senator of distinguished eminence, and one of the most illustrious of Americans." [12] Sumner was one of the last of the giants of the prewar era, and if he appears in retrospect to be something of a grotesque comic representation of a senator, still in many respects America had moved to the cadences of his vituperative speech. His dogmatic stands had come to represent considerable public sentiment.

Grant was going, too. Already, in 1874, there were strident voices in the land calling for a renunciation, clear and positive, of any aspirations for a third term. The shades of Washington, Jefferson, Madison, and Jackson were invoked, the storied traditions of America's national history were sounded, to establish finally that Ulysses S. Grant should not seek an additional term as president. Grant's historical knowledge was not profound, and his understanding of unwritten constitutional limitations was deficient; he really very much liked being president. He said nothing in response to the clamor against a third term, but his silence itself fed the uproar, and the widespread and determined opposition served by its very nature to answer the question. Roscoe Conkling would never join those who would deny a third term to General Grant. As far as he was concerned, if Grant wanted to remain president he would find the senior senator from New York a loyal and effective worker.

Conkling stood up one May day in the Senate and, in the course of his remarks, said

This is an era of reform; or if not an era of reform, it is an era of restlessness and change. I know of nothing that exists which there is not a disposition somewhere to revolutionize. If Pope were living now he would never dare to say that "whatever is, is right." If he wished to conform to the prevailing spirit he would have to reverse it and affirm that whatever is, is wrong.[13]

Conkling, however, resisted this spirit whenever he could. There were times, of course, as in the moieties repeal, when there was nothing to do but to abide inevitable change. In essential matters, though, Roscoe

[12] *Cong. Rec.*, 43d Cong., 1st sess., p. 2142.
[13] *Ibid.*, p. 4233, May 25, 1874.

Conkling would fight change for the sake of change, and he meant to defend with zeal and determination the political strengths which he had developed. He was, at this time, at the very height of his powers. He was forty-four years of age, strong, handsome, healthy, the good right arm of the Grant administration, sure enough of himself with his new six-year term in the Senate to turn down the highest judicial post in the land. His organization was dominant in New York's turbulent political waters, and he was one of the two or three strongest leaders of his party in the Senate. *The Nation,* as early as January 29, could say that Conkling "is a candidate for the Presidential succession in full training." Though the chatter about no third term was distressing, Conkling was not worried about it. He was for Grant, but if it could not be Grant, he would go after the prize himself.

In the spring of 1874, the premier social event of the season was the wedding of President Grant's daughter Nellie on May 21. She married a young Englishman named Algernon Sartoris, and though the match with a foreigner (no matter how estimable) seemed a trifle strange at first to the doughty Midwesterner who was the father of the bride, it appeared just fine to his more cultivated and cosmopolitan friend, the senator from New York. Bessie Conkling, the senator's only child, was one of Nellie's eight bridesmaids, and her parents beamed with pride and delight as Bessie played her role in the ceremonies. One observer said, "They looked like angels as they came down the long corridor . . . they were all so fair and sweet." [14] Julia had come down from Utica in one of her rare visits to Washington to aid Bessie in her preparations. The gay family gathering appears as one of the few bright spots in an otherwise rather gray domestic scene. For over a month Conkling's wife and daughter were with him in the capital, to appear in the fashionable dining spots, to call upon the proper people, to share the pew for which he paid rent in St. John's Church (his religion, according to what he had, he once said, cost him the most of any man in town [15]). Mrs. Sprague kept discreetly in the background, while wife and daughter occupied the idle hours of the senator and Julia renewed the fitful acquaintances she had made on other abbreviated visits to Washington. It was no doubt confining to him, but for over a month, thanks to Nellie and Algernon, Roscoe Conkling had a family.

Later on, in August, Grant made an effort to bring the whole Conkling

14 W. H. Crook, *Through Five Administrations,* p. 184.
15 *Cong. Rec.,* 42d Cong., 3d sess., p. 1950, Feb. 28, 1873.

family to the summer White House, his spacious and unpretentious home at Long Branch. The President, no doubt egged on by his wife, whose sympathies were with her friend Julia when the senator carried on with Kate Sprague in Washington, wrote puckishly to Julia on August 5: "Mrs. Grant and I will be pleased if we can have you and Miss Bessie spend next week with us at the Branch, when we will try to make your time pass pleasantly. Bring the Senator too, *just for company while traveling,* and to look after the baggage." [16]

In the summer, thoughts turned to the political campaign for that fall, with the governor's chair the major prize at issue. John A. Dix was the incumbent, and, though now over seventy-five, he desired renomination. He had performed the duties of the office in a capable manner, and he retained the wide popularity among his fellow citizens which had first won him the post. Dix had spent most of his life in and about politics, and he was not yet ready to step aside. Still, there were rumblings of discontent in the Republican organization, and it was noised about that the Conkling people were unhappy about the prospect of another run by Dix. The governor, at his age and with his separate following, considered himself somewhat independent of the Republican party and was definitely not subservient to Conkling, though he remained on good terms with the senator.

With the approach of the Republican state convention, to be held in Utica on September 23, there appeared to be two major items of business, the selection of a ticket and the adoption or not of an anti-third-term resolution. John Bigelow, the wartime minister to France, was one of those who wrote to Conkling, urging that the convention go on record in opposition to a third term for President Grant.[17] Conkling would have none of such an action, and the convention as a result was sternly silent on the question.

When the delegates gathered in Utica, there was no opposition to Dix, though the reporters said that the "officeholders," by which they meant Conkling's federal employees, were not enthusiastic about the governor. When the convention opened, George H. Sharpe, surveyor at the Custom House, Conkling lieutenant, and "officeholder" beyond a doubt, moved the nomination by acclamation of John A. Dix for governor,

---

[16] Conkling Papers, Library of Congress. See also I. Ross, *General's Wife,* pp. 229-231, despite some slight confusion over identities.

[17] Bigelow, V, 166. See also Bigelow to W. Reid, Oct. 27, 1874, Reid Papers.

which was quickly done. In like manner, the other two incumbents, John C. Robinson and Canal Commissioner Barkley, were nominated by acclamation also.

Roscoe Conkling was then introduced amid great cheers, and he delivered "a vigorous and effective speech" which ran for some seventy minutes, entitled "The Condition of Affairs in Louisiana." Though his talk dealt primarily with national issues, he did toward the end rip into the New York Democrats as well. Then the convention adjourned, liberating its members to refresh themselves in the manner customarily followed by politicians at such gatherings, to the profit of the saloons and taverns of Utica, and thence to proceed to their home districts to work for the success of the ticket against the Democrats.[18]

The Democrats, in the face of the opposition of the Canal Ring and what was left of Tammany Hall, nominated as their candidate for governor the crafty, sagacious lawyer from Gramercy Park in New York City, Samuel J. Tilden. Tilden, whose devious, secretive mind fitted him for the railroad reorganization and financing which became the backbone of his practice and the source of his immense fortune, had been a leader of the New York Democracy since prewar days when he had been a prominent Barnburner (along with John A. Dix). He had counseled Seymour in his constitutional opposition to Lincoln from 1863 to 1865, and had, as chairman of the New York State Democratic committee after 1866, first worked with and then been instrumental in overthrowing the Tweed Ring. It was on the basis of this latter achievement, for which the normally unpublicized Tilden had received probably more of the credit than was really due him, that he was nominated for governor in 1874.

The campaign did not go well for the Republicans. The Democrats were very happy to present a resolution deploring another term for Grant, thus contrasting with the awkward silence of the Republicans. Times were still bad, employment down, money scarce, and the Republicans appeared to be doing little about it. Tilden was riding the crest of a popular wave of approbation for the jailing of Tweed and his cohorts. Dix was charged with nepotism and wastefulness, and the Democrats brought up the fact that he had been president of the Union Pacific Railroad at the time when Oakes Ames's contract was made, and this oblique association with Credit Mobilier hurt. Finally, the Republican organization, from Conkling down, did little to help Dix. The governor's

18 N.Y. Times, Sept. 23, 1874; also *The Republic,* Nov. 1874.

independent conduct in Albany had been a pointed reminder of the fact that Dix really considered himself a Democrat, though he was happy to run on the Republican ticket, and that he did not subscribe to hard and fast party lines. The result was that he received only half-hearted, apathetic support from the politicians.

When the votes were counted in November, the Democrats were jubilant. Samuel Tilden was elected governor by 50,000 votes, the assembly was Democratic, eighteen of the state's thirty-three congressmen were Democrats, and the election of a Democratic successor to Fenton's Senate seat was assured. New York Republicans could not even turn elsewhere for cheer, for the Democrats had won control of the national House of Representatives. Bad times and bad government, the depression and Caesarism, had combined to give the Democracy control of one house of Congress for the first time since before the Civil War. Prospects looked gloomy for the beleaguered Republican party for 1876, and they would soon look worse.[19]

When Congress reconvened in December 1874, its members were very much aware that there remained but three months in which the Republican party would control the presidency and both houses of Congress. After that, for at least the foreseeable future, the responsibilities of government would be divided between the parties. What this would mean no one, least of all those Republicans who had lorded it over the opposition in the days of overwhelming majorities, could know.

The old problem of Louisiana resurfaced at this point, and the embroilments over rival state governments, who did what to whom in the local elections, and the role of the United States Army, were dragged forth and thrashed out once again.

On January 5, 1875, Thurman introduced a resolution asking the president to notify the Senate whether any elements of the Army had interfered with the organization of the Louisiana legislature the day before, and Conkling suggested that of course Thurman had meant to preface his inquiry with the standard phrase, "if in his judgment not incompatible with the public interest." Thurman flared up, saying, "It is not a case in which the public can suffer any detriment, in which the Government can suffer any detriment from the Senate of the United States knowing fully what are the facts of the case, and by what warrant of law or pretense of law this intervention, if it has taken place, has been made."

[19] Election coverage in Flick and Lobrano, p. 248, and Hudson, pp. 39–41.

Oh, no, rejoined Conkling, this is just such a case where the standard form *should* be used. The resolution related, he said, "to the serious disorder of a great community in one of the states of this Union." He recited the precedents and the background for the "if not incompatible" phrase, and then assured Thurman "that he is no more anxious than I am that the truth, the very truth to the uttermost, shall be known seasonably and in order, touching the doings in the State of Louisiana and the mighty murders that have there proceeded."

Thurman replied that he was sure Conkling would be heard when debate took place on the question, "for power never yet lacked advocates, and we all know that the Senator from New York is the leader here on the side of power." [20]

The problem in Louisiana, with dual legislative bodies and governments, each side claiming that the other was elected and formed by fraud, was aggravated by the presence in New Orleans of General Phil Sheridan as commander of the federal troops. Sheridan was shamelessly partisan, devoted to the Republican cause, and subject to all the frustrations military men frequently feel when confronted with complex political problems. The general's military mind conceived the simple solution to the unrest to be the wholesale military seizure and court-martial of everyone opposed to the Republican carpetbag government. On the same day that Thurman and Conkling were tangling in the Senate, Sheridan sent a wire to the secretary of war suggesting that Congress or the president declare the dissidents "banditti" so "they could be tried by a military commission." [21]

The debate, bad-tempered and not very constructive, continued throughout the month, and on January 28 and 29 Roscoe Conkling made a long speech on the topic. His speech was not much more enlightening, but it allowed Conkling to treat the Senate and the galleries to a prime example of his spread-eagle oratory which the galleries, at least, loved so well. "The presidential campaign of 1876 has been formally opened," he said. "It has been opened in the Senate, and legislation waits. It has been opened with somewhat of dramatic effect," turning toward Thurman, "and much of sensational awfulness." He scorned Thurman's four-hour speech of the day before as "carping criticism." There is a wide difference, he said, "between a critic and an architect.

---

[20] *Cong. Rec.*, 43d Cong., 2d sess., pp. 238–239, 243, 244.
[21] *Ibid.*, p. 311. When Secretary of War Belknap wired Sheridan that the cabinet had approved his course, Fish immediately wrote Conkling that the wire certainly did not speak for him. Conkling Papers, Library of Congress.

It is easier to pull down than to build up." The policy of the Democrats, he suggested, "consists only in denouncing whatever is done by those charged with public affairs." Conkling found occasion to raise the defense of his friend, General Sheridan, reminding his listeners that "Sheridan's sword was not the sword of an assassin, stabbing the humble and the helpless, but the sword of a soldier fighting that free government might not perish from the earth." [22]

And so it went on. No one was willing to admit that the problem of Louisiana would continue so long as the federal government determined to sustain the Republican carpetbag government there, against the will of the white populace, but this was clearly the crux of the situation. Louisiana was one of the few remaining Southern states which had not been "redeemed" by the white Democrats, "redeemed" from the carpetbagger, the black, and the Republican. In the meantime the wrangles of the state poisoned the air of the national legislative halls from time to time, as they had done for years.

There was some legislative business carried out in the short session. The most important was the Resumption Act. When Congress had reconvened in December, there was a general feeling, among the Republican members as well as some of the Democrats, that "the remedy for existing evils," as John Sherman put it, "was the return to specie payments." The various experiments in paper money were all well and good, usually necessary when made, and justified from time to time by the exigencies of the nation. Sometime, however, and this was a theme which Conkling had sounded for twelve or thirteen years now, all these promises to pay must be made good, the paper money must be made redeemable, the country must, in short, return to a specie basis for its currency.

The mistake of the previous spring, when the currency bill was debated and shaped on the floor of the Senate, much to the dismay of the leadership and the hard-money men, was not repeated. This time a measure would be drafted, presented, and passed without appreciable change. A committee of eleven Republican senators, chaired by Sherman and composed of the party's Senate leadership, was established to sit and to draft the desired legislation. The *ad hoc* committee's product was presented to the Senate Finance Committee as the unanimous act of the Republican membership, was reported out of committee on December 21, 1874, and was passed after a brief debate, mostly by Democrats.

[22] *Cong. Rec.,* 43d Cong., 2d sess., pp. 835–850.

When the House passed the bill unchanged, it was sent on to Grant, who signed it January 14. Under the act, the amount of greenbacks in circulation was to be reduced gradually to $300,000,000, and refunding in specie was to commence on the first day of 1879. Roscoe Conkling could rejoice that his efforts, as much as anyone's, had brought about this result.[23]

Conkling was one of a number of senators who called attention to the necessity for a better mode of counting the electoral votes for president than was currently provided by the twenty-second joint rule. This rule, which had been adopted by the two houses in 1865, provided that no vote should be counted, if there was a dispute about it, unless both houses agreed to count it. No one knew what the situation might be at the next election, or even whether there would be a problem, but everyone knew that the two houses would be under different political control, and the twenty-second joint rule could very well work to the partisan benefit of one party or the other; the aggravating factor, the factor which made it all a blindman's buff, was that no one knew which party would be in which situation.

Conkling, on January 21, predicted with uncomfortable accuracy that, "if there be serious importance in this subject, all Senators will agree that its gravity is as likely to be illustrated at the next Presidential election as at any election we can now forecast." This, obviously, was because the Republicans still had federal troops and carpetbag governments in several Southern states, which meant that the Negroes in those states would vote Republican in roughly equal proportions with the whites who would vote Democratic. This approximate numerical equality would then be compounded by the possibility of rival state governments, Republican and Democratic, claiming legitimacy for their respective electoral slates.

The senator from New York went on to analyze the words of the Constitution relating to counting the votes, and he said: "That language is very spare. The words are very few. It is certainly wanting in many an amplification which would be . . . convenient to a legislator looking for ways in which it might be enforced." But he found, in the constitutional phrase, "the votes shall then be counted," "appropriate domain, for legislative discretion, either by legislation or by a joint rule, if concurrent action between the two Houses rather than legislative action be

---

[23] J. Sherman, I, 509–511. The *ad hoc* committee members besides Sherman were Conkling, Boutwell, Allison, Howe, Edmunds, Thomas Ferry, Frelinghuysen, Logan, Morton, and Aaron Sargent. See also Sage, pp. 133–134.

preferred." In any event, he said, "We fall short in an urgent and imminent duty if the 4th of March witnesses a dissolution of these two Houses without their having devised some mode better than the twenty-second joint rule" for counting the electoral votes.[24]

Alas, when a bill finally did come to the floor of the Senate in the closing days of the session, a bill providing that any vote should be counted unless both houses joined in rejecting it, Conkling found this even "more likely to forecast disturbance and trouble" than the twenty-second joint rule. It was still blindman's buff. He voted against it. The bill in question passed, 28 to 20, but it died in the House, so the country was destined to move into the presidential election year with this question still unresolved.[25]

As the Forty-third Congress was drawing to a close, Conkling presented the credentials of New York's Senator-elect. We can be sure that he did this with mixed feelings, for, though it signaled the close of Reuben Fenton's senatorial career, Conkling would have much preferred to replace his old adversary with a Republican of his own choice. Instead, the credentials testified to the election of the first Democratic senator from New York since 1845. Yet the bitterness of this was tempered somewhat for Conkling, because the new senator was his old mentor, a two-time congressional opponent, Francis Kernan of Utica. Conkling could work better with him than he could with Fenton.[26]

[24] *Cong. Rec.*, 43d Cong., 2d sess., pp. 633–634.

[25] *Ibid.*, pp. 1777–1778, Feb. 25, 1875.

[26] There had been some movement afoot in New York Democratic circles to replace Fenton with Seymour, but the ex-Governor firmly squelched that and made it quite clear that he was for Kernan. See letters of Seymour of Nov. 14, 1874, to unnamed addressee, and Nov. 16, 1874, to J. J. Maslett, Seymour Papers.

CHAPTER 14

DARK SIDE OF THE MOON

In 1871, Whitelaw Reid had written to his friend John Bigelow, "All Administrations, I suppose, are more or less corrupt; certainly the depth of corruption this one has reached is scarcely suspected as yet, even by its enemies." [1] Whether Reid, who as Greeley's right hand shared his boss's ill feeling toward Grant, knew what he was talking about or was merely guessing makes little difference; by 1875 he had been proven appallingly correct.

The roster of scandals is dreadfully long: starting with Credit Mobilier, which broke during Grant's tenure but cannot truly be charged to his administration, it continued through the Whiskey Ring, the Emma Mine, Belknap's trading post, the DeGolyer paving contract in Washington, Williams and the justice department contingency funds, Navy Secretary Robeson and the Cattell grain matters, Richardson and the Sanborn contract, and so on. The details are distasteful, sometimes repetitive, and always discreditable to the Grant administration. In most cases, the victim was the American taxpayer, but not always. The Emma Mine, for example, was a speculative mining venture to which Robert C. Schenck, the rather popular minister to England, lent his name so that shares could be sold to the British public on the basis of a fraudulent prospectus. Grant tried to save Schenck, a former Republican congressman from Ohio, but he was not able to do so, and he had to bring him home in disgrace. The A. G. Cattell and Company connection with Secretary Robeson resulted in a tribute being levied upon the contracts of other flour firms with the Navy.

Possibly the most brazen of the scandals under Grant was the Whiskey Ring. Though there had long been charges and suspicions of frauds in collection of the whiskey tax, it was not until 1870 that General John

[1] Cortissoz, I, 204.

A. McDonald, appointed supervisor of internal revenue at St. Louis, was able to systematize the thievery. The Ring, when formed, was composed of internal revenue agents and distillers, with accomplices in important places in Washington. Numerous politicians in Missouri, Illinois and Wisconsin were also involved, for the Ring was used for several years to raise funds for the Republican party in those states. William Avery, the chief clerk of the internal revenue office at Washington, and Orville E. Babcock, Grant's private secretary of San Domingo fame, were the chief protectors of the Ring at Washington.

McDonald and his accomplices made huge profits through abatements of the whiskey tax combined with false and fraudulent returns. Two-fifths of these profits went to the high government officials involved in the swindle. While the complacent Boutwell and Richardson were at the head of the treasury department, the Ring and its members were safe and prosperous. In 1874, however, the incompetent Richardson was implicated in the Sanborn scandal, a messy bit of business in which John D. Sanborn, a crony of Ben Butler, was awarded a contract to collect delinquent taxes owed the government and to pocket half of the collections. All of this was contrary to law, particularly in light of the fact that no such action was required to collect most of the accounts anyway. Richardson was forced to resign as a result (though Grant rewarded him for his services with appointment to the court of claims, of all places). On June 1, 1874, Benjamin H. Bristow, a distinguished Kentucky lawyer and a Union veteran of Fort Donelson and Shiloh, was appointed secretary of the treasury. Bristow, who had been the nation's first solicitor-general from 1870 to 1872, was honest and fearless, and he was also shrewd, conscientious, and a good administrator.

It did not take Bristow long to discover a great discrepancy between the amount of liquor consumed and shipped and the amount on which taxes were paid. As the new secretary started to dig into the facts and figures, Babcock and Columbus Delano, the somewhat shadowy secretary of the interior, opened a campaign to get Bristow out of the cabinet.

Months of minute and necessarily very secret investigations pinpointed for Bristow the trouble spots—Chicago, Peoria, Milwaukee, Indianapolis, New Orleans, and mainly St. Louis. Since prior investigations had been tipped off in advance by Avery and his cohorts in the capital, Bristow had to recruit a brand new team of agents to work for him. On May 10, 1875, Bristow had his facts in order, and on that day his agents suddenly swooped down upon the custom houses in St. Louis, Chicago, and Milwaukee, gathering in their raids further incriminating evidence showing that millions of dollars had been stolen from the treasury.

The complacent Grant, after the raids, said to Bristow, "Well, Mr. Bristow, there is at least one honest man in St. Louis on whom we can rely—John McDonald. I know that because he is an intimate acquaintance and confidential friend of Babcock's." Disgusted with such naïveté, Bristow replied that "McDonald is the head and centre of all the frauds." [2]

Grant's crude and successful efforts to prevent the conviction of Babcock, after his initial directive to "let no guilty man escape," did little to raise the prestige of the chief executive. In its total effect, the Whiskey Ring story shattered public confidence in the administration.[3]

Finally, the Belknap scandal wore away whatever faith may have remained in the general honesty of Grant's associates. William H. Belknap, an Iowa lawyer, was appointed secretary of war after the untimely death of Rawlins in 1869. In 1870, his wife entered into an arrangement with Caleb P. Marsh of New York under which he would apply for the lucrative Indian post tradership at Fort Sill in the Indian Territory. Mrs. Belknap would see that he was awarded the place, and he would turn over half the profits to her. A tidy way indeed to put away some extra dollars! It worked out even more easily than that. The trader on the spot paid Marsh $12,000 a year to stay away, and he paid $6,000 to Mrs. Belknap. Even her subsequent death did not interfere with the arrangement, for the bereaved secretary shortly and very conveniently married her sister, "Puss," who ratified the compact with Marsh. He thereafter paid her share to Belknap, who passed it on to his wife. Ultimately, of course, word leaked out, and Marsh recited the whole tale to a House investigating committee. When impeachment proceedings against Belknap were initiated, the secretary hastened to the White House and tendered his resignation to Grant. The president, in-

[2] Nevins, *Fish,* II, 769. Material on the Whiskey Ring can be found in *ibid.,* II, 762–769, and Bowers, pp. 465–468. See also L. D. White, pp. 369–371, for other aspects of the corruption.

[3] Former Senator John B. Henderson, the special prosecutor, was dismissed after he indicated, in the trial of Avery, that Babcock was implicated. Grant's attorney general, Edwards Pierrepont, refused to grant immunity to witnesses turning state's evidence at Babcock's trial, so a number of potential witnesses against him never testified. Grant himself submitted a deposition on Babcock's behalf, and finally the trial judge virtually directed a verdict of "not guilty." See Pierrepont to D. P. Dyer, U.S. Attorney at St. Louis, Dec. 9, 1875, Pierrepont Papers.

credibly, accepted it, and Belknap was technically free of the danger of impeachment, being no longer a government officer. The House went ahead with the impeachment articles, but there was now a cloud over the proceedings. Belknap's sole serious defense was that he was a private citizen when the House impeached him, and Conkling raised the same point before the Senate. Though a majority of the Senate voted to sustain the jurisdiction of the Senate to try the impeachment, it was obvious that no conviction could be had. In the end, the vote to convict was 35 to 20, far less than the required two-thirds, and many of the twenty voted, as Conkling did, "on the ground that in this country by the Constitution private citizens are not impeachable." [4] Belknap thus got off the hook, but Grant did not.

Abused and defamed as he was by his cabinet and lesser associates, Grant never seemed to learn. When it came time to replace Delano in the interior department, the best he could do was ex-Senator Zach Chandler of Michigan. The president concealed his choice from the cabinet until it was made on October 19, 1875, since he named Chandler apparently at the urging of Babcock. The New York *Times* said: "We believe he has the reputation of being a 'first-rate story-teller,' and an amusing man to sit up with o'nights," but it knew of no better recommendation Chandler might have for the office. Chandler was crude and coarse, though affable, and the public was well aware of his limitations.[5]

Later on, Grant made J. Don Cameron his secretary of war. Cameron, at 43, had never held any office, was unknown to the public and was known even to politicians only as the son of old Simon Cameron of Pennsylvania, whose reputation for probity was always somewhat suspect. Young Cameron was a friend of Conkling, though, and Conkling suggested him to the president. This was enough.

With the record of the administration in Washington as a burden to carry, and the well-publicized activities of the Tilden administration in Albany as an additional handicap, Conkling needed a respite before launching into another campaign. During this summer of 1875, he took a trip to Europe and thus divorced himself for the time being from government, politics, and political activities.

It was a sagacious move. In the existing state of public sentiment to-

[4] *Cong. Rec.,* 44th Cong., Proceedings, p. 344, Aug. 1, 1876. See also Bowers, pp. 471–476.

[5] Nevins, *Fish,* II, 779–780; N.Y. *Times,* Oct. 20, 1875.

ward the Grant administration, it is doubtful if even Roscoe Conkling could have held the Republican state convention in line, when Republicans all over the country were trying for pure self-preservation to disconnect themselves from Grant. The convention, held in Saratoga in early September, was noticeable, it was said, "for the lack of all wire-pulling" and the delegates demonstrated that they were "controlled by no political clique." Resolutions calling for forbearance to the South, no third term for President Grant, and commendation for the correctors of public abuses were adopted, and a good ticket was nominated.[6]

When Senator Conkling returned from abroad in October, he pitched into the campaign with a ready will. He had three objectives in taking a major part in the canvass. He wished to counter the abuse and criticism directed at the Grant administration, not excusing its derelictions but pointing proudly to what he considered its chief accomplishments. He wished to slow down the surge of popular acclaim for Governor Tilden; the latter had added to his Tweed Ring renown by cracking down hard at the outset of his administration on the upstate Canal Ring, and his reformer reputation was growing apace. Finally, with the "no third term" movement clearly having removed Grant from further consideration, Conkling planned now to run for president in 1876, and a victory in New York in the face of the odds against it would add impetus to his candidacy.

Tilden was drawing immense crowds when he appeared during the campaign, but all would of course have to make way for the Empire State's champion orator, the senator from Utica. Conkling's first appearance, before a densely packed gathering in Albany, took place on October 18, and he treated his listeners to a "clear exposition of the reform movement and the characters most prominently connected therewith." With Conkling's known views on reformers, it is not astonishing that he gave the movement short shrift. He dwelt also upon "honest money and the safety of the free schools," and he occasioned "much speculation and surprise" when he said nothing about the third term, though why this should have surprised any knowledgable reporter is not clear.[7]

The Albany speech set the tone for Conkling's tour and reinvigorated the Republican hosts. An active contest followed, and even Conkling ad-

[6] N.Y. *Times,* Sept. 9, 1875. For full convention coverage, see Sept. 3–9.
[7] *Ibid.,* Oct. 19. When Tilden learned that Conkling planned to exert himself in the campaign, he endeavored to recruit Kernan and Horatio Seymour to do the same. Tilden to F. Kernan, Oct. 12, 1875, Kernan Papers.

mitted that "the personalities and scandals of this campaign are too general and numerous to be followed." The senator was the party's greatest asset in New York State, though he tried to deflect the credit to Cornell, and he spent himself to the utmost in this canvass.[8]

Though the Republicans started out the campaign with everything against them, the election of November 2 was a success. Though they lost the state-wide contests narrowly, they regained control of the state senate and the assembly. For this surprising outcome, the stump-speaking of Roscoe Conkling, which even *The Nation* saluted on October 28 as "the bright blade of his eloquence with its keen satiric edge," must be given major credit.

The Forty-fourth Congress convened for its first session on December 6, 1875, and the nation could watch for the first time in many years how the Democratic party could handle a majority in one house of Congress. The Senate, still Republican, had convened for its customary special session from March 5 to March 24, but this had produced little of note, except the appearance as the new senator from Tennessee of former President Andrew Johnson. There were several notable newcomers on that March 5, Kernan replacing Fenton of New York; Ambrose E. Burnside of Rhode Island in place of the despised Sprague; Blanche K. Bruce, a shy, quiet black man representing the state of Mississippi; and Isaac P. Christiancy of Michigan, who had sidetracked Zach Chandler. All eyes, however, were focused on Johnson as he strode into the chamber where he had been tried for high crimes and misdemeanors seven years earlier. Older but otherwise unchanged and as fearless and doughty as ever, he marched forward with firm step to take his seat. Among those who remained from his foes in that day past, O. P. Morton and John Sherman shook the hand of the former president, but Roscoe Conkling buried himself in a letter, only glancing at Johnson from the corner of his eye.[9]

Johnson during the special session delivered one lengthy and vigorous speech on the Louisiana question, giving notice to one and all that he returned to Washington not as a colorless elder statesman but as a de-

---

[8] Conkling to Sidney Fairchild, Oct. 31, 1875, Charles S. Fairchild Papers; Conkling to Pierrepont, Nov. 8, 1875, Pierrepont Papers.

[9] G. F. Milton, *Age of Hate*, p. 670. Burnside was the incompetent general who led the Union army into a catastrophic defeat at Fredericksburg. His major contribution to American culture was giving his name (slightly revised) to a type of whiskers.

termined and hardy partisan who had lost none of his storied zest for battle. However, he passed away during the summer, and his supporters had to be content with the vindication of his return to the Senate.

Thomas W. Ferry of Michigan, the president pro tem, had another sad announcement to make, that of the death of Vice-President Henry Wilson, the "Cobbler of Natick," a long-time laborer in the Whig and Republican vineyards, a fair and respected presiding officer, his long record scarred only by involvement with Credit Mobilier. For those who had their eyes on the counting of the electoral votes a year hence, it meant that Ferry had been elevated to the constitutional position of the person who "shall, in the presence of the Senate and House of Representatives, open all certificates."

Once again, the Senate, well aware of the imperfections in the applicable methods of counting electoral votes, struggled with the problem. Unhappily, Roscoe Conkling's part, though he said that "nobody is more thoroughly convinced than I am of the impropriety of the twenty-second joint rule, of the peril of that rule, of the objections to it," consisted primarily of waiting for someone else to come up with a new scheme. "Any plan of arriving at a true solution of it," he said, "shall have my vote always." [10] With the House of Representatives now Democratic, chances of achieving effective action were now more remote than ever, and nothing was done, except that the Senate failed to renew the twenty-second joint rule. By inaction, the members of Congress sowed a seed from which they would reap a frightening harvest.

With the presidential election coming on, the election which Democrats confidently expected to turn over to them the White House and full control of Congress, there was not much in the way of major legislative achievement in the session which ran on into August. There was a full quota of electioneering speeches, of course. Democrats shouted and hallooed about the iniquities of the Grant administration, the corruption and falsity of the president's chief ministers, the so-called power-hunger of the chief executive and his military clique, the brutal terrorization of the South, and the despair and hard times of the nation. The Republicans hit at their opponents for their inflationary fiscal schemes, for their connivance in Southern brutality toward the black man, and, again and again, for the whole panoply of crimes connected with the Rebellion. 1876 was to be one of the last and most vehement examples of that good Republican exercise known as "waving the bloody shirt."

[10] *Cong. Rec.,* 44th Cong., 1st sess., p. 603, Jan. 25, 1876.

Though it was Blaine in the House who carried this on in the crudest manner, examples of this questionable form of debate flourished in the upper chamber as well. Witness Roscoe Conkling, in an otherwise insignificant passage with Maxey of Texas on a Rivers and Harbors bill, trumpeting suddenly of "the hour when half a continent, including Texas, stood under the uplifted banners of revolt." [11]

The bloody shirt, though, served the Republicans as a mask, besides being an electoral device. By ascribing to the present-day Democratic party all the vices of slavery and rebellion, the Republican could cover up the fact that there was really little difference between the parties on current issues. As Reconstruction drew slowly to a close, both parties were more and more in thrall to major economic interests—to the railroads, to burgeoning industry, and to the big money-men who financed them. To avoid talking about these facts, political campaigns tended to focus on extrinsic issues, a development in which the public press generally cooperated.

[11] *Ibid.*, p. 4657, July 17, 1876.

CHAPTER 15

CONKLING FOR PRESIDENT—
AND AFTER

A presidential election in which there is no incumbent running always seems to have an additional measure of excitement and interest; perhaps it is the assured knowledge that there is to be a change at the helm of the nation, perhaps just the injection of new and (hopefully) fresh faces into the American political consciousness. Such a year was 1876; the widespread feeling against an additional term for President Grant had finally resulted in his being taken out of consideration, and a myriad of candidates sprang up to replace him.

Observers felt they knew who the Democratic nominee would be. A governor of New York, the largest state and the largest bloc of electoral votes, had always to be considered a potent factor at a nominating convention, and when that governor was also a strong figure with a nation-wide reputation as a reformer in a year when the desire for reform was considered very strong, he had to be rated a strong contender for the nomination. Thus, Tilden, who was also considered safe by the large financial and business interests of the East, stood out above his party colleagues as the probable Democratic candidate.

With the Republicans, matters were not so sure. With Grant out of the running, there appeared to be four major candidates and probably at least three "favorite sons." Of the major possibilities, Conkling and Oliver P. Morton would most likely share and divide the administration support, former Speaker James G. Blaine was the favorite of the non-Grant regulars, together with his own developing "Blaine Legion" of devotees, and Treasury Secretary Bristow was clearly marking out as his own the reform element of the party. The possible favorite sons were Governor John F. Hartranft of Pennsylvania, Governor Rutherford B. Hayes of Ohio, and Postmaster General Marshall Jewell of Connecticut. It promised to be an interesting struggle.

229

Blaine, of course, was the breezy ex-newspaperman from Maine, the "magnetic" man, the man of whom George Frisbie Hoar said, "There has never been a man in our history upon whom so few people looked with indifference. He was born to be loved or hated. Nobody occupied a middle ground as to him." [1] Blaine had increased his contacts with the interests of money and capital, and he had, too, augmented his own fortune in what some people felt was a remarkable degree. Blaine appeared to most observers to be the front-runner for the nomination.

Though Conkling hated Blaine, he had little better feeling toward Morton. Morton in turn detested Conkling and had long been suspicious of the New Yorker's influence with the president. The two senators worked for Grant and the administration on the floor, but on parallel tracks rather than in harmony. When Conkling on occasion engaged Morton in debate in the Senate, the barbs and bitter sarcasm of his words demonstrated his true feelings toward the Hoosier senator. Whitelaw Reid once called Morton "an unprincipled demagogue, of large ability and utter unscrupulousness," while Blaine thought him "extremely ambitious and selfish" with neither moral nor political principle.[2] Morton had been a powerful and successful governor of Indiana through the Civil War, and he had, like Conkling, promptly assumed a leading place in the Senate when he entered that body in 1867. He was conceded by all to be financially honest and unswayed by material things, but his bold, audacious, and forceful conduct of Senate business made him few friends. His position on currency matters was considerably softer than that of Conkling and most easterners, and his health was a factor to be considered in the contest for the nomination. He had suffered a paralytic stroke in 1865, from which he had never recovered. His presence in the race would split and weaken the influence of the administration and its followers, to the joint detriment of himself and Conkling.

The other serious candidate, besides Roscoe Conkling, was Bristow. His was a name hardly known outside his native Kentucky until less than a year previous, but his prosecution of the Whiskey Ring and his call for honesty in government led to an instant boom for him of some

---

[1] Hoar, I, 200.

[2] Cortissoz, I, 145; Nevins, *Fish*, II, 495. Even Zach Chandler felt that Morton was on all sides of the leading issues at once, and John Hay wrote, "The nomination of Morton is positively dreaded by the best men in the party." Hay to Blaine, Jan. 27, 1876, Blaine Papers.

proportions. The Bristow candidacy was remarkable for the fact that it was driven almost completely by what he stood for and not by the person or personality of the candidate. Though the secretary was honest and intelligent, he was not the man to capture the imagination of the people by any personal force or attraction. He was large and broad-shouldered, with piercing eyes; he wore his hair short, maintained a closely cropped beard and a drooping mustache. He was forty-four years old, a true son of the border, and the possessor of a creditable military record in the war. With his short but brilliant record in the cabinet, he stood out as an honest man who would fight for the honesty of the government, and in 1876 that was enough to make Benjamin H. Bristow a serious candidate for president.[3]

Roscoe Conkling had once spoken of the "hot-house air in the Senate which breeds candidates for the Presidency, but makes them past bearing, and kills them off before they get their growth." [4] But that was said at a time when he had no thought himself of running for the office; in 1876 he was in the struggle and he must avoid being killed off before he got *his* growth. His first task was to get the state of New York behind him.

Tom Platt later said, "I made it my pleasure and task to so help to organize the Empire State Republicans, that we might have a solid delegation for Conkling." In this regard the comment of the *Times,* that Conkling, like many presidential candidates, had "more to dread from his superserviceable friends than from his opponents," might be noted.[5]

March 22, at Syracuse, was established as the time for the state convention to select delegates-at-large to the national convention and to give to the delegation whatever instructions might be found desirable. To work up to this, of course, district meetings had to be held and district delegates chosen. The organization made sure that these were Conkling meetings which chose Conkling delegates. One of the earliest of them was a meeting of the Utica Conkling Club on March 2, where the speaker spoke of the hometown favorite "in the full maturity and plen-

---

[3] For Bristow, see Nevins, *Fish,* II, 716; C. Judah and G. W. Smith, *The Unchosen,* pp. 51, 55–60. As secretary of the treasury, Bristow had even put into effect a reduction in force at the New York Custom House, which had been bitterly deplored by Chester Arthur; for example, see letter of Arthur to Bristow, Jan. 16, 1875, Arthur Papers, New-York Historical Society.

[4] *Cong. Globe,* 42d Cong., 2d sess., p. 356, Jan. 11, 1872.

[5] Platt, p. 72; N.Y. *Times,* March 2, 1876.

itude of his powers, with a most commanding presence and a robust physique, fortified and preserved by a life of temperance," compared him favorably with Choate, Clay, and Webster, and called him "the acknowledged leader of a great party, its most sturdy champion, and its ablest and most uncompromising defender." [6]

A hitch developed, though, when, on March 9, the Union League Club of New York, a blue-blooded, relatively liberal, and definitely non-Conkling Republican organization, passed resolutions denouncing the plan to send an instructed delegation to the national convention at Cincinnati as "a gross violation of the first principles of republican institutions." The delegation, they said, must be "wholly unpacked and unpledged . . . and free to choose from among all the candidates who may be brought before the convention." Their resolutions called for "a President who shall be deservedly recognized as a reformer as well as a Republican." This was obviously not Conkling.[7]

The action of the Union League Club struck a responsive chord with Republicans all over the state, and sentiment grew against instructing a united delegation in favor of Conkling. Cornell did not help the senator's cause when he sent Conkling a wire, which shortly became very public, calling the Union League Club declarations "impudent." [8]

Nevertheless, the district meetings, filled in many instances by custom-house workers, letter carriers, and other patronage employees, did on the whole select pro-Conkling delegates, both to Syracuse and to Cincinnati. But things were just not going as they should have. More and more the press and Republican groups were talking about an unpledged delegation, although urged to give Roscoe Conkling strong consideration for the presidency. The *Times* made the intolerable assertion that "hardly any of his friends suppose that he had the slightest possible chance of securing the prize," and that "when he is out of the question," the delegates would still have to look around at the other contenders.[9]

The newspapers, shortly before the Syracuse gathering, reported that ex-governors Dix and Morgan were one with Curtis and the Union League crowd in opposing a pledged delegation. There was considerable speculation that Conkling wanted a pledged delegation, not with any real expectation of receiving the nomination, but as a bargaining counter to be thrown at the appropriate moment to that candidate (always excluding Blaine) who would promise Conkling continued control over the

[6] A. R. Conkling, pp. 495–496.   [7] N.Y. *Times,* March 10, 1876.
[8] *Ibid.,* March 19.   [9] *Ibid.,* March 19.

federal patronage of New York. The final *Times* dispatch from Syracuse before the convention said, "The Republican State Convention which meets in this city tomorrow will be completely in the hands of the friends of Sen. Conkling, and yet it is probably perfectly safe to say that a majority of the members of that body, if left to themselves, would prefer to indorse some other Republican as their candidate for President of the United States."

When the convention met, it chose Alonzo B. Cornell as the head of the delegation to Cincinnati and it selected other pro-Conkling delegates-at-large. In the face of a long anti-Conkling speech by George William Curtis, rebutted by Congressman Elbridge G. Lapham, the assemblage faltered as far as instructions were concerned. The resolution which was finally adopted read: "We present Roscoe Conkling to the National Republican Convention as our choice for President. We give assurance that the nomination of our candidate will secure beyond question the thirty-five electoral votes of New York for the Republican electoral ticket." [10]

Far from an instruction to the delegates, to disobey at their peril, as a mere "presentation" of Conkling to the convention the resolution was open to the interpretation, which Curtis quickly seized upon, that it was not even a request to vote for the senator but left every delegate free to do as he pleased. In truth, as the *Times* pointed out editorially, the convention at Syracuse was "a very hollow victory, which every shrewd observer will recognize as a substantial defeat." The paper further said that the party had shown itself "at last ready to cast off the shackles of self-appointed managers." Perhaps so; perhaps the increasingly noisy opposition to Conkling in his home state dated from this showing at Syracuse that a state convention, apparently so composed as to do his bidding, was not willing to go down the line for Conkling for president.

Why did Conkling not succeed at Syracuse as he should have? The delegates were mostly his people, or ostensibly so, but his managers could not keep them in line. Grant's unpopularity, the remoteness of Conkling's possible nomination, the idea of the senator's ulterior purpose in binding the delegation, the public and press clamor for a reformer; all these were involved, but possibly it was a secret resentment at the senator's domination or inability to visualize the proud, sneering, quarreling Roscoe Conkling as president of the United States.

The Syracuse convention was a positive hindrance to the Conkling

10 Platt, p. 72.

people when they went after delegates in other states. New Yorkers could hardly point to it as a sign that his home state was solidly behind the senator, and outsiders mentioned it as an illustration of the result of Conkling's policies and politics through the years.

Conkling became increasingly aggravated at Morton's candidacy. It was clear that Grant intended to take no position between the two, and Conkling felt cheated of the administration support that should have been his. Probably the president hoped for Conkling's success, but as he was unable to put this private desire into any kind of positive action it made not the least difference. Morton, too, garnered a larger share of the Southern carpetbagger delegates than Conkling, and here again the proud New Yorker felt that he was deprived of votes which were rightfully his. Morton was reaping the harvest of his years of total support of the Southern Republicans in every situation, no matter what its merits; Conkling's backing had been qualified on occasion by constitutional, legal, or ethical scruples. In the spring, Conkling complained to the two New Yorkers in the cabinet, Attorney General Edwards Pierrepont (a Conkling follower) and Fish, that he was receiving no help from the administration and that he had never received the proper amount of patronage. This was clearly petulance resulting from the continued Morton campaign. But Morton was going to stay in the race.[11]

What of the other candidates? Ohio on March 29 instructed its delegation for Governor Hayes, but he professed disinterest as to the nomination one way or the other: "I have discountenanced all efforts at organization, or management in my interest. I have said the whole talk about me is on the score of availability. Let availability do the work then." [12]

Bristow's campaign had to consist of picking and snatching delegates here and there, wherever there was sentiment for thoroughgoing reform (which, of course, meant only unyielding honesty in government, not any kind of social or economic reform). The revulsion against Grantism was so great that Bristow was able to appear a grave threat to the more orthodox politicos in the race. Bristow's campaign manager, future Supreme Court Justice John Marshall Harlan, wrote to him on January 24 that "Blaine cannot be nominated—nor can Conkling—nor can Morton" and that the choice would be between Bristow and Hayes.[13]

11 Nevins, *Fish,* II, 827.   12 T. H. Williams, ed., *Hayes,* pp. 15–16.
13 H. Barnard, *Rutherford B. Hayes,* p. 281.

More realistic observers felt that Blaine was ahead and gaining on the number of votes needed to insure his nomination. However, Blaine had stirred up a hornets' nest in the House, of which he stood to be the chief victim. On January 10, he proposed an amendment to a comprehensive amnesty bill, excepting from its operation Jefferson Davis, and used this amendment as a hook upon which to hang a vigorous harangue arraigning Davis for the "atrocities" at Andersonville prison, with all the gory and ghastly detail he could wring from the subject. It was bloody-shirt waving at its crudest and most irresponsible, and it threw the Democrats into transports of rage. It was a strong indication of the type of presidential campaign that could be expected from Blaine, and the Democrats were anxious to injure him if the opportunity arose. Unluckily for Blaine, some unsavory dealings from his own past soon made this possible, combined with the covert activities of the partisans of one of his rivals.

As it developed, Blaine had been involved in some discreditable transactions with certain railroad securities in 1869, when he had been Speaker of the House. He made handsome profits on the sale of bonds of the Little Rock and Ft. Smith Railroad to friends, after he had aided the road by a ruling from the chair on a land-grant bill in the House. When it developed that the securities were virtually worthless, Blaine stood in great danger of exposure for his part in swindling his friends, until suddenly the Union Pacific and two other railroads took him off the hook by purchasing the bonds at heavily inflated prices, thus obligating the Maine statesman to those interests.

Early in April 1876, rumblings about these transactions were heard about Washington, and when a news report alleged Blaine's involvement in the affairs of the Little Rock and Ft. Smith, the congressman took the floor of the House and, with a sweeping denial, branded the whole story as untrue. This was supposed to quiet the stir, but it did not. A newspaper friend of Hayes in Chicago heard of the existence of certain incriminating correspondence, the "Mulligan letters," so named because James Mulligan, a former partner in the Boston brokerage firm through which the sales had been handled, had lifted the letters from the files of the firm. Handling the story delicately, lest the blame for leaking it should fall upon his candidate, the Hayes man managed to have the story published through the New York *Sun,* and Blaine never connected Hayes with it. Indeed, he thought Bristow responsible. An investigation was initiated by the House, and Mulligan, complete with letters, was called to testify. Just before he began, a Blaine man on the committee pleaded illness and requested adjournment to the morrow.

That afternoon, Blaine met in a hotel room with Mulligan, Warren Fisher (the addressee of the letters), and a Union Pacific director, to plead for the return of the letters. When this was refused, Blaine asked to be allowed to see them, on the promise to return them. This Mulligan agreed to, but when Blaine got his hands on them, he reneged on his promise and refused to give them back. He refused also the demand of the House investigation committee to see the letters.

Some days later he rose in the House to a question of personal privilege. He denounced the investigation as a retaliation for his recent attack upon the Rebellion. He invoked the inviolability of private correspondence. Then, with a striking gesture, he said:

I have defied the power of the House to compel me to produce those letters. . . . But . . . I am not afraid to show the letters. Thank God Almighty, I am not ashamed to show them. There they are! [Holding them over his head] There is the very original package. And with some sense of humiliation, with a mortification I do not pretend to conceal, with a sense of outrage I think any man in my position would feel, I invite the confidence of forty-four million of my countrymen while I read those letters from this desk.

The leading Republican candidate for the presidential nomination then proceeded to read from the letters, in part, at random, omitting large chunks, so that the reading gave a quite erroneous impression of the contents of the whole. Blaine closed his speech with a cheap and sharp theatrical trick at the expense of the chairman of the committee investigating him, and sat down, to great applause. This all took place on June 4, and, with the Cincinnati convention only nine days away, perhaps Blaine had succeeded in muffling the attack.[14]

To top everything off, on the Sunday following his effort in the House, Blaine collapsed on the steps of his church in Washington and was rushed to the hospital. It was a very dramatic swoon, but there was nothing seriously wrong with him.

The effect that all of this had on Blaine's candidacy is problematical;

[14] The complex story of the Mulligan Letters can be followed in C. E. Russell, pp. 275–310, and D. S. Muzzey, *James G. Blaine*, pp. 83–98. The June 5 speech, with other excerpts from the record, is in a pamphlet found in the Blaine Papers. After this episode, there were multitudes who never trusted Blaine again for the rest of his political life. It was similar to the feeling many people have shared about Richard Nixon since disclosure of his secret fund in 1952, the Checkers speech, and his red-baiting campaigns of the same era.

perhaps it did not cost him any of his first-ballot votes at the convention, but the attack upon his honesty, which acute observers could see was not really explained away, probably slowed down the accretion of additional votes. Hayes, who was everyone's choice for second spot on the ticket, wrote a friend that he would not run with Blaine, "a man whose record as an upright public man is to be in question—to be defended from beginning to end." [15] And the Bristow men, the reform element, would find it distasteful to swing over to one whose personal honesty was so questionable.

An element which had been overlooked but which started to play a considerable importance as the delegates gathered in Cincinnati was the site of the convention. The Queen City of the West had originally been sought as the host by the backers of Morton and Bristow, for the benefits that proximity to their respective home bases would bring. As it developed, Cincinnati was Hayes's home town, and the governor received a great amount of publicity, both in the newspapers and by word of mouth, in and around the convention site which he never could have received elsewhere. This, one of his biographers maintains, conditioned the delegates to their eventual acceptance of him. [16]

Cincinnati, the old capital of the Northwest Territory, a major manufacturing and transport center whose primacy was slowly slipping away, the home of a large and industrious German populace, welcomed in June 1876 the delegates and workers, the leaders and the hangers-on, of the Republican party. The party, virtually supreme in the country for over a decade and a half, knew that its position was sorely threatened and that a mighty effort would be required to retain the White House in November. That effort had to start in Cincinnati.

The candidate picture was still jumbled as the delegates gathered. Blaine was still considered the leader, but his friends wondered, with Governor Kirkwood of Iowa, "Will Blaine come out of the fire unscorched?" [17] There now seemed to be four major candidates—Blaine, Bristow, Morton, and Conkling—and one, Hayes, who was somewhere between a major contender and a favorite son. Hartranft and Jewell were dismissed easily, but Hayes was not. Former Governor Edward F. Noyes of Ohio was on the spot and managing the campaign for Hayes, with the help of Senator John Sherman, and moving so well that Hayes was soon considered the second choice of a large number of delegates.

[15] June 14, 1876, C. R. Williams, ed., *Diary and Letters of Hayes*, III, 325.
[16] H. J. Eckenrode, *R. B. Hayes*, pp. 121–122. [17] Barnard, p. 287.

Chester Arthur arrived with some of the Conkling supporters on June 8, and took over the Grand Hotel for the New York delegation. Only the most presentable members of the organization, it was said, were permitted to come to Cincinnati. Conkling himself, who had never attended a national convention, stayed away from this one too, but left his interests in the hands of Arthur and Cornell. Blue Conkling badges were handed out to all takers at the hotel, a brass band played stirring airs, and the New Yorkers paraded in the streets and in the hotel lobbies. "The machine is in the very best working order," wrote a reporter. A huge banner was strung across the street in front of the hotel, reading: "ROSCOE CONKLING'S NOMINATION ASSURES THE THIRTY-FIVE ELECTORAL VOTES OF NEW YORK." In the meantime, Arthur and the New York leaders spent their time talking to delegates, primarily from the South and the West, pleading, bargaining, seeking votes or promises of support. With Tilden's nomination by the Democrats almost assured, New York's large bloc of electoral votes was put in jeopardy, and Conkling's men told the delegates that only Conkling could keep Tilden from sweeping the state. Unfortunately, people kept pointing to the Syracuse convention, throwing doubt upon even this claim. Though his managers worked hard, they made little headway in the pre-convention maneuvering. The Conkling people professed great confidence of success on the third or fourth ballot, but they were unable to point out to skeptical questioners where they expected their additional strength to come from.[18]

Two days before the convention opened, it was reported that Blaine was dead if he did not win on the first or second ballot, that Morton's votes would fall to Conkling, that Cameron and Logan had made deals to throw Pennsylvania and Illinois to Conkling, and that the only one who might beat the New Yorker was Hayes. All this was apparently reaction to the admiration and fear stirred up by the smooth operation of the Conkling organization. The next day, it was said that Conkling "has shot a little to the front." On June 14, however, the day the convention opened, the *Times* reporter, having found that Pennsylvania was *not* coming over, said, "Mr. Conkling is practically out of the Convention." Indeed, the opposition from back home was plaguing him again;

[18] Howe, pp. 56–57; Alexander, III, 333; N.Y. *Times,* June 12, 1876. In an effort to attract the Ohio votes, there was even a New York singing group, entertaining with a ditty that ran,

"Conkling and Hayes
  Is the ticket that pays."

Needless to say, it didn't; Barnard, p. 289.

just before the start of the convention, Theodore Roosevelt of New York City, father of a future president, on behalf of a Republican reform delegation instructed "to fight Conkling at all events," made a vivid speech against the senator from the balcony of the Gibson House. This certainly weakened Conkling further.[19]

At noon on the 14th, Edwin D. Morgan, the national chairman, called the convention to order in Exposition Hall, a huge barn of a building, and on the 15th, the gathering prepared for nominating speeches for the candidates. Stewart Woodford, the best orator in the Conkling camp outside the senator himself, was chosen to make the speech presenting Roscoe Conkling to the delegates. His speech was a good, workmanlike effort, but nothing exciting:

Broad in culture, eloquent in debate, wise in council, fearless in leadership, and as true to the old Republican party as the needle to the pole—Roscoe Conkling needs no defense nor eulogy. He is a positive quantity in our politics . . . the faithful and true friend of Ulysses S. Grant. . . . Give us a candidate with whom and under whom we can achieve victory; that means honesty in finance, loyalty in government and absolute protection to the lowliest and humblest under the flag of our fathers.

"Let us not nominate with our hearts," he said, "but with our heads." Not for Roscoe Conkling, "but for the ideas of the Republican party; for the cause." [20] He was politely applauded, but not a word of it was remembered. Besides, Woodford was following a tough act, one of the great convention speeches of our history.

After Bristow had been nominated, Colonel Robert G. Ingersoll, one of the country's most famous orators, a lawyer, lecturer, and agnostic (not necessarily in that order), took the rostrum a few moments before Woodford, to place Blaine in nomination. Ingersoll knew how to work up a gathering like this one, and as he proceeded he grappled his listeners to him in a thrall of excitement. The people, he said:

demand a statesman; they demand a reformer after as well as before the election . . . a man of superb moral courage. . . . They demand a man whose political reputation is as spotless as a star; but they do not demand that their candidate shall have a certificate of moral character signed by a confederate congress. The man who has, in full, heaped and rounded measure, all these splendid qualifications, is the present grand and gallant

[19] N.Y. *Times,* June 13, 14, 15, 1876. V. L. Shores, "The Hayes-Conkling Controversy," p. 248, quoting the Springfield *Republican,* Oct. 18, 1877.

[20] *Official Proceedings of the Republican National Conventions of 1868, 1872, 1876, and 1880* (hereafter just *Proceedings*), pp. 297–298.

leader of the Republican party—James G. Blaine. [The people of the nation] call for the man who has torn from the throat of treason the tongue of slander—for the man who has snatched the mask of Democracy from the hideous face of rebellion; for this man who, like an intellectual athlete, has stood in the arena of debate and challenged all comers, and who is still a total stranger to defeat. Like an armed warrior, like a plumed knight, James G. Blaine marched down the halls of the American Congress and threw his shining lance full and fair against the brazen foreheads of the defamers of his country and the maligners of his honor.

In the name of the Republic, in the name of her soldiers living and dead, in the name of those who perished in the prison camps at Andersonville and Libby, Ingersoll called for the nomination of "that prince of parliamentarians—that leader of leaders," James G. Blaine.[21]

The rafters rang with the cheers! Men pounded each other on the back and said it was the greatest thing they had ever heard. Though it was hard to recognize Blaine in it, it was a mighty speech, belonging, as a convention speech, probably in a class with Conkling in 1880, Bryan in 1896, and McCarthy in 1960. If the voting had started that day, Blaine's chances might have improved strikingly. But the lighting system in the hall failed—Blaine men spoke darkly of sabotage—and the convention was adjourned to the following day. The other camps had a chance to regroup their forces, and Ingersoll's oratorical triumph wore off.

When the delegates came together to ballot, the general expectation was that Blaine would be in the lead. He was, with 285 votes, far ahead of Morton's 124, Bristow's 113, and the 99 for Roscoe Conkling. Hayes had 61, Hartranft 58, Jewell 11 (for the first ballot only; he received no votes thereafter), and 3 for Congressman William A. Wheeler of upstate New York.[22] On the second ballot, Blaine went up to 296, but the other men held relatively firm; Conkling slid to 93. On the third, Blaine declined to 293, Bristow with 121 passed Morton as he fell off to 113, and Conkling totaled only 90. On the fourth ballot, Blaine again declined, with 292, Bristow picked up to 126, a gain but not enough of one, Morton and Conkling fell off farther, while the favorite sons,

[21] Col. R. G. Ingersoll's Famous Speeches Complete, pp. 116–120; Proceedings, pp. 295–296. Ingersoll's oratory was as vivid but not as stately as that of Roscoe Conkling.

[22] Conkling's first ballot votes were spread as follows: 1 each from California, Michigan, Mississippi, and Missouri; 2 from Nevada; 3 each from Florida, Texas, and Virginia; 7 from North Carolina; 8 from Georgia; and 69 out of 70 from New York. George William Curtis voted for Bristow.

Hartranft and Hayes, were holding firm at 71 and 68 respectively. The break came on the fifth ballot; Zach Chandler switched Michigan's 22 votes to Hayes and, with some additional gains from the other candidates, the Ohio governor surged. On the sixth ballot, the trend was becoming very clear, as Hayes, everyone's second choice, pulled closer to Blaine. Before the seventh ballot, Indiana switched to Hayes as Morton withdrew; Conkling, Platt said, "knew it was all up with him then." [23] Shortly thereafter, Harlan withdrew Bristow's name (without authorization and against Bristow's wishes, as it turned out, but it would have made little difference); no one took the trouble to withdraw Conkling, but he received no votes on the seventh ballot anyway. Of the New York 70, 61 switched to Hayes (9 went to Blaine), as the Ohio governor was nominated with 384 to Blaine's 351; Bristow still received 21 votes to the end.[24]

Because the big bloc of New York votes had ultimately nominated Hayes, the Ohio men wanted a New Yorker for the vice-presidential slot. The majority of the delegation wanted Woodford, and Platt placed his name in nomination. The anti-Conkling people, however, pushed for Wheeler, the congressman from Malone in the far northern part of the state, and a long-time opponent of Conkling. Luke Poland of Vermont nominated Wheeler, and he took an immediate and sizable lead on the first ballot. New York hastily withdrew Woodford, but it was still a galling defeat.[25]

[23] Platt, p. 75. This seems doubtful; probably at this point things were happening so rapidly that Conkling, back in New York, was unable to keep up with events.

[24] For the details of the voting, see McClure, p. 249, and *Proceedings,* pp. 304 to 327, which gives the individual state totals on each ballot as well as the interruptions and squabbles during the balloting.

[25] Eckenrode, whose intense historical animosity toward Conkling shines brightly through his biography of Hayes, tells an unlikely story related by Webb Hayes, the nominee's son, who was allegedly present (p. 135). When the New Yorkers were told they could have the vice-presidential nomination, they jokingly bandied it about among themselves, saying, "Take it, Chet," "You take it, Cornell," and finally, "Let's give it to Wheeler." This story completely overlooks the Woodford candidacy. Besides, Wheeler was no intimate of the organization. It was said that Wheeler was once told by Conkling, "Wheeler, if you will act with us, there is nothing in the gift of the State of New York to which you may not reasonably aspire." Wheeler answered, "Mr. Conkling, there is nothing in the gift of the State of New York which will compensate me for the forfeiture of my self-respect." The Wheeler colloquy with Conkling is recited by Allan Nevins in his foreword to the Inaugural Edition of John F. Kennedy's *Profiles in Courage* (New York: Harper and Row, 1961).

Thus ended the only effort of Roscoe Conkling for the highest office in the land. Platt said that Conkling "took his defeat much to heart." He could take cold comfort from the fact that his great enemy Blaine had not won, that Morton, who never should have been in the race, had not won, that Bristow, who had defamed the administration of which he had been part, had not won. He knew little about Hayes. He wired Cornell at Cincinnati, that he had "just heard of the nomination of Gov. Hayes and deem it good and wise." He thanked his friends for their efforts in his behalf. But it was still to him a shocking thing.[26]

The Democrats, as expected, nominated Tilden, and the nation settled back to examine the two candidates and await the campaign. Tilden the people knew something about. They knew that he had routed Tweed and, as governor of New York, was cleaning up the infamous Canal Ring. They knew that he was a dry, rich, corporation lawyer, and a bachelor. They chuckled when they heard Bob Ingersoll go after Tilden: "Think of a man surrounded by beautiful women, dimpled cheeks, coral lips, pearly teeth, shining eyes; think of a man throwing them all away for the embrace of the Democratic party. Such a man does not even know the value of time." [27]

They knew a good bit about Tilden; they did not know anything about Hayes, to whom Curtis wrote "Your nomination at this juncture is as fortunate for the country as that of Mr. Lincoln in 1860." [28] Who was he? What kind of a man was he? How had the Republican party, with all of its famous men, nominated him for the presidency?

Rutherford Birchard Hayes was born in Ohio in 1822, educated at a Connecticut prep school, Kenyon College, and Harvard Law School. He practiced law and Whig politics in Lower Sandusky (now Fremont) and Cincinnati, got into Republican politics, and served four years in the Union army in the war, receiving a commission as a major and leaving the service as a major general. Hayes was wounded five times, once seriously, and spent most of the war in the unglamorous campaigns of western Virginia. He was elected to Congress in 1864, while away in the

[26] Platt, pp. 75–76; N.Y. *Times,* June 17, 1876. The *Times* said that Cornell was "perhaps the only disappointed man in Ohio tonight," while even Arthur was now "one of Gov. Hayes' most enthusiastic supporters." This may be taken with a grain of salt.

[27] Speech at Indianapolis, Sept. 21, 1876, in Ingersoll, *Famous Speeches,* p. 148.

[28] Milne, p. 151.

army, and re-elected in 1866. He voted with the radicals in Congress, but he said little and was hardly noticed; he himself felt that Roscoe Conkling was one of "the noticeable men on our side of the house." In 1867, Hayes returned to Ohio to start a string of victories over the best Democratic vote-getters in the state; he was elected governor in 1867 over Thurman; he won re-election in 1869 over Congressman George Pendleton; and in a political comeback in 1875 he toppled the very popular Governor William Allen. In the interim, he was soundly beaten for a congressional seat in Cincinnati in 1872, refused Grant's appointment as assistant secretary of the treasury for the Cincinnati district in 1873, and shortly thereafter moved back to Fremont. He declined in 1873 to oppose John Sherman for re-election to the Senate, even though he was promised a majority, and, by so doing, he earned Sherman's gratitude and able assistance at the 1876 convention.[29]

Hayes was not religious, though he was a lifelong church-goer, a strong temperance man, and appeared to people to be very pious. He never joined a church. He had political principles, but he was willing to let them go if the majority ruled against him. Though he hoped that the Republican party would be ranged on the side of right, he would stick by the party even if wrong. He wrote, in March, 1875, "I do not sympathize with a large share of the party leaders. I hate the corruptionists of whom Butler is leader. I doubt the ultra measures relating to the South, and I am opposed to the course of Gen. Grant on the 3d term, the Civil Service, and the appointment of unfit men on partisan or personal grounds." [30]

Yet the Republican party, most of its leaders never suspecting that Hayes harbored such views, nominated him for president. Conkling had been unhappy with the outcome of the Cincinnati convention, to be sure, but this feeling would have been greatly compounded had he known the nominee was writing to George William Curtis for advice in the preparation of his letter of acceptance. Curtis recommended "a bold, unequivocal statement" that the civil service system "should be radically reformed." Conkling would have been unhappier still if he had known that Hayes was writing to Carl Schurz on June 27: "I now think as you do—probably precisely as you do—on the civil service reform part of our

---

[29] C. R. Williams, III, 9–10 (letter of Dec. 7, 1865); the best background on Hayes is from Barnard's excellent biography, pp. 211–275; see also Eckenrode, pp. 51–103.

[30] T. H. Williams, ed., p. 2.

platform. I want to make that *the* issue of the canvass—to be perfectly explicit, decided, and square, but *brief* in regard to it."

Schurz egged the governor on with his reply: "To fight for such a programme would, even in case of defeat, be glorious enough. But to succeed with it in the election, as I trust you will, and then faithfully to carry out such a reform, will place him who does it, in the first rank of the best names in American history." [31]

True to his word, Hayes did include a strong and unequivocal statement on civil service reform in his letter of acceptance. But then a curious thing happened. Hayes almost disappeared from the fall campaign. The Republicans had not the least interest in waging the canvass on a civil-service-reform platform; instead, they conducted the last of the virulent "bloody-shirt" campaigns, counterpointed by a vicious series of slanders against Tilden. Zach Chandler had replaced Morgan as national chairman, and Chandler had no intention of listening to Hayes for ideas on how to run the campaign. Hayes decried the macing of officeholders, wrote complacently that "I trust the committee will have nothing to do with it," and sat home in Fremont happily unaware of the vast assessments made and collected.[32]

Sam Tilden directed the Democratic campaign, which concentrated on the scandals of the Republican party under Grant, attacked the Republicans as a party, and practically ignored Hayes. The Republicans, with Ingersoll as their leading spokesman, ignored Hayes too. Ingersoll was too busy with passages like this: "Every man that starved Union soldiers and refused them in the extremity of death a crust was a Democrat. Every man that loved slavery better than liberty was a Democrat. . . . Every man that raised blood-hounds to pursue human beings was a Democrat. Every man that clutched from shrieking, shuddering, crouching mothers babes from their breasts and sold them into slavery was a Democrat." [33]

The Republicans hardly needed good, gray Governor Hayes with rhetoric like that.

Roscoe Conkling had received a letter from Hayes, dated August 15, asking for speeches in at least two or three cities in each of Ohio and Indiana, as well as in Chicago and Milwaukee. "Your speeches in the

[31] Milne, p. 152; C. R. Williams, III, 329–330.
[32] T. H. Williams, ed., pp. 35–36; Eckenrode, pp. 139–151.
[33] Ingersoll, *Famous Speeches,* pp. 121–122.

West," Hayes wrote, "will attract great attention. They will be polished and strengthen us in all parts of the U.S." He referred to Conkling's great Cooper Union speech of 1872, and said, "Your presence here will impart to our canvass life and enthusiasm, and insure that energetic effort which brings out a full vote and commands success." If Conkling would make the speeches requested, "I shall feel that you have placed the country and all of us under great obligations." [34]

Whether Conkling even responded to this or not we do not know; he made only one speech during the campaign, in the Utica Opera House on October 3. He was throughout this late summer and fall suffering from a malarial infection which affected his eyes, and he spent seven weeks in a darkened room. In the speech which he did give, "a sorry attempt, with a screaming voice," as the senator himself said, he made no mention of Hayes, or Wheeler, or civil service reform. He was unhappy with the candidates presented by the Cincinnati convention, he was unhappy with the work of the Saratoga convention in New York, and he was sick.[35]

Saratoga had been a sore disappointment. Conkling, the infection sapping his strength, had been absent, and his cohorts were troubled because they did not know why he was not there. Roscoe, proud of his robust vigor and health, would not advise his political associates of the purely physical weakness creeping over him. The machine's plan had been to push Cornell for governor. Before the convention, the New York reform element had announced the candidacy of William M. Evarts, who was anathema to Conkling. Shortly before the gathering on August 23, it became known that Thurlow Weed, a voice from the past here making his final effort at political management, was pushing the candidacy of former Governor Morgan. Morgan's name caught on quickly, and it became apparent that Evarts might ride to victory over the equiposed forces of Morgan and Cornell. A couple of days before the convention, "great curiosity" was reported "as to whether Sen. Conkling will come to the convention, and what he will do if he does." He did not come, but he could see from a distance the ineptitude of the canvass for Cornell; Arthur, he could see, with his old loyalties to Morgan, his original political patron, was particularly torn. Conkling even required assurance from Arthur that he would support Cornell. So, even though Conkling had been very suspicious of Morgan's indifference regarding his own presi-

[34] C. R. Williams, III, 347.
[35] Conkling to Pierrepont, Oct. 20, 1876, Pierrepont Papers.

dential candidacy, he ordered the Cornell forces to withdraw and support Morgan, in order to insure the defeat of Evarts. Morgan won on the first ballot, with 242 votes to 126 for Evarts. Unfortunately, without further guidance from the senator, Cornell was brought forth as a candidate for lieutenant governor; he then suffered the humiliating defeat he had avoided in the gubernatorial contest. State Senator Sherman S. Rogers of Erie, a reformer and foe of Conkling, was nominated.[36]

One report which should be of interest was the statement of the *Times* reporter in Saratoga on August 23 that Arthur and Sharpe had all along been "secretly opposed" to Cornell; while this rumor may have been founded on nothing more than the very real fact of Arthur's longtime obligation to Morgan, it prefigured the divergence which would arise in Conkling's machine more than four years in the future.

His nephew says that Roscoe Conkling planned four major speeches for the Republican slate during the campaign of 1876; illness prevented him from fulfilling more than one of the projected engagements. Nevertheless, four speeches for a major party figure like Conkling, a close contender for the presidential nomination, was a rather modest total. It is evident that, even without his illness, Roscoe Conkling was not going to put himself out for either the national or state ticket in 1876.

Morgan struggled from the beginning in his canvass. He came under sharp attack from the Democrats because of his obvious connection with Weed (old and toothless bogeymen are still sometimes the best) and because of his business involvement. The Republicans in New York ignored Lucius Robinson, the Democratic candidate, and concentrated their fire upon Tilden. Large sums of money were raised, a great deal of it from Morgan himself, and outside speakers were brought in, but the campaign did not go well without the aid of New York's greatest Republican voice. Morgan was hopeful, but as Election Day approached all could see that his fate depended on the effect of the Tilden campaign.[37]

Nationally, prospects were dark for the Republicans. They had hoped, with their "bloody-shirt" campaign, to carry all the Northern states, thus

[36] Rawley, pp. 254–255; Barrows, pp. 297–298; N.Y. *Times,* July 7 to Aug. 24, 1876. See Arthur's letter to Conkling of July 11, 1876, assuring the senator of his support for Cornell and a bit miffed that he had not heard from Cornell; Arthur Papers, New-York Historical Society.

[37] Rawley, pp. 256–258.

avoiding the need to carry any Southern states at all. In the state election in October, however, the Democrats carried Indiana, defeating Benjamin Harrison for governor. New York was shaky, and the Democrats expected Tilden to carry his home state. Indiana and New York, combined with a solid South, would elect Tilden president. It suddenly became essential to Republican victory to carry the three Southern states still under carpetbag rule—Florida, South Carolina, and Louisiana.

Hayes wrote in his diary that he meant "to go through cheerfully and firmly, and with clean hands." [38] He seemed blissfully unaware of how dirty his party's hands had become to that point, or into what mire they would shortly be thrust.

[38] T. H. Williams, ed., pp. 28–29.

CHAPTER 16

THE STATESMAN
ABOVE THE MIRE

The election looked black for the Republicans as the returns came in. Tilden carried New York by a big margin (Morgan's gubernatorial bid was clearly lost), he carried New Jersey and Connecticut, Indiana as expected went for him, and with the South it appeared that he was the new president. Most Republican newspapers conceded the result before they were put to bed for the night. Zach Chandler, the national chairman, went to sleep; why stay up and listen to more bad news? Late that night, when there appeared to be little more to be done, the New York *Times* received an inquiry from W. H. Barnum, a high official in the Democratic National Committee, asking whether the paper had any figures on South Carolina, Florida, and Louisiana. John Reid, the editor of the *Times,* a man who hated Democrats with a burning passion (he had been a prisoner of the Confederates during the war), quickly calculated that these three states, all of which had been informally conceded to Tilden, could give Hayes an electoral majority of one vote; yet the Democrats themselves were not sure of them!

The late night edition of the *Times* went to press, merely calling the election "doubtful." Reid then started to work, setting out in search of Zach Chandler. He first found William Chandler of New Hampshire (no relation), a shrewd and guileful party functionary, explained the situation to him, and then with him went up to the chairman's hotel room. The two awakened Chandler, set forth the possibilities of the situation to him, and were told sleepily to do what they thought best. They then dispatched telegrams to Republican leaders in the three carpetbag states, telling them to "hold your state," warning them not to be cheated by the Democrats. Each state Republican leader was assured that the election depended on his state—and it did. Reid and Chandler were confident that the recipients of the wires would be resourceful enough to do what had to be done.[1]

Even though, several days later, Hayes could still write in his diary, "The election has resulted in the defeat of the Republicans after a very close contest," [2] the wheels had been put into motion to reverse that verdict. Grant sent a deputation of dignitaries, all of them Republicans, to Louisiana and the other states to "watch" the count of the votes, and Abram S. Hewitt, the Democratic national chairman, did likewise. These gentlemen were all lumped together under one euphemistic designation as "visiting statesmen." "Visiting" they certainly were, but their actions on the whole were anything but statesmanlike.

The facts of the election in the disputed states apparently came to this: Tilden had a clear majority in Florida and would have carried it by even more without the use of federal troops to hold down his vote; Hayes carried South Carolina (Tilden was not friendly with Wade Hampton, the Democratic candidate for governor, and in some places "Hampton and Hayes" tickets were pushed [3]); and Tilden had a majority in Louisiana which might have been wiped out had not the whites forcibly prevented many Negroes from voting, "by murder, and hellish cruelties," Hayes thought.[4] This of course is speculation and extrapolation and could very well be wrong; within a short time after the election, the facts of the voting became rather academic anyway. The problem for the Republicans was that they could not concede a single state; they must have each of the three for Hayes to give him a 185 to 184 edge in the electoral college.

An additional bother came from Oregon. There was no doubt that Hayes had carried the state and its three electoral votes. One of the three electors, however, was a postmaster and therefore ineligible to serve; the Democratic governor promptly certified the two remaining Republicans and one Democrat as Oregon's electors. That one Democratic vote, if counted, would elect Tilden. The two remaining Republican electors thereupon chose a third Republican to fill what they contended was a vacancy. This of course would also be contested.

While the Republican "returning boards" in the South were doing

[1] Elmer Davis, *New York Times,* pp. 130–142; Bowers, pp. 522–523.

[2] Hayes diary, Nov. 11, 1876; T. H. Williams, ed., p. 47.

[3] Barnard, pp. 322–323.

[4] Hayes diary entry, Nov. 30, 1876; T. H. Williams, ed., pp. 51–52. See the Hayes biographies of Eckenrode, pp. 189–194, and Barnard, pp. 322–323, for speculation on the actual voting results.

their work, throwing out Democratic votes here, parishes there, counties elsewhere, all on the basis of the alleged fraud and intimidation practiced by the belligerent whites against the Negro Hayes voters, turning, particularly in Louisiana and Florida, Tilden majorities into Hayes majorities, Governor Hayes sat in Fremont and wondered what should be done. At first he was cautious: "We are not to allow our friends to defeat one outrage and fraud by another. There must be nothing crooked on our part. Let Mr. Tilden have the place by violence, intimidation and fraud, rather than undertake to prevent it by means that will not bear the severest scrutiny."

Others were cautious, too; Kirkwood of Iowa, though regarding a possible Tilden presidency as a public misfortune, would prefer it to "another civil war or a dual presidency." Grant scotched reports that the administration would seat Hayes by force, saying he would be bound by the determination of Congress; if Congress tells him that Tilden has been elected, "this department will see that Mr. Tilden peacefully takes possession of the President's house." [5]

Shortly, however, Hayes was convinced of the rightness of the Republican course of action. He closed his eyes to the saturnalia of fraud and corruption that attended the certification of votes in the three Southern states. On December 5, Sherman, Garfield and a number of other "visiting statesmen" stopped to see Hayes upon their return from Louisiana, and "they emphatically endorsed the general fairness and honesty of the Board's conduct." This was the Louisiana returning board, made up of four rascally Republicans who allowed themselves to be bought and sold repeatedly in the "performance" of their duties, who connived and cheated and worked very hard to throw out enough Tilden votes, with or without justifying evidence, and whose chairman, J. Madison Wells, was described even by General Phil Sheridan as "a political trickster and a dishonest man." The next day, Hayes piously wrote to Schurz that "I have no doubt that we are justly and legally entitled to the Presidency. My conversations with Sherman, Garfield . . . and others settled the question in my mind as to Louisiana." [6]

With the work of the returning boards done, it was assured that docu-

[5] Barnard, pp. 334–335; Sage, p. 146; Hudson, p. 83. O. P. Morton, on the other hand, was for installing Hayes and Wheeler by using all the federal force necessary; Hoar, II, 74.

[6] T. H. Williams, ed., pp. 54–55; Bowers, p. 526; Barnard, p. 335. There was supposed to be one Democrat at least on the Louisiana returning board, but this spot was vacant and the Republican members simply refused to fill it.

ments certifying the legitimacy of Republican electors would be placed before Congress when the time came to count the presidential votes as ordained by the Constitution. There would also be certificates of Democratic electors, furnished in each case other than Oregon by a Democratic state official who was not formally the person to make such return. This then put the issue squarely up to Congress; everyone knew that a searching inquiry into the methods used by the Southern boards would cast grave doubt upon the worth of their returns, but who was to make the decision of which return to count, and how, and what was to be done with the other returns?

The Constitution provided that "the President of the Senate shall, in the presence of the Senate and the House of Representatives, open all certificates and the votes shall then be counted." Which votes? Hard-line Republicans took the position that the president of the Senate, Ferry of Michigan, a Republican, had the power to determine which votes should be counted and then to count them. No Democrat subscribed to such a view, and many Republicans, led by Roscoe Conkling, felt that the assumption of such a power by Ferry would be an unconstitutional usurpation.[7] The Democrats contended that the twenty-second joint rule, which the Senate had not re-enacted, was nevertheless still in effect and that a contested vote would not be counted unless both houses agreed to count it. This really was empty theorizing, because they could not put over an argument like that, which would clearly win the election for Tilden. The lost days of the prior couple of years, when everyone had talked in Congress about doing something to make the vote-counting certain but had done nothing, were mourned now, but it was too late to go back. The crisis was upon the nation, and feelings were rising.

Democrats were furious at the thought that the election might be stolen from them; after all, nobody denied the fact that Tilden received roughly a quarter of a million more popular votes than Hayes. He had carried major Northern states as well as the South, and now sleazy characters like J. Madison Wells and his cronies were being used to take the victory away. Threats of violence were muttered throughout the land, and talk of a new civil war. Ten or eleven years after the war there were a great many Americans on both sides of the political fence who were accustomed to the use of arms, and a lot of them now talked of using them to make sure right triumphed in this contest. But how was the right to be decided? It was a vexing and demanding problem.

[7] Conkling to Pierrepont, Feb. 8, 1877, Pierrepont Papers.

Meanwhile, Roscoe Conkling was under attack from Hayes and from those around Hayes for two separate but related matters; first, the disappearance of Conkling from the fall campaign, combined with apparent disinterest on the part of the machine workers, and, second, Conkling's course and feelings as the electoral crisis deepened.

On November 11, Hayes wrote that the last reports from New York before the election "were very encouraging—full of confidence." Cornell, he said, told him that "he had never seen prospects brighter on the eve of an election." But, Hayes wrote, we all knew that with the tremendous registration against us in New York City and in Brooklyn we should not be too confident.[8]

This early realism soon came under pressure, however. In early December, two members of the Republican Reform Club of New York came to Fremont and filled Hayes with tales of the "coolness and neglect, (perhaps treachery) on the part of the New York managers of the canvass—meaning Cornell, some of the Federal officers, generally I suppose friends of Conkling." Hayes added, characteristically, that the facts were "not very conclusive, but tended to show a lack of hearty support."[9]

On December 17, Hayes received a very different kind of visitor. Col. Albert D. Shaw, consul at Toronto and a friend of Senator Conkling, arrived at Fremont on the heels of a letter to Hayes from Sherman advising him to receive Shaw cordially and listen to what he had to say. Shaw described the feeling of the "regulars" that Hayes would be in the hands of the "reform" element and the fears of the Southern Republican senators that the Hayes "policy of conciliation" would leave them out in the cold. Shaw said pointedly that Hayes might lose the "support of enough Senators on the approaching struggle in the Senate to change the result of the Presidential election, and bring in Mr. Tilden." Hayes, however, told him that he stood on his letter of acceptance, that he had "no private views or pledges to give," and that in appointments he would try to give "first consideration" to "all sections" of the party. Shaw then

showed the reasons why Mr. Conkling took no active part in the canvass— that his health was broken—and his eyes required that he should remain in a dark room. He explained the bad faith of Curtis toward C—of Bristow towards C and Grant—of Morton towards C., &c&c&c. He urged the appointment of C, (or rather of his being offered the appt) as Secretary of State. Spoke well of Platt—of Morrill of Me—of Secy of War—and in disparagement of Chandler, Blaine and Jewell.

[8] T. H. Williams, ed., p. 47.   [9] *Ibid.,* p. 54.

After this enlightening discussion (perhaps for the first time Hayes became fully aware of the bitterly contending factions in the party over which he might be called upon to preside), he wrote that Shaw departed, "pleased with what I told him . . . professing to think he could overcome difficulties at Washington." [10]

Shortly, however, the governor started receiving reports concerning Conkling's attitude toward the electoral count. John Sherman told Hayes that he doubted that Conkling would vote "that you have either Florida or Louisiana." Wheeler, William E. Chandler, and others wrote to him that "Conkling is decidedly hostile, and that he has enough followers to pass through the Senate a compromise measure." The effect of such a measure, Hayes thought, "is to change the result in all probability." The wording of that is strange, since there was no "result" as yet to be changed, except in the eyes of those such as Hayes for whom the corrupt Southern returning boards had established eternal truths. It is curious, too, to note the antagonism of the Republican leaders to a compromise measure of some sort, since there existed no other lawful way out of the imbroglio. Once again, the suspicion must be strong that they hoped to seat Hayes by force of arms, if necessary, ignoring completely the baneful and incalculable effects of such a course.

Matthew Quay of Pennsylvania, who had been a "visiting statesman," wrote Hayes on January 20: "Conkling is undoubtedly faithless and Col. McClure of Philadelphia assures me he is in correspondence with Tilden." A few days earlier, Whitelaw Reid wrote to Blaine that he had it on good authority that Conkling was being blackmailed to support Tilden. The details of this bizarre tale involved William Tweed, now languishing in prison, who had revealed the fact that he had paid the money to have Conkling elected to the Senate in 1867. After Conkling had Tilden inaugurated, so Reid's story went, Tilden would then have Tweed released from jail, and the ex-Boss would keep quiet about Conkling. Needless to say, nothing more was ever heard of the whole fabrication.[11]

There can be little doubt that Conkling, individually and privately, expressed himself on several occasions to the effect that he felt Tilden had fairly won the election. He felt that the Democrats had carried Florida and Louisiana and he wondered at the relative passivity the

[10] *Ibid.*, pp. 58–59. Conkling, presumably, would have had no interest in the state portfolio.
[11] Bowers, p. 533; T. H. Williams, ed., p. 69; Barnard, p. 348. Reid to Blaine, Jan. 10, 1877, Reid Papers.

Democratic party showed in asserting its rights. A Democrat from Utica, a friend of the senator, wrote Tilden a couple of weeks after the election that he had spoken at length with Conkling and that the senator had asked whether the Democrats meant "to act upon the *good boy* principle of submission, or whether we mean to have it understood that Tilden has been elected and, by the Eternal, he shall be inaugurated." [12]

Though Conkling believed Tilden had won, and he certainly abhorred the idea some Republicans had of installing Hayes by force, he was careful to keep his thoughts private. He never made any public profession of a Tilden victory, and he never committed such a view to writing. He was, after all, a good Republican; however, he intended to take no part in the contentious struggle for Hayes. The Democrats kept interpreting his private expressions of opinion coupled with his public silence as assurance that at the appropriate time he would come out publicly for Tilden; some Republicans did so, too. It seems clear that he never intended any such thing.

Congress was in a quandary over the situation, so its leaders appointed a special joint committee, composed of seven members from each house and seven members from each party. The four Senate Republicans named were Edmunds, Morton, Frelinghuysen, and Logan. Logan, however, was engaged in a fierce struggle for re-election back in Springfield, so he declined to serve. Roscoe Conkling was named in his place.[13]

The only idea that seemed to have much support was some sort of independent commission. There was, however, a great deal of opposition

[12] J. T. Spriggs to Tilden; Bowers, p. 533. On Jan. 10, 1877, J. C. Welling, president of Columbian College in Washington, wrote to Manton Marble, a journalist who was close to Tilden, that he had "the best of reasons for believing that Senator Conkling is disposed to 'do justice' in the matter of the electoral canvass and count, but is somewhat restrained by the fear that his action in that direction may be ascribed to political pique rather than honest conviction." Apparently Welling had this from a third party, to whom Conkling had spoken of the circumstances which had won him the suspicion of being a "sorehead" in the party. Conkling further asked why the lawyers of the country did not involve themselves in the electoral question, without leaving the whole burden upon the politicians. Tansill, p. 168.

[13] M. H. Northrup, "A Grave Crisis," p. 924. The House members on the committee, named Dec. 22, 1876, were Henry Payne, Eppa Hunton, Abram Hewitt, and W. M. Springer, Democrats, and George McCrary, Hoar, and George Willard, Republicans. The Democratic senators named were Thurman, Bayard, and M. W. Ransom of North Carolina. Flick and Lobrano, pp. 365–366.

to it as well. At this time Grant sent for Conkling. The president told the senator, earnestly, "This matter is a serious one, and the people feel it deeply. I think this Electoral Commission ought to be appointed."

Conkling replied, "Mr. President, Senator Morton is opposed to it and to your efforts; but if you wish the Commission carried, I can do it."

Grant closed the discussion by saying, "I wish it done." [14]

Thereupon, Conkling drafted a bill providing for an electoral commission to consist of the chief justice and four associate justices, to be chosen by lot. The commission would be charged with the responsibility of deciding which set of returns to count where the two houses were unable to agree. This bill was presented to the House committee members on January 3 and agreed to in principle, though there was to be considerable revision of the actual membership of the commission.[15]

In the meetings of the joint committee, Conkling played a calm and most constructive part. Still struggling over the membership question, on January 16, he proposed a commission of five from the House, five from the Senate, and five from the Supreme Court, the four senior judges (Clifford, Davis, Swayne, and Miller) together with a fifth to be named by them. He explained this the next day, saying: "My idea was, in suggesting that four justices name the fifth, that one judge would say, 'Here is Justice Field; why not take him?' Another, 'Here's Judge Strong; why not take him?' But one is a Democrat, the other a Republican. Probably in the end they would say, 'Both are good men; put them in a hat and draw out one.' " [16] Conkling's jurisdictional theory for the commission was that "the Constitution requires Congress to declare a President. The two houses employ this tribunal as auxiliary, as eyes and hands. We don't delegate this power. We keep it all. This is our own ministration."

When the committee report was sent to the two houses, proposing a commission of five senators, five congressmen, and five justices, with four of these designated by specific circuit numbers in order to include the only two Democrats on the bench, Field and Clifford, it was contemplated that the fifth member from the Court would be David Davis of Illinois. Davis was nominally and historically a Republican, but he

---

[14] A. M. Gibson, *A Political Crime,* p. 29. The basis for this account is what Grant told George W. Childs, a close friend and publisher of the Philadelphia *Ledger.*

[15] Flick and Lobrano, p. 367.   [16] Northrup, pp. 928–931.

was extremely independent and was actually more satisfactory to the Democrats than to the Republicans. Morton, "who had frowned darkly upon every step taken," refused to sign the committee report.[17]

Conkling, meanwhile, who usually drew nothing but grief from White-law Reid's *Tribune,* received a series of kindly notices in that journal as January progressed. On the 4th: "Messrs. Conkling, Blaine, & other Senators who have been withholding their opinions until the facts were all before them, have inspired the country with confidence that they will in the end act impartially and conscientiously." On the 5th: "The Tribune has had occasion before now to say what it thought of Mr. Conkling's attitude as a Senator in terms the reverse of complimentary; but for his present course it can have no words but those of commendation." And on the 17th it said that all the rumors about Conkling's position "unite on one point, namely, that they don't know anything about what he will or will not do."

The test was yet to come. The electoral commission bill had to be passed through both houses. There was staunch opposition to it among a number of prominent Republicans, taking their lead from Morton, Sherman, and Garfield. Billy Hudson of the Brooklyn *Eagle* one day met Kate Chase Sprague at the Washington railroad station, and, after she swore him to secrecy, she told him, "Senator Conkling will support the Commission with a speech." [18]

On January 23, Conkling gained the floor for his speech in support of the electoral commission bill. Always, in a moment of need, Conkling felt that the right and the good would prevail if only he could make a speech, setting forth at necessary length what the right and the good happened to be. Now, with threats of violence and disunion flying about, with Democratic newspapermen of the border states urging "100,000 Democrats" to converge on Washington to see to the inauguration of Tilden, with his own position being misrepresented by both sides, and with leaders of his party urging acquiescence in a course designed to

[17] *Ibid.,* p. 932. Northrup was secretary of the special House committee and thus an eye-witness of the committee's deliberations. While Conkling was laboring to frame the only logical way out of the crisis, Garfield of Ohio was writing back home, "Everything is going well here except the behavior of some of our Senators. It now looks as though Senator Conkling were going to break with us and be able to carry off several Senators." F. A. Henry, *Captain Henry,* p. 273. The conduct of some of the Ohio men throughout the struggle was less than glorious.

[18] Hudson, pp. 22–23.

bring the crisis to a fierce boil, Roscoe Conkling made a speech. Though perhaps not the most eloquent or most polished effort of his career, it was a well-worked speech, closely reasoned and finely documented, and in its effect it may have contributed more than anything else to a peaceful settlement of the Hayes-Tilden controversy. It was probably Roscoe Conkling's finest moment.

When Conkling started his speech, before packed and expectant galleries, he could still hear the echoes of Sherman's protest, just before he began, against "introducing into the sacred urn of our electoral system the blind goddess of chance." He knew that the Democrats distrusted him, because of his many years of stalwart opposition to their party; he knew that the Republicans worried that, vexed and aggrieved in his own disappointment, he had somehow bargained his support away to Tilden's cause. But he plunged forthrightly ahead, concerned only with winning as many adherents as possible to the bill. "Mr. President," he began, "before reaching the details of this measure or its advantages or wisdom, we must make sure of the power, in some mode, to subject the verification and count of electoral votes to the action of the two Houses." He then proceeded with a minute and thorough examination and exposition of the historical modes of interpreting, so far as they had been interpreted, the words of the Constitution dealing with the count of the votes. First, the function of the president of the Senate. "If, by the Constitution, the Senate and House are only spectators of the count, there is an end of the matter as to them." If the president of the Senate determines what votes to count, and counts them, there is no problem. But he showed conclusively that no such power was ever invested in the president of the Senate, and no such officer had ever presumed to possess such power. "Authority to act as custodian of papers, does not confer license to exercise transcendent powers of sovereignty, or of supreme ultimate political and public determination. . . . Breaking the seals is merely prefatory to a wholly different proceeding."

The Senator dwelt at length upon the proceedings of the Congress with the first presidential election, that of Washington, and upon the course later of Aaron Burr, always grasping for power and prerogative, when he was the presiding officer of the Senate in 1805 and made no such claim of power for himself. Morton had cited Chancellor Kent's *Commentaries* as ground for the Senate president's right to count the votes, but Conkling showed that this was merely a presumption on Kent's part, hedged about with the phrase, "in the absence of all legislative provision on the subject." As Conkling launched into a review of the practice of the nation from 1793 to 1877, he suddenly became weak and faint, the sign of the tenacious grip of his infection of the previous fall. Edmunds asked that Conkling be excused and, as the New Yorker was helped from the chamber, the Senate adjourned for the day.[19]

When the members assembled on the 24th for the start of the day's activities, Conkling was not present. While waiting for him, Aaron Sargent, a Republican from California, was given the floor; his speech in opposition to the measure was summed up when he said, "I consider this bill not a compromise, and not a victory, but a surrender." [20]

After Sargent finished, Roscoe Conkling, having entered the chamber, resumed the floor. Those who had heard the opening salvoes of his mighty blast the day before were back again in force in the galleries, as the famous senator drew himself up to his full six feet, three inches, hooked his thumb in his vest pocket, and took up the thread of his speech once more. He always spoke in slow, measured tones, accenting the vowels, and now he was in his best form.

He started by reading a petition from thirty-seven leading citizens of Indianapolis, Indiana, almost all of them Republicans, including Benjamin Harrison, favoring the compromise bill; this was a little touch which sent Morton into a rage, feeling that Conkling was trying to show him up, which of course he was. But Conkling was into the body of his talk again, citing the precedents established by statutory enactment and actual usage over the years. He was able to marshal in favor of his position the storied names of the past, a compendium of American history, names like Van Buren, Webster, Clay, Douglas, and Crittenden.

We have been told this morning that the measure before the Senate is a surrender of the rights of the Republican party. . . . Why, it is a surrender because it guards the vote of every state against rejection, until both Houses, by a common tribunal, the fairest, the most learned, the most fit, the most impartial that ingenuity can invent, have investigated and found the law and the facts, and, in the light of day, with a full statement of the reasons to be spread before the world, have come to a deliberate judgment that the Constitution forbids the vote to be received.

Scoring those who eight months before had passed a bill which would have permitted either house to reject the votes of a state, he said, "I am

---

[19] Conkling's speech that first day, as well as the close of Sherman's, is in *Cong. Rec.*, 44th Cong., 2d sess., pp. 825–831.

[20] *Ibid.*, p. 869.

willing to let these two surrenders stand side by side, while the nation compares them with each other."

But, Conkling went on, what was the answer of the bill's opponents to this "broad, deep, irresistible stream of historic precept and example?" Morton, he said, had given it: "If nothing is done, a condition of affairs will exist in which the President of the Senate, to prevent a deadlock, must act from necessity." This plea of necessity he scorned as "a political Hell Gate paved and honeycombed with dynamite. . . . Mr. President," he cried, " 'necessity knows no law.' Who is to decide whether he is called and chosen by necessity to be the master of an opportunity?" He denounced necessity as "that arch fiend and foe of government, that prolific mother and apology of anarchy, revolution, despotism, and fraud," and he implored, "Let not the representatives of American States, in this century year, connive at bringing about a necessity, they know not what, fraught with consequences they cannot order or foresee."

He said that any president so inaugurated would be regarded as a usurper; because he believed Hayes a patriot not wishing injury to his country, "I would have his title so clear that it can never be challenged with a pretext for believing that he, and they who supported him, meant to clutch usurped power, or dared not submit to a fair and constitutional examination of the truth of the election." Conkling concluded by asking for passage of the bill: "Adopted, it composes the country in an hour. The mists which have gathered in our land will be quickly dispelled; business will no longer falter before uncertainty or apprehension. . . . The measure will be a herald of order and calmness, from sea to sea; it will once again proclaim to the world that America is great enough, and wise enough, to do all things decently and in order." [21]

Morton replied, denouncing the bill as "a method of counting this vote, by which the Republican party is to be the loser and the Democratic party is to be the gainer." He thundered and roared, but Conkling's speech had had the effect he had promised Grant. Well into the next morning the vote was taken and the bill passed the Senate, 47 to 17.[22]

The next day, in a stunning development, the Illinois legislature elected David Davis to the Senate in place of Logan, and Davis immedi-

[21] The second day of Conkling's speech is in *ibid.*, pp. 870–878.

[22] Morton's statement is in *ibid.*, p. 894. The vote is on p. 913. Edmunds, Allison, Boutwell, Burnside, Dawes, Frelinghuysen, Howe, Jones of Nevada, Morrill, and Windom of Minnesota were among the Republicans joining Conkling in voting for the bill.

ately resigned from the Supreme Court. However, despite fears that the compromise might now go up in smoke, there was by this time too much impetus committed to the bill as the only way out of the impasse; the House quickly adopted it, mainly with Democratic votes, and the electoral commission was set up right after Grant signed the bill. Democratic Chairman Hewitt consulted Conkling on the choice of a fifth justice. Of those available, Conkling advised against both Justices Swayne and Hunt. Swayne was from Ohio, and the senator's old friend Hunt, aware of Conkling's belief that Tilden had been elected, might lean over backward against the Democrat to show his independence of Conkling. The only one left, Justice Joseph P. Bradley, a Republican from New Jersey, was thus designated the fifteenth member of the commission. The House named three Democrats and two Republicans, the Senate three Republicans and two Democrats, and with the five justices the political makeup of the commission was eight Republicans and seven Democrats.[23]

While the nation waited for the count to begin, praise for his speech came showering in upon Roscoe Conkling. The *Tribune* said, "Whatever Mr. Conkling's critics may say of his mannerisms or of his somewhat melodramatic form of delivery, they will not deny to his speech the praise due to a great effort." General Sherman, congratulating Conkling for his part in passing a bill which the General's brother had opposed, sent on a letter from General John M. Schofield, avowing that "those who have gained this victory in the interest of Peace, justice, and Law will be no less highly honored than those who saved the Country from disunion in the last decade." And, most surprisingly, *The Nation* wrote of "Mr. Conkling here making his first appearance as a politician of the highest class," and stated flatly that "the great event of the Senate debate was, of course, Mr. Conkling's speech." [24]

While the kudos were being composed for Conkling, Morton and Edmunds clashed on the question of making him one of the Senate members of the commission, Morton still not feeling confidence in Conkling's unyielding fidelity to the Hayes cause. The New Yorker eventually resolved the issue by firmly declining to serve even if chosen.

Hayes finally accepted the idea of the commission: "I trust the mea-

[23] A. Nevins, *Abram S. Hewitt*, p. 367.

[24] N.Y. *Tribune*, Jan. 25, 1877; Conkling Papers, Library of Congress, for Schofield and W. T. Sherman; *The Nation*, Feb. 1, 1877. Bancroft, the historian, wrote Conkling thanking him for his speech, "so thorough in research, so clear in statement." Scott, p. 195.

sure will turn out well. It is a great relief to me." [25] The work of the commission, after its first decision, was anti-climactical. The eagerly anticipated first decision, that on Florida, confirmed the worst fears of the Democrats. After hearing argument from distinguished counsel on both sides, the commission, by a straight-party 8 to 7 vote, Bradley voting with the rest of the Republicans, determined that it was without power to go behind the certificates. Thus, the count of the Republican returning board was accepted without question, and Florida was counted for Hayes. The provision of the enabling act was that a decision of the commission was to be final unless both houses voted to overturn it, and the Senate of course sustained the commission.

Ironically, this decision, holding in effect that a federal body had no right to go behind the returns submitted by the state authorities, good, bona fide states rights doctrine, led directly and in short order to the Solid South. When all the Southern states resumed control of their own destinies, the decision of the electoral commission was a handy and valuable precedent to cite when anyone mentioned the fact that Negroes were not permitted to vote in Southern elections. We hold our elections in our own way, they said, we send our returns on to Washington in properly certified form, and the federal government has no right to go behind the returns.

There was no doubt, after the Florida decision, that Hayes was in. Louisiana, Oregon, and South Carolina were all referred in turn to the commission, and by the identical 8 to 7 margin the commission voted to count the Hayes electors.

It was not to be as simple as that, of course. The Democrats in the House, hard losers as they saw Tilden's quarter-million vote triumph snatched away by a party-line vote on the electoral commission, started a filibuster to try to delay the completion of the count beyond March 4. Connected with this effort were all sorts of wild rumors about the course which Senator Conkling would take. Why had Conkling not been on the commission? All the assurances of Conkling's conviction that Tilden had really won were now retailed around Washington, along with the stories of the great speech he was going to make against accepting the corrupt return from Louisiana. He would sweep several other Republicans along

[25] T. H. Williams, ed., pp. 70–71. The Senate members of the Commission were Morton, Edmunds, Frelinghuysen, Thurman, and Bayard. From the House came Payne, Hunton, and Josiah Abbott of Massachusetts, Democrats, and Republicans Garfield and Hoar.

with him, and Louisiana would go to Tilden without even being referred to the commission or for Tilden even after the commission had ruled. When Louisiana came up, however, Conkling was in Baltimore, visiting friends, and no revolt was led. John Bigelow wrote: "Conkling has been trusted by our people to do something for Tilden; to at least enter his protest against giving a congressional sanction to the operations of the Louisiana returning board. Our friends have been fearfully deceived by him." [26]

Perhaps. Much more likely is it that they were deceived by themselves, by their own utterly unrealistic hopes. Equally unrealistic was the rumor, spread about by Whitelaw Reid and his *Tribune,* that Conkling was to be elected president of the Senate, that his friends were to combine with the Democrats to prevent the completion of the vote by March 4, and that Conkling would then become president of the United States for some unmentioned period of time.[27]

The Democratic filibuster was called off after representatives of Louisiana and South Carolina received assurances, from duly deputed representatives of Hayes (Sherman, Foster, Dennison, Garfield, and Stanley Matthews—Ohioans all), that the new administration would withdraw federal troops from those last carpetbag states. This done, of course, the Republican governments would collapse, and lily-white Democratic regimes would be installed in their places, though this of course was not stated. Bland assurances were given and accepted that all the rights of the Negroes would be respected by the Democrats, pledges which were dishonored as soon as the federal government lost the power to enforce them. There was also an understanding about a federal subsidy for a proposed Texas and Pacific Railroad. This agreement was reached at Wormley's Hotel, in the rooms of Evarts. Some Republicans, when they learned later of the conference at Wormley's, which produced the only tangible benefits for the Democrats from an election they had apparently won, felt that the Republican party had

[26] Bigelow, V, 301. Also Wall, p. 159. McClure and later Billy Hudson related a story that Conkling would have made his great speech on Louisiana but for the influence of Kate Chase Sprague, still bitter at Tilden for his part in denying her father the Democratic nomination for president in 1868. This story can safely be discarded as an utter fantasy; McClure, p. 269; Hudson, pp. 22–23; Ross, *Proud Kate,* pp. 238–239.

[27] Reid to Evarts, March 1, 1877, Cortissoz, I, 360; N.Y. *Tribune,* Feb. 24, 1877; Barnard, p. 384.

been somehow disgraced; William Chandler, for example, wrote that the conference was "almost too infamous for belief." [28]

Nevertheless, the pact cleaned up the last possible impediment to the completion of the count. On March 2, Hayes was officially proclaimed president-elect, and at midnight of March 3 (the 4th being a Sunday), he was secretly sworn in as president at the White House, the oath to be publicly repeated on Monday.

Rutherford B. Hayes was the nineteenth president of the United States, but it took a mighty effort to make him so, peacefully; Roscoe Conkling was entitled to a major part of the credit for achieving that result.

[28] Chandler to Reid, Dec. 30, 1877, Reid Papers.

CHAPTER 17

DIVERGENT LINES

Hayes had no sooner taken office as the beneficiary of a great effort of the Republican party, to which he had contributed very little, than he contrived to alienate many of the leaders of the party. There had naturally been some gossip around Washington about the future Hayes cabinet, but this was swallowed up in the general hubbub over the electoral votes. A Tilden cabinet seemed just as likely for some time. Shortly after Hayes was finally installed in the White House, though, observers had an actual cabinet to contemplate.

For the leading place as secretary of state, Hayes, in what Tom Platt called "a straight-arm blow at the regular organization in our State," named William M. Evarts. Evarts was undoubtedly highly qualified; he was, as one commentator wrote, "eloquent in advocacy, subtle in counsel, irresistible in social life." As another factor in his selection, however, Hayes wished to establish the anti-Conkling element in New York, and Evarts's inclusion in the cabinet would tend to that result. Ellis Roberts, no longer a friend of Conkling, told Evarts he could "put an end to the despotism which has ruled through federal spoils, and republicans may be republicans without wearing one man's collar." [1]

Conkling was furious. He had some time before the inauguration suggested that the New York member of the cabinet might very well be Tom Platt, and he had petitions to the president to that effect circulated among the members of the New York legislature. Evarts he regarded not only as an opponent in New York but one "whose record as a Republican has been more than doubtful." [2]

Sherman was named for the treasury. Sherman was a veteran senator,

[1] Platt, pp. 83–84; J. D. Cox, "The Hayes Administration," p. 825; Roberts to Evarts, March 10, 1877, Evarts Papers.
[2] N.Y. *Tribune*, Feb. 28, 1877, and March 2, 1877; Barrows, p. 311.

a long-time political pro, Hayes's manager at the convention, and a "visiting statesman" in Louisiana and staunch ally during the electoral count. No one could quarrel with that appointment.

Hayes had been under strong pressure through February to name Congressman George W. McCrary of Keokuk, Iowa, to a spot. Senator Allison was particularly anxious, because he regarded McCrary as a potentially dangerous rival for his Senate seat the following year. McCrary also had strong railroad connections, among men like Tom Scott of the Pennsylvania who had supported Hayes. Hayes had intended to name former Confederate General Joseph E. Johnston as secretary of war, in a striking demonstration of reconciliation. General Sherman, who had battled Johnston from Chattanooga to Atlanta, had doubts about this but ultimately said that he could take orders from his old adversary. By the time Hayes reached Washington, however, he had been convinced by his advisers that the war department in the hands of an ex-rebel might be a little too much for nervous Northerners, who had just gone through a "bloody-shirt" campaign; confirmation by the Senate would be unlikely. So he named McCrary, and he appointed a former Confederate colonel, a Democrat and Tilden backer, Senator David M. Key of Tennessee, as postmaster general.[3]

The president wanted a Massachusetts man in the cabinet and asked George Hoar who it should be. Hoar suggested his former law partner, Charles Devens, a jurist with a creditable military record but otherwise undistinguished except as a raconteur, and Hayes made him attorney general.

Hayes wanted someone from Indiana, as a tribute to Morton, and he suggested to the Indiana senator the selection of Benjamin Harrison, whose losing gubernatorial campaign in 1876 had elevated him to prominence. Morton was not interested in creating rivals for his leadership, so he turned thumbs down on Harrison and asked instead for a post for a puppet of his named Richard W. Thompson. Thompson was an old-time Whig and Know-Nothing politician from Terre Haute, who, in the navy department, was to become known as "The Ancient Mariner of the Wabash." Even Grant had once refused to appoint him to the cabinet because of his alleged connection with a land fraud. Hayes now named Thompson secretary of the navy, though the new appointee knew nothing of the navy and had his full share of midwestern prejudices against the seagoing arm of the military service. It was said, per-

[3] Sage, p. 147; Cox, p. 827.

haps apocryphally, that the first time he saw a ship, he cried in amazement, "Why the durned thing's hollow!" [4]

Finally, for the interior department, Hayes picked Carl Schurz.

When the slate was sent to the Senate, the lords of that chamber were horrified. Evarts was bad enough. McCrary, Devens, and Thompson were mediocrities. Key was a Democrat, and a rebel, too. But Carl Schurz! That was too much for any group of thick-and-thin Republican politicians to swallow, and Blaine and Conkling joined in moving that all the nominations be referred to committee. Sherman and Key as senators (and even Schurz as a former senator) might have been confirmed on the spot, and there was really no objection to Sherman, but he was in bad company. The reference to committee was an unprecedented action, but Hayes had been pretty unprecedented too, they thought. Conkling had wanted Platt in the cabinet, Simon Cameron wanted his son Don (who was just learning the job) continued as secretary of war, and Blaine had wanted William P. Frye, one of his followers from Maine, put in somewhere. Everyone thought a spot should have been found for good old "Black Jack" Logan, who had been so unceremoniously dumped out of the Senate by the Illinois legislature, and needed the money, but he was still unemployed. Cameron snarled, "A Republican President should appoint Republicans." The Senate leaders, as Hayes quickly learned, "were very bitter." [5]

The nominations were sent to committee on March 7. On March 8, a group of outraged businessmen led by John Jay held a rally on the steps of the Subtreasury Building in New York to support the right of the president to pick his own cabinet, and shortly the Senate was being swamped by protests from across the country, indicating clearly that public opinion was strongly opposed to that chamber's course. "The masses were getting up to the boiling heat of indignation," wrote one correspondent. Ellis Roberts in Utica called it "inexcusable delay." The Senate caved in after three days, brought the nominations back from committee, and confirmed them all with near unanimity. Hayes had surprisingly won an easy victory over the Senate without even seeking the contest.[6]

[4] Hoar, II, 9–10; Barnard, pp. 416–417; L. D. White, pp. 155–156; Eckenrode, p. 242. With the moribund state of the U.S. Navy in 1877, Thompson's appointment made little difference.

[5] W. E. Binkley, pp. 187–190; Barnard, p. 419; Hoar, II, 7; T. H. Williams, ed., pp. 80–81.

[6] Barrows, p. 312; Barnard, p. 419; W. E. Caldwell to Evarts, Ellis Roberts to Evarts, both March 10, 1877, Evarts Papers.

The president set right to work on redeeming his pledge to pull federal troops out of South Carolina and Louisiana. He tried at first, through emissaries, to persuade Chamberlain and Packard, the Republican gubernatorial claimants in those two states, to withdraw voluntarily and let the Democratic regimes of Hampton in South Carolina and Francis T. Nicholls in Louisiana move in to their places. These efforts were unsuccessful, and Hayes sent a commission to Louisiana to study the situation, while he invited Chamberlain and Hampton to Washington for a conference. In the meantime, Hayes was writing in his diary, on March 23, "It is not the duty of the President of the United States to use the military power of the Nation to decide contested elections in the States." He advised Chamberlain that the troops were to be withdrawn, and that settled the question in South Carolina. From April 3 through 10, the U.S. Army pulled out of the Palmetto State.

Louisiana, as always, was more complicated, made so particularly by people like Blaine, who said that Packard held his seat "by a title as valid as that which . . . seated Rutherford B. Hayes in the Presidential chair." The president's commission advised that the Nicholls government was the legal one, so the troops were removed on April 24 from the state house and Packard handed over his powers.[7]

Reconstruction was over.

After ordering the last of the troops out of Louisiana, Rutherford B. Hayes wrote in his diary, "Now for Civil Service Reform." In his inaugural address, Hayes had called attention "to the paramount necessity of reform in our civil service . . . a reform that shall be thorough, radical, and complete." He affirmed that "public officers should owe their whole service to the Government and to the people." [8] Hayes here was under the influence of Curtis and Schurz, who had written him that a president with public opinion at his back need have no fear of the Senate; "my own experience in the Senate convinces me that by a determined vigorous start you will rather avoid long antagonisms than provoke them." Schurz, it will be seen, was both right and wrong in his views, but he was delighted to egg Hayes on into a fight with the Senate powers. There could be no question that civil service reform

[7] Barnard, pp. 422–432; T. H. Williams, ed., pp. 85–86; Blaine's statement was in a letter to the Boston *Herald* of April 11, 1877, Blaine Papers. Blaine wrote Reid on April 12, "I can't go the new policy. Every instinct of my nature rebels against it." Reid Papers.

[8] Richardson, ed., VII, 444.

would run into trouble in the Senate; it would run into Roscoe Conkling.[9]

Civil service reform, as a political issue, first came to notice toward the end of the Civil War, when Congressman Thomas A. Jenckes, a Republican from Rhode Island, introduced bills providing for reform of the appointment and tenure of the federal civil service. Though Jenckes was unsuccessful, agitation for his proposed reforms continued, achieving a partial victory on the last day of the last session of the Forty-first Congress, March 3, 1871. A rider to the Sundry Civil Appropriations Bill, authorizing the president to make rules and regulations for the civil service, was offered by Lyman Trumbull and squeaked through the Senate. The House concurred, and Grant was given $10,000 to implement the idea. George William Curtis, who, since 1869, had included a lecture on civil service reform in his lyceum tour repertoire, was named by Grant as chairman of the new civil service commission. The commission furnished Grant with rules and regulations for appointments to office, and these were put into effect starting January 1, 1872. Grant's commitment to the idea of civil service reform was lackadaisical at best, particularly after most of those howling loudest for changes went whooping off after Horace Greeley in the campaign that fall, and the implementation of Curtis's rules was spotty, though Arthur put them into effect in the New York Custom House. Even Roscoe Conkling, though, was willing at that time to see how they worked out; "I have no thought," he wrote, "of doing anything to baffle a fair trial of the experiment. Moreover I am *for anything that will improve the matter of appointments to office.*" He later changed his mind. It may have been the system, or it may have been the men who most loudly championed reform.[10]

On March 18, 1873, just after George Sharpe was appointed surveyor of the New York Custom House without reference to the civil service rules, Curtis fired off a huffy letter, stating that he was resigning, "as the circumstances under which several important appointments have been recently made seem to me to show an abandonment both of the spirit and

[9] T. H. Williams, ed., p. 87; C. Schurz, *Speeches, Correspondence, and Political Papers of Carl Schurz,* III, 317. Conkling on March 27, 1877, wrote Edwards Pierrepont, "Some of the surprises hereabout have been very amusing—were I as worldly as you are I should have enjoyed them." Pierrepont Papers.

[10] Conkling to A. D. White, Jan. 31, 1872, A. D. White Papers. On Feb. 19, 1871, he had written in the same vein to Pierrepont, deploring the "exaltation" of patronage "over everything else" as the chief bane of the party; Pierrepont Papers.

the letter of the Civil Service regulations." This was not really fair, for Curtis, Arthur, and Jackson S. Schultz had been named a committee to select a surveyor, and Curtis had begged off on grounds of ill health. Grant shrugged and named Dorman B. Eaton as chairman to succeed him. Eaton, a hard-working Vermonter, was an assiduous advocate of the reform, but his commission was left in limbo when Congress cut off its appropriation in 1874. On December 7, 1874, in his annual message, Grant said, "If Congress adjourns without positive legislation on the subject of 'civil-service reform,' I will regard such action as a disapproval of the system, and will abandon it." Congress, of course, did adjourn without further action, and on March 9, 1875, the civil service rules and regulations were abolished.[11] The clamor did not cease, however, and both parties included pledges of reform in their 1876 platforms, though it may be seriously doubted whether they intended to keep them.

There was some debate on the merits of the spoils system, its defenders pronouncing it a means for citizen participation in the government, but the great rush for jobs at the inception of a new administration, the standard assessments of the salaries of jobholders for the means of running political campaigns, and the use of jobholders to sustain particular party factions had long since discredited the existing system. The navy yards, for example, employed about 5,000 men, all of them patronage appointees; when it is remembered that very little shipbuilding was done prior to 1883, it will be seen that these were handy spots for political hacks. There were 53,000 persons on the federal civilian payroll in 1871; ten years later this figure was increased to 107,000. The magnitude of the problem can be seen. Yet, even after he left office, General Grant could state complacently:

As to competitive examinations, they are of questionable utility. . . . The way to achieve the best civil service is, first to influence Congressmen, and induce them to refrain from pressure upon the Executive; then pass laws giving each office a special tenure; then keep the Republican party in power until the process of education is complete. As it is now, the only danger I see to civil service reform is in the triumph of the Democratic party.[12]

---

[11] L. D. White, pp. 281–284; Milne, p. 145; Arthur to Curtis and Schultz, Feb. 21, 1873, Arthur to Schultz, March 1, 1873, Arthur to Curtis, March 14, 1873, Arthur Papers, New-York Historical Society; Richardson, ed., VII, 301, 327.

[12] McClure, pp. 250, 256; L. D. White, pp. 18, 172, 286; J. R. Young, *Around the World,* II, 268. Senator John J. Ingalls said that he sought to get rid of all

Hayes was tackling a hardy institution.

The day after Hayes penned his note to himself that the time to work on the reform of the civil service had arrived, Sherman appointed a three-man commission to investigate the conditions in the New York Custom House. Sherman said that it was his suggestion that the major custom houses of the country—New York, Philadelphia, New Orleans, San Francisco—be checked into, but the basic idea behind the move looks much more like Hayes's than that of his secretary, who was more of a practical politician.

The theory behind the probe was to have it conducted by local businessmen where possible, and in New York the three members of the commission were supposed to represent the merchants, the officers of the port, and the treasury department. This was not quite the way things worked out; John A. Dix was originally to represent the merchants, but he told Arthur on April 16, 1877, that he was unable to assume the task. After a second nominee also declined, Arthur asked ex-Governor Morgan for advice, and Morgan suggested a young Democratic businessman named Lawrence Turnure of Moses Taylor and Company. Sherman named the assistant solicitor of the treasury department, J. H. Robinson, and the third member and chairman was John Jay, the grandson of the Revolutionary patriot and first chief justice. Jay was a querulous busybody, formerly active in antislavery circles, and very hostile to Roscoe Conkling. He had been a sore disappointment as minister to Austria under Grant. John Bigelow called him "a quarrelsome and treacherous dog . . . bound to make a mess of any public business he puts his hands to," and the mild-mannered Hamilton Fish, upon hearing of Jay's appointment to investigate the custom house, was driven to write: "No one is better fitted than he to perform a duty similar to that which on the Channel steamers is assigned to one of the stewards, of holding a bowl in which anyone may relieve himself of any uncomfortable matter on his stomach." [13]

The Jay commission started to work immediately, taking complaints,

---

Democrats in office in Kansas "as with a fine-toothed comb." Hoar, II, 83. On assessments, see the letter of Arthur to Curtis of Oct. 11, 1872, in which he says, "I have not thought it either my duty or my right to interfere with such contributions or solicitations, or the use which my subordinates voluntarily make of their own money." Arthur Papers, New-York Historical Society.

[13] Sherman, II, 673; G. F. Howe, "New York Custom-House Controversy," p. 351; John Bigelow to Whitelaw Reid, May 12, 1873, Reid Papers; Arthur to Sherman, April 16, 17, 1877, Arthur Papers, New-York Historical Society;

soliciting witnesses, receiving letters. Collector Arthur came before the probers, citing the changes and improvements in procedures which he had inaugurated, and defending his administration. Arthur pointed out that new employees were taken on probation, and the chiefs of divisions and the surveyor had to report cases of incapacity and dishonesty. "The best only remain and the others are gradually dropped. This is the real check on the system of appointments." [14]

On May 15, as the investigation was getting underway, the *Tribune,* usually anti-Conkling and anti-custom house, said of Arthur "that his administration has been a great improvement upon that of any of his recent predecessors, and that the mercantile community generally believe him to be honestly seeking to administer the office in the interests of the commerce of New York."

The commission rendered its first partial report on May 24, 1877, and it became clear that the commission members had to a great extent ignored or disbelieved what Arthur told them, had drawn conclusions more sweeping than what could validly be based upon the evidence before them, had, as Arthur put it, given too much credence to "common report" and had perhaps been led by the political bias of the chairman. The commission denounced the "settled practice" of making appointments for political reasons, though Arthur had testified that only 217 new appointments had been made outside of the civil service rules in his five and a half years. The commission called the system "unsound in principle, dangerous in practice, demoralizing in its influence on . . . the customs service, and calculated to encourage . . . official ignorance, inefficiency, and corruption." It reported inefficiency in every department together with some dishonesty, and called for a flat 20 per cent reduction in force.[15]

On the 26th, Hayes wrote to Sherman, advising on the basis of the partial report that it was his wish "that the collection of the revenues

---

Nevins, *Fish,* II, 902. See also Arthur to Sherman, Nov. 23, 1877, House Executive Documents, 45th Cong., 2d sess., No. 25, p. 7. It should be noted that none of the three members of the Jay commission represented the port officers.

[14] N.Y. *Tribune,* May 26, 1877. *The Nation,* on May 24, 1877, said of Arthur and his cohorts: "A custom-house without politics is to them like a tavern without liquor or a dairy without milk. The first step in reform is, in short, to get rid of them and the like of them."

[15] House Exec. Doc., 45th Cong., 1st sess., No. 8, p. 15. It was noted that, as Arthur carried out these rules, those persons whom he wished to employ were almost always found to be qualified; examinations were said to be "farcical." T. C. Reeves, "Silas Burt and Chester Arthur," p. 330.

should be free from partisan control, and organized on a strictly business basis." Then he got to the heart of what he wanted to enforce.

Party leaders should have no more influence in appointments than other equally respectable citizens. No assessments for political purposes on officers or subordinates should be allowed. No useless officer or employee should be retained. No officer should be required or permitted to take part in the management of political organizations, caucuses, conventions, or election campaigns. Their right to vote and to express their views on public questions, either orally or through the press, is not denied, provided it does not interfere with the discharge of their official duties.[16]

Two days later, Sherman instructed Arthur to reduce the force of the custom house by the recommended 20 per cent by June 30. The collector promptly asked the Jay commission for advice on specific unfit employees, but he was ignored once again.[17]

Meanwhile, the press of New York was cheering the commission on; people like Reid and Godkin felt that *they* knew what was really going on at the custom house and that the commission's conclusions were fully warranted. The *Tribune* applauded on May 3 that "the Commission seems to be getting thru the crust of the Custom-house," and laughed at Sherman's desire to make the place "the best-managed agency of the Government." It is already, said the paper, "but managed in the wrong way, by the wrong men, for the wrong purposes." Godkin in *The Nation,* never satisfied, complained that the president's letter was not strong enough, and that Arthur was retained; "on the whole, therefore, while the Committee's report is to be commended as excellent, so far as it goes, the action taken in consequence of it is not nearly so satisfactory." [18]

16 House Exec. Doc., 45th Cong., 1st sess., No. 8, p. 17.

17 Arthur to Jay, Turnure, and Robinson, June 12, 1877, Arthur Papers, New-York Historical Society; Arthur to Sherman, Nov. 23, 1877, on the commission's failure to respond, House Exec. Doc., 45th Cong., 2d sess., No. 25, p. 14.

18 N.Y. *Tribune,* May 29, 1877; *The Nation,* May 31, 1877. Sherman's letter to Arthur of May 28, 1877, was almost apologetic in its tone, shifting the responsibility for its message to Hayes: "Naturally in a government like ours, other things being equal, those will be preferred who sympathize with the party in power; but persons in office ought not to be expected to serve their party to the neglect of official duty, or to promote the interests of particular candidates . . . or to run caucuses or conventions. Such activity of office-holders is offensive to the great mass of people who hold no office, and gives rise to complaints and irritation. If any have been appointed for purely political reasons, without regard to their efficiency, now is a good time to get rid of them." He also told Arthur that the success of the reform depended mainly "upon your good sense and discretion." House Exec. Doc., 45th Cong., 1st sess., No. 8, pp. 19–20.

Additional reports were filed by the Jay commission on July 4, July 21, and August 31. These dealt with specific departments of the establishment, and all were marked by the same broad brushstrokes, making sweeping conclusions on the basis of less than adequate evidence, and giving little weight to the reports and documentary evidence furnished to the commission by Chester Arthur.[19]

In June, the *Tribune* published a rumor that Arthur's dismissal was impending, pointed out that the Democratic party managed to stay "pretty lively" without federal officeholders to run its affairs, and wondered "why one side should have the privilege of laying the country under contribution and not the other." A week later, it said that George Sharpe, in making the mandated reductions in his office, was firing his best clerks and keeping on the politicians. He had only himself to blame for this suspicion, it said: "He has made it his business to pull wires, and must not be surprised if people suspect that he goes on pulling them behind a mask of civil service reform." [20]

On June 22, meanwhile, Hayes had transformed his earlier letter to Sherman into his Executive Order No. 1, applying to all federal offices the rules he had set down for the New York Custom House. He apparently believed that those who held both a federal job and a position within a party organization would resign one or the other; if not, the violator would not be reappointed when his term expired. This passive course naturally stirred up criticism from the reform elements, which looked for whole-hog cleanouts immediately after the order was promulgated.[21]

Everyone knew that the New York Custom House was supposed to be run for the benefit of Roscoe Conkling. What was the senator doing during all this? John Jay was an enemy for whom Conkling had the utmost contempt; he was truly representative of the upper-class reformers that Conkling held responsible for most of the troubles of the Republican party. The Hayes letter and executive order were aimed squarely at Arthur, Cornell, Sharpe, and the officeholders who did most of the day-to-day work of the organization, the grassroots, down-to-earth labor of making sure that enough of the right type of delegates and candidates were selected, in wards and precincts throughout the state. This was an attack upon Conkling, by a president clearly under the influence of Evarts, Schurz, Curtis, and their kind.

[19] House Exec. Doc., 45th Cong., 1st sess., No. 8, pp. 36–42, 50–53, 58–68.
[20] N.Y. *Tribune*, June 25, 27, July 3, 1877.   [21] Barnard, pp. 451–452.

For a while, Conkling did nothing. He said very little publicly about the investigation, for he knew that Chester Arthur could handle as well as possible any questions about the actual operation of the custom house. Though Arthur was plainly stamped as Conkling's man, people did not get emotional about him as they did with Conkling. If anyone could disarm criticism, it would be Chester Alan Arthur, who had really done a remarkable job in running the custom house, serving the mercantile and commercial interests in a relatively efficient manner, while continuing the political aspects of the place at the same time. While a vast amount of his time was taken up with patronage matters, he still found opportunities to work improvements into the mechanics of the establishment.

After it became clear that the Jay commission's work was to be sharply critical, Conkling continued quietly to watch the implementation of all the high-sounding manifestoes flowing from the pen of Rutherford B. Hayes. There was talk of naming James Husted or Edwin Merritt to replace Sharpe, whose term as surveyor had expired, but nothing happened, so the senator went ahead with his planned trip to Europe, leaving on June 16, 1877, with a warm send-off from friends and supporters in New York. Edwards Pierrepont, still minister to England, had particularly urged Conkling to make the voyage. His prime purpose in taking the trip, on which Julia did not accompany him, was to overcome the effects of the malarial attack which had laid him low the year before. Gossips noted, however, that Mrs. Sprague was sojourning in Paris.

Conkling saw much of the Grants in London; the ex-president and his wife were on the first lap of a lengthy tour which would take them around the world. He also spent time looking around England on his own, away from the crowds which pointed and whispered about the famous American senator. On July 1, he wrote Bessie a long and chatty letter about his trip, a letter which is one of the few in existence showing Roscoe Conkling as a human being, as a father, rather than as a public figure.

He told Bessie, with the tourist's proud but weary air, "here I have been on the go night and day." At table one night, he related, Mrs. Grant said, "not to me but to the table," that "of all the great women she had seen not one was so easy or knew so well the right thing to do as Mrs. Fish or Mrs. Conkling." Without even seeing the other women, "I agreed with her, as to your mother especially." He wrote about the daring young ladies riding their horses in the streets, and he said that some of their horses were like Bessie's Charley—"none better." Her mother, he thought, "would faint if she saw you do what the girls there do, and yet you ride as well as any of them, & look a great deal better—and have considerably more sense."

"By myself I poke into all the by places. Franklin's house, Johnson's house, Crosby Hall (palace of Richard III, now a coffee house), Goldsmith's grave, etc.—(most of these places not sought by travellers) the tavern where Shakespeare & Ben Jonson drank ale. I have found all these & many other things."

He described Westminster Abbey—"the effigy of that monster Elizabeth"—and the Albert Museum—"the greatest thing I have seen in London." He complained that everyone, large and small, was concerned with moneymaking. "Everything which can be charged for is not free."

For Bessie, he summed up his England: "I could not have believed that on any spot of earth could dwell together so much majesty & littleness, so much grandeur & absurdity, so much power & weakness, so much wisdom & folly. I shall not settle in England." [22]

He left England for Paris and the Continent, where it is presumed he spent some time with Kate. When his tour was finished, the senator returned to New York on the *Neckar,* and was received on August 10 by a large crowd of enthusiasts, to whom he gave a short speech. It is obvious that the organization seized upon Conkling's homecoming as an occasion for a hearty demonstration of support. Some members of the crowd called out, "What about Hayes?" or "What about civil service reform?" but the senator intended to speak about these things at his own time. He was greeted in the same enthusiastic manner in Albany, Schenectady, Little Falls, and of course Utica, where he received a tumultuous welcome. It was a great triumph, even with the prearrangements, but one onlooker commented that Conkling "looked very anxious and troubled." [23]

Throughout the month of August, it was a matter for great speculation around New York what Conkling would say when he finally de-

[22] Conkling Papers, Library of Congress.

[23] N.Y. *Tribune,* Aug. 11, 1877; Ross, *Proud Kate,* p. 242. J. M. Bundy, publisher of the new *Evening Mail,* which Evarts was trying to establish as an administration organ in New York, to Evarts, Aug. 18, 1877, Evarts Papers. *The Nation,* on Aug. 16, 1877, said he was greeted "by a band of patriots, among whom we notice some of our most prominent appraisers, postmasters, weighers, gaugers, and inspectors." The *Neckar* actually docked at Hoboken, and he boarded the *Thomas Collyer* for the final leg of the journey to New York.

livered himself of an opinion on the Hayes administration. The *Tribune,* for example, opined one day that "if Senator Conkling should develop into a good Hayes Republican, it would be a great disappointment to the Democrats." Two weeks later, *The Nation* reported, "There is apparently an open breach between the Administration and Mr. Conkling." [24]

The first major issue seemed to be Cornell's retention of his position as chairman of the Republican state committee. This was in clear defiance of Hayes's dictum about officeholders with political functions, and the press would not let Hayes forget it. Cornell himself said the Hayes order was "an unwarranted and degrading invasion of his personal rights and liberty of citizenship." Peacemakers assured the president that Cornell had no more to do than to call the state convention to order on September 26 and then retire and the conflict would be at an end. Agitators claimed that he was holding the post in order to test the presidential order; the *Tribune* on August 13 said, "This is in the nature of a challenge to the President, and Mr. Cornell ought to know that Mr. Hayes is not a safe man to treat in that way." Godkin called Cornell's refusal "almost a national scandal," and further assured Hayes that "in this city the reform of the customs service by Mr. Arthur is regarded as a huge joke." [25]

Early in September, finally, after receipt of the last Jay commission report, Hayes, at the instigation of Evarts, decided to remove the three incumbent officers of the port. Sherman attempted, through an intermediary, to swap Arthur the consulship at Paris in exchange for a quiet resignation from the collectorship, and the efforts to consummate the withdrawals of the three officers occupied the month of September. [26]

The senator knew what was going on, and he had no love for Hayes. He selected the Republican state convention, to be held at Rochester on

[24] N.Y. *Tribune,* Aug. 22, 1877; *The Nation,* Sept. 6, 1877.

[25] Autobiographical sketch, Cornell Papers. *The Nation,* Sept. 6, 1877, Aug. 23, 1877. The N.Y. *Herald* on Sept. 1, 1877, pointed out that if Hayes would just "wait for a short time" about Cornell, "the pending difficulty will be removed." That is, until he called the convention to order. On the other hand, David Wells wrote a letter to Schurz the same day, complaining of "timidity" in civil service reform, and hoping "there will be no hesitation in meeting the defiance apparently shown by Cornell at New York." A Hoogenboom, *Outlawing the Spoils,* p. 158.

[26] Sherman, II, 681, where he said, "But for Evarts, Pres't Hayes would never have had the New York Custom House controversy." He wrote the same thing to Hayes on March 8, 1881. Barrows, p. 326.

September 26, for his rebuttal. The newspaper editors made their usual predictions beforehand, hoping that Senator Conkling would let sweet harmony and brotherhood prevail; Ellis Roberts, his erstwhile friend and follower, editor of the Utica *Herald* and successor to the Conkling congressional seat until toppled from it by a revolt caused by his split with Conkling, told an interviewer that the convention "will not dare to condemn the good work which Pres. Hayes is doing." Conkling, he said, "must choose for himself what his future will be. He cannot determine the future of the Republican Party."

One reporter wrote of Conkling: "He has not had the reputation of having a conciliatory disposition; but he has been esteemed a shrewd and sagacious politician, and he must certainly see that a policy of conciliation is essential," while another wrote that, though he would run the convention, "it would be an unwarranted inference to suppose that he will put it into open opposition, or even into covert opposition, to the President. He is too sagacious a politician." [27]

One thing which everyone agreed on: Conkling had absolute control of the convention, "like clay in the hands of a potter," the New York *Herald* said on September 25, mentioning also that the senator had been "unusually affable" in the hotel lobby, with "a pleasant word for everyone." Most Republicans hoped he would stay in such a happy mood. Many had heard George William Curtis, upon his arrival, insist that he would introduce a resolution fully endorsing President Hayes.

Cornell, a living symbol of the antagonism to Hayes, called the convention to order and then turned the gavel over to Tom Platt, who had been named temporary chairman. Platt, it was reported, had prepared two speeches, one hostile and harsh, the other mild and conciliatory, and presented them to Conkling. The senator chose the hard one, and it was this speech which Platt now delivered. He hit at Evarts, not by name but by crystal-clear inference, as a "demagogue" who was "conniving at the dissolution of the Republican party." He denounced the "political Pecksniffs and tricksters," but said their influence was not large. "The great Republican masses are sound and true." There was one subject, he said

which demagogues have magnified into unseemly proportions. I refer to the incessant cry which is raised that "the Republican party is pledged to reform in the civil service." Hungry expectants of office stand on street corners and shout the shibboleth until they are hoarse and weary. The in-

[27] N.Y. *Tribune,* Sept. 26, 1877; N.Y. *Herald,* Sept. 18, 24, 1877.

dependent journalist rolls it as a sweet morsel under his tongue, and daily blurts it in the face of a nauseated public.[28]

The delegates cheered; Conkling clapped his hands high over his head and waved his handkerchief. The senator was scheduled to assume the reins as permanent chairman of the convention, but now he moved to continue Platt as chairman; in view of the speech just concluded by Platt, this was a calculated insult to the president. The motion carried, 311 to 110. The platform was reported; its plank on the civil service, as drafted by the Conkling men, called for fit men, fixed terms, fair compensation, faithful performance of duty, frugality in the number of employees, freedom of political action (here was the crux of the conflict with Hayes), and no party assessments. The platform as reported did not mention any endorsement of the president, and George William Curtis soon had the floor. Things were about to blow up.

Curtis flung his defiance into the face of the organization, offering a resolution beginning with the declaration that "the lawful title of Rutherford B. Hayes to the Presidency is as clear and perfect as that of George Washington." It continued with commendation for the president's Southern policy "and for the correction of evils and abuses in the Civil Service" as fulfilling his own pledges and those of the platform at Cincinnati. Curtis supported his resolution with a speech which was, in its polite and precious way, denunciatory of Roscoe Conkling and of all those who opposed the president within the Republican party. He struck a foul blow when he said that Conkling always won his cases in the federal courts because he was trying against attorneys and before judges who owed their appointments to him. Besides being untrue, the canard was most unwise, for surely it justified Conkling in the attack which shortly followed.[29]

Conkling took the rostrum for a reply. Though it seemed certainly a speech in answer to the one just heard from Curtis, in reality the senator had worked on the speech for a long time.[30] When the right time came, just the right time, Conkling had his speech all ready. Now, in Rochester, he saw the appropriate moment to demolish George William Curtis and, beyond Curtis, the element in the Republican party that he represented.

He began by asserting that the delegates were gathered on state business, and that it was not the function of state political conventions to dally with national issues. And anyway, he went on, "Who are these men who, in newspapers or elsewhere, are cracking their whips over me

[28] Platt, pp. 87–89; Gosnell, p. 22.   [29] Milne, pp. 154–155.
[30] Depew, *Memories,* pp. 80–81.

and playing schoolmaster to the party? They are of various sorts and conditions. Some of them are the man-milliners, the dilettante and carpet knights of politics, whose efforts have been expended in denouncing and ridiculing and accusing honest men."

The Conkling delegates, fully alive to the show now after Platt's opening speech, Curtis's effort, and the beginning of the Boss's talk, loved the crack about "man-milliners." They all knew that *Harper's* was now running fashion articles, and they laughed with delight at the thrust.

Some of them are men who, when they could work themselves into conventions, have attempted to belittle and befoul Republican administrations and to parade their own thin veneering of superior purity. Some of them are men who, by insisting that it is corrupt and bad for men in office to take part in politics, are striving to prove that the Republican party has been unclean and vicious all its life. . . . Some of these worthies masquerade as reformers. Their vocation and ministry is to lament the sins of other people. Their stock in trade is rancid, canting self-righteousness. They are wolves in sheep's clothing. Their real object is office and plunder. When Dr. Johnson defined patriotism as the last refuge of a scoundrel, he was unconscious of the then undeveloped capabilities and uses of the word reform.

Chauncey Depew was sitting next to Curtis, who, under the rules of the convention, would have no opportunity to reply. Curtis's only reaction was to exclaim, at various points, "Remarkable!" "What an exhibition!" "Bad temper!" and "Very bad temper!" He later wrote to a friend that "no one can imagine the Mephistophelean leer and spite . . . the venom." [31]

Conkling, though, was pounding on: "Some of these new-found party overseers . . . forget that parties are not built up by deportment, or by ladies' magazines, or gush. . . . For extreme license in criticisms of administrations and of everybody connected with them, broad arguments can no doubt be found in the files of the journal made famous by the pencil of Nast." As the delegates roared, the senator continued, throwing everything in his armory of invective, sarcasm, and ridicule at Curtis. Depew called it "oratory of a high order," and Tom Platt said the senator "was rarely in more superb form." One reporter said his speech "was bristling with good points," but he also went on to say that it was the opinion of observers afterward "that there will not be the shadow of a chance to elect a State ticket this fall." [32]

31 *Ibid.*, p. 80; E. Cary, *G. W. Curtis*, pp. 257–258.
32 Depew, *Memories*, p. 79; Platt, p. 85; N.Y. *Herald*, Sept. 27, 1877.

A state ticket was nominated, after the formality of voting down Curtis's resolution was tended to, but when the convention was over no one talked about anything but Conkling and his speech. Curtis wrote to a friend: "It was the saddest sight I ever knew, that man glaring at me in a fury of hate, and storming out his foolish blackguardism. I was all pity. I had not thought him great, but I had not suspected how small he was." [33]

The New York *Herald* said, "He has not only drawn the sword and thrown away the scabbard; he has dipped his weapon in venom. . . . He used his personal triumph for flinging a firebrand of discord into the Republican party. . . . The Senator has acted the part of a blind and infuriate Samson who crushed himself beneath the edifice against whose pillars he leaned his mighty shoulders."

The *Tribune* said that "the Soreheads Convention at Rochester does not represent the Republican party." It called his attack "an incident without parallel" in the recent political history of New York and said that he had made a great mistake: "Before that speech he was stronger with the Republican party of the State . . . then he had been in years before." [34]

The Samson image seemed apt. No one could remember a state leader, a great party leader, like Conkling, placing himself and his state organization in hostile opposition to a president of his own party at the start of that president's term; old-timers went back to Douglas and Buchanan for a comparison, but "popular sovereignty" and the rights of Kansas seemed, in retrospect, to have been more pressing reasons for such a fight than Conkling's apparent motive, the right to run a federal custom house without interference from the federal government.

Men shook their heads and wondered what would come of the fight. They knew that Senator Conkling referred sneeringly to "snivel service" and that he discounted Hayes as "His Fraudulency" and "Rutherfraud B. Hayes," from the manner of his election victory. But all that was in private; it was another thing to take on the administration publicly, to hurl down a challenge like the one at Rochester.

After Rochester, though, the deed was done. Roscoe Conkling intended to fight Hayes. He felt that he had no alternative; in his eyes, it was Hayes who had declared war upon him—Evarts, Schurz, Curtis, now this business with the custom house, *his* custom house.

[33] Cary, pp. 257–258.
[34] N.Y. *Herald*, Sept. 27, 1877; N.Y. *Tribune*, Sept. 28, 1877.

CHAPTER 18

———◄••►———

CONKLING TRIUMPHANT

Evarts was primarily responsible for the decision to replace Arthur, Cornell, and Sharpe in the New York Custom House; indeed, a cabinet meeting called to discuss the matter was postponed until the secretary of state could be present. When the decision was made, early in September 1877, Sherman was instructed to make efforts to secure the voluntary resignations of the three officers. This effort was unsuccessful, as we have seen, and Conkling, at Rochester in late September, let the administration know what sort of a fight it was in for.

A protest came to the president on October 6, from Edwin D. Morgan, seeking the reversal of the decision to fire his old protégé and close friend, Chester Arthur: "Gen'l Arthur . . . is entitled, on his merits, to remain til the expiration of his term. . . . He is strong and popular with the merchants and business men of both parties. He is an able lawyer, an excellent man of business, kind and generous to all, and liberal in furnishing the 'sinews of war.' " [1]

Even intercession from so respectable a source did not help the embattled port officers. Hayes, his nerve steeled by Evarts and Schurz within the cabinet and Curtis without, was determined to make the changes; he was not interested in reasons why the incumbents should be retained. Resignation was out of the question; Arthur told John Sherman, "The treatment of the whole matter has been so unfortunate that I feel I cannot now resign." On October 19, four days into a special session of Congress, Hayes sent to the Senate his nominations for the custom house offices. For collector, he nominated Theodore Roosevelt, the father of a future president, a bitter enemy of Roscoe Conkling, the man who had led a delegation of New Yorkers to Cincinnati in 1876

---

[1] Barrows, p. 327; Rawley, p. 260. Liberality in furnishing the "sinews of war" was certainly not likely to interest Hayes.

with the avowed purpose of blocking Conkling's nomination. *The Nation* said that Roosevelt had "wealth above the temptations of any office, character, great business experience," and the merchants of New York would not "lightly brook" his rejection by the Senate. Godkin overlooked, of course, the fact that the merchants did not favor the dismissal of Arthur, who would remain in office if Roosevelt were rejected.[2]

L. Bradford Prince, a lawyer and a long-time politician from Queens, not a Conkling man, was nominated for Cornell's place as naval officer, and General Edwin A. Merritt, an old Fenton follower, was slated for surveyor in place of George Sharpe. The nominations were greeted in the Senate with "derisive laughter," and referred to the Senate commerce committee for consideration; the committee chairman was the senior senator from New York, Roscoe Conkling, the fox in charge of the hen house.[3]

Sharpe's term of office had expired, and he, seeing the handwriting on the wall, had withdrawn his application to the president for reappointment. Replacements for Arthur and Cornell had also been expected, though the actual names of the new nominees were not known till submitted; still it came as a shock to old Washington hands to see a president directly challenge a leading senator on a matter of senatorial privilege like this. The capital had become accustomed to a string of weak or powerless presidents since the election of Zachary Taylor, broken only by Lincoln, who had so many problems with the conduct of the war that he could not afford the luxury of battling with Congress on matters of prerogative and form. The Senate's authority had not often been put to the test, and, when it had been, the Senate generally won.

Hayes let it be known that his reason for turning out the old officers was his desire to have a new slate in the custom house to implement the reforms and recommendations of the Jay commission; this stand avoided a confrontation on the issue of Cornell's holding his position as Republican state chairman, and it got around the fact that there was very weak substantiation to any claim of incompetence on the part of the incumbents. This was very disappointing to the more vocal reformists,

2 Arthur to Sherman, Oct. 19, 1877, Arthur Papers, New-York Historical Society; *The Nation*, Nov. 1, 1877.
3 Binkley, p. 191.

who wanted an immediate issue made of the political activity of Arthur, Cornell, and Sharpe. Beside that, there was no doubt that Arthur had set to work implementing some of the more feasible proposals of the Jay commission, at Sherman's request, and the secretary, as he later wrote, "preferred to try to execute the proposed reforms with him in office rather than a stranger." [4] In addition, the removals coming after the investigation led the public to assume that they were made because of something revealed by the probe reflecting on Arthur, Cornell, and Sharpe. When nothing of this sort was ever produced, the president's case was weakened.

The New York *Herald's* correspondent wrote hopefully from Washington on November 2 that "Senatorial courtesy," the old custom of refusing to confirm appointments obnoxious to a senator of the president's party in that senator's state, would not prevail, and "it is doubtful whether any Senator will be so absurd as to try it on." A week later, the same reporter was writing more realistically that the port appointments "will cause strife" in the Senate. By that time, too, Conkling's commerce committee had not yet held any meetings in consideration of the nominations.

Under the amended Tenure of Office Act still in effect, after the abortive repeal in the early days of General Grant's first term, an officer held his position until a successor was confirmed, if Congress was in session; if it was not, he could be suspended and a successor named, but he went back into the office if the successor was not confirmed by the next session of the Senate.

Conkling's committee sat on the nominations until November 30, when they were reported to the floor with an adverse recommendation. Since the Senate, guided by Conkling, then refused Thurman's motion to go into executive session, nothing further was done before the end of the session on December 3. This was called "a signal victory for Mr. Conkling . . . adroitly won." [5]

Conkling had been busy in the interim. A bristling interview purported to be with him appeared in the New York *Herald* on November 9, in which the senator took a fair number of cracks at Hayes and inter-

[4] Sherman, II, 684, letter to Justin S. Morrill.
[5] N.Y. *Herald,* Dec. 1, 1877. Shores felt that Conkling's skillful management kept the nominations from coming up in the special session, when some observers felt that they would surely be confirmed. Shores, p. 242.

jected several comments pointedly praising former Governor Tilden. He sneered at his enemies, the "better elements," the reformers, in New York City:

There are about three hundred persons here who believe themselves to occupy the solar walk and milky way, and even up there they lift their skirts very carefully for fear even the heavens might stain them. Some of these people would vote against a man because he had been nominated. The mere fact of nomination and selection reduces him in their estimation. They would have people fill the offices by nothing less than divine selection.

On November 12, the senator rose in the Senate to make a half-hearted disclaimer of the interview, but it looked to be so much his in style, tone, and content that no one took the disclaimer very seriously. The editor of the *Herald* predicted "breezy times in Washington after Mr. Conkling's return."

A caucus of Republican senators was called by the New Yorker on November 10, marked by some bitter exchanges but an amicable outcome, as most members took a stand in favor of "senatorial courtesy" and against the president's determination to ride roughshod over it. A caucus committee headed by Edmunds called on Hayes to make him aware of the danger of the split between himself and the Senate Republicans, but Hayes merely reminded them that he was "President of the whole country, not of any party." Edmunds reported back sadly to the caucus that Hayes's views were "more suggestive of a political dreamer than of the sober sense of a statesman." [6]

Conkling had Arthur write Sherman a long letter, a draft of which went to Conkling on November 21, and the final version to the secretary on November 23, reviewing completely the methods and conclusions of the Jay commission, to that body's disfavor, and recalling to the secretary that as to the recommended actions, "those which are not repetitions of recommendations long since made by me are chiefly unwise or impracticable, while one of them is in direct violation of the law." [7]

[6] N.Y. *Herald,* Nov. 11, 1877; Barnard, p. 455. Curiously, even Democrats were uneasy about the changes. Horatio Seymour wrote on Nov. 19, 1877, to Kernan, warning him that "we should not bring back the Fenton influence in this state. . . . I do not know that Messrs. Roosevelt and Prince represent that faction but Gen. Merritt does." Kernan Papers.

[7] Arthur to Conkling, Nov. 21, 1877, Arthur Papers, New-York Historical Society; House Exec. Doc., 45th Cong., 2d sess., No. 25, p. 10. Arthur's full letter covers pages 7–16.

A New York *Herald* reporter on the same day predicted that the nominations would be rejected: "The lash of Mr. Conkling has been too vigorously applied. He has gained a moral ascendency over the Senators, if any there were, who might have stood against him, which now, it is believed, disables them." Conkling, it was said, "holds the Republican part of the Senate in his grip." The friends of the administration, by hesitation and irresolution, showed Conkling their weak point, "a mortal dread lest he might read them out of the Republican party." In the Senate, said the *Tribune* on December 3, "they seem to think Mr. Conkling has New York behind him. In New York it certainly looks as if he had the Senate behind him." Signs pointed, so it was said, to his victory in the custom house appointments.

Undaunted, Hayes resubmitted his nominations to the new session of the Congress, sending them to the Senate on December 6, and writing to a friend in Chicago two days later, "The Senatorial usurpation is now the question; the immediate result is in doubt." [8]

On December 11, the commerce committee reported the nominations to the Senate, Roosevelt and Prince adversely, Merritt favorably (Sharpe's term had expired so there was a vacancy in the surveyor's office, and Conkling never seems to have had any personal feeling against Merritt). The next day the Senate held an executive session lasting from 2:30 to 8:30. Over an hour of this time was occupied with a long speech by Roscoe Conkling. Bayard of Delaware, Gordon of Georgia, and Hayes's old friend Stanley Matthews of Ohio were among those speaking in favor of the nominations, but the only speech that really counted was Conkling's.

His speech contained three parts: first, a general discussion of the policy factors in removals and appointments; second, a lecture on where the political duties of such officers began and ended; and, third, an analysis of these particular nominations. His speech was described by his nephew as one of his three greatest oratorical efforts. Conkling said that the appointments were designed to "dishonor him politically." He described at length the exalted characters of Chester Arthur and A. B. Cornell, and the way in which Arthur had carried out many reforms and recommended others, not failing to mention Sherman's policy of pushing through the reforms with Arthur's assistance. He spoke of the many inconsistencies of Hayes in his treatment of the civil service, a matter about which many of the loudest reformers were complaining, and he

[8] To William Henry Smith; Barnard, p. 455.

said that neither Hayes nor Sherman had read the Jay commission reports. He denied that the New York Custom House was a political machine, and he attacked Theodore Roosevelt as a bitter personal enemy. He was well aware that the administration, blithely confident of success, had done virtually nothing to see to the confirmation of its nominees, and he knew that his voice would be the most important one raised before the Senate on either side of this question; he took full advantage of this fact. It was a powerful and convincing speech, and when the Senate voted on the nominations it rejected Roosevelt and Prince by votes of 31 to 25. Merritt was confirmed without opposition, but Hayes was staggered by the blow. All but five of the Republican members of the Senate voted with Conkling to reject the nominations of a Republican president.[9]

Arthur wrote to his champion, "I cannot tell you how gratified I am at the splendid victory you have won—apart from & way beyond any personal considerations of my own." All New York, he said, was excited by the event and feeling was with Conkling. He closed by thanking the senator for his "vindication of my official character." [10]

John Sherman, who should have taken care of the confirmations and as a practical politician was made to look absurd by the result, sputtered:

This action of the Senate was indefensible. There was not the slightest objection to Roosevelt or Prince, and none was made. The reasons for a change were given in the report of the Jay Commission. . . . The motive of Mr. Conkling was hostility to President Hayes and his inborn desire to domineer. The chief embarrassment fell upon me. . . . The office was held in pronounced contempt of the President.[11]

But the president sat in his study in the White House and wrote calmly: "In the language of the press 'Senator Conkling has won a

[9] N.Y. *Herald,* Dec. 13, 1877; N.Y. *Tribune,* Dec. 13, 1877; A. R. Conkling, p. 374. The other two of his three best speeches, according to his nephew, were the one on Murphy against Fenton, and one on Belknap's impeachment. All three of these, curiously, were in executive sessions of the Senate, where Conkling clearly had tremendous power. Stephen W. Dorsey, a carpetbag senator from Arkansas, was quoted as saying, "nobody will ever know the degree of Conkling's power in executive sessions. He has immense strength, when the spectators have gone, upon the minds of his peers." A. R. Conkling, p. 559, quoting the Philadelphia *Times.*

[10] Arthur to Conkling, Dec. 13, 1877, Conkling Papers, Library of Congress.

[11] Sherman, II, 682; Sherman, of course, overlooked his own part in hanging the Tenure of Office Act around Andrew Johnson's neck. He made further statements about Arthur not giving cooperation in the reforms, and about charges of unfitness made against Arthur, which were just not true.

great victory over the Administration.' My N.Y. nominations were rejected 31 to 25. But the end is not yet. I am right, and shall not give up the contest." [12]

And right there was the heart of the problem for Roscoe Conkling. His victory sent new life and heart surging through his organization. The great Senate lords, led by the greatest and most unflinching of them all, had stood up to this grayish, unknown president, and they had beaten him. Arthur and Cornell retained their posts in the custom house, and Conkling reigned supreme. But someday, sooner or later, Arthur's term was going to expire, and Cornell's too. There was no way that Roscoe Conkling or any combination of Senate chieftains could force Hayes to re-nominate Chester Arthur once his term ended. In the meantime, Hayes was telling himself that he would eventually get Arthur and Cornell as far out of the custom house as George Sharpe now was. It would be a long, grim struggle, and there had to be a ray of hope for Conkling's machine at the end of that struggle. Without that hope, his followers would be likely to creep silently away in the night.

There was now no turning back for Roscoe Conkling. He had long since marked out his own kind of political career; he had declared his war on Rutherford B. Hayes; the reformers, the do-gooders, the people occupying that solar walk he spoke of would have nothing to do with him. His way was the practical way; he controlled the caucuses and the conventions, so that the do-gooders were faced with a choice of voting for his candidates or for the Democrats, and seldom would they go *that* far. Now, at one of the most exhilarating highspots of his career, when he had, almost by himself, humbled a despised president of his own party, he must have realized that the "practical" way might not be the smartest way at all.

[12] T. H. Williams, ed., p. 107.

CHAPTER 19

———◆◆◆◆◆———

HAYES PERSISTENT

After Roosevelt and Prince were rejected, Godkin wrote:

It only remains for us to congratulate this great State on the kind of "senior Senator" it has. An ordinary man in that place would be occupied with the coarser interests of this busy commercial community—the currency, the national credit, the port, the tariff, the revenue system, the municipal administration—all of which have so much to do with its purely mundane prosperity. On this low class of questions the great man hardly seems to bestow a thought.[1]

Conkling left himself open to such attacks because, in truth, he took little apparent interest in the major problems with which the country was occupied. The year had been one of general labor unrest, capped by a far-flung railroad strike which led to violence and which President Hayes, at the request of several state governors, put down by the use of armed force. This strike, chillingly ominous in its implications of future labor and class strife, dismayed the conservative elements of American society, long fed one-sided reports of the horrors of the Paris Commune and the red-flag agitators of Europe, but it seems not to have bothered Roscoe Conkling. Agitation over the currency was continuing, and, though the nation was pulling itself out of the depression with which it had been plagued for a number of years, poverty, squalor, and misery were still widespread. The Nez Perce War of mid-1877, resulting in the capture of Chief Joseph and his band at the Bear Paw Mountains in northern Montana, drew the attention of the public, as the Indians stood off and frequently befuddled overwhelming units of the United States Army, and symbolized the failure of the nation's policies toward the Indian

[1] *The Nation,* Dec. 13, 1877.

tribes. On all of these questions, Roscoe Conkling said very little, initiated nothing, and lent no weight of support.[2]

Conkling was active in certain areas, however; primarily he was concerned about the proposed changes in the New York Custom House and the duplicity and mendacity of Hayes on civil service reform. He also kept up running squabbles with several of the Democratic senators from the South, touchy ex-brigadiers from the Confederate army, who found in a foe like Conkling a kindred spirit—proud, eloquent, sensitive, and given to assuming poses and attitudes.

The day after the Hayes nominations for the custom house were defeated, Conkling became engaged in a difference with Senator John B. Gordon of Georgia which threatened for a time to blow up into a duel. Gordon, a Confederate army hero, was the leader of the Southerners in the Senate and had attempted to win confirmation for Roosevelt and Prince. The trouble apparently grew out of a very minor passage over the Senate calendar, after which Gordon accused Conkling of giving orders to the vice-president in the chair. Conkling said the statement was untrue, and Gordon retorted, "We will settle this elsewhere." The next thing anyone knew, both senators had "seconds" who bustled about making arrangements and composing differences; the outcome was a statement signed by the seconds, advising that "the remarks of either should be treated as if never uttered, and . . . are mutually and simultaneously withdrawn." Much ado about very little, obviously, but it added its bit to the Conkling legend.[3]

The New Yorker had earlier taken an active part in the extended debate throughout the fall on the admission to a Senate seat of M. C. Butler, a former rebel general from South Carolina, who was challenged on the ground that he had personally participated in the lynching and terrorism of Negro voters in his state. Despite the opposition, Butler was ultimately admitted to his seat and sworn in on November 30. The Solid South, that spectre which had haunted the Republicans since the

[2] Excellent treatment of the Nez Perce problem can be found in A. Josephy, *The Nez Perce Indians and the Opening of the Northwest* (New Haven: Yale University Press, 1965).

[3] A. R. Conkling, pp. 560–562. The senator's "seconds" were Timothy Howe of Wisconsin and Hannibal Hamlin of Maine. Tom Platt shortly thereafter wrote that at the time of the affair, Senator Lucius Q. C. Lamar of Mississippi (of whom we shall hear more later) "armed himself and declared he should seek to avenge Gordon's insult on sight." Platt to W. Reid, Jan. 18, 1878, Reid Papers. General report had it that Conkling usually carried a pistol.

end of the war, was slowly taking shape, even so soon after the inauguration of Hayes and the withdrawal of the last of the troops.

One of those who had fought hardest to keep the South from becoming
solidly Democratic—with whatever weapons, legitimate or otherwise,
were at his disposal—passed away. On January 17, 1878, Conkling
delivered a eulogy on his old rival and co-worker, Morton of Indiana,
who had died November 1. The old enmities and jealousies were hidden
from view: "He needs no epitaph but his name; and though brass may
corrode, and marble moulder, men will still remember Oliver Perry
Morton as a leading and manful defender of the Republic in the
Republic's most dire and heroic age." [4]

Congressman Richard P. Bland of Missouri, "Silver Dick" Bland,
introduced a bill in late 1877 calling for the remonetization and free
coinage of silver. "The Crime of '73," the bill which had deleted the
silver dollar from the list of minted coins, the fictional conspiracy among
the great international financial interests against the poor debtors of the
West, was to be reversed and justice restored to the currency market.
A fatuous panacea? Perhaps; but millions of people in the West believed
fervently in silver as the issue out of all their troubles, and for two
decades regarded the two national parties as tweedledum-tweedledee
allies of Eastern gold. Bland's bill passed the House on November 5,
1877. Two weeks later, Allison of Iowa reported the measure, now
known as the Bland-Allison bill, out of the Senate finance committee
with amendments added to limit the amount of silver to be coined and
to restrict somewhat the inflationary aspect of the project. The bill
came up for consideration in the Senate in February 1878; here
was a measure into which Roscoe Conkling would surely sink his
teeth!

On February 5, Conkling presented to the Senate a large number of
printed form petitions submitted to him calling for remonetization of
the silver dollar, and he then advised his listeners that such petitions
"do not represent the opinions and convictions of a majority of the
people of the State of New York." The legislature, he said, had recently
"declared that gold is the standard," and "the people of New York look
with deep apprehension upon any experiment exposing the finances of
the country to fresh disturbance and vicissitude." Conkling endorsed
the sentiment expressed in one petition from which he quoted that those
pushing measures for remonetization of silver were "a nearly equal

[4] *Cong. Rec.*, 45th Cong., 2d sess., p. 377.

mixture of idiots and knaves," adding pleasantly, "present company is always excepted." [5]

It was a short speech and very general in its import. Those who had heard Conkling's major efforts through the years on behalf of sound money waited expectantly for his assumption of the leadership of the foes of the bill, for the mighty speech with which he would dispel the fogs of inflation and fiscal irresponsibility. Curiously, they waited in vain. Roscoe Conkling never made an important speech during the debates on the bill, though he was generally present and he voted for amendments (usually unsuccessful) to soften its inflationary impact. On February 15, the bill passed the Senate, 48 to 21, with Conkling and his colleague Kernan both voting "nay". The House concurred in the Senate amendments and sent it on to the White House, where it met a veto by Hayes, who said the bill "authorizes the violation of sacred obligations." Conkling then apparently tried to prevent hasty action on the veto, appealing to certain senators to let things cool for a while. This effort was completely unsuccessful. Both Houses easily overrode the veto, and the Bland-Allison Act became law, without the voice of Roscoe Conkling ever being raised in serious opposition to it, at least not the ferocious and determined opposition he could bring to bear upon such things as custom house appointments.[6]

He may have been oppressed at this time by the ambivalence of his position, as leader of the Republicans in the Senate, yet in fierce defiance of a Republican president on certain matters he deemed crucial to himself. Hayes was basically as conservative as he was, particularly on fiscal matters, and they were in general agreement on such questions, but they could not communicate, even when they were in accord. Thus there was no correlation of effort, and Conkling may very well have felt reluctant to take an advanced position in support of Hayes on any particular point while the president and his hated advisers were chipping away at Conkling's machine.

He was in opposition much of the time now. He fought against the Rivers and Harbors bill, because he believed that "many of these appropriations are utterly unwarrantable in fact and utterly unwarranted

[5] *Ibid.*, p. 749.

[6] *Ibid.*, p. 1112; Richardson, ed., VII, 487–489 (veto message of Feb. 28, 1878). Sage, pp. 152–157. A Platt letter to Whitelaw Reid on May 6, 1878, retails Conkling's story of his efforts for delay, including the fact that "he was hooted by every Senator he approached." Reid Papers.

upon any sustainable theory of law . . . within any true construction of the Constitution." [7]

He fought against the first of those riders to appropriation bills with which the Democratic majorities, first in the House of Representatives alone, later in both houses, bedeviled the president, in attempts to repudiate Reconstruction action and legislation by oblique attack. The provision in question in June of 1878, tacked on the Army Appropriation bill by the House, rendered unlawful the employment of the U.S. Army as a *posse comitatus* for the purpose of executing the laws, except as provided by the Constitution or acts of Congress. Conkling attacked it; though standing by itself, he said, it might be harmless enough, still one must look at the imputation of the amendment: "It is . . . adapted to make those who vote for it put a *cognovit* on the record, to make them plead in substance that things have been done in derogation of this principle, that they so admit that they regret it, and that they affirm by their votes that the time has come when a disapproval ought to be recorded." Perhaps, he said, some one in the army has done something of which not all would approve. But: "To vote for the provision now would, however, imply that some special occasion in this regard has arisen."

I shall not be suspected, Mr. President, of being too partial to the present national administration. . . . [Yet] if the head of any administration in ancient or in modern times has so conducted himself as to avoid reasonable suspicion of his intention to do that which this section denounces, I think I may say the head of the present administration has so conducted himself. . . . I do not feel bound, in the absence of any summons in this regard, to put on the statute-book such a denunciation.

The rider eventually amounted to little, but it was not the last that Hayes, Conkling, and the beleaguered Republican party would hear of it and its fellows.[8]

Congress adjourned on June 20, 1878. Hayes lost little time thereafter in resuming his efforts to oust the incumbent officers from the New York Custom House. Theodore Roosevelt had died in February, so the president had to find a new man.

On July 10, Sherman stopped in to the custom house and told Arthur that he was being supplanted by Edwin Merritt. The latter, after lunching

---

[7] *Cong. Rec.*, 45th Cong., 2d sess., p. 4423, June 11, 1878. This was precisely the position for which Arthur was to receive such acclaim as president.

[8] *Ibid.*, pp. 4303, 4304, June 8, 1878.

with the secretary at Delmonico's, told the press that he had "neither sought nor desired the Collectorship" and said that he was "placed in an embarrassing position." City politicians were thunderstruck by the move, and one bitterly said that the suspensions after the adjournment of the Senate showed that Hayes and Evarts "hadn't sufficient nerve to make a square fight." [9]

The next day, Hayes sent to Arthur and Cornell notices of suspension from their offices; he designated Merritt as the new collector, and Silas W. Burt as naval officer. Merritt, considered a man of high ability, had served in the legislature, in the state quartermaster and commissary departments, and had some prior experience in the custom house, having lost his job as naval officer, ironically, when Tom Murphy took over in 1870. Merritt had followed his mentor Fenton into the Liberal Republican party in 1872, but he had been received back into the party with no apparent ill feeling in 1874. Burt, who had been at Union College with Arthur, was a civil engineer who had been in the naval office since 1869. Now deputy naval officer, gossips said that he already performed Cornell's work.[10]

There was little personal criticism of Merritt and Burt, except from George Sharpe, who was quoted in the *World* on July 12 as saying, "If there were a thousand applicants for the collectorship, each worse than the other, nine hundred and ninety-nine would be picked out before General Merritt would be touched."

Late in the afternoon of July 19, Merritt showed up at the custom house with his letter of appointment from Sherman. He and Arthur chatted pleasantly for a while, and then Arthur gathered up his things, said good-bye to his deputies, and left. The action would move back to the Senate chamber, when Hayes submitted his nominations for confirmation.

After the malign and divisive Rochester convention of 1877, and the continued hostility since that time of Senator Conkling toward the

[9] N.Y. *Sun,* July 12, 1878.

[10] Arthur Papers, Library of Congress; W. Hartman, "Pioneer in Civil Service Reform," pp. 369–372. Interestingly, the supposedly simon-pure Whitelaw Reid had written to Sherman, after Roosevelt's death, that a new collector "be a man equal to all the practical duties of the place, which are necessarily and essentially political as well as mercantile," and Sherman wrote back that he "fully concurred" in Reid's views. When Conkling complained that he was assailed by a pack of hypocrites, he was not far wrong. See Howe, p. 83, for references to the Reid-Sherman exchange.

Hayes administration, Republican observers looked to the 1878 political activities in New York State with gloomy and fearful forebodings. If Conkling and his men, maddened by the outright suspension of Arthur and Cornell from the custom house, and exhilarated by the triumph over Hayes won by Conkling in the Senate, with the prospect of another to follow, chose to conduct the campaign in the same spirit, then disaster stalked the party. Journals like the New York *Tribune* opposed the call for a state convention, having only too clear a recollection of the one held a year earlier. Hayes reported on a talk he had with a New Yorker who advised him that "the enemies of the Administration have the organization in their hands, and will control the party in the State," even though "a majority of the good citizens outside of the politicians are sound" and in time "will control the organization." Evarts wrote to the president that "the way out of the malignant politics of N.Y. State is by frank and open treatment of both sides," a policy which the secretary of state had not begun to espouse until after the administration had come to disaster in following the brutal and abrupt methods he had earlier recommended. Everyone was clearly worried about New York.[11]

By this time, indeed, it appeared that 1878 was going to be an election year of more than ordinary off-year significance. Two years before, a new party commonly called the Greenback party, with a basic program of opposition to the resumption of specie payments, had nominated New York philanthropist and manufacturer Peter Cooper for president, and had won about 80,000 votes. By 1878, the new party had taken up hostility to the demonetization of silver, advocacy of restrictions upon the legal hours of labor, and other ideas designed to win wider popular approval for its candidates. Primarily, however, the Greenbackers campaigned against the impending resumption of specie payment, now scheduled for the beginning of 1879, setting forth in graphic terms the misery it would cause the poor working classes. Conservatives in the two older parties were alarmed at the possibilities of major gains for the Greenbackers, and the vast amount of scorn and denunciation poured upon their leaders in the press serves as a measure of this alarm. It was regarded as inevitable that the new party would win a few con-

[11] T. H. Williams, ed., p. 161, a diary entry of Aug. 12, 1878, concerning a meeting with George H. Forster, a New York City lawyer. Barrows, p. 328, for Evarts's letter of Aug. 24, 1878. See also the letter of Reid to James Garfield of March 16, 1878, stating that someone was needed (he suggested Fenton!) "to organize and pull together our factions." Reid Papers.

gressional seats in the West, but Republican strategists feared a division of the Republican hard-money forces between Conkling and Hayes wings which would deliver seats in the New York delegation into the hands of the soft-money advocates.

The platform of the New York Democratic party, adopted in its convention at Syracuse, was so vague in its stand on the currency that in places throughout the state Democratic forces were able to ally with Greenback candidates. This Democratic party, however, was still led by Samuel J. Tilden, and Sam Tilden was nobody's radical. He was still the same secretive legal wizard who had built himself an immense fortune through railroad manipulations—just the kind of activities which the Greenbackers and their progeny, the Populists, so bitterly detested. Tilden was committed to the gold standard, Senator Kernan was committed to the gold standard, and Governor Robinson was wholly committed to Tilden. Though Tilden still held the reins of the party in New York State, his control was not unchallenged. The new Tammany boss, John Kelly, tagged "Honest John" Kelly to emphasize the complete break in control between Tweed and his successor, hated Tilden. Kelly was smooth and polished and had been untouched by the Tweed scandals, since he had been in Europe from 1861 to 1871, though he had prior to that been in Congress and had served as sheriff. He had come back and taken control of Tammany, reorganizing and invigorating the old machine, hopefully fumigating it as well. But it was still Tammany, and it hated Tilden, who thought he was too good for the machine and who, it was felt, had vastly exaggerated its sins in order to make his own name greater. Kelly had fought Tilden in the state convention of 1877, and he fought him again at Syracuse in 1878, leaving a residue of bitterness after Tilden's narrow victory.

There was no state-wide race in 1878. Besides the congressional contests, however, a mayor of New York City was to be elected, and for this Arthur united the Republicans with anti-Tammany Democrats behind Edward Cooper, Peter Cooper's son, against Kelly's man, Auguste Schell. Kelly was vulnerable to intraparty rebellions within the city, where he was trying to get his man elected; it was a lesson he would remember the next year, when Tilden was trying to get *his* man re-elected on a state-wide level.

Along with the threat of the Greenbackers and the opportunity presented in the city by the Democratic split was another important fact; the legislature elected in November 1878 would elect a United States senator in January 1879. Not just any United States senator, either; it was Roscoe Conkling's seat with which the legislature would be dealing.

The Republican convention met at Saratoga on September 26. Roscoe Conkling had himself made permanent chairman of the gathering, and he made a speech, a "masterly and every way admirable address," said the *Tribune* the next day, supporting Hayes and his administration, with particular attention paid, to be sure, to its stand in favor of sound money and against the financial lunacies, as he saw them, of the Greenbackers, the free-silverites, and a large number of Democrats. Tom Platt said that Conkling's speech "strengthened weak knees everywhere." Even Curtis applauded the senator and made a little speech in support of his position. Peace and sweet unity swept over the Republican party of New York, and it stayed that way throughout the campaign that followed.[12]

Conkling worked hard in the campaign, and so did his supporters. There had been rumors during the summer of an impending divorce action to be instituted against the senator by his wife (all of which had been denied), but he did not let these bother him. Stewart Woodford was a frequent speaker on behalf of Cooper and various Republican congressional candidates, and Arthur was so closely connected with the canvass that Cooper was accused of being his puppet. As the campaign progressed, sound money slipped somewhat as a target for Republican orators behind the wickedness of the Democrats of the South, who had disenfranchised the Negro, were pushing for payment of the rebel war claims, and wanted to disarm the U.S. Army with attacks upon it in Congress. There was just enough truth behind these attacks, or just enough wild Southern rhetoric, to give them some plausibility. It was a bad year for the Republicans nationally. The Greenbackers won a large number of votes and a large number of congressmen, either members of the party or elected with its support; the Democrats retained control of the House (though by a slightly reduced margin); and the Democrats won enough state legislatures to make their control of the Senate sure. But 1878 was a good year for the Republican party in New York. Cooper was elected mayor of New York; twenty-six of the thirty-three New York congressmen would be Republicans; and the assembly went heavily Republican. They were the right kind of Republicans, too, and this last item virtually insured the re-election of Roscoe Conkling to the Senate.[13]

12 Platt to Reid, Sept. 27, 1878, Reid Papers.
13 P. H. Buck, *Road to Reunion*, pp. 115–116; Alexander, III, 407.

At the time the replacements were made at the custom house in the summer of 1878, Evarts told Hayes that the changes were so "useful to the public service and to the unity of the party" that he anticipated no prolonged opposition. Surely he could not have been so giddily optimistic as to suppose that Conkling would acquiesce in the removal of Arthur and Cornell. On December 3, the names of Merritt and Burt were sent in to the Senate, this time with Sherman vowing that he would resign if the nominations were rejected.[14]

Conkling, as expected, announced his opposition to the new nominees, and Hayes recorded in his diary:

The political event of the last week is the opposition of Conkling to the N. Y. appointments. This is a test case. The Senators generally prefer to confirm. . . . But many, perhaps a majority, will not oppose Conkling on the question. Senatorial courtesy, the Senatorial prerogative, and the fear of C's vengeance in future control them. He is like Butler, more powerful because he is vindictive and not restrained by conscience.[15]

Meanwhile, Merritt himself spent much of the month lobbying in Albany, at the suggestion of Sherman, trying to win support among the Republican members of the new legislature, in an endeavor to outflank Conkling and put pressure upon him from an unexpected source. This lobbying did not interfere with the senator's re-election, which took place as planned and with little overt opposition.

The question of the New York nominations was momentous not only for Conkling but for all those who were solicitous of Republican success in 1880. The twist was the gubernatorial election in New York in 1879; it was conceded that victory in the Empire State in 1879 was probably essential to Republican victory in the nation the following year. But how would victory be attained in New York if the conflict between Hayes and Conkling, allayed in 1878, was to be aggravated again?

Sherman sent to the Senate on January 15 a letter making more specific charges of inefficiency against Arthur and Cornell. He said that Arthur habitually came late to his office, did little while there, and let his deputy Lydecker perform his functions, while Cornell was alleged to have done none of the work of the naval office, leaving it all to Burt. Dispatch of this letter marked the assumption of a more aggressive line

[14] Evarts letter of July 13, 1878, Howe, p. 84; N.Y. *Tribune,* Dec. 4, 1878; Sherman, II, 683.

[15] T. H. Williams, ed., pp. 176–177, entry of Dec. 16, 1878. The "Butler" referred to here, of course, is Benjamin F. Butler of Massachusetts.

on the part of the administration and underscored Sherman's personal determination not to be beaten again on the appointments. Conkling, for the commerce committee, opposed publication of Sherman's letter and had it sent on to Arthur and Cornell for their use "in making such answer as you deem proper." [16]

Arthur responded with a strong defense of his administration of the office on January 21, denying that he gave less time than necessary to his duties, asserting that the collection of the revenues had prospered during his term, and adding that he had made suggestions for reforms upon which Sherman had failed to act. It was a substantial reply to Sherman, and the feeling obtained that it had largely neutralized the secretary's effort.

Sherman had written to Merritt on January 18: "It will be a warm contest." Events now bore him out. Conkling secured a solid vote of the Republican members of his committee to send the nominations to the floor with an unfavorable recommendation. On January 27, the Senate took up Merritt and Burt, and the letters of Sherman and of Arthur were ordered printed; the matter was set over, to the 29th, and at that time, against Conkling's wishes, to the 31st. On that day, Sherman sent another letter to the Senate, along with one from Hayes, charging that the suspended officers regarded the duties of their offices "as of subordinate importance to their partisan work," and that "they have made the custom-house a center of partisan political management." [17]

Conkling presented another statement from Arthur, but he wanted a vote on the 31st. However, a motion to postpone to the following Monday, February 3, carried. Sherman was busy in the interim. On January 31, he wrote to Allison for support, saying:

If the restoration of Arthur is insisted upon, the whole liberal element will be against us without doing a particle of good. . . . It will be a personal reproach to me, and merely to gratify the insane hate of Conkling, who in this respect disregards the express wishes of the Republican Members from New York, of the great body of Republicans, and, as I personally know, runs in antagonism to his nearest and best friends in the Senate.

The same day, the secretary wrote an even longer letter along the same line to Justin S. Morrill. What Sherman never acknowledged was the initial and renewed folly, urged by the impractical Evarts but not really opposed by the supposedly hardheaded Sherman, of blithely sail-

---

[16] Howe, pp. 86–87; Arthur Papers, Library of Congress; Shores, pp. 257–258.
[17] Howe, "Controversy," p. 360. Richardson, ed., VII, 511.

ing into such a contest without the faintest idea of where the votes would come from to confirm. This naïveté, along with the intransigency of Conkling, was responsible for stretching out over two years a dispute so injurious to the Republican party.[18]

Hayes was justly being scored for inconsistency in his implementation of civil service reform. Chauncey I. Filley, a notorious spoilsman, had been reappointed postmaster at St. Louis. Collector William Simmons of Boston, the unsavory henchman of Ben Butler, had even been permitted to place himself on the commission investigating the Boston Custom House. Most of those who had taken part in the transactions in the South during the contested election found places on the federal payroll. It began to appear as if only those unfortunate enough to have enemies in the cabinet, as Conkling did, could expect to have civil service reform administered to them.

Indeed, the sustained attack on Conkling was a curious affair. Conkling's major sin seems to have been that he was the most successful, most important machine leader, rather than that his machine was worse than others. Actually, the Conkling organization, to the extent by which it existed in a symbiotic relationship with the public payroll, appears to have been better than most. Once Murphy was displaced (and Conkling, after all, had not selected Murphy for his office), the two major federal installations in New York, the custom house and the post office, were run with efficiency by Arthur and James, both Conkling men. The public business was forwarded in a consistent manner. The political work was done, to be sure, but seldom in a way that interfered with the governmental functions of those establishments. Too, Conkling shied away from the kind of disreputable leadership existing at federal offices in places like Boston, New Orleans, and St. Louis.

The suspicion remains that Hayes was animated primarily by personal pique against the senator. Conkling had sat on his hands throughout the 1876 campaign and had no doubt given Hayes sleepless nights with the uncertainty of his intentions during the electoral dispute. In personality the two men were opposites, and Conkling loathed the type of men from whom the president drew his closest friends and advisers. Two such men, old-time adversaries of the senator, agitated Hayes from their cabinet positions while another, Curtis, needled him with letters from Staten Island.

The press felt the nominations would most likely be rejected. The reporter for the *Tribune* stated on January 31, Conkling "generally knows

18 Sherman, II, 684.

where his votes are to come from when he enters a contest such as this, and rarely forces the fighting until he is sure of winning. The eagerness with which he now proposes to push the Senate to a vote inspires his friends with the greatest confidence."

Yet prospects did not look so rosy to the senator. He really had wanted to vote on the 31st, and he was shaken by the vote on the motion to postpone. Ten Republicans had voted against him, and further delay might add to this number. The night before the decisive vote, Hayes wrote in his diary that the contest "is close and as yet undecided," but he felt that "we seem to be gaining." [19]

The Senate met at 1:00 P.M. on February 3, and, when it went into executive session, Conkling submitted another letter from Arthur in further reply to Sherman. After more debate, it suddenly appeared to Conkling that some of the Democratic votes upon which he had been relying were slipping away from him. When Senator Cockrell, a Democrat from Missouri, moved that the new letter from Arthur, together with all other documentary evidence on the matter, be returned to the commerce committee, with further instructions to investigate the conduct of the custom house under Merritt, Conkling supported the motion. The recommittal was carried by a voice vote, but then someone asked for a roll call. Before the roll was taken, Conkling decided to make a speech.

This was Conkling's milieu; in executive session, where he was supposed to be at his best, a good powerful speech might nail things down. This was a miscalculation; it was a powerful speech, "one of the best arguments he ever made," the *World* said the next day, but ineffective. He took two hours, and his words were bitter and eloquent. He angered some members by reading personal letters, letters written to Arthur by cabinet members and others close to Hayes, soliciting positions in the custom house. Sherman wrote several letters, in January and February of 1878, even while Arthur was under attack by the administration, asking for a job for the son of Justice Bradley (he of the fifteenth vote on the electoral commission). Logically, Conkling should have prevailed; he had exposed the hypocrisy of the reform pretensions of the Hayes administration, and he had made it look ridiculous. Some members laughed at the heavy Conklinian sarcasm which accompanied the letters. But it seemed as embarrassing to the listeners as to Hayes and his people, and many were offended by the reading of such personal correspondence, especially since it must have been furnished to Conkling

[19] T. H. Williams, ed., pp. 184–185.

by Chester Arthur. By the time Conkling's vituperative oration was over, the calm, reasoned arguments of Thomas Bayard in favor of confirmation seemed more and more convincing, especially to Republicans who dreaded a possible repetition of such a scene. The voice vote in favor of recommittal was turned around on roll call to a vote of 32-25 not to recommit. Quickly, then, a second roll call confirmed Merritt by 40 to 30, and a third confirmed Burt, 31 to 19. Fifteen Republicans had joined 25 Democrats to confirm Merritt, while Conkling could add to his loyal 23 Republicans (including Blaine) only 7 Democrats in opposition. It was shocking and hard to believe, but it had happened; Roscoe Conkling had been vanquished in executive session on a matter of New York patronage.[20]

Hayes wrote, "We are successful," while Conkling told Arthur of the "unjust result . . . reached in the dishonest war waged against you." Whichever position it was viewed from, the contest over the New York Custom House was done, and most Republicans were glad to put the problem behind them.[21]

Shortly thereafter, Conkling found himself again in the minority, this time an extremely small minority, on the bill to provide for taking the 1880 census. Conkling opposed it, taking the position as he had successfully ten years earlier that the Census Act of 1850 was "wise and adequate to its purpose . . . to count the people of the United States for the purpose of determining representation." He denounced the plans to use the census machinery for gathering all sorts of collateral statistics about the populace, admitting himself to be "an old fogy" with "a sort of preference for the ancient ways." Though the additional information to be collected would surely be of great aid to a busy commercial and industrial complex like New York, still he opposed it as wasteful and extravagant. From this Census Act of 1879 grew the existing system for taking the census, controversial though it may sometimes be, but Roscoe Conkling faced defiantly back toward 1850.[22]

[20] Howe, pp. 88–92; Alexander, III, 410; Howe, "Controversy," p. 362. Shores, pp. 256–264. The Sherman letters on young Bradley are in Arthur Papers, Library of Congress. The Democrats gleefully tried to have the letters to Arthur made public, but Conkling stuffed them in his pocket and stalked away.

[21] T. H. Williams, ed., p. 185; letter of Feb. 6, 1879, Arthur Papers, Library of Congress.

[22] *Cong. Rec.*, 45th Cong., 3d sess., pp. 1051–1052, Feb. 6, 1879, and 2290–2291, March 3, 1879.

Conkling found himself involved in the effort, instigated by West Coast agitators, to abrogate the Burlingame Treaty with China, to cut off the influx of Chinese laborers into the United States; the Senate, he said, should not "turn a deaf ear or a regardless sense to the judgment, the feelings, the interests, and as they believe the rights of those communities on the Pacific sea who . . . are deeply concerned and deeply indignant in this regard." But Conkling's plan was not the peremptory one called for by Senator Sargent of California; he proposed an effort to work out changes with the Emperor of China before determining upon the harsh step of unilateral abrogation. Blaine, on several occasions, took a demagogic line on Chinese immigration, a line clearly calculated to appeal to the baser fears of racial enmity. Conkling's position was less discreditable. Ultimately, the following year, a modification of the treaty was negotiated with China, certainly a more civilized mode of treating the subject than abrupt abrogation.[23]

At this time, too, Roscoe Conkling woke up to the fact that a vast and legalized raid on the treasury was taking place in the guise of pension legislation for Union army veterans and their dependents—what he later called "a great procession of mourners and of cripples." Voting against pension bills was a hazardous step to take in any event, and the G.A.R. had a loud and effective lobby in Washington. The Cummings Pension Arrears Bill was passed in 1879, with opposition, but not strenuous, from Roscoe Conkling, shepherded through the Senate by the chairman of the pensions committee, Ingalls of Kansas, who clearly did not understand what the bill was all about. He gave some vague assurances about costs in the floor debate, and the bill passed and was signed by the president. The whole matter came up again in February, when it was realized that no appropriation was included in the Cummings Bill, and a separate act was now required to pay for the authorized arrears. Conkling, who said, "I have no doubt that arrears of pension bill is going to cost a great deal more than any Senator supposed," angrily tried to pin Ingalls down on what the Kansan had meant in his earlier assurances of costs, but he was unsuccessful. The only thing he did accomplish was to demonstrate clearly the sublime ignorance under which Ingalls was proceeding. The pension money was voted through regardless. Though the Senate attempted to place some limit upon the total amounts to be poured out to pension claimants, the return

[23] *Ibid.*, pp. 1307–1308, Feb. 14, 1879.

of national prosperity ultimately made it possible to pay out almost limitless amounts of benefits.[24]

The life of the Forty-fifth Congress finally ended as it adjourned sine die on March 3, 1879, with vital appropriation bills still unpassed. The Democratic House persisted in attaching unacceptable riders to the measures, and the Republican Senate declined to acquiesce in them. The result was to make inevitable a special session of the new Congress, which Hayes called for March 18. The difference was that the new Congress would be controlled in both houses by the Democratic party.[25]

The special session lasted to the first of July, and it was a bitter and mostly bad-tempered Senate which sat. The Democrats gloried in their newly won control, and a party caucus kept a tight rein upon the majority members. The Republicans, led by Conkling, squirmed in their unaccustomed minority position, and various Democratic speakers were happy from time to time to jab a needle into the sensitive New Yorker about his loss of power.

The Democrats, in full control of Congress for the first time since prewar days, decided to attempt to repeal Reconstruction, or at least those parts of it open to some kind of repeal. It was an unwise policy, for, even had it succeeded, its results would have been symbolic only, and it managed to drive the divergent wings of the Republican party temporarily back together. Besides, the Democrats had no two-thirds majorities, and without them they were helpless and frustrated in the face of the vetoes which Hayes kept hurling back at them from the other end of Pennsylvania Avenue.

The main battle of the session was on the army appropriation bill, to which the Democrats had attached a rider which provided a $5,000 fine and five years imprisonment for a president or any other officer who interfered (by the use of soldiers) in any election. In the last session of the Forty-fifth Congress, the Democrats were able to prevent the passage of the army appropriations because they had a majority in the House. Now, it was their design to pass the bills with such riders, hopefully forcing the president to sign them, in effect condemning the past course of the Republican administration under Grant. Conkling

24 *Ibid.*, 46th Cong., 3d sess., p. 1350, Feb. 8, 1881, and 45th Cong., 3d sess., p. 2050, Feb. 28, 1879.
25 Richardson, ed., VII, 520.

fought the bill in the Senate. He delivered a major speech on the subject on March 24, 1879, in the course of which he thundered that when it is declared that "unless another species of legislation is agreed to, the money of the people, paid for that purpose, shall not be used to maintain their Government and to enforce the laws . . . the threat is revolutionary and its execution is treasonable." He denounced the plan to compel the president "to give up his convictions, his duty, and his oath, as the price to be paid a political party for allowing the Government to live."

What would the Democrats do if the president refused to give in to their coercion? Conkling knew something of Hayes's stubbornness in the face of challenge to his executive prerogatives: "The actors in this scheme have managed themselves and their party into a predicament, and unless the President lets them out they will and they must back out."

He treated his colleagues to a colorful rhetorical picture of election day in New York City if the Democratic rider were passed: "In the city of New York, all the thugs and shoulder-hitters and repeaters, all the carriers of slung-shot, dirks, and bludgeons, all the fraternity of the bucket-shops, the rat-pits, the hells and the slums, all the graduates of the nurseries of modern so-called democracy, all those who employ and incite them, from Kings Bridge to the Battery," are to be advised in advance that no federal soldier or authority can touch them on election day.

Conkling then reviewed at length the party, "dominated . . . by violence and fraud," which was pressing the rider, "that party under whose sway, in several States, not only the right to vote, but the right to be, is now trampled under foot: Such is the source of an insulting summons to the Executive to become *particeps criminis* in prostrating wholesome laws, and this is the condition on which the money of the people, paid by the people, shall be permitted to be used for the purposes for which the people paid it." [26]

But Roscoe Conkling's eloquence could not stop a determined Senate majority operating under a strict party whip; the riders were firmly attached to the appropriation bills when they went to the White House. They were still attached when the first of a series of vetoes by the president brought the army appropriation bill back to the House on April 29, with the statement, in a long veto message, that "the enact-

[26] *Cong. Rec.,* 46th Cong., 1st sess., pp. 802–805.

ment of this bill into a law will establish a precedent which will tend to destroy the equal independence of the several branches of the Government." Hayes denied the right of the House of Representatives, Commons-like, to "withhold supplies" in the absence of substantive legislation it might desire. He bored through quickly to the heart of the dispute, and persisted in his position with five separate vetoes of the repeated Democratic enactments, until finally the embarrassed majority party, under strong public pressure, did at last, as Conkling had predicted, "back out." [27]

Before they did, however, one long, hot night witnessed one of the most ill-tempered sessions of the Senate in years, featuring a bitter exchange between Conkling and Lucius Q. C. Lamar of Mississippi. Lamar was normally a mild-mannered, conciliatory man, and his 1874 eulogy of Charles Sumner in the House was regarded as a major milestone in the reunion of the sections. Lamar was no pushover, however; he had been a Confederate general and he had fought his way to the front politically while helping the white Democracy reclaim his state. He had broken off all relations with Conkling after the New Yorker's incident with John Gordon of Georgia two years before, and he had just recently complained to a friend, "I know Conkling is going to jump on me, and I wish he'd keep off. My conservative speeches and positions have irritated him, and he will try to make me lose my temper and say something foolish and rash." We have seen that Conkling was chafing under the weight of the Democratic majority. The stage was set for an explosion.[28]

On June 18 the Democrats kept the Senate in session until noon the next day in an attempt to ram through the final version of the army appropriation bill complete with rider. The Republican minority, which wanted to adjourn, resorted to all the time-honored delaying tactics of a minority, and Conkling pointed out that way back at the beginning of the day he had allowed Lamar to take up a bill on the understanding that there would be no vote that day on the army bill. When the time came, however, the Democrats voted in a body against adjournment and made it quite clear that they intended to run the bill.

Conkling sputtered with rage: "When I heard every democratic Senator vote to commit such an outrage as that upon the minority of

[27] Richardson, ed., VII, 531. The veto messages run from 523 to 547.
[28] Lamar to E. C. Walthall, in E. Mayes, *Lucius Q. C. Lamar*, p. 379. Mayes was Lamar's son-in-law, and his book was an "authorized" biography.

this body. . . . I do not deny that I felt my full share of indignation. . . . I say, Mr. President (and I measure my expression) that it was an act not only insulting but an act of bad faith. I mean that."

Tempers were wearing thin. The sensitive Lamar flared back:

With reference to the charge of bad faith that the Senator from New York has intimated toward those of us who have been engaged in opposing these motions to adjourn, I have only to say that if I am not superior to such attacks from such a source, I have lived in vain. It is not my habit to indulge in personalities; but I desire to say here to the Senator that in intimating anything inconsistent, as he has done, with perfect good faith, I pronounce his statement a falsehood, which I repel with all the unmitigated contempt that I feel for the author of it.

The galleries were hushed now, as Conkling rose to speak once again, his face pale, his manner agitated, and his eyes flashing daggers at the Southerner:

Mr. President, this not being the place to measure with any man the capacity to violate decency, to violate the rules of the Senate, or to commit any of the improprieties of life, I have only to say that if the Senator—the member, from Mississippi, did impute or intended to impute to me a falsehood, nothing except the fact that this is the Senate would prevent my denouncing him as a blackguard and a coward.

The galleries erupted, and the presiding officer reproved the spectators. Conkling refused to yield to Lamar and continued:

Let me be more specific, Mr. President. Should the member from Mississippi, except in the presence of the Senate, charge me, by intimation or otherwise, with falsehood, I would denounce him as a blackguard, as a coward, and a liar; and understanding what he said as I have, the rules and proprieties of the Senate are the only restraint upon me.

I do not think I need to say anything else, Mr. President.

Lamar was on his feet for the last word, as the onlookers gasped with dismay: "Mr. President, I have only to say that the Senator from New York understood me correctly. I did mean to say just precisely the words, and all that they imported. I beg pardon to the Senate for the unparliamentary language. It was very harsh; it was very severe; it was such as no good man would deserve and no brave man would wear."

The night passed with no further fireworks between Conkling and Lamar, though it was stormy enough, with the New York Republican in the thick of the battle for his side; and ultimately, when a bone-weary

Senate convened at noon the next day, a minute after adjourning the previous day's session, good sense prevailed and a time was set for the vote.[29]

Washington was awash, though, with rumors of a duel or some kind of hostile engagement between Conkling and his Mississippi adversary. Kate Sprague, watching from the gallery, was said to have come near fainting from worry over her champion, and senators waited expectantly for news of another encounter. Blaine, leaving the Capitol after the recess at noon, told a friend, "O, it was exceedingly rich! I don't think I ever saw Conkling's wattles quite so red." One of Lamar's Democratic colleagues, who expected to be a second in any duel that might be fought, said scornfully, "I don't think Conkling will fight. I don't regard him as a man of courage. Lamar will only be delighted to have Conkling challenge him. Of course everything rests with Conkling, as he is the insulted party." When a reporter tracked down the senator to ask him what came next, Conkling laughed and said that in New York they had a different method of settling personal controversies; he did not propose to be trapped into a duel by an ambitious Southerner. Lamar himself said that "I doubt if he has yet made up his mind what he will do." He cautioned that Conkling "is no ordinary man, either in intellect or energy of purpose, or physical strength and animal spirits." However, he went on, "for once in my life I feel that I am *right,* even in the most extreme alternative." [30]

As it became clear that no duel would be fought, the quarrel died away. Clearly, Lamar was the winner of the exchange, for he had responded to Conkling's challenge in the debate, had given him the lie in unmistakable terms, and had been required to face no further consequences. Most press comment, North and South, frowned upon the brutal language used by the New Yorker, even though Northern papers generally deplored as well the "plantation" manner shown by Lamar. No one, it might be added, apparently bothered to check into the accuracy of Conkling's original bad-faith charge.

The snarling set-to with Lamar was a fitting climax, though, for Conkling, who had functioned at his pugnacious best throughout the session and who, a few days earlier, had been angrily likened by Allen Thurman to "one of those genii in the Arabian Nights, who when the

[29] The Conkling-Lamar affair is in *Cong. Rec.,* 46th Cong., 1st sess., pp. 2142–2144.
[30] Lamar to E. C. Walthall, in Mayes, p. 387. The other quotes are on p. 386.

cork was taken out of the bottle rose out, away up to the clouds, to the utter amazement and astonishment of all beholders." [31]

Eventually, Congress passed the appropriations needed to run the government, without the Democratic riders, and adjourned until its regular session in December. Roscoe Conkling could turn his attention back to New York. This year was to be a very surprising one for him.

[31] *Cong. Rec.,* 46th Cong., 1st sess., p. 1823, June 6, 1879.

CHAPTER 20

FROM CANONCHET TO THE STATE HOUSE

The highly public romance between Roscoe Conkling and Kate Chase Sprague was flourishing in 1879. Even in the capital, where gossipy tongues were at their sharpest, the two defied convention by making no attempt to conceal their relations; Kate's carriage was frequently seen outside the senator's home, while he was often observed entering Edgewood, the old Chase family home. The fact that neither party was hindered by a spouse on the scene undoubtedly facilitated the liaison. During the spring session in 1879 Kate was usually found in the Senate gallery if Conkling was on the floor, and they openly exchanged notes and glances on many occasions; she frequently furnished flowers for the senator's desk. Everyone in town talked about their conduct, but they seemed to care not a whit.[1]

In early August, however, matters came to a head. On the 6th, just after Sprague had left Canonchet, his rambling mansion at Narragansett Pier, for a trip of about a week to Portland, Maine, a yacht bearing Roscoe Conkling nosed into the town wharf, where it was met by Mrs. Sprague. The senator, it was said, had been cruising off Newport and had stopped by on a professional visit to see Governor Sprague. It later developed that he had received an invitation from Kate. In any event, Sprague was not present, though several other guests were. Roscoe moved in.

The next night, Sprague returned. His arrival, at 3:00 A.M., was completely unexpected, especially to Kate and Roscoe; legend had it that a servant warned her mistress of the return just in time for the senior senator from New York to escape her bedroom through a

[1] Phelps, pp. 246–250.

window, with underwear hastily donned and his trousers over his shoulder.

Unaware of these heroics, however, Sprague went to bed. In the morning he got up early and went to town, where for the first time he learned that Conkling had been his wife's guest for several days. Then, in what the townspeople later described as an "uncontrollable" passion, he headed back to Canonchet.

Upon reaching the mansion, Sprague fetched his shotgun. The first person he encountered, however, was not Conkling but an elderly German tutor named George Linck, to whose presence Sprague had earlier objected, apparently because of the extravagance entailed by his employment. Waving the shotgun, the governor chased Linck away and resumed his search for Conkling.

He found Roscoe and Kate enjoying their breakfast, the senator sitting on a lounge coolly reading a newspaper. Sprague peremptorily demanded to know if Conkling was armed, and when the latter replied that he was not, Sprague ordered him off the premises, giving him five minutes to be gone or he would "blow his brains out."

Conkling then strode over to Kate and told her, "Mrs. Sprague, your husband is very much excited, and I think it better for all of us if I should withdraw. If my departure puts you in any danger, so say, and I will stay, whatever the consequence." Kate assured him that she would be all right, saying it would not do to argue with her overwrought husband.

With this, Conkling left Canonchet. Shortly thereafter the irate husband must have had second thoughts about allowing him to escape, because he took off for town in pursuit. He found Conkling outside a restaurant named Billington's. Whatever privacy the whole affair still retained to that point now vanished. A noisy confrontation between the two was witnessed by a number of the townspeople. After Sprague at length departed, Conkling entered the restaurant and had a brief meal of crackers and milk (another version had a bucket of steamed clams). While waiting for the train to Providence, he poked about on the beach and also spoke with Kate when she drove up.

Sprague, after the scene at Billington's, had returned to his home to find that his wife and three daughters had also departed. Kate left for Providence, but returned the following week to the Tower House at Narragansett, a famous hotel designed by Stanford White. Her husband visited her in the town, another angry scene ensued, and in the evening she was brought back to Canonchet, where Sprague held her in close confinement.

Roscoe Conkling, meanwhile, was worrying about his public image. After escaping to Providence, he refused to talk about the encounter at all. He was successful at first in silencing most of the New York press. Three days after the incident, however, the *Sun* picked up a story from a Boston paper, dealing with Sprague's angry eviction of the German tutor, a story in which Conkling figured only as a bystander. The *Sun* did take the precaution, though, of checking with Utica, where it was said that "the scandals or slanders from the outside have not broken the peace" of Conkling's household and it was stated that "Mrs. Conkling will institute no divorce proceedings." Even the contemplation of divorce seemed a little odd if the senator's part in the matter was only what was reported. The public was alerted for further details.

The *Sun* stayed with the story and two days later had penetrated the original cover story (said by some observers to have been concocted by Conkling). On August 13, it made it very clear that the episode with Herr Linck was merely incidental to the confrontation between Sprague and Conkling; it detailed Sprague's complaints about the conduct of Kate and Roscoe in Washington, it recounted the public argument between the two men at Narragansett Pier, and it quoted Sprague as saying, "He has tried to do here for my home what he did in Washington." Conkling, who arrived back in Utica that day, no doubt to a chilly reception, declined to say anything at all about the affair.

Kate tried to stem the tide of growing public interest with a letter which appeared in the Providence *Journal,* bemoaning "Governor Sprague's dissolute life and dissipated habits" which had "long ago interrupted our marital relations," but to no avail. Finally, on August 16, at Kate's request, a reporter from the *Sun* showed up at Canonchet for an interview to give her version of the story, which was in brief that Conkling had come to Narragansett on legal business and had intended to stay until he could discuss it with Sprague. She specifically and categorically denied that Conkling had ever "paid me any attention that a wife could not honorably receive from her husband's friend" and she also denied "the stories of my remaining out at late hours and meeting Mr. Conkling at the Capitol." Nobody believed her, and Conkling, rather than backing up her story with a statement of his own, stayed resolutely silent.[2]

2 The best coverage of the Conkling-Sprague encounter is in the New York

The *Times,* on the 19th, ignored Kate's story and interpreted the scant facts in its own way:

Sen. Conkling's presence at Canonchet has not been accounted for, and he is known to have waited at Newport until it was certain the ex-Governor was absent. Then he went to Canonchet. He was received at the landing by Mrs. Sprague, and how he installed himself at Canonchet is testified to by the German teacher, by the children, and by the servants. Ex-Governor Sprague has shown by his actions how he viewed this intrusion.

Though Kate was not able to escape from her virtual imprisonment in the eighty-room mansion until the end of August, most public attention was focused on Conkling, much to the senator's disgust. The reaction of the press may be summed up in an editorial which appeared in the Cincinnati *Commercial:*

There is a good deal of levity about Senator Conkling's law business at Narragansett Pier. . . . It is lucky for the Senator that his career was not terminated by a shot then and there, and his composure in partaking of clams and spurning all communications with the press is to be commended. The Senator has reached years of discretion, and has had a warning, a very loud one. He should wind up his legal business with the Spragues.[3]

The senator's reaction to the entire affair was not that of a gallant swain flying to the defense of his lady love. He complained to his friend Senator Jones of his distress at "hideous calumnies," adding that this was "not for my own sake chiefly as you will readily believe." [4] But he kept a stony public silence. He said and did nothing to help Kate out of her problems with her husband and the press. On the contrary, he acted on the assumption, correct as it turned out, that if he said absolutely nothing the whole furor would die down and be forgotten shortly. Romantics have long been disappointed to find that Roscoe brought his affair with Mrs. Sprague to an abrupt end and though he may have seen her occasionally thereafter, it was on a much more formal basis. The romance was ended.

Sun, from August 11 to August 17, 1879. The reporters of the *Sun* made a determined effort to stay on top of the story, to sift through the conflicting versions which various participants and bystanders put out and to reach the actual facts. The paper's editorial comment on August 13 was, "It would certainly have been a ridiculous as well as tragic ending of Senator Conkling's proud career if he had died at the mouth of a shotgun in the hands of an enraged husband."

[3] Ross, *Proud Kate,* p. 255.

[4] Conkling to J. P. Jones, Sept. 18, 1879, Conkling Letters.

Kate was crushed; she had clearly committed her heart to the handsome senator, and she did not quickly recover from the blow to her self-esteem in being dropped so unceremoniously. She who had been the belle of Washington for so long, still beautiful, still seductive, was cast aside without a thought. It was humiliating. Two and a half years later, she was still writing letters extolling the virtues of the New Yorker and damning the turpitude of his enemies, this even after he was out of the Senate and after she had commenced a sensational divorce action, but she waited in vain for any indication from Conkling that their relationship might resume its former course.[5]

For Conkling, the sudden and virtually complete termination of the affair with Kate Chase Sprague is revealing. His long relationship with her was based on intellectual compatibility and physical attraction—he picked her out as the brightest, wittiest, and sexiest girl available to him in Washington—but it clearly had for him no deeper significance; there was no question of love involved, so that as soon as it became inconvenient or embarrassing politically he cut the affair off without a qualm, without a backward glance, and apparently with regret only that he was made to look silly in the public eye. The suspicion is strong that Conkling was too enamoured of himself, his attention too centered upon his own person, to be capable of love for another. He had cronies, followers, allies, but it is hard to find anyone with whom he had a relationship that could be termed "love." He moved emotionally away from his wife shortly after their marriage, and there was very little pretense of meaningful communication between them. When she was young, his daughter Bessie was a source of great satisfaction, but this may well have been a narcissistic delight in a handsome reflection. This very spring, 1879, Bessie had married a young man named Walter Oakman of whom the senator disapproved; though his family was of acceptable social status, the young man had worked as a common laborer on the railroad in an effort to learn the business in which he would later assume an executive responsibility, and Roscoe Conkling sneered at such a lowering. When Bessie and Walter were married, the senator

---

[5] Letter of Oct. 15, 1881, Kate Sprague to Sen. Samuel C. Pomeroy, Arthur Papers, Library of Congress. Also, Ross, *Proud Kate,* pp. 261–262, for her divorce action. Several of Kate's letters now in the Arthur Papers, Library of Congress, give inferences that she may have seen her erstwhile lover on a couple of occasions, and a Conkling letter of August 11, 1883, to A. Blanchard at Washington, inquired about the delivery of a package he had sent to Mrs. K. Chase at Edgewood; Conkling Letters.

was not present, and he thereafter frequently referred to her as "Mrs. Conkling's daughter." Hardly a tale of deep devotion.

Finally, the outcome of the hitherto torrid affair with Kate Sprague indicates once again that Roscoe Conkling always kept a reserve, a restraint on his feelings, a final unwillingness to commit himself to another, when such a commitment would take away the ultimate freedom he cherished for himself. He was known, justifiably, for his hatreds, not for his loves, and only in those hatreds could he release the tethers on his emotions.

The senator was badly in need of a triumph of some sort. So far, 1879 had been a bad year. The Lamar encounter in the Senate had not shown him at his best, he had been made to look foolish by the Sprague affair, and his political vulnerability had been demonstrated a few months earlier, when the president's New York appointments were confirmed. With the custom house gone, Roscoe was ruling his organization on the premise that his power would return in a short time; such a premise could not survive too many personal setbacks. Conkling would find his organization crumbling about him if he could not reassert his power in some striking way; his enemies in New York scented a chance for a kill.

For the first time in New York's history, 1879 would witness the election of all of the chief state officers at one time. This was Conkling's opportunity, though it was just as much an opportunity for his opponents.

Governor Lucius Robinson said in the spring that he did not care to run for a second term, that "all the glory there was in the gubernatorial office was in having once occupied it well." Late in the summer, however, John Kelly, the Tammany boss, announced loudly and repeatedly that he would not *permit* the renomination of Governor Robinson. He was aggrieved at Robinson's refusal to yield to his ever-increasing demands for patronage, capped by the discharge of a Tammany sachem as county clerk of New York. After a sufficient amount of Kelly's billingsgate, Robinson announced that he would run again after all, on the theory that though he was quite willing to give up the office he would not be driven out by Kelly's denunciations.[6]

---

[6] Hudson, p. 89. On August 1, 1879, the *Sun* printed an interview with Kelly in which he said "not under any circumstances" would Tammany support Robinson.

While Kelly and Tammany Hall battled against the governor and his eminent sponsor, Samuel J. Tilden, the Republicans were not dormant. An active canvass for the gubernatorial nomination had been conducted through August, even while Roscoe Conkling was off on his celebrated visit to Rhode Island.

The leading candidates for the nomination were Frank Hiscock and Theodore M. Pomeroy from the central part of the state, Robertson from Westchester, Congressman John H. Starin from the Saratoga area, and Cornell. The latter, of course, was the organization candidate, while the other four divided the anti-Conkling strength, though Starin himself was not particularly unfriendly to the machine. Cornell had been denied the nomination three years before, but this time the organization worked full blast to win a sufficient number of delegates for him. Lou Payn, who was most adept at this sort of thing, took personal charge of several county and district meetings to ensure selection of pro-Cornell delegates.

It was not easy; even supporters of the machine were found balking at Cornell. One reporter wrote that

Mr. Cornell, faithful friend though he be to a few personal followers, is in every sense of the term an unpopular man. In his manner he is cold and repelling, and there is nothing about him which attracts a stranger or a casual acquaintance. . . . Still further than this, he has, within his own party, more active, outspoken, and influential enemies than any other man in the State.[7]

The big question in everyone's mind as the time for the convention at Saratoga drew near was the course which would be pursued by Senator Conkling. There was varied speculation about this. One of Conkling's friends in Utica was quoted to the effect that the senator would not make any overt effort for Cornell; that "he will, of course, favor him in a quiet way, but that his main object in going to the convention is to show to the country that recent events in the home of his Rhode Island connection do not compel him to keep aloof from public affairs."

Others felt, with equal logic, that Conkling at this point was virtually compelled to achieve a victory or see his control of the party organization slip away from him. Besides, since "Mr. Cornell and the interests which he represents are particularly obnoxious at Washington," this obviously presented Conkling with something of an opportunity.[8]

[7] N.Y. *Times,* Sept. 1, 1879.   [8] *Ibid.,* Aug. 28; N.Y. *Sun,* Aug. 16, 1879.

One thing was clear: if the senator did not make the effort, Cornell would not win the nomination. The New York *Times* reporter wrote on September 1,

It is no exaggeration to say that the political prominence of A. B. Cornell is due entirely to accidents of birth and association. He inherited the name of a distinguished and honored man; he served Senator Conkling, who, in return, gives him the support of a well-drilled and obedient political organization. Here Mr. Cornell's qualifications to be the nominee of the Republican Convention begin and end. What light he has is entirely reflected.

Godkin in *The Nation* suggested that Cornell's nomination would be a "striking bit of defiance to the reform element in the party," but he concluded that "there is nothing in the results of Mr. Conkling's past experiments on the party to forbid his trying this one." [9] "When it is said," wrote the *Times* just before the convention opened on September 3, "that Senator Conkling has chosen to make Mr. Cornell the depository of his favors and his confidence, everything has been said which is needed to explain Mr. Cornell's public career." [10] One major theme and one minor theme thus resounded through the press as the convention opened: first, Cornell's complete dependence upon Conkling, and, second, Cornell's own lack of qualification.

Roscoe Conkling had himself named temporary chairman at the start of the convention in Saratoga, though he was not feeling well physically, and he set the tone of the gathering with a relatively short speech emphasizing the need to carry New York in 1879 to gear up the Republican presidential effort for 1880 and calling for harmony in the Republican ranks.

Vice-President Wheeler was named the permanent chairman and gave a speech which "wearied the audience." When he mentioned Grant, Senator Conkling, sitting on the stage, clapped vigorously but at the mention of President Hayes it was noted that the senator was busy fanning himself. The meeting then got down to business promptly after a number of short speeches. As the first ballot for governor came on, the organization henchmen cracked their whips efficiently, and the small machine majority told the story. With 226 votes needed for nomination, Cornell received on the first ballot 234, with his rivals splitting the opposition vote among them. The Conkling people then made sure to fill the rest of the slate with out-and-out organization candidates;

[9] *The Nation,* Sept. 4, 1879.   [10] N.Y. *Times,* Sept. 2, 1879.

why, the thinking went, apologize for Cornell by putting his enemies on the ticket with him? The *Times* editorially called the rest of the slate "certain gentlemen whose brilliancy will not perceptibly outshine the lustre of the head of the ticket." [11]

There was much wringing of hands and moaning among the anti-Conkling people over Cornell's nomination. Evarts called it a "frog-in-the-well" selection, and Godkin felt that Conkling had caused it for his own vindication, after his setbacks in Rhode Island and the custom house: "The greater Cornell's unfitness for the place, judged by the ordinary standards, the more valuable is the nomination as a proof of his patron's ascendancy." He said that Conkling's machine "is probably the most perfect instrument of its kind in existence," and pointed out another key factor in the senator's victory:

No one can deny his skill as a Machinist, and the party believes that as soon as Mr. Hayes goes out the Machine will work again with the old gearing; that the Custom House belt will be again put on the wheel, and all go on as before; and that if his successor is a Republican, Mr. Conkling will again wield his old power in the State. Men who care, therefore, for political activity, and fancy they have a political future, refuse to quarrel with him.[12]

The *Sun* called it "a great personal victory" for the senator, and warned: "Men may hate Roscoe Conkling; let no man henceforth affect to despise him." [13]

On September 5, a young journalist named Richard R. Bowker wrote a letter to the New York *Evening Post* urging Republicans to vote for all the members of the ticket except Cornell and Howard Soule, the candidate for state engineer, who was attacked as being incompetent and corrupt; Bowker's theory was that if the rest of the ticket could be elected without Cornell it would be a "moral victory in the hands of patriotic and not machine Republicans." Bowker put together an amateur organization called the Young Republican Committee, devoted to cutting Cornell and Soule, with a slogan, "We propose not to bolt but to scratch!" [14]

[11] N.Y. *Sun,* N.Y. *Times,* both Sept. 4, 1879. Soule, the candidate for state engineer, was particularly denigrated. For Conkling being "ill at Saratoga, & much more ill immediately thereafter," see Conkling to L. P. Morton, Morton Papers.

[12] *The Nation,* Sept. 11, 1879; Barrows, p. 330.

[13] N.Y. *Sun,* Sept. 5, 1879.

[14] E. M. Fleming, "The Young Scratcher Campaign of 1879," pp. 323–324.

Bowker and his Scratchers made themselves an important factor in the campaign. So, fortunately for Conkling, did John Kelly. The Tammany boss, "a paranoid with fierce pride and ungovernable temper," according to one writer, was determined to fight Tilden and Robinson to the end. On September 6, a Tammany meeting run by Kelly passed a resolution declaring that the entire Tammany delegation would bolt the state convention if Governor Robinson was renominated. On September 11, when the state convention at Saratoga defied Kelly and did renominate Robinson, Tammany marched out in an angry body, formed its own rump convention across the street, and nominated Honest John Kelly for governor.[15]

So as A. B. Cornell and Lucius Robinson squared off for the 1879 campaign, each with his powerful sponsor, Conkling for the one, Tilden for the other, each was confronted with an active and potentially dangerous intraparty defection. No one knew, in September, whether Bowker's Scratchers would have any real impact upon the usual Republican vote; no one knew, in September, whether Kelly would indulge his pique to the point of staying in the race, although all the experts recognized that a serious Tammany defection could guarantee a Republican victory.

Young Bowker was able to raise over $5,000 to publicize the anti-Cornell effort, and he got editorial support from Curtis and Godkin. There were others whose support he expected, however, who attacked him and his group. Chief among these were the two members of the Hayes cabinet who had been most instrumental in sacking Cornell, William Evarts and John Sherman.[16]

Bowker wrote to Evarts on October 16 that his support of Cornell would be "a direct blow at the permanent interests of the party" and that the secretary would be best advised to keep "a significant silence" in the campaign. Instead, Evarts came to Cooper Institute on October 21 and supported Cornell with a speech of over an hour and a half. He derided the Scratchers: "It is bad enough to have to vote under circumstances where your vote won't be counted, but it is a great deal worse to vote so that your vote can't count at all. Well now, gentlemen, we don't vote in the air." [17]

---

[15] L. Dinnerstein, "The Impact of Tammany Hall," 237–238. Kelly showed that he had learned his lesson well when the Tilden group had come into New York City the year before to back Edward Cooper and defeat Tammany.
[16] Fleming, p. 325.   [17] N.Y. *Times,* Oct. 22, 1879; Barrows, p. 330.

The *Herald* the next day called it an abdication of self-respect for Evarts to speak in favor of Cornell, and the two reformist editors were beside themselves. Godkin in *The Nation* called Evarts's speech "indecent" and Curtis called the secretary "unspeakable." [18]

A week later, Sherman, who had finally put his job on the line to secure the ouster of Cornell from the custom house, came to New York, at the invitation of Arthur, who was running the campaign, and spoke on Cornell's behalf. Sherman's speech was his usual dry-as-dust discussion of financial issues, but it was the fact of his presence more than what he said that counted. As he closed the speech, he threw in the president's support, too: "I can say for the President that . . . he has openly expressed his desire for the success of the entire Republican ticket. As for myself, I regard the election of Mr. Cornell as of the highest national importance, and if I had a thousand votes and a thousand voices they would all be for him." [19]

In addition, on October 23, Vice-President Wheeler had spoken at Ogdensburg, saying that "Mr. Cornell is a man of spotless integrity, of rare good judgment, and of high executive ability." [20]

So although Sherman and Evarts in particular made themselves look slightly ridiculous in doing so, the big guns of the Republican administration wheeled into line behind Conkling's candidate, while young Richard Bowker learned a lesson that political rebels have had to learn from time to time, that factional leaders of substance will not necessarily go flying off the party reservation for any forlorn though gallant cause that may come along.

Conkling, in the meantime, was stumping the state for his protégé, obliterating the machine issue with a vivid discussion of the conduct of the Southern members of Congress trying to undo the results of the war and Reconstruction. He emphasized again and again the national importance of the election and its crucial bearing upon 1880.

While the Republicans paraded their party unity and worked to minimize the effect of the Scratcher campaign, the Democrats could do nothing with Kelly. He was clearly in the race to stay and this spelled disaster to his party. The *World,* on October 17, published a despairing little bit of doggerel:

> John Kelly. Oh! John Kelly!
> We read you like a book;

[18] Barrows, pp. 331–332.   [19] N.Y. *Times,* Oct. 28, 1879.
[20] *Ibid.,* Oct. 24.

> We've got plain country common-sense,
>   Though homely we may look;
> And we know each vote you beg, John,
>   Is only begged to sell;
> You are but the tool of Conkling,
>   And bargained to Cornell.

There was no bargain, though. There was no need of one. The Republicans made it their business to keep Kelly stirred up throughout the campaign, knowing they could trust to his Celtic temper to do their work for them.

The Nation assured its readers that "better scratching than Cornell they will never meet with," but Evarts, Sherman, and Hayes urged support of the entire ticket, and the eminent divine, Henry Ward Beecher, still listened to despite the sensational adultery case he was then mired in, said, "I intend to do no scratching." [21]

The figures on election day told the story clearly. Cornell ran 20,000 votes behind the rest of the Republican ticket, but John Kelly piled up 77,000 votes which would otherwise have gone to Governor Robinson. Cornell received 418,000 votes, enough for a comfortable margin of victory over Robinson's 375,000.

Curtis, sorely disappointed at the failure of the Scratcher campaign, tried to salvage something for his side; he wrote, "Among the mortally wounded is Conkling. Everybody here feels that it is he who has 'engineered' the ridiculous result of a Republican governor elected by Tammany Hall." [22] The editor overlooked, however, those factors that made it in reality a solid triumph for the senator. In the wake of a serious defeat in the Senate over the custom house nominations and with the public guffawing over the thought of Conkling climbing out a bedroom window in his drawers, he had nominated and elected as governor of the largest state in the Union one of his scorned henchmen, he had vindicated Cornell after the custom house dismissal, and he had brought Evarts and Sherman, and by implication Hayes, into New York to speak for Cornell in a campaign managed by Arthur. It was a considerable victory for Roscoe Conkling, no matter how achieved.

[21] *The Nation,* Oct. 9, 1879; P. Hibben, *Henry Ward Beecher,* p. 287.
[22] Cary, p. 269.

CHAPTER 21

GRANT IN THE HANDS
OF HIS FRIENDS

As the election of 1879 faded away, as the assessments and recriminations, credits and losses, were forgotten, the thoughts of politicians turned naturally to the subject of the upcoming presidential nomination and election. For the Republicans, there would be a change, without a doubt; Hayes had announced when he ran in 1876 that he would not seek a second term. The Republican leaders were happy to take him at his word, and no serious effort was made to reverse the decision. This of course left an inviting void, into which a number of aspiring Republicans were eager to plunge.

The name which was heard most often, however, was the familiar one of Grant. After he was succeeded by Hayes in 1877, the general and his family took off on a round-the-world trip which lasted over two years. Before the general's cigar aroma was aired out of the White House, however, his name was figuring in long-range speculation for 1880. Conkling, in May 1877, wrote that "Gen. Grant is now the strongest man in the nation with the people" and deplored "the obvious effort to disparage his acts." In June, *The Nation* wrote that the Republican machine politicians, the ones most disenchanted with the quasi-reform administration of Hayes, were looking to Grant for 1880 as "the one who is most likely to restore their fallen fortunes. . . . That hopes and expectations of this sort will grow during the next three years we have no doubt." [1]

The ex-president's name was kept before the American public while he was abroad, because the New York *Herald* sent one of its top reporters, John Russell Young, to cover the tour almost daily. In the

[1] Conkling to Pierrepont, May 12, 1877, Pierrepont Papers; *The Nation,* June 28, 1877.

capitals of Europe, Ulysses S. Grant was not the lackluster and unsuccessful president; he was the glorious Hero of Appomattox. As Young
relayed the reports of Grant's triumphs, popular affection for the great
soldier once more overwhelmed public disdain for the patronage politician, and the Grant boom took real shape, at least in the calculations
of his political friends.

The Grants returned to the United States in September 1879, landing to a tumultuous welcome in San Francisco. From his arrival until
January 1880, Grant was feted across the country with parades, ban-
quets, testimonials, and receptions of all kinds. At no time did he
mention publicly his candidacy, but there was no doubt that he desired
another term. However, the nimbus of glory with which the world tour
had reinvested him seemed to shrink day by day on American soil. The
boom faded rapidly, and the general's advisers shipped him off to Cuba
and Mexico to receive more plaudits. Probably there never was any real
public demand for Grant's return to the presidency. Popular feeling
was that of affection and enthusiasm for the silent, steadfast war hero.[2]

The principal sponsor of the Grant boom was Roscoe Conkling, aided
by John Logan of Illinois and Don Cameron of Pennsylvania. These
three men were the leading practitioners of old-line, patronage, machine
politics. Their motives were transparent:

No supporter of the movement has thought it necessary up to the present
to give any reason for thinking that should General Grant be again elected
these men will not resume their old places. That Conkling believes he will
resume his, he does not in the least attempt to conceal. That General Grant,
in a two-years' tour in foreign countries, of only one of which he understood the language, at the ripe age of fifty-seven learned to distrust his
old advisers, is a purely gratuitous assumption.[3]

In February, the New York *Times,* which favored Grant, wrote that if
the movement for the old general was subsiding, "it is due to the fact
that politicians have taken it in hand. . . . Many of those who desired
Grant . . . do not want him as the candidate of the Camerons and
Conklings, secured by manipulated caucuses and pledged delegations." [4]

By that time, Cameron had already held his state convention in Pennsylvania. The national convention was scheduled to open in Chicago on
June 2, but the Republican state convention met in Harrisburg on

[2] Hesseltine, pp. 432–436. See Badeau, p. 317, on Grant's return, and generally,
J. R. Young and the New York *Herald* for the duration of the trip.
[3] *The Nation,* Oct. 9, 1879. [4] N.Y. *Times,* Feb. 22, 1880.

February 4. Many voices were raised, asking why such a meeting had to be called so early, but the answer was clear. The leaders of the Stalwarts, as the pro-Grant forces came to be called, wanted to take advantage of the waning Grant enthusiasm, before it disappeared altogether. Conkling's convention, set for Utica, was called for February 25, for the same reason.

In Harrisburg, Don Cameron wheeled his troops into line and the delegation was instructed to vote as a unit for General Grant. People in New York waited to see if Conkling would do the same.

The other contenders for the nomination were Blaine and Sherman. The secretary of the treasury, whose enthusiasm for civil service reform had never matched that of his chief, had recently been wielding the patronage powers of his office in a manner clearly designed to advance his candidacy, and the newspapers of the country were ringing with denunciations of Sherman power plays. In addition, the treasury contingent fund was being used to cover some of the secretary's campaign expenses.[5]

Sherman was a cold and crusty person, not a popular man, and his hopes for the nomination had to rest on recognition among the delegates of his ability and achievements. He forfeited this possibility with his blatant political maneuvers. His speeches in 1879 for Cornell were so obviously designed to placate Conkling and advance his own presidential candidacy that many who might have supported Sherman were disgusted. Besides, Conkling was clearly unimpressed; the *Times* on February 6 commented that "the ghosts of Arthur and Cornell begin to haunt the Secretary of the Treasury." Sherman would be a major factor in the convention, but he would probably not win.

The "plumed knight," James G. Blaine, the disappointed warrior who led all through the convention in 1876 only to have the prize snatched away at the end by Hayes, was another matter. Though he formally took a position that he was not an active candidate (in December 1879, he wrote Whitelaw Reid that "I will never again fight an aggressive battle— horses cannot drag me into it"), Blaine was soon in the contest with all his vigor. His adherents were no less numerous than they were four years earlier, and they were determined this time to win. William E. Chandler led the Blaine forces, though he complained that perhaps "the beloved don't like a fight as well as he used to." The Mulligan letters

[5] L. D. White, pp. 375–376. This came out in a Senate investigation in 1881–1882. Sherman himself denied any knowledge of the diversion of funds.

were now four years behind him, they hoped, and a sort of political statute of limitations might excuse Blaine from the transgressions they had brought to light.[6]

Four years before, though, he had not been contending against U. S. Grant. The solution to Blaine's problem was obvious: coalition with Sherman. However, an indiscreet raid by the Blaine people upon Sherman's Ohio delegation made the secretary of the treasury furious and ruled out all hopes of a combination. Nine district delegates announced their support for Blaine, while Sherman was exposed to the comment that if he could not even control his own state his chances must be slim indeed. Blaine resented the Ohioan's candidacy; he wrote bitterly, "Had he cleared the track I would have beaten Grant ten to one in Ohio and then ploughed him under in Illinois with ease. . . . Sherman's remaining in the field is the bête noir of the Campaign." Sherman's reaction was understandable. Thus, it began to appear that neither of the other two contenders could muster a majority.[7]

When the Utica convention met in late February, Conkling had a safe but not overwhelming majority. He used it well, however, and the convention followed his lead. The four delegates-at-large were solid: Arthur, Governor Cornell, James D. Warren, and Roscoe Conkling, who was going to make his first appearance ever at a national convention. The goal in this one was too important for the welfare of the machine to entrust leadership to anyone else.

In his speech at Utica, Conkling spoke forcefully of the necessity of district delegates honoring the instructions of the state convention, rather than their own districts. No one challenged him when he finished, and the resolution he introduced, binding all the delegates "to use their most earnest and united efforts to secure the nomination of Ulysses S. Grant," was adopted. When a speaker mentioned the name of Blaine, cheers came down from the galleries, but they were squelched by Conkling, who scornfully quoted a line from Raleigh's poem, "The Silent Lover," "The shallows murmur but the deeps are dumb."

When the districts reported the names of their chosen delegates, those who were suspected of harboring pro-Blaine feelings were called upon to affirm their submission to the convention's instructions for Grant.

---

[6] Blaine to Reid, Dec. 10, 1879, Reid Papers; Chandler to Mrs. J. G. Blaine, Dec. 13, 1879, Blaine Papers.

[7] J. Sherman, II, 773; N.Y. *Times,* April 29, 1880; Blaine to Reid, April 25, 1880, Reid Papers.

All did so, including even Curtis. The Utica convention was a complete success for Conkling; New York now seemed safely in line for Grant.[8]

The Utica convention produced one disgruntled machine man—Tom Platt. Afterwards he wrote to Cornell:

Senator Conkling sneered and snubbed me at the Convention till I made up my mind I was an idiot or he was crazy—& that in either case I had better disavow all future claims to leadership. It seems to me that the more one tries to serve him & execute his purposes the more certain he is to tyrannise over him. I don't enjoy it. While bowing to his transcendent talents & powers I do not think he possesses all the practical common sense that the State has ever produced & I believe the opinions of pigmies, like myself, are entitled to respect. I have my own views & when I am satisfied I am right I am quite as tenacious as he. This of course I shall never say to any other human being but—Enough.[9]

Platt stored these feelings away, but he did not dismiss them.

As the lines of battle formed, there were three other contenders for the Republican nomination. Elihu B. Washburne, Grant's original congressional sponsor, later secretary of state and minister to France by Grant's appointment, now entered the lists himself, much to the chagrin of the former president's supporters. Senator George F. Edmunds of Vermont and Senator William Windom of Minnesota were also candidates, not so much as active contestants but as men who held themselves available for consideration in the event of a deadlock. Given the posture of the major candidates, a deadlock appeared quite possible.

High hopes in the Grant camp had been held for the addition of Massachusetts to the strong nucleus of New York, Pennsylvania, and Illinois. Four ex-governors, representing different factions within the state, endorsed Grant. But the "better elements" of Massachusetts Republicanism remembered that Grant had delivered their state over to Ben Butler and his henchman, William A. Simmons, collector of Boston, and they wanted no repetition; George Hoar said, "No personal respect for General Grant could induce the Massachusetts Republicans to run the risk of having again a President who was subjected to personal in-

[8] Alexander, III, 432–433. The N.Y. *Times,* on Feb. 26, commented that "in years past there has been no fairer, more open, or honestly conducted a convention than that which met here today." The *Times,* of course, was supporting Grant.

[9] Platt to Cornell, March 3, 1880, Cornell Papers.

fluences like these." Blaine was equally distasteful to them. Casting about for a repository for their support until such time as the course of the convention became clear, the Massachusetts delegates settled upon Edmunds, though they recognized that he was "not a person calculated to inspire much popular enthusiasm." In the meantime, they would work with the Blaine and Sherman men to block an early nomination of Grant.[10]

The outline of the anti-Grant strategy was now clear: cooperation on preliminary questions, even if consolidation on one candidate was impossible. John Logan arrived in Washington on April 26 and set forth very clearly in an interview what the Grant leaders intended: "You may rest assured of one thing—General Grant will not withdraw, nor be withdrawn, under any circumstances. . . . General Grant is in the hands of his friends, and they will not withdraw him until he is beaten, no matter how many ballots are taken. That is the whole case." [11]

With General Grant in the hands of his friends, of course, he did not need many enemies. Many long-time admirers of the silent but persistent soldier, hopeful that a new Grant administration would be led by a new Grant, were deeply saddened to find it made unmistakably clear that the general was still under exactly the same influences as he had been in the White House. The campaign for his nomination was to be one strictly of political contrivances, in the best Conkling manner; there was no longer much in the way of popular support for Grant's nomination, nor was it felt necessary by the Grant leaders. It was all very disheartening for those who cherished the general's fame and achievements as a national treasure.

The Blaine people frankly cared little whether it was a new Grant or an old Grant. On May 6, the New York delegation, carefully instructed to vote as a unit for Grant by the Utica convention, cracked. Senator William H. Robertson wrote a letter to the Albany *Evening Journal,* stating that "a district delegate should represent the wishes of the Republicans of his district." In his district, he said, they preferred

---

[10] Hoar, I, 385–386. A letter from Schurz to young Henry Cabot Lodge on May 23, 1880, described the cooperation of Massachusetts as "vital." He went on: "Let not the Massachusetts delegates put any obstacle in the way of such co-operation on account of their fear of Blaine." Schurz, *Papers,* III, 506.

[11] N.Y. *Times,* April 27, 1880.

Blaine, so at Chicago he would vote for Blaine. The letter stirred up great excitement, and the Grant forces attempted to put down any revolt. The *Times* the next day scornfully wondered that "the hitherto timid Judge should have mustered up courage enough" to repudiate the instructions of the convention.

By that time, however, the rebellion had spread. William Woodin rose in the state senate to announce that, though he would consider himself bound by the pledge he had made at Utica, he was going to let his alternate cast his vote at the convention for Blaine. Senators Loren B. Sessions and John Birdsall also denied that they were in any way bound by the action of the state convention, and they would vote as they saw fit in Chicago.[12]

Interestingly, Senator Dennis McCarthy of Onondaga, a wealthy Syracuse salt merchant, who usually followed the lead of Robertson and his cronies, said on May 8, "I see no reason why I should not abide by the instructions of the Republican State Convention. I feel honorably bound to do so."

Nevertheless, the defection in the New York delegation soon reached the level of about fifteen or sixteen. There was some doubt, however, that the rebels, now called "Half Breeds," would be able to make good their defiance, for Conkling and the other Stalwart leaders intended to enforce the unit rule upon their delegations at Chicago. The Blaine managers would attempt to overthrow the unit rule, in order to free a considerable number of Blaine votes in the three large delegations instructed to vote as a bloc, New York, Pennsylvania, and Illinois. This would be one of the most crucial contests at Chicago and a key test of the cooperation among the anti-Grant forces.

As the convention drew near, the candidates made their final preparations, assessed their chances, and counted heads.

Blaine, his troops led by seasoned political campaigners like Chandler of New Hampshire and his own Maine lieutenants, Eugene Hale and William P. Frye, was confident of ultimate victory. He introduced an innovation into presidential conventioneering by setting up a telegraph wire from his home direct to the convention. He was still Blaine, warm and breezy, ostensibly frank and open but with calculation governing his every move. As the man from Maine was attempting to exert his

12 *Ibid.*, May 8, 10, 1880.

magnetic spell upon the delegates, James A. Garfield was writing, "I like Blaine, always have, and yet there is an element in him which I distrust," and Godkin, writing in *The Nation,* said

The public ought to be reminded just now that Mr. Blaine enjoys the miserable distinction of being the one Speaker of a great legislative assembly who, in all parliamentary history, has been convicted, on the evidence of his own letter pitifully claiming his reward, of having ruled in the chair in favor of speculators, with the object of being considered a partner in their venture.[13]

Sherman, too, was working hard to get everything organized for Chicago. He recognized that he would stand third on the first ballot, but good organization, perseverence, and availability might still enable him to carry off the nomination. One of the things which Sherman had considered of cardinal importance he had accomplished; Garfield had agreed to serve as his convention floor manager. Garfield, from Mentor, in Ohio's Western Reserve, a long-time congressman and now senator-elect, was a clever politician. He was a fine speaker and would no doubt make a good nominating speech. What Sherman had been concerned about, though, was a Garfield candidacy for president, draining off Ohio support and leaving the secretary of the treasury high and dry. With Garfield firmly tied down, he could forget about that worry. When Garfield sat down with the candidate on May 25 to find out what strong points Sherman thought should be stressed in presenting him to the convention, Sherman "suggested that the chief characteristic of his life from boyhood up had been courageous persistence in any cause he had adopted." Fine, said Garfield in effect, and he set out to work on the speech. Curiously, in 1871, Garfield had written of Sherman, "The fact that he has studied the popular current and floated with the tide and drifted with the wind of popular opinion is undeniable." [14]

In the White House, Hayes was still waiting for some kind of a draft movement to start, a vindication of his administration that he could respectfully decline. Nothing happened; politically, the president was dead. Bob Ingersoll said that Hayes "couldn't be elected if no one ran against him. . . . There would be enough scattering votes to defeat

---

[13] Garfield's diary entry of April 14, 1880, T. C. Smith, *Life and Letters of Garfield,* II, 956–957; *The Nation,* Feb. 5, 1880, referring of course to the Little Rock and Ft. Smith affair and one of Blaine's letters to Warren Fisher, Mulligan's employer.

[14] Smith, II, 957; I, 475, 476.

him if he was the only candidate in the field." This was cruel, but it expressed Republican sentiment, at least among the politicians who would run the convention.[15]

The Grant leaders were supremely confident. On May 21, the New York *Times* called his nomination "certain," and on June 2 it quoted "a politician of national importance" who added up 380 votes for Grant, even spelling out in detail where they were coming from. Senator Conkling was coming to Chicago to take personal charge of the convention, and at the Plymouth Church in Brooklyn the Reverend Henry Ward Beecher was offering up prayers for the success of Ulysses S. Grant. All the auspices were favorable, the skies were bright, the troops were in order, their shoes shined and their buttons polished; Ulysses S. Grant was in the hands of his friends.

[15] Barnard, p. 487; C. H. Cramer, *Royal Bob,* p. 192.

CHAPTER 22

ROSCOE CONKLING'S
CONVENTION

Chicago was a good town for the Republican party. It had met there twice before, in 1860, when Lincoln was first nominated, and in 1868, when Grant was selected for the first time. These had been good times for the party, palmy days when the faithful knew they were going to win. Now, twelve years later, the Republicans were back in the Windy City, with prospects of a slam-bang convention, though their hopes for the November election were not as high as in past years.

Chicago, the rail center of the nation, was already a great commercial city. Rebuilt after the famous fire of 1871, the city had little time for culture, beauty, or art; it was the second city of the nation, and it concentrated on making money. Its great names were McCormick, Pullman, Armour, Marshall Field, Joseph Medill, and Potter Palmer. The town was lusty, booming with the nation's renewed prosperity, larger than life. It welcomed the tough, coarse, no-nonsense men who led the majority party of the nation in the Gilded Age. It was the perfect spot for the battle of giants called the Republican National Convention of 1880.

From the time Roscoe Conkling set foot in Chicago, he was the outstanding figure of the convention. This was his first national convention and his first major political gathering west of the Alleghenies. With his tall frame and striking appearance, his renown as a bold, fighting senator, heedless alike of foes within and without his own party, and his leadership of the Grant forces on the convention floor, Conkling dominated the gathering. Indeed, General Grant himself came to seem incidental. It was the climax of the senator's career. An early dispatch affirmed:

It is no exaggeration to say that Senator Conkling attracts more curiosity and interest than any of the assemblage of remarkable men now in attendance on this Convention. When his lofty and well-proportioned form is descried in the lobby, or street, all other occupation ceases for the time, and men and women point him out to each other as the lion of the occasion, and their remarks never indicate disappointment. . . . The Senator has not created the impression of imperiousness with the people here which he has elsewhere enjoyed. . . . The universal verdict of the delegates who attended the Grant caucus last night, most of whom had never seen him before, is that never had they met a leader whose personal methods inspired such confidence.[1]

Even Blaine acknowledged that Conkling, "by intellectual force, by ardent zeal and earnest advocacy, and by common recognition," was the "master spirit" of the Grant supporters.[2]

Prior to the start of the convention, Conkling took part in a meeting of the leaders of the various camps, to select a chairman for the convention who could be trusted to be impartial among the contending candidates. Senator Hannibal Hamlin of Maine suggested George Hoar of Massachusetts, who was supporting Edmunds; Hoar was opposed to both Grant and Blaine and presumably could be trusted to be fair. Conkling, who never got along with Hoar, snorted that such a proposal was an insult. Hamlin replied, "I guess I can stand the insult," but the discussion then ranged over some other names. The choice was finally narrowed down to Benjamin Harrison of Indiana, Augustus Brandegee of Connecticut, and Hoar, none of whom were very satisfactory to the Stalwarts, and Conkling reluctantly went along with Hoar.[3]

Don Cameron was chairman of the national committee, and there was talk that he was going to ram the unit rule into effect by fiat, without reference to the sentiment of the convention. He probably would have, too, were it not for the fact that the members of the national committee, at a stormy meeting on May 31, let him know, in an informal but unmistakable manner, that they were prepared to oust him from his position if he tried any such nonsense. Unfortunately for Conkling and the Stalwart Grant leaders, that put an end to that tactic; the issue would have to be decided by the convention itself, where the outcome would not be nearly as sure.[4]

[1] N.Y. *Times,* June 3, 1880.
[2] J. G. Blaine, *Twenty Years of Congress,* p. 660.
[3] Hoar, I, 392; F. H. Gillett, *G. F. Hoar,* p. 102.
[4] T. C. Smith, II, 964, mentions the fear that Cameron might try to impose the unit rule by fiat. See also H. J. Clancy, *The Presidential Election of 1880,* pp. 85–86.

The convention was called to order by Cameron on Friday, June 2; shortly thereafter the gavel was turned over to Hoar as the chairman. The Massachusetts senator delivered his address, nothing memorable, and the business of the convention got underway.

The important work was being done in the rules committee. Here George Sharpe was Conkling's New York representative and the Stalwart leader. Garfield, in the absence of any pre-eminent Blaine leader, was quickly becoming the captain of the anti-Grant coalition; he was the committee chairman. The group haggled and argued and debated over the question of the unit rule, for on this might depend the outcome of the convention. There were roughly 50 votes in the three big Stalwart delegations which would be freed from Grant if the unit rule were barred; 50 votes in a convention which promised to be as close and hard-fought as this one was a big chunk of delegates, more than two or three good-sized states. The committee voted, after three hours, to report against the unit rule. Garfield, as chairman, would present the committee's recommendation; Sharpe would have a minority report.

During the Saturday afternoon recess, the delegation leaders worked feverishly toward winning votes on the major question to come up that evening, the report on the unit rule. The lines were drawn pretty tightly, however, as Conkling discovered in his whispered conferences with anti-Grant delegates. Unless you were for Grant, you were against the unit rule; it became that simple. As convention questions so often do, the real merits of the proposition became lost in the implications that success or failure might have for particular candidacies. Garfield wrote to his wife that afternoon that his report would "encounter the fury of the Grant men," because "the fate of Grant and the possible success of Conkling happen to be involved in this and hence we expect a fierce fight which I must probably bear the brunt of." [5]

When the convention reconvened, the rules committee struggle was put off to take up a credentials committee report on Illinois, which knocked out several of John Logan's hand-picked delegates. The fight on this matter went against the Stalwarts, which boded ill for the unit rule. Finally, the big battle came; Garfield and Sharpe led their respective forces, and when it was over the unit rule was killed, by a vote of 449 to 306. Conkling and his allies had Sunday to lick their wounds, but they had suffered a serious setback. An anti-Grant majority in the convention had been clearly shown. If that majority could coalesce upon a single candidate it could nominate him. The senator from New York

[5] T. C. Smith, II, 967.

still felt that when a move was made to a new contender, a dark horse, a sufficient number of Blaine and Sherman delegates would fall off to Grant to nominate the old general. Others were not so confident.

On Monday, Conkling involved himself in a bit of foolishness that emboldened the enemy. He offered a resolution that every member of the convention be bound in honor to support the nominee, whoever he may be, "and that no man should hold a seat here who is not ready so to agree." A harmless enough proposition, which passed overwhelmingly on a voice vote after desultory discussion. Brandegee of Connecticut asked for a roll call vote, and was supported by Conkling, who asked "that we may know who it is in a Republican Convention that votes 'no' on such a pledge." When the roll was called, the 716-3 vote showed three negative votes cast by West Virginia, and Conkling then offered a further resolution that the dissenters "do not deserve and have forfeited their votes in this Convention."

The chairman of the West Virginia delegation stormed to his feet in outrage; he asserted that though West Virginia meant to support the nominee, it denied the convention's right to dictate to its delegates. He was supported by others including Garfield. The Ohioan's speech meant two things to Conkling. He sent over to Garfield a message saying, "New York requests that Ohio's real candidate and dark horse come forward," and he realized that his resolution to oust the West Virginians was lost. When Hoar ordered the roll called, Conkling had no other recourse but to withdraw his resolution, while the Blaine people guffawed.[6]

That evening, a number of delegates visited Conkling to offer their support to him if General Grant were out of the race. Presumably the tradition against a third term was too strong, when combined with the failures of Grant's previous administration. On the other hand, the striking effect of Conkling's appearance and conduct in Chicago might win him great support among the delegates. We do not know who the delegates were who came to Conkling or what states or interests they represented or whether there was ever any chance of Conkling winning the nomination. In any event, they were speaking to the wrong man. Conkling retorted:

Gentlemen, I appreciate your kind proposition. I could not be nominated in any event, for if I were to receive every other vote in the Convention, my own would still be lacking, and that I would not give. I am here as the

6 *Proceedings,* pp. 410–417; Clancy, p. 92. For the "dark horse" note, slightly jumbled, A. R. Conkling, p. 592, and Platt, p. 103. See Gillett, p. 103.

agent of New York to support General Grant to the end. *Any man who would forsake him under such conditions does not deserve to be elected, and could not be elected.*[7]

The next day was to be the big one for Roscoe Conkling. He would deliver a speech, nominating Grant and destroying his opponents. First, though, there was some leftover business to take care of, including the platform, which mildly endorsed the Hayes administration as "efficient, just, and courteous," and which had to be amended from the floor with a civil service reform plank because the platform committee had left one out. The convention then recessed until 7:00 P.M., when the serious business of nominating a president could begin.[8]

The first nomination was that of Blaine, presented in speech of indifferent caliber by James Joy, a Michigan industrialist, who even garbled the name of his candidate at the climactic moment, calling for support for "James S. Blaine."

Senator Windom was nominated by a fellow Minnesotan, and then New York was called. Roscoe Conkling stepped forward, jumped up on a reporters' table just in front of the platform, and paused dramatically, while all eyes riveted upon him and the vast assemblage was reduced to silence. Then he began, with a familiar bit of doggerel from the postwar period.

> When asked what state he hails from,
>   Our sole reply shall be,
> He comes from Appomattox,
>   And its famous apple-tree.

The hall exploded; the reference to Appomattox set off a wild ten-minute demonstration while the senator looked on, approvingly, waiting for the uproar to end.

In obedience to instructions I should never dare to disregard—expressing, also, my own firm convictions—I rise to propose a nomination with which the country and the Republican party can grandly win. The election before us is to be the Austerlitz of American politics. It will decide, for many years, whether the country shall be Republican or Cossack. . . . The need that presses upon this convention is of a candidate who can carry doubtful states both North and South. And believing that he, more surely than any other man, can carry New York against any opponent, and can carry not

[7] A. R. Conkling, p. 605; G. C. Gorham, *Roscoe Conkling Vindicated*, p. 6.
[8] Barnard, pp. 492–493; McClure, pp. 276–277.

only the North, but several States of the South, New York is for Ulysses S. Grant. Never defeated in peace or in war, his name is the most illustrious borne by living man.

The delegates cheered again, as the great warrior's name came to his champion's lips, but they quieted quickly, as Conkling resumed with a review of Grant's merits:

Never having had a policy to enforce against the will of the people, he never betrayed a cause or a friend, and the people will never desert nor betray him. . . . He has studied the needs and defects of many systems of government, and he has returned a better American than ever, with a wealth of knowledge and experience added to the hard common sense which shone so conspicuously in all the fierce light that beat upon him during sixteen years, the most trying, the most portentous, the most perilous in the nation's history.

Grant, he said, had withstood all the assaults of his enemies.

Calumny's ammunition has all been exploded; the powder has all been burned once; its force is spent; and the name of Grant will glitter a bright and imperishable star in the diadem of the republic when those who have tried to tarnish that name have moldered in forgotten graves, and when their memories and their epitaphs have vanished utterly.

Conkling celebrated the magnanimous terms of peace offered to Lee, and the great service to the nation in vetoing the inflation bill; Grant, he said, "would hew to the line of right, let the chips fly where they may. . . . With him as our leader we shall have no defensive campaign. No! We shall have nothing to explain away. We shall have no apologies to make. The shafts and the arrows have all been aimed at him, and they lie broken and harmless at his feet."

But what of the argument heard in all corners of Chicago in this convention, the hallowed tradition of the Fathers, that no man shall serve a third term as president?

His integrity, his common sense, his courage, his unequaled experience, are the qualities offered to his country. The only argument, the only one that the wit of man or the stress of politics has devised is one which would dumfounder Solomon, because he thought there was nothing new under the sun. Having tried Grant twice and found him faithful, we are told that we must not, even after an interval of years, trust him again. . . . Who dares—who dares to put fetters on that free choice and judgment which is the birthright of the American people?

Being Roscoe Conkling, of course, he could not forego the opportunity to make a couple of cracks about Sherman and Blaine and about the "independents," whom he loathed.

Can it be said that Grant has used official power and place to perpetuate his term? He has no place, and official power has not been used for *him*. Without patronage and without emissaries, without committees, without bureaus, without telegraph wires running from his house to this Convention, or running from his house anywhere else, this man is the candidate whose friends have never threatened to bolt unless this Convention did as they said. He is a Republican who never wavers. He and his friends stand by the creed and the candidates of the Republican party. They hold the rightful rule of the majority as the very essence of their faith, and they mean to uphold that faith against not only the common enemy, but against the charlatans, jayhawkers, tramps, and guerrillas—the men who deploy between the lines, and forage now on one side and then on the other.

As the senator worked through to the end of his speech, excitement mounted in the hall; as the majestic phrases rolled from the front to the back of the vast crowd, all seemed to be caught up in it, as Conkling's perfect delivery and timing gripped them.

This Convention is master of a supreme opportunity. It can name the next President. It can make sure of his election. It can make sure not only of his election, but of his certain and peaceful inauguration. . . . Gentlemen, we have only to listen above the din and look beyond the dust of an hour to behold the Republican party advancing with its ensigns resplendent with illustrious achievements, marching to certain and lasting victory with its greatest Marshal at its head.[9]

The crowd erupted once again as he closed, and the cheering continued for fifteen or twenty minutes; "the friends of Grant," said the *Times* the next day, "threw away the characteristics of age and became boys once more." But it was not just the Grant partisans who cheered; most of the people in the convention recognized it as great oratory and applauded it to the rafters, so well had Conkling swept them up in his message. Colonel McClure later wrote that Conkling's speech was second only to Ingersoll's in 1876 of all the many convention speeches he had heard. Men talked about it with admiration for years.[10]

There were unfortunate echoes in the speech, however, which remained with some of the delegates when the cheering was done. Primarily, these were the unnecessary slams at Sherman and Blaine and

[9] Conkling's speech is in *Proceedings,* pp. 550–553.
[10] McClure, pp. 270–271.

their modes of conducting the canvass. Even Conkling's friends and Grant's supporters regretted his inclusion of these references; George Boutwell said, "Whatever he said that was in support of his cause, affirmatively, was of the highest order of dramatic eloquence. When he dealt with his opponents, his speech was not advanced in quality and its influence was diminished." The *Times* realistically said that these references were "impolitic and tending to repel delegates who have held the ex-President as a second choice." [11]

Thus Conkling's speech solidified the Grant sentiment, without a doubt, but it also added to the inflexibility, the rigidity of position, which so characterized the 1880 convention and which led, inevitably, to deadlock.

Garfield, again, still dogging Conkling's footsteps, followed the New York senator with a speech nominating John Sherman. He never had gotten around to writing out his effort, but he said later that night that "Conkling's extraordinary speech gave me the idea of carrying the mind of the convention in a different direction." [12]

"I have witnessed the extraordinary scenes of this Convention with deep solicitude," he began, while the clamor and excitement of the Grant enthusiasm was still dying down.

As I sat in my seat and witnessed this demonstration, this assemblage seemed to me a human ocean tossed in tempest . . . but I remember that it is not the billows but the calm level of the sea from which all heights and depths are measured. . . . Gentlemen of the Convention, your present temper may not mark the healthful pulse of our people. When your enthusiasm has passed, we shall find below the storm and passion that calm level of public opinion from which the thoughts of a mighty people are to be measured.

Conkling stalked out, sneering to a reporter as he left that he felt "sea-sick" from Garfield's speech. But the Ohioan had brought the delegates back down to earth, a considerable achievement after Conkling's speech and the Grant demonstration. In addition, he made a masterful speech (though the *Times* sourly called it "too ornamental and elaborate") which, though not really doing much for John Sherman, did a great deal for James A. Garfield. The man's name was on many lips as a possible compromise choice.[13]

[11] Boutwell, II, 268; N.Y. *Times,* June 7, 1880.   [12] T. C. Smith, II, 977.
[13] Garfield's speech is in *Proceedings,* pp. 554–557. A. R. Conkling, p. 604, for the "sea-sick" remark; N.Y. *Times,* June 7, 1880.

After Garfield's speech, Edmunds and Washburne were also placed in nomination, and the delegates went back to their hotels. The next morning, balloting would begin.

In almost any political convention, the tense night before the voting starts usually witnesses fevered activity on the part of the managers for the different candidates, as well as a ferment of conversation among the delegates, as factions and alliances are woven together and come apart, as dreams of success blossom and fade, and as the constituents of the convention mill about in search of the right man and a winner. That evening of June 6, 1880, was marked by the almost complete absence of such activity. The rival camps were separated by too much bitterness, too much frustrated promise, too much personal jealousy and animosity, to consider intercourse among the factions. The coalition of Blaine, Sherman, and independent forces which had prevailed against the Stalwart leaders on the preliminary issues fell apart as soon as the necessity for its existence disappeared. Sherman felt that Blaine's raid which prevented a united Ohio delegation had been a grievous blow, and he would not countenance talk of his people going over to the Maine man. Blaine's people, on the other hand, felt they had been cheated out of their rightful prize in 1876, and they intended to stand fast this time. Those supporting Windom, Edmunds, and Washburne saw clearly the impending deadlock, and they would do nothing to remove their men from positions of availability.

In this spirit, the convention met on Wednesday, and Chairman Hoar ordered the call of the roll of the states. When the state of New York was called, Conkling ordered the clerk to poll his delegation. The renegades, led by John Birdsall, were forced to proclaim their apostasy to the world, with the senator glaring at them from a few feet away. They all swallowed and did it, however, and the delegation's vote broke down to Grant 51, Blaine 17, and Sherman 2.[14]

On that first ballot, General Grant led with 304, Blaine had 284, Sherman had 93, Edmunds had 34, Washburne had 31, and Windom had 10. On the second ballot, Grant picked up another vote, but he was far from the 378 necessary for nomination. Ballot after ballot followed, with virtually no fluctuation in the totals of any of the candidates. Grant got as high as 309, Blaine got up to only 285 and finally fell back into the 270's, Sherman reached 97 at one point, while the three minor candidates stayed virtually stationary. Windom got his 10 Minnesota votes

14 *Proceedings*, pp. 569–570.

all day. On some ballots one or two delegates voted for Garfield, Hayes got a vote on three successive ballots in the middle of the session, and once, on the thirteenth ballot, somebody voted for Conkling. The senator turned and glared in the direction of the miscreant, and the latter did not repeat the vote.

Twenty-eight ballots were taken that day, and when the day ended, Grant had 307, Blaine 279, Sherman 91, Washburne 35, Edmunds 31, Windom 10, and Garfield 2. There had been practically no movement. The weary delegates went back to their hotels, to caucus, to eat, to drink (almost a necessity, after such a day), and to ponder the day's events.

One of the things they remarked upon was the wonderful sneer that Roscoe Conkling put in his voice as he announced his delegation's vote: "Two delegates are said to be for Sherman, seventeen are said to be for Blaine, and fifty-one *are* for Grant." On the seventeenth ballot, he was forced to vary his routine slightly, for Dennis McCarthy of Syracuse apparently decided he was no longer "honorably bound," as he had put it before, to obey the instructions of the Utica convention; he switched to Blaine and stayed with him thereafter.

When the balloting resumed the next day, it quickly became obvious that the deadlock still existed. On the first ballot of the day (the twenty-ninth of the convention), some of the Edmunds and Windom delegates switched to Sherman, pushing the Ohioan up to 116, but the hoped-for stampede never developed. The lines stayed firm, and the wearying procession of ballots continued. Only a few delegates seemed interested in trying to get their fellows to break the stalemate; one vote was cast on the thirtieth ballot for General Phil Sheridan, and another vote for Conkling cropped up on the next ballot, but no one else picked up the challenge.

Finally, however, at the end of the thirty-fourth ballot, Wisconsin switched its 16 votes from Washburne to Garfield, the leader earlier of the anti-Grant coalition. Garfield quickly got to his feet:

GARFIELD: Mr. President—
HOAR: For what purpose does the gentleman rise?
GARFIELD: I rise to a question of order.
HOAR: The gentleman from Ohio rises to a question of order.
GARFIELD: I challenge the correctness of the announcement. The announcement contains votes for me. No man has a right, without the consent of the person voted for, to announce that person's name, and vote for him, in this convention. Such consent I have not given—
HOAR: The gentleman from Ohio is not stating a question of order. He

will resume his seat. No person having received a majority of the votes cast . . .[15]

Hoar later said that "I was terribly afraid that he would say something that would make his nomination impossible, or his acceptance impossible, if it were made." Probably Hoar worried needlessly; the Garfield effort had all the earmarks of a grandiose bit of drama to draw attention to the sanctimonious Ohioan. He had been receiving one or two votes since the second ballot, the day before, and he never made any attempt to disclaim them.[16]

On the next ballot, Grant reached his high-water mark at 313, as the Blaine and Sherman blocs finally started to crack, but those votes were going to Garfield, who now had 50.

As the thirty-sixth ballot started, Conkling stood in the aisle, calmly assuring the Grant delegates, "Keep steady, boys; Grant is going to win on this ballot." The Garfield vote was climbing, however, and when Maine, Blaine's state, threw all its votes to Garfield, Conkling realized something had to be done. He sent word to his lieutenants for delay, and John Creswell, the Stalwart head of the Maryland delegation, called for a poll of his state. While the poll was taken, Conkling and the other Grant leaders did what they could to pick up some of the newly liberated votes, but to no avail. All but fifty of the anti-Grant votes swung over to Garfield, as he nosed past the majority mark with 399. Incredibly, though, with everything smashing down around them, with the tide of the convention clear, the Stalwarts still polled 306 votes for Grant.[17]

Conkling was the first to rise, then, and move that the nomination of Garfield be made unanimous, which was promptly done, as the delegates cheered wildly—whether for the selection of Garfield or for the selection of anybody at all. Conkling stormed out angrily, in a classic rage.[18]

People around the convention had been talking for days about Garfield as a compromise choice; all it took was the proper length of the deadlock, the right degree of weariness on the part of the delegates, and

---

[15] *Ibid.*, p. 622.

[16] Hoar, I, 397. Garfield may have been trying to protect his rear against the predictably angry John Sherman. McClure says that Wisconsin held a caucus to see where it should throw its votes, and decided on Garfield by only a slight majority over William Windom. McClure, p. 273.

[17] Henry, p. 296.

[18] Conkling's motion for unanimity, together with a plea for unity against the Democrats, is in *Proceedings*, p. 628. A capsule rundown of the thirty-six ballots is in McClure, pp. 272–273, while they are set out at length in *Proceedings*, pp. 568–628.

a large enough clump of votes to start the big swing. Circumstances all combined on the thirty-sixth ballot—but that did not sweeten Roscoe Conkling's disposition. He had made the supreme effort of his life for this convention—much more so than four years earlier when he himself was a candidate. This time he had pulled all the wires, cashed all the political I.O.U.'s, taken all the steps. But because of Blaine and Garfield and the New York renegades, Conkling had lost.

The Ohio men, with the presidential nomination suddenly dropped in their laps, quickly decided upon a New Yorker for the second spot on the ticket, to bring Conkling into the campaign and generate some enthusiasm in the one state they would have to carry. Conkling's obvious intransigence was distressing to them, so they took the one step immediately available to appease him.

The first choice of Garfield and Governor Foster of Ohio was Congressman L. P. Morton, an eminent financier, a staunch member of the Conkling organization, and also a personal friend of Garfield. Morton had previously been mentioned as a possible vice-presidential candidate. He had tossed the question about in conversations and letters with Cornell, wondering whether the office was not "the fifth wheel to the coach," but he had still not resolved it in his own mind. He was contacted while still on the floor of the convention, before a recess was taken, and offered the spot. Morton asked for time to consult with his associates, and instantly went to look for Conkling.

When he found the senator, Morton told him of the offer, and Conkling frostily replied: "If you think the ticket will be elected, if you think you will be happy in the association, accept."

Morton said, "I have more confidence in your judgment than in my own."

"Governor Boutwell of Massachusetts is a great friend of yours," Conkling rejoined. "Why don't you talk with him?"

Morton did so, and Boutwell, as Conkling expected, advised him to reject the offer. Morton dutifully declined.[19]

This, of course, left the Ohio people without a candidate. They may have contacted Stewart Woodford, but he, with Conkling's "I hope no sincere friend of mine will accept it" ringing in his ears, would not entertain such a notion. Besides, Woodford had been burned on the same griddle four years before. The Ohio men next offered the nomination to

[19] Alexander, III, 444, based on a letter from Morton to Alexander twenty-eight years later. See also undated letter, Morton to Cornell, Cornell Papers.

Chester Arthur, though surely this must have been a move of desperation, in view of Arthur's unfortunate public image at the time.

Arthur, according to an eyewitness, found Conkling in an empty room, much perturbed, and approached him gingerly: "I have been hunting everywhere for you, Senator."

"Well, sir," growled Conkling, who may have heard why his chief aide was looking for him.

"The Ohio men have offered me the Vice Presidency."

"Well, sir, you should drop it as you would a red hot shoe from the forge," Conkling cried, indignantly.

Arthur stood his ground: "I sought you to consult, not—"

"What is there to consult about?" the angry Senator retorted. "This trickster of Mentor will be defeated before the country."

Still Arthur persisted, though Conkling was obviously working into a rage. "There is something else to be said," he went on.

"What, sir, you think of accepting?" Conkling shouted at him.

Arthur gulped and said, "The office of the Vice President is a greater honor than I ever dreamed of attaining. A barren nomination would be a great honor. In a calmer moment you will look at this differently."

"If you wish for my favor and my respect you will contemptuously decline it."

"Senator Conkling," Arthur said defiantly, "I shall accept the nomination and I shall carry with me the majority of the delegation."

Conkling glowered and then stalked away from him; it was clear to the senator that he and he only knew the meaning of ultimate commitment. When you gave yourself to a cause, you stuck with it to the end. Garfield had been an enemy throughout the convention, was still the enemy, as far as Roscoe Conkling was concerned; yet here were Morton and even Chester Arthur willing, nay, eager, to run with him. Their commitment, he now knew, was not total. No wonder; in truth, the cause was more than Grant, more than Stalwart Republicanism— the cause really was Roscoe Conkling's own peculiar psychoses, his hatred and implacable enmity, for Garfield, for Blaine, for Hayes, for anyone who crossed him.[20]

---

[20] Hudson, pp. 97–99. Hudson claims to have been present but unnoticed at the Arthur-Conkling confrontation. Morton, in his letter to Alexander of Sept. 14, 1908, mentioned earlier, confirms the fact of Arthur and Conkling being closeted together during the vice-presidential discussions. And a letter of Depew to A. B. Samford, June 3, 1920, describes roughly the same occurrence, without, of course, Hudson's colorful details; Depew Papers.

Chester Alan Arthur was placed in nomination by Woodford and seconded by former Governor Dennison of Ohio, to show Garfield's choice. Despite an effort for Washburne, Arthur was easily chosen on the first ballot.[21]

The convention sent out to the country James A. Garfield of Ohio for president and Chester A. Arthur of New York for vice-president; the weary delegates then adjourned. Let the party do with the ticket what it chose.

[21] One delegate, opposing Arthur, reminded the convention of the civil service reform plank and warned, "Let us not stultify ourselves before the country." *Proceedings*, p. 643.

CHAPTER 23

RALLY ROUND
GARFIELD AND ARTHUR

Reactions to the work of the Chicago convention were spotty. Most Republicans recognized the divisions in the party, and not many were overly enthusiastic about the candidate. There were few who found fault directly with the nomination of Garfield, though some worried what the Democrats would do with his tainted past, but many applauded his selection only because he was not one of the other candidates. The New York *Times,* the day after the convention, observed that "the obstinacy of the Grant leaders has saved the party from the candidacy of Blaine, and that is a service of no slight magnitude." *The Nation* congratulated the party, and said Garfield's choice was bad news for the Democrats, "to whose hands the nomination of either the Silent Man or the Magnetic Man would undoubtedly have given the battle." Rutherford B. Hayes, seeking comfort from the convention that had so studiously ignored him, called Garfield's nomination "the best that was possible . . . altogether good." [1]

There was very little happiness for John Sherman. The secretary felt privately that Governor Foster of Ohio had betrayed him at the convention, and he had his suspicions about Garfield. A couple of weeks later, he wrote sourly to Foster:

The nomination of Garfield is entirely satisfactory to me. The only shade that rests on this feeling is the fact that Garfield went there by my selection to represent me and comes from the convention with the honor that I sought. I will do him the justice to say that I have seen no evidence that he has contributed to this result except by his good conduct in the presence of the convention.

[1] N.Y. *Times,* June 9, 1880; *The Nation,* June 10, 1880; T. H. Williams, ed., p. 278.

344

Sherman was mortified, too, by the nomination of Arthur. Cornell as governor of New York was bad enough, but he had swallowed that; Arthur for vice-president of the whole United States was a real slap at him and at the policy of the president. Sherman called Arthur's nomination "a ridiculous burlesque . . . inspired by a desire to beat the ticket." Later he said it was "rather a scandalous proceeding." The only reason for Arthur's nomination, Sherman said, "was that he was discharged from an office that he was unfit to fill." [2]

The New York rebels were unhappy about Arthur, too. John Birdsall told a reporter that they all thought Robertson, who had caused the initial breach in the Grant phalanx, should have received the nomination, rather than "a Conkling heeler." But, he concluded, "they'll get over it. We made our kick and pledges have been made. The judge will have a big place in the Cabinet or something as good." Time would show that pledges were Garfield's stock in trade.

The big question was: Is the Garfield-Arthur ticket electable? Many politicians felt that Garfield was a beaten man as he left Chicago. The bitterness and rancor of the convention hung on, and Garfield's managers worried about the inflexibility shown at Chicago—particularly since the most inflexible of all, the senior senator from New York, had it in his power to defeat the ticket, and he had shown no signs of relaxing his rigorous posture.[3]

The Democrats met in Cincinnati on June 22. It had been assumed for several years that the Democrats in 1880 would offer the country the "Old Ticket," Tilden for president and Hendricks of Indiana for vice-president, as in 1876, to capitalize on the great electoral mess of that year. Events conspired against this, though. Tilden's name was implicated in a House investigation of some of the unsavory dealings after the 1876 election (much to the chagrin of the Democrats who set up the investigation, hoping to dig up Republican dirt). Hendricks felt that

[2] J. Sherman, II, 777–778; Burton, pp. 296–297; Howe, pp. 112–113. Young Henry Cabot Lodge wrote that "such a nomination on general principles is thoroughly bad and a direct insult to the present administration," but he said that it was a strong political move. "No one will abandon Garfield on account of Arthur," and the ticket would get the benefit of the "direction of the shrewdest political manager in the country." C. M. Fuess, *Carl Schurz*, pp. 272–273.

[3] "There were elements that were resentful and in an ugly temper." Hudson, pp. 104–105. Conkling was heard to say that Garfield's nomination was "a public calamity."

he should be considered a candidate for the presidency this time, so coolness developed between his partisans and the supporters of Tilden. The former New York governor was in less than robust health, and, most importantly, an announced intention on the part of John Kelly and Tammany to defect from a Tilden nomination made his chances of carrying New York look slim indeed. This presented the Democrats with a dilemma, for the only way they could capitalize on the Great Fraud of 1876 was to run the Great Defrauded again for president.

Before the convention met, Tilden gave his brother Henry a letter addressed to the New York delegation, to be used if and when circumstances made his nomination appear impossible, withdrawing from the running. Unfortunately, word of the letter of withdrawal leaked out before the convention even began, and Tilden's chances evaporated. On the second ballot, General Winfield Scott Hancock of Pennsylvania, the good Democratic general even through the trying days of Reconstruction, was nominated, and William H. English of Indiana, a relic of prewar battles between Douglas and Buchanan, was named for the vice-presidency. No one really knew whether Tilden wanted to run again or not, but the fumbling course of his managers at Cincinnati assured that the convention would pick another.[4]

The Democratic party, with the threat of a Tammany defection in New York averted, was reasonably united as it headed into the 1880 campaign, while the Republicans were badly splintered. The Democratic candidate was a genuine Union army hero, the savior of Gettysburg, and obviously not about to deliver the country into the hands of the old Confederacy; even the Republican stump-speakers held off on such a charge. The Republican presidential candidate, for all his long and generally progressive service in the House, still carried the stain of his involvement with Credit Mobilier. Though the affair had been whitewashed in 1873, Garfield's part in it, even so much as had been revealed to the public, still looked unsavory. In addition, he had been mixed up in a paving contract scandal in Washington. The Republican vice-presidential nominee appeared to the country as a very glaring example of the thing civil service reform was all about. Of Arthur's good qualities and of the relatively efficient manner in which he had run the

---

[4] Wall, p. 169; Dinnerstein, pp. 239–240; Hudson, pp. 108–109; McClure, pp. 278–279. Fernando Wood felt that Horatio Seymour should be the candidate; Wood to Seymour, June 10, 1880, Seymour Papers.

custom house, the people knew nothing. He was a spoilsman and a henchman of Roscoe Conkling. The Democrats were expected to emphasize that the two heads of the Republican ticket symbolized the party perfectly, with corruption as one and the spoils system as the other. The Democrats felt confident in 1880; they had last won the White House in 1856, but now they felt victory coming.

All was not lost for the Republicans, however. Prosperity had returned to the nation; the grinding depression following the Panic of 1873 had finally lifted, and times were good again. This had to help the party in power. There was little real difference between the two parties, and correspondingly no national need to turn from one to the other. The Hayes administration, no matter how little thought of by the Republican politicians, was apparently well regarded by the people; there had been no scandals, resumption had taken place without a hitch, the bitter problem of Southern state governments supported by federal troops was gone, and the very blandness of the president's personality had a calming influence upon the nation. The Democrats, who had controlled both houses of Congress since the 1878 elections, had not given very impressive evidence of their ability to govern, and public sympathy had generally been with Hayes in the battle over the appropriation riders. All of these factors had to count as pluses for the Republicans. The big problem, however, remained; how to win an election if half the party workers and leaders sit on their hands?

The situation was not improved when, back in Washington, Conkling called upon Garfield in mid-June, as a courtesy visit, presumably, found the nominee absent, and later learned that at that very time Garfield was riding with Carl Schurz. Garfield, when he got back, quickly dispatched a note to Conkling at Wormley's, where the senator was staying, apologizing for missing him and asking Conkling to name a time the next day when they could get together. Conkling scornfully declined to answer, snorting, we can well imagine, at the thought of holding commerce with a man who would be seen publicly with Schurz; the breach widened.[5]

In the meantime, Garfield was trying to draft a letter of acceptance which would satisfy both the Grant and Blaine wings of the party. The

[5] Reid to Garfield, June 26, 1880, Reid Papers; the Garfield note to Conkling, dated June 17, 1880, is in Conkling Papers, Library of Congress. For explanation of Conkling's reaction after missing Garfield, from a close friend of the Senator, see Gorham, p. 7.

wobbly result, which was published on July 10, pleased very few. *The Nation* scorched it, saying, "The unworthy phrases in which Mr. Garfield's ideas are concealed or his old-time professions recanted betray a want of backbone." [6]

This last charge was a real problem for Garfield. He was easily swayed from one position to another, and his disposition usually inclined him to follow the line of least resistance. Though he was a handsome man and a fine speaker, these qualities were not really enough. John Sherman said that "his will power was not equal to his personal magnetism. He easily changed his mind, and honestly veered from one impulse to another." A more charitable view was that his "sympathetic mind so often mirrored the changing views of the community in which he lived." [7]

Garfield was forty-nine years old in 1880. He had grown up on a farm in the Western Reserve of Ohio, but he had gone to college at Williams in Massachusetts. He had been president of Hiram College in Ohio as well an an evangelist before the Civil War, and he got into politics as a member of the Ohio state senate. This political background enabled him to get a commission in the army, and he eventually rose to the rank of brigadier general. He served with distinction on the staff of General W. S. Rosecrans with the Army of the Cumberland, winning commendation for his work at the battle of Chickamauga. Elected to Congress in 1862, he left the army the next year to take his seat in Washington.

The Nineteenth District of Ohio was New England in background and unwaveringly Republican in its politics, though Garfield periodically worried about his re-election. He was re-elected eight times, and in 1880 was elected to the Senate, though he was destined never to take his seat in the upper house. He assumed a position of leadership in the House, and the creditable service he performed there tended to obscure the scandals in which he was mildly implicated, scandals into which he was drawn probably because of his inclination to go along with things before he realized what he was into. He was a fine parliamentarian, a good orator, and, even to Tom Platt, "a most attractive man to meet." But he was a weather vane.[8]

[6] July 22, 1880. A letter from Garfield to Whitelaw Reid on June 29, 1880, set forth his hopes to pacify everyone; Reid Papers.

[7] J. Sherman, II, 807; R. G. Caldwell, *James A. Garfield,* p. 180.

[8] Platt, p. 125.

Garfield suggested that any of four possibilities would be acceptable to him as national chairman: Eugene Hale, William E. Chandler, R. C. McCormick, and Marshall Jewell. Jewell of Connecticut was named.

Garfield also suggested Platt as secretary of the national committee, but at the behest of John Logan, Stephen W. Dorsey, former carpetbag senator from Arkansas, a Stalwart, and an ingenious thief, was selected for this post. Dorsey took as his personal responsibility Indiana, which had a pivotal state election in October. There were in Indiana enough purchasable votes to swing the election, and in each election one side or the other purchased them. It was Stephen Dorsey's kind of state.[9]

None of this touched Garfield's major problem: Roscoe Conkling. After the failure of communications in Washington in mid-June, the angry senator went off to the Thousand Islands to go fishing, and he took the vice-presidential candidate with him. Schurz wrote Garfield that "the regular machine elements do not like you because they know that at heart you do not belong to them, whatever you say." This was obvious to the nominee, but it did nothing to solve his problem. "If Conkling himself sulks," Schurz went on, "his following will go on without him and he will lose it." Perhaps, but Garfield was chary of taking the chance that Schurz was right; if he was not, there was a presidential election lost.[10]

As July wore on, Conkling's silence became ever more ominous. On the 23rd, the *Times* reported an extensive speaking tour for the senator on behalf of the ticket, but this was a rumor without any basis in fact. Those on the inside, the pros like Chandler and Dorsey who knew Conkling, knew that as of that time there was no indication that the senator intended to do anything at all for the ticket. They knew, as Tom Platt later confirmed, that by the end of July nothing had been done by the state committee in New York. They knew that Conkling was still boiling mad about the outcome of the convention and Garfield's part in it, and they had a pretty good idea what he would require to pacify him and put him to work.

Dorsey, who was nothing if not a practical politician, conceived the idea of a meeting in New York between Garfield and Conkling, and he told Garfield firmly that it had to be: "I insist that a conference with Gov. Cornell and Sen. Conkling is an absolute essential to success in this campaign." When Garfield asked naïvely what they wanted to see him about, Dorsey told him plainly enough,

---

[9] T. C. Smith, II, 999–1000.   [10] Schurz, *Papers,* IV, 3.

they want to know whether the Republicans of the State of New York are to be recognized . . . or whether the "Scratchers" and Independents and "featherheads" are to ride over the Republican party of this state as they have for the last four years. They not only want to know that but they intend to know it and they can only be satisfied by a personal conference with you.[11]

Garfield, as usual, wavered and vacillated. One day he wrote Reid that "I really think it will be better not to go" (Reid had told him not to run after the malcontents; "let them run after you"), and then he wrote Chandler that "I am entirely willing and indeed should be glad, to see Mr. Conkling." He was sure that Conkling would not ask "any unreasonable thing." He wrote in his journal, "It is an unreasonable demand that so much effort should be made to conciliate one man," and then added, characteristically, "but to resist the opinion of the whole Committee would be ungracious and perhaps unwise." Finally, he decided to make the effort, though he wrote to President Hayes on July 31 that "if any part of the purpose of this meeting is to secure any concession to the N. Y. men who are sulking, they will find no help in me beyond what I should give to any Republican." That Garfield could have had any misunderstanding of the purpose of the proposed meeting after the representations made to him of the necessity for holding it is hardly credible. The comment to Hayes looks like the careful preparation of an escape hatch.[12]

It was finally decided to arrange a meeting of the national committee and all the prominent national leaders as a cover for the crucial conference between Garfield and Conkling. The nominee's advisers felt that an obvious confrontation between the two men would lower Garfield in public estimation, so the large gathering was set up for public consumption.

Garfield left Mentor on August 3 to head for New York, and his train made some twenty stops between Buffalo and the metropolis, as the candidate made speeches and welcomed New York Republican leaders as they climbed aboard his train. The receptions at the various stops were good and must have encouraged the nervous candidate. The *Times* noted that they showed "no suggestion of Republican apathy."

[11] Dorsey to Garfield, July 26, 1880, T. C. Smith, II, 1010.

[12] For the various reactions of Garfield and his correspondents, see *ibid.*, II, 1008–1011; correspondence in Reid Papers; and Henry, p. 303, for the advice of a long-time close friend of the candidate, spelling out clearly why Conkling had to be conciliated.

Conkling arrived in the city on the evening of August 2, going directly to the Fifth Avenue Hotel, though the usual cloud of rumor and speculation trailed behind him. Garfield's train pulled into New York on the evening of August 4, and he went to a meeting to discuss finances with some of the leading money men. The outcome of this meeting was a tentative undertaking by L. P. Morton to chair a committee to raise sizable sums of cash for Garfield's campaign, for expenditure where it might be most needed.[13]

At noon the following day, August 5, the large conference of the national committee and leading Republicans was held at the Fifth Avenue Hotel. The meeting was just window dressing although there was one unforeseen development. The *Times* said the next morning that "Senator Conkling was conspicuously absent from the Republican conference yesterday," but it concluded that this was "doubtless, due to his sincere desire for party harmony." A charitable view, but one not shared by the presidential nominee. Garfield wrote in his journal that evening: "The absence of Sen. Conkling gave rise to unpleasant surmises as to his attitude." Conkling's friends, he thought, "were embarrassed and somewhat indignant." Additionally, as he prepared for the important session the next day, Garfield assured himself staunchly: "There shall neither be nor appear to be, if I can prevent it, any mortgaging of my future freedom." Then he casually mentioned the obvious source of this last-minute bracing when he said that he "had a long and friendly talk with Blaine," whom he called "the prince of good fellows." [14]

Where was Roscoe Conkling? No one seemed to know; his supporters appeared to be as much in the dark as Garfield and his entourage. He had apparently moved in with his brother Frederick for the duration of the conclave, but he told no one. Why had he taken off? There were several theories. His nephew later said that the senator was "unwilling to trust to Mr. Garfield's imperfect memory of a private conversation, however unimportant." Platt said that Conkling told Dorsey roughly the same thing when he heard about the proposed conference and "refused absolutely to become a party to it," though he would abide by the decisions of his friends. Reid suggested to Garfield later that it was the pres-

13 N.Y. *Times,* Aug. 3, 1880, for Conkling's arrival. McElroy, pp. 109–110. Conkling seemed unconcerned about the meeting when he wrote to Morton on Aug. 1, mostly about stock prices, and casually added that he would be in town by the 9th; Morton Papers.

14 T. C. Smith, II, 1012.

ence of Curtis that kept the senator away. Whatever it was, it soon became clear that he had left plenipotentiary powers with his aides, to treat for him with the enemy and to make such commitments as they thought wise. He had confidence in these men, and he was aware they knew quite well his goals for the meeting with Garfield. Still, it was unusual to see Conkling put himself unreservedly in their hands.[15]

The next afternoon, the presidential candidate sat down with Arthur, Crowley, Morton, and Platt in Morton's room at the hotel. It was a long meeting, and when it was over the Stalwart leaders were obviously pleased and satisfied. Curiously, Garfield's entry in his diary about the conference was brief and unspecific, only the following: "Had, in the afternoon a long interview with Morton, Crowley, Arthur and Platt." The only other participant who left a record of the meeting is Platt, in his autobiography written many years later. Though he may have embellished his own role, and in spite of the fact that his book is suspect in numerous items, there seems no reason to doubt his general description of the meeting, substantiated as it is by events, logic, and common sense.[16]

There was an initial uncomfortable silence when the five men got down to business, according to Platt, broken by Garfield's expression of indignation at the senator's absence. Excuses were made on Conkling's behalf, and then Platt opened up, stating that the question to be decided before any work was done was whether a Garfield administration would be similar to that of Hayes; "whether," as Platt put it, "you are going to recognize and reward the men who must do the work in this State, and bear the brunt of the battle in this campaign; or whether you are to counsel with and be guided by the advice of the seventeen men who rebelled from the delegation at Chicago." If the latter, Platt said, the New York Stalwarts would take no part in the active work of the canvass. "We cannot afford to do the work, and let others reap the reward."

In the discussion that followed, according to Platt, Garfield denied any intention to follow the Hayes path, acknowledged Conkling's primacy in the state of New York, and "assured us that the wishes of the element of the party we represented should be paramount with him touching all questions of patronage." Pressed particularly on the status

---

[15] A. R. Conkling, p. 611; Platt, p. 127; Reid to Garfield, Aug. 13, 1880, Reid Papers.

[16] T. C. Smith, II, 1012. Platt's version is in Platt, pp. 129–132.

of the Chicago rebels, Garfield said he would consult with the Stalwarts and do for Robertson and his friends only what the Conkling wing approved. (One harkens back to what John Birdsall said after the convention, "Pledges have been made." It all depended on who spoke with Garfield last.) One final item of business was taken care of in an inner room, by Platt's story, where Morton and Garfield met privately and straightened out Morton's future status if he took care of Garfield's financial needs. Morton, it was settled, should have his choice of several appropriate positions, including secretary of the treasury.

Platt's story of the meeting with Garfield rings true. He and his fellow Stalwart lieutenants were shrewd political bargainers, had been in the game for a long time, and had a clear idea of what they wanted to achieve. They did not enter into alliances lightly, and knew only too well they would have to account to Roscoe Conkling. Indeed, what they had to offer was not only the good offices of the machine in New York but also the oratorical splendor of the state's Republican senator, for service on behalf of the ticket where it would do the most good. The subsequent work of the organization, along with Conkling's speaking tour, demonstrates that Arthur and his confederates felt that they were fulfilling their side of a bargain, a bargain struck on August 6 in the Fifth Avenue Hotel. They were not shy and had few political illusions, so it is difficult to believe that their terms were less than clear to Garfield. What they wanted as the price of the Conkling machine's cooperation and assistance was control of patronage in New York, and a veto over rewards to the renegades at Chicago, though they acknowledged that some form of recognition would have to be given. As a minor corollary, because of the specialized work to be performed by Morton, they wanted a specific understanding as to his status. They felt that they achieved appropriate understandings with Garfield on all three items, so they went to work.

The four Conkling negotiators would undoubtedly have been startled had they seen the entry Garfield made in his journal on August 9, when he returned from his New York trip: "Very weary but feeling that no serious mistake has been made and probably much good has been done. No trades, no shackles and as well fitted for defeat or victory." This was a curious note; it means that Garfield did not appreciate the significance of the concessions made to the New Yorkers, or was fooling himself, or made none of the agreements which the Conkling men later claimed, but rather laid down the law on the obligations of party leadership. The last possibility seems too far-fetched to consider; it is just not Garfield. The other thought is that Garfield purposely or subconsciously misunderstood or misinterpreted words in the standard political lexicon, such as "recognition" and "reward" and "approval," words with specific political meanings, so as to distort and unshape the agreement made in New York. Reid wrote the candidate on July 30, preparing him for the New York conference, "It is going to be a case for careful phrasing coupled with the utmost appearance of good will and cordiality." If that was the mental set which Garfield brought to the meeting, his unspoken reservations, if there were such, led to bitter results.[17]

Roscoe Conkling had no doubts about the outcome of the meeting. Later on he told a newsman, referring to the conference of August 6: "How willing Garfield then was, when everything looked blue and certain defeat seemed to stare him in the face; how willing he was to concede anything and everything to the Stalwarts if they would only rush to the rescue and save the day!" [18]

One strange event took place which went completely unnoticed in the general excitement of the nominee's visit. On the evening of the 6th, a big rally was held by the Boys in Blue, a Republican veterans organization; among the speakers recorded by the *Times* the next morning were, of course, Garfield and Arthur, George Sharpe, Logan, Pierrepont, Benjamin Harrison, and, way down at the end of the program, one Charles Guiteau of Illinois. Garfield went back to Ohio freighted with trouble for the future, but with his campaign looking healthy for the first time.

And so Roscoe Conkling got into the campaign of 1880 at last. The prospects for the Republican ticket, before Conkling's entry, were gloomy. The Democrats were united, to a degree, and working hard. They counted upon a Solid South and all the Border states. They expected to win New Jersey and the Far Western states of California, Nevada, and Oregon, and then either New York or the combination

[17] T. C. Smith, II, 1015. Reid Papers. On July 4, 1883, Andrew D. White noted in his diary a talk with Platt which anticipated the version of the Fifth Avenue Hotel conference that Platt would record many years later; Ogden, ed., p. 233.

[18] T. B. Connery, "Secret History of the Garfield-Conkling Tragedy," p. 150. A close friend of the candidate, the editor of the Cleveland *Leader,* asked Garfield point-blank and in confidence if there was anything to the wide-spread rumors of a deal with Conkling; he never received a reply; Clancy, p. 192.

of Ohio and Indiana would assure Hancock the presidency. In late summer it appeared very likely that all of these states would go Democratic, along with some others like Maine and perhaps Hancock's native Pennsylvania. The Democrats were floundering in some measure on the tariff question, because their platform called for "a tariff for revenue only" at a time when much of the nation was in favor of protection. This was something Conkling could sink his teeth into. Various Democratic leaders attempted to dodge the implications of the platform plank, until General Hancock delivered himself of the opinion that the tariff was "a local issue" and should not be in the presidential campaign. This caused snickers among the knowing, and Hancock looked slightly foolish. Still, he seemed to be well ahead, and his advisers would try to keep him quiet for the rest of the campaign. Roscoe Conkling's task was immense, if he hoped to stem the Democratic tide.

He visited the national committee about a week after Garfield's trip to New York, sat down for some time with Dorsey, and arranged his itinerary for the canvass. He needed some time, since he was accustomed to spending a great deal of time and effort upon a speech, and he had some personal business and some legal clients to take care of before he could begin. On August 29, he wrote, "I am working hard to get to the point where I can get time to read up and get ready for the campaign." He had to return some $18,000 worth of retainers already paid before he could start his campaign business. That must have hurt, because the senator was not wealthy. But he did pitch right in to save the Republican party and to fulfill his part of the compact with Garfield. He knew he was needed, and he acted the part without hesitation. Young John Hay wrote to Reid in late August about "Conkling's demeanor." "He really thinks he is the Savior of the Situation," wrote Hay, "and makes no bones about it." [19]

The senator's first speech was made on September 17 in the Academy of Music in New York, where an overflow throng heard him speak for three hours and forty minutes.

I hold up the record since 1860, when the bloody drama of the rebellion opened, and I say that the Democratic party has been wrong and beaten on all the great issues of the century.

A triumphant Nationality—a regenerated Constitution—a free Republic —an unbroken country—untarnished credit—solvent finances—unparalleled

[19] Cortissoz, II, 38; Conkling to L. P. Morton, Aug. 29, 1880, Morton Papers; A. R. Conkling, p. 614, on the $18,000 worth of retainers.

prosperity—all these are ours, despite the policy and the efforts of the Democratic party.

Near the close, Conkling even deigned to give a brief mention to the presidential nominee:

Some service with him in Congress has made me well acquainted with General Garfield. That he has the intelligence, experience, and habits of mind which fit a man for the Presidential office, I think I know. Without early advantages, he, years ago, achieved prominence among the leading men in public life, and that prominence he has maintained ever since in all the collisions between individuals and parties. That he is competent to the duties before him, there seems to me no reason to doubt.[20]

This grudging tribute was hardly of the type to stir men's souls for Garfield, but Conkling had never promised to extol the candidate. He was working for the ticket and the party, and Garfield would have to be an incidental beneficiary of his work. The important thing was that Conkling was in the field; his speeches and his very presence would stir up the faithful and illuminate the issues of the campaign.

After the Academy of Music, the senator went on tour. On September 28, he spoke in Warren, Ohio, again barely mentioning Garfield, and followed his speech with a visit to Garfield's Mentor home, at the invitation of the candidate. Tom Platt, who was not there, later told a charming tale of Conkling's arrival in a downpour, with Garfield rushing off the porch to embrace him, exclaiming: "Conkling, you have saved me. Whatever man can do for man that will I do for you!" Whereupon Conkling, according to Platt, exacted from the nominee a pledge of approval for all New York patronage. It's a nice story, but it probably did not happen. Garfield's private secretary denied vehemently that any such exchange ever took place. There was no opportunity for a private meeting between the two men, Conkling surely would not have wanted any such meeting and, after the arrangements at the Fifth Avenue Hotel, Conkling presumably would have felt no need for any further pledges. If Garfield would not keep the promises he had already made, new ones would have been useless.[21]

[20] N.Y. *Times*, Sept. 18, 1880. This speech was also included in a collection of *Great Republican Speeches of 1880.*

[21] Garfield's letter of invitation to Conkling and his party, which included Morton, Simon Cameron, and General Grant, is in Conkling Papers, Library of Congress. Platt's version is in Platt, pp. 134–135; the contradiction by J. Stanley-Brown, Garfield's private secretary, is in T. C. Smith, II, 1033–1034.

After Garfield received reports on the Warren speech, he complained of the "narrow and unmanly" way in which Conkling made "such a manifest effort . . . to avoid mentioning the head of the ticket in any generous way." He called Conkling "a singular compound of a very brilliant man and an exceedingly petulant spoiled child." [22] But it did not matter. Conkling had gone on his way, doing heavy work for Garfield in spite of himself. He spoke on September 29 in Cleveland, scoring heavily against Hancock and the Democrats on the tariff, and attracted a huge crowd in Cincinnati, where he spoke on the sectional issue, the newly Solid South and what it meant, in a city strongly oriented commercially toward the South.[23]

The senator swung on into the critical state of Indiana, drawing big and enthusiastic crowds everywhere he visited. There was little doubt that Conkling's efforts, together with Dorsey's, helped tremendously in holding the Hoosier State for the Republicans in October, which in turn invigorated the party nation-wide for November.

Conkling came back home for the rest of the campaign, for New York was the most important state of all. Though he knew the tide had been turned, he came back with few illusions. When Platt asked him, "Have you any faith in Garfield?" the senator responded, wryly, "Not much, but we will try him out." He even wrote to Morton that "my heart is I fear as much turned on money making as yours on contry [sic] making." There was little choice now but to go on, to carry out his part of the bargain, and hope that Garfield might carry out his. As Conkling toured the state, prospects for the Republican ticket brightened considerably.[24]

The perceptive Godkin, who had little belief in Conkling's disinterested devotion to the party, put his finger upon one of the apparent enigmas of the campaign when he wrote, in his October 21 issue:

Mr. Conkling has been "supporting the ticket" with so much zeal and energy, though on the tariff issue mainly . . . and in this way is making his conduct in this campaign so much of a contrast to his conduct in the Hayes campaign and to his sulky attitude when Mr. Garfield was in New York, that it is reported that he must have concluded a satisfactory "bargain" with the Republican candidate. . . . Mr. Garfield has, however,

[22] T. C. Smith, II, 1032.

[23] S. P. Hirshson, *Farewell to the Bloody Shirt,* pp. 85–86, quoting the Cincinnati *Gazette,* Oct. 2, 1880.

[24] Platt, pp. 134–135; Conkling to L. P. Morton, Oct. 14, 1880, Morton Papers; A. R. Conkling, p. 626.

given emphatic assurances that he will make no bargains or promises of the kind which Mr. Conkling most delights in; so that we have before us the alternative of believing that Mr. Garfield has been making false representations, or that Mr. Conkling's friends do him injustice when they admit that he never really "works" in a canvass until he knows what his pay is to be.

One of the major skeins tying our early history to the present is the quadrennial presidential election. The size of the electorate may have increased, and styles of campaiging may have changed, but the basic institution remains unaltered—the ebb and flow of party fortunes, the interchange of issues and personalities, and the interlocking of local, state, and national politics. So it was in 1880. The Democrats trotted out a clumsy forgery, called the "Morey letter," to tar Garfield in the West with pro-Chinese sentiments, but it was easily seen through and there was enough time to counteract it. President Hayes took off on a nonpolitical trip to the Far West, returning to Fremont on the very eve of the election. When Hayes did something nonpolitical, it was *really* nonpolitical, but even this was good; an incumbent president can easily get in the way of his would-be successor, with statements or actions of one kind or another, and the nominee has no control over them. Hayes did not get in Garfield's way. Dorsey spread money lavishly and judiciously in the right parts of Indiana, with the full knowledge of Garfield, who had obviously convinced himself that the Indiana electoral votes were worth fighting fire with fire.

And in New York, Garfield got a final, unexpected boost. John Kelly, who hated Tilden, probably wanted to see Hancock win. In spite of this, Kelly nominated an Irish Catholic named William Grace for Mayor of New York City (over the protests of many Democratic leaders, who saw only too well what would happen); Grace's candidacy immediately alienated the German voters and raised the old issue of diversion of funds from the free public schools. It brought out an anti-Catholic vote in the city, and this was Republican. Grace's candidacy was of incalculable help to Garfield, who carried the state of New York by only 21,000 votes.

With New York went the election. It was an anxious election night, but it finally brought the Republicans good news. Garfield carried New York, Ohio, and Indiana, and with them an electoral victory of 214–155. His popular vote plurality in the nation was less then 10,000 votes, but he won the crucial states where Conkling worked for him, and with them the presidency.[25]

Garfield was now president-elect. For a man of his temperament, it was a dangerous status. Even his friends recognized the problem. Shortly before the election, John Hay had written the candidate, "Beware of your own generosity!" He further advised Garfield that, after being elected, "it will pay you to keep a cheap friend to drone continually in your ear, 'It was *you* who were nominated at Chicago and elected by the people.' " Garfield's travail was about to begin.[26]

[25] Barnard, p. 494, for Hayes's trip. Dinnerstein, pp. 241–242, and A. Nevins, *Grover Cleveland*, p. 96, on the Grace nomination. Grace won the mayoralty by 3,000 votes, but he clearly cost Hancock the state and the nation. For election results, see McClure, pp. 283–284. On Indiana, Garfield wrote Reid, "It is hardly possible for anyone to have a fuller knowledge of the forces now at work in Indiana than I. The most minute and comprehensive reports are brought to me daily of the operations there." Sept. 2, 1880, Reid Papers.

[26] Hay to Garfield, Oct. 18, 1880, *Letters of John Hay*, II, 52.

CHAPTER 24

---◆◈◈◗---

CABINETMAKING

Filling the cabinet and the leading positions of a new administration has always been a difficult task for a president-elect; there are so many aspirants and so few jobs. Seldom has the problem been more difficult than it was for James Abram Garfield—and for this his own peculiarly malleable personality was to blame. Eager to please, Garfield solicited and took advice from everyone. All sorts of diverse and miscellaneous Republican politicians came away from discussions with him thinking that he had agreed to put a particular friend of the caller into the new cabinet. Yet there were only seven cabinet ministries available.

One of these was marked out from the beginning. Garfield decided early upon Blaine, that "prince of good fellows," for the state department. This selection he stuck with throughout—expect for one time late in the interregnum period when, desperate for a solution of his New York problem, he toyed with the idea of making Roscoe Conkling secretary of state and asking Blaine to move over to some other job, probably treasury! The prospect of the intimate meetings of such a cabinet staggers the imagination. Blaine quickly squashed the idea.

Garfield's efforts to construct a cabinet embracing all the elements of the Republican party were futile, as it turned out. In the process, the president-elect showed only a faint recognition of the immensity of the split in the party, causing one to wonder if Garfield truly appreciated the significance of what had taken place at the convention in Chicago. The Stalwarts were aggrieved as soon as they heard of the choice of Blaine for secretary of state, and Garfield's efforts to satisfy Conkling, Logan, and their crowd thoroughly alarmed the Half Breeds, the wing of the party grouped roughly around Blaine, to say nothing of the professional reformers, who generally felt that even selecting Blaine was going quite far enough to satisfy the politicians. The reform element

360

had filled two of the posts in the Hayes cabinet, with Evarts and Schurz, and considered itself entitled to representation with Garfield. Besides, the reformers were hard-pressed to draw distinctions between Conkling politicians and Blaine politicians. With all this, Garfield received a stream of advice and admonitions from young men like Whitelaw Reid and John Hay, warning with dire predictions against concessions to Conkling and the Grant wing; Reid and Hay kept telling one another that they had to keep doing this to stiffen Garfield's backbone, to keep him from making dangerous concessions, to keep him from handing over control of his administration to Roscoe Conkling, which they apparently had no doubt he would do unless they could save him from his own good nature and weakness. It was curious treatment of a man who had just been elected president of the United States, but they knew Garfield only too well. They were probably right, too.

The press had a field day with Garfield's cabinet difficulties, dutifully recording all the rumors, offers, and vacillations. On January 18, 1881, the *Times* said, "If all reports are true, Pres. Garfield's Cabinet will contain about one hundred twenty-five persons." This followed that paper's earlier advice to Garfield, on December 29, that "the shortest path to lunacy" was to "undertake to appoint a Cabinet which will satisfy everybody." It was becoming pretty clear, though, Garfield was trying to do just that.

For the six cabinet positions that were left there were quite a few names prominently in circulation. Senators Howe, Allison, and Windom were all mentioned for the treasury. Governor Foster of Ohio, Robert Lincoln (Abe's son), Judge Hunt of Louisiana, Wayne MacVeagh (Don Cameron's brother-in-law)—these too were mentioned as being in the running for positions. Garfield suggested that he wanted someone from Iowa, and the Republicans of that state responded with the names of Allison, Samuel J. Kirkwood, and James F. Wilson. None of the three were very anxious for the honor, since Allison and Kirkwood wanted to remain in the Senate, and Wilson preferred to succeed whoever moved up. Also put in the running were Postmaster Tom James of New York and Judge Charles Folger, as representatives of the Conkling machine; however, the party line of the New York Stalwarts, a position which would cause Garfield all sorts of problems and poison the air between him and Conkling, was that the treasury had been pledged to L. P. Morton and that no less would suffice.[1]

[1] Sage, pp. 169–173.

While Garfield's tribulations continued, Albany, New York, was the scene of some internecine squabbling which would have serious consequences later.

The Half Breeds in New York were spoiling for a fight. Garfield's hopes for the success of his national administration centered upon a strategy of keeping the Stalwarts and the Half Breeds away from each other's throats, which involved pacifying Roscoe Conkling. The Blaine people in New York, who hated Conkling—men like Reid, Robertson, Woodin and their followers—wanted no part of such a design. They had been kept under the Conkling thumb for so long, had suffered so many indignities at his hands, and had made so many predictions, both public and private, of how different things would be once Garfield became president, that a policy of peace was for them a disaster. They grumbled that peace in New York would be on Conkling's terms, even though this might insure peace within the Republican party on a national scale, and they were quite prepared to sacrifice Garfield's hopes in order to stir up a little strife on the New York front.

Blaine's role in New York affairs was curious. As presumptive secretary of state, he no doubt wished for the success and good fortune of the Garfield administration, and recognized that Garfield's political policy was based upon conciliation of the Stalwarts, including that group's leader, the senator from New York. Yet Blaine could always be diverted from the direct approach by a minor opportunity to score a partisan point or two; it was a major weakness of the man and contributed to the mistrust he aroused in many Republicans throughout the country. He showed this trait in New York in January of 1881. Clearly, he felt that a group of his supporters, going out to pick a fight with Roscoe Conkling and his henchmen, should receive the backing, indeed the encouragement, of their leader, even though this immediately involved the incoming administration and threw a sickly glow of disbelief upon Garfield's protestations of harmony. Blaine did get himself involved.

There were two contests which would be decided by the legislature in January. First was the speakership of the assembly. George Sharpe was a candidate for re-election to this post; he not only had the full backing of the Conkling organization, of which he was a leader, but he had also that backing which comes from a job well done. Sharpe had been a good presiding officer; he could make a speech of more than passing quality, he was fair and judicious, and the door to his office was generally open to members of the assembly who had problems. Though his breadth of vision was limited by his narrow background and ambitions, George Sharpe was an expert politician. He had already exercised the whip of committee assignments before, and it required a measure of political recklessness to defy him just before he would presumably hand out these plums once again. A Half Breed named Skinner was selected to oppose Sharpe, and taken around by Whitelaw Reid among groups of legislators gathering together to talk about the upcoming session, but he was clearly outclassed in the contest.

The second struggle would be for United States senator. The term of Francis Kernan was expiring, and the solidly Republican legislature would elect his successor. Conkling had a clear majority in the Republican caucus and could hand-pick the man. Until the previous summer, there had been little doubt upon whom Conkling would confer a Senate seat if he had one available. Particularly after Cornell's election as governor, the only logical choice for the Senate, as well as the most able man available, was Chester Alan Arthur. Probably, Conkling was grooming Arthur for the position and thus did not run him for governor. Now, though, Arthur was vice-president-elect, and no longer in consideration for the Senate. The race was open. Three candidates from the ranks of the Stalwarts soon came to the fore: Richard Crowley, Tom Platt, and L. P. Morton. There is no doubt that Roscoe Conkling could happily have supported any one of the three to be his colleague in Washington; what was equally clear was that a choice among them by the senator might have dire repercussions within the organization. All three were more or less publicly committed to the race, so that a withdrawal would be sticky. This problem of Conkling's, though, was not widely recognized. The wise heads in Albany expected that soon enough Conkling would speak, and his words would be followed by discreet retreats upon the part of the disappointed candidates; after all, they could see the intensity of the drive to place Morton in the cabinet, thereby drawing off some of the pressure of the senatorial race.[2]

Into this situation was inserted the deft and sinister hand of James G. Blaine. On January 3, a double-leaded editorial, which hardly any-

[2] Howe, p. 98; McElroy, pp. 121–122. Reid, in a letter to Garfield during the campaign, Aug. 30, 1880, suggested that Platt, Payn, and Cornell were opposed to Arthur being the senator in any event, though presumably this did not include a firm decision by Conkling; Reid Papers.

one took the trouble to conceal as proceeding from the pen of Blaine, appeared in the New York *Tribune,* proclaiming the policy of the incoming administration:

It is not to be used as a make-weight, in pending Senatorial contests, whether in New York or elsewhere. We are fully authorized to say this, and the words are entitled to their full significance.

It is proper to say, further, that the incoming Administration will see to it that the men from New York and from other States, who had the courage at Chicago to obey the wishes of their districts in the balloting for President, and who thus finally voted for Garfield, shall not suffer for it, nor lose by it. . . . Gentlemen at Albany, who are said to have been threatened with a different course at Washington, may reassure themselves. The Administration of President Garfield is to be an Administration for the whole Republican party. It will foment no quarrels; it will most earnestly seek the things that make for peace, and for the best interests of the party it represents. But it will not permit its friends to be persecuted for their friendship.

Garfield, when he saw the *Tribune* editorial, wrote to Reid characteristically, saying, "This article is all right and may do good." What it would do for the hoped-for party harmony appeared somewhat murky. It is no wonder that Conkling trusted neither Garfield nor Blaine. "What is to be after March 4," Conkling wrote a friend, "no one can yet forecast." When George Boutwell told Conkling he had heard Blaine say that the New York Stalwarts would be treated fairly, Conkling asked, "Do you believe one word of that?"

Boutwell said, "Yes, I believe Mr. Blaine."

Conkling, sneering, said, "I don't." [3]

The attempt to rouse up the assemblymen against George Sharpe failed miserably. The same day that Blaine's editorial blossomed forth in the *Tribune,* Sharpe was overwhelmingly re-elected; the *Times* editorially called Reid a "ridiculous coxcomb." [4]

In the meantime the Senate canvass continued. Morton's candidacy languished, as Conkling stepped up pressure on Garfield to appoint the financier to the treasury. Morton was thus somewhat involuntarily sidelined in Albany. But Crowley and Platt stayed in the race, and a third

---

[3] Boutwell, II, 273; Garfield's letter to Reid, Jan. 3, 1881, Reid Papers; Conkling to J. S. Crosby, Jan. 25, 1881, Conkling Papers, New-York Historical Society.

[4] N.Y. *Times,* Jan. 4, 1881.

aspirant joined them. This was Chauncey Depew, who was invited into the contest by (who else?) James G. Blaine. Blaine came to New York to see Depew and to insist that the railroad man, who himself felt that "election would have been a personal calamity" and who was in little danger of it, announce his availability as a stand-in for the Garfield administration.[5]

Depew's entry into the race complicated matters for the Stalwart contenders, for it now became apparent that a majority in the caucus might be exceedingly difficult to achieve. Though Crowley and Platt continued on apparent good terms with one another throughout the struggle, some of their supporters did not. The jealousy between Arthur and Cornell which had first been manifested at Saratoga in 1876, when Arthur had been lukewarm in his support of Cornell against E. D. Morgan, was now discussed openly as a major element in the Senate race. The two men, so different in personality, had never been particularly close, but now the divergence started to affect the organization. Some of the rivets in the machine were working loose.

Cornell had been a revelation as governor. Even some of those who had derided him the most now conceded that he was doing a surprisingly good job. He was liberal with the use of his veto power, and sparing with the use of his pardoning power. No one really expected imaginative programs, but few were prepared for his square, stubborn resistance to measures he thought wrong. He had demonstrated independence of thought and action, and some of the most optimistic of the Conkling-haters saw signs that Cornell was about to "set up on his own." Whether this was true or no, the governor did have a definite preference for the U.S. Senate seat. He was for Tom Platt, and he put at Platt's service most of his state appointees. Lou Payn was for Tom Platt, too, and if there was one thing Lou Payn knew it was the New York legislature. Between the governor and his patronage appointees and Lou Payn and his ability to manipulate the legislature, Platt's campaign was a serious one.

Crowley's effort, too, was in earnest. He was supported by the vice-president-elect, by Speaker Sharpe, by Judge Folger, Tom Murphy, John Starin, and John F. Smyth, who was considered to be almost as adroit a wire-puller as Lou Payn. Sharpe started to try the old routine of withholding committee appointments, but the tactic stirred up resentment

[5] Depew, *Memories,* p. 112; C. M. Depew, *Orations, Addresses, and Speeches,* II, 212–213.

when used against fellow machine-members. Crowley had some problems, though. He was a poor man. Platt had parlayed his political contacts into a tidy fortune, but Dick Crowley was only a country lawyer who lived on his fees. This made a difference with practical politicians in 1881, in the midst of the Gilded Age, and they talked about Crowley with a touch of condescension. How can he be a proper senator if he can't make it as a lawyer, they wondered. Roscoe Conkling was not wealthy either, of course, but everyone *knew* he could make a lot of money if he were not so busy with his political career (a theory amply justified later); Crowley had had the time to make his fortune, and he just had not done so. On top of everything, in the midst of the canvass, Crowley's law office back in Lockport burned down. Another thing: Dick Crowley was a Roman Catholic. "That fact," wrote one reporter, "makes some unreasonable prejudice against him." [6] But he had lots of friends, too. Crowley was forty-six at the time, good-natured, keen, intelligent. He had served four years in the state senate, a term in Congress, and eight years as United States attorney for the Northern District of New York. He had served his apprenticeship, and he was a loyal follower of Roscoe Conkling. He wanted to go to the United States Senate, and he and his friends felt that Richard Crowley looked more like a senator than did Tom Platt.

Morton, who had no one on the scene pushing his candidacy, made one last effort for the prize. He wrote Conkling a letter, asking the senator to pull Platt out of the race and to support him. Conkling wrote back on January 10, saying that Platt would certainly have no right to ask him to pull Morton out, "and I can see no right of mine to ask Mr. P. to withdraw." He said that it seemed to him "wholly inadmissible for me to attempt by my request to prevent any friend who pleases from submitting his claim to party friends." That seemed to take care of any possibility that the senator would intervene to determine the Senate race.[7]

On the afternoon of January 11, Cornell made an effort at mediation, proposing that Morton, Crowley, and Platt each pick three men to sit down in a group, thrash out the issues, and decide upon a candidate, with the others withdrawing. Both Morton and Crowley agreed to the governor's idea, but Platt declined. He had something else going for him.[8]

[6] N.Y. *Tribune,* Jan. 4, 1881.   [7] McElroy, p. 123.
[8] N.Y. *Times,* Jan. 13, 1881.

One day during the canvass, Robertson proposed to the Crowley camp that the Half Breed votes—currently pledged to Depew, but holding the balance of power between Crowley and Platt—could be secured by that candidate who would give assurances of protection to the Chicago rebels and support for any patronage appointments of those men made by the new president. Arthur, for Crowley, "promptly and indignantly" turned the suggestion down. Afterwards, though, they could only guess that the same offer would be made to Platt; they knew not whether he would treat it in the same manner. It was, and he did not. Platt, it developed, was willing to strike out, a little bit, on his own. Depew approached Platt first and, receiving a tentative acceptance of the proposition, then arranged a meeting of Platt with himself, Woodin, McCarthy, Birdsall, and Robertson. At this conference, the candidate pledged himself to "countenance no effort at crushing or ignoring the Chicago bolters," to allow "their fair share of patronage," to "do all in his power to help" the confirmation of any of them before the Senate, even Robertson, "though much opposed to such a nomination," and to "do all he could (not much, probably) to keep Conkling reasonable." Depew then dropped out of the race and, at the caucus, the Half-Breed votes went to Platt, Robertson telling a reporter, "I believe in giving them all the Cornell they want." Of the total vote of 105, 54 went to Platt, so the devious politician from Owego was elected to the Senate.[9]

Conkling sent his new colleague a message saying: "I congratulate the Republican party in the State of New York on the choice of a Senator who never apologized for being a 'Stalwart.' " Conkling should have examined more closely the composition of Platt's majority in the caucus and perhaps have been suspicious of the motives of some of those who voted for the victor. Perhaps, though, he knew what had happened—surely Arthur told him about the Robertson proposal to Crowley—but decided that nothing could be done about it now. Conkling's actions, since the Chicago convention, betray a slight indication of fatalism, of weariness with the struggle, of accepting whatever came his way. The spectacle of a Stalwart senator being elected as a result of a secret bargain with the Half Breeds came about solely because of Conkling's refusal to indicate a clear choice. Now, he had a colleague of whom

[9] *Ibid.*, Jan. 14, 15. Reid Papers, Library of Congress, for the Reid letter to Garfield on Jan. 16, detailing Platt's promises; see also Depew, *Orations,* II, 212–213; Alexander, III, 468.

one Half-Breed leader said, "We shall not need a step-ladder to reach his ear." [10]

The *Tribune,* which had seldom had a kind word for Platt in all his previous years on the New York political scene, suddenly reversed its field, now that the covenant was made, and called the new senator "the victim of an unreasonable prejudice . . . a faithful and zealous Republican," and predicted that he would be "an industrious, capable, and efficient business Senator." It also ventured the remarkable opinion that "Mr. Conkling will be quite as likely to be advised by Mr. Platt as he by Mr. Conkling." [11]

Harper's, however, felt that Platt's election did nothing but give Conkling two votes, while *The Nation* said, "We presume that no man has ever gone from this State to the United States Senate with so little mental baggage of any kind as Mr. Platt." [12]

Meanwhile, Whitelaw Reid was writing to John Hay that "Platt's last words to me were, 'I am yours to command; draw on me at sight.'" Making due allowance for Reid's penchant for overdramatization, it is still clear that Platt had set himself up for a lively career as a senator, once all his promises came into collision with the absolute fidelity which Roscoe Conkling would demand. [13]

Meanwhile, Garfield had not gotten much farther than Blaine for the state department in his cabinetmaking. If the question of the New York Stalwart in the cabinet could be settled, the rest of the list would follow fairly easily. But the problem of Conkling's man was a vexatious one.

Conkling and his people took the position, obviously as a result of the conference at the Fifth Avenue Hotel in August, that there was no problem. The treasury department had been pledged by Garfield to L. P. Morton, and all that needed to be done was for Garfield to honor his

[10] Platt, p. 142; Alexander, III, 468. The Reid Papers contain an exchange of telegrams of Jan. 12 and 13 between Reid and Platt in which Reid asked "how fully I and interests I represent could depend on you," and Platt responded that he had given Reid's go-between "assurances . . . which I believe will be satisfactory."

[11] N.Y. *Tribune,* Jan. 14, 1881. An "efficient business Senator" was, of course, the ideal of the Gilded Age; an "efficient business Senator" was one who did not interfere with or ask questions about the booming industrialization of the country but helped it along when necessary.

[12] *Harper's Weekly,* Jan. 29, 1881; *The Nation,* Jan. 27, 1881.

[13] Cortissoz, II, 51.

commitment. Morton himself wrote that "during the canvass, Genl. Garfield said to me that he would like to have me in the Cabinet as Secy. of the Treasury." [14]

Yet Garfield stoutly denied any such promise. In late November 1880, he sent for Morton to visit him in Washington, to discuss what post might be acceptable to the New York congressman. After the meeting, the president-elect observed in his diary that Morton was "under the misapprehension that Secretary of the Treasury is promised to N. Y." This he called "wholly inadmissible" as "a congestion of financial power at the money centre," even though Morton indicated a willingness to sever all his financial ties. The next day he told Morton: "I will not tolerate nor act upon any understanding that anything has been pledged to any party, state or person." This conversation suddenly made it very clear to the New York Stalwarts how much faith they could put in the understanding reached with Garfield in the dark days of summer, now that fall had brought his election to the presidency.[15]

On December 13, Cornell, Crowley, and Payn visited Garfield at Mentor, with the objective of pushing Morton's claims. They were similarly rebuffed, and they left after being snowed in for two days, in a very unhappy frame of mind. Even when Dick Crowley suggested that Senator Conkling hoped to sustain the new administration and help win Garfield a second term, the Ohioan returned a self-righteous and ungracious answer.[16]

Several days later, Stephen Dorsey wrote to Garfield, reminding him of the pledges made to the New York men at the Fifth Avenue Hotel during the summer, and affirming Conkling's desire to support Garfield's administration as he had that of Grant. Garfield's comment on this letter referred only to the latter point, with no reference at all to the former reminder of his promises. The man was clearly torn. He wanted Conkling's support, for he had watched the mounting troubles of Hayes with no firm base in the Senate and with the Republican party of New York hostile to the administration. Yet he wanted that support without yielding anything for it. It was obvious that Garfield intended his administration to be Blaine-oriented, and this would hardly be possible

14 McElroy, p. 121.   15 T. C. Smith, II, 1047.
16 *Ibid.*, II, 1053. Reid's Dec. 20, 1880, letter to Garfield chuckled about the president-elect "entertaining them with your views about the Cabinet for two days among the snow drift." Reid Papers.

with a Conkling New Yorker in one of the two major cabinet positions. As a result, he spent virtually the entire four months of the interim period blowing this way and that on the cabinet makeup.[17]

The stalemate continued on into January, as Garfield listened to advice, often conflicting, from many different sources while he attempted to find a Stalwart to include in his cabinet. At one point he even persuaded Hayes to appoint L. P. Morton to the existing navy vacancy with the understanding that Garfield would keep him on after March 4, but Morton squelched that plan by declining. On January 17, Garfield suggested Tom James for postmaster general, but Blaine, Sherman, and Dorsey scorned the idea. Blaine and Sherman both said James would be nothing but a spy for Conkling, while Dorsey called James "not fit for this great place . . . the merest tool of scheming men." We will see that Dorsey had his own ideas about the post office department. He was pushing the name of Judge Charles Folger for secretary of the treasury.[18]

Whitelaw Reid in New York kept the pot boiling, as he attempted to "brace" his friend Garfield. The president-elect's wife was staying at Reid's home in the city, and on January 21, she retailed to her husband some hearsay fed her by the editor:

Mr. Reid told me this morning that Morton had been very ugly in his talk about you, using the expression that seems to be so gratifying to the Conkling clique, "That Ohio man cannot be relied upon to stand by his pledges." . . . You will never have anything from those men but their assured contempt, until you fight them *dead*. You can put every one of them in his political grave if you are a mind to & that is the only place where they can be kept peaceable.[19]

Still being helpful, Reid on January 25 forwarded to Garfield at Mentor an agitating letter he had just received from William Robertson: "With two 'Stalwart' Senators and Vice-President from the State, the incoming Administration could in no other way so effectually put our independent delegates to the Chicago Convention in a political metallic casket, hermetically sealed, as by placing in the Cabinet a 'Stalwart' from New York." [20]

[17] T. C. Smith, II, 1054–1055.

[18] N.Y. *Times,* Jan. 2, 1881; T. C. Smith, II, 1075.

[19] T. C. Smith, II, 1074. Lucretia Garfield may not have understood the plans for a "harmony" administration, fomenting no quarrels.

[20] Cortissoz, II, 52; T. C. Smith, II, 1074.

Sherman, on the 23rd, wrote Garfield that Conkling was "greatly overrated, with egotism . . . unbounded . . . sensible to criticism and ridicule." Conkling, he said, "never interests himself in anything but personal antagonisms, he never rises above a Custom House or a Post Office." Because of his position, Sherman went on, he was entitled to consideration and full recognition, "but if you ever yield to him so that he thinks you fear him, he becomes overbearing." If differences should arise, "then the only way is to give him blow for blow." He added that "the Executive always has power to command the respect even if it cannot win the favor of members of Congress."

Bolstered by all this counsel, Garfield still wavered. On January 28, two months after telling Morton that the treasury could not go to New York because of the concentration of money power, he wrote in his diary: "If I could find a large true man in New York for the Treasury, I would take him. Perhaps Judge Folger would do." The next day, he met with Cornell and Platt and asked them who should get the treasury. When they mentioned only Morton, he asked them what they thought of Folger for treasury or justice. "They said he was a good man but could not safely be spared." It was all very confusing.[21]

Finally, getting nowhere, Garfield wrote on January 31 to Conkling, inviting him to Mentor to consult "on several subjects relating to the next administration—and especially in reference to New York interests."[22] The same day, he wrote to Blaine, suggesting that since "a fight at short range," if there had to be a fight, was "better than from behind the intrenchments of an executive session," he was thinking of offering a portfolio to Conkling! "What would you say to exchanging seats—you for the Treasury, he for State."

What would he say, indeed! Blaine's reply was prompt: "His appointment would act like strychnine upon your administration—first bring contortions & then be followed by death." He wanted *no* Conkling men in the cabinet; his view of the proper treatment of the Stalwarts was that "they must not be knocked down with bludgeons; they must have their throats cut with a feather."[23]

Conkling took his time about rushing off to Mentor. After a week he wrote back to the president-elect, accepting the invitation and stating,

---

[21] T. C. Smith, II, 1075–1077, 1082.

[22] Conkling Papers, Library of Congress.

[23] T. C. Smith, II, 1077–1078; the "throat-cutting" letter from Blaine to Garfield was Dec. 16, 1880.

in cleverly double-edged phrases: "I need hardly say that your administration cannot be more successful than I wish it to be, nor can it be more satisfactory to you, to the country, and to the party than I will labor to make it." [24]

The senator showed up on February 16 and had what Garfield called "a full conversation on the cabinet and kindred subjects." Both men have left recollections of this meeting, not really in conflict as to the outline of the discussion.

Garfield wrote in his diary:

His knowledge of men is fuller and more accurate than I had expected and, in the main, his judgment is sound. He appeared to be frank and friendly. Urged the importance of recognizing N. Y. and thought Morton would do well in the Treasury. I told him I thought the objections insuperable. I asked his opinion of Folger & he spoke highly of him, but thought it would be dangerous to the party in N. Y. to take him from the Chief Justiceship. I told him I wanted his friendship & believed we could work together with independence and mutual respect, but I could not give Morton more than the War or Navy.

He wrote a report of the meeting to Blaine, saying Conkling had said "it would be better all around, to appoint no cabinet officer from New York than to take one for a minor place." Conkling felt "New York ought not to have a less place than the Treasury, Interior, or P. O.," the three patronage departments, by no coincidence. He spoke of James for the post office, Garfield said, "but closed by preferring Morton."

Conkling's version is in an interview he gave later in which he described his amazement at "the trifling and undecided manner of his host." Garfield told him he could not appoint Morton, and he had heard that Folger drank whiskey (an idea implanted by Whitelaw Reid).

I told General Garfield that I had always known Folger as a man of honor, and I asked him why Folger's character was brought into question. Do you contemplate offering him a cabinet position? If such is your purpose, I would like to advise that the Treasury is the only post which would satisfy New York, and that our state would prefer to be passed altogether if it could not obtain the department to which its rank and service entitled it.

To his question, Conkling said, Garfield gave no direct answer.[25]

[24] *Ibid.,* II, 1078. Garfield wrote Reid on Feb. 14, 1881, that "the tone of his letter is much more friendly than I expected." Reid Papers.

[25] Garfield's version is in T. C. Smith, II, 1082–1083; Conkling's is in Connery, p. 151.

The public and the press wondered what had transpired between Conkling and Garfield at Mentor. Mostly it was guessing. The New York *Times* carried a statement from an anonymous friend of Garfield, affirming hopefully that "Gen. Garfield and Senator Conkling have always been on good terms, and any intimation that there is to be trouble between them has no foundation beyond the imagination of those who would be pleased to have it so." The Utica *Herald,* no longer friendly to its eminent townsman, said, "General Garfield does well to discover the spirit which he may expect to meet from quarters where President Hayes has found bitter hostility and unremitting obstruction." And one of Garfield's close friends wrote him that he was surprised to see Mohammed visit the Mountain.[26]

Garfield now asked Charles J. Folger to visit him at Mentor. When the New York chief justice arrived on February 19, Garfield "was greatly pleased with his spirit and his manifest great ability." He thereupon offered Folger the office of attorney general, a position of little activity or power, but the wary New Yorker said he could not give an answer until he reached home. The rumor reached New York City the following day that Folger was to be secretary of the treasury, and Blaine instantly dispatched a letter to Mentor, saying the story had created a panic among Garfield's friends; "in N. Y. it is understood to be the original concoction of Dorsey, Tom Murphy, and a whole nest of unclean birds who wish to go in for loot and booty." Though this letter crossed in the mails one from Garfield to Blaine, calling Folger "far more independent than any mere follower of Conkling can be," the whole matter soon proved to be of no consequence. When Folger returned to New York, presumably after consultation with Roscoe Conkling, he declined on February 23 the tender of the justice department.[27]

The whole Folger episode only served to weaken Conkling's faith in the new president's good intentions. After all, he had told Garfield that Folger would take nothing but the treasury. "Was it only to find out what I would like, and then do just the opposite," Conkling raged, "that this man Garfield called me to Mentor? Was it only to make his indifference to my wishes more marked that he summoned Folger, whose

[26] N.Y. *Times,* Feb. 20, 1881; Utica *Morning Herald,* Feb. 18, 1881; Hinsdale to Garfield, Feb. 17, 1881, M. L. Hinsdale, ed., *Garfield-Hinsdale Letters,* p. 480.
[27] T. C. Smith, II, 1085–1086; N.Y. *Times,* Feb. 20, 21, 22, 23, 1881. It might be noted that Blaine was considered by many to be something of an expert on loot, booty, and unclean birds.

character he had impugned, the moment my back was turned, to offer him an office lesser in dignity than that which I had said New York was entitled to?" Roscoe Conkling was becoming progressively more disenchanted with the whole crew of Garfield, and Blaine, and Reid, and Robertson.[28]

The business about Dorsey and Folger and loot and booty was one of the most bizarre aspects of Garfield's cabinet problems. Stephen Dorsey's whole concern about the cabinet was the post office and who was to head it. The former carpetbag senator was deeply involved in what came to be known as the Star Route frauds in the postal service.

In the spacious western states and territories, contracts for carrying the mails were awarded to the lowest bidders who would agree to do so with "certainty, celerity, and security." These three words were indicated on the postal registers by three small stars, from which the routes derived their collective name. The basic concept behind the Star Route contracts, which were for four-year periods, was that changes in the rates of compensation were to be allowed in the interest of greater speed or improved service. The department was given the authority to make these changes, and in the hierarchy of the department responsibility rested in Second Assistant Postmaster General Thomas J. Brady, who was appointed by Grant in 1876 and kept on through succeeding administrations. Brady was the key to the entire system. The scheme which Dorsey, Brady, and several co-conspirators worked up was simple: their contractors won the routes with bids far too low for any responsible competitor to match, and then they "improved" their service, receiving tremendous increases from the compliant Brady. There were approximately one hundred thirty-five Star Routes involved in the frauds, and the graft totalled hundreds of thousands of dollars each year. One of Dorsey's routes in Dakota and Montana, for example, had been raised from $2,350 to $72,350 per year.[29]

It is easy to see why Dorsey was interested in protecting such a lucrative racket. But how was Folger involved with it? There was no doubt that Stephen Dorsey was pushing hard for Folger's inclusion in the Garfield cabinet; yet Folger was reputed an honorable man, a hardworking, upright jurist. The answer was simple. Dorsey was for Folger, or Morton, or anyone who appeared to have a chance to win the New York cabinet seat, so long as it was not in the post office. For if New

[28] Connery, p. 152.
[29] L. D. White, pp. 376–378; Carpenter, p. 171; Cramer, pp. 201–210.

York got the post office, there could be only one man for that job, Thomas L. James. Dorsey and his cronies knew enough about James to know that their whole plot would be in serious jeopardy if the postmaster of New York were elevated to the head of the department. James in New York had been an avowed enemy of all forms of graft, thievery, or dishonesty, and he would surely require little time to discover the Star Route frauds. So Dorsey pushed for any other New Yorker who might be available.

The amazing thing was that this man, about whom few had any illusions, who was widely reputed to have helped to bankrupt the state of Arkansas to his own gain while he and his friends had control of it, who was known to have "bought" Indiana in 1880, and who was the object of a great deal of open suspicion about his connection with the Star Routes, should have been one of Garfield's close advisers during the interim period, one of those who was frequently consulted about cabinet prospects. Garfield apparently had no worries about Stephen Dorsey, though he was wary as the plague of Roscoe Conkling.

A singular episode took place at Delmonico's in New York on February 11. A great feast was given as a testimonial for Dorsey, attended by the cream of the Republican party. General Grant presided, and among the guests were Henry Ward Beecher, Hamilton Fish, Morton, Senator-elect Platt, Senator Frelinghuysen of New Jersey, Chauncey Depew, Robertson, Sharpe, John Jay, Thurlow Weed, Collector Merritt, Jay Gould (who knew another thief when he saw one), J. P. Morgan, Collis P. Huntington, and many others. Letters of regret were read from Cornell, Blaine, Attorney General Devens, both Camerons, and Robert Lincoln. The dinner was generally understood to be designed to further Dorsey's aims, whatever they were, and it certainly appeared to enlist behind him much of the respectability of the party. The main speech, given by Vice-President-elect Arthur, was so disjointed, indiscreet, and fatuous as to raise the suspicion that he had indulged in too much of Delmonico's excellent wine. At one point he said:

I don't think we had better go into the minute secrets of the campaign, so far as I know them, because I see the reporters present, who are taking it all down. . . . Indiana was really, I suppose, a Democratic State. It had always been put down in the book as a State that might be carried by close and careful and perfect organization and a great deal of—

Here he paused, meaningfully, and someone in the audience shouted "soap!" as everyone laughed.

I see the reporters here, and therefore I will simply say that everybody showed a great deal of interest in the occasion, and distributed tracts and political documents all through the country. [Laughter.] If it were not for the reporters I would tell you the truth, because I know you are intimate friends and devoted adherents to the Republican party.

The Delmonico's dinner confirmed the impression that a great many people had of Chester Arthur, and it linked many Republican leaders much more closely than they should have liked with a shady figure like Stephen Dorsey.[30]

As February passed away, Garfield *had* to come up with a cabinet. And he still wanted very much to have a Conkling-type New Yorker in it. Conkling, however, wanted only the treasury department. The reason for this, of course, was that the secretary of the treasury was the superior of the collector of New York. On February 26, Garfield wrote to Morton, offering him once again the navy portfolio. This time Morton accepted, and Whitelaw Reid was able to crow in a letter to his fiancée, "So we have carried our exact point there, and Conkling is at once utterly foiled and left without any cause of quarrel." Conkling was not yet through, however; he telegraphed Platt that "our unwise friend is making a great deal of trouble for us." John H. Starin was sent to fetch Morton; he roused the would-be secretary out of bed at 1:00 A.M. on the morning of March 2 and brought him to Conkling's rooms; they talked to him through the night. In the morning, Garfield had in his hands a message that because of "embarrassments connected with my acceptance" Morton was declining the navy department. Scratch one New Yorker. Morton, in a rare display of political loyalty, had now declined both the vice-presidency and a cabinet ministry at the behest of Roscoe Conkling. Garfield told Reid at this point "that he was tempted to appoint Judge Robertson himself, the very head and front of the anti-Conkling people." But that, even Reid conceded, "will surely not be done."[31]

Finally, Thomas James was decided upon. All the evidence indicates that this was the doing of Blaine and Reid, with Garfield a more or less passive onlooker, though he had checked on James earlier. The name

---

[30] N.Y. *Times*, Feb. 12, 16, 1881. Among others present at the dinner were John J. Astor, Boutwell, William Windom of Minnesota (soon to be secretary of the treasury), Noah Davis, Warner Miller, Edwards Pierrepont, and George Jones, editor of the *Times*.

[31] McElroy, pp. 127–128; Connery, p. 152; Reid Papers.

of the New York postmaster had been involved in cabinet speculation from the start, since he was notoriously the most capable man in the whole department. Invariably, though, he was eliminated from consideration by reason of his well-known loyalty to and friendship with Roscoe Conkling. However, as time ebbed away, Tom James suddenly became an important factor. James had always wanted the head job, and now the incoming administration realized it wanted him. Reid said that Blaine "patched up a new deal" involving James. "The policy," Reid wrote, "is to detach James from Conkling and make him feel that he owes his appointment to that." [32]

In any event, James was sent for, secretly. Whitelaw Reid, in a letter to his fiancee on March 3, described being awakened at 8:00 A.M. by the "embryo Post Master General" just in from New York. Reid took him to meet Garfield. "Next I had to get Platt," he went on, "and make him say that, while Conkling had nothing to do with this, and knew nothing of it, and had refused to recommend James or even mention him, he could not object with any reason, which he (Platt) fully approved. This I did—taking Platt up and asking the questions myself in Garfield's presence. G. is greatly pleased."

Garfield himself wrote that James "seemed firm and earnest." However, this last eventful day before the inauguration was not over for the man from Mentor. Platt made a second visit to Garfield's rooms that day, this time with Conkling and Arthur, "the former," Garfield wrote, "full of apprehension that he had been or was to be cheated." A stormy scene ensued, in the course of which Conkling became very angry and abusive of the man who was on the morrow to become president of the United States.[33]

Nonetheless, James was in the cabinet to stay, and the question of New York Stalwart representation was settled. With this taken care of, at long last, the rest of the cabinet could fall into place. On March 3, Allison agreed to become secretary of the treasury, but the following morning he pulled out again, and it finally went to Senator Windom of Minnesota. Kirkwood, in the interior department, became Iowa's cabinet member. Wayne MacVeagh of Pennsylvania was named attorney general, while Robert T. Lincoln headed the war department. William H. Hunt of Louisiana, a judge of the court of claims, a Whig and a Know-Nothing before the war, a Republican after, was named secretary of the navy, to the surprise of all.

The appointment of James was hailed in the liberal press as a master

[32] Reid Papers.   [33] Reid Papers; T. C. Smith, II, 1092–1093.

stroke, a concession to Conkling, yet a highly respectable nomination. But others were not as happy. Grant wrote to Conkling on March 5 that, having just learned the composition of the cabinet, "I confess to much disappointment." And Conkling himself was hardly reassured by the conduct of Garfield and his friends during the interregnum.[34]

Garfield, Blaine, Reid, and their associates gave pretty shabby treatment to the man who more than anyone made Garfield's election possible. If the new president truly hoped for the friendship and cordial support of Conkling and his organization, he demonstrated that desire in rather peculiar ways during the interim period, even apart from ignoring the pledges he had made in August at New York. The correspondence of Garfield and his friends concerning the construction of the cabinet shows a consistent effort to work out some way of putting in a New Yorker with whom Conkling would be unhappy but about whom he could make no public complaint. From Blaine's interference in the Senate election to the underhanded manner in which James's assent to a cabinet position was gained, the whole Garfield coterie showed any gratitude it may have felt in a rather ungenerous way.

[34] The Springfield *Republican,* March 5, 1881, and *The Nation,* March 10, 1881, were among those applauding James. The Grant letter is in Conkling Papers, Library of Congress.

CHAPTER 25

ROBERTSON

Garfield was sworn in on March 4, with Roscoe Conkling standing directly behind him on the platform, and things then settled down to a period of quiet—of rather ominous quiet, perhaps. Garfield was left to handle a veritable army of office-seekers who descended upon him, "a Spartan band," he called them, "who drew papers on me as highwaymen draw pistols," and no doubt he recalled wearily what he had told the press back in January, that "I sometimes think of myself as a man going to prison." He would obey all the rules of the presidency, he said, "and then come back and 'live it down.' " [1]

The Senate convened in its special session on March 4, under the gavel of the new vice-president, and immediately fell into a fearful row which utterly prevented its organization. The new Senate was composed of thirty-seven Republicans, thirty-seven Democrats, one Independent, David Davis of Illinois, who had announced that he would vote with the Democrats in the organization of the chamber, and William Mahone of Virginia. Mahone was a former Confederate general who had been elected by a group in Virginia called the Readjuster-Democrats, winners of a majority in the legislature with a program calling for repudiation of a portion of the state debt. Before 1880, Mahone had been a regular Democrat, but the new party with which he was affiliated had won control in a struggle against the regular Democratic party. No one was quite sure with whom he would vote, but his vote was essential to the Republicans and Conkling set out to get it.

Matters were complicated further for the Republicans when three of their members, Blaine, Windom, and Kirkwood, resigned to accept cabinet commissions, and a fourth, Matt Carpenter of Wisconsin, died on February 24. All of these positions would be filled by Republicans,

[1] T. C. Smith, II, 1146; N.Y. *Tribune,* Jan. 2, 1881.

but not right away; even when they were, Mahone's vote would still be crucial to create a tie, which Vice-President Arthur could then break in the Republicans' favor.

The president hesitated at an alliance with a debt repudiator, but the political necessities were imperative. Conkling worked out the details, and bland assurances that the Virginia debt would be honestly settled soon won Garfield over. Mahone's price for assuring the Republican party control of the Senate was steep: his friend (and Conkling's) George C. Gorham was selected secretary of the Senate; his Virginia ally Harrison H. Riddleberger was to be named sergeant at arms; Mahone was given control over the patronage in Virginia; and the Republican ticket was to be withdrawn from future elections in the Old Dominion.

The Democrats were infuriated at the treachery of Mahone, and they at once launched a filibuster to prevent confirmation of Gorham and Riddleberger. The Republicans refused to allow any executive sessions to consider appointments, so the United States Senate was totally stalemated.[2]

As the deadlock developed, it was more and more Conkling of New York and Ben Hill of Georgia who led their respective arrays, lashing the opposition with bitter invective and sarcasm. But while the Senate sank into inaction, developments on another front quickly seized the attention of the nation.

On March 20, Garfield invited Conkling and Platt to visit him at the White House to discuss patronage appointments in the state of New York. Platt was in New York City, but Conkling showed up, explaining that the presence of his colleague was not essential to the conversation since Platt, he said, would go along with any decisions reached. The president and the senator spent two and a half hours going over the situation in New York, with inconclusive results, though even Conkling agreed that the meeting was amicable.

Garfield appeared willing enough to continue and renew the appointments of several of Conkling's followers, so the status of these men was not a problem. He indicated, though that he wanted to recognize the

---

[2] For Mahone, the Readjusters, and the Senate stalemate, see generally, N. M. Blake, *William Mahone of Virginia;* Rothman, pp. 32–33; Hirshson, pp. 95–97; and *Cong. Rec.,* 47th Cong., spec. sess. Reid in a letter to Garfield of Jan. 31, 1881, quotes C. P. Huntington as calling Mahone "an unscrupulous and utterly treacherous demagogue." Reid Papers. Even a whiff of debt repudiation stirred up storms in the capitalist circles.

Robertson–Half-Breed element which, by contributing to the deadlock, had made Garfield's nomination possible in Chicago. "I told him," the president wrote, "I must recognize some of the men who had supported me at Chicago." Conkling helpfully suggested foreign appointments, but Garfield said they deserved not "exile but rather a place in the affairs of their own state." Conkling can hardly have been happy to hear a sentiment like that. The senator later said that Garfield suggested that he, Platt, Arthur, and Cornell devise a workable plan to take care of the New York Half Breeds, and that he agreed to do so.

As Conkling was leaving, he asked, "Mr. President, what do you propose about the collectorship of New York?"

Garfield reassured him: "We will leave that for another time." Since Merritt's term had another two years to go, this certainly seemed reasonable, and undoubtedly Conkling dismissed the Port of New York from his mind.[3]

The next day, Garfield sent to the Senate, still wallowing in procedural confusion, nine re-appointments in New York, all of them men backing Conkling. They included Lou Payn as U. S. marshall, Woodford as U. S. attorney for the Southern District of New York, and several other U. S. attorneys and postmasters. The president had already appointed L. P. Morton to be minister to France, so it appeared that he was fulfilling, at least to some extent, the pledges made to the Stalwart wing of the party.

The small but noisy anti-Conkling element in New York immediately emitted loud howls of outrage and distress, full of such charged words as "weakness" and "surrender" and "ingratitude." The shock waves reached Washington, as they were designed to do, and Garfield reacted characteristically. On the afternoon of March 23, as the filibuster in the Senate droned on, an emissary from the president entered the chamber, advanced to the chair, and handed a message to Vice-President Arthur. The vice-president read through it with obvious consternation, and then summoned a page, who delivered the paper to the senior senator from New York. Conkling read over the message slowly but with clear indications of mounting wrath. When several other senators wandered over to

[3] Garfield's diary entry concerning the meeting of March 20, dated that day, is in T. C. Smith, II, 1104. Conkling's version of the same meeting is in Connery, pp. 153–154, and Boutwell, II, 273. Platt, p. 149, also mentions it, but his story appears to have strayed far from the path of accuracy. Conkling told his friend George Gorham the meeting was pleasant; N.Y. *Herald*, June 4, 1888.

see what it was that was causing such a reaction, Conkling showed them the paper without a word. The president, in a complicated series of office-jugglings, had created and filled a vacancy in the office of collector of the Port of New York. He had sent Edwin A. Merritt to London as consul general and had named as collector the man that he and everyone knew to be Conkling's most virulent enemy in the state, William H. Robertson.[4]

Once again, the New York Custom House was to serve as the pivot of Conkling's power, the test of his control over the United States Senate and over the Republican party of his state. Merritt had been collector since the summer of 1878, and Conkling's dominance in New York had not been lessened. Merritt was a good administrator with no existing political connections (since the forced retirement of his patron, Reuben Fenton), and he had ignored all requests for political utilization of the custom house. Thus, while Conkling suffered some loss by the inability to manipulate the custom house as theretofore, no other faction gained, and the machine remained by far the most powerful element in New York Republican politics.

Now, Merritt was to be displaced and the control of the establishment was to be turned over to a rabid partisan of Blaine, a man who had never shown any interest in nonpolitical administration of the civil service, and who was a staunch foe of Roscoe Conkling. Robertson's legislative career in Albany had been undistinguished, except for an active solicitude for major business enterprises when public control over them was sought. He had been an avid office-seeker for many years, and his slavish support of Blaine was now to be rewarded. Garfield apparently thought that Conkling would acquiesce in the changes, but the senator certainly never considered doing so. Responsibility for the Robertson appointment has never been positively fixed. Garfield claimed the work as his own, but most observers thought it was too audacious a stroke for the man. Garfield told Marshall Jewell, who passed it on to Boutwell, that the reaction to the nine Stalwart appointments caused him to nominate Robertson "without delay and without consultation with anyone." Blaine, too, told Boutwell that he had not known of the appointment until it was announced. But Blaine had spent two hours

---

[4] Howe, p. 139. The chain reaction from the Robertson nomination moved Merritt to London as consul general, General Adam Badeau from that position to Copenhagen as minister, one Cramer from there to Switzerland, and Nicholas Fish (Hamilton's son), chargé d'affaires in Switzerland, was left out in the cold.

with Garfield the night before the Robertson nomination was sent in, and it is incomprehensible that Garfield would hide from his chief adviser a contemplated selection of such magnitude. Besides, Thomas Nichol, Garfield's private secretary, told Merritt that the topic of the meeting was appointments and that Blaine had "insisted upon" Robertson. It seems likely, and it tallies with Blaine's whole course of conduct relative to New York political affairs.[5]

Reactions to the Robertson gambit were varied, as might have been expected, with the unfavorable in predominance. Three members of the president's own cabinet were unhappy with the nominations. James, of course, as a Conkling supporter was displeased, and told Garfield he would probably have to resign "to make his friends understand that he was not a party to the appointment." Windom, the secretary of the treasury, was angry because Garfield had not even mentioned to him the proposed changes in one of the most important establishments in his department. And Wayne MacVeagh, the attorney general, opposed Robertson because in the same general shake-up another Blaine man, William E. Chandler, was named solicitor general, against MacVeagh's wishes.[6]

Robertson himself issued a mendacious statement:

This nomination is especially gratifying to me because it comes to me unsought. No friend of mine, to my knowledge, has solicited for me any place under President Garfield's Administration. . . . I have no doubt about my confirmation. . . . I assume that I shall have the support of both the Senators from New York. I interpret the nominations of President Garfield as an indication that he intends to reward the men who made possible his nomination at Chicago.[7]

Ellis Roberts' Utica *Herald,* completely pro-Blaine now, complained that the "party and the country have been made to suffer from the irascible temper and the distracting attitude of this Senator" during the entire Hayes administration and that such an attack should not be repeated; besides, the nomination of Robertson "is in itself eminently proper and commendable," which was not of course universally conceded. Blaine, as might have been expected, wrote Garfield: "Your work of today creates a splendid impression. Your own friends in N. Y. who

[5] Boutwell, II, 274; Merritt, p. 136.
[6] T. C. Smith, II, 1111; Merritt, p. 136; Connery, p. 154. Chandler was ultimately rejected by the Senate.
[7] N.Y. *Tribune,* March 24, 1881.

had waited without a complaint for a single recognition of their great labors for you are amply rewarded." This was odd, since everyone thought that these were *Blaine's* friends who had labored for *Blaine,* not for Garfield, who was little more than the accidental beneficiary of their efforts. Mrs. Blaine wrote to her son, suggesting that the nominations meant "business and strength." Garfield himself said that "the sensation produced by the nomination was very great but I think the Senate will approve." [8]

Others were not so happy with the appointment. John Sherman, who would later undertake to direct the drive for confirmation in the Senate, was at this time opposed. He suggested to Merritt that the change ought to be resisted; if he himself acquiesced in it, the ex-secretary wrote on March 31, it would put him in the position of upholding Merritt against Conkling but deserting him when his removal was pushed by Garfield. Sherman, of course, good old staunch, steadfast John Sherman, soon overcame his scruples. Opposition to Conkling came to seem more important than the good of the civil service.[9]

The New York *Times,* which habitually treated Robertson with scorn and contempt, interpreted the nomination as the end of civil service reform in the custom house and the disposition of the patronage to Blaine. It is ridiculous, the *Times* said several days later, "to pretend that Judge Robertson represents anything but the Blaine faction in this State. . . . What is to be expected from Mr. Robertson can only be inferred from the character of his political 'backer' in the Cabinet. There is nothing in the legislative record of Senator Robertson to show that he is a man of any real force or independence of character." [10] Godkin suddenly found himself alongside Roscoe Conkling in opposing the nomination, although for completely different reasons, and even Garfield's old friend Hinsdale wrote the president on March 30 that the nomination of Robertson was "unwise." [11]

Garfield, however, got a boost from an unexpected source when both houses of the New York legislature passed a resolution calling for the confirmation of Robertson as collector. This was generally considered an aberration produced by lack of communication with Senator Conkling in

[8] Utica *Morning Herald,* March 28, 1881; T. C. Smith, II, 1110–1111; H. S. B. Beale, ed., *Letters of Mrs. James G. Blaine,* I, 197.
[9] Merritt, pp. 124–126.   [10] N.Y. *Times, March* 24, 29, 30, 1881.
[11] Hinsdale, ed., pp. 486–487.

Washington and Robertson's membership in the state senate. Nevertheless, it foreshadowed some strange events in the near future. No one in the Stalwart camp got the message in this resolution of the disinclination of politicians to spend four full years fighting their own administration.

On March 26, Senator Allison of Iowa had a long talk with Conkling about New York politics, and the next day he passed the substance of it on to the president. Though Garfield interpreted it to mean that his offense was in not "consulting" with the senator before the appointment was made, this did not cause any variation in the president's stance. Indeed, the president "joyfully" considered the Robertson appointment to be *"casus belli."* He had just been bolstered by a wire from Reid to Hay, to be given to him, affirming that the nomination was "the turning point of his whole Administration. . . . If he surrenders now, Conkling is President for the rest of the term and Garfield becomes a laughing stock. On the other hand he has only to stand firm to succeed." The New York legislature, he said, supported Robertson because the members believed that "Garfield, unlike Hayes, meant to defend his own administration. The Assembly is overwhelmingly Conkling, but they did not dare to go on record against Robertson, so long as they thought the Administration meant business." [12]

The editor soon received a letter from Garfield which must have been very reassuring; it meant that the president was still standing firm. He defended the removal of Merritt, as his choice between "a worrying struggle of two years or a decisive settlement of the question now. It better be known in the outset whether the President is the head of the govt., or the registering clerk of the Senate." Somehow, this did not seem very logical, this picking a fight long before there was any need for it, a fight which could have been easily avoided by the retention of Merritt, both in 1881 and two years later, but apparently it made sense to Garfield and perhaps even to Whitelaw Reid, though the latter was interested mainly in fighting Roscoe Conkling, much less in administrative consistency. Surely it made sense to Blaine, who wrote that for Garfield to back down would be "a deep damnation personally and politically." [13] March ended with the nominations still on the vice-president's desk.

12 Sage, pp. 175–176; T. C. Smith, II, 1112; Cortissoz, II, 60.
13 Garfield to Reid, March 30, 1881, and Blaine to Reid, March 31, 1881, Reid Papers.

Most of the Republican senators were with Conkling as the fight over Robertson got underway. Each one could easily picture the situation in which *he* would need the protection of senatorial courtesy to fend off an undesirable appointment. Blaine's writ obviously ran at large in the country. To have the executive ignoring such a salutary principle, particularly at the outset of his term, was a dangerous thing.

John Hay wrote to his friend Reid on April 4 that the Republican caucus held that day was "completely under Conkling's thumb. . . . It would amaze you to see the pusillanimity of some of our great men. Conkling seems to have a magic influence over them. They talk as bold as lions to me . . . and then they go into caucus, or the Senate, and if he looks at them they are like Little Billee of the ballad. . . . Senators who owe him nothing, now or prospectively, are eager to lick his boots." [14]

Even Frye of Maine, who had taken his mentor Blaine's seat in the Senate, told the president the next day that the nomination was dangerous, but Garfield merely recorded this in his diary. In the meantime, efforts were being made to compromise the situation.

Initially, on March 24, the day after the nomination, upon the intercession of Thomas James and Wayne MacVeagh, there appeared to be a possibility of Garfield backing off, assigning Robertson the federal attorney's job and sending Woodford to Portugal. A meeting was arranged to work out the details, and James, Platt, MacVeagh, Arthur, and Conkling were about to leave for the White House to sit down with Garfield, when a telegram arrived from Albany. The wire was addressed to Roscoe Conkling from Governor Cornell, urging him "to desist from further opposition to Robertson for the sake of harmony." The presumption, the absurdity, the utter treachery of such a wire so enraged Roscoe Conkling that he absolutely refused to have anything to do with any meeting in the White House! From that time on, relations between Conkling and Cornell, his former protégé, deteriorated.

Without Conkling, there was not much point in the peace conference at the White House, so James and MacVeagh went alone and told the president what had happened. Now Garfield went into a rage: "I must remember that I am President of the United States. I owe something to the dignity of my office and to my own self-respect, and you may say to this senator that now, rather than withdraw Robertson's nomination, I will suffer myself to be dragged by wild horses." After Conkling scuttled

[14] Reid Papers.

this meeting, Tom James considered himself absolved of any duty to resign his cabinet post.[15]

Shortly afterwards, a formal remonstrance, signed by Arthur, Platt, James, and Conkling, was presented to the president, calling for the withdrawal of Robertson, but this had no more effect than any other protest. The best chance for peace, for a settlement, had been lost in Conkling's fury on March 24. Even without the telegram from Cornell, of course, the possibility of compromise may have been largely illusory. Garfield's advisers wanted no settlement.

Arthur, on April 14, met with Garfield and told the president that Robertson's confirmation would inevitably defeat the party in New York. The split in the party was becoming a chasm. Garfield's reaction to Arthur's message was the bellicose statement that he did not want war, "but if it is brought to my door the bringers will find me at home." [16]

Platt still had it in his head that there was a possibility of moving Robertson over to the post of U. S. attorney, and some such maneuver was clearly the only salvation for the junior senator. Platt was becoming very nervous about the impending collision of his promises to the Half Breeds, which had gotten him elected, and his fidelity to Conkling. He visited Garfield and suggested the switch, but Garfield told him that he would have to make the arrangements. Platt, apparently still entertaining hopes of finding Robertson reasonable, then called upon the nominee, to see if he would agree to the change. Robertson, as might have been expected, gave a scornful refusal. He went further and composed a letter to Reid, with the full understanding that the editor would send it on to Garfield: "Under no circumstances will I ask Pres. Garfield to withdraw my nomination . . . nor will I consent to its withdrawal . . . as the withdrawal of my name at his instance would make him Conkling's abject slave for the residue of his term." [17]

T. B. Connery, the editor of the New York *Herald,* came down to Washington to see what he could do for Roscoe Conkling, the good friend of his absentee publisher, James Gordon Bennett. He met first with Arthur, who gave him a fairly balanced statement of grievances.

[15] Connery, p. 157. Also N.Y. *Times,* May 31, 1881. Cornell later wrote to his son Charles, Feb. 11, 1896, that he advised Conkling not to fight Robertson "as a matter of political expediency, but it was of no use. He was irreconcilable and would not listen to any pacific advice." Cornell Papers.

[16] Garfield to Reid, April 18, 1881, Reid Papers.

[17] T. C. Smith, II, 1118–1119.

Arthur said that Garfield had not been "square," or "honorable," or "truthful" with Conkling, and that he had broken every pledge made to the Stalwarts, "in a most offensive way." Garfield, he said, was "too easily led" by Blaine.

Then Conkling came in, and gave Connery *his* version of affairs. Garfield and Robertson both, he said, were nothing but puppets of Blaine, who had instigated and stirred up all of the trouble. This thought touched off a two-hour harangue. Near the end, he read to Connery the *Tribune* editorial of January 3, the one Blaine concocted, and said:

So you see, sir, how long ago this base ingratitude of Garfield was contemplated. You will observe also that the administration's idea of the best way to "foment no quarrels" is to make war—war, sir!—war upon the larger branch of the Republican party of the Empire State. What was the meaning of that article? What was the meaning of it, if not to give me timely warning that the men who had voted faithfully for Grant—the men who clung to their pledges and their honor—need expect no quarter from the administration, while the men who had basely violated their pledges by abandoning Grant for Garfield, and thereby turned the tide of voting in favor of Garfield, were to be rewarded for their treachery? [18]

Senator Conkling was sore and unhappy over a matter which he could do nothing about. Garfield had made pledges and had shamelessly violated them; he had turned upon his benefactor and delivered over unto his enemies the citadel of power. Even without pledges, if we accept for a moment the premise that the Conkling machine rolled into operation in the middle of the 1880 campaign without any promises of recognition, consultation, or patronage, the ingratitude shown by Garfield in selecting a sworn enemy for the custom house was colossal. But there it was; Garfield was president, thanks in large part to Roscoe Conkling, but there was no way that the senator could rescind what he had done. The election was over, the votes all counted, with no way to say that some of them were Conkling's, some others Garfield's. Roscoe Conkling would march forward as before, but his growing fatalism would march beside him.

Lou Payn felt it. Payn had a long talk with Whitelaw Reid, in which he admitted that the boys in the organization, the vital cogs in the machine, were scared. It was not just the leaders who were frightened for the future, but also medium level politicos like Canal Commissioner

[18] Connery, pp. 146–150.

Silas Dutcher, New York Police Commissioner Stephen French, young Elihu Root, and others, who had committed their political futures to this organization. Conkling, Payn told Reid, had decided to get out of politics at the end of his term, to go to work, to make some big money. This thought is corroborated by some of the letters Conkling had written in this period to J. P. Jones and to Morton, letters devoted principally to inquiries about Conkling's investments. Payn said the senator had utterly abandoned the idea of the presidency or of any future in politics at all—he was over fifty now, getting a little tired, and the Grant defeat had really hit him hard—and he planned to spend the next four years "simply in wreaking his revenges." Platt and Payn and Cornell, of course, felt that they still had political futures, and they did not really care to be caught in the rubble of the collapsing Conkling machine.[19]

There may be an element of exaggeration in all this, since Reid used it in one of his bracing letters to Garfield, but there is no doubt much truth in the story. From the moment that Grant went down, the moment when Garfield was nominated over the opposition of the Stalwart 306, Conkling appeared to be almost sleepwalking, to be doing the things expected of him, even to the extent of the rages and the sulks, without much possibility that his actions would profit him. He expected little from Garfield, though this did not reduce the extent of the perfidy, and he expected nothing from Blaine. After Chicago, Grant was definitely a retired politician, and Roscoe Conkling was a senator with four years left in his term. He was extremely powerful still in the Senate, but the means of maintaining his hegemony in New York had slipped away that June day in Chicago. He did what he could, he did what he had to do, but he was looking around to private life. The knife was being sharpened for him, and he knew it. Bad as Hayes had been, he was not vindictive, and he ran his own administration. Conkling could see that James G. Blaine would run Garfield's.

Grant did what he could, not much, really, for his old supporter. He wrote to Garfield on April 24, protesting against the punishment of "my personal friends" because of their "friendship and support." When Garfield would do nothing for him, the old general wrote to his friend Adam Badeau, who was one of the diplomatic appointees being shuffled around the map of Europe to make room for Robertson in the New York

19 Reid to Garfield, April 11, 1881, Reid Papers.

Custom House, that "Garfield has shown that he is not possessed of the backbone of an angle-worm. I hope his nominations may be defeated." [20]

As April passed into May the deadlock in the Senate gave signs of being resolved, and at a Republican caucus on May 2, it was decided that when executive sessions were held treaties and uncontested nominations would be considered before any more controversial matters (like the collector of New York) were taken up. A five-man committee of conciliation, headed by Henry Dawes of Massachusetts, was set up in a futile effort to try to work out a compromise between Garfield and Conkling. Conkling appeared before the committee and delivered a stirring oration of two and a half hours, detailing his grievances against Garfield, Blaine, and Robertson. Dawes, who had heard him speak for years, said that "he surpassed himself in all those elements of oratorical power for which he was so distinguished."

The close of Conkling's speech caused much anxiety and excitement among the members of the committee: "I have in my pocket an autograph letter of this President . . . which, I pray God I may never be compelled in self-defense to make public; but if that time shall ever come, I declare to you, his friends, he will bite the dust."

Dawes rushed to the White House to see what the president knew about the dreaded letter, and was startled to hear Garfield pass it off as just another one of several indiscreet letters he had written during the late campaign urging the macing of federal employees for funds. Dawes suggested that Garfield publish it to forestall any sensational use of it as Conkling was talking about, and the president was going to do so, when Blaine entered.

"Here, Blaine," said Garfield, "is where I have been slopping over again." He showed the letter to Blaine, who, as solicitous of the sanctity of private correspondence as ever, advised strongly against publication. Conkling never mentioned it again, but the threat did not show him in a very attractive light. [21]

Later, Dawes ran into Conkling on the street and informally advised him to forgive personal differences in the interest of party harmony.

[20] T. C. Smith, II, 1132–1134. Badeau had written on April 9 to Henry B. Carrington that as he had earlier declined better posts than Denmark he "was not likely to accept" that one; Carrington Family Collection.

[21] H. L. Dawes, "Garfield and Conkling," p. 343. Thomas Bayard wrote Francis Kernan on May 12, 1881, that "there is no art of the baser kind of politics which is being left untried to defeat Robertson"; Kernan Papers.

This, the Massachusetts senator said, would bring Conkling great respect and favor in the Senate. Conkling replied sadly that that was no solution:

Your medicine, Dawes, is much easier to prescribe than to take. . . . Why, you have no idea of the bitterness of the feeling in New York in condemnation of these men. If I should take the course you suggest, I should myself go under and should be burned in effigy from Buffalo to Montauk Point, and could not be elected a delegate to a county convention in Oneida County.[22]

On May 4, the Senate problems were settled, and an executive session was finally held. One of the Stalwart appointments was confirmed that day, so the following day Garfield withdrew from the Senate the five major New York Stalwart appointments. The possibility that all of the Stalwart nominees could be confirmed and the Senate then adjourn without taking any action on Robertson was thus foreclosed. "This," Garfield wrote, "will bring the Robertson nomination to an issue. It may end in his defeat but it will protect me against being finessed out of a test." In the Senate, when the message was read, Tom Platt hung his head. His escape hatches were rapidly being sealed up.[23]

On May 9, the Robertson issue came up in the Republican caucus. George Edmunds moved to postpone consideration of the nomination until December; Conkling, who clearly was not sure of enough votes to defeat Robertson now, supported the motion with a long speech. The magic was not there, however. The next day, Edmunds' caucus resolution was withdrawn, in the face of impending defeat, and a temporary delay was adopted instead—to give more time to work out a compromise, or to save face for Roscoe Conkling. On Friday the 13th, another caucus was held, it became obvious that no adjustment was possible, and a reference of the nomination to an executive session for a vote was adopted. Conkling stormed angrily out of the room, vowing never again to go into a Republican caucus.

Where was Conkling's support going? One Republican senator told the press: "He has assumed to dictate to the President and to bully his colleagues into supporting him, by threatening to bring defeat and disaster to the Republican party of New York, unless he is permitted to

[22] Dawes, p. 344. In light of later developments, it would appear that Conkling was the one who had no idea of the feeling in New York.

[23] T. C. Smith, II, 1124–1125; M. P. Breen, *Thirty Years of New York Politics,* p. 656.

have his own way." He concluded that Conkling's defeat would rather add to than decrease Republican strength in New York. "No one," he concluded, "will be so bitterly disappointed as Mr. Conkling should he attempt to execute his threats." [24]

Regardless of Conkling's threats, the Senate had now cleared the decks for an early consideration of the Robertson nomination. Roscoe Conkling—and Tom Platt—stood with their backs to the wall.

[24] N.Y. *Times,* May 3, 1881. The *Times,* on May 10, 1881, said that, contrary to the expectation of several weeks before, "it is now certain that Mr. Conkling will not receive much support from the Democratic side."

CHAPTER 26

RESIGNATION AND
REJECTION

The following Monday, May 16, as the Senate prepared for the week's business, Vice-President Arthur asked the clerk to read to the body a message just received, advising the Senate "that my resignation as Senator of the United States from the State of New York has been forwarded to the governor of that State." It was signed by Roscoe Conkling. As the dumbfounded senators, inattentive to this point, stared at the podium, trying to grasp what they had just heard, the clerk read a second and identical communication, this one from Tom Platt.[1]

There was then no doubt of it, after a few minutes: Roscoe Conkling had thrown up his commission as a senator, had chucked it all, was now a private citizen. Senator Conkling was no more. But why? What was the point of it? What could a resignation accomplish? What were the political implications? What did it mean, that Conkling's senatorial echo, his second vote, had tendered up the seat he had worked so hard to win a few short months earlier?

What happened now?

No one knew at the moment, just as only three or four of Conkling's friends had known that the resignations were coming. Clearly, for the bitterly torn Republican party, harmony was farther away than ever. The great senator's colleagues were astounded. George Vest of Missouri proclaimed, "Conkling has made a fool of himself," and most of his fellow senators agreed that the course of Conkling and Platt was a great mistake.

The *Times* said, with perhaps a touch of exaggeration, that "the sensation created today by the announcement of the resignations . . . was not exceeded by any event that occurred in the most exciting days of the

[1] *Cong. Rec.,* 47th Cong., spec. sess., p. 459.

rebellion." Mrs. Blaine, on the other hand, wrote that "the sensational resignations of Conkling and Platt . . . produce no excitement here, and I have yet to hear one criticism complimentary of Conkling, though I have seen all sorts of people and of every shade of cowardice." [2]

Garfield wrote that their "very weak attempt at the heroic . . . will be received with guffaws of laughter," and, indeed, at Albany, the rejoicing among the Half Breeds, whether premature or not, was widespread. Rutherford Hayes, back in Ohio, expected the two Stalwarts to be re-elected as Republicans opposed to the administration and called it "a wretched business." And the Utica *Herald* suggested that "the men who sneeze when Mr. Conkling takes snuff will be surprised this morning to find that the world has not gone to smash, nor the earth varied from the usual time of its revolution." [3]

Why Conkling quit the Senate is still somewhat of a mystery. As is so often the case, unfortunately, we have no record of Conkling's private thoughts leading him to this course. Thomas Platt later claimed it was all his idea, "to rebuke the President by immediately turning in our resignations," and then to be vindicated by re-election. Perhaps, but the mind boggles at the thought of the secretive Tom Platt counseling Roscoe Conkling, the great and magnificent, "the becurled, perfumed grandee gazed at by gallery gapers in the Senate," suggesting to Conkling that resignation was the only course open to them. It certainly may have appealed to Platt as a way out of his personal dilemma, and he may have suggested it, meekly, to his boss, but he had recently seen the anger and scorn which Conkling visited upon Cornell's presumptuous attempt to give advice. Given the situation and the personalities involved, we can hardly credit Tom Platt as the author of such a bold stroke. Obviously, by the testimony of Reid's description of his talk with Lou Payn a month before, Conkling was thinking of getting out. He was still relatively poor, and the time for enrichment at the bar was slipping away. The pliant Garfield was in for four years, with Blaine at his elbow, and the course of the administration was clear. Robertson was

[2] N.Y. *Times,* May 17, 1881; H. S. B. Beale, ed., I, 199. Former Governor Morgan said the office of U.S. senator was one "no man ought to be allowed to trifle with." The ancient Thurlow Weed said of Conkling, "he and his serf Platt are trifling with a great national issue, and they ought to be rebuked."

[3] T. C. Smith, II, 1134; C. R. Williams, ed., IV, 19; Utica *Morning Herald,* May 17, 1881. The hometown paper also pointed out, recalling Kernan, that three months before Utica had had two U.S. Senators and now suddenly had none at all.

about to be confirmed—of that, there was no longer any doubt—and he would surely embark at once upon a fierce course of proscription of his political enemies. Even Conkling's followers were wavering, for self-preservation is a powerful instinct among politicians, and they could read the signs as well as the senator could. Well, then, why not do the thing up in a bold Conklinian way, bow out with a flourish, and capture the dramatic imagination of the public one last time? [4]

Unfortunately, the public laughed. "The apparent expectation," wrote *Harper's,* "was that the country and the Senate would be aghast. . . . The country, instead of terror, has shown only the most genuine amusement." The Senate, the next day, confirmed Robertson without audible dissent. "This leaves Conkling's attitude ridiculous," wrote Garfield. "His row is with the Senate equally with me." [5]

Godkin, unable to believe the good fortune which had befallen him and his fellow Conkling-haters, fairly leaped into print: "Persons of this temper are not fit for public life. The proper sphere for them is a monastery, or some solitary pursuit like metaphysics or sheep-herding. . . . Who can name any good cause or public policy that will be injured by Conkling's lapsing into utter obscurity and silence for the rest of his days?" [6] The Conkling resignation projected the cleavage in the Republican party into the public limelight as never before. Clearly, the split had now become irremediable; the Garfield nomination had merely papered over, if that, the bitter differences. Conkling's resignation meant war to the end between the Republican factions—the war that had been implicit all along in the stand of the Stalwarts at Chicago.

In Albany, matters were moving swiftly. Reaction in the state capital was almost uniformly negative; no spontaneous move to send the two senators back to Washington developed. Instead, even the Stalwart leaders in the legislature were forced to concede to reporters that the double resignation was "childish," and they were instantly thrown on the defensive. The Stalwarts were hard-pressed to give reasons why Conkling and Platt should be restored to the offices they had just vacated, for no very good purposes, and, even more disabling, they did not

[4] For Platt's version, Platt, p. 151. The "grandee" quote is from Eckenrode, p. 280. One Democratic senator said Conkling had told him sometime before "that he was tired of service in the Senate, and that he felt disposed to resign from that body." N.Y. *Times,* May 17, 1881.

[5] *Harper's Weekly,* June 4, 1881; T. C. Smith, II, 1135.

[6] *The Nation,* May 19, 1881.

even know whether or not the two ex-senators *desired* re-election. Wires and letters were shipped off to Conkling in Washington, but none were answered. Dead silence prevailed.

In the face of this, sentiment built rapidly for the permanent retirement of the longtime senator and his echo.

The Conkling men are all at sea, losing strength every hour, partly through the absence of leaders, but more clearly because the Conkling men have no purpose except to re-elect the men who have resigned, while it is believed that Mr. Conkling does not wish to be re-elected, and Mr. Platt is declared to be out of the race. . . . The general impression is that Conkling's fight is ended.[7]

John Hay, running the *Tribune* during Reid's honeymoon, wrote the absent editor: "I will not indulge in prophecy with *half* a dozen cables between us, but to speak of certainties Roscoe is finished. That Olympian brow will never again garner up the thousands of yore." It was, said Hay, "a freak of insanity on the part of a man who has lost sight of his true relations with the rest of the world." [8]

The Half-Breed leaders were tireless in working on doubtful members, including some who were considered Stalwarts, and letters and resolutions from individuals and civic and political groups poured in to the capital, almost all urging the legislature to stand firm against Conkling and Platt. The surge of public opinion was clearly against the two men.

In the meantime, a parliamentary stratagem worked by the Half Breeds postponed action on the vacancies for a week, during which the anti-Conkling elements had time to augment their strength. Under the law, a Senate vacancy was to be filled by the legislature meeting in joint session on the second Tuesday after the declaration of the vacancy. The resignations had been announced on Monday, May 16, and Governor Cornell intended to notify the legislature in its session that evening, so that the vote would take place on May 24. Instead of sending two messengers, however, the governor sent only one. When that worthy reached the senate, having gone first to the assembly, he found the upper house in adjournment. At the stroke of eight, Senator Loren Sessions, one of the Half-Breed leaders, had taken the chair and, as soon as the prayer was concluded, heard a motion to adjourn by Woodin, gavelled it through on a voice vote, and declared the senate adjourned until the next

[7] N.Y. *Times,* May 19, 1881.
[8] Hay to Reid, May 26, 1881, John Hay, *Letters,* II, 63–64.

day, while Robert Strahan, the Conkling leader, and several other Stalwarts clamored fruitlessly for recognition. Ten minutes later the governor's courier arrived.

By this trick, the anti-Conkling men put off the voting until May 31. In the meantime, they would sound the changes on one theme: Conkling's power was gone, and Blaine and Garfield had it now. "Stand by the Administration" was the watchword, with all the implications that worried politicians could read into it.

It is speculation, of course, to think that Conkling and Platt would have done better on the 24th than the 31st; the Stalwart forces were so disorganized and defensive that the results might have been exactly the same. But the parliamentary coup helped to inspire the Half Breeds with a feeling of having already put one over on the machine.

The machine leaders, who were anxious to do what Senator Conkling wished them to do, were still in the dark as to his intentions. One Stalwart, weary of the constant anti-Conkling talk of the Half Breeds, said wistfully, "Why, if he would only come here and walk through the hall of the Delevan, he would make the half-breeds up stairs tremble." But still no word came from Washington, where, presumably, the ex-senator had withdrawn from public view.[9]

On May 20, Conkling left Washington on the 2:00 P.M. train for New York, accompanied by his faithful friend, Senator J. P. Jones of Nevada. Rumors of the "he will—he won't" type swirled around New York and Albany, but most observers decided that good sense dictated a discreet retirement to a private law practice. The *Times*, for example, pointed out that it would be "somewhat of an anti-climax to his dramatic stroke of resignation" for Conkling to have to make a canvass for re-election, and it was now quite clear that an active and probably bitter contest would be required.[10]

Conkling checked into the Fifth Avenue Hotel on Friday evening, leaving word at the desk that he was not to be disturbed. Vice-President Arthur arrived in New York at roughly the same time. At this juncture, Arthur was more the machine lieutenant than the vice-president. On

[9] N.Y. *Times*, May 17, 1881, May 20, 1881. Billy Hudson describes the Sessions coup graphically in Hudson, pp. 116–117. Sessions, incidentally, was later indicted by the Albany Grand Jury for alleged bribery of a pro-Conkling legislator named Bradley from Cattaraugus. Things got rough in this battle.

[10] N.Y. *Times*, May 21, 1881; Lucius Q. C. Lamar was quoted in the Vicksburg *Herald* as saying, "Mr. Conkling does not need to hold official place to wield vast influence in the United States." Mayes, p. 391.

Saturday, Conkling stayed in his room most of the day, receiving callers, except for a forty-five minute stroll around sundown. Among those he saw were Platt, Jones, Tom Murphy, Senator Strahan, and Elihu Root.

The next morning, Conkling and Platt were driven to Arthur's home on Lexington Avenue for a conference of Stalwart leaders which the *Times* said "was suggested and arranged by the Governor." The governor's position was felt to be important, since he had to that time made no public announcement of his own sentiments and some of the Half Breeds were suggesting that they could support Cornell for one of the vacancies. Cornell, according to report, promised to try to attend the Sunday morning meeting, but he never did so. Present, however, were the vice-president, Speaker Sharpe, Senator Strahan, Police Commissioner Stephen B. French, Insurance Commissioner John F. Smyth, Lou Payn, and A. B. Johnson, an old friend from Utica.

Conkling opened by stating that he preferred to go back to private life; now that he was out of the Senate, he would stay out, go into law, and make some money. Most of those present, though, urged a different course; they felt that the only way to hold the Senate seats was with the name of Roscoe Conkling. He must go to Albany and lead the fight for re-election. He owed it to his loyal supporters, to the continued existence of the organization he had built. He had to be there, to put his name into the fight; no one thought Tom Platt's name could rally the hosts. They argued, persuaded, cajoled, and finally Conkling agreed, apparently reluctantly, to do what his friends wanted, to lead the battle, provided that Platt was supported, too. The two of them had left the Senate together; as a matter of principle, they had to go back together.

When the conversation got around to Garfield, Conkling excitedly interrupted again. It was clear that Conkling, who had always been so scornful and heedless of public opinion, was deeply chagrined that Garfield had been able to turn a blatant violation of good civil service principles into a struggle against the domination of a wicked senator. This feature of the Robertson affair may very well have been what drew Conkling back to Albany. He, Conkling said, had not tried to steal the patronage of the state; Garfield had done it. Pointing to a hat on the table, he drew a parallel:

Suppose a man should come in here and attempt to take that hat, and one of you gentlemen should say to him, "Don't do that; the hat is not yours," and a squabble should arise, and then suppose the man who was trying to take it should accuse the man who was endeavoring to prevent him of being a thief, and assert that he was the man who was doing the wrong. That is an exactly parallel case to this of my trouble with the President. I have not tried to steal the Collectorship. I have tried to keep it in the hands of the man who has a right to it until his term expires, but I am the man accused of being a thief. I am accused of grabbing for patronage. I have simply tried to prevent others from succeeding in their grab for patronage.

Roscoe Conkling as a defender of the sanctity of the civil service never managed to come across with much conviction, and the reasons for his resignation, set forth in a long letter to Governor Cornell which accompanied the letters of resignation, failed to gain much public approval. Louis Payn, who had been in Albany during the past week, knew this; he understood the pressures bearing upon all of the legislators, from their constituents, from the press, and from the national administration. He recognized that these pressures would be intensified over the weekend, when the members would be home and would hear first-hand the adverse public reaction to Conkling's move. Lou Payn knew his legislature, and he predicted that both Conkling and Platt would be defeated. In one version of the meeting, George Sharpe, who should have known better, allegedly scoffed, "We shall win this battle without any trouble." Payn turned on him and snarled, "Huh, but you will be the first to desert us." Part of this, of course, was a trace of lingering ill feeling from the January Senate battle, but it should have been worrisome.

No one evidently made the point that even a hard-fought victory, under the best circumstances now foreseeable, would hardly constitute "vindication" for the senators' course against the President. This was a delicate point that the power-brokers of the disintegrating machine could hardly worry about. They now needed Conkling more for their own purposes than for Conkling's. Payn's prediction represented the sudden injection into the meeting of the reality of Albany, but Conkling chose to ignore it. In his pride and disdain, Roscoe Conkling could not envision defeat. He would go to Albany. It was a dreadful mistake, worse even than the decision to resign.[11]

The announcement that the two ex-senators would indeed be candidates to succeed themselves came as a surprise to many experts who

[11] N.Y. *Times,* May 23, 1881; Platt, pp. 159–160; Howe, p. 147. Platt is the authority for Sharpe's over-confident remark, which makes it somewhat suspect. Sharpe had been in Albany all week; it is hard to imagine such a shrewd politico blindly ignoring the visible signs of trouble. Sharpe, it should be remembered, had worked for Crowley in January, so it is in character for Platt to attempt to throw the onus of defeat upon him.

could plainly see the disposition of the legislature, who were familiar with Conkling's overbearing pride, and who knew of his oft-expressed desire to earn some money outside of politics. These things all added up to a quiet withdrawal into private life, not a contentious campaign for the Senate vacancy.

The *Times,* in a May 23 editorial entitled "The Conkling Episode," called it incredible "that a man who has a reputation as a statesman to maintain should resign his seat in the United States Senate for the mere purpose of being re-elected." The paper called the whole episode "one of the most undignified and inexcusable in recent political history."

Nevertheless, Conkling arrived in Albany on the mid-afternoon train on May 24, to take personal charge of the canvass. When he arrived at the Delevan House, instead of following his usual custom of sweeping upstairs and leaving his retainers to take care of the detail work of checking in, he marched over to the desk and grandly signed the register, shaking every hand he could reach along the way. He was all cheer and affability. Gone was the proud, distant, terrifying personage the politicians all knew. "Nothing could have been more gracious than his manner," wrote one reporter, "and no statesman ever wore a more winning smile." After he rested for an hour, he held a reception in his parlor for anyone who wanted to see him. This was all so unlike Roscoe Conkling that it was painful to watch. Conkling had never begged for anything; even when he was dealing with Garfield over offices and cabinet posts, he never begged. Now he was begging for votes in a contest he had not even wanted to enter.

Later, he had a long consultation in his rooms with Cornell and Arthur, and ultimately Platt joined them. The strategy decided upon was to call a caucus for Thursday evening, the 26th, and bind the entire Republican vote with a majority in the caucus. This plan itself was a confession of defeat for two senators who had resigned in order to be "vindicated" by the legislature, but that was not the worst of it. The Senate caucus committee, headed by Dennis McCarthy of Syracuse, refused to issue a call, and the signatures on a Stalwart petition for a call accumulated slowly at best. The Half Breeds had determined to avoid a caucus, and the machine's efforts to force one were so far unsuccessful.

Blaine, who had written a friend on May 18 that "everything possible or impossible must be done to beat those fellows at Albany," had recruited Chauncey Depew back into the Senate race and even made a trip to New York City on May 24 to coordinate strategy. Prospects were looking unbelievably good for the secretary and his friends. His great political enemy was unaccountably eliminating himself from national Republican affairs, leaving the way clear for a successful Garfield administration, dominated by Blaine, to be succeeded in natural course by a Blaine administration. Just follow through in Albany, clearly, and that man with the "turkey-gobbler strut" was finished forever.

On May 26, the *Times* reported that "the cause of the ex-Senators had not been as rapidly successful as their friends had predicted," and pointed out that the drive for names on the caucus-call petition had ground to a halt.[12]

On the 25th, Conkling spent most of his time in his room at the Delevan, and it was noted that he had dropped his "cordial, affectionate manner" of the day before. Cornell came again in the evening and met with the ex-senators and Arthur. The reporters by this time were more interested in what Cornell might say than in Conkling. The governor was still being spoken of as a possible senator, while the press had just about written off the chances of the two ex-senators, whom the *Times* called "a pair of political bushwhackers." Indeed, on Thursday the 26th, it was said that the election of Conkling and Platt by Republican votes was now impossible, though rumors were circulating that a deal was being cooked up with the Democratic minority to send Conkling and a Democrat to Washington. Conkling, it is now clear, never considered any such thing. Still, Conkling was clearly losing ground; no more did his supporters talk about routing the opposition with an appearance in the Delevan lobby.[13]

Still, though reason, pride, and personal inclination must have told him to pull out, to get away while it could still be done with some dignity, Roscoe Conkling stuck. It was painful to him, and embarrassing, to send for old supporters, let alone opponents, to ask for their votes, and to be turned down. Four years in opposition to the Garfield administration did not appeal to many, not when the folks back home were daily giving evidence they were against such a folly. Old Elbridge Lapham, who had carved out a nice career as a congressman through Conkling's favor, was now making himself available for the Senate, letting the word out that he would not fight the administration. Cornell's course was a mystery; he told his friends to vote for Conkling and Platt, he told them he was not a candidate, but he said nothing publicly and he scrupulously kept the state machinery out of the contest. No matter what his privately expressed views, when so prominent a beneficiary of Conkling's support

---

[12] Blaine to Stephen Elkins, May 18, 1881, Rothman, p. 179; N.Y. *Times,* May 26, 1881.

[13] N.Y. *Times,* May 25, 26, 1881.

took no public position, it served the same as open opposition. Cornell found the situation "extremely embarrassing." He wrote later that he was "loyally anxious to render them all possible support," but this conflicted with "the constraint of the proprieties of his official position." The governor had not hesitated to use state patronage for Platt in January, but now he took a stand on principle. It was an inconvenient time for such scruples, and many who had suspected Cornell of "setting up" on his own found their suspicions confirmed. Unlike Cornell, Chester Arthur stuck by his boss, at some further cost to his own reputation; Godkin said that Arthur's "open and active conspiring" with the two ex-senators heightened "the indecency of the present situation." [14]

On Friday morning, a long meeting was held among Conkling, Arthur, Payn, French, and Elihu Root, and this was followed by a half-hour conference early in the afternoon of Conkling, Sharpe, and Cornell. The meetings were producing nothing of consequence. Conkling and most of the Stalwart leaders departed for New York City on Friday afternoon, and still no state patronage was being wielded for the ex-senators' benefit. Conkling, said one politician, "was in a desperate mood." He had now begun to refer privately to Alonzo Cornell as "the lizard on the hill."

When Conkling arrived in New York, there was little in the way of reception for him, and no one pressed forward to shake his hand. As he checked quietly into the Fifth Avenue Hotel, accompanied only by A. B. Johnson of Utica, a reporter wrote, "It was painfully evident that he had ceased to be a lion."

His week in Albany had been a disaster:

He has not shrunk from all the common methods of conventions and canvasses, but has sat up late and got up early to pour into the ears of members the story of his grievances. . . . During his brief stay here any man, let him be ever so dull, or never so much opposed to Conkling's re-election, could, by speaking the word, be accorded a private interview with him, and command his time for a half-hour, an hour, or longer. . . . Strange as it may seem, and mortifying as it must have been to Mr. Conkling, there came an hour when he was driven to the extremity of writing invitations to members, requesting them, as a personal favor, to grant him the boon of a few moments' conversation with them.[15]

On Sunday night, May 29, Conkling and his party went back to Albany by boat, apparently to avoid reporters. The bitterness of the feel-

[14] Autobiographical sketch, Cornell Papers; *The Nation,* May 26, 1881.
[15] N.Y. *Times,* May 28, 1881.

ing toward Cornell now began to creep out into the open. One anonymous Stalwart complained of the governor's lack of assistance as contrasted with Conkling's support of Cornell when he was seeking the gubernatorial nomination. "While Mr. Conkling does not doubt the loyalty of the Governor," he said, "his lukewarmness and seeming indifference are unaccountable to him." [16]

On Monday evening the Stalwarts made an unsuccessful attempt to call a caucus, but it was so poorly attended that any decision it made would have been a nullity. The Democrats caucused, but the Republicans would go into the balloting on Tuesday free to do as they pleased.

When the joint session convened and voted on Tuesday, May 31, the magnitude of Roscoe Conkling's folly in going to Albany was fully revealed. The brutal arithmetic of the balloting told the story. John C. Jacobs, the Democratic Senate leader, got 53 Democratic votes in the voting for the short term, while the Republicans split all over the place. Conkling's 35 was the highest single total, while the other 71 votes were scattered among nineteen individuals, the highest being former Vice-President Wheeler with 19.

On the ballot for the long term, Kernan got 54 Democratic votes, and Platt's 29 Republican votes led his party, but seventeen persons split up the other 76 votes. Depew had the next highest total with 21.

Ominously, on both ballots there were numerous votes for other Stalwarts such as Cornell, Folger, Crowley, Lapham, Silas Dutcher, and Morton, with the governor having the highest totals. Clearly, the machine had lost its balance wheel when Conkling threw up his Senate seat, and it was now in the process of flying apart. In the protracted deadlock that followed, neither Conkling nor Platt was ever able to rise higher than his first-ballot figure.

A *Times* editorial remarked that Conkling had long confused "Republicanism and Conklingism" and had now made the mistake of letting the Republicans of the state choose between them. "The result must have astonished him." [17]

Garfield, in Washington, wrote in his diary, "And this is the 'vindication' he appealed for!" Whitelaw Reid's *Tribune,* pointing out that two-thirds of the Republican members of the legislature had declared

[16] *Ibid.,* May 30.

[17] *Ibid.,* June 1. The first ballot totals, for the long term, were Kernan (the Democrat) 54, Platt 29, Depew 21, Cornell 12, Lapham 8, Miller 5, Crowley 3, others 25. For the short term it was Jacobs (the Democrat) 53, Conkling 39, Wheeler 19, Cornell 9, Crowley 5, others 38.

against him, suggested that "the time has come for him to withdraw from a contest in which there can be nothing but humiliation for him." Good advice—but the series of horrendous political decisions in which Conkling had become enmeshed continued. He chose to stay in the race, dooming the legislature to a long and unseemly stalemate and condemning himself to a painfully extended agony of self-abasement.[18]

Throughout June the balloting continued, with no real break in the patterns, except that Depew very quickly took the lead over Platt on the Republican side for the long term, and by the end of the month Wheeler was running ahead of Conkling. Conkling's old friend General Grant tried to help out in an interview, when he said, "He has been shamefully treated, Sir, and for no cause whatsoever that I can discover," but it had no effect whatever. It became brutally clear that neither Conkling nor Platt could possibly be re-elected to the Senate, but Conkling insisted that his thirty or so votes stand obstinately clear of any compromise on any other candidate. There was talk that Conkling and his supporters wanted to prevent the election of anyone, so the legislature could adjourn and later return to send Conkling and Platt to Washington, but this was clearly nonsense. Perhaps it was the 306-standing-firm-for-Grant all over again, but if that was the reason it fell far short of the mark. The stand of the Stalwarts at Chicago had borne some elements of the heroic, the glorious, but the stand at Albany had none. Most people found it simply the wanton arrogance, the hubris, of Roscoe Conkling's whole career elevated (or lowered) to its utmost degree.[19]

Toward the end of June, a boom started for Richard Crowley, without his approval, of course, while Conkling was off in New York City. It offered Roscoe a possible way out, a way to withdraw while procuring the election of a loyal supporter. Conkling came back to Albany and instantly killed the movement for Crowley. The struggle would go on.

Early in July, two events occurred which promised to bring an end, finally, to the Senate struggle. First, Platt withdrew from the race. He said later that "by remaining in the field I was very much injuring Conkling's chances for re-election." But Conkling, of course, had no chance

---

[18] T. C. Smith, II, 1137; N.Y. *Tribune,* June 1, 1881.

[19] Grant's interview was in N.Y. *Times,* June 4, 1881, while the old General was in New Orleans. Depew many years later wrote that he several times turned down offers of enough Democratic votes to elect him; this may or may not be accurate. Depew to D. S. Alexander, Dec. 16, 1908, Depew Papers.

of re-election at this time. What had really happened was that a group of Half Breeds on a stepladder had peered through an open transom into a hotel room where they observed Platt and a lady of the town in bed together, disporting themselves in a way which did not quite seem fitting for a pillar of the Methodist Church, former U. S. Senator, and president of the United States Express Company. Soon, everybody in Albany knew about the scene, and when oblique references to it began appearing in the papers Tom Platt pulled out.[20]

The same morning that Platt's withdrawal was read to the joint legislature, July 2, President Garfield and Secretary Blaine went to the Baltimore and Potomac railroad station in Washington to take a train for New England. Garfield was planning to attend a reunion at Williams College. While walking through the station he was suddenly attacked by a nondescript-looking man, slim, dark-bearded, and dressed in shabby clothes, who pulled out a revolver and shot the President twice. One bullet hit Garfield's arm, but the other went into his spinal column. The president fell unconscious to the floor, apparently dead, while his assailant turned and walked rapidly away. A policeman at one of the station exits, hearing the shots, apprehended the man as he tried to hurry past. The suspect was Charles Julius Guiteau, "a half-crazed, pettifogging lawyer" from Illinois, or, as he styled himself in one of the letters found on his person after his arrest, "a lawyer, a theologian, and a politician." Guiteau said that he had taken upon himself the "political necessity" of "removing" Garfield, much as he himself regretted it; and he made it crystal clear that he was a Stalwart and that his intention was to make Arthur president.[21]

Garfield was not dead. He was taken back to the White House and

[20] Platt, pp. 160–161. The Albany *Argus,* of July 2, 1881, contained such a reference, as did the New York *World* of the same date, referring to "a half-breed committee of inspection established on step-ladders in the hotel at Albany." See Gosnell, p. 28.

[21] *The Independent,* July 7, 1881; N.Y. *Times,* July 3, 1881. Cyrus W. Field to Blaine, June 24, 1881, for details of the proposed Garfield trip; Blaine Papers. Guiteau will be remembered as one of the speakers at the rally in New York after the conference at the Fifth Avenue Hotel the previous August. See also H. G. and C. J. Hayes, eds., *A Complete History of the Trial of Guiteau,* pp. 17–18, for Guiteau's letters. One of the persistent legends of American history is that Guiteau, at the moment of firing, shouted "I am a Stalwart of the Stalwarts! Arthur is President now!" This story is pretty well laid to rest in an excellent new study of the assassination and its aftermath, C. E. Rosenberg, *The Trial of the Assassin Guiteau* (Chicago and London: University of Chicago Press, 1968).

turned over to the ministrations of a high-powered team of physicians. Indignation and hatred toward Conkling and Chester Arthur, as the possible beneficiary of Guiteau's act, boiled over in the land. Arthur, severely shaken, met with Conkling three separate times after hearing of the news. The next day he left for Washington.

Andrew D. White, then minister in Berlin, but long familiar with New York politics, said that his first reaction to the news was one of "stupefaction" at the possible succession of Arthur: "Chet Arthur President of the United States! Good God!" [22]

Mainly, though, the opprobrium fell upon Conkling. One man said, "This is the result of placating bosses. If Conkling had not been placated at Chicago, President Garfield would not now be lying on his deathbed." Others were even more denunciatory. Conkling himself complained privately of the "incendiary calumnies" with which he was assaulted. The press, long before the shooting, had been drumming into its readers the wickedness of Conkling's course toward Garfield and the administration, and the confessed motivation of the demented assassin added the finishing touches to Roscoe's evil image. Guiteau, who talked incessantly, said that his decision to "remove" Garfield (his word—the thought of killing as such was apparently distasteful to him) came out of his depression on May 18 caused by Conkling's resignation. For many people, Guiteau was merely a Conkling agent, and the New Yorker might as well have pulled the trigger himself. On top of that, even after Conkling's vengeance was wreaked upon Garfield, to have his flunky Arthur become president was almost obscene. That Guiteau was undoubtedly suffering from mental illness—pronounced by modern psychiatrists "a common garden variety of paranoid schizophrenia"— that he was a two-bit politician desperate because he could not procure a job from the Garfield administration, that he was in fact totally unknown to Roscoe Conkling (he complained that "My Lord Roscoe," always on his "high horse," had snubbed him)—all of these factors were resolutely ignored by the public in fixing the blame for the attempt on Garfield's life. Roscoe Conkling had none of the warm, human qualities of a James Garfield; he was distant, proud, and overbearing. He personified the side of evil in the struggle with Garfield, and the assassination by one of his "followers" merely clinched the identification.[23]

[22] A. D. White, I, 193.

[23] Rosenberg, p. xiii, for the psychiatric verdict. Conkling to A. T. Brown, July 9, 1881, Roscoe Conkling Letters. H. G. and C. J. Hayes, eds., pp. 428, 450; N.Y. *Times,* July 3, 1881.

The assault upon the president stretched the Republican party to its greatest extreme. The amazing thing is that, when analyzed, this split was not one of issues, or of policies—it was mainly one of personalities —and, more than any other, Roscoe's Conkling's personality. Almost unaided, Conkling severed the Republican party.

Garfield lingered for two and a half months. For a long time, it seemed that he would pull through, and he fought for life tenaciously and with good spirit. His gallant battle won him public respect and admiration which his fumbling course as president had not earned. His medical care, though, was incompetent, and ultimately, on September 19, at Elberon, New Jersey, where he had been taken for the bracing effect of the sea air, James A. Garfield died.

Roscoe Conkling sent messages of regret to the president during his confinement and even called at the White House to offer his hopes for Garfield's recovery. After Garfield died, though, Conkling's lips were closed. "How can I speak into a grave?" he asked. "How can I battle with a shroud? Silence is a duty and a doom." [24]

Arthur's reputation had been refurbished somewhat during Garfield's agony by wide circulation of an adulatory statement by the highly respected Edwin D. Morgan on the vice-president's character and capacities. When news of Garfield's death came, Arthur was more prepared— and the country was more prepared—than if Guiteau's bullets had done their intended work on July 2. But no one certified to Roscoe Conkling's high character or services, and the major qualification in the public's acceptance of Arthur was concern for the probable over-influence of the former senator.[25]

By the time Garfield died, Roscoe Conkling was definitely and irrevocably a former senator. After the shooting on July 2, the stalemate in Albany started to break up. There had been two reasons for the deadlock: the intransigence of the Conkling followers, obeying the dictates of the Boss, was one, but the inability of the forces opposing Conkling to unite on two candidates for the two seats was certainly another. The ambition of former Vice-President Wheeler was a major contributing

[24] H. L. Stoddard, *As I Knew Them,* p. 114. T. C. Smith, II, 1196, refers to Conkling's efforts toward the dying man.
[25] Rawley, p. 261. Arthur was at home on Lexington Avenue when news of Garfield's death came. One of those present, who helped to find a judge to swear in the new president, was Elihu Root, who was also to be with Theodore Roosevelt twenty years later at the moment that vice-president was informed of McKinley's death by an assassin's bullet. P. Jessup, *Elihu Root,* I, 119.

cause, as well as opposition to Depew for his railroad connections. Finally, on July 8, a Republican caucus was held—called by the opponents of Conkling, boycotted by the twenty-eight remaining supporters of the ex-senator. The caucus members had reached agreement that one of the two seats was to go to a Half Breed, the other to a Stalwart. The caucus picked the men.

For the long term, it took three ballots to select Congressman Warner Miller of Herkimer as the caucus candidate for the Half-Breed seat, primarily over the opposition of Wheeler. Only two ballots were required to pick a Stalwart for the other seat. Elbridge Lapham of Canandaigua, the elderly congressman from Ontario County, who was clearly no threat for a long tenure, won out over Cornell. Miller and Lapham were now officially the caucus candidates, but they would have to win over some of the remaining Conkling votes to win a majority.

On July 16, George Sharpe gave way; though he had not participated in the meeting, he announced that he would vote for both the caucus candidates as the only way out of the stalemate. He was violently attacked by Lou Payn and some other remaining Conkling men, but the Speaker's defection was enough to have Miller elected to the long term to succeed Platt. The ordeal continued, though, for Roscoe Conkling, who refused to release his other supporters.

A few days later there were reports that Conkling was about to withdraw, but when Roscoe heard that possibly Cornell might be elected his successor he backed off; "while he had little admiration for Mr. Lapham, he had none at all for Gov. Cornell." A couple of days after that, though, the weary Stalwarts finally conceded and went into a caucus. On July 22 Lapham achieved a majority in the legislature, receiving on the 56th ballot, 92 votes to 42 to Clarkson N. Potter, the Democrat. Elbridge G. Lapham, one of the first deserters, succeeded Roscoe Conkling in the Senate of the United States.

That evening, Conkling took a short stroll from his hotel room in New York but declined to be interrogated. The next day, "moody and fretful," he checked out and left town.[26]

The *Times* morosely commented on July 23 that "New York has got two Senators of no remarkable ability," but has at least "got rid of two Senators by whom it was conspicuously misrepresented." In Washington, from his sickbed, Garfield said, "I am glad it is over. I am sorry

[26] N.Y. *Times*, July 23, 24, 1881. The July 23 headline in the *Times* was simply "Roscoe Conkling Beaten."

for Conkling. He has made a great mistake, in my judgment. I will offer him any favor he may ask, or any appointment he may desire."

But it was sure that Conkling would never ask. He had "had his day as a public man," as another observer commented.[27] He could now take up that private practice of law of which he had spoken so often. Whatever aberrant streak in his psyche forced him to the degradation and humiliation of the summer of stalemate in Albany history can hardly tell, but it was done. He was tricked, deceived, reviled, deserted, and cast aside. He was also now a private citizen, with no money and no following.

The astonishing crash of Roscoe Conkling's political career from such an eminence, and so suddenly, startled and amazed the public. Americans were not accustomed to seeing their giants topple so shockingly. They expected to see their pre-eminent leaders die in the saddle, in the battle to the end—like Calhoun, Webster, Douglas, Stevens—or to become at least elder statesmen, like Jackson, Adams, Jefferson, and Seward. Historical purists may object to comparing Conkling to figures like these, but the New York senator's political power and public influence had been dramatically demonstrated within the year at Chicago and in the campaign that followed, while his contemporary enemies as well as later historians have testified to the control Conkling wielded over his Senate colleagues. Even Lucius Lamar, no friend, said, "As the people esteemed and honored Clay, Calhoun, and Webster in their day, and as they honor Seymour now, they honor Conkling." *He* was one of the major issues of the day. Conkling, for what he was more than for what he had done, was a giant of his time, and now he was gone. Moreover, he had thrown his influence away himself. And by going to Albany, by staying in the struggle to the very bitter end, he had cast away the meaning that the majesty of his personality might still have held; he could not even be an elder statesman.[28]

[27] D. W. Bliss, "The Story of President Garfield's Illness," p. 302; *The Independent,* July 28, 1881.
[28] Mayes, p. 391.

CHAPTER 27

PROFITABLE TWILIGHT

By the time that Elbridge Lapham was elected to the United States Senate, Roscoe Conkling was frozen into his historical niche, and he now had to provide for the future, to take up the occupation of an ex-politician. And this was what Roscoe Conkling now was; the Washington *Critic* quoted him, after the Albany battle: "I am done with politics now and forever. This fight is over, and I shall hereafter devote my time and purpose of life to my law practice." [1] No one really believed that, but he meant it, and he meant to make it stick.

First, though, he had to regain his health. The great, tall, muscular senator had suffered recurring sieges of ill health since the malarial infection of 1876, and the brutal two months in Albany, following hard on the heels of the pressure-packed weeks of the cabinet squabbles and the Robertson nomination, laid him low once again. He may have been more exhausted than anything else, but he was certainly in no condition to venture forth, marked man as he was, emotionally drained by the bitter summer, into the competitive world of private legal practice.[2]

Conkling spent the rest of the summer at home in Utica, back in the gray stone house in Rutger Park. Sitting in the house, or out on the spacious lawn, staring down John Street toward the Mohawk, alone with his thoughts, Roscoe must on occasion have looked back with regret on some of the events of the recent past, but if he harbored any such feel-

[1] Quoted in *The Independent,* Aug. 4, 1881. See letters of Conkling to A. T. Brown on his disinclination to speak or take much interest in politics, Aug. 4, 1884, Conkling Letters; April 1, 1886, Conkling Papers, New-York Historical Society.

[2] See letter of Conkling to Joseph C. G. Kennedy of Oct. 24, 1881, referring to his illness, "And tho better I am the worse for the visitation." Conkling Letters.

ings he always kept them well concealed from public view. He never made any attempt to explain, to justify, to correct the record. He had exposed too much of himself to the world in the dreadful days at Albany. Now he retreated behind an impenetrable wall of personal containment. The world must take him as it would.

One unfortunate strain to which Conkling was subjected was the old Kate Chase Sprague matter. Though Julia had been compliant and acquiesced in his philandering while the affair persisted, she gave Roscoe some difficulty about it in the early summer of 1881. Kate filed for divorce from her husband that spring, and the litigation was pounced on by the press; for a while it was a sensational staple of the gazettes, and of course the name of Roscoe Conkling was bandied about freely.[3] This was most painful to Julia, and she apparently commented to friends on a few occasions about her part in the Conkling domestic situation. In the midst of his ordeal at Albany, on June 29, Roscoe wrote his wife a sternly chiding letter:

Do you not think it better to abstain with acquaintances from discussing family affairs of a private nature? Your habit *was* not to do so, and any modification of it has not I think been for the better. . . . Then, too, we understand some affairs quite differently, and unless onesided statements are allowed to go without comment we may get into the predicament of contradicting each other. No answer to this is needed. I suggest it for your consideration only.

This remarkable letter was just too much for Julia. After all, she recalled that it had been he who had cuckolded his former Senate colleague, who had been chased from his mistress's bedroom in a state of undress, who had carried on a heedlessly public love affair, while she tended her gardens and her clubs in Utica. Dare he task her with flaunting the Conkling home life in public? She had long been meek and submissive, but now she too took pen in hand:

I cannot agree that no answer is needed to your letter. I confess I feel dismayed that years of well tested loyalty fail to outweigh the stories of talebearers or mischief makers & that I am subjected to criticism on their account. I do not discuss private affairs with acquaintances. . . . My course has been to live quietly, & endeavor to sustain my dignity and yours by pursuing the even tenor of my way in silence. These "family difficulties"—a

[3] I. Ross, *Proud Kate,* pp. 261–262. After a while, the publicity was calmed down, and a discreet settlement worked out.

phrase I copy from the newspapers, have not been of my making, & my most strenuous efforts have been made to avert comment.[4]

After his final defeat for the Senate, Roscoe came back to Utica and made his peace with Julia. There was clearly, after a quarter-century of an unfortunate marriage, no love remaining. Perhaps Conkling felt he could ill afford at this time a domestic contretemps on top of everything else. In any event, he spent no more time in Utica than previously, for his law practice was in Manhattan, but he never thereafter involved the family name in any personal scandal. He still came back to Utica to vote. And, in the summer of 1883, when Conkling went west again, touring the Yellowstone country by rail, Julia accompanied him.

Late in the fall, Conkling left once again for New York City to resume the practice of law. Still ailing, in debt, an object of public hatred and scorn from recent events, his prospects did not look bright. Roscoe, though, remembered one fact that his critics and detractors overlooked: he knew that he was a good lawyer. He was, as ever, confident of success. Though his long absence from the bar may have dulled his attention to close and intricate legal reasoning, Roscoe Conkling was very intelligent, he was an excellent speaker, he knew a great many important and wealthy people, and, in spite of his recent troubles, he still carried himself with an air which demanded victory. His career at the New York bar over the next six and a half years was astonishing in the magnitude of its brilliance for such a late starting date, but it should not have surprised those who knew Roscoe Conkling as more than the washed-up political boss depicted by the newspapers.

Conkling took up lodgings on West 29th Street, next door to the offices of the New York Bar Association, and he opened a small office on Nassau Street, where he shared a law library with another lawyer. He refused several offers of partnership; he had always been essentially a loner, and he would succeed or fail by his own efforts. He found at first that he was physically unable to work more than half a day, and he tailored his efforts to his available strength. But clients sought him out.

Jay Gould came to see him, and so did young Thomas Alva Edison. Edison needed legal aid in some patent problems, and Gould always

---

[4] Both letters are in Conkling Papers, Library of Congress. Julia added that, when blamed by Roscoe's friends for not accompanying him to Washington, she had stated that "you preferred I should remain in Utica—that press of public affairs interfered with domestic life."

needed a good lawyer. The sly, imaginative, unscrupulous financier was usually up to his neck in legal tangles, and he was constantly on the lookout for a lawyer with an analytical touch for the complex corporate and financial webs that he wove. In Conkling, Gould found a master of corporate law, and until Roscoe's death he was Gould's attorney. Jay Gould was no angel, to say the least, but a lawyer is not required to judge his client. The experts who kept predicting Roscoe Conkling's impending return to the politcial wars might have stopped to recognize that representation of the unsavory financier would have been a considerable handicap for a practicing politician.[5]

About a year after he started, Conkling's gain in health made an even more active practice possible, and he moved his offices to larger quarters at the corner of Wall Street and Broadway and had his own law library brought down from Utica. He was building a practice in equity litigation, which in effect meant corporate law.

Conkling appeared as counsel in many important cases in the New York and federal courts, as his legal reputation grew. He was getting excellent results for his clients, and the word got around quickly. His old friend Collis P. Huntington, the West Coast railroad baron, retained him, and he defended the New York *World,* which as a Democratic paper had abused him down through the years, in several libel actions (the *World* had come under the control of Jay Gould). He appeared as counsel for the contestant in a famous and lengthy suit to break the will of Jesse Hoyt, a self-made grain merchant, who left the income but no principal of a $7,000,000 estate to his eccentric daughter, Conkling's client. Conkling here had the pleasure of battling in court against his old enemy Evarts.[6]

One of the judges before whom Conkling practiced later wrote, in words reminiscent of John Hay's complaint about Conkling's dominance over his senatorial colleagues: "Mr. Conkling was unquestionably one of the greatest trial lawyers that the State ever produced, and as an advocate he had few, if any, equals in the country. Give him the last speech to a jury, and if the case was evenly balanced on the evidence, he would win a verdict. He did not persuade the jury, he overpowered

[5] The best background on Conkling's return to the law is in Scott, pp. 197–198. See also Ross, *Proud Kate,* p. 264.

[6] Scott, p. 199; Barrows, pp. 234–236. After Conkling's death, his client in the Hoyt case was represented by Benjamin F. Butler and Roger Pryor, and eventually she lost the case. As a further ironic note, Evarts wes elected to succeed Lapham in the U.S. Senate in 1885—to Conkling's old seat.

them and made his will theirs." Summing up, the judge said, "Take him all and all, as a lawyer and advocate, his equal has rarely been seen in the country." [7]

Meanwhile, affairs of state continued in Washington, though they were of little immediate interest to Conkling. After Garfield's death and the inauguration of his successor, the new president showed his first signs of independence in a stout refusal to live in the White House until the mansion had undergone an extensive cleaning and redecoration. Chester Arthur's home on Lexington Avenue had accustomed him to comfortable, elegant living, and his expert eye immediately told him that the White House, for all the glory of the place, was a frowsy establishment. Arthur got rid of a lot of the seedier furnishing and set to work to spruce the house up. In the meantime he moved in with Senator J. P. Jones of Nevada, a close friend of both Conkling and Arthur.

The knowledge of the new president's temporary domicile caused some public dismay when, during the week after Arthur's inauguration, Jones journeyed off to Utica to visit with Roscoe Conkling. All of the forces which had long been opposed to the Stalwarts bemoaned the Jones visit as an indication that there was really to be a barely disguised Conkling administration. Speculation of this nature swelled when Conkling himself went to Washington on October 8 and had a long visit with President Arthur.

Conkling, though, really intended to leave politics. He did not desire to be the power behind the throne of Chester Arthur, and the role would not have suited him, though it would be several years before his old enemies would acquit him of devious participation in the political affairs of the day. Roscoe Conkling always led from in front, where he could be on the firing-line. All he wanted from Arthur was Robertson's discharge as collector. But Chester Arthur, at least, had learned a great deal in those eventful months since the Chicago convention, those months of bitter fraternal warfare within the Republican party, mostly inspired or led by Roscoe Conkling. The blood-letting must come to an end, and if it was to do so it must start now. Robertson, for his symbolic value if for no other reason, must stay; it was for just the same symbolic value that Conkling wanted him to go. For Roscoe Conkling, the discharge of Robertson would be a semblance of vindication of the last meaningful act of his political career. The request showed that he

[7] A. Chester, ed., *Legal and Judicial History of New York*, III, 223.

cared hardly at all about the fate of Arthur's administration, for such a discharge would have doomed any hopes of Republican reconciliation under the new president's guidance.

Arthur told his old mentor that the demand was outrageous and that Robertson would be kept on. Conkling became enraged, accused Arthur of disloyalty, and swore that all of his friends had turned traitor to him. The scene was ugly, and it destroyed an old friendship. But Robertson stayed.[8]

Arthur was a better president than was expected—or feared. He worked hard at the job, rising late in the morning but working long into the night, often over a convivial glass with his advisers. He tried to keep in mind that his constituency was now the American people. He once said: "For the Vice-Presidency I was indebted to Mr. Conkling, but for the Presidency of the United States my debt is to the Almighty." [9]

In his first annual message, on December 6, 1881, Arthur asked for legislation toward the reform of the civil service, and this request eventually turned into the Pendleton Act, which the president signed into law on January 16, 1883, the first comprehensive legislative step toward rational control of the civil service in the nation's history. Irony lay in the fact that this measure was signed by a president who had been discharged from a subordinate position for alleged patronage abuses.[10]

Arthur took courageous though unsuccessful stands in vetoing a treaty-breaching Chinese exclusion bill and an over-stuffed rivers-and-harbors bill. His veto of the "pork-barrel" bill generated much public acclaim, but Congress went ahead and passed it over his veto.[11]

[8] Howe, p. 158. Hudson, pp. 126–127. Interestingly, while Arthur refused Conkling's request to fire Robertson, Blaine was writing to Whitelaw Reid on Dec. 21, 1881, "I tell you Arthur means death and political destruction to every Garfield man. The more licks you get in quickly the better." Reid Papers.

[9] A. D. White, I, 194. Arthur's wife Ellen died Jan. 12, 1880, prior to his gaining the vice-presidency, so that Arthur was denied that solace in his lonely new job.

[10] On Dec. 10, 1881, Rutherford Hayes confided to his diary that Arthur's message to Congress indicated that he "has no faith in the reform, but in deference to public sentiment he yields." C. R. Williams, ed., IV, 52.

[11] State Papers of Chester A. Arthur, President of the United States, pp. 73–82, for the veto of the Chinese exclusion bill, and pp. 113–117 for the "pork-barrel" veto. In his message, Arthur (who followed good Conklinian doctrine here) pointed out that because of the log-rolling and back-scratching aspects of rivers-and-harbors legislation, "As the bill becomes more objectionable, it secures more support."

In another noteworthy development, Arthur's administration took the lead in modernizing and rebuilding the United States Navy, which had fallen into sad disrepair after the Civil War. The president emphasized the need for an up-to-date navy again and again. The establishment of a powerful fleet was a lengthy process, but it had its start during Arthur's presidency.

One of the least creditable aspects of Arthur's presidency was the less than vigorous prosecution of the Star Route swindlers. Actions begun by James and Wayne MacVeagh under Garfield were left to fizzle out under the new administration.

Many of Arthur's old opponents were won over by his independent course as president. Down in Louisville, Henry Watterson, who rarely had a civil word for any Republican, said that he found Chester Alan Arthur to be "a man of surpassing sweetness and grace." [12]

But Roscoe Conkling was no longer charmed by his former aide. When Roscoe's old crony Ward Hunt retired from the U.S. Supreme Court on January 7, 1882, after several years of disability, Arthur on February 24 named Conkling to the vacancy, incurring the disapproval of much of the nation. Chief Justice Waite was definitely not enchanted with the prospect of having Roscoe as a colleague. *Harper's* said the appointment caused "universal amazement," and Godkin attacked Conkling as "a lawyer only in name" who "must make a poor judge." Besides, "he has been offered the Chief Justiceship of the same Court once before, and declined it as beneath his notice." Nevertheless, the Senate on March 2 confirmed the nomination by a vote of 39 to 12, whereupon, for a second time, Conkling turned down a place on the nation's highest court. Arthur's next appointment, Samuel Blatchford of New York, received more general approval and was confirmed as well. The president's handling of the court vacancy was widely criticized, but he had, with the Supreme Court nomination, discharged his obligations to his old leader.[13]

Conkling was not pacified by the appointment, however; he was angry that Arthur chose not to run an unashamed Stalwart administration. He was heard to refer to Arthur from time to time as "the stalled ox of the White House." He sneered at him as "His Accidency," and a statement he gave to a reporter for the Cincinnati *Commercial-Gazette,* printed on

[12] Wall, p. 187.

[13] *The Nation,* March 2, 1882. *Harper's Weekly,* March 11, 1882. Warren, II, 623–624; Howe, p. 195.

April 12, 1883, was widely quoted: "I have but one annoyance with the Administration of President Arthur, and that is, that, in contrast with it, the Administration of Hayes becomes respectable, if not heroic." [14]

In any event, Conkling's interest was focused on an important piece of litigation in which he was involved. Huntington's Southern Pacific Railroad was having tax troubles out in California. San Mateo County, just south of San Francisco, started suit in the county court in April 1882, to collect a tax claim levied against the railroad. The line filed an answer, saying the tax was discriminatory and illegal, and had the case removed to the federal court. On September 25, 1882, judgment was entered in favor of the defendant, and the county immediately took a writ of error to the U.S. Supreme Court. There the case was "elaborately argued" on December 19, 1882, on the railroad's behalf by Roscoe Conkling and George Edmunds, still a U.S. senator.[15]

Edmunds carried a small part of the burden, but the spectacular portion of the argument was Conkling's. Conkling always performed well before the high court; Mr. Justice Miller once said, "for the discussion of the law and the facts of the case Mr. Conkling is the best lawyer who comes into our court." [16] He set out to demonstrate to the court that the tax upon which the suit was brought, admittedly assessed only against railroads, was discriminatory and contrary to "due process" as applied to the states by the Fourteenth Amendment. The task was not an easy one, for the Supreme Court, in 1872, had ruled in the *Slaughter-House Cases,* 16 Wallace 36, that the intent of the Fourteenth Amendment "due process" clause was the protection of black freedmen— period. Roscoe Conkling had to overturn this opinion, to convince particularly Justice Miller, who had written the earlier opinion and still sat on the court, that corporate bodies were entitled to due process of law. The economic implications, though, were immense. Conkling's point, if carried, would have ramifications far beyond those of the particular case.

"The people of all the States in Congress assembled," he said, "and the people of the States themselves, went to the trouble of so amending the National Constitution as to forbid, and as far as they could to pre-

[14] *Ibid.,* pp. 215, 244. See also Merritt, p. 148. Conkling was but one of the old members of the machine to break with Arthur. Cornell, Platt, Woodford, Morton and Crowley were also found in the same situation.

[15] *San Mateo County v. Southern Pacific Railroad Company,* 116 U.S. 138 (1885), No. 1063, Oct. Term 1882.

[16] Boutwell, II, 265.

vent, the very thing which boisterous agitation drove California to do."
Conkling's argument was that the Fourteenth Amendment provision,
"nor shall any State deprive any person of life, liberty, or property,
without due process of law," was intended to protect not only the im-
pecunious Negro freedman but also those juridical entities, those legal
"persons," business corporations.

This was the section which John Bingham of Ohio had worked into
the amendment, even though Roscoe Conkling had shown very little interest in it at the time. Now, however, Roscoe was very interested, and
he had a surprise ready for the august judges of the Supreme Court.

During his argument, Conkling produced a musty old book, which
turned out to be a copy of the unpublished "Journal of the Joint Committee on Reconstruction," of which he had been a member. In the
course of his discussion, he quoted passages from the journal in an
attempt to prove his point. The members of the committee, Conkling
argued, *meant* to include within the amendment's protection corporate
bodies equally with individuals. "From Runnymede to Appomattox,"
he said, "the jewel for which civilized man has fought has been the law
of the land and equality before the law."

Individuals and joint stock companies were appealing for congressional
and administrative protection against invidious and discriminating state and
local taxes. . . . Those who devised the Fourteenth Amendment wrote in
grave sincerity. They planted in the Constitution a monumental truth. . . .
That truth is but the Golden Rule, so entrenched as to curb the many who
would do to the few as they would not have the few do to them.[17]

The importance of Conkling's argument was that it aided in the creation by the Supreme Court of the doctrine of "substantive due process,"
under which for decades states were forbidden to tamper with the industrial and financial monoliths which grew up within their boundaries.
Though historians have on occasion been inclined to accord too much
credit to the single argument, it is clear that Roscoe Conkling, speaking
with the insider's authority and presuming on that fact for the benefit
of his client, pointed the way for a court which was only too eager to
follow, and state regulation of business abuses was set back decisively.

---

[17] *Transcript of Records, U. S. Supreme Court,* vol. 536, Conkling Argument
pp. 1–64; Conkling's commentary on the Fourteenth Amendment is discussed
as well in Stampp, p. 137; H. K. Beale, p. 218; Warren, II, 541; and in the
introduction to Kendrick. No evidence has been found that really supports
Conkling's argument. Andrew C. McLaughlin, in his scholarly analysis of the

"Substantive due process" lived on to bedevil Franklin D. Roosevelt and his New Deal, but the change in the Supreme Court starting in the late 1930's finally dealt the concept a death blow. The doctrine flourished for many years, however, years in which the economic destiny of the country was shaped, and Roscoe Conkling bears much of the responsibility for giving it a respectable birth, in his argument in the *San Mateo* case. It is ironic that Conkling, who was often criticized during his long Senate career for showing little interest in the business and commercial sectors of the community, accomplished so much in these areas indirectly through his legal career.

The actual disposition of the *San Mateo* case was anticlimactical. The railroad made some payments, and the court decided that these satisfied whatever claim the county had. The case was declared moot.

Conkling took no part in the state convention of 1881. Indeed, his name was even rejected as a contesting delegate from Oneida County by the convention, which was firmly controlled by his enemies. There is no evidence, though, that the senator had anything to do with the presentation of his name. The disaster prefigured in the bitter struggle of the spring and summer overtook the party in the fall. The Republicans were overwhelmed in the November elections, as the Stalwart–Half-Breed war continued on another field. Many Republicans supported Democrats in preference to their intraparty rivals.

Conkling had no official part in the Republicans' 1882 blood-letting. In the convention that year, Alonzo B. Cornell sought a well-deserved renomination, but a scandalously rigged convention gave the position to Judge Folger. Arthur had not forgotten Cornell's indifference in the summer of 1881, and he put the weight of the national administration behind Folger. Conkling was for Folger, too, because the jurist, who had gone into Arthur's cabinet as secretary of the treasury (the post Garfield had declined to offer him), had remained loyal to him and because Cornell, in his eyes, had not. Jay Gould was against Cornell, because the governor had vetoed an elevated railways bill which Gould had shepherded through the legislature. Cornell later claimed that both Gould and his lawyer, Conkling, would have been for him if not for the veto, but this seems unlikely. Gould might have been, but Roscoe Conkling

Conkling argument in the *San Mateo* case, concludes that "Conkling's handling of the material was not altogether commendable." A. C. McLaughlin, "The Court, the Corporation, and Conkling," p. 55.

was not the kind to forget disloyalty such as Cornell had perpetrated.[18]

Arthur's major foray into intraparty politics during his term as president, the Folger nomination turned out disastrously. The scandal about the state convention and the lingering split in the party were too much for Folger. He was swamped by the little-known mayor of Buffalo, Grover Cleveland, going under by 190,000 votes. New York's Republicans were in complete disarray.

Two years later, this same Grover Cleveland, now the well-known governor of New York, was the Democratic candidate for president. The struggle for the Republican nomination at the party convention in Chicago was between Arthur and Blaine, who had left the state department shortly after Garfield's death. Arthur felt that his services as president entitled him to a second term, but Stalwart dissatisfaction at his failure to institute a campaign of reprisal when he became president deprived him of many votes which he expected, while the well-organized Blaine ranks stayed intact. One of the seconding speeches for Blaine was given by Tom Platt, of all people. It took four ballots, but the man from Maine finally achieved his nomination, though many in the reform elements of the party warned that they would not support Blaine. Down through the years Blaine had had too many questionable involvements and had left too many unresolved suspicions. The man had an unhealthy air about him of lust for money. 1884 was to be the year of the Mugwumps.

It was an intensely dirty campaign. As was so often true, there were few party issues of any importance, so the campaign orators were able to concentrate on personalities. For a while, this was an uneven contest, for Cleveland's rigid integrity contrasted sharply with Blaine's checkered past. Then someone came up with the story of the Widow Halpin and the illegitimate child which Cleveland may or may not have fathered, and the mudslinging started in earnest.

Blaine recognized that his toughest task would be to carry New York, with its shattered Republican party. He and his advisers felt that the best way to win the Empire State would be to enlist Roscoe Conkling in his behalf. One day a group of Blaine workers called upon the former senator, to ask if he would consent to speak for Blaine. Conkling, savoring the moment, surely must have toted up in his mind the indignities

[18] See Alexander, III, 493, and Gosnell, pp. 30–31, for Cornell's theory that the veto cost him Conkling's support. See also letter from J. N. Matthews, editor of the Buffalo *Express,* to Cornell, Oct. 31, 1882, referring to communications from Conkling to Matthews about Cornell that "might surprise if not pain you." Cornell Papers.

suffered at the hands of the Republican nominee—from the "turkey-gobbler strut" to Robertson and the humiliation at Albany—as he drew himself up and replied, "No, thank you, I don't engage in criminal practice." [19]

Additionally, Conkling was said to have passed the word among his friends in Utica to support the Democratic candidate. When Blaine came barnstorming through Utica, he received a very chilly reception, including a shout, when his train started to pull out, "All aboard for Little Rock!" The New York *World,* for which Conkling was counsel, printed savage attacks on Blaine, the manuscript of one of which was later alleged to have been in Conkling's handwriting. The press spoke openly of Stalwart distaste for Blaine; and a group of Stalwart Republicans in Oneida County, perhaps inspired by Roscoe Conkling, came out openly for Cleveland.[20]

What part Conkling played in these various endeavors is open to conjecture, but it is undeniable that Blaine lost the election because he lost New York State by some 1,049 votes. The Reverend Burchard, and his classic allusion to "Rum, Romanism, and Rebellion," cost a lot of votes, as did Blaine's ill-advised attendance at a feast at Delmonico's with "the money kings." Yet he still could have won the state. Look, though, at another statistic: Oneida County, which had gone Republican for Garfield in 1880 by 2,053 votes, went to Cleveland by 19. Blaine and the insiders knew that Conkling had squared accounts. Roscoe Conkling surely must have smiled.[21]

With Blaine brought to grief, Conkling continued his growing legal career. "He was employed in a great many important causes," wrote one observer. "His clients ranked him, and rated the value of his ser-

[19] Mitchell, p. 548.

[20] Nevins, *Cleveland,* 178; Mitchell, p. 548. Billy Hudson of the Brooklyn *Eagle* tells a long story about a trip he was sent on to Boston by Conkling and Senator Arthur Gorman of the Democratic national committee. Hudson picked up a package of papers which he delivered unopened to Gorman, but he always suspected they were the second batch of Mulligan Letters, released to the press shortly thereafter; Hudson, pp. 199–204. Afterwards, the New York *World* reported on Nov. 11, 1884, that Conkling was serving as counsel to the Democrats during the count of the vote in New York.

[21] Lucretia Garfield wrote a note of sympathy to Mrs. Blaine on Nov. 18, 1884, in which she demonstrated the extreme bitterness toward Conkling which still animated her: "For you personally, my dear friend, I cannot be sorry. The treacherous foe did not lurk in camp to help elect Mr. Blaine, and with his diabolic hatred then arm the assassin. Your husband is spared to you." Blaine Papers.

vices very high." And, indeed, he charged heavy fees; "my father," he said, "would denounce me if he knew what charges I am making." His income grew tremendously, and he was able to lead a comfortable life in New York. He even treated himself in 1885 to a three-month vacation in Europe.[22]

Conkling had always been a loner; always intolerant of those he considered inferior to himself, he honestly believed that most men fit into this category. He lived a solitary existence in New York, though his social life was as active as he desired it to be. As a famous personage, and as a famous lawyer, he was frequently invited to the elegant gatherings of Manhattan society, but he picked his functions with care. He dined often with Hamilton Fish in the ex-secretary's tastefully elegant home on Stuyvesant Square, where the two men could discuss the good old days of the Grant administration. Most of the time, though, Conkling kept to himself.[23]

On occasion, Roscoe would sit in the tavern at the Hoffman House, of which his apartment was an annex, observing humanity as it passed by. He always drank sparingly, and he continued that rule. Probably, he was merely passing time.

One evening in 1885, Conkling attended the eightieth birthday party given in honor of the eminent lawyer David Dudley Field at the Gramercy Park home of Field's brother Cyrus. An onlooker described Conkling: "He looks even taller and straighter and more muscular than ever. . . . His hair has turned quite gray and the famous hyacinthine curl above his forehead has entirely vanished. His voice is smooth and rich; his words are measured and deliberate, carrying the weight of a special personal authority. But he . . . does not glow with love for the human race."

The same onlooker then tells of a reporter from Boston being presented to Conkling and saying, effusively, "Senator! I have known and admired you so as a public man that I have very much wished to meet you."

Conkling, however, answered superciliously, "Ah! There was a time, sir, when that confession would have deeply moved me; but now I am impassive and have scarcely any longer, as the Declaration of Independence says, 'a decent regard for the opinions of mankind.' "

[22] Shipman, p. 80; "His fees were enormous," N.Y. *Tribune,* April 18, 1888. Boutwell, II, 265.
[23] Nevins, *Fish,* II, 901.

The Boston reporter turned away, crushed. Roscoe Conkling had not changed, even though he was out of politics.[24]

In February, 1886, Conkling suddenly appeared as counsel to a special committee of the state senate investigating the circumstances surrounding the franchising of the Broadway Surface Railway. This surprising role for Conkling was thought by many to be a step back into politics, but they were wrong. Simply, the investigation was a challenge, it was a job that needed doing, and he was paid for it. Whatever his motives, Conkling and his co-counsel, Clarence Seward, did a masterly job. An energetic traction entrepreneur named Jacob Sharp had dispensed bribes amounting to a half million dollars to the New York Board of Aldermen, receiving in return the franchise for the Broadway line. The "boodle aldermen," as they were commonly called, were confident that nothing could be pinned on them; they called Conkling and the committee members "a big lot of stuffs" when it looked as if no actual evidence of bribery could be produced. Ultimately, however, Conkling's persistence and skill paid off, and those aldermen who had not fled the jurisdiction were arrested one by one for accepting bribes. Though, as it turned out, evidence sufficient for courtroom convictions of the aldermen was lacking, Sharp himself was jailed and the legislature passed bills drafted by Conkling and Seward annulling the charter given to Sharp and his company. Conkling's calm competence and forensic brilliance won him much praise from press and public.[25]

Death was depleting the ranks of Conkling's old political associates. Horatio Seymour died on February 12, 1886, in the midst of the Broad-

[24] W. A. Croffut, *An American Procession: 1855–1914*, pp. 257–258. The Field brothers, who gave the party, were an impressive lot. David, the oldest, was one of the most eminent lawyers in the U.S., famous for the major cases he had handled and for his codifications of New York and international law. Stephen, the next oldest, was an associate justice of the United States Supreme Court. Cyrus, among his other accomplishments, promoted the first Atlantic cable. The youngest brother, Henry, a Presbyterian minister, was the well-known author of several travel books and biographies of his brothers David and Cyrus.

[25] The speculation about Conkling's motive on taking the post as counsel was in N.Y. *Times,* Feb. 23, 1886, and the "lot of stuffs" comment was in N.Y. *Times,* March 4, 1886. The investigation went on through the spring of 1886 and produced interesting items like the incrimination of one man by letters written by his son to the son's girlfriend, later rejected. The disappointed young lady, at the appropriate time, shipped the letters off to Conkling. See also Jessup, I, 149–150.

way Railroad investigation, but Conkling did not return to Utica until
the day of the funeral itself, though his brother-in-law's death had occurred in the house in Rutger Park. Roscoe's older brother Frederick
was asked to be a pallbearer, but Roscoe was not. The Seymours generally were not as forgiving as Julia was.

Later in the year, on November 18, Chester Alan Arthur died of a
cerebral hemorrhage and Bright's disease. Because of the estrangement
during Arthur's presidential years, there was fear that Conkling would
not attend the funeral, but he showed up and sat directly behind Alonzo
Cornell, showing, it is said, sincere grief.[26]

Reuben Fenton had died the year before, and Grant had too, just
after finishing his memoirs while waging a courageous battle against
cancer. The memoirs, covering only the general's war years, were tremendously successful, and Adam Badeau became involved in litigation
with Mrs. Grant, claiming an interest in the authorship and in the profits. She did what her husband had done so often when in trouble and
turned to Roscoe Conkling. He was representing her in defending against
Badeau's claim at the time of his own death.[27] Even for Grant, though,
Conkling would not break the self-imposed ban on speaking engagements. When asked to deliver a eulogy upon his old leader, he declined;
his speeches were made only in court now.

Another old associate, Andrew D. White, who had twenty years earlier called for the election of Conkling to the Senate to give New York
a voice in that body, gave a long interview to a New York *Tribune* reporter on the subject of civil service reform. In the course of his talk,
which was published on September 12, 1887, White recalled telling
Senator Conkling, at a time when the latter reigned supreme in New
York through Grant's favor, that his use of patronage hurt him more
than it helped. If there are forty applicants for a job, he remembered
saying to Conkling, only one can be satisfied, while thirty-nine become
enemies. But, he continued, Conkling "thought differently and went on
making the appointments. The years went on and his political enemies
within the Republican party grew larger and larger in number. He kept
them under for a long time by his will, but finally they rose up and
crushed him."

For some reason, Conkling, who generally ignored what was said by
the press about him, was infuriated by the White article. He wrote three

[26] Howe, p. 287.   [27] Ross, *General's Wife,* p. 318.

letters to White, who characterized them as "outrageous," and "long and abusive." White replied, even consulting Alonzo Cornell at one point. The exchange continued until the end of October.[28]

The letters were eventually destroyed by the correspondents, so we can only conjecture as to their contents. Perhaps Conkling reiterated what he had said over the years, that he was not interested in patronage, since he made recommendations for only a very few fairly high offices. This was somewhat disingenuous, of course, since the holders of these offices, the collectors and the postmasters, knew very well what to do with the jobs at *their* disposal. It was also not really accurate; Arthur corresponded frequently with Conkling and others about the senator's preferences concerning various available appointments. It may have been that Conkling wrote to correct White's misunderstanding about the nature of the perfidious enemies in the party who had finally compassed the senator's overthrow. Roscoe's candid thoughts about these old adversaries may well have curled the edges of his letter paper. Cornell, perhaps, came in for such abuse as the former senator might choose to hurl at an ingrate and traitor. Whatever the subject of Conkling's letters, it is clear that he expressed himself with the bitter invective of old, startling even a man of the world like Andrew White. These three letters, too, may have been Roscoe Conkling's only attempt at a justification of his career to posterity. Unfortunately, we shall never know.

[28] See Ogden, ed., pp. 272–274, for White's side of what he called "my Conkling imbroglio." White destroyed his file of the correspondence on Aug. 29, 1901, as did Conkling shortly before his death. As White said later, "It became angry on both sides" (p. 372).

CHAPTER 28

DEATH RIDES A BLIZZARD

Sunday, March 11, 1888, was a miserable day in New York City. "Early in the afternoon," wrote a reporter, "the rain fell upon the just and the unjust with no discrimination except such as resulted from the interposition of umbrellas . . . and the starless night gave little indication of brighter hours in the near future." The forecast for March 12 was "clearing and colder, preceded by light snow." [1]

This prediction was seen by very few, though, for when New Yorkers awoke on Monday morning, their newspapers were covered by a vast blanket of snow or blown away by a howling wind. The heavy rain of the evening before had turned to sleet as the temperature dropped sharply, and at ten minutes after midnight it turned to snow. This was the start of the Blizzard of '88. [2]

The conjunction of two low-pressure centers, one coming east from the Rockies, the other north from Georgia, caused the storm. Instead of blowing out to sea, as each might normally have done, they joined and formed a mammoth storm area off the Jersey coast. This storm center was then held stationary over Block Island by a mass of freezing Canadian air, while the blizzard raged over the East Coast and New England. The results were devastating.

New York was simply "knocked out," "paralyzed," and reduced to a condition of suspended animation. Traffic was practically stopped, and business abandoned. The elevated railway service broke down completely . . . the street-cars were valueless; the suburban railways were blocked; telegraph communications were cut; the Exchanges did nothing; the Mayor didn't

[1] N.Y. *Tribune,* March 12, 1888.
[2] Most of the material on the Blizzard is from I. Werstein, *The Blizzard of '88,* and the New York *Tribune* for the days following the storm.

visit his office; the city was left to run itself; chaos reigned, and the proud, boastful metropolis was reduced to the condition of a primitive settlement.[3]

"The wind and the snow did it all," wrote one reporter, adding that "never before" was there "such a terrific combination" of the two.

At seven in the morning, the storm, already a heavy snowfall, got worse. The wind shrieked and howled in gusts up to 75 miles per hour. The fierce gale only intensified the cold, and that was bad enough, with temperatures ranging from eleven degrees above to one degree below zero. Sixteen and a half inches of snow fell in New York on Monday, and four inches more on Tuesday. This total did not match the fifty inches which piled up on Connecticut and eastern Massachusetts, but it was quite sufficient to tie up the city as never before.

The wind built up huge drifts which became impassable because there was no chance for them to be packed down. The drifting snow cut off almost all means of transportation in the city, with the exception of an occasional sturdy carriage driver, who raised his rates to compensate for his extraordinary efforts. Those people who had somehow made it downtown to work in the morning soon found themselves with no way to get home again. The grog shops, cigar shops, and "gent's furnishing" stores (where earmuffs and scarfs and an extra sweater might be purchased, at sharply increased prices) did good business, but everything else came to a standstill. The elevated railway trains were also blocked, but their passengers could leave their roosts only at peril of life and limb. Live electrical wires were down all over the streets, making an additional hazard for beleaguered pedestrians.

Roscoe Conkling had a hearing in court. He represented the proponent of the will of the widow of A. T. Stewart, the merchant, and he was defending it against attempts to break it. It was an important case, with a great deal of money involved, and large legal fees as well. He showed up in court on Monday morning, undaunted by the snowfall, and prepared to go on with the case. Word was received from the judge, however, that he was snowbound and the hearing was set over to the next day.

Roscoe went back to his office and worked for several hours. Just because it was snowing outside was no reason for a man to shirk his practice. Late in the afternoon, though, he decided perhaps he had better get an early start home. As he left his office he hailed a cab and

[3] N.Y. *Tribune,* March 13, 1888.

asked the driver to take him to the New York Club, at Madison Square. The driver told him that the trip would cost $50, and Conkling indignantly refused to pay any such fare. He set out on foot to walk the two and half miles. "I had an ugly tramp in the dark," he wrote later, describing "drifts so high that my head bumped against the signs, and . . . fallen, snarled telegraph wires." The blizzard in front made it hard to stand, and it was "so cold as to close the eyes with ice. . . . Bumps and falls and strains and tugs made it quite an interesting excursion." [4]

It must have been quite a sight—the tall, vigorous warrior, now 59, plowing resolutely forward in the great storm, heedless of the buffeting and slips. "It was dark and it was useless to pick out a path," Conkling said later, "so I went magnificently along, shouldering through drifts and headed for the north." At Union Square, "pretty well exhausted," as he put it, Conkling cut through the park and blundered into a huge drift, in which he was buried up to his armpits. He exhausted himself in an hour's struggle to break free from the snowbank, and when he finally reached his club, "covered all over with ice and packed snow," he pitched over unconscious after crossing the threshhold. He had been three hours battling the storm.[5]

Notwithstanding his collapse, Roscoe Conkling was back in court the next morning, though the blizzard was still raging. His narrow escape, as it was thought, was regarded as one of the more interesting items from the storm. For several weeks, Roscoe pursued his active career in the courts, devoting most of his time to the Stewart will case, with some attention to the preparation and filing of an answer on behalf of Mrs. Grant in Badeau's suit.

On the evening of March 30, however, after he had spent the day in a hearing held in a room which was inadequately heated, Conkling complained of a pain in his head. When this pain became severe, he sent for his personal physician, Dr. Fordyce Barker, who examined him and found an abscess in the inner right ear. Dr. Barker was of the opinion

[4] *Ibid.*, April 18.

[5] Conkling told his story to the New York *World*, March 14, 1888. Many years later, William Sulzer, a future mayor but in 1888 a young lawyer with offices on the same floor as Conkling's, remembered that he had marched along in the snow behind Conkling as far as the Astor House, where he quit and tried to persuade Roscoe to do so too. Sulzer to D. A. Woodhouse, Aug. 6, 1934, "Blizzard Men of 1888—Reminiscences," New-York Historical Society.

that the cause of this malady was the exposure suffered by Conkling in the blizzard, coupled with exhaustion. Barker put his patient to bed and summoned Dr. D. Hayes Agnew of Philadelphia, an eminent physician who had, ironically, been a member of the team treating Garfield after his shooting.

There were complications, primarily an inflammation of the adjacent brain membranes. A very high temperature, reaching 104½ at one point, alarmed the physicians, and Conkling became "mildly delirious." After several days of complete isolation, during which not even Julia or Bessie was allowed to see him, Conkling rallied, to the point where Dr. Barker told the press on April 7 that the ex-senator "would soon be himself again."

The next day, though, Roscoe suddenly became much worse, and the *Tribune* led off the front-page article by saying that "his life hangs in the balance." His temperature soared again, his pulse rate quickened alarmingly, and he was in a constant state of delirium, leaping out of bed and pacing wildly around his room and one adjoining. Doctors and friends were hardly able to subdue the patient. Finally, they decided upon an operation "to relieve the brain of the pressure of pus on it," as the *Tribune* put it on April 10. Dr. Barker, now aided by four additional physicians despite losing Agnew to an illness of his own, felt that the operation was necessary to save Conkling's life. Dr. Henry B. Sands performed the actual surgery, drilling a hole into the skull with mallet and chisel to remove about an ounce of pus. The pressure was relieved, though the surgeon said privately he doubted that the patient could live more than forty-eight hours.

On the tenth, no improvement was shown, although Dr. Barker was happy that Conkling was able to sleep without narcotics. He was a difficult patient, though; Ned Stokes, the owner of the Hoffman House, was the only one who had much success in getting medication into him.[6]

The next day, Conkling took a turn for the better. His delirium lessened, and he asked Julia, "Don't you think I'm better? I think I am."

Dr. Barker told the press that day: "Mr. Conkling's constitution is marvellous. No ordinary man could have stood what he has. He has wonderful vitality. Since he has been sick he has suffered not only from

[6] N.Y. *Tribune,* April 11, 1888. Stokes's last brush with fame had come when he shot and killed Jim Fisk, in an altercation over Stokes's mistress, one Josie Mansfield. Stokes served four years at Sing Sing for the murder.

the wasting due to the disease but from the wear and tear of brain and muscular tissue due to his excited condition and frequent restless pacing of the floor." [7]

On the twelfth, the doctor was complaining again about his difficult patient. Conkling kept tearing the bandage away from his head wound, and four strong men were required to get him into bed. In order to treat the wound the doctor was forced to use ether on his patient.

On Friday the 13th Conkling suffered another relapse, one which his depleted constitution could not afford. His extremities started twitching uncontrollably, and the doctor expressed the fear that Roscoe's nerves were going. The following day the head wound began suppurating again, and on Sunday bronchitis set in, bringing with it racking coughing spells. Still the amazing vitality of the man kept him alive.

As Roscoe Conkling's fight for life continued, messages and visits came from old political friends and foes alike. When a wire sent by all the Democratic members of the U. S. Senate was read to him, Conkling's eyes twinkled. It was pleasing to him, too, to receive many messages from ordinary citizens, people who remembered him from the days of his battles against the political forces of his day, urging him to overcome this last adversary.

On April 17, Conkling lapsed into a coma around noon, and Dr. Barker said he had "advanced pulmonary edema from heart failure." The press said, "The last hope for ex-Senator Conkling's recovery has departed." There was nothing more to be done. At 2:00 A.M. on the morning of April 18, 1888, Roscoe Conkling breathed his last.

The New York *Tribune,* one of his ancient enemies, said: "Peace to his ashes! A great Republican has fallen, a man among men has passed on." [8]

A memorial service was preached at the Trinity Church in New York by the Reverend Morgan Dix, New York's pre-eminent Episcopal divine. The remains were then taken by train, courtesy of Chauncey Depew's New York Central, for the last journey to Utica. A large crowd

[7] *Ibid.,* April 12. Doctor Barker, incidentally, was a very versatile physician. Although he was Conkling's doctor, his specialty was gynecology; yet he had been a star witness for the prosecution in the trial of Charles Guiteau for the murder of Garfield, testifying that the defendant was legally sane. He was a highly respected leader of the American medical profession. For a summary of Barker's testimony on Guiteau, see Rosenberg, pp. 166–169.

[8] N.Y. *Tribune,* April 18, 1888.

of the old senator's townspeople poured out to pay their last respects. In Utica, he was still the senator; some 24 per cent of the people of Oneida County had answered a survey early in 1888 by saying that their candidate for president of the United States was Roscoe Conkling. Another service was conducted, and he was laid to rest in the Forest Hill Cemetery.[9]

A little later Robert Ingersoll came to Albany at the request of the legislature—that body which had had so much to do with Roscoe Conkling's ups and downs, though he had never served in it—and delivered the eulogy:

He stood for independence, for courage, and above all for absolute integrity. . . . Roscoe Conkling was an absolutely honest man. . . . He not only acted without fear, but he had that fortitude of soul that bears the consequences of the course pursued without complaint. He was charged with being proud. The charge was true—he was proud. His knees were as inflexible as the "unwedgeable and gnarled oak," but he was not vain. Vanity rests on the opinion of others—pride, on our own. . . . And as he lived he died. Proudly he entered the darkness—or the dawn—that we call death. . . . And he has left with us his wealth of thought and deed—the memory of a brave, imperious, honest man, who bowed alone to death.[10]

"Brave, imperious, honest"—that was no doubt the way Roscoe Conkling would have wanted to be remembered.

[9] The survey was in *ibid.*, April 7. Conkling was second; Chauncey Depew had the highest total.

[10] R. G. Ingersoll, pp. 17–28. Back before Ingersoll's break with Blaine, he had called Conkling "a swill politician;" Cramer, p. 289.

CHAPTER 29

---◆◆◆◆◆---

A MAN OF HIS TIME

On January 18, 1879, when Conkling was elected to his third term in the United States Senate, the New York *Times* called him "a typical American statesman—a man by whose career and character the future will judge of the political standards of the present." This is a fascinating thought, but closer examination throws doubt upon such a pronouncement. Though his career was in certain ways representative of the era's sometimes empty partisanship, we can hardly call Roscoe Conkling "typical." His was a one-of-a-kind personality, cut to no mold but his own.

He inspired loathing and hatred among many: a fledgling lawyer named Clarence Darrow once said that Conkling was "a cold, selfish man, who had no right to live except to prey upon his fellowmen." But there were times when he showed kindliness and humanity, as in 1875, when a young Negro named Blanche K. Bruce took his seat as United States Senator from the state of Mississippi. The trembling Bruce was resolutely ignored by his new colleagues until Roscoe Conkling, the haughtiest and most aloof member of the body, strode over to him and warmly grasped his hand. Conkling was friendly toward Bruce throughout his term. Even Mrs. Blaine was startled one evening at a dinner party, at which she learned with consternation that Senator Conkling had been assigned as her table partner, to find him both charming and thoughtful; she later said that she "had never had a more agreeable evening." And another of his enemies, speaking years before Conkling's death, said, "Many superficial observers do not get beyond Mr. Conkling's mere personal peculiarities. . . . These are mere specks on the portrait of a really great man." [1]

[1] Cramer, p. 232; B. K. Bruce to Conkling, Sept. 21, 1879, Conkling Papers, Library of Congress. Bruce named his first son after Conkling. T. H. Sherman,

In short, there was a real person behind the façade of the public figure, though the senator did his best to conceal it from his contemporaries
and from posterity. He could be gracious and cordial at times, though
almost always in a stiff, unbending manner, but he clearly made no
special effort to be kind. Besides, the private variances from his public
image were relatively few—he *was* irascible and proud and given to un-
dying hatreds, just as the outside world saw him. He was cold and self-
centered, as his relations with those to whom he should have been
closest make clear. There is no evidence that his lonely last years were
uncongenial to Conkling; though out of politics, he still lived by his
own rules.

Andrew White, who was both a supporter and opponent of Conkling
in his time, wrote of him when he heard the senator was dying:

He was a man of much ability and too proud to sham or steal, but overbearing and vain—not constructive on anything, but destructive—a political
gladiator—nothing more. Quarreling with everybody—even to his wife
and daughter, his only child. . . . Hardly worthy to be called a statesman,
and as an orator very pompous and inflated, yet strong and wonderful at
times in his rhetoric.[2]

Another critic said, "there is not the slightest evidence that his soul
has ever risen above pap and patronage." He was called "this patriot of
the flesh-pots." [3]

A few short years before, however, General John M. Schofield had
predicted that those who procured the passage of the compromise electoral commission bill in 1877, and he meant primarily Roscoe Conkling—"those," as he called them, "who have gained this victory in the
interest of Peace, justice and law"—would be "no less highly honored
than those who saved the Country from disunion in the last decade."
Schofield, a good general, was a poor prophet. History has given little
credit to Conkling and the others who saved the country from a dangerous political and sectional impasse in 1877, and the interesting question arises as to how much acclaim might have been given Lincoln by
posterity if he had been able to avert the Civil War by peaceful nego-
tiations in 1861.

The electoral commission was by no means Conkling's only contribu-

---

Twenty Years with James G. Blaine, pp. 29–30. Also Lucius Q. C. Lamar on
Conkling in 1881, Mayes, p. 391.
[2] Ogden, ed. p, 283.   [3] N.Y. *Tribune,* May 14, 1881.

tion from his seat in the United States Senate. His stalwart opposition to the Inflation Bill of 1874, and his influence which led Grant to veto the measure, worked to shore up and maintain the nation's credit. He was consistent, too, in his opposition to inflationary ideas and theories and his support of any measure that would tend to harden the nation's money.

Conkling's congressional record otherwise, however, is not marked by any great outpouring of creative initiatives. He worked hard in the Reconstruction committee on the formulation of the Fourteenth Amendment, but most of the original thoughts that went into it came from others. Congressional Reconstruction bore little of the Conkling stamp; his time of leadership came afterwards. There was too much ideology in Reconstruction; Roscoe Conkling was never much for ideology. He frequently played a very active role in consideration of other men's bills; he fought measures he was against, he amended bills, he helped to steer them through the House and the Senate, he led debates; but there is no Conkling Act on the books, and the senator did not seem particularly disposed to press for one. He sometimes offered the opinion in debate that there was no need for more and more new legislation, and his frequent opposition to measures propounded by leaders of both parties was concrete evidence of this feeling.

No one doubted, though, that he was one of the pre-eminent leaders of the Republican side of the Senate—virtually unchallenged in leadership after Oliver Morton's death. Political power was his forte. He controlled the party in the nation's largest state; he had Grant's ear; and he assumed the national leadership of a sizable faction of the party. He had a coterie of supporters in the Senate who nearly always followed his lead—men like Timothy Howe, J. P. Jones, Henry Anthony, the Camerons, Bruce, and most of the carpetbag Southern senators such as Simon Conover and George Spencer. But his leadership in the upper chamber was expended mostly on political rather than legislative issues, and he wore away the patience and sympathy of his colleagues with his snarling defiance of both Hayes and Garfield.

Conkling's machine in New York was one of the wonders of the age. Politicians and would-be bosses across the country viewed it with awe and envy, and all agreed that Roscoe Conkling had constructed the greatest organization of its kind in our history. Just before the machine crumbled, it appeared to be at its most powerful. Conkling had procured the election of Garfield as president, and the latter was tied down with the commitments of the previous August at the Fifth Avenue Hotel; both U.S. senators from New York were Stalwarts; the nation's vice-president was one of the machine's most skillful leaders; the governor of New York was a loyal adherent, owing his nomination and election solely to Conkling; the postmaster general of the United States was a devoted follower; the New York legislature was safely Republican and strongly Stalwart; and machine leaders were securely tucked into important and prestigious jobs both in New York and overseas, men like Payn, Woodford, and Morton. But the edifice was a hollow shell. Conkling knew it; Blaine had the new president's ear, and surely it was a matter only of time before an attack came. In the twinkling of an eye both senators were gone, the legislature was in rebellion, Governor Cornell had turned neutral, the jobs were in jeopardy, Robertson was in the custom house, and the whole machine had smashed.

The power of the presidency was never more clearly shown than in the toppling of the mighty Conkling machine by two mediocre presidents, simply because they had the office and a portion at least of the Republican party. Conkling knew this, too; the machine really came apart when his desperate bid for Grant failed at Chicago in the summer of 1880. The following spring it collapsed in disarray.

It has been said that Conkling pulled the Republican party over on top of him when he fell, and to a great extent this is true. Certainly the bitter Stalwart–Half-Breed split, only thinly covered over by the Arthur administration and brought once again to the fore by the 1884 nomination of Blaine, contributed mightily to the Democratic victory, which undoubtedly would have been much greater but for the incalculable effect of Cleveland's indiscretions with Maria Halpin. Historians have made much of the hatred between Roscoe Conkling and James Blaine, and clearly it affected the political history of the 1870's and 1880's to an astonishing degree.

Why, though, should this have been so? There have been politicians on the national scene before and since who have had enmities within their party without wrecking that party. Why should these two have done so? How was it that for the last few years of the 1870's and the first year or so of the following decade the major though unspoken issue in Republican politics seemed so often to be Roscoe Conkling's personality?

Conkling, patronage, his machine, his feud with Blaine, the whole struggle for civil service reform: all of these were really obscurantic issues in these decades after the Civil War. Twentieth-century America was building during this time, but not on the front pages of the newspapers where the ramifications of Blaine's and Conkling's mutual animosity were detailed. Rather it was in the back pages, where the dry statistics of finance and business were piled up one upon another in the daily financial columns. The development of capital agglomerations with marketing and industrial know-how which were to mark the country's economic future took place in this period; new names like Rockefeller, Pullman, Westinghouse, McCormick, and Wanamaker stood out on the business landscape. America, shoved ahead by the Civil War and the transportation boom which preceded and accompanied it, was undergoing rapid industrialization and financial consolidation, all the while that Roscoe Conkling was defending his right to have the last word in the appointment of weighers and gaugers in the New York Custom House.

Many of the economic devices and methods used in the developing industrial growth, however, could not stand close scrutiny. The patron saints of Amercan capitalism were many of them cutthroat pirates, and the standards of practice they condoned and encouraged were often, where not clearly illegal, plainly and unmistakably unethical. Every once in a while these things would come to light, in the exposure of a Gould or a Fisk, or in the investigation of some of the more brazen railroad transactions, but most of the business development was carried on out of the public limelight. All that was asked from government was tariff protection and a hands-off policy; beyond the tariff comparatively little notice was taken of business growth.

The press helped in this screening process with the inordinate attention given to the purely political, *ad hominem,* doings of public figures like Roscoe Conkling. Readers were interested in the conduct and battles of Blaine and Conkling, Schurz and Sumner, Morton and Thurman, and their colleagues on both sides of the aisle and both ends of the Capitol, because they put on a good show. They were interesting people. "The Senate took the place of Shakespeare," wrote Henry Adams, "and offered real Brutuses and Bolingbrokes, Jack Cades, Falstaffs, and Malvolios—endless varieties of human nature nowhere else to be studied." The oratorical heroics of speakers like Conkling were valued more for their histrionic than for their historical content.[4]

While the politicians amused the people, they fought election battles

4 H. Adams, p. 394.

with no issues and presented party platforms with no differences. Democrat or Republican, no one was much concerned with the tremendous implications for the future posed by the industrial concentrations; politicians fought long and hard over the spoils system and whether or not a man would be required to take a test before he was tendered a government job. They fought over control of their parties, with little at stake other than the guardianship of the status quo. Roscoe Conkling struggled fiercely against two successive presidents for the integrity of his machine, but the machine existed only to perpetuate itself and its leaders. Conkling seldom gave voice to any but the conventional wisdom of the day, and this wisdom included no concern for the economic future of the nation. It was not until the two Cleveland administrations showed the almost total identity of Democratic and Republican economic views that any substantial demand for alternatives developed within the major party structures. This came slowly, but at least it finally appeared.

Conkling's issues with Hayes and Garfield served to dramatize, however, the resurrection of the presidency from the nadir of the Johnson years. Grant had done little for the majesty of the office, deferring time after time to his advisers in the Senate. The fights with the two Ohioans over the collectorship, though, turned the corner for the presidency. Notice was served that henceforth the most powerful and arrogant senator must yield to the chief executive over matters like appointments. Conkling threatened to make Garfield "bite the dust," as he put it, but it was he who ultimately gave way.

Though Roscoe Conkling contributed to the obscuring of the true issues of the day from the American people, we can hardly say that he did so consciously. For him the maintenance and perpetuation of his organization was without doubt his primary objective, followed closely by the punishment of his enemies. The combative nature of the man unfortunately found in these limited aims sufficient scope for his considerable talents. Pressing home his attacks on these fronts occupied him satisfactorily, so he simply ignored more substantive problems. He was above such things, and he was above the carping of his critics, the milksops like Godkin and Curtis, who kept asking what he had ever done of any importance. It was a shame, because both in his legislative and legal careers he demonstrated a good mind, organizational talent, and command of the art of persuasion. Given his powers, Conkling could have made a great contribution to the nation by facing up boldly to the hazed-over issues of the future. He might even have attempted a more subtle approach to the problems of the black man in a white society, something more lasting and effective than the crude mechanisms of Reconstruction. But, obviously, Conkling was not interested in such things as the future economic development of American society. He presented no solutions to the racial conflict inherent in America, professing reliance upon the measures passed by Republican congresses under Johnson and Grant. He gave lip service to the rights of the black man, but he never went beyond the consensus of his colleagues in implementing those rights. He had his own interests, and these are what he dealt with.

Why this was so we are hardly in a position to determine. The answer lies in Roscoe Conkling's singular character. In his career in the House of Representatives, Conkling pursued the major public questions of the day, but he grew away from this kind of interest in the Senate. Editorial writers occasionally made the comment that it was a sad day for Conkling when he became involved in a contest with Fenton for control of the Republican party of New York. If he had not become enmeshed in patronage and machine politics, so this thesis went, how much more productive his career might well have been. Perhaps; it might also have been a great deal shorter. Edwin Morgan stayed away from power politics, and Reuben Fenton brought a premature end to his Senate career in 1869. Conkling's domineering personality would have chafed in any event at relegation to a subordinate position. Perhaps the nature of New York politics mandated the course of Conkling's Senate career. Yet, as matters stood, Conkling *had* the control, he *had* the power, and he *was* elected to three terms in the United States Senate. The question recurs: why did he hold himself relatively aloof from the problems of the day and, more importantly, the problems which, left unattended, shaped the nation's future? The answer thrusts itself upon us and just as surely thrusts us into the realm of psychology: something in the depths of Conkling's mind impelled him to the course he took, something which accounts as well for his narcissism, his stiffness, his combativeness; from the evidence available, we may have some but certainly not all of the clues to that something. Whatever the answer, it is clear as well that Roscoe Conkling was very much a man of his time.

It was a strange time, the period we call the Gilded Age, and Roscoe Conkling was one of its strangest characters. In an era of almost unbelievable corruption, he was above all suspicion of dishonesty. Roscoe Conkling did not steal, which made him rare in itself, and an orator referring to his legendary honesty could make the senator glow with pride and satisfaction. His personal life left much to be desired in conventional eyes, but here again he was honest, with himself and with the world. He did not sneak around corners or carry on clandestine affairs. When Roscoe Conkling engaged in adultery, all of Washington knew it.

He had an unusual personality; hardly what one would expect in a politician. Civility he clearly did not consider one of the cardinal virtues. In his eyes, disloyalty was a mortal sin, but he was so extremely sensitive to slights that he marked off as traitors any of his followers who chose not to accompany him in his self-immolation. He loved a fight more than anything, and he generally rejected conciliation or compromise. Even the Electoral Commission in 1877 was a conciliation of somebody else's fight; Conkling hardly cared whether Tilden or Hayes won. In 1878. Congressman Garfield wrote: "Conkling is very strong, a great fighter, inspired more by his hates than his loves; desires and has followers rather than friends. He will be of more service in a minority than in a majority." [5]

Garfield never could understand a politician who refused to bend and sway with the shifting winds of popular opinion. Conkling scorned such actions. He had been a popular public figure in his congressional days as well as in his early Senate career, but when he left the Senate, he was hated by many across the nation. Yet he had not changed; the public had. Limited though he may have been in his dedication to righting the wrongs of the world, Roscoe Conkling marched straight ahead, looking neither to left nor right.

He was a man of exceptional talent, of remarkable ability. Both his political and legal careers showed it. But his personality was sadly flawed. He attained a position of great prominence and power, but he let himself be caught up in inconsequentials. Conkling's was not a case of the man whose talents are wasted because he never reaches a place where he can put them to use. His story is far more distressing; it is that of the man of great ability, placed in a position of authority, who still somehow fritters away his opportunities. This is ultimately the tragedy of Roscoe Conkling.

[5] T. C. Smith, II, 670.

SELECTED BIBLIOGRAPHY

Manuscript Collections

Arthur, Chester Alan. Papers. Library of Congress.
——. Papers. New-York Historical Society.
Blaine, James G. Papers. Library of Congress.
Blizzard Men of 1888—Reminiscences. New-York Historical Society.
Burt, Silas W. Papers. New-York Historical Society.
Carrington Family Collection. Yale University Library.
Conkling, Roscoe. Papers. Library of Congress.
——. Papers. New-York Historical Society.
——. Letters. Photostats from originals owned by Harold J. Jonas, New York Public Library.
——. Miscellaneous Papers. New York Public Library.
Cornell, Alonzo Barton. Papers. Cornell University Library.
Depew, Chauncey M. Papers. Yale University Library.
Evarts, William Maxwell. Papers. Library of Congress.
Fairchild, Charles Stebbins. Papers. New-York Historical Society.
Greeley, Horace. Papers. New-York Historical Society.
——. Papers. New York Public Library.
Jones, George E. Papers. New York Public Library.
Kernan, Francis. Papers. Cornell University Library.
Morton, Levi Parsons. Papers. New York Public Library.
Penniman Collection. Yale University Library.
Pierce, Elbridge Bancroft, Collection. Yale University Library.
Pierrepont, Edwards. Papers. Yale University Library.
Reid, Whitelaw. Papers. Library of Congress.
Seymour, Horatio. Papers. New-York Historical Society.
Sigel, Franz. Papers. New-York Historical Society.
Webb, Alexander Stewart. Papers. Yale University Library.
White, Andrew Dickson. Papers. Cornell University Library.
Woolsey Family Correspondence. Yale University Library.

Newspapers and Journals

Congressional Globe, 1859–1863, 1865–1873
Congressional Record, 1873–1881
Harper's Weekly, 1867–1881
The Independent, 1880–1881
The Nation, 1867–1881
New York *Herald,* 1875–1881, 1888
New York *Sun,* 1878–1880
New York *Times,* 1862–1882, 1884–1888
New York *Tribune,* 1864–1881, 1887–1888
New York *World,* 1874–1881, 1884, 1888
Oneida *Morning Herald,* 1849–1850
Utica *Morning Herald,* 1858–1867, 1881

Published Primary Sources

Adams, Henry. *The Education of Henry Adams.* New York: Random House (Modern Library ed.), 1931.

Arthur, Chester Alan. *State Papers of Chester A. Arthur, President of the United States.* Washington: 1885.

Badeau, Adam. *Grant in Peace: From Appomattox to Mount McGregor.* Hartford, Conn.: S. S. Scranton, 1887.

Beale, Harriet Stanwood Blaine, ed. *Letters of Mrs. James G. Blaine.* 2 vols. New York: Duffield, 1908.

Bigelow, John. *Retrospections of an Active Life.* 5 vols. New York: Baker and Taylor, 1909–1913.

Blaine, James G. *Twenty Years of Congress: From Lincoln to Garfield.* 2 vols. Norwich, Conn.: Henry Bill, 1886.

Bliss, D. W. "The Story of President Garfield's Illness." *Century Magazine,* vol. 23 (Dec. 1881).

Boutwell, George S. *Reminiscences of Sixty Years in Public Affairs.* 2 vols. New York: McClure, Phillips, 1902.

Breen, Matthew P. *Thirty Years of New York Politics.* New York: published by the author, 1899.

Brown, Harry James, and Frederick D. Williams, eds. *The Diary of James A. Garfield.* Vols I–II. East Lansing, Mich.: Michigan State University Press, 1967.

Butler, Benjamin F. *Butler's Book: Autobiography and Personal Reminiscences of Major-General Benj. F. Butler.* Boston: A. M. Thayer, 1892.

Carpenter, Frank G. *Carp's Washington.* Arranged and edited by Frances Carpenter. New York: McGraw-Hill, 1960.

Clews, Henry. *Twenty-Eight Years in Wall Street.* New York: Irving, 1888.

Conkling, Alfred R. *The Life and Letters of Roscoe Conkling, Orator, Statesman, Advocate.* New York: Charles L. Webster, 1889.

Conkling, Roscoe. *The True Issue.* Pamphlet of October 8, 1879, speech. New York: 1879.

Connery, T. B. "Secret History of the Garfield-Conkling Tragedy." *Cosmopolitan Magazine,* vol. 23 (June 1897).

Cox, Jacob Dolson. "The Hayes Administration." *Atlantic Monthly,* vol. 71 (June 1893).

Croffut, William A. *An American Procession, 1855–1914.* Boston: Little, Brown, 1931.

Crook, William H. *Through Five Administrations.* Margarita Spalding Gerry, ed. New York: Harper and Bros., 1910.

Crowley, Julia M. *Echoes from Niagara.* Buffalo: C. W. Moulton, 1890.

Dana, Charles A. *Recollections of the Civil War.* New York: Collier Books, 1963.

Davis, J. C. Bancroft, ed. *United States Reports.* Vol. 116. New York and Albany: 1886.

Dawes, Henry L. "Garfield and Conkling." *Century Magazine,* vol. 47 (Jan. 1894).

Depew, Chauncey M. *My Memories of Eighty Years.* New York: Chas. Scribner's Sons, 1922.

——. *Orations, Addresses, and Speeches.* John Denison Champlin, ed. 8 vols. New York: Privately printed, 1910.

Draper, Andrew S. "General Grant's Veto of the 'Inflation Bill.' " *Century Magazine,* vol. 54 (July 1897).

Eaton, Dorman B. *True Significance of the National Civil Service Act.* Pamphlet. Washington: 1893.

Gorham, George C. *Roscoe Conkling Vindicated.* Pamphlet. New York: 1888.

Great Republican Speeches of the Campaign of 1880. New York: Stapleton, 1881.

Halstead, Murat. "The Tragedy of Garfield's Administration." *McClure's Magazine,* vol. 6 (Feb. 1896).

Hay, John. *Letters of John Hay and Extracts from Diary.* 3 vols. Washington: 1908.

Hayes, H. G. and C. J., eds. *A Complete History of the Trial of Guiteau, Assassin of President Garfield.* Philadelphia: Hubbard, 1882.

Hinsdale, Mary L., ed. *Garfield-Hinsdale Letters: Correspondence between James Abram Garfield and Burke Aaron Hinsdale.* Ann Arbor, Mich.: University of Michigan Press, 1949.

Hoar, George Frisbie. *Autobiography of Seventy Years.* 2 vols. New York: Chas. Scribner's Sons, 1903.

House Executive Documents, Forty-Fifth Congress, First Session, No. 8. "Commissions to Examine Certain Custom-Houses of the United States." Washington: Government Printing Office, 1877.

House Executive Documents, Forty-Fifth Congress, Second Session, vol. X, No. 25. "Investigation of the Customs Service." Washington: Government Printing Office, 1878.

Hudson, William C. *Random Recollections of an Old Political Reporter.* New York: Cupples & Leon, 1911.

Ingalls, John J. "The Stormy Days of the Electoral Commission." *Saturday Evening Post,* vol. 172, no. 39 (March 24, 1900).

Ingersoll, Robert G. *Memorial Address on Roscoe Conkling.* Albany: J. B. Lyon, 1888.

——. *Col. R. G. Ingersoll's Famous Speeches Complete.* New York: L. Lipkind, 1906.

Kasson, John A. "A Veto by Grant." *Century Magazine,* vol. 53 (April 1897).

Kendrick, Benjamin B., ed. "The Journal of the Joint Committee of Fifteen On Reconstruction." *Columbia University Studies,* vol. 62. New York: 1914.

Lincoln, Charles Z., ed. *State of New York: Messages from the Governors.* Vol. VII (1877–1884). Albany: J. B. Lyon, 1909.

McCulloch, Hugh. *Men and Measures of Half a Century.* New York: Chas. Scribner's Sons, 1889.

Merritt, Edwin Atkins. *Recollections, 1828–1911.* Albany: J. B. Lyon, 1911.

Mushkat, Jerome. "The Impeachment of Andrew Johnson: A Contemporary View." (The journal of Congressman John V. L. Pruyn of New York.) *New York History,* vol. 48 (July 1967).

Nicolay, John G., and John Hay. *Abraham Lincoln.* 10 vols. New York: Century, 1890.

Northrup, Milton Harlow. "A Grave Crisis in American History." *Century Magazine,* vol. 62 (Sept. 1901).

Norton, Charles Eliot, ed. *Orations and Addresses of George William Curtis.* 3 vols. New York: Harper and Bros., 1894.

Official Proceedings of the Republican National Conventions of 1868, 1872, 1876, and 1880. Minneapolis: Charles W. Johnson, 1903.

Ogden, Robert Morris, ed. *The Diaries of Andrew D. White.* Ithaca, N. Y.: Cornell University Library, 1959.

Pedder, Henry C. *Garfield's Place in History.* New York: G. P. Putnam's Sons, 1882.

Platt, Thomas Collier. *The Autobiography of Thomas Collier Platt.* Louis J. Lang, ed. New York: B. W. Dodge, 1910.

Richardson, James D., ed. *Messages and Papers of the Presidents, 1789–1908*. Vol. VII. Washington: Bureau of National Literature and Art, 1908.

Rockwell, A. F. "From Mentor to Elberon." *Century Magazine*, vol. 23 (Jan. 1882).

Root, Elihu. *Addresses on Government and Citizenship*. Cambridge, Mass.: Harvard University Press, 1916.

Schurz, Carl. *The Reminiscences of Carl Schurz*. 3 vols. New York: McClure, 1907–1908.

——. *Speeches, Correspondence, and Political Papers of Carl Schurz*. 6 vols. New York: G. P. Putnam's Sons, 1913.

Sherman, John. *Recollections of Forty Years in the House, Senate, and Cabinet*. 2 vols. Chicago and New York: Werner, 1895.

Sherman, Thomas H. *Twenty Years with James G. Blaine*. New York: Grafton Press, 1928.

Shipman, William B. "A Memorial of the Late Roscoe Conkling, Presented and Adopted on December 10, 1889." Association of the Bar of the City of New York, *Twentieth Annual Report*. New York: 1890.

Stanton, Elizabeth Cady. *Eighty Years and More (1815–1897)*. New York: European, 1898.

Stewart, William M. *Reminiscences of Senator William M. Stewart of Nevada*. New York and Washington: Neale, 1908.

Stoddard, Henry L. *As I Knew Them*. New York: Harper and Bros., 1927.

United States Supreme Court. *Transcripts of Records, 1885*. DXXXVI (116 U.S. 138–161).

Utica City Directory. Utica: 1847–1848 to 1882.

Weed, Thurlow. *Autobiography*. Harriet A. Weed, ed. Boston: Houghton Mifflin, 1884.

Welles, Gideon. *Diary of Gideon Welles, Secretary of the Navy under Lincoln and Johnson*. 3 vols. Boston and New York: Houghton Mifflin, 1911.

White, Andrew Dickson. *Autobiography of Andrew Dickson White*. 2 vols. New York: Century, 1905.

Williams, Charles Richard, ed. *Diary and Letters of Rutherford Birchard Hayes*. 5 vols. Columbus, Ohio: The Ohio State Archaeological and Historical Society, 1922–1926.

Williams, T. Harry, ed. *Hayes: The Diary of a President, 1875–1881*. New York: David McKay, 1964.

Secondary Books

Adams, Charles Francis. *Charles Francis Adams*. Boston and New York: Houghton Mifflin, 1900.

Adler, Selig. *The Senatorial Career of George Franklin Edmunds, 1866–1891*. (Pamphlet). Urbana, Illinois: 1934.

Alexander, De Alva Stanwood. *A Political History of the State of New York*. 3 vols. New York: Henry Holt, 1909.

Bagg, Moses M., M.D., ed. *Memorial History of Utica, N.Y.* Syracuse: D. Mason, 1892.

Barnard, Harry. *Rutherford B. Hayes and His America*. New York and Indianapolis: Bobbs-Merrill, 1954.

Barrows, Chester L. *William M. Evarts: Lawyer, Diplomat, Statesman*. Chapel Hill, N.C.: University of North Carolina Press, 1941.

Beale, Howard K. *The Critical Year: A Study of Andrew Johnson and Reconstruction*. New York: Harcourt Brace, 1930; F. Ungar, 1958.

Binkley, Wilfred E. *President and Congress*. New York: Vintage Books, 1962 (originally published in 1937 by Doubleday, Doran, as *The Powers of the President*).

Blake, Nelson Morehouse. *William Mahone of Virginia, Soldier and Political Insurgent*. Richmond: Garrett & Massie, 1935.

Bowen, Croswell. *The Elegant Oakey*. New York: Oxford University Press, 1956.

Bowers, Claude G. *The Tragic Era: The Revolution after Lincoln*. New York: Houghton Mifflin, 1929.

Brown, Dee. *The Year of the Century: 1876*. New York: Chas. Scribner's Sons, 1966.

Brown, Francis. *Raymond of The Times*. New York: W. W. Norton, 1951.

Buck, Paul H. *The Road to Reunion, 1865–1900*. New York: Little, Brown, 1937; Vintage Books, 1959.

Burgess, John W. *The Administration of President Hayes*. New York: Chas. Scribner's Sons, 1916.

Burton, Theodore E. *John Sherman*. Boston and New York: Houghton Mifflin, 1906.

Caldwell, Robert Granville. *James A. Garfield: Party Chieftain*. New York: Dodd, Mead, 1931.

Cary, Edward. *George William Curtis*. Boston and New York: Houghton Mifflin, 1894.

Cate, Wirt Armistead. *Lucius Q. C. Lamar: Secession and Reunion*. Chapel Hill, N.C.: University of North Carolina Press, 1935.

Chester, Alden, ed. *Legal and Judicial History of New York*. 3 vols. New York: National Americana Society, 1911.

Chidsey, Donald Barr. *The Gentleman from New York: A Life of Roscoe Conkling*. New Haven, Conn.: Yale University Press, 1935.

Clancy, Herbert J., S.J. *The Presidential Election of 1880*. Chicago: Loyola University Press, 1958.

Cochran, Thomas C., and William Miller. *The Age of Enterprise*. New York and Evanston, Illinois: Macmillan, 1942; Harper & Row (Harper Torch Books edition), 1961.

Coleman, Charles H. *The Election of 1868: The Democratic Effort to Regain Control*. New York: Columbia University Press, 1933.

Conkling, Ira Broadwell. *The Conklings in America*. Washington, D.C.: Charles H. Potter, 1913.

Cortissoz, Royal. *The Life of Whitelaw Reid*. 2 vols. New York: Chas. Scribner's Sons, 1921.

Cramer, C. H. *Royal Bob: The Life of Robert G. Ingersoll*. Indianapolis and New York: Bobbs-Merrill, 1952.

Davis, Elmer. *History of the New York Times, 1851–1921*. New York: New York Times, 1921.

Dodge, Mary Abigail (Gail Hamilton). *Biography of James G. Blaine*. Norwich, Conn.: Henry Bill, 1895.

Dorf, Philip. *The Builder: A Biography of Ezra Cornell*. New York: Macmillan, 1952.

Eckenrode, Hamilton J. *Rutherford B. Hayes: Statesman of Reunion*. New York: Dodd, Mead, 1930.

Fish, Carl Russell. *The Civil Service and the Patronage*. Cambridge, Mass.: Harvard University Press, 1904.

Flick, Alexander C., ed. *History of the State of New York*. 10 vols. New York: Columbia University Press, 1933–1937.

———, and G. S. Lobrano. *Samuel Jones Tilden: A Study in Political Sagacity*. New York: Dodd, Mead, 1939.

Foulke, William Dudley. *Fighting the Spoilsmen*. New York: G. P. Putnam's Sons, 1919.

———. *Life of Oliver P. Morton*. 2 vols. Indianapolis and Kansas City: Bowen-Merrill, 1899.

Fuess, Claude Moore. *Carl Schurz, Reformer*. New York: Dodd, Mead, 1932.

Gibson, A. M. *A Political Crime: The History of the Great Fraud*. New York: Gottsberger, 1885.

Gillett, Frederick H. *George Frisbie Hoar*. Boston and New York: Houghton Mifflin, 1934.

Goldman, Eric F. *Rendezvous with Destiny*. New York: Alfred A. Knopf, 1953.

Gosnell, Harold F. *Boss Platt and His New York Machine*. Chicago: University of Chicago Press, 1924.

Harding, Rev. John R., ed. *One Hundred Years of Trinity Church, Utica, N.Y.* Utica: T. J. Griffiths, 1898.

Hatch, Alden. *The Wadsworths of the Genesee.* New York: Coward-Mc-Cann, 1959.

Haworth, Paul L. *The Hayes-Tilden Election.* 2d ed. Indianapolis: Bobbs-Merrill, 1927.

Henry, Frederick A. *Captain Henry of Geauga.* Cleveland: Gates Press, 1942.

Hesseltine, William B. *Ulysses S. Grant, Politician.* New York: Dodd, Mead, 1935.

Hibben, Paxton. *Henry Ward Beecher: An American Portrait.* New York: The Press of the Readers Club, 1942.

Hirshson, Stanley P. *Farewell to the Bloody Shirt: Northern Republicans and the Southern Negro, 1877–1893.* Bloomington, Ind.: Indiana University Press, 1962.

Hofstadter, Richard. *The American Political Tradition and the Men Who Made It.* New York: Alfred A. Knopf, 1948.

Hoogenboom, Ari. *Outlawing the Spoils: A History of the Civil Service Reform Movement, 1865–1883.* Urbana, Ill.: University of Illinois Press, 1961.

Howe, George Frederick. *Chester A. Arthur: A Quarter Century of Machine Politics.* New York: Dodd, Mead, 1934.

Hyman, Harold Melvin. *Era of the Oath: Northern Loyalty Tests during the Civil War and Reconstruction.* Philadelphia: University of Pennsylvania Press, 1954.

——, ed. *New Frontiers of the American Reconstruction.* Chicago: University of Illinois Press, 1966.

James, Joseph B. *The Framing of the Fourteenth Amendment.* Illinois Studies in the Social Sciences, vol. XXXVII. Urbana, Ill.: 1956.

Jessup, Philip C. *Elihu Root.* 2 vols. New York: Dodd, Mead, 1938.

Josephson, Matthew. *The Politicos, 1865–1896.* New York: Harcourt Brace, 1938.

Judah, Charles, and George Winston Smith. *The Unchosen.* New York: Coward-McCann, 1962.

Kavaler, Lucy. *The Astors: A Family Chronicle of Pomp and Power.* New York: Dodd, Mead, 1966.

Keller, Morton. *The Art and Politics of Thomas Nast.* New York: Oxford University Press, 1968.

Korngold, Ralph. *Thaddeus Stevens: A Being Darkly Wise and Rudely Great.* New York: Harcourt Brace, 1955.

Levin, Peter R. *Seven by Chance: The Accidental Presidents.* New York: Farrar, Straus, 1948.

McCall, Samuel W. *Thaddeus Stevens*. Boston and New York: Houghton Mifflin, 1899.

McClure, Alexander K. *Our Presidents and How We Make Them*. New York: Harper and Bros., 1900.

McElroy, Robert. *Levi Parsons Morton: Banker, Diplomat, and Statesman*. New York: G. P. Putnam's Sons, 1930.

McKitrick, Eric L. *Andrew Johnson and Reconstruction*. Chicago: University of Chicago Press, 1960.

McMahon, Helen G. *Chautauqua County: A History*. Buffalo: H. Stewart, 1958.

Magrath, C. Peter. *Morrison R. Waite: The Triumph of Character*. New York: Macmillan, 1963.

Mayes, Edward. *Lucius Q. C. Lamar: His Life, Times, and Speeches*. Nashville, Tenn.: Publishing House of the Methodist Episcopal Church, South, 1896.

Merrill, Horace Samuel. *Bourbon Leader: Grover Cleveland and the Democratic Party*. Boston and Toronto: Little, Brown, 1957.

Milne, Gordon. *George William Curtis and the Genteel Tradition*. Bloomington, Ind.: Indiana University Press, 1956.

Milton, George Fort. *The Age of Hate: Andrew Johnson and the Radicals*. New York: Coward-McCann, 1930.

Mitchell, Stewart. *Horatio Seymour of New York*. Cambridge, Mass.: Harvard University Press, 1938.

Muzzey, David Saville. *James G. Blaine: A Political Idol of Other Days*. New York: Dodd, Mead, 1934.

Nevins, Allan. *Abram S. Hewitt, with Some Account of Peter Cooper*. New York: Harper and Bros., 1938.

———. *Grover Cleveland: A Study in Courage*. New York: Dodd, Mead, 1932.

———. *Hamilton Fish: The Inner History of the Grant Administration*. 2 vols. New York: Dodd, Mead, 1936.

Oberholtzer, Ellis Paxson. *Jay Cooke: Financier of the Civil War*. 2 vols. Philadelphia: Geo. W. Jacobs, 1907.

Paine, Albert Bigelow. *Th. Nast: His Period and His Pictures*. New York: Macmillan, 1904.

Patrick, Rembert W. *The Reconstruction of the Nation*. New York: Oxford University Press, 1967.

Phelps, Mary Merwin. *Kate Chase: Dominant Daughter*. New York: Thomas Y. Crowell, 1935.

Randall, J. G. *The Civil War and Reconstruction*. Boston and New York: D. C. Heath, 1937.

Rawley, James A. *Edwin D. Morgan, 1811–1883: Merchant in Politics.* New York: Columbia University Press, 1955.

Ross, Earle Dudley. *The Liberal Republican Movement.* New York: Henry Holt, 1919.

Ross, Ishbel. *The General's Wife: The Life of Mrs. Ulysses S. Grant.* New York: Dodd, Mead, 1959.

——. *Proud Kate: Portrait of an Ambitious Woman.* New York: Harper and Bros., 1953.

Rothman, David J. *Politics and Power: The United States Senate, 1869–1901.* Cambridge, Mass.: Harvard University Press, 1966.

Russell, Charles Edward. *Blaine of Maine: His Life and Times.* New York: Cosmopolitan, 1931.

Sage, Leland L. *William Boyd Allison: A Study in Practical Politics.* Iowa City, Iowa: State Historical Society of Iowa, 1956.

Scott, Henry W. *Distinguished American Lawyers.* New York: C. L. Webster, 1891.

Smith, Theodore Clark. *The Life and Letters of James Abram Garfield.* 2 vols. New Haven, Conn.: Yale University Press, 1925.

Stampp, Kenneth M. *The Era of Reconstruction, 1865–1877.* New York: Alfred A. Knopf, 1966.

Stanwood, Edward. *James Gillespie Blaine.* Boston and New York: Houghton Mifflin, 1905.

Stein, Charles W. *The Third Term Tradition: Its Rise and Collapse in American Politics.* New York: Columbia University Press, 1943.

Stoddard, William O. *Men of Business.* New York: Chas. Scribner's Sons, 1893.

Storey, Moorfield, and Edward W. Emerson. *Ebenezer Rockwood Hoar: A Memoir.* Boston and New York: Houghton Mifflin, 1911.

Tansill, Charles Callan. *The Congressional Career of Thomas Francis Bayard, 1869–1885.* Washington, D.C.: Georgetown University Press, 1946.

Thayer, William Roscoe. *The Life and Letters of John Hay.* 2 vols. Boston and New York: Houghton Mifflin, 1915.

Thomas, Benjamin P., and Harold M. Hyman. *Stanton: The Life and Times of Lincoln's Secretary of War.* New York: Alfred A. Knopf, 1962.

Thompson, E. Bruce. *Matthew Hale Carpenter: Webster of the West.* Madison, Wis.: State Historical Society of Wisconsin, 1954.

Van Deusen, Glyndon G. *Horace Greeley.* Philadelphia: University of Pennsylvania Press, 1953.

——. *Thurlow Weed: Wizard of the Lobby.* Boston: Little, Brown. 1947.

——. *William Henry Seward.* New York: Oxford University Press, 1967.

Wall, Joseph Frazier. *Henry Watterson*. New York: Oxford University Press, 1956.

Walter, George W. *Chips and Shavings: Stories of Upstate New York*. Sherburne, N.Y.: Heritage Press, 1966.

Warren, Charles. *The Supreme Court in United States History*. 2 vols., rev. ed. Boston and Toronto: Little, Brown, 1922, 1926.

Werstein, Irving. *The Blizzard of '88*. New York: Thomas Y. Crowell, 1960.

White, Leonard D. *The Republican Era, 1869–1901*. New York: Macmillan, 1958.

Whyte, James H. *The Uncivil War: Washington during the Reconstruction, 1865–1878*. New York: Twayne, 1958.

Writers' Program of Works Progress Administration in the State of New York. *New York: A Guide to the Empire State*. New York: Oxford University Press, 1940.

Secondary Articles

Belden, Marva R., and Thomas G. "Kate Was Too Ambitious." *American Heritage*, vol. 7 (Aug. 1956).

Bronner, Frederick L., George F. Howe, and Hiram C. Todd. "Chester Alan Arthur." *Union Worthies*, no. 3, Union College, Schenectady, New York (1948).

Dinnerstein, Leonard. "The Impact of Tammany Hall on State and National Politics in the Eighteen-Eighties." *New York History*, vol. 42 (July 1961).

Fleming, E. McClung. "The Young Scratcher Campaign of 1879: The Birth of the Mugwumps." *New York History*, vol. 23 (1942).

Goff, John S. "President Arthur's Domestic Legislative Program." *New-York Historical Society Quarterly*, vol. 44 (April 1960).

Hartman, William. "The New York Custom House: Seat of Spoils Politics." *New York History*, vol. 34 (April 1953).

———. "Pioneer in Civil Service Reform: Silas W. Burt and the New York Custom House." *New-York Historical Society Quarterly*, vol. 39 (Oct. 1955).

Howe, George F. "The New York Custom-House Controversy, 1877–1879." *Mississippi Valley Historical Review*, vol. 18 (Dec. 1931).

Jonas, Harold J. "Alfred Conkling, Jurist and Gentleman." *New York History*, vol. 20 (July 1939).

McLaughlin, Andrew C. "The Court, The Corporation, and Conkling." *American Historical Review*, vol. 46 (Oct. 1940).

Newcomer, Lee. "Chester A. Arthur: the Factors Involved in His Removal from the New York Customhouse." *New York History,* vol. 18 (1937).

Reeves, Thomas C. "Silas Burt and Chester Arthur: A Reformer's View of the Twenty-first President." *New-York Historical Society Quarterly,* vol. 54 (Oct. 1970).

Resseguie, Harry E. "Federal Conflict of Interest: The A. T. Stewart Case." *New York History,* vol. 47 (July 1966).

Shores, Venila Lovina. "The Hayes-Conkling Controversy." *Smith College Studies in History,* vol. 4, Department of History of Smith College, Northampton, Mass. (1919).

Stebbins, Homer Adolph. "A Political History of the State of New York, 1865–1869." *Studies in History, Economics, and Public Law,* Columbia University, vol. 55, no. 1 (1913).

Wheatley, R. "The New York Custom-House." *Harper's New Monthly,* vol. 69 (June 1884).

White, William Allen. "Platt." *McClure's Magazine,* vol. 18 (Dec. 1901).

INDEX

462   INDEX